ACCOUNTING FOR MANAGERS

Interpreting accounting information for decision-making

Second Edition

Paul M. Collier

Monash University, Melbourne
previously Aston Business School, Birmingham

JOHN WILEY & SONS, LTD

Other Wiley Editorial Offices

John Wiley & Sons, Inc., 111 River Street, Hoboken, NJ 07030, USA

Jossey-Bass, 989 Market Street, San Francisco, CA 94103-1741, USA

Wiley-VCH Verlag GmbH, Boschstr. 12, D-69469 Weinheim, Germany

John Wiley & Sons Australia Ltd, 42 McDougall Street, Milton, Queensland 4064, Australia

John Wiley & Sons (Asia) Pte Ltd, 2 Clementi Loop #02-01, Jin Xing Distripark, Singapore 129809

John Wiley & Sons Canada Ltd, 22 Worcester Road, Etobicoke, Ontario, Canada M9W 1L1

Wiley also publishes its books in a variety of electronic formats. Some content that appears
in print may not be available in electronic books.

Library of Congress Cataloging-in-Publication Data

Collier, Paul M.
   Accounting for managers ; interpreting accounting information for
decision-making / Paul M. Collier. – 2nd ed.
      p. cm.
   Includes bibliographical references and index.
   ISBN-13: 978-0-470-01609-1 (pbk. : alk. paper)
   ISBN-10: 0-470-01609-4 (pbk. : alk. paper)
   1. Managerial accounting.   I. Title.
HF5657.4.C647 2006
658.15'11 – dc22

British Library Cataloguing in Publication Data

A catalogue record for this book is available from the British Library

ISBN-13 978-0-470-01609-1
ISBN-10 0-470-01609-4

Typeset in 10/12pt Photina by Originator, Gt Yarmouth, Norfolk
Printed and bound in Great Britain by Scotprint, Haddington, East Lothian
This book is printed on acid-free paper responsibly manufactured from sustainable forestry
in which at least two trees are planted for each one used for paper production.

For Loredana and Alexis

CONTENTS

PREFACE TO THE SECOND EDITION

The second edition builds on the success of the original but has been updated in particular to expand the coverage of financial statements, particularly reflecting the introduction of International Financial Reporting Standards (IFRS) and the increased emphasis on corporate governance. This has resulted in two new chapters: Chapters 8 and 9 and a revision of much of chapters 6 and 7. The structure of the book has been altered to accommodate the changes. Part I provides the context of accounting. Part II is concerned with financial statements. Part III, which remains largely unchanged concentrates on management accounting information for planning, decision-making and control, while Part IV provides the supporting information. In Part IV the Glossary has been substantially increased to provide a single point of reference for accounting terminology used in the book. Part V contains a variety of questions and case studies with solutions.

RATIONALE FOR THE BOOK

This book was motivated by my experience in teaching accounting at postgraduate level (MBA and MSc) at Aston Business School and providing in-house training for non-financial managers in many organizations to introduce them to the use of financial tools and techniques.

My own education as an accountant was aimed at achieving professional recognition and emphasized an uncritical acceptance of the tools and techniques that I was taught. It was only after moving from financial to a general management position in industry that I began to see the limitations and questionable assumptions that underlay these tools and techniques. When I returned to study later in my career, I was exposed for the first time to alternative paradigms from which to view accounting. This book is therefore as much a result of my practical experience as a producer and user of accounting information as it is a result of my teaching and training experience.

As accounting increasingly becomes decentred from the accounting department in organizations, line managers in all functional areas of business are expected to be able to prepare budgets, develop business cases for capital investment, and exercise cost control to ensure that profit targets are achieved. Managers are also expected to be able to analyse and interpret accounting information so that marketing, operations and human resource decisions are made in the light of an understanding of the financial implications of those decisions.

I was disappointed by the books available to support teaching and training because most books on accounting have a similar format that is *accounting-centric*: chapters typically cover accounting techniques rather than the types of decisions made by non-financial managers. The emphasis in those books, many of which are designed for people whose career aspirations are to become accountants, is on *doing* accounting rather than *using* accounting. This book has been written for the vast majority of undergraduate and postgraduate students and practising managers who do not want to become professional accountants. The book therefore has a *practitioner–manager orientation*.

The title of the book, *Accounting for Managers: Interpreting accounting information for decision-making*, emphasizes the focus on accounting to meet the needs of managers. The material contained in the book stresses the interpretation (rather than the construction) of accounting information as well as a critical (rather than unthinking) acceptance of the underlying assumptions behind accounting. It is suitable for postgraduate and undergraduate students who are undertaking courses in accounting that do not lead to professional accreditation, and to practising non-financial managers who need a better understanding of the role of accounting in their organizations.

There is a focus in most accounting books on manufacturing organizations, perhaps because many of those books have been issued as revised editions for many years and have not adequately reflected the changing nature of the economies in the developed world. The growth of service businesses and the knowledge economy is not sufficiently explored in most accounting texts. This book uses examples, case studies and questions that are more equally balanced between the needs of organizations in manufacturing, retail and services.

In most accounting books there is also insufficient attention to theory, particularly for postgraduate students who should have a *wider theoretical underpinning* of accounting as it is used in organizations. Theory should encourage the reader to enquire more deeply into the alternative theoretical positions underlying accounting as well as its social and behavioural consequences, both within their own organizations and in the wider society. This book therefore introduces the reader to some of the journal literature that is either fundamental to the role of accounting or is path breaking. The book is not intended to be deeply theoretical, but rather provides, through the ample references in each chapter, an accessible route for those who want to reach into the wider literature.

Accounting books are often inaccessible to those from non-English-speaking backgrounds, because of the complexity of the language used. Many of the examples and questions in typical accounting books rely on a strong knowledge of the nuances of the English language to interpret what the question is asking, before students can make any attempt to answer them. This book adopts a more plain English style that *addresses the needs of European and Asian students*.

Finally, the examples in most accounting books focus on the calculations that accountants perform to construct accounting reports, rather than on the *interpretive needs* of managers who use those reports. While some calculation questions are needed to ensure that readers understand how information is produced, the emphasis for the non-financial manager should be on *critical understanding and questioning* of the accounting numbers and of the underlying assumptions behind those numbers, and on the need to supplement accounting reports with non-financial performance measures and broader perspectives than satisfying shareholder wealth alone.

OUTLINE OF THE BOOK

The book is arranged in five parts. The first part describes the context and role of accounting in business. Some theoretical frameworks are provided. It is hoped that this will provide a foundation for readers' understanding that accounting is more than a technical subject but is grounded in competing theories. These theories are themselves rooted in historical, political, economic and social causes. The theoretical framework should help to make the subject more meaningful to students and practitioners alike. Although the reader is encouraged to read Part I, the arrangement of the book is such that the reader can commence in Part II, where the analysis and interpretation of accounting information begins.

For example, those readers with a good business understanding may omit Chapters 1 and 2. Those who understand the basics of accounting can omit Chapter 3. These first three chapters are provided for those students who are coming to a business studies course for the first time, although even the experienced reader will find some value in them. Readers may not want to read the theoretical Chapters 4 and 5 until they are further into Part II and Part III; however, the theory in each of the chapters in those Parts will be more understandable after reading Chapters 4 and 5.

Those readers who have undertaken a course in financial accounting may have already covered much of the material in Part II (Chapters 6 through 9). Again, this book is intended to be a complete coverage of the subject for students and readers with no prior experience of accounting and Chapters 6 through 9 provide an important basis for understanding management accounting.

In this second edition, Chapters 8 and 9 have been added. Some of the feedback from course leaders in institutions around the world has been that insufficient coverage of financial statements was included for students studying at postgraduate level. While the text was always intended to help managers, whose day-to-day roles are largely unaffected by reporting to parties external to the organization, practicing managers do appreciate a more in-depth coverage of financial statements. The introduction of International Financial Reporting Standards (IFRS) and the Operating and Financial Review (OFR) and the increased attention to corporate governance provided the impetus in this second edition to broaden the coverage in Part II.

The third part of the book shows the reader how accounting information is used in decision-making, planning and control. In this third part the accounting tools and techniques are explained, illustrated by straight forward examples. Case studies, drawn mainly from real business examples, help draw out the concepts. Theory is integrated with the tools and techniques and the use of quotations from original sources should encourage the reader to access the academic accounting literature. A critical approach to the assumptions underlying financial information is presented, building on the theoretical framework provided in Chapters 4 and 5.

The fourth part provides a wealth of supporting material. Chapter 18 suggests an approach to research in accounting. Chapter 19 introduces four readings from the accounting literature. These cover the spectrum of the literature and support the most important concepts in the book. They present four different yet complementary perspectives on accounting in organizations. Each reading has several questions that the reader should think about and try to answer in order to help understand the concepts.

The fourth part contains an extensive glossary of accounting terms. The use of blue keywords in the text highlights that the meaning of the term is outlined in the glossary.

The fifth part of the book contains an appendix of questions and case studies to enable readers to test their understanding of the concepts described in the book.

The questions in Appendix 1 cover each chapter and rely on knowledge gained from reading that and preceding chapters. Consequently, there is a greater level of detail involved in questions about the later chapters. Attempting these questions will help the reader to understand how accountants produce information needed by non-accounting managers. An understanding of accounting tools and techniques is important in using the results of these tools and techniques for decision-making. Appendix 2 contains answers for all the questions.

The case studies in Appendix 3 help in developing the ability to interpret and analyse financial information produced by an accountant for use by non-accounting managers in decision-making. Each is identified with the chapters that will aid under-standing, interpretation and critical analysis of the case. Appendix 4 contains a suggested answer for each case, although the nature of such cases is that there is rarely a single correct answer, as different approaches to the problem can highlight different aspects of the case and a range of possible solutions.

ACKNOWLEDGEMENTS

The author acknowledges the indirect contribution of Stan Brignall and Stuart Cooper at Aston to this text, which is in no small part the result of team teaching at Aston over the last five years. The author is also grateful for the helpful suggestions made by Amanda Nayak of Birmingham and Mike Tayles of Bradford in relation to the first edition and a number of academics throughout the world who provided feedback on the first edition, much of which has been incorporated into this updated and revised second edition. He also thanks Steve Hardman, Rachel Goodyear and Mark Styles at John Wiley & Sons for their support and helpful advice throughout the writing of the book.

ABOUT THE AUTHOR

Dr Paul Collier Ph.D. (Warwick), B.Bus. (NSWIT), M.Comm. (NSW), Grad.Dip.Ed. (UTS), CPA (Aust.) is a senior lecturer in management accounting at Monash University in Melbourne and was previously at Aston Business School in Birmingham. Paul has worked in senior financial and general management roles in the UK and Australia. He was financial controller/company secretary and subsequently general manager (operations) for one of Australia's largest printing companies before moving to the UK in 1993. The book uses material developed by the author based on his experience as a practitioner, in his teaching at Aston and elsewhere, and in delivering financial training to non-financial managers in diverse industries over many years. Paul's research interests are in the use of management accounting and non-financial performance information in decision-making and the behavioural aspects of management accounting. He has published a large number of articles in academic journals and is an examiner for the Chartered Institute of Management Accountants.

PART I

CONTEXT OF ACCOUNTING

Part I describes the context and role of accounting in business and provides some theoretical frameworks. It is hoped that this will offer a foundation for readers' understanding that accounting is more than a technical subject and is grounded in competing theories. These theories are themselves rooted in historical, political, economic and social causes. The theoretical framework should help to make the subject more meaningful to students and practitioners alike.

Chapter 1 provides an introduction to accounting, and an overview of accounting history as well as describing how the role of accounting has changed, including the influence that this changed role has had on non-financial managers.

Chapter 2 describes the context in which management accounting operates: the capital market emphasis on shareholder value, and the strategic necessity of organizing complex businesses through divisions.

Chapter 3 describes how transactions are recorded by accounting systems and the limitations that are imposed by these methods.

Chapter 4 covers the traditional theoretical approach to management accounting and control, while Chapter 5 offers alternative perspectives on accounting. The theoretical framework in Chapters 4 and 5 is important to support the interpretive analysis and critical perspective taken by this book.

1 INTRODUCTION TO ACCOUNTING

This chapter introduces accounting and provides a short history of management accounting. It describes the early role of the management accountant and recent developments that have influenced the role of non-financial managers in relation to the use of financial information. The chapter concludes with a critical perspective on accounting history.

ACCOUNTING, ACCOUNTABILITY AND THE ACCOUNT

Businesses exist to provide goods or services to customers in exchange for a financial reward. Public-sector and not-for-profit organizations also provide services, although their funding comes not from customers but from government or charitable donations. While this book is primarily concerned with profit-oriented businesses, most of the principles are equally applicable to the public and not-for-profit sectors. Business is not about accounting. It is about markets, people and operations (the delivery of products or services), although accounting is implicated in all of these decisions because it is the financial representation of business activity.

The American Accounting Association defined accounting in 1966 as:

> The process of identifying, measuring and communicating economic information to permit informed judgements and decisions by users of the information.

This is an important definition because:

- it recognizes that accounting is a process: that process is concerned with capturing business events, recording their financial effect, summarizing and reporting the result of those effects, and interpreting those results (we cover this in Chapter 3);
- it is concerned with economic information: while this is predominantly financial, it also allows for non-financial information (which is covered in Chapter 4);

■ its purpose is to support 'informed judgements and decisions' by users: this empha-sizes the decision usefulness of accounting information and the broad spectrum of 'users' of that information. While the primary concern of this book is the use of accounting information for decision-making, the book takes a stakeholder perspec-tive that users of accounting information include all those who may have an interest in the survival, profitability and growth of a business: shareholders, employees, customers, suppliers, financiers, government and society as a whole.

The notion of accounting for a narrow (shareholders and financiers) or a broad (societal) group of users is an important philosophical debate to which we will return throughout this book. This debate derives from questions of accountability: to whom is the business accountable and for what, and what is the role of accounting in that accountability?

Boland and Schultze (1996) defined accountability as:

The capacity and willingness to give explanations for conduct, stating how one has discharged one's responsibilities, an explaining of conduct with a credible story of what happened, and a calculation and balancing of competing obligations, includ-ing moral ones. (p. 62)

Hoskin (1996) suggested that accountability is:

more total and insistent . . . [it] ranges more freely over space and time, focusing as much on future potential as past accomplishment. (p. 265)

Boland and Schultze argued that accountability entails both a narration of what transpired and a reckoning of money, both meanings deriving from the original meanings of the word *account*.

Accounting is a collection of systems and processes used to record, report and inter-pret business transactions. Accounting provides an **account** – *an explanation or report in financial terms* – about the transactions of an organization. It enables managers to satisfy the *stakeholders* in the organization (owners, government, financiers, suppliers, customers, employees etc.) that they have acted in the best interests of stakeholders rather than themselves. This is the notion of **accountability** to others, a result of the *stewardship* function of managers that takes place through the process of accounting. Stewardship is an important concept because in all but very small businesses, the owners of businesses are not the same as the managers. This separation of ownership from control makes accounting particularly influential due to the emphasis given to increasing shareholder wealth (or shareholder value). Accountability results in the production of financial statements, primarily for those interested parties who are external to the business. This function is called **financial accounting**.

Accounting is traditionally seen as fulfilling three functions:

■ *Scorekeeping*: capturing, recording, summarizing and reporting financial performance.
■ *Attention-directing*: drawing the attention of managers to, and assisting in the inter-

pretation of, business performance, particularly in terms of the comparison between actual and planned performance.

■ *Problem-solving*: identifying the best choice from a range of alternative actions.

In this book, we acknowledge the role of the scorekeeping function in Chapters 6 through 9, while emphasizing attention-directing and problem-solving as taking place through three inter-related functions (covered in Chapters 10 through 17), all part of the role of non-financial (marketing, operations, human resources, etc.) as well as financial managers:

■ *Planning*: establishing goals and strategies to achieve those goals.
■ *Decision-making*: using financial information to make decisions consistent with those goals and strategies.
■ *Control*: using financial information to maintain performance as close as possible to plan, or using the information to modify the plan itself.

Planning, decision-making and control are particularly relevant as increasingly businesses have been decentralized into many business units, where much of the planning, decision-making and control is focused. Managers need financial and non-financial information to develop and implement strategy by planning for the future (budgeting); making decisions about products, services, prices and what costs to incur (decision-making using cost information); and ensuring that plans are put into action and are achieved (control). This function is called **management accounting**.

This book is primarily concerned with the planning, decision-making and control aspects, i.e. management accounting. However, it begins by setting the role of the manager and the use of accounting information in the context of financial accounting.

A SHORT HISTORY OF ACCOUNTING

The history of accounting is intertwined with the development of trade between tribes and there are records of commercial transactions on stone tablets dating back to 3600 BC (Stone, 1969). The early accountants were 'scribes' who also practised law. Stone (1969) noted:

> In ancient Egypt in the pharaoh's central finance department . . . scribes prepared records of receipts and disbursements of silver, corn and other commodities. One recorded on papyrus the amount brought to the warehouse and another checked the emptying of the containers on the roof as it was poured into the storage building. Audit was performed by a third scribe who compared these two records. (p. 284)

However, accounting as we know it today began in the fourteenth century in the Italian city-states of Florence, Genoa and Venice as a result of the growth of maritime trade and banking institutions. The first bank with customer facilities opened in

Venice in 1149. The Lombards were Italian merchants who were established as money-lenders in England at the end of the twelfth century.

Balance sheets were evident from around 1400 and the Medici family (who were Lombards) had accounting records of 'cloth manufactured and sold'. The first treatise on accounting (although it was contained within a book on mathematics) was the work of a monk, Luca Pacioli, in 1494. The first professional accounting body was formed in Venice in 1581.

Much of the language of accounting is derived from Latin roots. 'Debtor' comes from the Latin *debitum*, something that is owed; 'assets' from the Latin *ad + satis*, to enough, i.e. to pay obligations; 'liability' from *ligare*, to bind; 'capital' from *caput*, a head (of wealth). Even 'account' derives initially from the Latin *computare*, to count, while 'profit' comes from *profectus*, advance or progress. 'Sterling' and 'shilling' came from the Italian *sterlino* and *scellino*, while the pre-decimal currency abbreviation 'LSD' (pounds, shillings and pence) stood for *lire, soldi, denarii*.

Chandler (1990) traced the development of the modern industrial enterprise from its agricultural and commercial roots as a result of the Industrial Revolution in the last half of the nineteenth century. By 1870, the leading industrial nations – the United States, Great Britain and Germany – accounted for two-thirds of the world's industrial output. One of the consequences of growth was the separation of ownership from management. Although the corporation, as distinct from its owners, had been in existence in Britain since 1650, the separation of ownership and control was enabled by the first British Companies Act, which formalized the law in relation to 'joint stock companies' and introduced the limited liability of shareholders during the 1850s. The London Stock Exchange had been formed earlier in 1773 by stockbrokers, who had previously worked from coffee houses.

The second consequence of growth was the creation of new organizational forms. Based on his extensive historical analysis, Chandler (1962) found that in large firms structure followed strategy and strategic growth and diversification led to the creation of decentralized, multidivisional corporations like General Motors, where remotely located managers made decisions on behalf of absent owners and central head office functions. Ansoff (1988) emphasized that success in the first 30 years of the mass-production era went to firms that had the lowest prices. However, in the 1930s General Motors 'triggered a shift from production to a market focus' (p. 11).

In large firms such as General Motors, budgets were developed to co-ordinate diverse activities. In the first decades of the twentieth century, the DuPont company developed a model to measure the return on investment (ROI). ROI (see Chapters 7, 14 and 15) was used to make capital investment decisions and to evaluate the performance of business units, including the managerial responsibility to use capital efficiently.

THE ROLE OF MANAGEMENT ACCOUNTING

The advent of mechanized production following the Industrial Revolution increased the size and complexity of production processes, which employed more people and required larger sums of capital to finance machinery. Accounting historians suggest that the increase in the number of limited companies that led to the separation of ownership from control caused an increase in attention to what was called 'cost accounting' (the forerunner of 'management accounting') in order to determine cost and exercise control by absent owners over their managers. Reflecting this emergence, the earlier title of management accountants was cost or works accountants. Typically situated in factories, these accountants tended to know the business and advised non-financial managers in relation to operational decisions. Cost accounting was concerned with determining the cost of an object, whether a product, an activity, a division of the organization or market segment. The first book on cost accounting is believed to be Garcke and Fell's *Factory Accounts*, which was published in 1897.

Historians have argued that the new corporate structures that were developed in the twentieth century – multidivisional organizations, conglomerates and multinationals – placed increased demands on accounting. These demands included divisional performance evaluation and budgeting. It has also been suggested that developments in cost accounting were driven by government demands for cost information during both World Wars. It appears that 'management accounting' is a term used only after the Second World War.

In their acclaimed book *Relevance Lost*, Johnson and Kaplan (1987) traced the development of management accounting from its origins in the Industrial Revolution supporting process-type industries such as textile and steel conversion, transportation and distribution. These systems were concerned with evaluating the efficiency of internal processes, rather than measuring organizational profitability. Financial reports were produced using a separate transactions-based system that reported financial performance. Johnson and Kaplan (1987) argued that by 1925 'virtually all management accounting practices used today had been developed' (p. 12).

They also described how the early manufacturing firms attempted to improve performance via economies of scale by reducing unit cost through increasing the volume of output. This led to a concern with measuring the efficiency of the production process. Calculating the cost of different products was unnecessary because the product range was homogeneous.

Over time, the product range expanded and businesses sought economies of scope through producing two or more products in a single facility. This led to the need for better information about how the mix of products could improve total profits. However, after 1900 the production of accounting information was largely for external reporting to shareholders and not to assist managerial decision making.

Johnson and Kaplan (1987) described how:

a management accounting system must provide timely and accurate information to facilitate efforts to control costs, to measure and improve productivity, and to devise improved production processes. The management accounting system must also report accurate product costs so that pricing decisions, introduction of new products, abandonment of obsolete products, and response to rival products can be made. (p. 4)

The Chartered Institute of Management Accountants' definition of the core activities of management accounting includes:

■ participation in the planning process at both strategic and operational levels, involving the establishment of policies and the formulation of budgets;

■ the initiation of and provision of guidance for management decisions, involving the generation, analysis, presentation and interpretation of relevant information;

■ contributing to the monitoring and control of performance through the provision of reports including comparisons of actual with budgeted performance, and their analysis and interpretation.

One of the earliest writers on management accounting described 'different costs for different purposes' (Clark, 1923). This theme was developed by one of the earliest texts on management accounting (Vatter, 1950). Vatter distinguished the information needs of managers from those of external shareholders and emphasized that it was preferable to get less precise data to managers quickly than complete information too late to influence decision-making. Johnson and Kaplan (1987) commented that even today, organizations

> with access to far more computational power ... rarely distinguish between information needed promptly for managerial control and information provided periodically for summary financial statements. (p. 161)

They argued that the developments in accounting theory in the first decades of the twentieth century came about by academics who

> emphasized simple decision-making models in highly simplified firms – those producing one or only a few products, usually in a one stage production process. The academics developed their ideas by logic and deductive reasoning. They did not attempt to study the problems actually faced by managers of organizations producing hundreds or thousands of products in complex production processes. (p. 175)

They concluded:

> Not surprisingly, in this situation actual management accounting systems provided few benefits to organizations. In some instances, the information reported by existing management accounting systems not only inhibited good decision-making by managers, it might actually have encouraged bad decisions. (p. 177)

Johnson and Kaplan (1987) described how the global competition that has taken place since the 1980s has left management accounting behind in terms of its decision usefulness. Developments such as total quality management, just-in-time inventory, computer-integrated manufacturing, shorter product life cycles (see Chapter 11) and the decline of manufacturing and rise of service industries have led to the need for 'accurate knowledge of product costs, excellent cost control, and coherent performance measurement' (p. 220). And 'the challenge for today's competitive environment is to develop new and more flexible approaches to the design of effective cost accounting, management control, and performance measurement systems' (p. 224).

RECENT DEVELOPMENTS IN MANAGEMENT ACCOUNTING

Partly as a result of the stimulus of *Relevance Lost* but perhaps more so as a consequence of rapidly changing business conditions, management accounting has moved beyond its traditional concern with a narrow range of numbers to incorporate wider issues of performance measurement and management. Management accounting is now implicated, to greater or lesser degrees in different organizations, with:

■ value-based management;
■ non-financial performance measurement systems;
■ quality management approaches;
■ activity-based management; and
■ strategic management accounting.

Value-based management is more fully described in Chapter 2, but is in brief a concern with improving the value of the business to its shareholders. Management accounting is implicated in this, as a fundamental role of non-financial managers is to make decisions that contribute to increasing the value of the business.

The limitations of accounting information, particularly as a lagging indicator of performance, have led to an increasing emphasis on non-financial performance measures, which are described more fully in Chapter 4. Non-financial measures are a major concern of both accountants and non-financial managers, as they tend to be leading indicators of the financial performance that will be reported at some future time.

Improving the quality of products and services is also a major concern, since advances in production technology and the need to improve performance by reducing waste have led to management tools such as total quality management (TQM), just-in-time (JIT), business process re-engineering (BPR) and continuous improvement processes such as Six Sigma and the Business Excellence model. Management accounting has a role to play in these techniques (introduced in Chapters 11 and 17) and non-financial managers need to understand the relationships between accounting and new management techniques.

Activity-based management is an approach that emphasizes the underlying business processes that are required to produce goods and services and the need to identify the drivers or causes of those activities in order to be able to budget for and control costs more effectively. Activity-based approaches are introduced throughout Part III.

Strategic management accounting, which is described more fully in Chapter 4, is an attempt to shift the perceptions of accountants and non-financial managers from an inward-looking to an outward-looking one, recognizing the need to look beyond the business along the value chain to its suppliers and customers and to seek ways of achieving and maintaining competitive advantage.

These changes to the narrow view of accountants, from 'bean-counters' to more active participants in formulating and implementing business strategy, have been accompanied by a shift in the collection, reporting and analysis of routine financial information from accountants to non-financial line managers. This decentring of accounting is evidenced by the delegation of responsibility for budgets and cost control to line managers and is the underlying reason that non-financial managers need a better understanding of accounting information and how that information can be used in decision-making.

A CRITICAL PERSPECTIVE

Although the concepts and assumptions underlying accounting are yet to be introduced, having begun this book with an introduction to accounting history it is worthwhile considering a contrasting viewpoint. While this viewpoint is one that may not be accepted by many practising managers, it is worth knowing, because it does lie at the very basis of the capitalist economic system in which we live, and in which accounting plays such an important role.

The Marxist historian Hobsbawm (1962) argued that colonialism had been created by the cotton industry that dominated the UK economy, and this resulted in a shift from domestic production to factory production. Sales increased but profits shrank, so labour (which was three times the cost of materials) was replaced by mechanization during the Industrial Revolution.

Entrepreneurs started with borrowings and small items of machinery and growth was largely financed by borrowings. The Industrial Revolution produced 'such vast quantities and at such rapidly diminishing cost, as to be no longer dependent on existing demand, but to create its own market' (Hobsbawm, 1962, p. 32).

Advances in mass production followed the development of the assembly line, supported by railways and shipping to transport goods, and communications through the electric telegraph. At the same time, agriculture diminished in importance. Due to the appetite of the railways for iron and steel, coal, heavy machinery, labour and capital investment, 'the comfortable and rich classes accumulated income so fast and in such vast quantities as to exceed all available possibilities of spending and investment' (Hobsbawm, 1962, p. 45).

While the rich accumulated profits, labour was exploited with wages at subsistence levels. Labour had to learn how to work, unlike agriculture or craft industries, in a manner suited to industry, and the result was a draconian master/servant relationship. In the 1840s a depression led to unemployment and high food prices and 1848 saw the rise of the labouring poor in European cities, who threatened both the weak and obsolete regimes and the rich.

This resulted in a clash between the political (French) and industrial (British) revolutions, the 'triumph of bourgeois-liberal capitalism' and the domination of the globe by a few western regimes, especially the British in the mid-nineteenth century, which became a 'world hegemony' (Hobsbawm, 1962).

This 'global triumph' of capitalism in the 1850s (Hobsbawm, 1975) was a consequence of the combination of cheap capital and rising prices. Stability and prosperity overtook political questions about the legitimacy of existing dynasties and technology cheapened manufactured products. There was high demand but the cost of living did not fall, so labour became dominated by the interests of the new owners of the means of production. 'Economic liberalism' became the recipe for economic growth as the market ruled labour and helped national economic expansion. Industrialization made wealth and industrial capacity decisive in international power, especially in the US, Japan and Germany.

This 'British' capitalist system was exported throughout the world, not least with the support of a colonial expansionist Empire that lent large sums of money in return for adopting the British system. This system has since been taken over by multinational corporations, largely based in the United States.

Armstrong (1987) traced the historical factors behind the comparative (in relation to other professions) pre-eminence of accountants in British management hierarchies and the emphasis on financial control. He concluded that accounting controls were installed by accountants as a result of their power base in global capital markets, which was achieved through their role in the allocation of the profit surplus to share-holders. Armstrong argued that mergers led to control problems that were tackled by:

> American management consultants who tended to recommend the multidivisional form of organization ... [which] entirely divorce headquarters management from operations. Functional departments and their managers are subjected to a battery of financial indicators and budgetary controls ... [and] a subordination of opera-tional to financial decision-making and a major influx of accountants into senior management positions. (p. 433)

Roberts (1996) suggested that organizational accounting embodies the separation of instrumental and moral consequences, which is questionable. He argued:

> The mystification of accounting information helps to fix, elevate and then impose upon others its own particular instrumental interests, without regard to the wider social and environmental consequences of the pursuit of such interests. Accounting thus serves as a vehicle whereby others are called to account, while the interests it embodies escape such accountability. (p. 59)

This is a more critical perspective than that associated with the traditional notion of ac-counting as a report to shareholders and managers, which is a result of the historical development of capitalism in the West.

CONCLUSION

While this book is designed to help non-financial managers understand the tools and techniques of accounting, it is also intended to make readers think critically about the role of accounting and the limitations of accounting, some of which have been historically defined. One intention is to reinforce to readers that:

> accounting information provides a window through which the real activities of the organization may be monitored, but it should be noted also that other windows are used that do not rely upon accounting information. (Otley and Berry, 1994, p. 46)

REFERENCES

American Accounting Association (1996). *A Statement of Basic Accounting Theory*. Saratosa, FL: American Accounting Association.

Ansoff, H. I. (1988). *The New Corporate Strategy*. New York: John Wiley & Sons.

Armstrong, P. (1987). The rise of accounting controls in British capitalist enterprises. *Accounting, Organizations and Society*, **12**(5), 415–36.

Boland, R. J. and Schultze, U. (1996). Narrating accountability: Cognition and the production of the accountable self. In R. Munro and J. Mouritsen (eds), *Accountability: Power, Ethos and the Technologies of Managing*, London: International Thomson Business Press.

Chandler, A. D. J. (1962). *Strategy and Structure: Chapters in the History of the American Industrial Enterprise*. Cambridge, MA: Harvard University Press.

Chandler, A. D. J. (1990). *Scale and Scope: The Dynamics of Industrial Capitalism*. Cambridge, MA: Harvard University Press.

Clark, J. M. (1923). *Studies in the Economics of Overhead Costs*. Chicago, IL: University of Chicago Press.

Hobsbawm, E. (1962). *The Age of Revolution: Europe 1789–1848*. London: Phoenix Press.

Hobsbawm, E. (1975). *The Age of Capital: 1848–1875*. London: Phoenix Press.

Hoskin, K. (ed.) (1996). The 'awful idea of accountability': Inscribing people into the measurement of objects. In R. Munro and J. Mouritsen (eds), *Accountability: Power, Ethos and the Technologies of Managing*, London: International Thomson Business Press.

Johnson, H. T. and Kaplan, R. S. (1987). *Relevance Lost: The Rise and Fall of Management Accounting*. Boston, MA: Harvard Business School Press.

Otley, D. T. and Berry, A. J. (1994). Case study research in management accounting and control. *Management Accounting Research*, **5**, 45–65.

Roberts, J. (ed.) (1996). From discipline to dialogue: Individualizing and socializing forms of accountability. In R. Munro and J. Mouritsen (eds), *Accountability: Power, Ethos and the Technologies of Managing*, London: International Thomson Business Press.

Stone, W. E. (1969). Antecedents of the accounting profession. *The Accounting Review*, April, 284–91.

Vatter, W. J. (1950). *Managerial Accounting*. New York, NY: Prentice Hall.

2 ACCOUNTING AND ITS RELATIONSHIP TO SHAREHOLDER VALUE AND BUSINESS STRUCTURE

This chapter develops the two themes that were identified in Chapter 1 as being important to the content of this book: the separation of ownership from control and the divisionalized form of business. The first is implicated in the emergence of capital markets and value-based management, the subject of this chapter, in which several tools for measuring shareholder value are described. The link between shareholder value, strategy and accounting is then introduced.

The second theme is the shift towards a decentralized, multidivisional business structure and the measurement and management of divisional (i.e. business unit) performance that has influenced the development of management accounting. This chapter introduces the structure of business organizations, with emphasis on the divisionalized structure and decentralized profit responsibility. Part III develops the divisional performance issue in much greater detail.

The chapter concludes with a critical perspective that questions the focus on shareholders alone and raises issues concerning accounting in the divisionalized organization.

CAPITAL AND PRODUCT MARKETS

Since the seventeenth century, companies have been formed by shareholders in order to consolidate resources and invest in opportunities. Shareholders had *limited liability* through which their personal liability in the event of business failure was limited to their investment in shares. Shareholders appointed directors to manage the business, who in turn employed managers. Shareholders have few direct rights in relation to the conduct of the business. Their main powers are to elect the directors and appoint the auditors in an annual general meeting of shareholders. They are also entitled to an annual report containing details of the company's financial performance (see Chapters 7 and 9).

The market in which investors buy and sell the shares of companies is called the capital market, which is normally associated with the Stock Exchange. Companies obtain funds raised from shareholders (equity) and borrowings from financiers (debt). Both of these constitute the capital employed in the business.

The cost of capital represents the cost incurred by the organization to fund all its investments, comprising the cost of equity and the cost of debt weighted by the mix of debt and equity. The cost of debt is interest, which is the price charged by the lender. The cost of equity is partly dividend and partly capital growth, because most shareholders expect both regular income from profits (the dividend) and an increase in the value of their shares over time in the capital market. Thus the different costs of each form of capital, weighted by the proportions of different forms of debt and equity, constitute the weighted average cost of capital. The management of the business relationship with capital markets is called *financial management* or corporate finance.

Companies use their capital to invest in technologies, people and materials in order to make, buy and sell products or services to customers. This is called the product market. The focus of shareholder wealth, according to Rappaport (1998), is to obtain funds at competitive rates from capital markets and invest those funds to exploit imperfections in product markets. Where this takes place, shareholder wealth is increased through dividends and increases in the share price. The 1990s saw a growing concern with the role of accounting in improving shareholder wealth.

The relationship between capital markets and product markets is shown in Figure 2.1.

VALUE-BASED MANAGEMENT

Since the mid-1980s, there has been more and more emphasis on increasing the value of the business to its shareholders. Traditionally, business performance has been measured through accounting ratios such as return on capital employed (ROCE), return on investment (ROI), earnings per share and so on (which are described in Chapter 7). However, it has been argued that these are historical rather than current measures, and they vary between companies as a result of different accounting treatments.

Rappaport (1998) described how companies with strong cash flows diversified in the mid-twentieth century, often into uneconomic businesses, which led to the 'value gap' – the difference between the market value of the shares and the value of the business if it had been managed to maximize shareholder value. The consequence was the takeover movement and subsequent asset stripping of the 1980s, which provided a powerful incentive for managers to focus on creating value for shareholders. The takeover movement itself led to problems as high acquisition premiums (the excess paid over and above the calculated value of the business, i.e. the goodwill) were paid to the owners and financed by high levels of debt. During the 1990s institutional investors (pension funds, insurance companies, investment trusts etc.), through their dominance of share ownership, increased their pressure on management to improve the financial performance of companies.

Value-based management (VBM) emphasizes shareholder value, on the assumption that this is the primary goal of every business. VBM approaches include total

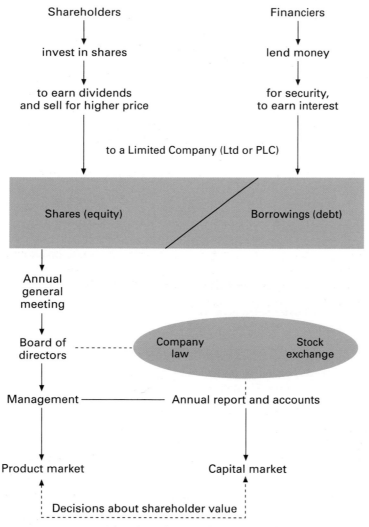

Figure 2.1 Capital and product market structure and interaction

shareholder return, market value added, shareholder value added and economic value added. Recent research into the use of value-based management approaches by UK companies is covered by Cooper *et al.* (2001).

Total shareholder return (TSR) compares the dividends received by shareholders and the increase in the share price with the original shareholder investment, expressing the TSR as a percentage of the initial investment.

Market value added (MVA) is the difference between total market capitalization (number of shares issued times share price plus the market value of debt) and the total capital invested in the business by debt and equity providers. This is a measure of the value generated by managers for shareholders.

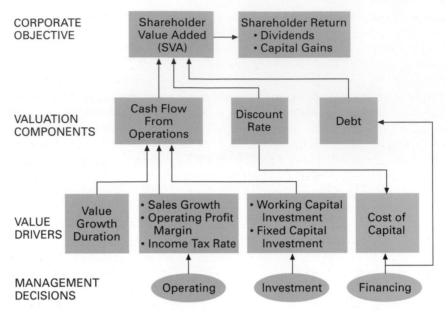

Figure 2.2   The shareholder value network

Reprinted from Rappaport, A. (1998). *Creating Shareholder Value: A Guide for Managers and Investors*. (Revd. edn). New York, NY: Free Press.

Rappaport (1998) coined *shareholder value added (SVA)* to refer to the increase in shareholder value over time. He defines shareholder value as the economic value of an investment, which can be calculated by using the cost of capital to discount forecast future cash flows (which he called *free cash flows*) into present values (discounted cash flow techniques are described in detail in Chapter 14). The business must generate profits in product markets that exceed the cost of capital in the capital market for value to be created (if not, shareholder value is eroded).

Rappaport developed a shareholder value network (see Figure 2.2). Through this diagram, he identified seven drivers of shareholder value: sales growth rate, operating profit margin, income tax rate, working capital investment, fixed capital investment, cost of capital and forecast duration. Managers make three types of decisions that influence these value drivers and lead to shareholder value:

■ Operating decisions – product mix, pricing, promotion, customer service etc., which are then reflected in the sales growth rate, operating profit margin and income tax rate.

■ Investment decisions – in both inventory and capacity, which are then reflected in both working capital and fixed capital investment.

■ Financing decisions – the mix of debt and equity and the choice of financial instrument determine the cost of capital, which is assessed by capital markets in terms of business risk.

The value growth duration is the estimated number of years over which the return from investments is expected to exceed the cost of capital.

The seven value drivers determine the cash flow from operations, the level of debt and the cost of capital, all of which determine shareholder value. A detrimental consequence of the emphasis on shareholder value is that it has led to a continued focus on short-term financial performance at the expense of longer-term strategy.

Economic Value Added^{TM} (EVA) is a financial performance measure developed by consultants Stern Stewart & Co. It claims to capture the economic profit of a business that leads to shareholder value creation. In simple terms, EVA is net operating profit after deducting a charge to cover the opportunity cost of the capital invested in the business (when by taking one action you lose the opportunity to undertake any alternative; described in more detail in Chapter 3). EVA's 'economic profit' is the amount by which earnings exceed (or fall short of) the minimum rate of return that shareholders and financiers could get by investing in other securities with a comparable risk (see Stern Stewart's website at www.sternstewart.com).

EVA accepts the assumption that the primary financial objective of any business is to maximize the wealth of its shareholders. The value of the business depends on the extent to which investors expect future profits to be greater or less than the cost of capital. Returns over and above the cost of capital increase shareholder wealth, while returns below the cost of capital erode shareholder wealth. Stern Stewart argues that managers understand this measure because it is based on operating profits. By introducing a notional charge based on assets held by the business, managers (whether at a corporate or divisional level) manage those assets as well as the profit generated.

EVA also has its critics. For example, the calculation of EVA allows up to 164 adjustments to reported accounting profits in order to remove distortions caused by arbitrary accounting rules and estimates the risk-adjusted cost of capital, both of which can be argued as subjective, although Stern Stewart argues that most organizations need only about a dozen of these. The increase in shareholder value is reflected in compensation strategies for managers whose goals, argues Stern Stewart, are aligned to increasing shareholder wealth through bonus and share option schemes that are paid over a period of time to ensure consistent future performance.

SHAREHOLDER VALUE ANALYSIS

Shareholder (or strategic) value analysis emphasizes the processes by which shareholder value is achieved. In practice, the pursuit of shareholder value (or economic value added) can be achieved through the introduction of new or redesigned products and services; the management of costs; the development of performance measurement systems; and through improved decision-making. This form of value analysis compares cost with the value to the customer. Consequently, improving shareholder value is inextricably linked with both strategy and accounting.

ACCOUNTING AND STRATEGY

This book treats accounting as part of the broader business context of strategy, marketing, operations and human resources. The focus of accounting in business organizations is shareholder value – increasing the value of the business to its share-holders – through dividends from profits and/or through capital growth. Strategy both influences and is influenced by shareholder value. Strategy is reflected in the functional business areas of marketing, operations and human resources, through the actions the business wants to take to achieve, maintain and improve competitive advantage. The relationship between these elements is shown in Figure 2.3.

Financial management (which is outside the scope of this book) is concerned with raising funds from shareholders or financiers to provide the capital the business needs to sell and produce goods and services. Financial accounting represents the stewardship function, that managers are accountable to those with a financial interest in the business and produce financial reports to satisfy that accountability (Chapters 6 through 9). Management accounting provides the information for planning, decision-making and control (Chapters 10 through 17). Therefore, the main content of this book is the interaction between the functional areas of marketing, operations and human resources – driven by strategy – and how accounting provides a set of tools and techniques to assist functional managers. Management accounting both influences and is influenced by the functional areas and by business strategy.

The importance of strategy for management accounting and the information it provides is that a strategic perspective involves taking a longer-term view about the business than is usually provided by traditional accounting reports. Management accounting comprises a set of tools and techniques to support planning, decision-making and control in business organizations. Accounting is – or at least should be – integrated with business strategy. However, these same accounting tools and techniques can be used to help evaluate the performance of customers, suppliers and competitors in order to improve competitive advantage. This is called strategic management accounting, which is described in Chapter 4.

Accounting should also extend beyond a narrow concern with financial measurement and encompass non-financial performance measurement, a subject of steadily increasing importance for those managers who are responsible for achieving performance targets, as well as for accountants (performance measurement is also described in Chapter 4).

Strategy is concerned with long-term direction, achieving and maintaining competitive advantage, identifying the scope and boundaries of the organization and matching the activities of the organization to its environment. Strategy is also about building on resources and competences to create new opportunities and take advantage

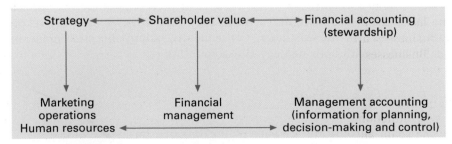

Figure 2.3   Shareholder value, strategy and accounting

of those opportunities and manage change within the organization. There is also a link between strategy and operational decisions in order to turn strategy formulation into strategy implementation (for a fuller description, see for example Johnson and Scholes, 1997).

An economic perspective is added by Grant (1998), who saw the value created by firms distributed among customers, suppliers and equity risk-takers. In order to provide this value, business firms establish profit as the single dominant objective. The purpose of strategy 'is to pursue profit over the long term' (p. 34). Strategy is thus linked to performance by setting performance targets (both financial and non-financial) for the business as a whole and for individual business units and then measuring performance against those targets (this is the subject of Chapter 4).

It is to the divisionalized organizational form that we now turn.

STRUCTURE OF BUSINESS ORGANIZATIONS

Organizations are typically considered to be of three types:

- the private sector, comprising businesses whose prime goal is profit;
- the public sector, which is government funded (through various kinds of taxation), providing services for the public, such as in health, education, law and order etc.; and
- the 'third sector' of not-for-profit (or often, non-profit-distributing) organizations, providing a range of charitable or social services, funded by donations, lottery grants etc.

The accounting described in this book is primarily concerned with for-profit businesses, although many of the concepts are equally applicable to the other two sectors. Business organizations can be further subdivided into a number of major types:

- agriculture, or primary production;
- manufacturing, or secondary production;
- services, or tertiary production.

Again, our concern is with all businesses other than agriculture as the means of production and the accounting requirements of agriculture are significantly different from the latter two, which in any event dominate the economy. Manufacturing and service businesses are concerned with satisfying customer demand for products or services. Businesses produce products/services through a variety of organizational forms, but predominantly through either a functional structure or a divisionalized structure.

The *functional structure* locates decision-making at the top of the corporate hierarchy, with functional responsibilities for marketing, operations, human resources, finance and so on allocated to *departments*, as shown in the typical organization chart in Figure 2.4.

Figure 2.4 Functional organization chart

In the functional structure, accounting provides a *staff* function to the *line* functions, simplified here as marketing, operations and human resources. Accounting knowledge tends to be centralized in the accounting department, which collects, produces, reports and analyses accounting information on behalf of its (internal) customer departments.

The functional structure may be suitable for smaller organizations with a narrow geographic spread and a limited product/service range, but it is not generally suitable for larger organizations.

The *divisional structure* is based on a head office with corporate specialists supporting the chief executive, with divisions established for major elements of the business. These divisions may be based on geographic territories or different products/services, and each division will typically have responsibility for all the functional areas: marketing, operations, human resources and accounting. A typical divisional structure is shown in Figure 2.5.

The advantage of the divisional structure is that while planning is centrally co-ordinated, the implementation of plans, decision-making and control is devolved to local management who should have a better understanding of their local operations. The divisions are often referred to as strategic business units (SBUs) to describe their devolved responsibility for a segment of the business. These SBUs are, in accounting, termed responsibility centres.

Responsibility centres, through their managers, are held responsible for achieving certain standards of performance (this is covered in more detail in Chapter 15). There are three types of responsibility centres:

- cost centres, which are responsible for controlling costs;
- profit centres, which are responsible for achieving profit targets; and

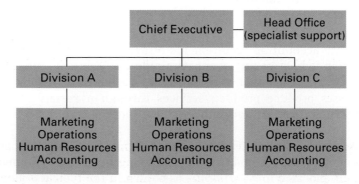

Figure 2.5 Divisional organization chart

■ investment centres, which are responsible for achieving an adequate return on the capital invested in the division.

Management within divisions will carry out a significant function in analysing and interpreting financial information as part of their local management responsibilities, typically supported by locally based accounting support staff. Accounting influences and is influenced by the structure adopted and the extent of managerial responsibility for business unit performance, a subject that will be developed further throughout Part III but in particular in Chapter 15, which considers how the performance of business units and their managers can be evaluated.

Emmanuel *et al.* (1990) described organizational structure as:

> a potent form of control because, by arranging people in a hierarchy with defined patterns of authority and responsibility, a great deal of their behaviour can be influenced or even pre-determined. (p. 39)

Child (1972) defined organizational structure as 'the formal allocation of work roles and the administrative mechanisms to control and integrate work activities' (p. 2), emphasizing that structure depends on the decision-makers' evaluation of environmental impacts, the standard of required performance and the level of performance actually achieved. This stresses the role of decision-makers, defined as the 'power-holding group' (p. 13).

Galbraith and Nathanson (1976) suggested that the choice of organizational form was the result of choices about five design variables: task, people, structure, reward systems and information and decision processes. These choices should be consistent with the firm's product-market strategy, i.e. there should be 'fit' or 'congruence'. Galbraith and Nathanson applied Chandler's (1962) four growth strategies – expansion of volume, geographic dispersion, vertical integration and product diversification – to see how each affects the form of organizational structure, based on Chandler's thesis that structure follows strategy. They argued:

> Variation in strategy should be matched with variation in processes and systems as well as in structure, in order for organizations to implement strategies successfully. (p. 10)

Galbraith and Nathanson further built on Chandler's research, adding that diversification leads to multidivisional forms, with competition as an important variable.

A CRITICAL PERSPECTIVE

The shareholder value movement has subsumed much consideration of the wider accountability of business to other stakeholders. Shareholders' interests dominate business and accountants occupy a privileged position as those who establish the rules and report business performance. This can be seen as an historical development.

Stakeholder theory looks beyond shareholders to those groups who influence, or are influenced by, the organization. Shareholders are not representative of society and stakes are held in the organization by employees, customers, suppliers, government and the community. Stakeholder theory is concerned with how the power of stakeholders, with their competing interests, is managed by the organization in terms of its broader accountability.

Dermer (1988) suggested a broader view of organizations with interdependent but conflicting stakeholders, arguing:

> Cognitive and/or political models view organizations as non-goal-oriented, non-instrumental social systems, enmeshed in broader socio-political contexts. (p. 29)

Dermer contrasted the presumption of managerial authority and unitary purpose with a pluralistic governance model comprising four elements: leadership (management); citizenship (stakeholders); institutions (formal and informal patterns of relating); and ideologies (patterns of belief).

Given that accountability (as we saw in Chapter 1) is the duty to provide an explanation – an account – of the actions for which an organization is responsible, this implies a *social accounting* and a *right to information* by various stakeholder groups in a democracy (which is discussed in Chapter 9).

Strategy is also open to criticism. Mintzberg (1994) was critical of strategic planning because it is a 'calculating style of management' resulting in strategies that are extrapolated from the past or copied from others. Rather, Mintzberg saw some strategy as deliberate but other strategy as an emergent process, which should lead to learning. He argued:

> Strategic planning often spoils strategic thinking, causing managers to confuse real vision with the manipulation of numbers. (p. 107)

A critical stance can also be applied to the divisionalized form of organization. Roberts and Scapens (1985) argued that in a divisionalized company there is distance between the division and the head office, such that 'the context within which accounting information is gathered will typically be quite different from the context in which it is interpreted' (p. 452). This may result in manipulating the appearance of accounting reports. Roberts and Scapens concluded:

> The image of an organization which is given through Accounts will be from a particular point of view, at a particular point in time and will be selective in its focus. Events, actions, etc. which are significant for the organization may be out of focus, or not in the picture at all ... the image conveyed by the Accounts may misrepresent the actual flow of events and practices that it is intended to record. (p. 454)

The separation of management from control, the creation of decentralized business units and the pursuit of shareholder value imply a particular goal-oriented, economic and rational theory of management behaviour and organizational action. We will consider the theoretical assumptions behind this perspective in Chapters 4 and 5.

CONCLUSION

While Chapter 1 provided an introduction to accounting, its history and the changing role of the management accountant, this chapter has provided the context in which the changing role of accounting and the accountant has taken shape. First, we considered the importance of capital markets and how they dictate the drive for shareholder value-based management. Second, we described how the strategy that is the result of the shareholder value approach has led to the divisionalized form of organization that dictates much of the way in which management accounting is organized. Finally, we have added a critical perspective that challenges shareholder value with a stakeholder view and raises concerns about strategy and divisionalization that will be developed in later chapters.

REFERENCES

Chardler, A. D. J. (1962). *Strategy and Structure: Chapters in the History of the American Industrial Enterprise.* Cambridge, MA: Harvard University Press.

Child, J. (1972). Organizational structure, environment and performance: The role of strategic choice. *Sociology*, **6**, 1–22.

Cooper, S., Crowther, D., Davies, M. and Davis, E. W. (2001). *Shareholder or Stakeholder Value: The Development of Indicators for the Control and Measurement of Performance.* London: Chartered Institute of Management Accountants.

Dermer, J. (1988). Control and organizational order. *Accounting, Organizations and Society*, **13**(1), 25–36.

Emmanuel, C., Otley, D. and Merchant, K. (1990). *Accounting for Management Control.* (2nd edn). London: Chapman & Hall.

Galbraith, J. R. and Nathanson, D. A. (1976). *Strategy Implementation: The Role of Structure and Process.* St Paul, MN: West Publishing Company.

Grant, R. M. (1998). *Contemporary Strategy Analysis: Concepts, Techniques, Applications.* Oxford: Blackwell Publishers.

Hopper, T., Otley, D. and Scapens, B. (2001). British management accounting research: Whence and whither: Opinions and recollections. *British Accounting Review*, **33**, 263–91.

Johnson, G. and Scholes, K. (1997). *Exploring Corporate Strategy.* London: Prentice Hall.

Mintzberg, H. (1994). The fall and rise of strategic planning. *Harvard Business Review*, Jan–Feb, 107–14.

Otley, D. (2001). Extending the boundaries of management accounting research: Developing systems for performance management. *British Accounting Review*, **33**, 243–61.

Rappaport, A. (1998). *Creating Shareholder Value: A Guide for Managers and Investors.* (Revd edn). New York, NY: Free Press.

Roberts, J. and Scapens, R. (1985). Accounting systems and systems of accountability – Understanding accounting practices in their organizational contexts. *Accounting, Organizations and Society*, **10**(4), 443–56.

3

RECORDING FINANCIAL TRANSACTIONS AND THE LIMITATIONS OF ACCOUNTING

In order to understand the scorekeeping process, we need to understand how accounting captures information that is subsequently used for planning, decision-making and control purposes. This chapter describes how business events are recorded as transactions into an accounting system using the double-entry method that is the foundation of accounting. In this chapter we also show how the principles underlying accounting can limit the usefulness of accounting information as a management tool. Finally, the chapter introduces the notion of cost, and how cost may be interpreted in multiple ways.

BUSINESS EVENTS, TRANSACTIONS AND THE ACCOUNTING SYSTEM

Businesses exist to make a profit. They do this by producing goods and services and selling those goods and services at a price that covers their cost. Conducting business involves a number of *business events* such as buying equipment, purchasing goods and services, paying expenses, making sales, distributing goods and services etc. In accounting terms, each of these business events is a transaction. A **transaction** is the financial description of each business event.

It is important to recognize that transactions are a financial representation of the business event, measured in monetary terms. This is only one perspective on business events, albeit the one considered most important for accounting purposes. A broader view is that business events can also be recorded in non-financial terms, such as measures of product/service quality, speed of delivery, customer satisfaction etc. These non-financial performance measures (which are described in detail in Chapter 4) are important elements of business events that are not captured by financial transactions. This is a limitation of accounting as a tool of business decision-making.

Each transaction is recorded on a **source document** that forms the basis for recording in a business's accounting system. Examples of source documents are invoices and cheques. The **accounting system**, typically computer based (except for very small businesses), comprises a set of accounts that summarize the transactions that have been recorded on source documents and entered into the accounting system. Accounts can be considered as 'buckets' within the accounting system containing similar transactions.

There are four types of accounts:

- Assets: things the business *owns*.
- Liabilities: debts the business *owes*.
- Income: the *revenue* generated from the *sale* of goods or services.
- Expenses: the *costs* incurred in *producing* the goods and services.

The main difference between these categories is that business profit is calculated as

$$profit = income - expenses$$

while the capital of the business (the owner's investment) is calculated as

$$capital = assets - liabilities$$

Financial reports – the Income Statement (or Profit and Loss account) and Balance Sheet (see Chapter 6) – are produced from the information in the accounts in the accounting system. Figure 3.1 shows the process of recording and reporting transactions in an accounting system.

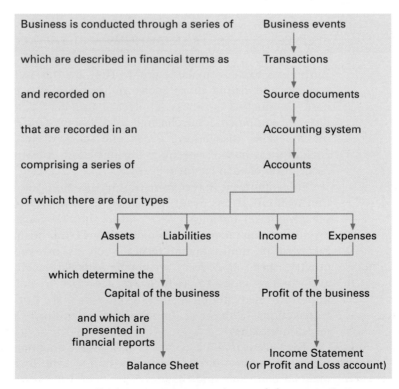

Figure 3.1 Business events, transactions and the accounting system

THE DOUBLE ENTRY: RECORDING TRANSACTIONS

Businesses use a system of accounting called double entry, which derives from the late fifteenth-century Italian city-states (see Chapter 1). The double entry means that every business transaction affects two accounts. Those accounts may *increase* or *decrease*. Accountants record the increases or decreases as debits or credits, but it is not necessary for non-accountants to understand this distinction.

Transactions may take place in one of two forms:

■ *Cash*: If the business *sells* goods/services for cash, the double entry is an increase in income and an increase in the bank account (an asset). If the business *buys* goods/services for cash, either an asset or an expense will increase (depending on what is bought) and the bank account will decrease.

■ *Credit*: If the business *sells* goods/services on credit, the double entry is an increase in debts owed *to* the business (called debtors, an asset) and an increase in income. If the business *buys* goods/services on credit, either an asset or an expense will increase (depending on what is bought) and the debts owed *by* the business will increase (called creditors, a liability).

When goods are bought, they become an asset called inventory (or stock). When the same goods are sold, there are two transactions:

1 The sale, either by cash or credit, as described above; and
2 The transfer of the cost of those goods, now sold, from inventory to an expense, called cost of sales.

In this way, the profit is the difference between the *price* at which the goods were sold (1 above) and the purchase *cost* of the same goods (2 above). Importantly, the purchase of goods into inventory does not affect profit until the goods are sold.

To record transactions, we need to decide:

■ what type of account is affected (asset, liability, income or expense); and
■ whether the transaction increases or decreases that account.

Some examples of business transactions and how the double entry affects the accounting system are shown in Table 3.1.

The accounts are all contained within a ledger, which is simply a collection of all the different accounts for the business. The ledger would summarize the transactions for each account, as shown in Table 3.2.

In the example in Table 3.2 there would be a separate account for each type of expense (wages, cost of sales, advertising), but for ease of presentation these accounts have been placed in a single column. The ledger is the source of the financial reports that present the performance of the business. However, the ledger would also contain the balance of each account brought forward from the previous period. In our simple example, assume that the business commenced with £50,000 in the bank account

Table 3.1   Business transactions and the double entry

Business event	Transaction	Source document	Accounts affected	Type of account	Increse or decrease	
Install new equipment for production	Buy equipment for cash £25,000	Cheque	Equipment	Asset	Increase	£25,000
			Bank	Asset	Decrease	£25,000
Receive stock of goods for resale	Purchase stock on credit £15,000	Invoice from supplier	Inventory	Asset	Increase	£15,000
			Creditor	Liability	Increase	£15,000
Pay weekly wages	Pay wages £3,000	Cheque	Wages	Expense	Increase	£3,000
			Bank	Asset	Decrease	£3,000
Sell goods to customer from stock	Sell stock on credit £9,000	Invoice to customer	Debtors	Asset	Increase	£9,000
			Sales	Income	Increase	£9,000
Deliver goods from stock	The goods that were sold for £9,000 cost £4,000 to buy	Goods delivery note	Cost of sales	Expense	Increase	£4,000
			Inventory	Asset	Decrease	£4,000
Advertising	Pay £1,000 for advertising	Cheque	Advertising	Expense	Increase	£1,000
			Bank	Asset	Decrease	£1,000
Receive payment from customer for earlier sale on credit	Receive £4,000 from debtor	Bank deposit	Bank	Asset	Increase	£4,000
			Debtor	Asset	Decrease	£4,000
Pay supplier for goods previously bought on credit	Pay £9,000 to creditor	Cheque	Bank	Asset	Decrease	£9,000
			Creditor	Liability	Decrease	£9,000

that had been contributed by the owner (the owner's *capital*). Table 3.3 shows the effect of the opening balances.

EXTRACTING FINANCIAL INFORMATION FROM THE ACCOUNTING SYSTEM

To produce financial reports we need to separate the accounts for income and expenses from those for assets and liabilities. In this example, we would produce a Profit and Loss based on the income and expenses:

Income		9,000
Less expenses:		
Cost of goods sold	4,000	
Wages	3,000	
Advertising	1,000	8,000
	————	————
Profit		1,000

Table 3.2 Summarizing business transactions in a ledger

Account transaction	Asset equipment	Asset inventory	Asset debtor	Asset bank	Liability: creditors	Income: sales	Expenses
Buy equipment for cash £25,000	+25,000			−25,000			
Purchase stock on credit £15,000		+15,000			+15,000		
Pay wages £3,000				−3,000			+3,000
Sell stock on credit £9,000			+9,000			+9,000	
The goods that were sold for £9,000 cost £4,000 to buy		−4,000					+4,000
Pay advertising £1,000				−1,000			+1,000
Receive £4,000 from debtor			−4,000	+4,000			
Pay £9,000 to creditor				−9,000	−9,000		
Total of transactions for this period	+25,000	+11,000	+5,000	−34,000	+6,000	+9,000	+8,000

Table 3.3 Summarizing business transactions with opening balances in a ledger

Account	Capital	Asset equipment	Asset inventory	Asset debtor	Asset bank	Liability: creditors	Income: sales	Expenses
Investment by owner	+50,000				+50,000			
Totals of transactions for this period		+25,000	+11,000	+5,000	−34,000	+6,000	+9,000	+8,000
Totals of each account at end of period	+50,000	+25,000	+1,000	+5,000	+16,000	+6,000	+9,000	+8,000

The Balance Sheet lists the assets and liabilities of the business, as shown in Table 3.4.

The Balance Sheet must *balance*, i.e. assets are equal to liabilities. Although shown separately, capital is a type of liability as it is owed by the business to its owners. The

Table 3.4   Balance sheet

Assets		Liabilities	
Equipment	25,000	Creditors	6,000
Inventory	11,000	Capital –	
Debtors	5,000	Owner's original investment	50,000
Bank	16,000	Plus profit for period	1,000
		Total capital	51,000
Total assets	57,000	Total liabilities plus capital	57,000

double-entry system records the profit earned by the business as an addition to the owner's investment in the business:

$$\text{assets} = \text{liabilities} + \text{capital}$$

This is called the **accounting equation**. However, a more common presentation of the Balance Sheet is in a vertical format, as follows:

Assets:
Equipment   25,000
Inventory   11,000
Debtors   5,000
Bank   16,000
                                      57,000
Less liabilities:
Creditors   6,000
                                      51,000

Capital:
Owner's original investment   50,000
Plus profit for period   1,000
                                      51,000

The accounting equation can therefore be restated as:

$$\text{capital}(£51,000) = \text{assets}(£57,000) - \text{liabilities}(£6,000)$$

There are some important points to note about the above example:

1   The purchase of equipment of £25,000 has not affected profit (although we will consider depreciation in Chapter 6).
2   Profit is not the same as cash flow. Although there has been a profit of £1,000, the bank balance has reduced by £34,000 (from £50,000 to £16,000).
3   Most of the cash has gone into the new equipment (£25,000), but some has gone

into working capital (again, this is covered in Chapter 6). Working capital is the investment in assets (less liabilities) that continually revolve in and out of the bank, comprising debtors, inventory, creditors and the bank balance itself (in this case £32,000 less £6,000 = £26,000).

The distinction between profit, cash flow and capital investment – the purchase of assets – is a crucial one for accounting. Whether a payment is treated as an expense (which affects profit) or as a Balance Sheet item (called capitalizing the expense, and therefore not affecting profit) is important, as it can have a significant impact on profit, which is one of the main measures of business performance.

Both the Income Statement (or Profit and Loss account) and the Balance Sheet are described in more detail in Chapter 6. In financial reporting, as Chapters 6 and 8 will show, there are strict requirements for the content and presentation of these financial statements. One of these requirements is that the reports (produced from the ledger accounts) are based on line items. Line items are the generic types of assets, liabilities, income and expenses that are common to all businesses. This is an important require-ment as all businesses arc required to report their expenses using the same accounts, such as rent, salaries, advertising, vehicle running costs etc. While this may not appear to be significant, it does cause a problem when a business is trying to make decisions based on cost information, because cost information is needed for products and services, rather than for line items.

PRINCIPLES AND LIMITATIONS OF ACCOUNTING

There are some basic accounting principles that are generally accepted by the account-ing profession as being essential for recording and reporting financial information. These are as follows.

Accounting entity

Financial reports are produced for the business, independent of the owners – the business and its owners are separate entities. This is particularly important for owner-managed businesses where the personal finance of the owner must be separated from the business finances. The problem caused by the entity principle is that complex organizational structures are not always clearly identifiable as an 'entity'. The treatment by Enron of joint-venture vehicles that were not part of the Enron group for financial reporting purposes enabled 'off-Balance Sheet' financing that was a cause of that company's collapse.

Accounting period

Financial information is produced for a financial year. The period is arbitrary and has no relationship with business cycles. Businesses typically end their financial year at the end of a calendar or national fiscal year. The business cycle is more important than the financial year, which after all is nothing more than the time taken for the Earth to revolve around the Sun. If we consider the early history of accounting, merchant ships did not produce monthly accounting reports. They reported to the ships' owners at the end of the business cycle, when the goods they had traded were all sold and profits could be calculated meaningfully.

Matching principle

Closely related is the matching (or accruals) principle, in which income is recognized when it is earned and expenses when they are incurred, rather than on a cash basis. The accruals method of accounting provides a more meaningful picture of the financial performance of a business from year to year. However, the preparation of accounting reports requires certain assumptions to be made about the recognition of income and expenses. One of the criticisms made of many companies is that they attempt to 'smooth' their reported performance to satisfy the expectations of stock market analysts in order to maintain shareholder value. This practice has become known as 'earnings management'. This has been particularly difficult in the telecoms industry, where income that should have been spread over several years has been taken up earlier, or where expenditure has been treated as an asset in order to improve reported profits. When this last practice was disclosed, it was a significant cause of the difficulties faced by WorldCom.

Monetary measurement

Despite the importance of market, human, technological and environmental factors, accounting records transactions and reports information in financial terms. This provides a limited though important perspective on business performance. The criticism of accounting numbers is that they are *lagging* indicators of performance. In Chapter 4 we consider non-financial measures of performance that are more likely to present *leading* indicators of performance. An emphasis on financial numbers tends to overlook important issues of customer satisfaction, product/service quality, innovation and employee morale, which have a major impact on business performance.

Historic cost

Accounting reports record transactions at their original cost less depreciation (which is explained in Chapter 6), not at market (realizable) value or at current (replacement) cost. The historic cost may be unrelated to market or replacement value. Under this principle, the Balance Sheet does not attempt to represent the value of the business and the owner's capital is merely a calculated figure rather than a valuation of the business. The Balance Sheet excludes assets that have not been purchased by businesses but have been built up over time, such as customer goodwill, brand names etc. The *market-to-book ratio (MBR)* is the market value of the business divided by the original capital invested. Major service-based companies such as Microsoft, which have enormous goodwill and intellectual property but a low asset base, have high MBRs because the stock market takes account of information that is not reflected in accounting reports.

Going concern

The financial statements are prepared on the basis that the business will continue in operation. Many businesses have failed soon after their financial reports have been prepared on a going concern basis, making the asset values in the Balance Sheet impossible to realize. As asset values after the liquidation of a business are unlikely to equal historic cost, the continued operation of a business is an important assumption.

Conservatism

Accounting is a prudent practice, in which the sometimes over-optimistic opinions of non-financial managers are discounted. A conservative approach tends to recognize the downside of events rather than the upside. However, as mentioned above, the pressure on listed companies from analysts to meet stock market expectations of profitability has resulted from time to time in 'creative' accounting practices (discussed in Chapter 7), such as those that led to problems at Enron and WorldCom.

Disclosure

The accounting standards and principles that have been applied in the financial statements are described in the financial reports. In the UK, there is a substantial body of principles governing what information is to be disclosed in financial reports (see Chapter 6), although in the US the disclosure requirements are rule based rather than principle based. As a result, it has been argued that it is easier to find ways to get around rules that are set in explicit terms than principles that are more general. The interpretation of the disclosure rules is important in auditing and led to criminal charges against accounting firm Arthur Andersen in the United States.

Consistency

The application of accounting standards and principles should be consistent from one year to the next. Where those principles vary, the effect on profits is separately reported under the disclosure principle. However, some businesses have tended to change their rules, even with disclosure, in order to improve their reported performance, explaining the change as a once-only event.

These principles are applied in the collection, recording and reporting of financial information. It therefore follows that information used by managers for decision-making is subject to the same principles, and therefore to the same limitations. One of the most important pieces of financial information for line managers is cost, which forms the basis for most of the following chapters. The calculation of cost is determined in large part by accounting principles and the requirements of financial reporting. The cost that is calculated under these assumptions may have limited decision usefulness.

Additional principles have been developed by the International Accounting Standards Board as a *Framework for the Preparation and Presentation of Financial Statements*. These are discussed in detail in Chapter 8.

COST TERMS AND CONCEPTS

Cost can be defined as 'a resource sacrificed or foregone to achieve a specific objective' (Horngren *et al.*, 1999, p. 31).

Accountants define costs in monetary terms, and while we will focus on monetary costs, readers should recognize that there are not only non-financial measures of performance but also human, social and environmental costs. For example, making employees redundant causes family problems (a human cost) and transfers to society the obligation to pay social security benefits (a social cost). Pollution causes long-term environmental costs that are also transferred to society. These are as important as (and perhaps more important than) financial costs, but they are not recorded by accounting systems (see Chapter 7 for a further discussion). The exclusion of human, social and environmental costs is a significant limitation of accounting.

For planning, decision-making and control purposes, cost is typically defined in relation to a cost object, which is anything for which a measurement of costs is required. While the cost object is often an *output* – a product or service – it may also be a resource (an *input* to the production process), a *process* of converting resources into outputs or an *area of responsibility* (a department or cost centre) within the organization. Examples of inputs are materials, labour, rent, marketing expenses etc. Examples of processes are purchasing, customer order processing, order fulfilment, despatch etc.

Businesses typically report in relation to line items (the resource inputs) and responsibility centres (departments or cost centres). This means that decisions requiring cost information on business processes and product/service outputs are difficult, because most accounting systems (except activity-based systems, as will be described in Chapter 13) do not provide adequate information about those cost objects. For example, in a project-based business, published financial reports do not provide cost and revenue information about each project, but instead report information about salaries, rental, office costs etc.

Businesses may adopt a system of management accounting to provide this information for management purposes, but rarely will this second system reconcile with the external financial reports because the management information system may not follow the same accounting principles described in this chapter. The requirement to produce financial reports based on line items, rather than cost objects, is a second limitation of accounting as a tool of decision-making.

The notion of cost is also problematic because we need to decide how cost is to be defined. If, as Horngren *et al.* defined it, cost is a resource sacrificed or forgone, then one of the questions we must ask is whether that definition implies a cash cost or an opportunity cost. A cash cost is the amount of cash expended (a valuable resource), whereas an opportunity cost is the lost opportunity of not doing something, which may be the loss of time or the loss of a customer, equally valuable resources. If it is the cash cost, is it the *historical* (past) cost or the *future* cost with which we should be concerned?

For example, is the cost of an employee:

■ the historical, cash cost of salaries and benefits, training, recruitment etc. paid? or
■ the future cash cost of salaries and benefits to be paid? or
■ the lost opportunity cost of what we could have done with the money had we not employed that person, e.g. the benefits that could have resulted from expenditure of the same money on advertising, computer equipment, external consulting services etc.?

Wilson and Chua (1988) quoted the economist Jevons, writing in 1871, that past costs were irrelevant to decisions about the future because they are 'gone and lost forever'. This is a difficult question, and the problematic nature of calculating costs may have been the source of the comment by Clark (1923) that there were 'different costs for different purposes'.

This, then, is our third limitation of accounting: what do we mean by cost and how do we calculate it?

CONCLUSION

This chapter has described how an accounting system captures, records, summarizes and reports financial information using the double-entry system of recording financial transactions in accounts. It has also identified how the principles underlying the accounting process can present limitations for managers in using financial information for decision-making. This has a particular effect in relation to cost, which as we will see throughout Part III is crucial for non-financial managers.

In this chapter we have also identified three particular limitations of accounting that result from the domination of the scorekeeping function:

■ the exclusion of the wider human, social and environmental costs from those reported by accounting systems;
■ the focus on line items rather than cost objects, despite the latter having more meaning for planning, decision-making and control; and
■ the problematic notion of defining cost as historic, future or opportunity.

Each of these is taken up in subsequent chapters.

REFERENCES

Clark, J. M. (1923). *Studies in the Economics of Overhead Costs*. Chicago, IL: University of Chicago Press.

Horngren, C. T., Bhimani, A., Foster, G. and Datar, S. M. (1999). *Management and Cost Accounting*. London: Prentice Hall Europe.

Wilson, R. M. S. and Chua, W. F. (1988). *Managerial Accounting: Method and Meaning*. London: VNR International.

4

MANAGEMENT CONTROL, MANAGEMENT ACCOUNTING AND ITS RATIONAL-ECONOMIC ASSUMPTIONS

Management accounting needs to be understood as part of the broader context of management control systems. In this chapter, we describe the theoretical background of management control and management accounting and its most recent developments: non-financial performance measurement and strategic management accounting.

MANAGEMENT CONTROL SYSTEMS

In his seminal work on the subject, Anthony (1965) defined management control as:

> The process by which managers assure that resources are obtained and used effectively and efficiently in the accomplishment of the organization's objectives.

Management control encompasses both financial and non-financial performance measurement. Anthony developed a model that differentiated three planning and control functions:

- Strategy formulation was concerned with goals, strategies and policies. This fed into
- Management control, which was concerned with the implementation of strategies and in turn led to
- Task control, which comprised the efficient and effective performance of individual tasks.

Anthony was primarily concerned with the middle function. Otley (1994) argued that such a separation was unrealistic and that management control was 'intimately bound up with both strategic decisions about positioning and operating decisions that ensure the effective implementation of such strategies' (p. 298).

Building on Anthony's earlier definition, Anthony and Govindarajan (2000) defined management control as a process by which managers at all levels ensure that the people they supervise implement their intended strategies (p. 4).

Berry *et al.* (1995) defined management control as:

> the process of guiding organizations into viable patterns of activity in a changing environment ... managers are concerned to influence the behaviour of other organizational participants so that some overall organizational goals are achieved. (p. 4)

Ouchi (1979) identified three mechanisms for control:

- the market in which prices convey the information necessary for decisions;
- bureaucracy, characterized by rules and supervision; and
- an informal social mechanism, called a clan, which operates through socialization processes that may result in the formation of an organizational culture.

In this chapter we are concerned with management control as a system (a collection of inter-related mechanisms) of rules.

Simons (1994) also took a broader view of management control systems in his description of them as:

> the formal, information-based routines and procedures used by managers to maintain or alter patterns in organizational activities. These systems are both pervasive and unobtrusive, but are rarely recognized as potentially significant levers of organizational change. (p. 185)

Simons described the actions taken by newly appointed top managers attempting revolutionary and evolutionary strategic change, all of whom used control systems to overcome inertia; communicate the substance of their agenda; structure implementation timetables; ensure continuing attention through incentives; and focus organizational learning on strategic uncertainties.

Simons (1990) developed a model of the relationship between strategy, control systems and organizational learning in order to reduce strategic uncertainty. The model is reproduced in Figure 4.1.

Research by Simons (1990) found that the choice by top managers to make certain control systems interactive provided signals to organizational participants about what should be monitored and where new ideas should be proposed and tested. This signal activates organizational learning.

We can distinguish systems for planning from systems for control. Planning systems interpret environmental demands and constraints and use a set of numbers to provide a 'common language which can be used to compare and contrast the results obtained by each activity' (Otley, 1987, p. 64). These numbers may be financial (resource allocations or performance expectations). They are represented in accounting

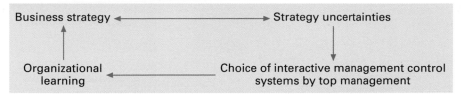

Figure 4.1 Process model of relationship between business strategy and management control systems
Reprinted from *Accounting, Organizations and Society*, Vol. 15, No. 1/2, R. Simons, The role of management control systems in creating competitive advantage, pp. 127–43, Copyright 1990, with permission from Elsevier Science.

and in non-financial performance measurement. Otley *et al.* (1995) noted that:

> accounting is still seen as a pre-eminent technology by which to integrate diverse activities from strategy to operations and with which to render accountability. (p. S39)

Control systems are concerned with feedback control, in which 'the observed error is fed back into the process to instigate action to cause its reduction' (Otley, 1987, p. 21). By contrast, planning systems are also concerned with feedforward control, 'because it is only an expected error that is used to stimulate the control process' (p. 21).

We can consider the management planning and control system as a single system in which both feedback and feedforward are concerned with reducing the performance gap (Downs, 1966). Downs defined this as 'the difference in utility [an individual] perceives between the actual and the satisfactory level of performance' (p. 169). According to Downs, the larger the gap, the greater the motivation to undertake more intensive search.

We can show this diagrammatically in Figure 4.2.

Feedforward is the process of determining, prospectively, whether strategies are likely to achieve the target results that are consistent with organizational goals.

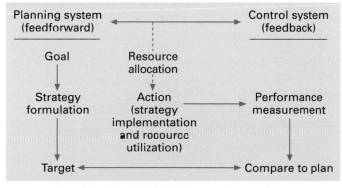

Figure 4.2 Model of planning and control system

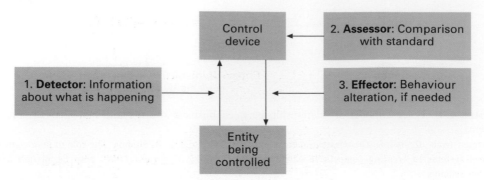

Figure 4.3   Elements of a control system
Reprinted from Anthony, R. N. and Govindarajan, V. (2000). *Management Control Systems*. (10th edn), McGraw-Hill Irwin.

Feedback is the retrospective process of measuring performance, comparing it with the plan and taking corrective action. The two systems need to be integrated as a management control system as they share common targets, the need for corrective action to be reflected either in goal adjustment or in changed behaviour, and the allocation or utilization of resources (i.e. budgeting and budgetary control, which are covered in Chapters 16 and 17).

According to Anthony and Govindarajan (2001), every control system has at least four elements:

1   A detector or sensor that measures what is happening.
2   An assessor that determines the significance of what is happening by comparing it with a standard or expectation.
3   An effector (feedback) that alters behaviour if the assessor indicates the need to do so.
4   A communication network that transmits information between the other elements.

This can be represented in the diagram in Figure 4.3.

There are five major standards against which performance can be compared (Emmanuel *et al.*, 1990):

1   Previous time periods.
2   Similar organizations.
3   Estimates of future organizational performance *ex ante*.
4   Estimates of what might have been achieved *ex post*.
5   The performance necessary to achieve defined goals.

Hofstede (1981) provided a typology for management control: routine, expert, trial-and-error, intuitive, judgemental or political. The first three are cybernetic and these are described in this chapter. Non-cybernetic controls are described in Chapter 5.

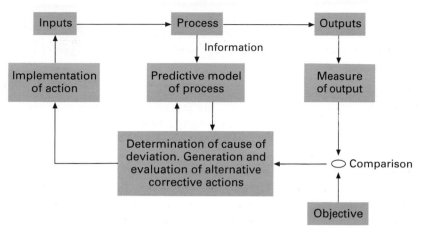

Figure 4.4   Necessary conditions for control
Reprinted from Emmanuel, C., Otley, D. and Merchant, K. (1990). *Accounting for Management Control* (2nd edn).
London: Chapman & Hall.

A *cybernetic control* process involves four conditions (Berry *et al.*, 1995, originally published in Otley and Berry, 1980):

1   The existence of an objective that is desired.
2   A means of measuring process outputs in terms of this objective.
3   The ability to predict the effect of potential control actions.
4   The ability to take actions to reduce deviations from the objective.

However, Otley and Berry (1980) recognized that:

> organizational objectives are often vague, ambiguous and change with time ... measures of achievement are possible only in correspondingly vague and often subjective terms ... predictive models of organizational behaviour are partial and unreliable, and ... different models may be held by different participants ... the ability to act is highly constrained for most groups of participants, including the so-called 'controllers'. (p. 241)

Based on work by Berry *et al.* (1995), Emmanuel *et al.* (1990) presented a simplified diagram of the control process as a regulator. This is contained in Figure 4.4.

This model differs from that by Anthony as it emphasizes the importance for control of a predictive model, which is necessary for both feedback (reactive) and feedforward (anticipatory) modes of control. The difficulty with each form of control is the reliability of the predictive model. A standard, such as a budget, requires a predictive model of the organization and how it interacts with its environment.

Otley and Berry (1980) defined four types of control:

1   First-order control adjusts system inputs and causes behaviour to alter.
2   Second-order control alters system objectives or the standards to be attained.

3   Internal learning amends the predictive model on the basis of past experience and the measurement and communication processes associated with it.
4   Systemic learning or adaptation changes the nature of the system itself – inputs, outputs and predictive models.

The problem of a predictive model is in understanding the complex and ambiguous relationship between means and ends, or inputs and outputs. Ouchi (1977) argued that there were 'only two phenomena which can be observed, monitored, and counted: behavior and the outputs which result from behavior' (p. 97).

To apply behaviour control, organizations need agreement or knowledge about means–ends relationships. To apply output control, a valid and reliable measure of the desired outputs must be available. Ouchi argued that as organizations grow larger and hierarchy increases, there is a shift from behaviour to output control.

MANAGEMENT PLANNING AND CONTROL SYSTEMS AND MANAGEMENT ACCOUNTING

Daft and Macintosh (1984) described six components of management control systems: strategic plan, long-range plan, annual operating budget, periodic statistical reports, performance appraisal, and policies and procedures. Management accounting should be understood in this broader context of management control. Emmanuel *et al.* (1990) believed that management accounting was important because it represents 'one of the few integrative mechanisms capable of summarizing the effect of an organization's actions in quantitative terms' (p. 4). Because management information can be expressed in monetary terms, it can be aggregated across time and diverse organizational units and provides a means of integrating activities.

Otley and Berry (1994) described how in management control:

accounting information provides a window through which the real activities of the organization may be monitored, but it should be noted also that other windows are used that do not rely upon accounting information. (p. 46)

Otley (1994) called for a wider view of management control, with less emphasis on accounting-based controls. Criticizing Anthony's model of planning and control, Otley argued that '[t]he split between strategic planning, management control and operational control, which was always tendentious, now becomes untenable' (p. 292).

Otley claimed that there was widespread agreement that undue emphasis was given to financial controls rather than to a more 'balanced scorecard' approach, hence the increasing importance given to non-financial (or multidimensional) performance management in the study of management control systems.

Otley *et al.* (1995) argued for expanding management control beyond accounting, distinguishing financial control from management control, the latter as:

a general management function concerned with the achievement of overall organizational aims and objectives ... management control is concerned with looking after the overall business with money being used as a convenient measure of a variety of other more complex dimensions, not as an end in itself. (p. S33)

Otley (1999) proposed a framework for management control systems around five central issues: objectives, strategies and plans, target-setting, incentive and reward structures, and information feedback loops. The framework was tested against three major systems of organizational control: budgeting, economic value added (EVA) and the Balanced Scorecard. Otley concluded that performance management provides an important integrating framework.

NON-FINANCIAL PERFORMANCE MEASUREMENT

The limitations of financial measures were identified most clearly by Johnson and Kaplan (1987), who argued that there was an excessive focus on short-term financial performance. They commented:

Managers discovered that profits could be 'earned' not just by selling more or producing for less, but also by engaging in a variety of non-productive activities: exploiting accounting conventions, engaging in financial entrepreneurship, and reducing discretionary expenditures. (p. 197)

such as:

R&D, promotion, distribution, quality improvement, applications engineering, human resources, and customer relations – all of which, of course, are vital to a company's long-term performance. The immediate effect of such reductions is to boost reported profitability, but at the expense of sacrificing the company's long-term competitive position. (p. 201)

Johnson and Kaplan (1987) emphasized the importance of non-financial indicators, arguing:

Short-term financial measures will have to be replaced by a variety of non-financial indicators that provide better targets and predictors for the firm's long-term profitability goals, signifying this as a return to the operations-based measures that were the origin of management accounting systems. (p. 259)

The development of the **Balanced Scorecard** (Kaplan and Norton, 1992; 1993; 1996; 2001) has received extensive coverage in the business press. It presents four different perspectives and complements traditional financial indicators with measures of performance for customers, internal processes and innovation/improvement.

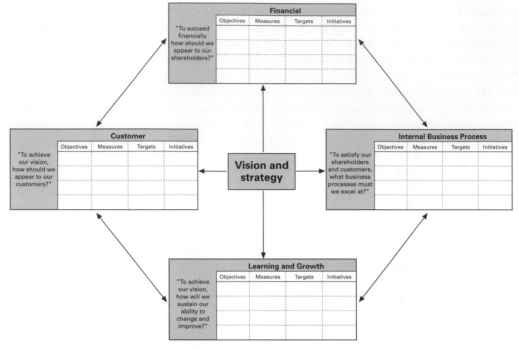

Figure 4.5 Translating vision and strategy: four perspectives

Reprinted by permission of *Harvard Business Review*. From 'Using the Balanced Scorecard as a strategic management system' by R. S. Kaplan and D. P. Norton, Jan–Feb 1996. Copyright 1996 by the Harvard Business Scholl Publishing Corporation; all rights reserved.

These measures are grounded in an organization's strategic objectives and competitive demands. The Balanced Scorecard is shown in Figure 4.5.

Kaplan and Norton (1996) argued that the Scorecard provided the ability to link a company's long-term strategy with its short-term actions, emphasizing that:

> meeting short-term financial targets should not constitute satisfactory performance when other measures indicate that the long-term strategy is either not working or not being implemented well. (p. 80)

The Balanced Scorecard took as a starting point the goal to generate long-term economic value, which required other than financial measures as drivers of long-term performance and growth. Kaplan (1994) described how:

> the new concepts and theories emerged from attempting to document, understand and subsequently influence the management accounting practices at innovating organizations. (p. 247)

There had been earlier attempts at non-financial performance measurement. Eccles (1991) argued that 'income-based financial figures are better at measuring the consequences of yesterday's decisions than they are at indicating tomorrow's performance'. Meyer (1994) proposed a 'dashboard' in contrast to Kaplan and Norton's Balanced Scorecard. He argued that traditional performance measurement systems don't work as they track what happens within not across functions. The few cross-functional 'results measures' are financial. In contrast, 'process measures' monitor the activities that produce given results.

Innes (1996) described the *tableaux de bord* that had been developed by 'sub-departments' in French factories. These comprise non-financial measures that managers identify as critical to success and that are developed and monitored locally, rather than being part of the formal reporting process.

There have been other efforts at Balanced Scorecard-type models, such as the *Performance Pyramid* of Lynch and Cross (1991). Although the initial concern of most Balanced Scorecard-type systems was with manufacturing businesses, Fitzgerald *et al.* (1991) emphasized the needs of service businesses and developed a *Results and Determinants Framework* containing six performance dimensions divided into two different categories. Competitiveness and financial performance as 'ends' reflected the success of the chosen strategy, while the others, the 'means', determined competitive success. They applied this model to three 'service archetypes' – professional services, service shops and mass services – using the number of customers handled as the differentiating factor. Figure 4.6 shows the Results and Determinants Framework.

	Dimensions of performance	Types of measures
Results	Competitiveness	Relative market share and position Sales growth Measures of the customer base
	Financial performance	Profitability Liquidity Capital structure Market ratios
Determinants	Quality of service	Reliability, responsiveness, appearance, comfort, cleanliness, friendliness, communication, courtesy, competence, access, availability, security
	Flexibility	Volume Delivery speed Specification
	Resource utilization	Productivity Efficiency
	Innovation	Innovation process Individual innovations

Figure 4.6   Results and Determinants Framework
Reprinted from Fitzgerald, L., Johnston, R., Brignall, S., Silvestro, R. and Voss, C. (1991). *Performance Measurement in Service Businesses*. London: Chartered Institute of Management Accountants.

A further model, reflected in the practitioner rather than the academic literature, is the 'Business Excellence' model developed by the European Foundation for Quality Management (EFQM). This is an integrated self-assessment tool comprising nine elements that are weighted and divided into two groups: results and enabling criteria. The results criteria are business results, people satisfaction, customer satisfaction and impact on society. The enablers are processes, people management, policy and strategy, resources and leadership.

Another model used in industry is the ISO 9000 quality model, while in the UK Chartermark is used in the public sector and Investors in People is used for human resource and training and development strategies. All require external assessment.

The difficulty with performance measurement systems is that multiple measures are a result of multiple stakeholders inside and outside the organization. There are inherent difficulties in the predictive model that a business explicitly or implicitly uses to obtain resources and implement processes in order to deliver product/services to customers.

The *Performance Prism* was developed at Cranfield University by Neely *et al.* (2002). It differs from other non-financial performance measurement systems in that it considers all stakeholders in the business, such as regulatory agencies, pressure groups and suppliers. This ensures that the performance measurement system used presents a balanced picture of business performance. It also differs from Balanced Scorecard-type systems in that the performance measures are not developed from strategy, as Kaplan and Norton (2001) suggest, but informs management whether the business is going in the strategic direction that is intended.

A research study by the Chartered Institute of Management Accountants (1993) found that most companies tend to make decisions primarily on financial monitors of performance. Boards, financiers and investors place overwhelming reliance – often exclusively – on financial indicators such as profit, turnover, cash flow and return on capital. Managers mostly support the view that non-financial performance information should only be used internally. There is no optimal mix of financial and non-financial performance measures and the non-financial indicators used are not fixed. The report argued that performance measures need to mirror operational complexity, but must be kept simple to be understood.

In order to compete in a global economy, manufacturers have had to move towards higher quality, shorter cycle times, smaller batch sizes, greater variety in product mix and cost reduction. The development of new manufacturing philosophies such as computer integrated manufacturing (CIM), flexible manufacturing systems (FMS), just-in-time (JIT), optimized production technology (OPT) and total quality management (TQM) has shifted the balance from financial to non-financial performance measurement.

However, Sinclair and Zairi (1995b) argued that performance measurement has been dominated by management control systems that are focused on 'control' rather than 'improvement'. They saw management accounting and financial performance as a limiting constraint rather than a tool for managing continuous improvement. Sinclair and Zairi (1995a) undertook a survey of performance measurement in companies implementing TQM and found that despite the aims of TQM being communicated to managers, performance measurement systems were inappropriate.

Research suggests that the management control paradigm may still be dominated by management accounting and that non-financial performance measurement is isolated from, rather than integrated with, management accounting. Despite the proliferation of non-financial measures, many remain rooted in short-term financial quantification.

Brignall and Ballantine (1996) described the concept and history of multi-dimensional performance measurement (PM):

PM systems are part of an attempt to give management accounting a more strategic, outward-looking focus, incorporating non-financial, competitor-centred and customer-focused information into the search for a sustainable competitive advantage in services. (p. 27)

Otley (1999, see earlier in this chapter) concluded that performance *management* (which he contrasted with performance *measurement*) goes beyond the boundaries of traditional management accounting. It could be achieved by accountants having a better understanding of the operational activities of the business and building this understanding into control systems design; connecting control systems with business strategy, which has to some extent been addressed by the proponents of strategic management accounting (see below); and focusing on the external environment within which the business operates, through a value-chain-based approach.

One avenue that may address the need for a holistic approach to performance management is provided by *strategic enterprise management (SEM)*. This is based on an information system that supports the strategic management process, and aims to overcome the difficulties of integrating information from diverse systems. It is based on the concept of a data warehouse holding large amounts of data that can be accessed by a range of analytical tools such as Balanced Scorecard-type measures, activity-based management, benchmarking or shareholder value measures. The end result is argued to be faster and better managerial decision-making throughout the organization using information captured both from inside and outside the organization. The weakness of the SEM approach is its cost, as it is a systems-based solution that requires integration of data typically held in many systems, often in different formats with overlapping and ambiguous connections.

This brings us to a further development in accounting that looks beyond the boundaries of the business organization.

STRATEGIC MANAGEMENT ACCOUNTING

In their book *Relevance Lost*, Johnson and Kaplan (1987) argued that management accounting and control systems could not cope with the information demands of the new manufacturing environment and the increased importance of service industries. The notion of **strategic management accounting (SMA)** is linked with business strategy and maintaining or increasing competitive advantage.

The term strategic management accounting was coined by Simmonds in 1981. Simmonds defined SMA as:

> the provision and analysis of management accounting data about a business and its competitors which is of use in the development and monitoring of the strategy of that business. (quoted in Drury, 2000, p. 924)

Simmonds argued that accounting should be more outward looking and help the firm evaluate its competitive position relative to its competitors by collecting and analysing data on costs, prices, sales volumes and market share, cash flows and resources for its main competitors. Simmonds emphasized the learning curve through early experience with new products that led to cost reductions and lower prices.

Bromwich (1990) argued that SMA is the management accountant's contribution to corporate strategy, while Bromwich and Bhimani (1994) drew attention to SMA as an area for future development. There is no comprehensive conceptual framework of what strategic management accounting is (Tomkins and Carr, 1996) or of how it relates to corporate strategy. Bromwich (1990) defined SMA as the:

> provision and analysis of financial information on the firm's product markets and competitors' costs and cost structures and the monitoring of the enterprise's strategies and those of its competitors in these markets over a number of periods. (p. 28)

Bromwich suggested that SMA should consider product benefits and how the cost of providing these benefits related to the price the customer was willing to pay.

Wilson (1995) identified SMA as:

> an approach to management accounting that explicitly highlights strategic issues and concerns. It sets management accounting in a broader context in which financial information is used to develop superior strategies as a means of achieving sustainable competitive advantage. (p. 162)

Lord (1996) summarized the characteristics of SMA:

- collection of competitor information: pricing, costs, volume, market share;
- exploitation of cost reduction opportunities: a focus on continuous improvement and on non-financial performance measures;
- matching the accounting emphasis with the firm's strategic position.

There are various classifications to identify the strategic positions of firms. The most recent contributions to SMA from the strategy literature are from Porter (1980; 1985):

- The four forces model (the threat of new entrants; the threat of substitutes; rivalry among firms; bargaining power of suppliers and customers) that assesses industry attractiveness from the perspective of long-term profitability.

■ The generic strategies (cost leadership; differentiation; focus in market segments) that lead to sustainable competitive advantage and the firm's relative position within its industry.

■ The value chain (the linked set of nine inter-related primary and support functions, see Chapter 11) that compares the price customers are willing to pay for features with the costs associated with providing them.

Lord (1996) argued that firms place more emphasis on particular accounting techniques depending on their strategic position. Dixon (1998) argued that strategy formulation and implementation:

> is carried out using the techniques and language of the management accountant. In turn, the strategic decision-making process can influence the procedures of management accounting and the design of management control systems. (p. 273)

SMA was a development of an earlier concern with *strategic cost management (SCM)*, which is based on value chain analysis and conceives of the business as the linked set of value-creating activities from raw material to the delivery of the product and its ancillary services to the final customer. The aim of SCM is:

> to expand the domain of management accounting horizontally to include critical elements external to the company with a particular emphasis on adding value for customers and suppliers. (Macintosh, 1994, pp. 204–5)

SCM also advocated lengthening the time horizon of management accounting reports over the entire life cycle of a product. Wilson (1995) suggested that SCM was a variation of SMA that 'aims to reduce unit costs continually in real terms over the long run' (p. 163).

However, Lord (1996) questioned the role of accountants in strategic management accounting, arguing that firms successfully collect and use competitor information without any input from the management accountant. Dixon (1998) argued that:

> the costs of capturing, collating, interpreting and analysing the appropriate data out-weighs the benefits . . . [and] that the collection and use of competitor information for strategic purposes can be achieved without implementing a formal SMA process. (p. 278)

One of the conclusions of research by Edwards, Collier and Shaw (2005) into knowledge management found that the focus of strategic management accounting has been external when it should have been internal. In ten organizations studied, all believed that knowledge acquired was not being effectively shared, retained or utilized. Management accountants do not recognize their role in broader issues of knowledge management, and top management does not appear to appreciate the link between knowledge management as a source of competitive advantage and financial performance.

A THEORETICAL FRAMEWORK FOR MANAGEMENT ACCOUNTING

In this chapter we have identified management accounting as part of a broader management control system that is driven by goals and strategy. We have also expanded the notion of management control to incorporate non-financial performance measurement and a strategic perspective that monitors the behaviour of other organizations in pursuit of competitive advantage. This description of management control systems implies a cybernetic system of control, with feedforward and feedback processes that influence behaviour.

There are certain assumptions underlying the cybernetic model that are based on what is called a rational or economic *paradigm*, or view of the world. *Rational* means following reasoning as opposed to experience or observation (which is called *empiricism*). The traditional approach to decision-making for management control and management accounting has been from an *economically rational* perspective. Under this perspective alternatives can be evaluated and decisions computed as a result of preferences.

March and Simon (1958) laid the basis for economic theories of the firm in distinguishing the neoclassical assumption that economic decisions were made by perfectly rational actors possessing relatively complete information aimed at *maximizing* with *satisficing* behaviour. Satisficing was based on *bounded rationality*: actors with general goals searching for whatever solution more or less attained those goals. March and Simon used the example of searching a haystack for the sharpest needle (maximizing) versus searching for a needle sharp enough to sew with (satisficing). March and Simon's notion of bounded rationality recognized that decision-makers have limited information and limited ability to process that information in an uncertain and complex environment.

Scott (1998) described three perspectives on organizations: as rational systems, natural systems and open systems. The *rational perspective* is based largely on classical management theory, which sees organizations as 'purposeful collectivities', i.e. the actions of participants are co-ordinated to achieve defined goals. Organizations are highly formalized with rules governing behaviour and roles determined independent of the attributes of the people occupying those roles. Scott argued that Taylor's scientific management, Fayol's administrative theory, Weber's bureaucracy and Simon's theory of administrative behaviour are all examples of rational systems. Rational systems are predicated on the division of labour and specialization of tasks, reducing transaction costs, efficiently processing information and monitoring the work of agents.

Within the rational perspective, accounting has been dominated by the notion of contract, which is reflected in two theories: agency and transaction cost economics. *Agency theory* (see Chapter 6) focuses on the contractual relationship between the owners and managers and on the cost of the information needed by owners to monitor contractual performance. The cost of information is also an important aspect of *transaction cost economics* (see Chapter 15), which considers whether transactions should take place in the marketplace or in an organizational hierarchy.

The rational perspective and the notion of contract will determine how organizational structures, and in particular the management accounting and control systems used by organizations, are viewed. However, different perspectives will suggest different interpretations of events, grounded in the different ways in which the preparers and users of accounting information may see the world. This is expanded in Chapter 5.

CONCLUSION

In his review of management accounting in the UK, Otley (2001) argued that we need to 'put the management back into management accounting' (p. 259). Otley reinforced the *Relevance Lost* argument (Johnson and Kaplan, 1987) that management accounting had become 'irrelevant to contemporary organizations, but worse that it was often actually counter-productive to good management decision-making' (p. 243). Otley remarked that Johnson gave up on accounting while Kaplan (with Cooper) 'has become a leader in the re-invention of management accounting practices' (p. 244), having developed activity-based costing (described later in this book).

Simultaneously, Kaplan and Norton developed the Balanced Scorecard, which in turn came into conflict with Stern Stewart's Economic Value Added, a shareholder value approach (see Chapter 2), although the two have to a large extent been reconciled as mutually reinforcing (Kaplan and Norton, 2001). Both activity-based costing and the Balanced Scorecard emphasize the transformation from the nineteenth-century Industrial Revolution to the twentieth-century Information Revolution and a shift in many western countries to a knowledge-based economy.

These techniques are, however, still rooted in the rational, economics-based paradigm, which emphasizes the goal orientation and control system based on feedback and feedforward described in this chapter. The next chapter provides alternative perspectives on the inter-relationship between accounting and organizations.

After you have read this chapter, you should read and think about Reading B. The Readings are in Part IV of this book.

REFERENCES

Anthony, R. N. (1965). *Planning and Control Systems: A Framework for Analysis*. Boston, MA: Harvard Business School Press.

Anthony, R. N. and Govindarajan, V. (2000). *Management Control Systems*. (10th international edn). New York, NY: McGraw-Hill Irwin.

Berry, A. J., Broadbent, J. and Otley, D. (1995). The domain of organizational control. In A. J. Berry, J. Broadbent and D. Otley (eds), *Management Control: Theories, Issues and Practices*, London: Macmillan.

Brignall, S. and Ballantine, J. (1996). Performance measurement in service businesses revisited. *International Journal of Service Industry Management*, **7**(1), 6–31.

Bromwich, M. (1990). The case for strategic management accounting: The role of accounting information for strategy in competitive markets. *Accounting, Organizations and Society*, **15**(1/2), 27–46.

Bromwich, M. and Bhimani, A. (1994). *Management Accounting: Pathways to Progress*. London: Chartered Institute of Management Accountants.

Chartered Institute of Management Accountants (1993). *Performance Measurement in the Manufacturing Sector*. London: Chartered Institute of Management Accountants.

Daft, R. L. and Macintosh, N. B. (1984). The nature and use of formal control systems for management control and strategy implementation. *Journal of Management*, **10**(1), 43–66.

Dixon, R. (1998). Accounting for strategic management: A practical application. *Long Range Planning*, **31**(2), 272–9.

Downs, A. (1966). *Inside Bureaucracy*. Boston, MA: Little, Brown and Company.

Drury, C. (2000). *Management and Cost Accounting*. (5th edn). London: Thomson Learning.

Eccles, R. G. (1991). *The Performance Measurement Manifesto, Getting Numbers You Can Trust: The New Accounting*. Boston, MA: Harvard Business Review Paperbacks.

Edwards, J., Collier, P. M. and Shaw, D. (2005). *Knowledge Management and Its Impact on the Management Accountant*. London: Chartered Institute of Management Accountants. ISBN 1-85974-569-9 available from *http://www.cimaglobal.com/cps/rde/xber/SID-OAAAC564-01C6258/live/Knowledge_Management_Full_Report_06-05.pdf*

Emmanuel, C., Otley, D. and Merchant, K. (1990). *Accounting for Management Control*. (2nd edn). London: Chapman & Hall.

Fitzgerald, L., Johnston, R., Brignall, S., Silvestro, R. and Voss, C. (1991). *Performance Measurement in Service Businesses*. London: Chartered Institute of Management Accountants.

Hofstede, G. (1981). Management control of public and not-for-profit activities. *Accounting, Organizations and Society*, **6**(3), 193–211.

Innes, J. (1996). Activity performance measures and tableaux de bord. In I. Lapsley and F. Mitchell (eds), *Accounting and Performance Measurement: Issues in the Private and Public Sectors*, London: Paul Chapman Publishing.

Johnson, H. T. and Kaplan, R. S. (1987). *Relevance Lost: The Rise and Fall of Management Accounting*. Boston, MA: Harvard Business School Press.

Kaplan, R. S. (1994). Management accounting (1984–1994): Development of new practice and theory. *Management Accounting Research*, **5**, 247–60.

Kaplan, R. S. and Norton, D. P. (1992). The Balanced Scorecard – Measures that drive performance. *Harvard Business Review*, Jan–Feb, 71–9.

Kaplan, R. S. and Norton, D. P. (1993). Putting the Balanced Scorecard to work. *Harvard Business Review*, Sept–Oct, 134–47.

Kaplan, R. S. and Norton, D. P. (1996). Using the Balanced Scorecard as a strategic management system. *Harvard Business Review*, Jan–Feb, 75–85.

Kaplan, R. S. and Norton, D. P. (2001). *The Strategy-Focused Organization: How Balanced Scorecard Companies Thrive in the New Business Environment*. Boston, MA: Harvard Business School Press.

Lord, B. R. (1996). Strategic management accounting: The emperor's new clothes? *Management Accounting Research*, **7**, 347–66.

Lynch, R. L. and Cross, K. F. (1991). *Measure Up! Yardsticks for Continuous Improvement*. Oxford: Blackwell.

Macintosh, N. B. (1994). *Management Accounting and Control Systems: An Organizational and Behavioral Approach*. Chichester: John Wiley & Sons.

March, J. G. and Simon, H. A. (1958). *Organizations*. Chichester: John Wiley & Sons.

Meyer, C. (1994). How the right measures help teams excel. *Harvard Business Review*, May–June, 95–103.

Neely, A., Adams, C. and Kennerly, M. (2002). *The Performance Prism: The Scorecard for Measuring and Managing Business Success*. London: Prentice Hall.

Otley, D. (1987). *Accounting Control and Organizational Behaviour*. London: Heinemann.

Otley, D. (1994). Management control in contemporary organizations: Towards a wider framework. *Management Accounting Research*, **5**, 289–99.

Otley, D. (1999). Performance management: A framework for management control systems research. *Management Accounting Research*, **10**, 363–82.

Otley, D. (2001). Extending the boundaries of management accounting research: Developing systems for performance management. *British Accounting Review*, **33**, 243–61.

Otley, D. T. and Berry, A. J. (1980). Control, organization and accounting. *Accounting, Organizations and Society*, **5**(2), 231–44.

Otley, D. T. and Berry, A. J. (1994). Case study research in management accounting and control. *Management Accounting Research*, **5**, 45–65.

Otley, D. T., Berry, A. J. and Broadbent, J. (1995). Research in management control: An overview of its development. *British Journal of Management*, **6**, Special Issue, S31–S44.

Ouchi, W. G. (1977). The relationship between organizational structure and organizational control. *Administrative Science Quarterly*, **22**, 95–113.

Ouchi, W. G. (1979). A conceptual framework for the design of organizational control mechanisms. *Management Science*, **25**(9), 833–48.

Porter, M. E. (1980). *Competitive Strategy: Techniques for Analyzing Industries and Competitors*. New York, NY: Free Press.

Porter, M. E. (1985). *Competitive Advantage: Creating and Sustaining Superior Performance*. New York, NY: Free Press.

Scott, W. R. (1998). *Organizations: Rational, Natural, and Open Systems*. (4th edn). Upper Saddle River, NJ: Prentice Hall International.

Simons, R. (1990). The role of management control systems in creating competitive advantage: New perspectives. *Accounting, Organizations and Society*, **15**(1/2), 127–43.

Simons, R. (1994). How new top managers use control systems as levers of strategic renewal. *Strategic Management Journal*, **15**, 169–89.

Sinclair, D. and Zairi, M. (1995a). Benchmarking best-practice performance measurement within companies. *Benchmarking for Quality Management and Technology*, **2**(3), 53–71.

Sinclair, D. and Zairi, M. (1995b). Effective process management through performance measurement. *Business Process Re-engineering Journal*, **1**(1), 75–88.

Tomkins, C. and Carr, C. (1996). Reflections on the papers in this issue and a commentary on the state of Strategic Management Accounting. *Management Accounting Research*, **7**, 271–80.

Wilson, R. M. S. (1995). Strategic management accounting. In D. Ashton, T. Hopper and R.W. Scapens (eds), *Issues in Management Accounting* (2nd edn), London: Prentice Hall.

A useful website on performance measurement and management is provided by the Performance Measurement Association at *www.performanceportal.org*

The Management Control Association promotes the study of management control and management accounting. Its website is *www.managementcontrolassociation.ac.uk*

5

INTERPRETIVE AND CRITICAL PERSPECTIVES ON ACCOUNTING AND DECISION-MAKING

In Chapter 4 we described the rational-economic paradigm that underpins management control systems in general and management accounting in particular. There are, however, alternative paradigms. For example, Otley and Berry (1980) questioned the usefulness of cybernetic control given the limitations of accounting systems as a result of organizational and environmental complexity. The problem with cybernetic control, they say:

> is the apparently inevitable division of labour between controllers and those who are controlled ... the primary function ascribed to the task of management is that of organization control. (p. 237)

While Chapter 4 assumed a rational paradigm, this chapter explores alternative conceptions of the role of accounting in management. We review the interpretive and the social constructionist paradigm and how organizational culture is implicated in accounting. We then consider the radical paradigm and how power is a major concern of critical accounting theory. These alternative perspectives to the rational-economic one described in Chapter 4 are an important focus of this book.

ALTERNATIVE PARADIGMS

One non-rational approach to decision-making is the 'garbage can', which March and Olsen (1976) described as the 'fortuitous confluence' whereby problems, solutions, participants and choice opportunities somehow come together. Cooper *et al.* (1981) detailed the rational model of financial and management accounting systems as planning and control devices that measure, report and evaluate individuals and business units. In the bounded rationality model (see Chapter 4), accounting systems are stabilizers, emphasizing consistency. By contrast, the garbage can view recognizes that systems provide an appearance of rationality and create an organizational history, but that 'the sequence whereby actions precede goals may well be a more accurate portrayal of organizational functioning than the more traditional goal-action paradigm' (p. 181) and 'accounting systems represent an ex post rationalization of actions, rather than an ex ante statement of organizational goals' (p. 188).

A non-rational (as opposed to irrational) paradigm has also been taken in relation to non-financial performance measurement. For example, Waggoner *et al.* (1999) took a multidisciplinary approach to the drivers of performance measurement systems and identified four categories of force that can influence the evolution of those systems: internal influences such as power relations and dominant coalition interests within the firm; external influences such as legislation and technology; process issues such as the implementation of innovation and the management of political processes; and transformational issues including the level of top-down support for and risks from change.

Bourne *et al.* (2000) developed a framework for analysing the implementation of a performance measurement system and interpreted three case studies of manufacturing companies against that framework. They identified problems in each company with IT infrastructure, resistance to measurement and management commitment that arose in designing, implementing, using and updating performance measurement systems.

These perspectives can be linked to Scott's (1998) conceptualization of organizations as rational, natural and open systems. Figure 5.1 shows the different perspectives in diagrammatic form. The *rational perspective* is of the organization as a goal-oriented collective that acts purposefully to achieve those goals through a formal structure governing behaviour and the roles of organizational members. The *natural perspective* is based on the human relations school and argues that rules and roles do not significantly influence the actions of people in organizations. In this natural perspective people are motivated by self-interest and the informal relations between them are more important than the formal organizational structure in understanding organizational behaviour. These informal relations emphasize the social aspect of organizations, which may operate in *consensus* where common goals are shared or in *conflict*. Conflictual approaches stress organizational structures as systems of power where the weaker groups are dominated by the more powerful ones.

Both rational and natural perspectives view the organization as a *closed system*, separate from its environment. By contrast, the *open systems perspective* emphasizes the impact of the environment on organizations. In the open perspective, organizations are seen as shifting coalitions of participants and a collection of interdependent activities that are tightly or loosely coupled.

Thompson (1967) contrasted the technical core of the organization with its goal achievement and control-oriented rationality, implying a closed system and the elimination of uncertainty, with the organization's dependency and lack of control at an institutional level where the greatest uncertainty existed, implying an open system. Thompson argued that at a managerial level there was mediation between the two, provided by a range of manoeuvring devices and organizational structures.

Within the open systems perspective, *contingency theory* (see Chapter 13) suggests that there is no one best way of exercising management control or of accounting. The appropriate systems emerge from the influence of the environment (which may be turbulent or static), technology, organizational size and need to fit with the organizational strategy, structure and culture. *Population ecology theory* is based on the biological analogy of natural selection and holds that environments select organiza-

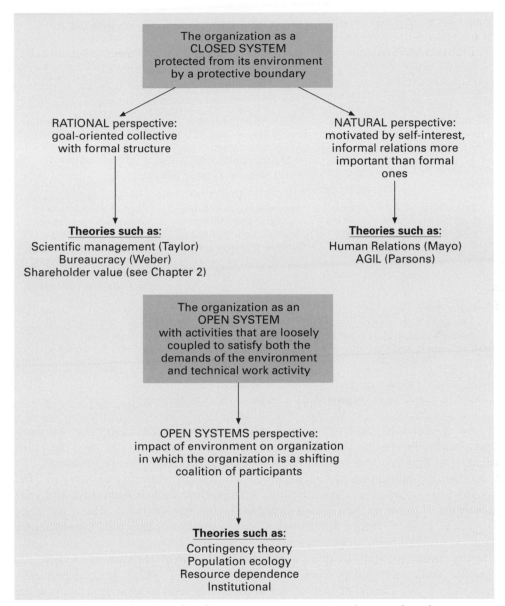

Figure 5.1 Organizations as closed or open systems: rational, natural and open systems perspectives
Based on Scott (1998).

tions for survival on the basis of the fit between the organizational form and the characteristics of the environment. *Resource dependence theory* emphasizes adaptation as organizations act to improve their opportunity to survive, particularly through the relationships of power that exist. *Institutional theory* (see Chapter 7) stresses the rules

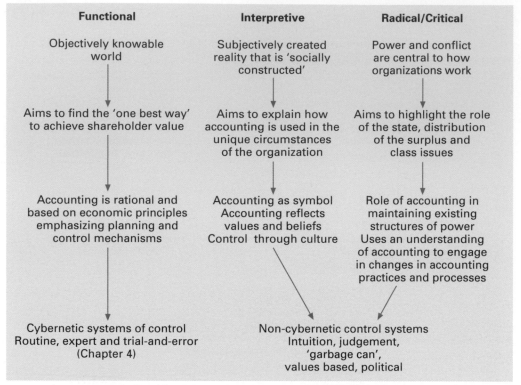

Figure 5.2   Paradigms of understanding

that are imposed by external parties, especially by government; the values and norms that are internalized in roles as part of socialization processes; and the cultural controls that underpin the belief systems that are supported by the professions.

In their categorization of the nature of knowledge, Burrell and Morgan (1979) proposed four paradigms – functionalist, interpretive, radical humanist and radical structuralist – based on two dimensions: one subjective–objective, the other regulation–radical change. Figure 5.2 shows a representation of rational, interpretive and radical (or critical) paradigms.

In his classification of the types of management control, Hofstede (1981) separated cybernetic (rational) models from non-cybernetic ones, which were dependent on values and rituals. The cybernetic model of control systems is located in the functional paradigm. Non-cybernetic systems are located in interpretive or critical paradigms.

The functional paradigm relies on an 'objectively knowable, empirically verifiable reality' (Boland and Pondy, 1983, p. 223), which has been described in Chapter 4.

THE INTERPRETIVE PARADIGM AND THE SOCIAL CONSTRUCTION PERSPECTIVE

The interpretive view reflects a subjectively created, emergent social reality, which Chua (1986) links to an understanding of 'accounting in action'. The interpretive approach offers 'accounts of what happens as opposed to what should happen' (Chua, 1988, p. 73).

Hopwood (1983) coined the term *accounting in action* to describe the 'ways in which accounting reflects, reinforces or even constrains the strategic postures adopted by particular organizations' (p. 302). Hopwood (1987) contrasted the constitutive as well as reflective roles of accounting.

The aim of the interpretive perspective is:

> to produce rich and deep understandings of how managers and employees in organizations understand, think about, interact with, and use management accounting and control systems. (Macintosh, 1994, p. 4)

Preston (1995) described the social constructionist model of behaviour not as a rational process but a product of the 'creative individual'. Individuals act towards things on the basis of the *meaning* that things have for them. Preston described the critical process that takes place between encountering a situation or event and interpreting it, in which the individual constructs a meaning of the situation or event and acts in accordance with that meaning. Meaning is not inherent, it is brought to the situation by the individual. These meanings are derived through social interaction, the ways in which people meet, talk, work and play together and in doing so construct and share meanings. These meanings are socially constructed, internalized and shared between individuals.

Preston (1995) added that the social constructionist perspective does not preclude the existence of organizational structures and processes, but suggests that these are symbolic representations of a particular view of organizational reality. These meanings are also expressed symbolically through language. In this context accounting information is a symbolic representation of reality. Individual behaviour is guided by the meanings, values and beliefs that are constructed and shared by organizational members. These symbols are then subject to interpretation by individuals, who act towards them on the basis of the meaning they have for them. However, Preston recognized that these structures and processes may influence the development of an organizational culture – the shared values, beliefs and meanings that are collectively held by organizational participants.

CULTURE, CONTROL AND ACCOUNTING

Allaire and Firsirotu (1984) contrasted a *sociostructural* system based on formal structures, strategies, policies and management processes with a *cultural* system based on myths, ideology, values and artefacts and shaped by society, the history of the organization and the contingency factors affecting it. Sociostructural and cultural systems were in a complex relationship, with potential for stress when an organization is subject to sudden pressures for change.

The review of research on organizational culture undertaken by Smircich (1983) reflected a convergence of views around culture as 'shared key values and beliefs'

(p. 345). These values and beliefs convey a sense of identity, generate commitment, enhance social system stability, and serve as a sense-making device to guide and shape behaviour. Smircich also identified the existence of multiple organization subcultures – a multiplicity of cultures within an organization, rather than one pervading culture.

Handy (1978) described four different organizational cultures: club, based on informal relationships; role, based on tightly defined jobs; task, a focus on solving problems; and existential, an orientation to individual purpose. Deal and Kennedy (1982) also identified four types of cultures: tough guy/macho (individualists who take high risks); work hard/play hard (fun and action with low risk); bet-your-company (big stakes decisions); and process (bureaucratic emphasis).

As we saw in Chapter 4, Ouchi (1979) identified three mechanisms for control: market (based on prices); bureaucracy (based on rules); and clan (based on tradition). Clan mechanisms are represented in professions, where different organizations have the same values. Ouchi used the example of a hospital, where a highly formalized and lengthy period of socialization leads to both skill and value training.

Schein (1988/1968) described the process that brings about change in the values and attitudes of different groups of people throughout their career as 'organizational socialization'. It occurs whenever an individual enters an organization, changes departments or is promoted. Socialization determines employee loyalty, commitment, productivity and turnover. It is the process whereby a new member learns the values, norms and behaviour patterns – the 'price of membership' (p. 54). These norms, values and behaviours are learned from organizational publications, from training, line managers, peers and role models, and from the rewards and punishments that exist. Where the values of the immediate group that the individual joins are out of line with the value system of the organization as a whole, the individual learns the values of the immediate group more quickly than those of the organization. The essence of management, according to Schein, is that managers must understand organizations as social systems that socialize their members, and then gain control over those forces.

Accounting can be one such element of control. Scott (1998) described accounting systems as 'one of the most important conventions connecting institutionally defined belief systems with technical activities' (p. 137). Scott argued that some organizations rely less on formal controls and more on developing a set of beliefs and norms to guide behaviour.

Langfield-Smith (1995) contrasted culture as the setting for control; as a control mechanism itself; and as a filter for perceiving the environment. Langfield-Smith described a model by Flamholtz, Das and Tsui in which culture facilitates control when the control system is consistent with the social norms of the organization, or inhibits control when it is at variance with those norms. As Ouchi (1977) showed, culture can lead to a ritual form of control where knowledge of the transformation process is imperfect and the ability to measure output is low. Langfield-Smith (1995) also described research by Birnberg and Snodgrass in which culture influences the effectiveness of a control system by influencing individual perceptions and value judgements about those perceptions.

Hofstede (1981) argued that control systems must be sensitive to organizational cultures and that those running counter to culture are unlikely to be successfully imposed. Markus and Pfeffer (1983) suggested that resistance to and failure of accounting control systems was common, arguing that control systems will be implemented when they are consistent with the dominant organizational culture and paradigm in their implications for values and beliefs.

THE RADICAL PARADIGM AND CRITICAL ACCOUNTING

Radical approaches (Burrell and Morgan, 1979) emphasize broader structural issues such as the role of the state, distribution of the surplus of production and class difference (Hopper *et al.*, 1987). Hopper and Powell (1985) claimed that the functional approach does not address issues of power and conflict and argued that interpretive approaches 'indicate how accounting systems may promote change, albeit within a managerial conception of the term, rather than being stabilizers' (p. 449).

Hopper *et al.* (2001) argued that under Thatcherism:

> accounting data and the consulting arms of accounting firms had been central to economic and policy debates, involving privatization, industrial restructuring, reform of the public sector, and worries about de-industrialization ... it appeared apparent that accounting had to be studied in its broader social, political and institutional context. (p. 276)

Those writers who sought a more radical interpretation than the interpretive one drew on the work of Marx. There are three groups within this perspective: political economy, labour process and critical theory (Roslender, 1995). All are concerned with promoting change in the *status quo*.

The *political economy* approach recognizes power and conflict in society and the effect that accounting has on the distribution of income, power and wealth. *Labour process* focuses on the corruption of human creativity in the pursuit of wealth, especially deskilling and management control as a reproducer of capitalism. Labour process theorists argue that:

> the driving force for social change in capitalist society is the development and displacement (i.e. of impediments to capital accumulation and their resolutions) ... [that] are inherent in the structural instabilities that characterize capitalism's unequal and antagonistic social relations. (Neimark and Tinker, 1986, p. 378)

Neimark and Tinker emphasized the 'on-going conflict among and between social classes over the disposition and division of the social surplus' (p. 379) and how '[s]ocial and organizational control systems are not neutral mechanisms in these struggles but are attached to and legitimate concrete power interests' (p. 380).

The third Marxist perspective, *critical theory*, emphasizes a critique of the *status quo* and emancipation towards a better life. Hopper and Powell (1985) argued that critical studies show how 'accounting measures alienate through subordinating behaviour to perceived imperatives which are in fact socially created' (p. 454).

Laughlin (1999) defined *critical accounting* as providing:

a critical understanding of the role of accounting processes and practices and the accounting profession in the functioning of society and organizations with an intention to use that understanding to engage (where appropriate) in changing these processes, practices and the profession. (p. 73)

An example of the application of critical theory is provided by Perrow (1991), who argued:

If one raised profits by externalizing many costs to the community, exploiting the workforce, evading government controls by corrupting officials, manipulating stock values, and controlling the market by forming quasi-cartels or other predatory practices – all common practices in the nineteenth and twentieth century – then profits will not reflect the efficient use of labor, capital, and natural resources. (p. 746)

Much of critical theory is concerned with opening up the discourse from a narrow economic-rational application of accounting to question its underlying assumptions and its (often dysfunctional) consequences. *Discourse* is a conversation, albeit an informed one, through which arguments and counter-arguments are considered. Accounting is implicated in discourse because in its written form, it presents 'facts' that contain implicit assumptions. An accounting discourse of profit and return on investment is dominated by an economic-rational logic. Thus, accounting 'serves to construct a particular field of visibility' (Miller and O'Leary, 1987, p. 239).

In promoting critical theory, Broadbent and Laughlin (1997) emphasized 'a recognition of the choice between seeking to develop change through meaningful debate [rather than] through the application of power or coercion' (p. 645).

POWER AND ACCOUNTING

We have seen how control systems and management accounting in particular are aimed at influencing behaviour. This is inextricably bound up with consideration of power. Pfeffer (1992) defined power as 'the potential ability to influence behavior, to change the course of events, to overcome resistance, and to get people to do things that they would not otherwise do' (p. 30).

Morgan (1986) identified power as either a resource or a social relation, defining it as 'the medium through which conflicts of interest are ultimately resolved' (p. 158). As a social relation, power is concerned with domination of one person (or group) over another. As a resource, power is concerned with the dependency of one party on particular allocations, and the control over the distribution of that resource by another party. By contrast, Giddens (1976) argued that power does not of itself imply conflict. Because power is linked to the pursuit of interest, it is only when interests do not coincide that power and conflict are related.

Power is implicit in organizational functioning and in the definition of what is important. Child (1972) concluded:

> When incorporating strategic choice in a theory of organization, one is recognizing the operation of an essentially political process in which constraints and opportunities are functions of the power exercised by decision-makers in the light of ideological values. (p. 16)

Cooper *et al.* (1981) saw accounting systems having:

> [an] impact on sustaining and influencing an organization's culture and language and in terms of their ideological and legitimizing influence in maintaining systems of power and control in organizations. (p. 175)

Emmanuel *et al.* (1990) described control as taking two forms: control as domination of one person or group over others; and control as regulation where the controller detects a variation between actual and planned results and creates a stimulus for corrective action. While the latter is associated with the cybernetic system described in Chapter 4, control as domination is relevant to the interpretive and critical perspective.

Markus and Pfeffer (1983) argued that accounting and control systems are related to intra-organizational power:

> because they collect and manipulate information used in decision-making . . . [and] because they are used to change the performance of individuals and the outcomes of organizational processes. (pp. 206–7)

Case Study 5.1: easyJet

easyJet provides an interesting and well known example to illustrate many of the aspects of management control described in Chapter 4. In this case we also draw on some of the issues raised in Chapters 4 and 5 to illustrate rational economic, interpretive and critical perspectives.

Background

easyJet, the low cost airline, floated on the stock exchange in late 2000, flying 30 aircraft to 19 destinations. easyJet acquired Go airline in 2002. In 2004, easyJet carried 24 million passengers and earned total revenue of £1,091 million with a profit before taxation of £85 million, generating cash of £180 million. The company had 187 routes and flew to 57 airports.

Cost advantages

The company's low cost strategy is based on various cost advantages:

- Lower administration, e.g. no ticketing costs, no seat allocations;
- Direct sales, avoiding travel agent commissions and third party reservation system costs;

- No free catering or in-flight amenities, which provides opportunity for on-board sales;
- Cost reductions by avoidance of exceptions that incur overheads, e.g. no unaccompanied children, no pets, no flexibility with late airport check-ins;
- Cheaper aircraft (easyJet pitched Boeing and Airbus in a battle to win orders):
- Lower crew costs through fast airport turnaround, hence higher productivity;
- Lower airport costs through use of secondary airports;
- Higher seat density – more seats per aircraft;
- Use of marginal pricing formula and yield management to maximize capacity utilization and revenue – the average load factor on their aircraft in 2004 was 84%.

Performance measurement

As well as cost control and revenue maximization, the key non-financial performance measures are likely to include:

- Number of sectors flown
- Number of kilometres flown
- Available seat kilometres (ASK)
- Number of passengers
- Revenue per ASK
- Revenue per passenger
- Revenue per seat
- Capacity utilization
- Turnaround time
- Market share.

Costs and revenues are likely to be monitored for each route, so that only profitable and strategically important routes are retained.

A rational-economic perspective

easyJet's approach to shareholder value is that it has never declared or paid any cash dividends on Ordinary Shares and does not anticipate paying cash dividends in the foreseeable future. At the time of writing, it is the directors' intention to retain earnings for use in easyJet's business for the foreseeable future.

An interpretive perspective

easyJet's culture favours an informal company culture with a very flat management structure, which eliminates unnecessary and wasteful layers of management. The low cost focus of easyJet means that it can be criticized. Frequent television documentaries from Luton and other airports reveal passenger complaints about easyJet's inflexibility, especially over late airport check-ins. However, it is the company's low cost culture that necessitates the avoidance of exceptions which are, in most businesses, expensive to handle.

A critical perspective

When easyJet listed on the Stock Exchange in 2000, its founder Stelios Haji-Ioannou was forced to stand down as Chairman of the board as investors did not consider him the appropriate person to head the company's future development. Even though Stelios remains a significant shareholder, this demonstrates the power of stock market investors.

CONCLUSION

We will return to interpretive and critical perspectives throughout this book. In particular, Chapter 8 applies these different perspectives to financial statements, Chapter 13 applies them to costs and Chapter 17 addresses budgets. However, a major difficulty in adopting a perspective other than the rational-economic one is that organizational discourse suggests that the rational-economic perspective of shareholder value is the only valid one, while individuals often act in the pursuit of power and self-interest.

Otley *et al.* (1995) suggested that while the definition of management control was 'managerialist in focus ... this should not preclude a critical stance and thus a broader choice of theoretical approaches' (p. S42).

The aim of critical management accounting is to promote a greater level of self-awareness in management accountants and so develop an improved form of management accounting that is more insightful as to its consequences (Roslender, 1995). Readers should also be aware of the concern expressed by Power (1991), who decried traditional accounting education and 'the institutionalization of a form of discourse in which critical and reflective practices are regarded as "waffle"' (p. 350).

An advantage in understanding interpretive and critical alternatives to the rational economic one is what Covaleski *et al.* (1996) called 'paradigmatic pluralism ... alternative ways of understanding the multiple roles played by management accounting in organizations and society' (p. 24). The full text of the Covaleski *et al.* paper is included as one of the readings in this book.

After you have read this chapter, you should read and think about Reading C. The Readings are in Part IV of this book.

REFERENCES

Allaire, Y. and Firsirotu, M. E. (1984). Theories of organizational culture. *Organization Studies*, **5**(3), 193–226.

Boland, J. R. J. and Pondy, L. R. (1983). Accounting in organizations: A union of natural and rational perspectives. *Accounting, Organizations and Society*, **8**(2/3), 223–34.

Bourne, M., Mills, J., Wilcox, M., Neely, A. and Platts, K. (2000). Designing, implementing and updating performance measurement systems. *International Journal of Operations and Production Management*, **20**(7), 754–71.

Broadbent, J. and Laughlin, R. (1997). Developing empirical research: An example informed by a Habermasian approach. *Accounting, Auditing and Accountability Journal*, **10**(5), 622–48.

Burrell, G. and Morgan, G. (1979). *Sociological Paradigms and Organizational Analysis*. London: Heinemann.

Child, J. (1972). Organizational structure, environment and performance: The role of strategic choice. *Sociology*, **6**, 1–22.

Chua, W. F. (1986). Radical developments in accounting thought. *Accounting Review*, **LXI**(4), 601–32.

Chua, W. F. (1988). Interpretive sociology and management accounting research – A critical review. *Accounting, Auditing and Accountability Journal*, **1**(2), 59–79.

Cooper, D. J., Hayes, D. and Wolf, F. (1981). Accounting in organized anarchies: Understanding and designing accounting systems in ambiguous situations. *Accounting, Organizations and Society*, **6**(3), 175–91.

Covaleski, M. A., Dirsmith, M. W. and Samuel, S. (1996). Managerial accounting research: The contributions of organizational and sociological theories. *Journal of Management Accounting Research*, **8**, 1–35.

Deal, T. E. and Kennedy, A. A. (1982). *Corporate Cultures*. Reading, MA: Addison-Wesley.

Emmanuel, C., Otley, D. and Merchant, K. (1990). *Accounting for Management Control*. (2nd edn). London: Chapman & Hall.

Giddens, A. (1976). *New Rules of Sociological Method: A Positive Critique of Interpretative Sociologies*. London: Hutchinson.

Handy, C. (1978). *Understanding Organizations*. Harmondsworth: Penguin.

Hofstede, G. (1981). Management control of public and not-for-profit activities. *Accounting, Organizations and Society*, **6**(3), 193–211.

Hopper, T. and Powell, A. (1985). Making sense of research into the organizational and social aspects of management accounting: A review of its underlying assumptions. *Journal of Management Studies*, **22**(5), 429–65.

Hopper, T., Otley, D. and Scapens, B. (2001). British management accounting research: Whence and whither: Opinions and recollections. *British Accounting Review*, **33**, 263–91.

Hopper, T., Storey, J. and Willmott, H. (1987). Accounting for accounting: Towards the development of a dialectical view. *Accounting, Organizations and Society*, **12**(5), 437–56.

Hopwood, A. G. (1983). On trying to study accounting in the contexts in which it operates. *Accounting, Organizations and Society*, **8**(2/3), 287–305.

Hopwood, A. G. (1987). The archaeology of accounting systems. *Accounting, Organizations and Society*, **12**(3), 207–34.

Langfield-Smith, K. (1995). Organizational culture and control. In A. J. Berry, J. Broadbent and D. Otley (eds), *Management Control: Theories, Issues and Practices*, London: Macmillan.

Laughlin, R. (1999). Critical accounting: Nature, progress and prognosis. *Accounting, Auditing and Accountability Journal*, **12**(1), 73–8.

Macintosh, N. B. (1994). *Management Accounting and Control Systems: An Organizational and Behavioral Approach*. Chichester: John Wiley & Sons.

March, J. G. and Olsen, J. P. (1976). *Ambiguity and Choice in Organizations*. Bergen: Universitets-forlagen.

Markus, M. L. and Pfeffer, J. (1983). Power and the design and implementation of accounting and control systems. *Accounting, Organizations and Society*, **8**(2/3), 205–18.

Miller, P. and O'Leary, T. (1987). Accounting and the construction of the governable person. *Accounting, Organizations and Society*, **12**(3), 235–65.

Morgan, G. (1986). *Images of Organization*. Newbury Park, CA: Sage Publications.

Neimark, M. and Tinker, T. (1986). The social construction of management control systems. *Accounting, Organizations and Society*, **11**(4/5), 369–95.

Otley, D. T. and Berry, A. J. (1980). Control, organization and accounting. *Accounting, Organizations and Society*, **5**(2), 231–44.

Otley, D. T., Berry, A. J. and Broadbent, J. (1995). Research in management control: An overview of its development. *British Journal of Management*, **6**, Special Issue, S31–S44.

Ouchi, W. G. (1977). The relationship between organizational structure and organizational control. *Administrative Science Quarterly*, **22**, 95–113.

Ouchi, W. G. (1979). A conceptual framework for the design of organizational control mechanisms. *Management Science*, **25**(9), 833–48.

Perrow, C. (1991). A society of organizations. *Theory and Society*, **20**(6), 725–62.

Pfeffer, J. (1992). *Managing with Power: Politics and Influence in Organizations.* Boston, MA: Harvard Business School Press.

Power, M. K. (1991). Educating accountants: Towards a critical ethnography. *Accounting, Organizations and Society,* **16**(4), 333–53.

Preston, A. (1995). Budgeting, creativity and culture. In D. Ashton, T. Hopper and R. W. Scapens (eds), *Issues in Management Accounting* (2nd edn), London: Prentice Hall.

Roslender, R. (1995). Critical management accounting. In D. Ashton, T. Hopper and R. W. Scapens (eds), *Issues in Management Accounting* (2nd edn), London: Prentice Hall.

Schein, E. H. (1988/1968). Organizational socialization and the profession of management. *Sloan Management Review,* Fall, 53–65.

Scott, W. R. (1998). *Organizations: Rational, Natural, and Open Systems.* (4th edn). Upper Saddle River, NJ: Prentice Hall International, Inc.

Smircich, L. (1983). Concepts of culture and organizational analysis. *Administrative Science Quarterly,* **28**, 339–58.

Thompson, J. (1967). *Organizations in Action: Social Science Bases of Administrative Theory.* New York, NY: McGraw-Hill.

Waggoner, D. B., Neely, A. D. and Kennerley, M. P. (1999). The forces that shape organizational performance measurement systems: an interdisciplinary review. *International Journal of Production Economics,* No. 60-61, pp. 53–60.

PART II

THE USE OF FINANCIAL STATEMENTS FOR DECISION-MAKING

Although the major concern of this book is with accounting information for decision-making, financial statements provide a crucial ingredient of decision-making due to the importance of shareholder value (as we saw in Chapter 2). Therefore, the concept of 'decision usefulness' – i.e. the value of information for making decisions, while largely based on notions of cost (the recurrent theme in Part III) is also intertwined with the value of the business as perceived by shareholders and capital markets. Thus the focus of Part II is on understanding and interpreting financial statements.

Chapter 6 shows how the most important financial reports are constructed. This introduction to financial accounting is an important building block for an understanding of management accounting.

Chapter 7 helps the reader to interpret the main financial statements using the tool of ratio analysis.

Chapter 8 introduces International Financial Reporting Standards in the context of global harmonization. It describes in some detail the *Framework for the Preparation and Presentation of Financial Statements* which sets out the concepts underlying the preparation and presentation of financial statements for external users.

Chapter 9 introduces the topic of corporate governance and sets the context of accounting through the regulation of companies, the responsibilities of directors, audit and the audit committee.

PART **II**

THE USE OF
FINANCIAL
INSTRUMENTS FOR
DECISION-MAKING

6

CONSTRUCTING FINANCIAL STATEMENTS AND THE FRAMEWORK OF ACCOUNTING

This chapter introduces each of the principal financial statements, beginning with the Income Statement (until recently this was called the Profit and Loss account) and Balance Sheet. It begins with an overview of the regulations governing financial statements and describes the matching principle, which emphasizes prepayments, accruals and provisions such as depreciation. The chapter then describes three important accounting treatments: value added tax, goodwill and leases. It introduces the Cash Flow statement and the management of working capital and concludes with an introduction to agency theory.

FINANCIAL ACCOUNTING

Accounting provides an **account** – an explanation or report in financial terms – about the transactions of an organization. Accounting enables managers to satisfy the *stakeholders* in the organization (owners, government, financiers, suppliers, customers, employees etc.) that they have acted in the best interests of stakeholders rather than themselves. Chapter 1 provided a more in-depth treatment of accountability.

These explanations are provided to stakeholders through financial statements or reports, often referred to as the company's 'accounts'. The main financial reports are the Income Statement (Profit and Loss account), the Balance Sheet and the Cash Flow statement. The first two of these were introduced briefly in Chapter 3.

The presentation of financial reports must comply with Schedule 4 to the Companies Act, 1985, which prescribes the form and content of accounts. Section 226 of the Act requires the financial reports to represent a *'true and fair view'* of the state of affairs of the company and its profits. The Companies Act requires directors to state whether the accounts have been prepared in accordance with accounting standards (described in detail in Chapter 8) and to explain any significant departures from those standards. For companies listed on the Stock Exchange, there are additional rules contained in the Listing Requirements, commonly known as the *Purple Book* (previously known as the *Yellow Book*), which requires the disclosure of additional information.

There is a legal requirement for the financial statements of companies (other than very small ones) to be *audited*. Auditors are professionally qualified accountants who have to conduct an *audit* – an independent examination of the financial statements – and form an opinion as to whether the financial statements form a true and fair view and have been prepared in accordance with the Companies Act. A Financial Reporting Review Panel has the power to seek revision of a company's accounts where those accounts do not comply with the standards and if necessary to seek a court order to ensure compliance.

The requirement for a true and fair view has never been tested at law, but it takes precedence over accounting standards. The notion of 'true and fair' is somewhat sub-jective and it can be argued that it encourages flexibility and can provide the potential to ignore accounting standards because of the 'true and fair view' override. By compar-ison, the equivalent US requirement is that financial statements be 'presented fairly and in accordance with generally accepted accounting principles'. In the UK, account-ing standards are said to be 'principles based' rather than the 'rules based' approach in the US. The rules based approached has been criticized following the failures of Enron and WorldCom.

Accounting standards are principles to which accounting reports should conform. They are aimed at:

■ achieving comparability between companies, through reducing the variety of accounting practice;
■ providing full disclosure of material (i.e. significant) factors through the judgements made by the preparers of those financial reports; and
■ ensuring that the information provided is meaningful for the users of financial reports.

From 2005, International Financial Reporting Standards (IFRSs) produced by the International Accounting Standards Board (IASB) take effect. The purpose of IFRSs is to achieve a set of global accounting standards for the recognition, measurement, presentation and disclosure of information in financial statements. These standards are dealt with in more detail in Chapter 8. They replace Financial Reporting Standards (FRSs) issued by the Accounting Standards Board (ASB) and Statements of Standard Accounting Practice (SSAPs) issued by the Accounting Standards Committee, which preceded the ASB. FRSs and SSAPs have governed many aspects of the presentation of financial statements and the disclosure of information, a role now carried out by IFRSs.

REPORTING PROFITABILITY

Businesses exist to make a profit. Thus, as we saw in Chapter 3, the basic accounting concept is that:

$$\textbf{profit} = \textbf{income} - \textbf{expenses}$$

However, business profitability is determined by the matching principle – *matching income earned with the expenses incurred in earning that income*. Income is the value of sales of goods or services produced by the business. The IFRS definition is that income is increases in economic benefits during the accounting period. Expenses are all the costs incurred in buying, making or providing those goods or services and all the marketing and selling, production, logistics, human resource, IT, financing, administration and management costs involved in operating the business. Expenses are decreases in economic benefits during the accounting period.

The profit (or loss) of a business for a financial period is reported in an Income Statement (known as a Profit and Loss account prior to the introduction of IFRS). This will typically appear as in Table 6.1.

It should be noted that published financial statements up until 2004 include a Profit and Loss account. After 2005, published financial statements will use the term Income Statement. For the purposes of this course, there is little difference, although the calculation of profits (as will be seen in Chapter 8) does have important differences under IFRS compared with previous methods, although these are largely beyond the scope of this text.

The turnover is the business income or sales of goods and services. The cost of sales is either:

■ the cost of providing a service; or
■ the cost of buying goods sold by a retailer; or
■ the cost of raw materials and production costs for a product manufacturer.

However, not all the goods bought by a retailer or used in production will have been sold in the same period as the sales are made. The matching principle requires that the business adjusts for increases or decreases in inventory – the stock of goods bought or produced for resale but not yet sold. Therefore, the cost of sales in the accounts is more properly described as the cost of goods *sold*, not the cost of goods *produced*. Because the production and sale of services are simultaneous, the cost of services

Table 6.1 Profit and Loss account

Turnover	2,000,000
Less: cost of sales	1,500,000
Gross profit	500,000
Less: selling, administration and finance expenses	400,000
Operating profit before interest and tax	100,000

produced always equals the cost of services sold (there is no such thing as an inventory of services). The treatment of inventory is covered in more detail in subsequent chapters. The distinction between cost of sales and expenses leads to two types of profit being reported: gross profit and operating profit.

Gross profit is the difference between the selling *price* and the purchase (or production) cost of the goods or services sold. Using a simple example, a retailer selling baked beans may buy each tin for 5p and sell it for 9p. The gross profit is 4p per tin.

$$\textbf{gross profit} = \textbf{sales} - \textbf{cost of sales}$$

Expenses will include all the other (selling, administration, finance etc.) costs of the business, that is those not directly concerned with buying, making or providing goods or services, but supporting that activity. The same retailer may treat the rent of the store, salaries of employees, distribution and computer costs and so on as expenses in order to determine the *operating profit*.

$$\textbf{operating profit} = \textbf{gross profit} - \textbf{expenses}$$

The operating profit is one of the most significant figures because it represents the profit generated from the ordinary operations of the business. It is also called **net profit**, **profit before interest and taxes (PBIT)** or **earnings before interest and taxes (EBIT)**.

The distinction between cost of sales and expenses can vary between industries and organizations. A single store may treat only the product cost as the cost of sales, and salaries and rent as expenses. A large retail chain may include the salaries of staff and the store rental as cost of sales with expenses covering distribution and corporate costs. For any particular business, it is important to determine the demarcation between cost of sales and expenses.

From operating profit, a company must pay *interest* to its lenders, *income tax* to the government and a *dividend* to shareholders (for their share of the profits as they – unlike lenders – do not receive an interest rate for their investment). The remaining profit is retained by the business as part of its *capital* (see Table 6.2).

Table 6.2   Income Statement (extended)

Operating profit before interest and tax	100,000
Less: interest	16,000
Profit before tax	**84,000**
Less: income tax	14,000
Profit after tax	**70,000**
Less: dividend	30,000
Retained profit	40,000

REPORTING FINANCIAL POSITION

Not all business transactions appear in the Income Statement. The second financial statement is the **Balance Sheet**. This shows the financial position of the business – its assets, liabilities and capital – at the *end* of a financial period. Some business payments are to acquire assets.

The IFRS definition of an **asset** is a resource controlled by an entity as a result of past events and from which future economic benefits are expected to flow to the entity. An entity acquires assets to produce goods or services capable of satisfying customer needs. Physical form is not essential. **Fixed assets** (or non-current assets) are things that the business *owns* and uses as part of its infrastructure. There are two types of fixed assets: tangible and intangible. *Tangible fixed assets* comprise those physical assets that can be seen and touched, such as buildings, machinery, vehicles, computers etc. *Intangible fixed assets* comprise non-physical assets such as the customer goodwill of a business or its intellectual property, e.g. its ownership of patents and trademarks.

Current assets include money in the bank, **debtors** (the sales to customers on credit, but unpaid) and **inventory** (the stock of goods bought or manufactured, but unsold). The word *current* in accounting means 12 months, so current assets are those that will change their form during the next year (see working capital later in this chapter). By contrast, non-current assets (see above) do not normally change their form in the ordinary course of business, as infrastructure they have a longer term role.

Sometimes assets are acquired or expenses incurred without paying for them immediately. In doing so, the business incurs liabilities. **Liabilities** are debts that the business *owes*. The IFRS definition of a liability is a present obligation of the entity arising from past events, the settlement of which is expected to result in an outflow from the entity of resources embodying economic benefits. Liabilities – called **creditors** in the Balance Sheet – may be *current liabilities* such as bank overdrafts, trade creditors (purchases of goods on credit, but unpaid) and amounts due for taxes etc. As for assets, the word current means that the liabilities will be repaid within 12 months. Current liabilities also form part of working capital.

Long-term liabilities or creditors due after more than one year cover loans to finance the business that are repayable after 12 months and certain kinds of provisions (see later in this chapter). **Capital** (or equity) is a particular kind of liability, as it is the money invested by the owners in the business. As mentioned above, capital is increased by the retained profits of the business (the profit after paying interest, tax and dividends). **Equity** is defined as the residual interest in the assets of the entity after deducting all its liabilities. In a company, capital or equity is usually called **shareholders' funds**.

The Balance Sheet will typically appear as in Table 6.3. In the Balance Sheet, the assets must agree with the total of liabilities and capital, because what the business owns is represented by what it owes to outsiders (liabilities) and to the owners (capital). This is called the accounting equation:

$$\textbf{assets} = \textbf{liabilities} + \textbf{capital}$$

or

$$\textbf{assets} - \textbf{liabilities} = \textbf{capital}$$

Table 6.3 Balance Sheet

Fixed assets	1,150,000
Current assets	
Debtors	300,000
Stock	200,000
	500,000
Less: creditors due within one year	
Creditors	300,000
Bank overdraft	50,000
	350,000
Net current assets	**150,000**
Total assets less current liabilities	**1,300,000**
Less: creditors due after one year	
Long-term loans	300,000
Total net assets	**1,000,000**
Capital and reserves	**1,000,000**

An older (but no longer used) format for the Balance Sheet is one where liabilities and capital appear on the left hand side while assets appear on the right hand side. Although this format is no longer in use, it may be helpful to picture that format as it is sometimes easier to understand the relationship of assets being equal to liabilities and capital. This format would show the Balance Sheet as:

Liabilities		**Assets**	
Current liabilities		Current assets	
Creditors	300,000	Debtors	300,000
Bank overdraft	50,000	Stock	200,000
	350,000		500,000
Long-term loans	300,000	Fixed assets	1,150,000
Total liabilities	650,000		
Capital	1,000,000		
	1,650,000		1,650,000

Importantly, the capital of the business does *not* represent the value of the business – it is the result of the application of a number of accounting principles. In addition to the accounting standards referred to earlier, there are some basic accounting principles that are generally accepted by the accounting profession as being important in preparing accounting reports. These were described in Chapter 3.

Disclosure

In the Income Statement, it is common practice to separate those items of income and expenses that arise in the ordinary course of business and those that do not.

The definition of income includes both revenue and gains. Revenue arises in the ordinary course of business (e.g. sales, fees, interest, dividends, royalties and rent). Gains represent other items such as income from the disposal of non-current assets or revaluations of investments. Gains are usually disclosed separately in the financial statements. The definition of expenses includes those expenses that arise in the ordinary course of business (e.g. salaries, advertising etc.) as well as losses. Losses represent other items such as those resulting from disasters such as fire and flood and following the disposal of non-current assets or losses following from changes in foreign exchange rates. Losses are usually disclosed separately in the financial statements.

ACCRUALS ACCOUNTING

An important principle that is particularly relevant to the interpretation of accounting reports is the matching principle.

The matching (or accruals) principle recognizes income when it is *earned* and recognizes expenses when they are *incurred*, not when money is received or paid out (a method called cash accounting). While cash is very important in business, the accruals method provides a more meaningful picture of the financial performance of a business from year to year.

Unlike a system of *cash accounting*, where receipts are treated as income and payments as expenses (which is common in not-for-profit organizations), the matching principle requires a system of *accrual accounting*, which takes account of the timing differences between receipts and payments and when those cash flows are treated as income earned and expenses incurred for the calculation of profit.

Accruals accounting makes adjustments for:

■ prepayments;
■ accruals; and
■ provisions.

The matching principle requires that certain cash payments made in advance are treated as prepayments, i.e. made in advance of when they are treated as an expense for profit purposes. Other expenses are accrued, i.e. treated as expenses for profit purposes even though no cash payment has yet been made.

Table 6.4   Prepayments and accruals

	Profit effect	Balance Sheet	Cash flow
Prepayment	Expense of £3,000	Prepayment (current asset) of £9,000	Cash outflow of £12,000
Accrual	Expense of £800	Accrual (creditor) of £800	No cash flow until quarterly bill received and paid

A good example of a prepayment is insurance, which is paid 12 months in advance. Assume that a business which has a financial year ending 31 March pays its 12 months insurance premium of £12,000 in advance on 1 January. At its year end, the business will only treat £3,000 (3/12 of £12,000) as an expense and will treat the remaining £9,000 as a prepayment (a current asset in the Balance Sheet).

A good example of an accrual is electricity, which like most utilities is paid (often quarterly) in arrears. If the same business usually receives its electricity bill in May (covering the period March to May) it will need to accrue an expense for the month of March, even if the bill has not yet been received. If the prior year's bill was £2,400 for the same quarter (allowing for seasonal fluctuations in usage) then the business will accrue £800 (1/3 of £2,400).

The effect of prepayments and accruals on profit, the Balance Sheet and cash flow is shown in Table 6.4.

A further example of the matching principle is in the creation of provisions. **Provisions** are estimates of possible liabilities that may arise, but where there is uncertainty as to timing or the amount of money. An example of a possible future liability is a provision for warranty claims that may be payable on sales of products. The estimate will be based on the likely costs to be incurred in the future.

Other types of provisions cover reductions in asset values. The main examples are:

■ *Doubtful debts*: customers may experience difficulty in paying their accounts and a provision may be made based on experience that a proportion of debtors will never pay.
■ *Inventory*: some stock may be obsolete but still held in the store. A provision reduces the value of the obsolete stock to its sale or scrap value (if any).
■ *Depreciation*: this is a charge against profits, intended to write off the value of each fixed asset over its useful life.

Provisions for likely future liabilities (e.g. warranty claims) are shown in the Balance Sheet as long-term liabilities, while provisions that reduce asset values (e.g. doubtful debts, inventory and depreciation) are shown as deductions from the cost of the asset. The most important provision, because it typically involves a large amount of money, is for depreciation.

DEPRECIATION

Fixed assets are **capitalized** in the Balance Sheet so that the purchase of fixed assets does not affect profit. However, depreciation is an expense that spreads the cost of the asset over its useful life. The following example illustrates the matching principle in relation to depreciation.

An asset costs £100,000. It is expected to have a life of four years and have a resale value of £20,000 at the end of that time. The depreciation charge is:

$$\frac{\text{asset cost} - \text{resale value}}{\text{expected life}} = \frac{100,000 - 20,000}{4} = 20,000 \, \text{p.a.}$$

It is important to recognize that the cash outflow of £100,000 occurs when the asset is bought. The depreciation charge of £20,000 per annum is a non-cash expense each year. However, the value of the asset in the Balance Sheet reduces each year as a result of the depreciation charge, as follows:

	Original asset cost	Provision for Depreciation	Net value in Balance Sheet
End of year 1	100,000	20,000	80,000
End of year 2	100,000	40,000	60,000
End of year 3	100,000	60,000	40,000
End of year 4	100,000	80,000	20,000

If the asset is then sold, any profit or loss on sale is treated as a separate item in the Income Statement (Profit and Loss account). Alternatively, the asset can be depreciated to a nil value in the Balance Sheet even though it is still in use.

A type of depreciation used for intangible assets, such as goodwill or leasehold property improvements, is called **amortization**, which has the same meaning and is calculated in the same way as depreciation. In reporting profits, some companies show the profit before depreciation (or amortization) is deducted, because it can be a substantial cost, but one that does not result in any cash flow. A variation of EBIT (see earlier in this chapter) is **EBITDA: earnings before interest, taxes, depreciation and amortization**.

Three accounting treatments are important for managers to understand and each is treated in turn:

■ Accounting for value added tax.
■ Accounting for goodwill.
■ Accounting for leases.

ACCOUNTING FOR VALUE ADDED TAX (VAT)

Value Added Tax (or VAT) is not shown in most financial statements (although an exception is in some retail businesses). VAT is added to sales by businesses selling goods and services. When businesses purchase goods and services, they have to pay VAT. The business must remit the difference between the VAT it recovers from customers and the VAT it pays its suppliers to the tax authorities. As a transaction, the receipts (from sales) equal the payments (to suppliers and to the tax authorities) and hence these are not shown in the Income Statement (Profit and Loss account) although the unremitted liability to the taxation authorities appears in the Balance Sheet as a creditor. In retail businesses, where VAT is more complex (some transactions are exempt from VAT) the VAT-inclusive and exclusive turnover may both be shown in the Income Statement.

ACCOUNTING FOR GOODWILL

Goodwill is an intangible asset. It arises where a company buys a business and pays more than the fair value of the tangible assets. Goodwill represents the value of brands, customer lists, location, reputation etc. and is reflected in the expectation of future profits. Goodwill cannot be created on a Balance Sheet from internally generated goodwill, but only on the acquisition of another business. Goodwill is amortized (amortization is the same principle as depreciation, but the term is used in relation to intangible assets) over a maximum of twenty years, although an annual assessment of impairment (see Chapter 8) must be carried out. The IFRS number IAS36 sets out the proper accounting treatment.

Example of goodwill

Negotiations are completed for the acquisition of a business for £1 million. The fair value of tangible assets purchased is £700,000. The goodwill is therefore £300,000 and the acquiring business decides to amortize the goodwill over 10 years. The annual amortization cost is therefore £30,000. At year end, the Balance Sheet will show:

Intangible asset – goodwill	£300,000
Less provision for amortization	30,000
	£270,000

The £30,000 annual charge will need to re-assessed annually to determine if the goodwill has been impaired. This is called an annual impairment test, although the detailed method of calculating impairment is beyond the scope of this book.

ACCOUNTING FOR LEASES

Leasing arose as a method of finance for equipment used by business organizations, in which a business needing equipment (the lessee) 'rented' that equipment from a financial institution (the lessor) which in turn paid the supplier for the equipment. The lessee pays a fixed monthly sum over a number of years to the lessor in payment of the debt. Historically, the lease payments were treated as a business expense. Most businesses finance much of their tangible non-current assets through leasing facilities. The IFRS number IAS17 sets out the proper accounting treatment.

There are two types of leases: operating and finance. The difference is that under a finance lease, all the risks and rewards are with the lessee. In the case of finance leases, the substance and economic reality are that the lessee acquires the economic benefits of the use of the leased asset for the major part of its useful life in return for entering into an obligation to pay an amount, usually in instalments, approximating the fair value of the asset and the interest cost. Finance leases satisfy the definition of an asset and liability and are therefore recognized as such in the lessee's Balance Sheet.

Payments made to the lessor are apportioned between the interest cost which is treated as an expense in the Income Statement and a reduction of the liability. The asset is depreciated in the Income Statement and reduces the Balance Sheet asset value as though it was owned.

Operating lease payments, where risk and rewards are maintained by the lessor, (the most common example is the company motor vehicle) are treated as an expense and are not capitalized in the Balance Sheet, although a disclosure of the lease liability must be made in the Notes to the financial statements.

Example of accounting for a lease

A company buys equipment on 1st April for £100,000 and enters a finance lease agreement with repayments of £25,000 per year over 5 years. The total interest cost is therefore £25,000 (5 years @ £25,000 = £125,000 – cost of equipment £100,000). Depreciation is charged over 5 years. The interest cost is not allocated equally as higher interest charges are allocated to the early years when the debt is highest. A common method for allocating interest costs over the loan period is the 'Rule of 78', the detailed calculation for which is beyond the scope of this text. However, applying this method, the interest cost is allocated over the lease term as

Year 1	£8,934
Year 2	£6,967
Years 3–5	£9,099 (in total)

When the equipment is first leased (on 1st April) the company's Balance Sheet will show:

		£
Fixed asset		100,000
Current liability	25,000 – interest 8,934	16,066
Long term liability	100,000 – interest 16,066	83,934
		100,000

Note that the interest is deducted from the repayment liability because it does not become an expense until future years, under the principle of accrual accounting.

At the end of the first year (on 31st March), the Income Statement will include expenses of

	£
Depreciation (£100,000/5)	20,000
Interest	8,934
Total expenses	28,934

At the end of the first year, the Balance Sheet will show:

Fixed asset		100,000
Less provision for depreciation		20,000
		80,000
Current liability	25,000 – interest 6,967	18,033
Long term liability	75,000 – interest 9,099	65,901
		83,934

There have been repayments to the lessor of £25,000 of which:

Interest	8,934
Principal repayment	16,066

The £16,066 is represented by the reduction in the total debt from £100,000 to £83,934. It may appear that the Balance Sheet at the end of the first year does not balance (assets are £80,000 and liabilities are £83,934, a difference of £3,934). However, this emphasizes the importance of the Cash Flow statement. The full picture is that in addition to these Balance Sheet figures, the Cash Flow will include expenses of £28,934 less repayments of £25,000 (a difference of £3,934).

REPORTING CASH FLOW

The third financial statement is the cash flow. The Cash Flow statement shows the movement in cash for the business during a financial period. It includes:

- cash flow from operations;
- interest receipts and payments;
- income taxes paid;
- capital expenditure (i.e. the purchase of new fixed assets);
- dividends paid to shareholders;
- new borrowings or repayment of borrowings.

Table 6.5 Cash Flow statement

Net cash inflow from operating activities (see Note 1)	115,000
Interest paid	−16,000
Taxation (see Note 2)	−12,000
Capital expenditure	−100,000
Dividends paid (see Note 2)	−25,000
Cash outflow before use of liquid resources and financing	−38,000
Additional borrowing	50,000
Increase in cash	12,000

Note 1:

Operating profit before interest and tax	100,000
Depreciation charge	20,000
Stock increase	(10,000)
Debtors' increase	(15,000)
Creditors' increase	20,000
Net cash flow from operating activities	115,000

Note 2:

Taxation and dividends are not the same as the amounts shown in the Profit and Loss account earlier in this chapter because of timing differences between when those items are treated as expenses and when the cash payment is made, which is normally after the end of the financial year.

The cash flow from operations differs from the operating profit because of:

■ depreciation, which as a non-cash expense is added back to profit (since operating profit is the result *after* depreciation is deducted);
■ increases (or decreases) in working capital (e.g. debtors, inventory, prepayments, creditors and accruals), which reduce (or increase) available cash.

An example of a cash flow statement is shown in Table 6.5.

The management of working capital is a crucial element of cash management.

WORKING CAPITAL

Working capital is the difference between current assets and current liabilities (or creditors). In practical terms, we are primarily concerned with stock and debtors, although prepayments are a further element of current assets. Current liabilities comprise creditors and accruals. The other element of working capital is **bank**, representing either surplus cash (a current asset) or short-term borrowing through a bank overdraft facility (a creditor).

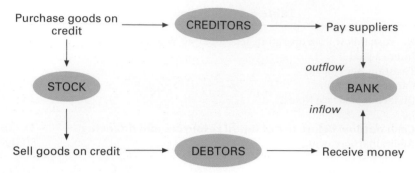

Figure 6.1   The working capital cycle

The working capital cycle is shown in Figure 6.1. Money tied up in debtors and stock puts pressure on the firm, either to reduce the level of that investment or to seek additional borrowings. Alternatively, cash surpluses can be invested to generate additional income through interest earned.

Managing working capital is essential for success, as the ability to avoid a cash crisis and pay debts as they fall due depends on:

■ managing debtors through effective credit approval, invoicing and collection activity;
■ managing stock through effective ordering, storage and identification of stock;
■ managing trade creditors by negotiation of trade terms and through taking advantage of settlement discounts; and
■ managing cash by effective forecasting, short-term borrowing and/or investment of surplus cash where possible.

Methods for managing and monitoring debtors, stock and creditors are described in Chapter 7.

A THEORETICAL PERSPECTIVE ON FINANCIAL STATEMENTS

A necessary ingredient for shareholder value (see Chapter 2), given the separation of ownership from control in most large business organizations, is the control of what managers actually do. Control is considered in the rational-economic paradigm (see Chapter 4) through the notion of *contract*, in which the role of control is to measure and reward performance such that there will be greater *goal congruence*, i.e. that individuals pursuing their own self-interest will also pursue the collective interest.

There are two main versions of contractual theory: agency theory and transaction cost economics. Agency theory sees the economy as a network of interlocking contracts. The transaction cost approach sees the economy as a mixture of markets and hierarchies (transaction cost economics is discussed further in Chapter 15).

AGENCY THEORY

Agency theory is concerned with contractual relationships within the firm, between a principal and an agent, whose rights and duties are specified by a contract of employment. This model recognizes the behaviour of an agent (the manager), whose actions the management accounting and control system seeks to influence and control. Both are assumed to be rational-economic persons motivated solely by self-interest, although they may differ with respect to their preferences, beliefs and information.

The principal wishes to influence what the agent does, but delegates tasks to the agent in an uncertain environment. The agent expends effort in the performance of these tasks. The outcome depends on both environmental factors and the effort expended by the agent. Under the *sharing rule*, the agent usually receives a reward, being a share of the outcome. The reward will depend on the information system used to measure the outcome. Consequently, financial reports play an important role in regulating the actions of agents. The assumption of agency theory is that the agent obtains utility (a benefit) from the reward but disutility from expending effort. Both principal and agent are assumed to be risk averse and utility maximizers.

The agency model involves seeking an employment contract that specifies the sharing rule and the information system. An accounting system can provide output measures from which an agent's efforts can be inferred, but the measures may not accurately reflect the effort expended. This leads to uncertainty about the relationship between the accounting measure and the agent's effort. If the principal cannot observe the agent's effort, or infer it from measured output, the agent may have an incentive to act in a manner different to the employment contract – this is called *moral hazard*. A principal who can observe the agent's effort but does not have access to all the information held by the agent does not know whether the effort expended has been based on the agent's information or whether the agent has 'shirked'. This is called *adverse selection*.

Moral hazard and adverse selection are a consequence of *information asymmetry*. This happens because principal and agent have different amounts of information. A function of accounting under agency theory is to improve efficiency by minimizing the losses caused through moral hazard and adverse selection.

Seal (1995) gives the example of renting a holiday home that is used by the owner only a few weeks of the year. The owner (the principal) may appoint a local agent to let out the home. The agency problem is how to motivate and monitor the agent in return for the commission earned by the agent. The owner will expect regular accounts of income and expenditure. Agency theorists use this reasoning to explain the development of financial accounting and auditing in more complex agency relationships.

There are problems with agency theory, however. It ignores the effect of capital markets by assuming a single owner rather than a group of owners. The model focuses on single-period behaviour; many individuals violate the assumptions of rational self-interested behaviour and the agency perspective is narrow because there is no regard given to power, trust, ethical issues or equity, all of which may affect behaviour. We consider alternative theories in the next chapter.

CONCLUSION

This chapter has covered the main financial statements. It has introduced the regulations and standards governing those statements and described the most important principles underlying the construction of accounts. Three important accounting treatments have also been described: value added tax, goodwill and leases. The chapter has also introduced the concept of working capital. The chapter concluded with an introduction to what has been historically one of the main theories underlying the construction of financial statements, agency theory. In the next chapter, we introduce the tools and techniques that are used to interpret financial statements and consider some alternative theoretical perspectives.

After you have read this chapter, you should:

■ Revise your understanding of the accounting terms. The Glossary in Part IV is a helpful aid.
■ Practice the Questions for this chapter and then check your answers against the solutions. Questions for each chapter are in Appendix 1. The solutions are in Appendix 2.

REFERENCES

Blake, J. (1997). *Accounting Standards*. (6th edn). London: Financial Times/Pitman Publishing.
Seal, W. (1995). Economics and control. In A. J. Berry, J. Broadbent and D. Otley (eds), *Management Control: Theories, Issues and Practices*, London: Macmillan.

7

INTERPRETING FINANCIAL STATEMENTS AND ALTERNATIVE THEORETICAL PERSPECTIVES

This chapter shows how ratio analysis can be used to interpret financial statements. This interpretation covers profitability, liquidity (cash flow), gearing (borrowings), activity/efficiency and shareholder return. A case study demonstrates how the use of ratios can look 'behind the numbers' contained in an Annual Report. The chapter concludes with several alternative theoretical frameworks on financial reporting.

RATIO ANALYSIS

The Income Statement (Profit and Loss account), Balance Sheet and Cash Flow statement can be studied using ratios. *Ratios* are typically two numbers, with one being expressed as a percentage of the other. **Ratio analysis** can be used to help interpret *trends* in performance year on year and by *benchmarking* to industry averages or to the performance of individual competitors. Ratio analysis can be used to interpret performance against five criteria:

- the rate of profitability;
- liquidity, i.e. cash flow;
- gearing, i.e. the proportion of borrowings to shareholders' investment;
- how efficiently assets are utilized; and
- the returns to shareholders.

There are different definitions that can be used for each ratio. However, it is important that whatever ratios are used, they are meaningful to the business and applied consistently. The most common ratios follow. The calculations refer to the example Income Statement (Profit and Loss account) and Balance Sheet in Chapter 6 and which are repeated below in Tables 7.1, 7.2 and 7.3.

Ratios are nearly always expressed as a percentage (by multiplying the answer by 100). In the following examples, only £'000 (thousands of pounds) are shown.

Table 7.1   Income Statement

Turnover	2,000,000
Less: cost of sales	1,500,000
Gross profit	500,000
Less: selling, administration and finance expenses	400,000
Operating profit before interest and tax	100,000

Table 7.2   Income Statement (extended)

Operating profit before interest and tax	100,000
Less: interest	16,000
Profit before tax	**84,000**
Less: income tax	14,000
Profit after tax	**70,000**
Less: dividend	30,000
Retained profit	40,000

Table 7.3   Balance Sheet

Fixed assets	1,150,000
Current assets	
Debtors	300,000
Stock	200,000
	500,000
Less: creditors due within one year	
Creditors	300,000
Bank overdraft	50,000
	350,000
Net current assets	**150,000**
Total assets less current liabilities	**1,300,000**
Less: creditors due after one year	
Long-term loans	300,000
Total net assets	**1,000,000**
Capital and reserves	**1,000,000**

PROFITABILITY

Return on (shareholders') investment (ROI)

$$\frac{\text{net profit after tax}}{\text{shareholders' funds}} = \frac{70}{1000} = 7\%$$

Return on capital employed (ROCE)

$$\frac{\text{operating profit before interest and tax}}{\text{shareholders' funds} + \text{long-term debt}} = \frac{100}{1,000 + 300} = 7.7\%$$

Operating margin (or operating profit/sales)

$$\frac{\text{operating profit before interest and tax}}{\text{sales}} = \frac{100}{2,000} = 5\%$$

Gross margin (or gross profit/sales)

$$\frac{\text{gross profit}}{\text{sales}} = \frac{500}{2,000} = 25\%$$

Overheads/sales

$$\frac{\text{overheads}}{\text{sales}} = \frac{400}{2,000} = 20\%$$

Each of the profitability ratios provides a different method of interpreting profitability. Satisfactory business performance requires an adequate return on shareholders' funds and total capital employed in the business (the total of the investment by shareholders and lenders). Profit must also be achieved as a percentage of sales, which must itself grow year on year. The operating profit and gross profit margins emphasize different elements of business performance.

A further method of interpreting performance is sales growth, which is simply

$$\frac{\text{sales in year 2 -- sales in year 1}}{\text{sales in year 1}}$$

Hence, had the sales in the previous year been 1,800 (not shown in the example), the sales growth would be

$$\frac{2,000 - 1,800}{1,800} = \frac{200}{1,800} = 11.1\%$$

Businesses and the stock market like to see increasing profitability but also increasing sales, which is an important measure of the long term sustainability of profits.

LIQUIDITY

Working capital

$$\frac{\text{current assets}}{\text{current liabilities}} = \frac{500}{350} = 143\%$$

Acid test (or quick ratio)

$$\frac{\text{current assets} - \text{inventory}}{\text{current liabilities}} = \frac{500 - 200}{350} = 86\%$$

A business that has an acid test of less than 100% may experience difficulty in paying its debts as they fall due. On the other hand, a company with too high a working capital ratio may not be utilizing its assets effectively.

GEARING

Gearing ratio

$$\frac{\text{long-term debt}}{\text{shareholders' funds} + \text{long-term debt}} = \frac{300}{1,000 + 300} = 23.1\%$$

Interest cover

$$\frac{\text{profit before interest and tax}}{\text{interest payable}} = \frac{100}{16} = 6.25 \text{ times}$$

The higher the gearing, the higher the risk of repaying debt and interest. The lower the interest cover, the more pressure there is on profits to fund interest charges.

However, because external funds are being used, the *rate of profit* earned by shareholders is higher where external funds are used. The relationship between risk and return is an important feature of interpreting business performance. Consider the example in Table 7.4 of risk and return for a business whose capital employed is derived from different mixes of debt and equity.

While in the example in Table 7.4 the return on capital employed is a constant 20% (an operating profit of £20,000 on capital employed of £100,000), the return on shareholders' funds increases as debt replaces equity. This improvement to the return to shareholders carries a risk, which increases as the proportion of profits taken by the interest charge increases (and is reflected in the interest cover ratio). If profits turn down, there are substantially more risks carried by the highly geared business.

Table 7.4   Risk and return – effect of different debt/equity mix

	100% equity	50% equity 50% debt	10% equity 90% debt
Capital employed	100,000	100,000	100,000
Equity	100,000	50,000	10,000
Debt	0	50,000	90,000
Operating profit before interest and tax	20,000	20,000	20,000
Interest at 10% on debt	0	5,000	9,000
Profit after interest	20,000	15,000	11,000
Tax at 30%	6,000	4,500	3,300
Profit after tax	14,000	10,500	7,700
Return on investment	14%	21%	77%

ACTIVITY/EFFICIENCY

Asset turnover

$$\frac{\text{sales}}{\text{total assets}} = \frac{2,000}{1,150 + 500} = 121\%$$

This is a measure of how efficiently assets are utilized to generate sales. Investment in assets has as its principal purpose the generation of sales.

MANAGING DEBTORS

The main measure of how effectively debtors are managed is the number of days' sales outstanding. Days' sales outstanding is:

$$\frac{\text{debtors}}{\text{average daily sales}}$$

The business has sales of £2 million and debtors of £300,000. Average daily sales are £5,479 (£2 million/365). There are therefore 54.75 average days' sales outstanding (£300,000/£5,479).

The target number of days' sales outstanding will be a function of the industry, the credit terms offered by the firm and its efficiency in both credit approval and collection activity. Management of debtors will aim to reduce days' sales outstanding over time and minimize bad debts.

Acceptance policies will aim to determine the creditworthiness of new customers before sales are made. This can be achieved by checking trade and bank references, searching company accounts and consulting a credit bureau for any adverse reports. Credit limits can be set for each customer.

Collection policy should ensure that invoices and statements are issued quickly and accurately, that any queries are investigated as soon as they are identified, and that continual follow-up (by telephone and post) of late-paying customers should take place. Discounts may be offered for settlement within credit terms. Bad debts may occur because a customer's business fails. For this reason, firms establish a provision (see earlier in this chapter) to cover the likelihood of customers not being able to pay their debts.

MANAGING STOCK

The main measure of how effectively stock is managed is the stock turnover (or stock turn). Stock turn is:

$$\frac{\text{cost of sales}}{\text{stock}}$$

In the example, cost of sales is £1.5 million and stock is £200,000. The stock turn is therefore 7.5 (£1,500,000/£200,000). This means that stock turns over 7.5 times per year, or on average every 49 days (365/7.5). Sound management of stock requires an accurate and up-to-date stock control system. Often in stock control the *Pareto principle* (also called the 80/20 rule) applies. This recognizes that a small proportion (often about 20%) of the number of stock items accounts for a relatively large proportion (say 80%) of the total value. In stock control, ABC analysis takes the approach that, rather than attempt to manage all stock items equally, efforts should be made to prioritize the 'A' items that account for most value, then 'B' items and only if time permits the many smaller-value 'C' items. Some businesses adopt *just-in-time (JIT)* methods to minimize stockholding, treating any stock as a wasted resource. JIT requires sophisticated production planning, inventory control and supply chain management so that stock is only received as it is required for production or sale.

Stock may be written off because of stock losses, obsolescence or damage. For this reason, firms establish a provision to cover the likelihood of writing off part of the value of stock.

MANAGING CREDITORS

Just as it is important to collect debts from customers, it is also essential to ensure that suppliers are paid within their credit terms. As for debtors, the main measure of how effectively creditors are managed is the number of days' purchases outstanding. Days' purchases outstanding is:

$$\frac{\text{creditors}}{\text{average daily purchases}}$$

The business has cost of sales (usually its main credit purchases, as many expenses – e.g. salaries, rent etc. – are not on credit) of £1.5 million and creditors of £300,000. Average daily purchases are £4,110 (£1.5 million/365). There are therefore 73 average days' purchases outstanding (£300,000/£4,110). This figure has to be reported in a company's annual report to shareholders (see Chapter 7).

The number of days' purchases outstanding will reflect credit terms offered by the supplier, any discounts that may be obtained for prompt payment and the collection action taken by the supplier. Failure to pay creditors may result in the loss or stoppage of supply, which can then affect the ability of a business to satisfy its customers' orders.

SHAREHOLDER RETURN

For these ratios we need some additional information:

Number of shares issued	100,000
Market value of shares	£2.50

Dividend per share

$$\frac{\text{dividends paid}}{\text{number of shares}} = \frac{30,000}{100,000} = fl0.30 \text{ per share}$$

Dividend payout ratio

$$\frac{\text{dividends paid}}{\text{profit after tax}} = \frac{30,000}{70,000} = 43\%$$

Dividend yield

$$\frac{\text{dividends paid per share}}{\text{market value per share}} = \frac{0.30}{2.50} = 12\%$$

Earnings per share

$$\frac{\text{profit after tax}}{\text{number of shares}} = \frac{70,000}{100,000} = fl0.70 \text{ per share}$$

Price/earnings (P/E) ratio

$$\frac{\text{market value per share}}{\text{earnings per share}} = \frac{2.50}{0.70} = 3.57 \text{ times}$$

The shareholder ratios are measures of returns to shareholders on their investment in the business. The dividend and earnings ratios reflect the annual return to shareholders, while the P/E ratio measures the number of years over which the investment in shares will be recovered through earnings.

INTERPRETING FINANCIAL INFORMATION USING RATIOS

The interpretation of any ratio depends on the industry. In particular, the ratio needs to be interpreted as a trend over time, or by comparison to industry averages or competitor ratios. These comparisons help determine whether performance is improving and where improvement may be necessary. Based on the understanding of the business context and competitive conditions, and the information provided by ratio analysis, users of financial statements can make judgements about the pattern of past performance and prospects for a company and its financial strength. Broadly speaking, businesses seek:

■ increasing rates of profit on shareholders' funds, capital employed and sales;
■ adequate liquidity (a ratio of current assets to liabilities of not less than 100%) to ensure that debts can be paid as they fall due, but not an excessive rate to suggest that funds are inefficiently used;
■ a level of debt commensurate with the business risk taken;
■ high efficiency as a result of maximizing sales from the business's investments; and
■ a satisfactory return on the investment made by shareholders.

When considering the movement in a ratio over two or more years, it is important to look at possible causes for the movement. These can be gained by understanding that either the numerator (top number in the ratio) or denominator (bottom number in the ratio) or both can influence the change.

Some of the possible explanations behind changes in ratios are described below.

Profitability

Improvements in the returns on shareholders' funds (ROI) and capital employed (ROCE) may either be because profits have increased and/or because the capital used to generate those profits has altered. When businesses are taken over by others, one way of improving ROI or ROCE is to increase profits by reducing costs (often as a result of economies of scale), but another is to maintain profits while reducing assets and repaying debt.

Improvements in operating profitability as a proportion of sales (PBIT or EBIT) are the result of profitability growing at a faster rate than sales growth, a result either of a higher gross margin or lower expenses. Note that sales growth may result in a higher profit but not necessarily in a higher rate of profit as a percentage of sales. Improvement in the rate of gross profit may be the result of higher selling prices, lower cost of sales, or changes in the mix of product/services sold or different market segments in which they are sold, which may reflect differential profitability.

Naturally, the opposite explanations hold true for deterioration in profitability.

Liquidity

Improvements in the working capital and acid test ratios are the result of changing the balance between current assets and current liabilities. As the working capital cycle in Figure 6.1 showed, money changes form between debtors, stock, bank and creditors. Borrowing over the long term in order to fund current assets will improve this ratio, as will profits that generate cash flow. By contrast, using liquid funds to repay long-term loans or incurring losses will reduce the working capital used to repay creditors.

Gearing

The gearing ratio reflects the balance between long-term debt and shareholders' equity. It changes as a result of changes in either shareholders' funds (more shares may be issued), raising new borrowings or repayments of debt. As debt increases in proportion to shareholders' funds, the gearing ratio will increase.

Interest cover may increase as a result of higher profits or lower borrowings (and reduce as a result of lower profits or higher borrowings), but even with constant borrowings changes in the interest rate paid will also influence this ratio.

Activity/efficiency

Asset turnover improves either because sales increase or the total assets used reduce, a similar situation to that described above for ROCE. The efficiency with which debtors are collected, inventory is managed and creditors paid is also an important measure.

Shareholder return

Decisions made by directors influence both the dividend per share and the dividend payout ratio. Dividends are a decision made by directors on the basis of the proportion of profits they want to distribute and the capital needed to be retained in the business to fund growth. Often, shareholder value considerations will dictate the level of dividends, which businesses do not like to reduce on a per share basis. This is sometimes at the cost of retaining fewer profits and then having to borrow additional funds to support growth strategies. However, the number of shares issued also affects this ratio, as share issues will result in a lower dividend *per share* unless the total dividend is increased. As companies have little influence over their share price, which is a result of market expectations as much as past performance, dividend yield, while influenced by the dividend paid per share, is more readily influenced by changes in the market price of the shares.

Earnings per share is influenced, as for profitability, by the profit but also (like dividends) by the number of shares issued. As for the dividend yield, the price/earnings (P/E) ratio is often more a result of changes in the share price than in the profits reflected in the earnings per share.

Explanations for changes in ratios are illustrated in the following case study.

Case Study 7.1:   Ottakar's – interpreting financial statements

Ottakar's has 74 bookshops and 900 employees. It is the second largest specialist bookseller in the UK after Waterstone's. The information in Tables 7.5 and 7.6 has been extracted from the company's annual report.

The number of shares issued was 20,121,000 in 2001 and 20,082,000 in 2000. Ratios for profitability are shown in Table 7.7.

There was a strong sales growth between 2000 and 2001. Despite this growth, the gross margin remained constant and operating profit to sales increased. This is because the proportion of sales consumed by overheads (selling, distribution and administration costs) reduced from 36.6% [(22,707 + 3,986)/72,922] to 34.8% [(26,219 + 3,797)/86,287]. Operating profit more than doubled (from £1,678 to £3,516) and profit after tax increased from £463 to £1,792 (all figures are in £'000). As shareholders' funds increased by only 10%

Table 7.5   Ottakar's Profit and Loss account

in £'000	2001	2000
Turnover	86,287	72,922
Cost of sales	−52,755	−44,551
Gross profit	33,532	28,371
Selling and distribution costs	−26,219	−22,707
Administration expenses	−3,797	−3,968
Operating profit	3,516	1,678
Profit/(loss) on disposal of fixed assets	4	−336
Profit before interest and taxation	3,520	1,342
Other interest receivable and similar income	3	2
Interest payable and similar charges	−727	−562
Profit on ordinary activities before taxation	2,796	782
Taxation on profit on ordinary activities	−1,004	−319
Profit for the financial period	1,792	463
Dividend and appropriations	−503	−302
Retained profit for the period for equity shareholders	1,289	161
Earnings per share	8.91p	2.31p

Note that the term Profit and Loss account has been used as this is a real financial statement produced before the introduction of IFRS.

Table 7.6 Ottakar's Balance Sheet

in £'000	2001	2000
Fixed assets		
Intangible assets	793	838
Tangible assets	17,692	17,187
	18,485	18,025
Current assets		
Stocks	14,692	13,601
Debtors[1]	2,798	2,612
Cash at bank and in hand	370	–
	17,860	16,213
Creditors:		
Amounts falling due within one year[2]	−14,379	−13,729
Net current assets	3,481	2,484
Total assets less current liabilities	21,966	20,509
Creditors:		
Amounts falling due after more than one year	−7,920	−7,948
Provision for liabilities and charges	−403	−207
Net assets	13,643	12,354
Capital and reserves		
Called-up share capital	1,006	1,006
Share premium account	6,041	6,041
Capital redemption reserve	512	512
Profit and loss account	6,084	4,795
Equity shareholders' funds	13,643	12,354

Notes　[1] The notes disclose that these are predominantly prepayments, with trade debtors comprising only £301,000.
[2] The notes disclose that of the current liabilities, £10,027 are trade creditors and £3,117 accruals (for the year 2000, trade creditors are £8,695).

and capital employed by only 6%, the return on both measures of investment showed a strong improvement.

　　Ratios for liquidity are shown in Table 7.8. While the working capital ratio is healthy, indicating that the company has adequate funds to pay its debts, the acid test reveals that after deducting inventory, the company has only about 22% of assets to cover its current liabilities. This means that it is dependent on sales of books in stock to pay suppliers for those books. The efficiency measures (see below) support this.

　　Ratios for gearing are shown in Table 7.9. These ratios reflect the reduction in long-term debt and the increase in shareholders' funds. Although there has been an increase in interest expense, the increase in operating profit has doubled the interest cover. Borrowings are one third of capital employed, which is fairly conservative, while the interest cover provides good security for lenders.

　　The ratio for activity/efficiency is shown in Table 7.10. Despite a higher asset base, the 18.3% sales increase resulted in an improved efficiency ratio. As reflected in the acid test

Table 7.7   Ottakar's profitability ratios

	2001	2000
Return on shareholders' funds	1,792	463
	$\dfrac{}{13,643}$ = 13.1%	$\dfrac{}{12,354}$ = 3.7%
Return on capital employed	3,516	1,678
	21,563 (13,643 + 7,920) = 16.3%	20,302 (12,354 + 7,948) = 8.3%
Operating profit/sales	3,516	1,678
	$\dfrac{}{86,287}$ = 4.1%	$\dfrac{}{72,922}$ = 2.3%
Gross profit/sales	33,532	28,371
	$\dfrac{}{86,287}$ = 38.9%	$\dfrac{}{72,922}$ = 38.9%
Sales growth	86,287 − 72,922	
	$\dfrac{}{72,922}$ = 18.3%	

Table 7.8   Ottakar's liquidity ratios

	2001	2000
Working capital	17,860	16,213
	$\dfrac{}{14,379}$ = 124.2%	$\dfrac{}{13,729}$ = 118.1%
Acid test	3,168 (17,860 − 14,692)	2,612 (16,213 − 13,601)
	$\dfrac{}{14,379}$ = 22.0%	$\dfrac{}{13,729}$ = 19.0%

Table 7.9   Ottakar's gearing ratios

	2001	2000
Gearing	7,920	7,948
	21,563 (13,643 + 7,920) = 36.7%	20,302 (7,948 + 12,354) = 39.1%
Interest cover	3,520	1,342
	$\dfrac{}{727}$ = 4.8 times	$\dfrac{}{562}$ = 2.4 times

Table 7.10 Ottakar's activity/efficiency ratio

	2001	2000
Asset turnover	86,287	72,922
	36,345 (18,485 + 17,860) = 237%	34,238 (18,025 + 16,213) = 213%
Stock turnover	52,755	44,551
	14,692 = 3.6 turns = 101 days (365/3.6)	13,601 = 3.27 turns = 112 days (365/3.27)
Creditors days	10,027	8,695
	145 (52,755/365) = 69 days	122 (44,551/365) = 71 days

Table 7.11 Ottakar's shareholder return ratios

	2001	2000
Dividend per share	503,000	302,000
	20,121,000 = 2.5p per share	20,082,000 = 1.5p per share
Dividend payout ratio	503	302
	1,792 = 28%	463 = 65%
Earnings per share (disclosed in Profit and Loss account)		

ratio (Table 7.8), working capital is affected significantly by the low stock turn (3.6 means that on average books are held for 101 days before they are sold). It is also reflected in the average time it takes to pay creditors (over two months). However, the ratios show a slight improvement between 2000 and 2001 as current assets increased more than current liabilities, stock turn is higher and creditor payments quicker. Note that there are virtually no trade debtors as the bookshops are a retail business, consequently the debtor days measure is somewhat meaningless.

The shareholder return ratios are shown in Table 7.11. The increase in profits between 2000 and 2001 resulted in increased earnings per share and a higher dividend payout in cash terms, although the percentage of profits paid out in dividends reduced.

As was indicated earlier in this chapter, two years is too short a period to draw any meaningful conclusions and we would need to look at the ratios over five years to identify any trends properly. Table 7.12 shows some of the information from the five-year summary of performance in Ottakar's annual report. These figures show the sales growth over the five years much more clearly than do the two-year ratios, although the increase in profits has been much lower. It also shows that the 2000 year experienced a fall in profits that was outside the trend. By calculating the ratios in Table 7.13 we can see this more clearly.

Table 7.12 Ottakar's five-year summary of performance

in £'000	1997	1998	1999	2000	2001
Turnover	23,710	38,649	57,316	72,922	86,287
Gross profit	9,100	14,988	22,343	28,371	33,532
Operating profit	1,276	2,619	3,312	1,678	3,516
Earnings per share	7.78p	10.61p	12.36p	2.31p	8.91p

Table 7.13 Ottakar's ratios based on five-year summary of performance

in £'000	1997	1998	1999	2000	2001
Sales growth		+63%	+48.3%	+27.2%	+18.3%
Gross margin	38.4%	38.8%	39.0%	38.9%	38.9%
Operating profit/sales	5.4%	6.8%	5.8%	2.3%	4.1%

Although sales continue to increase, the rate of sales growth is slowing. The rate of gross profit to sales is very steady (an indication of the margin allowed by book publishers), while operating profits fluctuated (probably a reflection of costs incurred in opening new bookshops, since location, in common with most retail businesses, is a key aspect of success). Ottakar's annual report explains that the book market should experience an annual growth of 4–5%, but that the larger chains should gain market share at the expense of their weaker competitors.

It is important to remember that ratio analysis can be undertaken not only in relation to the manager's own organization, but also in relation to the financial statements of competitors, customers and suppliers. This is an aspect of strategic management accounting that was discussed in Chapter 4.

LIMITATIONS OF RATIO ANALYSIS

As we have seen in relation to estimates such as accruals, depreciation, goodwill amortization and provisions (see Chapter 6), accounting reports contain information that is arrived at after estimates which involve significant subjectivity. There is also some flexibility in how accounting rules are applied (as we will see in Chapter 8). These judgements influence the numbers that are used in ratio analysis.

Financial statements are historical records and backwards-looking. Inflation can also impact on the values shown in financial statements, particularly where assets are held at historical cost in the Balance Sheet for many years. The Balance Sheet, it should be recognized, is merely a 'snapshot' of assets and liabilities on the last day of the financial year. Ratios are of little value unless calculated over several years when a trend can be identified, or in comparison with similar organizations for benchmarking purposes.

Finally, there are different definitions of ratios used in different textbooks and by different financial statement analysts. The consistent use of a ratio definition is more important than the particular definition selected. Consequently, care needs to be exercised in calculating and interpreting ratios and time needs to be spent understanding economic and competitive conditions and the context of the industry and organization for which ratios are being interpreted. This broader contextual understanding can be gained by reading the company's Annual Report (see Chapter 9), by reading the financial and trade press, internet reports, analyst reports etc. that provide broader information about economic change, the industry, competitive conditions, supply chain issues, customer behaviour, regulatory change etc.

ALTERNATIVE THEORETICAL PERSPECTIVES ON FINANCIAL STATEMENTS

Chapter 6 described the traditional theoretical perspective that has informed financial statements, that is agency theory. We now consider some alternative perspectives: intellectual capital and institutional theory. We also introduce creative accounting and ethics.

INTELLECTUAL CAPITAL

Edvinsson and Malone (1997) defined intellectual capital as 'the hidden dynamic factors that underlie the visible company' (p. 11). Stewart (1997) defined intellectual capital as 'formalized, captured and leveraged knowledge' (p. 68).

Intellectual capital is of particular interest to accountants in increasingly knowledge-based economies in which the limitations of traditional financial statements erode their value as a tool supporting meaningful decision-making (Guthrie, 2001). Three dimensions of intellectual capital have been identified in the literature: human (developing and leveraging individual knowledge and skills); organizational (internal structures, systems and procedures); and customer (loyalty, brand, image etc.). The disclosure of information about intellectual capital as an extension to financial reporting has been proposed by various accounting academics. The most publicized example is the *Skandia Navigator* (see Edvinsson and Malone, 1997).

While most businesses espouse a commitment to employees and the value of their knowledge, as well as to some form of social or environmental responsibility, this is often merely rhetoric, a facade to appease the interest groups of stakeholders. The *institutional* setting of organizations provides another perspective from which to view accounting and reporting.

INSTITUTIONAL THEORY

Institutional theory is valuable because it locates the organization within its historical and contextual setting. It is predicated on the need for *legitimation* and on isomorphic processes. Scott (1995) describes legitimation as the result of organizations being dependent, to a greater or lesser extent, on support from the environment for their survival and continued operation. Organizations need the support of governmental institutions where their operations are regulated (and few organizations are not regulated in some form or other). Organizations are also dependent on the acquisition of resources (labour, finance, technology etc.) for their purposes. If an organization is not legitimated, it may incur sanctions of a legal, economic or social nature.

The second significant aspect of institutional power is the operation of *isomorphism*, the tendency for different organizations to adopt similar characteristics. DiMaggio and Powell (1983) identified three forms of isomorphism: coercive, as a result of political influence and the need to gain legitimacy; mimetic, following from standard responses to uncertainty; and normative, associated with professionalization. They held that isomorphic tendencies between organizations were a result of wider belief systems and cultural frames of reference. Processes of education, inter-organizational movement of personnel and professionalization emphasize these belief systems and cultural values at an institutional level, and facilitate the mimetic processes that result in organizations imitating each other. Isomorphic tendencies exist because 'organizations compete not just for resources and customers, but for political power and institutional legitimacy, for social as well as economic fitness' (DiMaggio and Powell, 1983, p. 150).

These legitimating and isomorphic processes become taken for granted by organizations as they strive to satisfy the demands of external regulators, resource suppliers and professional groups. These taken-for-granted processes themselves become institutionalized in the systems and processes – including accounting and reporting – adopted by organizations. Meyer (1994) argued that accounting arises 'in response to the demands made by powerful elements in the environment on which organizations are dependent' (p. 122).

Institutional investors (insurance companies and pension funds, although this is not the only meaning of 'institution') own over a third of listed UK shares, with a further third being owned by overseas investors (half of these in the United States). In 1963, individuals owned 54% of the shares in UK companies but in 2003 this figure had fallen to 15%. One of the issues arising from this changing pattern of share ownership in the UK has been institutional investor activism, or rather the lack of it. This is beginning to change and some institutional investors are becoming more active in holding Boards more accountable for their performance. This has been at least in part a response to large corporate failures such as Enron and WorldCom and the increased importance given to corporate governance (see Chapter 9).

Each of these theoretical perspectives provides a different view of the role of preparers and the needs of users of financial statements. This perspective also follows through to the users of management accounting information. However, as we have suggested earlier in this book, accounting is not without its limitations. A case study serves to highlight these limitations.

Case Study 7.2:   Carrington Printers – an accounting critique

Carrington Printers was a privately owned, 100-year-old printing company employing about 100 people and operating out of its own premises in a medium-sized town. Although the company was heavily indebted and had been operating with a small loss for the past three years, it had a fairly strong Balance Sheet and a good customer base spread over a wide geographic area. Carrington's simplified Balance Sheet is shown in Table 7.14.

Table 7.14   Carrington Printers' Balance Sheet

Fixed assets	
Land and buildings at cost less depreciation	1,000,000
Plant and equipment at cost less depreciation	450,000
	1,450,000
Current assets	
Debtors	500,000
Inventory	450,000
	950,000
Less creditors due within one year	
Creditors	850,000
Bank overdraft	250,000
	1,100,000
Net current liabilities	−150,000
Total assets less current liabilities	1,300,000
Less creditors due after one year	−750,000
Total net assets	550,000
Capital and reserves	
Issued capital	100,000
Profit and loss account	450,000
Shareholders' funds	550,000

The nature of the printing industry at the time the accounts were prepared was that there was excess production capacity and over the previous year a price war had been fought between competitors in order to retain existing customers and win new customers. The effect of this had been that selling prices (and consequently profit margins) had fallen throughout the industry. Carrington's plant and equipment were, in the main, quite old and not suited to some of the work that it was winning. Consequently, some work was being produced inefficiently, with a detrimental impact on profit margins. Before the end of the year the sales director had left the company and had influenced many of Carrington's customers, with whom he had established a good relationship, to move to his new employer. Over several months, Carrington's sales began to drop significantly.

Lost sales and deteriorating margins on some of the business affected cash flow. Printing companies typically carry a large stock of paper in a range of weights, sizes and colours, while customers often take up to 60 days to pay their accounts. Because payment of taxes and employees takes priority, suppliers are often the last group to be paid. The major suppliers are paper merchants, who stop supplies when their customers do not pay on time. The consequence of Carrington's cash flow difficulties was that suppliers limited the supply of paper that Carrington needed to satisfy customer orders.

None of these events was reflected in the financial statements and the auditors, largely unaware of changing market conditions, had little understanding of the gradual detrimental impact on Carrington that had taken place at the time of the audit. Although aware of the cash flow tightening experienced by the company, the auditors signed the accounts, being satisfied that the business could be treated as a going concern.

As a result of the problems identified above, Carrington approached its bankers for additional loans. However, the bankers declined, believing that existing loans had reached the maximum percentage of the asset values against which they were prepared to lend. The company attempted a sale and leaseback of its land and buildings (through which a purchaser pays a market price for the property, with Carrington becoming a tenant on a long-term lease). However, investors interested in the property were not satisfied that Carrington was a viable tenant and the property was unable to be sold on that basis.

Cash flow pressures continued and the shareholders were approached to contribute additional capital. They were unable to do so and six months after the Balance Sheet was produced the company collapsed, and was placed into receivership and subsequently liquidation by its bankers.

The liquidators found, as is common in failed companies, that the values in the Balance Sheet were substantially higher than what the assets could be sold for. In particular:

- Land and buildings were sold for far less than an independent valuation had suggested, as the property would now be vacant.
- Plant and machinery were almost worthless given their age and condition and the excess capacity in the industry at the time.
- Debtors were collected with substantial amounts being written off as bad debts. Customers often refuse to pay accounts giving spurious reasons and it is often not worthwhile for the liquidator to pursue collection action through the courts.
- Inventory was discovered to be largely worthless. Substantial stocks of paper were found to have been held for long periods with little likelihood of ever being used and other printers were unwilling to pay more than a fraction of its cost.

As the bankers had security over most of Carrington's assets, there were virtually no funds remaining after repaying bank loans to pay the unsecured creditors.

This case raises some important issues about the value of audited financial statements:

1   The importance of understanding the context of the business, that is how its market conditions and its mix of products or services are changing over time, and how well (or in this case badly) the business is able to adapt to these changes.
2   The preparation of financial statements assumes a going concern, but the circumstances facing a business can change quickly and the Balance Sheet can become a meaningless document.
3   The auditors rely on information from the directors about significant risks affecting the company. The directors did not intentionally deceive the auditors, but genuinely believed that the business could be turned around into profit through winning back customers. They also believed that the large inventory would satisfy future customer orders. The directors also genuinely believed that the property could be sold in order to eliminate debt. This was unquestioned by the auditors.

CREATIVE ACCOUNTING AND ETHICS

Accounting choices according to Francis, are moral choices:

Accounting is important precisely to the extent the accountant can transform the world, can influence the lived experience of others in ways which cause that experience to differ from what it would be in the absence of accounting, or in the presence of an alternative kind of accounting (quoted in Gowthorpe and Blake, 1998, p. 3)

Creative accounting is a process of artificially manipulating accounting figures by taking advantage of loopholes in accounting standards or making estimates or judgements that are unrealistic, the purpose of which is to present financial statements in a way that shareholders or other stakeholders may prefer.

Creative accounting practices have been justified by managers for reasons of income smoothing, to bring profits closer to forecasts; changing accounting policies to distract attention from poor performance; or maintaining or boosting share prices (Gowthorpe and Blake, 1998).

Common methods of creative accounting include:

- Under or overstating inventory.
- Depreciating or amortising assets over shorter or longer periods.
- Capitalizing or not capitalizing expenditure (e.g. determining when an expense is a repair or the enhancement of an asset).
- Using accruals to create hidden reserves and/or shift profits between financial periods.
- Increasing or decreasing provisions (e.g. doubtful debts).

Despite the role of accounting standards and other regulations, creative accounting has always played a part in the efforts made by a few companies to present their performance in a better light. Griffiths (1986) commented on the power of financial analysts and investment advisers in the City (of London) and the aim of company directors to present the business as having steady growth in income and profits. This desire for a smoothing effect can be achieved by practices such as accruals, stock valuation, creating or reducing provisions, capitalizing or expensing costs (WorldCom fraudulently capitalized expenses as assets) and off-Balance Sheet financing (creating special purpose entities that hid liabilities from shareholders, which was the main factor in Enron's downfall in the United States). While creative accounting has been frowned on, earnings management has not. Under earnings management, directors aim to satisfy the market expectations influenced by stock analysts.

Smith (1992) described the techniques adopted by companies and claimed that 'much of the apparent growth in profits which had occurred in the 1980s was the result of accounting sleight of hand rather than genuine economic growth' (p. 4). However, although accounting standards continually improve, there are always loopholes that accountants seem to find as quickly as standards are produced.

Richardson and Richardson (1998) emphasized the role of accountants in organizations. They occupy special positions that privilege them to information that has the potential to reveal deviant top management behaviour, which can lead to social and emotional costs for innocent stakeholders and to corporate failures (such as those caused by Robert Maxwell and Polly Peck's Asil Nadir). As these conflicts are unlikely to be resolved internally, the authors argue for the ability to 'blow the whistle'.

However, as things stand, it is more likely that the accountant will simply leave the organization. The problem with *whistleblowing*, the authors comment, is that to some it is an act of subversion, while to others it is an act of citizenship. To the organization, it is an act of disloyalty.

CONCLUSION

This chapter has provided the tools for analysing financial information in terms of profitability, liquidity, gearing, efficiency and shareholder return, while also identifying some of the limitations of financial statement analysis. It has set financial statements in the context of alternative theoretical frameworks that can provide different perspectives on accounting information. In the words of Bebbington *et al.* (2001), accounting practice is the result of 'habit, history, law and expedience, as well as social, political and economic choice' (p. 8). These alternative perspectives continue throughout the third part of this book.

After you have read this chapter, you should:

- Revise your understanding of the accounting terms. The Glossary in Part IV is a helpful aid.
- Practice the Questions for this chapter and then check your answers against the solutions. Questions for each chapter are in Appendix 1. The solutions are in Appendix 2.
- Read Case Study 1. This will help you to interpret accounting information. Try to write an answer. The Case Studies are in Appendix 3 and suggested solutions are in Appendix 4.

REFERENCES

Bebbington, J., Gray, R. and Laughlin, R. (2001). *Financial Accounting: Practice and Principles* (3rd edn). London: Thomson Learning.

Blake, J. (1997). *Accounting Standards.* (6th edn). London: Financial Times/Pitman Publishing.

DiMaggio, P. J. and Powell, W. W. (1983). The iron cage revisited: Institutional isomorphism and collective rationality in organizational fields. *American Sociological Review*, **48**, 147–60.

Edvinsson, L. and Malone, M. S. (1997). *Intellectual Capital*. London: Piatkus.

Gowthorpe, C. and Blake, J. (eds) (1998). *Ethical Issues in Accounting*. London: Routledge.

Griffiths, I. (1986). *Creative Accounting: How to Make Your Profits What You Want Them to Be.* London: Waterstone.

Guthrie, J. (2001). The management, measurement and the reporting of intellectual capital. *Journal of Intellectual Capital*, **2**(1), 27–41.

Meyer, J. W. (1994). Social environments and organizational accounting. In W. R. Scott and J. W. Meyer (eds), *Institutional Environments and Organizations: Structural Complexity and Individuality*, Thousand Oaks, CA: Sage, Publications.

Richardson, S. and Richardson, B. (1998). The accountant as whistleblower. In C. Gowthorpe and J. Blake (eds), *Ethical Issues in Accounting*, London: Routledge.

Scott, W. R. (1995). *Institutions and Organizations*. Thousand Oaks, CA: Sage Publications.

Smith, T. (1992). *Accounting for Growth: Stripping the Camouflage from Company Accounts*. London: Century Business.

Stewart, T. A. (1997). *Intellectual Capital: The New Wealth of Organizations*. London: Nicholas Brealey Publishing.

INTERPRETING FINANCIAL STATEMENTS UNDER INTERNATIONAL FINANCIAL REPORTING STANDARDS (IFRSs)

This chapter introduces International Financial Reporting Standards in the context of global harmonization. It describes in some detail the *Framework for the Preparation and Presentation of Financial Statements* which sets out the concepts underlying the preparation and presentation of financial statements for external users. Specific IFRSs are also reviewed and criticisms of accounting standards are identified.

ACCOUNTING STANDARDS

International Financial Reporting Standards are published by the International Accounting Standards Board (IASB). The predecessor of the IASB was the Board of the International Accounting Standards Committee (IASC) which published International Accounting Standards (IASs). The term 'International Financial Reporting Standards (IFRSs)' includes both the newer IFRSs and the older IASs, together with interpretations issued under these standards.

GLOBAL HARMONIZATION OF ACCOUNTING STANDARDS

This move towards the harmonization of accounting standards between countries through the work of the International Accounting Standards Board (IASB) has been a consequence of the globalization of capital markets, with the consequent need for accounting rules that can be understood by international investors. The dominance of multinational corporations and the desire of companies to be listed on several stock exchanges have led to the need to rationalize different reporting practices in different countries.

The European Union has mandated that all companies must adopt IFRSs by 2005. The US equivalent of the true and fair view (see Chapter 6) is for financial statements to be presented fairly and in accordance with Generally

Accepted Accounting Principles (or GAAPs). This relies more on a rules-based approach than the principles-based approach in IFRSs.

The US has a Financial Accounting Standards Board which has not yet adopted IFRSs. However, at a joint IASB/FASB meeting in 2004, agreement was reached to develop a common conceptual framework (see later in this chapter for an explanation).

COMPLIANCE WITH IFRSs

The need to comply with IFRSs came into effect in 2005. Companies with a 31st December year-end need to comply with IFRS for the first time in December 2005. For companies with a 31st March 2006 year-end, those accounts must comply with IFRSs from that date. Companies will, however, need to show prior year comparative figures according to IFRSs, so the date for altering accounting policies is effectively December 2004 and March 2005, respectively. The changes in accounting policies will, however, also affect the opening Balance Sheet a year earlier.

IAS 1 *Presentation of Financial Statements* requires that an entity whose financial statements comply with IFRSs must make an explicit and unreserved statement of compliance in the Notes to the financial statements. The impact of changed accounting policies must also be shown in the financial statements.

STRUCTURE OF ACCOUNTING STANDARD-SETTING BODIES

The IASB was formed in 2001 and is based in London. The IASB is selected, overseen and funded by the International Accounting Standards Committee (IASC) Foundation with financial support coming from major accounting firms, private financial institutions and industrial companies throughout the world, as well as central and development banks. The IASC Foundation is directed by 19 trustees. Of these trustees:

■ 6 are from North America;
■ 6 are from Europe;
■ 4 are from Asia Pacific; and
■ 3 are from any area, provided geographical balance is maintained.

Of the 19 trustees, 5 represent the accounting profession while international organizations of preparers, users and academics are each represented by 1 trustee.

The IASB has sole responsibility for setting accounting standards. It comprises 14 individuals. Of these, at least 5 are practising auditors, at least 3 are preparers of financial statements, at least 3 are users of financial statements and at least 1 is an academic. The objectives of the IASB are:

■ to develop, in the public interest, a single set of high-quality, understandable and enforceable global accounting standards that require high-quality, transparent and comparable information in financial statements and other financial reporting to help participants in the various capital markets of the world and other users of the information to help make economic decisions;

■ to promote the use and rigorous application of these standards; and

■ to work actively with national standard-setters to bring about convergence of national accounting standards and IFRSs to high-quality solutions.

(Source: International Accounting Standards Board, 2004)

The Standards Advisory Committee (SAC) has 50 members and gives advice to the IASB about its priorities and informs the IASB about the implications of proposed standards for preparers and users of financial statements.

INTERNATIONAL FINANCIAL REPORTING STANDARDS (IFRSs) – AN OVERVIEW

IFRSs (or 'the Standards') set out recognition, measurement, presentation and disclosure requirements dealing with transactions and events that are important in general purpose financial statements, although some standards refer to specific industries. General purpose financial statements are directed towards the common information needs of a wide range of users.

IFRSs are designed for profit-oriented entities. Although they are not designed for not-for-profit activities in the private sector or for public sector or government, these entities may also find them appropriate, and many such entities will use IFRSs in the preparation of their financial statements.

The IASB has produced a *Framework for the Preparation and Presentation of Financial Statements*. While this is not part of IFRSs, the *Framework* is used when an accounting policy is needed and there is no appropriate Standard to choose. All IFRSs are based on the *Framework*.

FRAMEWORK FOR THE PREPARATION AND PRESENTATION OF FINANCIAL STATEMENTS

A complete set of financial statements includes a:

■ Balance Sheet;

■ Income Statement;

■ statement showing changes in equity (i.e. shareholders' funds);

■ Cash Flow Statement;

■ explanatory policies and explanatory Notes.

Information about financial position is primarily provided in a Balance Sheet. Information about performance is primarily provided in an Income Statement. Information about changes in financial position is provided by way of a separate financial statement, although the Cash Flow Statement is largely concerned with this.

Users are defined as:

- investors;
- employees;
- lenders;
- suppliers and trade creditors;
- customers;
- government and their agencies;
- public.

Importantly, management is not defined as a user in terms of financial statements. This is because management has the ability to determine the form and content of additional information to meet its needs. The reporting of information to meet the needs of management is beyond the scope of the *Framework*. Part III of this book is concerned with the information needs of managers, although, as we have seen in Chapter 7, the analysis and interpretation of performance trends and benchmarks through ratio analysis is important for managers in improving shareholder value.

The *Framework* sets out the concepts underlying the preparation and presentation of financial statements for external users. Where there is conflict between the requirements of a Standard and the *Framework*, the Standard prevails. The *Framework* is concerned with:

1 The objective of financial statements.
2 The qualitative characteristics that determine decision usefulness.
3 The definition, recognition and measurement of the elements from which financial statements are constructed.
4 Concepts of capital maintenance.

Each of these is considered in turn.

OBJECTIVE OF FINANCIAL STATEMENTS

The objective of financial statements is to provide information about the financial position, performance and changes in financial position (i.e. cash flow) of an entity that is useful to a wide range of users in making economic decisions (i.e. 'decision usefulness'). The financial statements show the results of the stewardship or accountability of management for the resources entrusted to them by shareholders.

QUALITATIVE CHARACTERISTICS OF FINANCIAL STATEMENTS

The underlying assumptions of financial statements are that they are prepared on an accruals basis and as a going concern (see Chapters 3 and 6). There are also qualitative characteristics that make the information useful to users. These are:

1   *Understandability*: Users are assumed to have a reasonable knowledge of business and economic activities and accounting.

2   *Relevance*: Information must be relevant to the decision-making needs of users. The relevance of information is affected by its nature and *materiality*. Information is material if its omission or mis-statement could influence the economic decisions of users taken on the basis of financial statements.

3   *Reliability*: Information is reliable when it is free from material error and bias and can be depended upon by users to *represent faithfully* that which it purports to represent. To be represented faithfully, it is necessary that transactions are accounted for and presented in accordance with their substance and economic reality and not merely their legal form, which may be contrived (this is called *substance over form* – see the case studies of Enron and WorldCom later in this chapter).

    Information may lose its relevance and reliability if there is undue delay in reporting.

4   *Comparability*: Users must be able to compare the financial statements of an entity through time and be able to compare the financial statements of different entities in order to evaluate their relative financial position, performance and changes in financial position. Measurement and presentation must, therefore, be consistent throughout an entity and over time (see Chapter 3). Importantly, users must be informed of the accounting policies employed in the preparation of financial statements, any changes in these policies and the effects of those changes. However, it is not appropriate for an entity to leave its accounting policies unchanged when more relevant and reliable alternatives exist. The corresponding information for the preceding period is essential for comparability.

Although the *Framework* does not deal directly with the need for a 'true and fair view' (see Chapter 6), the application of the above qualitative characteristics and of appropriate accounting standards normally results in financial statements that convey what is generally understood as a true and fair view.

ELEMENTS OF FINANCIAL STATEMENTS

Financial statements portray the financial effects of transactions by grouping them into broad classes according to their economic characteristics. These broad classes are the elements of financial statements. The elements related to the measurement of financial position in the Balance Sheet are assets, liabilities and equity. The elements related to the measurement of performance in the Income Statement are income and expenses.

Recognition is the process of incorporating in the Balance Sheet or Income Statement an item that meets the definition of an element. Recognition depicts an item in words and a monetary amount and the inclusion of that figure in the Balance Sheet or Income Statement totals. An item that meets the definition of an element should be recognized if:

■   it is probable that any future economic benefit associated with the item will flow to or from the entity; and

■   the item has a cost or value that can be measured with reliability.

An item that has the characteristics of an element but does not meet these criteria for recognition may warrant disclosure in a Note to the financial statements (see Chapter 9).

An asset is not recognized in the Balance Sheet when expenditure has been incurred for which it is considered improbable that economic benefits will flow to the entity beyond the current accounting period. This should be treated as an expense (see the WorldCom case study in this chapter for an example).

A liability is recognized in the Balance Sheet when it is probable that an outflow of resources which have economic benefit will result from the settlement of a present obligation.

MEASUREMENT OF THE ELEMENTS OF FINANCIAL STATEMENTS

Measurement is the process of determining the monetary amounts at which the elements of the financial statements are to be recognized and carried in the Balance Sheet and Income Statement. There are four bases of measurement:

■   *Historical cost*: Assets are recorded at the cash or fair value consideration given at the time of their acquisition.

■   *Current cost*: Assets are carried at the cash that would have to be paid if the same or equivalent asset was acquired currently.

■   *Realizable value*: Assets are carried at the cash that could currently be obtained by selling the asset.

■   *Present value*: Assets are carried at the present discounted value of the future net cash inflows that the item is expected to generate (see Chapter 14 for a full explanation of present value).

The most common measurement basis is historical cost. However:

■   inventories are usually carried at the lower of cost and net realizable value;

■   marketable investments may be carried at market value;

■   pension liabilities are carried at present value.

CONCEPTS OF CAPITAL MAINTENANCE

The *financial* concept of capital comprises invested money, being equal to net assets or the equity of a company. The *physical* concept of capital refers to the productive capacity of the business. The concept chosen indicates the goal to be attained in determining profit.

Capital maintenance provides the linkage between concepts of capital and profit because it provides the point of reference as to how profit is measured. Under *financial capital maintenance*, a profit is earned only if the financial amount of net assets at the end of a period exceeds the financial amount of net assets at the beginning of a period, excluding distributions to (i.e. dividends) and contributions from (i.e. share issues) shareholders.

Under *physical capital maintenance*, a profit is earned only if the physical productive capacity of the business at the end of a period exceeds the physical productive capacity at the beginning of a period, after excluding distributions to and contributions from shareholders.

The physical capital maintenance concept requires the adoption of the current cost basis of measurement, which is not a requirement of financial capital maintenance. The principal difference between the two concepts is the treatment of changes in the prices of assets and liabilities. For the purposes of this book, we will assume that the concept of financial capital maintenance applies.

SPECIFIC IFRSs

The full list of IFRSs and their predecessor IASs is contained in the Appendix to this chapter. Many relate to specific accounting treatments or specific industries that are beyond the scope of this book. However, some important standards are:

- IFRS 2 *Share-based payment*: Companies have increasingly used grants of shares through share options and share ownership plans to employees. Previously, these were not reflected in financial statements until such time as the option was exercised. There has been much criticism of this accounting treatment by shareholders. The Standard now requires an entity to reflect in its Income Statement the effects of share-based payment transactions based on the fair value of the equity instruments granted, measured at the date of the grant. Concern has been expressed that some companies may limit their share options in view of this change in accounting treatment.
- IAS 2 *Inventory*: Stock is valued at the lower of cost and net realizable value (i.e. sales proceeds less costs of sale). Importantly for the purposes of subsequent chapters, the cost of inventory includes all costs of purchase, costs of conversion and other costs incurred in bringing the inventory to its present location and condition. Costs of purchase include import duties and transport, less any discounts or rebates. Costs of conversion include direct labour and a systematic allocation of fixed and variable production overheads (this is covered in detail in Chapters 12 and 13).
- IAS 10 *Events after the Balance Sheet date*: Contrary to prior practice, companies that declare a final dividend after the Balance Sheet date do not recognize the liability for the dividend at the balance date.

- IAS 16 *Property, plant and equipment*: Assets are valued at either cost less accumulated depreciation or at a revaluation less depreciation. Depreciation was covered in detail in Chapter 6.
- IAS 19 *Employee benefits*: The stock market losses of recent years have resulted in pension fund liabilities (to pay pensions for retired employees) exceeding their assets. One of the earlier standards, FRS17, was introduced to require companies to recognize the liability for a deficit in their pension funds in their financial statements which is having a significant impact on reported performance, and has resulted in the closure of many corporate pension funds to new employees. In summary, the standard requires that pension scheme:
    - assets are measured using market values;
    - liabilities are measured using a prescribed method and discounted to present values at a specified rate;
    - surplus or deficit is recognized in full on the company's Balance Sheet, and that the movement in the scheme surplus or deficit is analysed into: current and past service costs which are recognized in operating profit; the interest cost and expected return on assets which are recognized as other finance costs; and actuarial gains and losses which are recognized in the statement of total recognized gains and losses.
- IAS 36 *Impairment of assets*: Impairment refers to the reduction in value of an intangible asset such as goodwill (see Chapter 6 for an example of goodwill). Impairment involves the annual assessment of the recoverable amount of an asset. *The recoverable amount* is the higher of its fair value less costs to sell; and the value in use – i.e. the present value of future cash flows (see Chapter 14 for the calculation of present value of cash flows). An increase in the amortization (the same as depreciation) provision would need to be made (reducing the goodwill carried in the Balance Sheet) if future cash flows were unable to justify the existing carrying value.
- IAS 37 *Provisions, contingent liabilities and contingent assets*: A provision is a liability of uncertain timing or amount (see Chapter 6 for examples). Examples include warranty obligations and retail policies for refunds. The amount recognized as a provision is the best estimate of the expenditure required to settle the obligation.
- IAS 38 *Intangible assets*: Internally generated goodwill, brands, customer lists etc. are not recognized as assets. Intangible assets arise when they are purchased (see Chapter 6 for the example of goodwill). These assets are carried at cost less amortization or at a revaluation less amortization, but see IAS 36 above re impairment. In companies that invest heavily in research and development (e.g. pharmaceuticals), expenditure on research is recognized as an expense although expenditure on development may be recognized as an asset provided specific criteria can be satisfied. Examples of research include activities aimed at gaining new knowledge and the search for evaluation and selection of alternative materials, products, processes, services etc. Examples of development include design, construction and testing of prototypes; design of tooling, moulds and dies; design, construction and operation of a pilot plant; and the design, construction and testing of a selected alternative for improved materials, products, processes, services etc.

There are also significant changes in accounting for financial instruments (IAS 39) such as hedging and changes in foreign exchange rates (IAS 21) but these are outside the scope of this book.

EFFECT OF IFRSs ON FINANCIAL STATEMENTS

An important presentational change is the change of name of the Profit and Loss account to the Income Statement, a requirement of the *Framework* document. However, most of the examples in this book, using real companies, retain the language Profit and Loss account as, at the date of writing, few companies have produced accounts under IFRSs. Although IFRSs will have an impact on both the Income Statement and the Balance Sheet, most of these changes are outside the scope of this text. However, by way of example, in May 2005 Cadbury Schweppes plc restated their 2004 financial statements taking into account the changes required by IFRSs.

Cadbury Schweppes revealed that:

■ Profit before tax had decreased by 5%.
■ Gross margin had decreased by 0.6%.
■ Earnings per share had decreased by 6%.
■ Net assets were £788 million lower.
■ There was no impact on cash flow.

These changes were primarily a result of:

■ Amortization of goodwill (IAS 38).
■ Inclusion of share-based payments as an expense (IFRS 2).
■ Inclusion of pension costs as an expense and a liability (IAS 19).
■ Timing of recognition of liability for final dividend (IAS 10).
■ Financial instruments, foreign exchange and hedging (IAS 21 and IAS 39).

CASE STUDIES

The emergence of IFRSs has been in part a response to the globalization of capital markets but also in part a response to the failure of accounting standards to provide early warning of corporate collapses. Although the highest profile failures (Enron and WorldCom) have been in the US, there have been many in other countries as well.

Case Study 8.1:   Enron

In December 2001, US energy trader Enron collapsed. Enron was the largest bankruptcy in US history. Even though the United States was believed by many to be the most regulated financial market in the world, it was evident from Enron's collapse that investors were not properly informed about the significance of off-Balance Sheet transactions.

Enron had taken out large loans that were created through special purpose entities such that they were not treated as liabilities in Enron's financial statements. It is believed that US accounting rules may have contributed to this, as they are concerned with the strict legal ownership of investment vehicles rather than with their control. By contrast, IFRSs follow the principle of 'substance over form' (see above).

In their comments on the failure of Enron, the Association of Certified Chartered Accountants recommended the need for global financial markets to have a global set of principles-based financial reporting standards and a global code of corporate governance, arguing that legalistic, rules-based standards encourage creative, loophole-based practice.

There were some indications that Enron may have actively lobbied against changing the treatment in US financial reporting of special purpose entities used in off-Balance Sheet financing. Overall, there was a clear need for greater transparency and trust in reporting.

Case Study 8.2 WorldCom

WorldCom filed for bankruptcy protection in June 2002. The company had used accounting tricks to conceal a deteriorating financial condition and to inflate profits. It was the biggest corporate fraud in history, largely a result of treating operating expenses as capital expenditure.

WorldCom admitted in March 2004 that the total amount by which it had misled investors over the previous 10 years was almost $US75 billion (£42 billion) and reduced its stated pre-tax profits for 2001 and 2002 by that amount.

Former WorldCom chief executive Bernie Ebbers was subsequently charged with conspiracy to commit securities fraud, securities fraud and filing misleading data with the Securities and Exchange Commission (SEC). Scott Sullivan, former chief financial officer, pleaded guilty to three criminal charges.

The SEC said WorldCom had committed 'accounting improprieties of unprecedented magnitude' – proof, it said, of the need for reform in the regulation of corporate accounting.

CRITICISMS OF ACCOUNTING STANDARDS

There have been various criticisms of accounting standards including:

- the almost continual introduction of new and amended standards;
- standards don't consider practical implementation issues – e.g. the impact of pension fund accounting (IAS 19) and accounting for stock options (IFRS 2), and the strong for and against arguments in relation to those particular standards;
- international standards do not yet include the US;
- the complexity of standards means that they are unlikely to be understood by anyone other than professional accountants, and their effect may be ignored by stock market analysts and confusing to lay investors;
- lobbying may influence the development of standards (there is evidence from the US of lobbyists for Enron attempting to influence standard setters);
- although implicit, there is little that is explicit about the relationship between the legal requirement for a true and fair view (see Chapter 6) and standards;

- it has been argued that standards are a remedy for creative accounting (see Chapter 7) but there is evidence that standards are likely to lead to more creative endeavours;
- standards have a narrow accounting focus rather than being inclusive of non-financial performance and broader accountability issues such as social and environmental reporting (see Chapter 9 for a discussion of these issues).

APPLYING DIFFERENT PERSPECTIVES TO FINANCIAL STATEMENTS

In Chapters 4 and 5, we considered rational-economic, interpretive and critical perspectives that help to provide multiple views about the world in which we live. Chapters 6, 7 and 8 have introduced many aspects of the construction and interpretation of financial statements.

Implicit in most of what is contained in the last three chapters is an acceptance of the rational-economic perspective described in Chapter 4. Financial statements support the agency model (see Chapter 6) by holding managers-as-agents accountable to shareholders-as-principals. The actions of managers, whose performance financial statements report, are oriented to increasing shareholder value and are crucial elements of the product and capital markets in which businesses operate. Financial statements are focused on profit (the Income Statement) and on cash flow (the Cash Flow Statement), both of which are (together with debt) the most significant contributors to shareholder value. In the shareholder value model, this is generally considered to be the only real way of viewing the world, especially when it is reinforced by bonuses and profit-sharing.

How then can the other perspectives inform the views we take about financial statements? The interpretive perspective relies on the notion of a reality that is socially constructed. This perspective accepts that shareholder value is a valid way of seeing the world, but it is not the only way of seeing the world. For example, a common phrase in many organizations is that people are our greatest asset, yet they do not appear in financial statements except in relation to salary expenses. Human resource managers often see the focus on financial performance rather than issues of employee selection, retention, training and motivation as equally important for long-term business success. Similarly, marketing managers will value customer retention and satisfaction. The brief discussion of intellectual capital in Chapter 7 reflected a different approach to reporting on these kinds of issues. Non-financial performance measures like the Balanced Scorecard (see Chapter 4) take a more interpretive perspective, yet they are not reflected in financial statements. The culture of (or multiple cultures within) an organization are consequences of the relative importance of financial and non-financial aspects of performance and the power (see below) of different groups within the organization.

The critical perspective questions the taken-for-granted assumptions behind financial statements and profit determination. At its extreme, this perspective questions why shareholders are in a privileged position and receive all the profits from business (in Chapter 3 we saw that the profit for a period is always transferred to shareholders' funds in the Balance Sheet). For example, Marxists ask why capital is more important than labour. A less extreme example is in relation to moral and ethical considerations. The discussion of creative accounting and ethics in Chapter 7 and the examples of WorldCom and Enron in this chapter reflect the dysfunctional consequences of the shareholder value model. Power is a central issue in the critical perspective, and institutional theory (see Chapter 7) shows how power reinforces the *status quo*, through the way capital markets work and the regulation of financial statements. This power is reinforced by top managers who use financial reports and rewards to reinforce their position. While this is to be expected under the rational-economic model, reinforcing the existing managerial hierarchy is not taken for granted in the critical perspective, which aims at questioning and if necessary changing these things.

A good example of the interpretive and critical perspective is in relation to the use of social and environmental accounting described in Chapter 9. This is a reflection both of wider perspectives on a business (interpretive) and power being exerted to require businesses to report in different ways, which by choice they are not likely to have done (critical). The Operating and Financial Review (OFR), also described in Chapter 9, expands the reporting of directors by including information, for example, about strategy, competitive position, non-financial performance measures, social and environmental issues. This is a good example of the application of (at least to some extent) an interpretive paradigm because company reports are being forced (a critical concept, as it relates to issues of power) to move away from the single focus on financial performance and report wider issues.

CONCLUSION

This chapter has introduced International Financial Reporting Standards (IFRSs). The adoption date of 2005 means that examples cannot be included in this text as few companies have as yet adopted the new IFRSs. However, the *Framework for the Preparation and Presentation of Financial Statements* which sets out the concepts underlying the preparation and presentation of financial statements provides a useful method by which the basic principles underlying IFRSs can be understood. Some specific IFRSs have also been overviewed together with the impact of IFRSs on financial statements. Criticisms of accounting standards have also been identified.

REFERENCES

The website of the International Accounting Standards Board is at *http://www.iasb.org/*

International Accounting Standards Board (2004a) *International Financial Reporting Standards (IFRSs) 2004*. London.

International Accounting Standards Board (2004b) *Framework for the Preparation and Presentation of Financial Statements*. London.

APPENDIX: LIST OF IFRSs AND IASs AT 31ST MARCH 2004

IFRS 1   First-time Adoption of International Financial Reporting Standards
IFRS 2   Share-based Payment
IFRS 3   Business Combinations
IFRS 4   Insurance Contracts
IFRS 5   Non-current Assets Held for Sale and Discontinued Operations
IAS 1   Presentation of Financial Statements
IAS 2   Inventories
IAS 7   Cash Flow Statements
IAS 8   Accounting Policies, Changes in Accounting Estimates and Errors
IAS 10   Events After the Balance Sheet Date
IAS 11   Construction Contracts
IAS 12   Income Taxes
IAS 14   Segment Reporting
IAS 16   Property, Plant and Equipment
IAS 17   Leases
IAS 18   Revenue
IAS 19   Employee Benefits
IAS 20   Accounting for Government Grants and Disclosure of Government Assistance
IAS 21   The Effects of Changes in Foreign Exchange Rates
IAS 23   Borrowing Costs
IAS 24   Related Party Disclosures
IAS 26   Accounting and Reporting by Retirement Benefit Plans
IAS 27   Consolidated and Separate Financial Statements
IAS 28   Investments in Associates
IAS 29   Financial Reporting in Hyperinflationary Economies
IAS 30   Disclosures in the Financial Statements of Banks and Similar Financial Institutions
IAS 31   Interests in Joint Ventures
IAS 32   Financial Instruments: Disclosure and Presentation
IAS 33   Earnings per Share
IAS 34   Interim Financial Reporting
IAS 36   Impairment of Assets
IAS 37   Provisions, Contingent Liabilities and Contingent Assets
IAS 38   Intangible Assets
IAS 39   Financial Instruments: Recognition and Measurement
IAS 40   Investment Property
IAS 41   Agriculture

For the updates list and access to summaries of each standard, see *http://www.iasb.org/standards/summaries.asp*

9

GOVERNANCE AND THE OPERATING & FINANCIAL REVIEW (OFR): UNDERSTANDING THE CONTEXT OF ACCOUNTING

This chapter introduces the regulation of companies as it applies to accounting, the content of a company's Annual Report and recent changes in relation to company law and the Operating and Financial Review (OFR) effective for companies from 2005. It then provides an overview of corporate governance and the responsibilities of directors, auditors and the audit committee. The chapter introduces risk and internal control and also covers in some detail the notion of social and environmental reporting, including sustainability.

THE REGULATION OF COMPANIES

The Companies Act of 1985 is the primary legislation governing companies. The Act sets out the effects of incorporation – i.e. the 'limited liability' of shareholders for any unpaid portion of their shares. In most cases, issued shares are fully paid and, therefore, shareholders have no liability beyond this in the event of a company's failure.

The Act sets out the need for companies to have a constitution, formally known as the *Memorandum of Association and Articles of Association*. Each company has a share capital, enabling ownership to be divided over many 'share holders' or members of the company. Shareholders appoint directors to manage the company on their behalf. These directors have various duties. They may authorize the company to borrow money. The directors must keep accounting records and produce financial statements in a specified format. If the company makes a profit, the directors may recommend that a dividend be paid out of profits. An auditor must be appointed to report annually to shareholders. Shareholders have no management rights. However, shareholders receive an Annual Report (see below) containing the financial statements and an annual general meeting of shareholders must be held which appoints directors, ratifies the dividend, etc.

STOCK EXCHANGE LISTING RULES

The primary aim of a Stock Exchange is to provide issuers, intermediaries and investors with attractive, efficient and well-regulated markets in which to raise capital and fulfil investment and trading requirements.

All companies are subject to the Companies Act, but publicly listed companies have to abide by additional regulations called the 'Listing Rules'. These were traditionally set by the Stock Exchange itself but are now administered by the Financial Services Authority (FSA) and effectively have the force of law. The Listing Rules (commonly called the *Purple Book* – previously known as the *Yellow Book*) dictate such matters as the contents of the prospectus on an initial public offering (IPO) of shares, and on-going obligations such as the disclosure of price-sensitive information, and communications on new share offers, rights issues, and potential or actual takeover bids for the company.

One of the major requirements for listed and unlisted companies is the annual report to shareholders.

ANNUAL REPORTS

For unlisted companies, the Companies Act requires the preparation of financial statements. Financial statements are an important part of a company's Annual Report, which is required for all companies listed on the Stock Exchange.

The Annual Report for a listed company typically contains:

- A financial summary – the key financial information.
- A list of the main advisers to the company: legal advisers, bankers, auditors etc.
- The chairman's or directors' report. This provides a useful summary of the key factors affecting the company's performance over the past year and its prospects for the future. It is important to read this information as it provides a background to the financial statements – in particular, the company's products and major market segments. The user must 'read between the lines' in this report, since the intention of the Annual Report is to paint a 'glossy' picture of the business. However, as competitors will also read the Annual Report, the company takes care not to disclose more than is necessary.
- The statutory reports (i.e. those required by the Companies Act) by the directors and auditors. These will contain a summary of financial performance, major policies, strategies and activities, details about the Board of Directors, and statements about corporate governance and internal control (see later in this chapter) and the responsibility of the Board for the financial statements.
- The audit report which will define the auditors' responsibility (see later in this chapter), an opinion as to whether the financial statements give a true and fair view and are compliant with the Companies Act and applicable accounting standards and the basis upon which that opinion has been formed.
- The financial statements: Income Statement (previously called the Profit and Loss account), Balance Sheet and Cash Flow Statement. Where consolidated figures are

provided, these should be used, as they are the total figures for the group of companies that comprise the whole business.

■ Notes, which provide detailed explanations to the financial statements, and usually run to many pages. As well as a breakdown of many of the figures contained in the Income Statement, Balance Sheet and Cash Flow Statement, the Notes will include details such as: the major accounting policies adopted; staff numbers and staff costs; directors' remuneration; depreciation of assets; investments; taxation; share capital; reconciliation between the profit in the Income Statement and the Cash Flow Statement; capital expenditure contracted for; pension liabilities; lease liabilities; subsidiaries; events occurring after the balance date (end of financial year).

■ A 5-year summary of key financial information (a Financial Services Authority *Purple Book* requirement).

The Accounting Standards Board recommends that listed companies also include an *operating and financial review* that provides 'a framework for the directors to discuss and analyse the business's performance and the factors underlying its results and financial position, in order to assist users to assess for themselves the future potential of the business' (quoted in Blake, 1997). The operating and financial review would replace much of the information contained in the chairman's or directors' reports (see above). The Operating and Financial Review becomes compulsory for financial years beginning after January 2005. It is described in more detail below.

COMPANY LAW REVIEW

The Company Law Review has carried out an independent review of company legislation. It found that company accounting and reporting was essentially backward-looking with insufficient reporting of the factors that underlie past and future performance such as strategy, prospects, opportunities and risks. The three principles that emerged from that review were:

■ the need to clarify directors' duties and to whom and how directors owe a duty of care;
■ the need to improve transparency and accountability; and
■ the need to encourage and enable shareholders to exercise more effective and responsible control over their companies.

The issue of transparency and accountability is largely addressed by the Operating and Financial Review (see below).

The Government published a White Paper 'Company Law Reform' in March 2005, setting out the Government's proposals for comprehensive reform of the UK company law framework to bring it in line with modern business needs. The proposed reforms build on the work of the Company Law Review and, pending results of a consultation, will be introduced through a Company Law Reform Bill. The draft Bill proposes four key changes:

■ Enhancing shareholder engagement and a long-term investment culture by promoting the wider participation of shareholders.
■ Ensuring that shareholders are informed and involved with decisions made based on the longer term view rather than just short-term profits. Ensuring better regulation because although the vast majority of UK companies are small, company law has been written with the large company in mind. Legislation needs to be easier for all to understand and use.
■ Removing unnecessary burdens to directors and preserve the UK's reputation as a favoured country in which to incorporate.
■ Providing flexibility for the future by allowing for updating and amendment of legislation as circumstances dictate.

THE OPERATING AND FINANCIAL REVIEW

Many company annual reports have grown in size over recent years from an average of 20–25 pages to 90 or more pages.

The Operating and Financial Review (or OFR) is mandatory for companies listed on the Stock Exchange with effect from financial years beginning on or after 1st January 2005. The OFR was a recommendation of the Company Law Review although a voluntary OFR has existed since 1993.

The objective of the OFR aims to provide a balanced and comprehensive analysis of:

■ the development and performance of the business during the financial year;
■ the position of the business at year end;
■ the main trends and factors underlying the development, performance and position of the business during the financial year;
■ the main trends and factors which are likely to affect its future development, performance and position.

The OFR sets out directors' analysis of the business in order to inform shareholders about the performance of the business. It should include:

■ analysis of the nature of the business, its objectives and strategies;
■ operating review of performance in the last period and influences on performance including expected trends and potential risks;
■ financial review of the company's financial position, capital structure and treasury policy.

The OFR is both retrospective and prospective, enabling shareholders to assess the effectiveness of past strategies as well as the potential for future strategies to be successful. Although there is a great deal of discretion for directors in what is contained within the OFR, it should also contain information about employees, environmental matters, and social and community issues if this information is needed for shareholders to assess the business strategies.

The Accounting Standards Board has produced its *Reporting Standard No. 1: Operating and Financial Review* which sets out the requirements for the OFR. They are required for OFRs relating to financial years beginning on or after 1st April 2005. The principles in the Reporting Standard require that the OFR: be an analysis of the business through the eyes of the board of directors; focus on matters that are relevant to shareholder interests; have a forward-looking orientation; complement and supplement financial statements; be comprehensive and understandable; be balanced and neutral; and be comparable over time.

The Reporting Standard includes a framework for disclosures in an OFR, intended to set out the key content elements that should be addressed within an OFR (para. 27, p. 11).

DISCLOSURE FRAMEWORK FOR THE OFR

The OFR provides information to assist shareholders to assess the organization's strategies and their potential to succeed. Paragraph 28 requires disclosure of:

- the nature of the business, description of the market, the competitive and regulatory environment, and the organization's objectives and strategies;
- the development and performance of the business in the last year and in the future;
- the resources, principal risks, uncertainties and relationships that may affect long-term value;
- description of the capital structure, treasury policies and objectives, and liquidity of the business in the last year and in the future.

To the extent necessary to meet the paragraph 28 requirements, the OFR must include information about:

a. Environmental matters.
b. Employees.
c. Social and community issues.
d. Persons with whom the business has contractual or other arrangements which are essential to the business.
e. Receipts from and returns to shareholders in respect of shares.
f. All other matters the directors consider to be relevant.

For each of (a) to (c) above, the OFR must include the policies of the organization and the extent to which those policies have been successfully implemented.

The OFR must also include:

- A description of the business and the external environment in which it operates.
- The objectives of the business to generate or preserve value over the longer term.
- The directors' strategies for achieving business objectives.
- Key performance indicators, both financial and non-financial, used by the directors to assess progress against objectives.
- The significant features of the development and performance of the business in the past year, focusing on those business segments that are relevant to an understanding of the development and performance as a whole.
- The main trends and factors that directors consider likely to impact future prospects.
- A description of the resources available to the business and how they are managed.
- A description of the principal risks and uncertainties facing the business and the directors' approach to them.
- Information about significant relationships with stakeholders other than shareholders which are likely to influence the performance of the business and its value.
- Details of distributions, capital raising and share repurchases in relation to shares held by shareholders.
- An analysis of the financial position of the business.
- The capital structure of the business.
- The treasury policies and objectives.
- The cash inflows and outflows during the financial year and the organization's ability to generate cash, to meet known or probable cash requirements and to fund growth.
- Current and prospective liquidity, including the level of borrowings and their seasonality and the maturity profile of borrowings and undrawn committed borrowing facilities.

For each key performance indicator (KPI) disclosed in the OFR, an explanation must be provided of its definition and calculation method, its purpose, the source of data and any assumptions, and quantification or commentary on future targets. A reconciliation between figures in the OFR and financial statements must be provided. Corresponding amounts for the prior year must be disclosed and any changes to KPIs must be disclosed.

Disclosure is not required about impending developments if the disclosure would, in the opinion of the directors, be seriously prejudicial to the interests of the entity. The OFR must include a statement as to whether it has been prepared in accordance with the Reporting Standard together with reasons for any departure from the Standard.

The Company Law Review and the OFR are both important elements of improving corporate governance for companies.

In November 2005, the Chancellor announced that the Government will abolish the requirement that all quoted companies must publish an Operating and Financial Review (OFR). This requirement had previously been mandated by Statutory Instrument 2005/1011.

Following the Chancellor's announcement, the Department for Trade & Industry announced that the OFR will be replaced by a requirement to publish a 'simpler Business Review', although no details are available at the time of writing.

Many commentators believe that the trend towards more extensive disclosure of business performance will continue, despite the Government's announcement that there is no longer a requirement for companies to produce an OFR.

Regardless of whether or not an OFR is a statutory requirement, the Accounting Standards Board's (ASB) view of best practice remains unchanged. The ASB has stated that its Reporting Standard 1 is the most up-to-date and authoritative good source of best practice guidance for companies to follow.

The ASB further argued that, despite the Chancellor's announcement, companies (and not just quoted companies) will still be required by law to publish an enhanced business review in the directors' report. This requires large and medium-sized (but not small) companies to provide a 'balanced and comprehensive analysis of the development and performance of the company's business and of its position, consistent with the size and complexity of the business.' The review must also include a description of the principal risks and uncertainties that a company faces.

A lot of the debate over the statutory OFR focused on the reporting of non-financial performance. The ASB stated that the law still requires that 'to the extent necessary for an understanding of the company's development, performance or position, the analysis shall include both financial and, where appropriate, non-financial key performance indicators relevant to the particular business, including information relating to environmental and employee matters.' Medium-sized companies do not have to provide the non-financial information.

INTRODUCTION TO CORPORATE GOVERNANCE

Corporate governance is the system by which companies are directed and controlled. Boards of directors are responsible for the governance of their companies. The shareholders' role is to appoint the directors and auditors (see later in this chapter). The responsibilities of the Board include setting the company's strategic goals, providing leadership to senior management, monitoring business performance and reporting to shareholders.

There are two models of corporate governance:

■ Shareholder value (see Chapter 2), which is based on agency theory (see Chapter 6).
■ Stakeholder model (introduced in Chapter 2, but described in more detail later in this chapter).

Each represents a different means by which the functioning of boards of directors and top management can be understood. In UK company law, there is no doubt that shareholders are in a privileged position compared with other stakeholders. Hence, corporate governance in the UK is founded on the shareholder value/agency model.

In the UK, the *Combined Code on Corporate Governance* (Financial Reporting Council, 2003) has applied for reporting years beginning on or after 1st November 2003. Stock Exchange Listing Rules require listed companies to disclose how they have applied the principles in the Code and to confirm either that the company complies with the

Code's provisions or, if it does not comply, to provide an explanation. This approach is known as 'comply or explain'. The Combined Code consists of a set of principles for corporate governance.

Even before the publication of the *Combined Code*, a growing number of institutional investors were starting to encourage greater disclosure of governance processes, emphasising the quality and sustainability of earnings, rather than short-term profits alone. Research has shown that an overwhelming majority of institutional investors are prepared to pay a significant premium for companies exhibiting high standards of corporate governance. The media has also increased its reporting of governance practices. The high-profile failures of companies, notably the press coverage given to Enron and WorldCom (see Chapter 8), brought corporate governance to worldwide attention. Major corporate collapses have been a feature of recent business history in the UK and elsewhere. In the UK failures have included the Maxwell publishing group, Bank of Commerce & Credit International (BCCI), Polly Peck and Marconi. Similar high-profile failures have occurred in most countries. The September 11 attacks in the United States also resulted in an increase in attention to risk. The resulting increased attention to corporate governance has been global.

The emergence of a renewed emphasis on corporate governance can be traced to:

■   an enforcement exercise in relation to past misdeeds;
■   changing financial markets including the rapid rise of institutional investors and their increasing desire to be more active investors; and
■   the growth of savings for pensions in most member countries and the dependence of an ageing population on pensions and savings which have been affected by declining confidence in stock markets.

In the United States, the introduction of the Sarbanes–Oxley Act in 2002 was the legislative response to the financial and accounting scandals of Enron and WorldCom and the misconduct at the accounting firm Arthur Andersen. Sarbanes–Oxley introduced the requirement to disclose all material off-Balance Sheet transactions. The Act requires the certification of annual and quarterly financial reports by the chief executive and chief financial officer of all companies with US securities registrations, with criminal penalties for knowingly making false certifications.

However, other models of governance take a broader view – e.g. that found in South Africa where the *King Report on Corporate Governance* provides an integrated approach to corporate governance in the interest of all stakeholders, embracing social, environmental and economic aspects of organizational activities. It therefore takes – to some extent at least – a broader stakeholder model of governance (this notion is developed later in this chapter). The *King Report* relies heavily on disclosure as a regulatory mechanism.

The benefits of applying good corporate governance are to reduce risk, stimulate performance, improve access to capital markets, enhance the marketability of product/services by creating confidence among stakeholders, improve leadership, and demonstrate transparency and accountability.

The Financial Reporting Council has announced a review of the UK *Combined Code* to identify whether it is working effectively and whether any amendments are required. The review was undertaken in the second half of 2005 (see earlier in this chapter).

PRINCIPLES OF CORPORATE GOVERNANCE

The role of a company's Board of Directors is to provide entrepreneurial leadership of the company within a framework of prudent and effective controls which enables risk to be assessed and managed. The Board should set the company's strategic aims and ensure that the necessary financial and human resources are in place for the company to meet its objectives and review management performance. The Board should set the company's values and standards and ensure that its obligations to its shareholders and others are understood and met.

The main principles of corporate governance found in the *Combined Code* are in relation to: roles and responsibilities of directors and their remuneration; accountability and audit; relations with shareholders and with institutional shareholders, in particular; and disclosure of governance arrangements in annual reports.

In relation to accountability and audit, the *Combined Code* recommends that the Board of Directors should:

■ present a balanced and understandable assessment of the company's position and prospects;
■ maintain a sound system of internal control to safeguard shareholders' investments and the company's assets; and
■ establish formal and transparent arrangements for considering how they should apply the financial reporting and internal control principles and for maintaining an appropriate relationship with the company's auditors.

The board as a whole has responsibility for ensuring that a satisfactory dialogue with shareholders takes place and the board should use the annual general meeting to communicate with investors and to encourage their participation.

RESPONSIBILITY OF DIRECTORS

Under Companies legislation, the financial statements of a company are the responsibility of directors. Directors are responsible for keeping proper accounting records which disclose with reasonable accuracy the financial position of the company at any time and to ensure that financial statements comply with the Companies Act. They are also responsible for safeguarding the company's assets and for taking reasonable steps to prevent and detect fraud.

The financial statements must show a true and fair view (see Chapter 6) of the state of affairs of the company and of the profit or loss for that year. In preparing the financial statements, directors: must select suitable accounting policies and apply them consistently; make judgements and estimates that are reasonable and prudent; and prepare financial statements on a going concern basis unless it is inappropriate to presume that the company will continue in business (see Chapter 3 for a discussion of these principles).

Although in practice these functions will be delegated to a company's managers, the responsibility cannot be delegated by the board of directors.

AUDIT

Audit is a periodic examination of the accounting records of a company carried out by an independent auditor to ensure that those records have been properly maintained and that the financial statements which are drawn up from those records give a true and fair view. An audit includes examination, on a test basis, of evidence relevant to the amounts and disclosures in financial statements. It also includes an assessment of significant estimates and judgements made by directors in the preparation of financial statements, and whether accounting policies are appropriate, consistent and adequately disclosed. Auditors carry out their audit in accordance with UK Auditing Standards, issued by the Auditing Standards Board.

Each year, the auditors present a report to shareholders, giving their opinion as to whether the financial statements give a true and fair view and are properly prepared in accordance with the Companies Act and applicable accounting standards. They also report if the Directors' Report is not consistent with the financial statements or if the company has not kept proper accounting records or if satisfactory explanations have not been provided to the auditors by directors.

AUDIT COMMITTEES

The audit committee is a committee of the board of directors. The *Combined Code* states that the board should establish an audit committee of at least three, or in the case of smaller companies (below FTSE 350) two members, who should all be independent non-executive directors. The Board should satisfy itself that at least one member of the audit committee has recent and relevant financial experience.

The main role and responsibilities of the audit committee include:

- Monitoring the integrity of the company's financial statements, significant judgements made in relation to the financial statements and formal announcements made by the company to the stock exchange.
- Reviewing the company's internal control and risk management systems.
- Monitoring and reviewing the effectiveness of the internal audit function.
- Making recommendations to the Board for the Board to place a resolution before shareholders in an annual general meeting for the appointment, re-appointment and removal of the external auditor and to approve the terms of engagement and remuneration of the external auditor.

■ Reviewing and monitoring the external auditor's independence and objectivity, and the effectiveness of the audit process.

■ Developing and implementing policy on the engagement of the external auditor to supply non-audit services in order to maintain auditor objectivity and independence.

RISK, INTERNAL CONTROL AND MANAGEMENT ACCOUNTING

The *Combined Code* takes a strong view in relation to risk, defining it as uncertain future events which could influence the achievement of the organization's strategic, operational and financial objectives. Risk may be: business or operational, arising from the normal course of business (loss of customers, failure of computer systems, poor-quality products, etc.); financial, arising from changes in interest rates, foreign currency exposure, poor credit control etc.; environmental, arising from changes in external economic, social, technological factors; or reputational. Risk may be considered in relation to downside factors ('bad things may happen') or upside factors ('good things may not happen'). This recognizes that taking risks is a necessary part of conducting business, with returns being the compensation for taking risks. The *Combined Code* requires that Boards of Directors institute a system of internal control based on the organization's risk appetite and the identification and assessment of risks facing the organization. This ensures appropriate risk responses, monitoring and reporting processes.

Internal control is the whole system of internal controls, financial and otherwise, established in order to provide: reasonable assurance of effective and efficient operation; internal financial control; and compliance with laws and regulations. The *Combined Code* provides that the Board should maintain a sound system of internal control to safeguard shareholders' investment and the company's assets. The Board should, at least annually, conduct a review of the effectiveness of the group's system of internal controls and should report to shareholders that they have done so. The review should cover all material controls, including financial, operational and compliance controls and risk management systems.

Although there are forms of control other than financial ones (see Chapter 4), internal financial controls are established to provide: reasonable assurance of the safeguarding of assets against unauthorized use or disposition; the maintenance of proper accounting records; and the reliability of financial information used within the business or for publication.

Accounting controls are important in all organizations. They include control over cash, debtors, inventory, fixed assets, creditors, loans, income and expenses.

Financial controls exist over:

■ product/service costing (Chapters 10–13);
■ Capital investment appraisal and divisional performance (Chapters 14 and 15);
■ budgets and budgetary control (Chapters 16 and 17).

Budgets (see Chapter 16) are one of the most visible forms of control. Budgets are established in line with strategy and a view can be taken for each budget year as to whether the budget will contribute to achieving the strategy (feed forward, see Chapter 4). Budgets hold managers accountable for achieving financial targets (revenue, cost, profit, return on investment etc.). Managers must explain variances between actual and budget performance (feedback, see Chapter 5). Management style will influence the level and extent of budgetary control in a particular organization.

Management accounting is an important form of internal control, and is the subject of Part III of this book, although the theoretical foundations have already been laid in Chapters 4 and 5.

Although this chapter has been concerned with statutory requirements for Annual Reports, the Operating and Financial Review and corporate governance, a critical approach questions this emphasis on the shareholder value/agency model. A broader perspective has been reflected in the South African *King Report* on corporate governance, and before leaving the subject of financial statements and annual reports, we should consider the issue of social and environmental reporting.

A CRITICAL VIEW: CORPORATE SOCIAL AND ENVIRONMENTAL REPORTING

The concern with stakeholders rather than shareholders (introduced in Chapter 2) began in the 1970s and is generally associated with the publication in 1975 of *The Corporate Report*, a publication by the Accounting Standards Steering Committee. Accounting academics began to question profit as the sole measure of business performance and suggested a wider social responsibility for business and a more *social accounting*.

Stakeholder theory argues that managers should serve the interests of anyone with a 'stake' in (i.e. anyone who is affected by) the organization. Stakeholders include shareholders, but also encompass employees, suppliers, customers, government and the communities in which the firm operates. Managers need to strike an appropriate balance between these interests when directing the firm's activities so that one stakeholder group is not satisfied to the detriment of others. Much of the argument behind stakeholder theory is that economic pressures to satisfy only shareholders is short-term thinking and organizations need to ensure their survival and success in the long term by satisfying other stakeholders as well – this is called *sustainability* (see below). A concern with stakeholders beyond shareholders has led to a wider view about the content of annual reports.

Concepts of *corporate social accounting* and *socially responsible accounting* – most recently corporate social and environmental reporting (CSR) – attempt to highlight the impact of organizations on society.

Jones (1995) suggested three reasons for this:

■   A moral imperative that business organizations were insufficiently aware of the social consequences of their activities.

■ External pressure from government and pressure groups and the demand by some institutional investors for ethical investments. This was linked to the role of accounting in demonstrating how well organizations were fulfilling their *social contract*, the implied contract between an organization and society.

■ Internal change taking place within organizations as a result of education and professionalization etc.

However, there has been little support for broader social accounting because accountants and managers have generally seen themselves as the agents of owners. Social reporting could be seen as undermining the power of shareholders and the foundation of the capitalist economic system. There are also technical difficulties associated with social reporting and a dominant belief among business leaders that government, and not business, has the responsibility to determine what is reported.

During the 1980s and 1990s environmental accounting (see, for example, Gray *et al.*, 1996) focused on responsibility for the natural environment and, in particular, on sustainability as a result of concerns about ozone depletion, the greenhouse effect and global warming. These concerns were associated with the growth of pressure groups such as Greenpeace and Friends of the Earth. Part of the appeal of environmental accounting was that issues of energy efficiency, recycling and reductions in packaging had cost-saving potential and, therefore, profits and social responsibility came to be seen as not necessarily mutually exclusive.

Zadek (1998) argued that social and ethical accounting, auditing and reporting together provide one of the few practical mechanisms for companies to integrate new patterns of civil accountability and governance with a business success model focused on stakeholders and core non-financial as well as financial values. Socially responsible businesses:

> find the spaces in the pipeline between investors and consumers where some choice in behaviour is possible ... [and] a far more ambitious agenda of shifting the basic boundaries by raising public awareness towards social and environmental agendas, and supporting the emergence of new forms of investors that take non-financial criteria into account. (p. 1439)

SUSTAINABILITY AND THE 'TRIPLE BOTTOM LINE'

The best-known definition of sustainability comes from *Our Common Future* (the so-called 'Brundtland Report') prepared under the auspices of the World Council on Environment and Development in 1987, which defines sustainable development as that which meets the needs of the present without compromising the ability of future generations to meet their own needs. In other words, sustainability is a condition where the demands placed upon the environment by people and business organizations can be met without reducing the capacity of the environment to provide for future generations. Some of the major sustainability issues are population, climate change, ecology and energy use.

An example is pollution. Pollution is normally a sign of poor technology and bad management, and reducing pollution through better technology will almost always lower cost or raise product value which will offset the cost of compliance with environmental standards, although doing so may require innovation.

The term 'triple bottom line' is credited to John Elkington and his consultancy firm SustainAbility to describe new types of markets and innovative business approaches that are needed to achieve success. The originators believe not only that profitable business must be socially and environmentally responsible, but further that social and environmental innovation is key to the new market opportunities of the future.

In its broadest sense, the triple bottom line captures the spectrum of values that organizations must embrace – economic, environmental and social. In practical terms, triple bottom line accounting means expanding the traditional company reporting framework to take into account not just financial outcomes but also environmental and social performance.

GLOBAL REPORTING INITIATIVE

The Global Reporting Initiative (GRI) is a multi-stakeholder process and independent institution whose mission is to develop and disseminate globally applicable Sustainability Reporting Guidelines. These Guidelines are for voluntary use by organizations for reporting on the economic, environmental and social dimensions of their activities, products and services. The GRI incorporates the active participation of representatives from business, accountancy, investment, environmental, human rights, research and labour organizations from around the world. Started in 1997, GRI became independent in 2002 and is an official collaborating centre of the United Nations Environment Programme (UNEP).

In broad terms, the GRI Sustainability Reporting Guidelines recommend specific information related to environmental, social and economic performance. It is structured around a CEO statement, key environmental, social and economic indicators, a profile of the reporting entity, descriptions of relevant policies and management systems, stakeholder relationships, management performance, operational performance, product performance and a sustainability overview. The GRI has developed a set of core performance measures, or metrics, intended to be applicable to all business enterprises, sets of sector-specific metrics for specific types of enterprises and a uniform format for reporting information integral to a company's sustainability performance.

The indicators are split into economic, environmental, social, human rights and workplace. For the GRI ambition to be realized, companies need to do three things:

■ describe factors which are genuinely about the health of the business and its relationship with various stakeholders;
■ cover all the different aspects of how the business has significant impacts on society;
■ contain measures of performance, not just management process.

CONCLUSION

The chapter has described the regulation of companies, the contents of company annual reports and the introduction of the Operating and Financial Review (OFR). It has also described corporate governance and the responsibilities of directors and auditors and the emerging area of risk and internal control. The chapter has also covered in some detail the notion of social and environmental reporting, sustainability and the Global Reporting Initiative (GRI).

REFERENCES

Accounting Standards Board (2005). *Reporting Standard No. 1: Operating and Financial Review.* London. Available from Financial Reporting Council website at *http://www.frc.org.uk/images/ uploaded/documents/Web%20optimized%20OFR%20REPORTING%20STANDARD.pdf*

Financial Reporting Council. (2003). *The Combined Code on Corporate Governance.*

Gray, R. II., Owen, D. L. and Adams, C. (1996). *Accounting and Accountability: Changes and Challenges in Corporate Social and Environmental Reporting.* London: Prentice Hall.

Jones, T. C. (1995). *Accounting and the Enterprise: A Social Analysis.* London: Routledge.

Zadek, S. (1998). Balancing performance, ethics, and accountability. *Journal of Business Ethics,* **17**(13), 1421–41.

Stock Exchange listing rules are produced by the Financial Services Authority, whose website is *http://www.fsa.gov.uk/Pages/index.shtml*

The website of the London Stock Exchange is *http://www.londonstockexchange.com/ en-gb/*

Latest details about the Company Law Review and the Operating and Financial Review can be obtained from *http://www.dti.gov.uk/index.html*

The website of SustainAbility is *http://www.sustainability.com/* and that of the Global Reporting Initiative is *http://www.globalreporting.org/*

APPENDIX: RESOURCES FOR ANNUAL REPORTS

Full annual reports are available on the Web for many companies.

Readers may like to search for annual reports in companies or industries in which they are interested. It will help in understanding the concepts in Part II of this book to look at:

J Sainsbury plc *http://www.j-sainsbury.co.uk/ar05/index.asp?pageid=64*
Management Consulting Group plc *http://ww6.investorrelations.co.uk/mcg/AnnualReport.shtml*
Ottakar's plc *http://www.ottakars.co.uk/Internet/about/pressreleases.jsp*
Cadbury Schweppes plc *http://www.cadburyschweppes.com/EN/InvestorCentre/*

Many of these annual reports contain an Operating and Financial Review.

PART III

USING ACCOUNTING INFORMATION FOR DECISION-MAKING, PLANNING AND CONTROL

Part II has been concerned with the use of financial information for decision-making, primarily for external reporting purposes. Part III shows the reader how accounting information is used by managers. While an analysis of financial statements is useful, particularly for external interested parties (shareholders, bankers and financiers, the government etc.), the information is of limited use to the internal management of the business because:

- it is aggregated to the corporate level, whereas managers require information at the business unit level;
- it is aggregated to annual figures, whereas managers require timely information, usually at not less than monthly intervals;
- it is aggregated to headline figures, whereas managers require information in much greater detail;
- it does not provide a comparison of plan to actual figures to provide a gauge on progress towards achieving business goals.

Consequently, the chapters in Part III are concerned with management accounting: the production of accounting information for use by managers. This information is disaggregated (to business unit level), more regular (typically monthly) and is more detailed for management decision-making, planning and control.

In Part III, the accounting tools and techniques are explained and illustrated by straightforward examples. Case studies, drawn mainly from real business examples, help draw out the concepts. Theory is integrated with the tools and techniques, and the use of quotations from the original sources should encourage readers to access the accounting academic literature that they may find of interest.

Chapters 10, 11 and 12 consider the accounting techniques that are of value in marketing, operations and human resource decisions respectively. These chapters do not take an approach to accounting that is common to other books. These chapters provide a practitioner- rather than an accounting-centred approach, demonstrating techniques that do not require any prior management accounting knowledge. The more traditional accounting focus is left to Chapter 13, by which time the reader should have little difficulty in understanding the more complex concepts. Chapter 14 focuses on strategic decisions such as capital investment and Chapter 15 on divisional performance measurement. Chapter 16 covers the subject of budgeting and Chapter 17 discusses budgetary control.

10 MARKETING DECISIONS

This chapter considers the use of accounting information in making marketing decisions. It begins with an overview of some of the key elements of marketing theory and introduces cost behaviour: the distinction between fixed and variable costs, average and marginal costs. Decisions involving the relationship between price and volume are covered through the technique of cost–volume–profit (CVP) analysis. Different approaches to pricing are covered: cost-plus pricing; target rate of return; the optimum selling price; special pricing decisions; and transfer pricing. The chapter concludes with an introduction to segmental profitability.

MARKETING STRATEGY

Porter (1980) identified five forces that affect an industry: the threat of new entrants, the bargaining power of customers, the bargaining power of suppliers, the threat of substitute product/ services, and rivalry among competitors in an industry, with each competitor developing strategies for success. In a later book, Porter (1985) identified three generic strategies that businesses can adopt in order to achieve a sustainable competitive advantage. The alternative strategies were to be a low-cost producer, a higher-cost producer that can differentiate its product/services, or to focus on a market niche. Consequently, the notion of cost is important in marketing decisions, particularly pricing decisions.

Marketing is the business function that aims to understand customer needs and satisfy those needs more effectively than competitors. Marketing can be achieved through a focus on selling products and services or through building lasting relationships with customers (customer relationship management). Marketing texts emphasize the importance of adding value through marketing activity. Adding value differentiates product/ services from competitors, and enables a price to be charged that equates to the benefits obtained by the customer. However, for any business to achieve profitability, customers must be prepared to pay more for the product/service benefit than the benefit costs to provide.

The price customers are willing to pay depends on what Doyle (1998) calls the 'factors which drive up the utility of an offer', which he divides into four groups. Product drivers include performance, features, reliability, operating costs and serviceability. Services drivers include ease of credit availability, ordering, delivery, installation, training, after-sales service and guarantees. Personnel drivers include the professionalism, courtesy, reliability and responsiveness of staff. Image drivers reflect the confidence of customers in the company or brand name, which is built through the other three drivers and by advertising and promotional activity. Doyle (1998) recognized that each of these value drivers has cost drivers.

The **sales mix** is the mix of product/services offered by the business, each of which may be aimed at satisfying different customer needs. Businesses develop marketing strategies to meet the needs of their customers in different *market segments*, each of which can be defined by its unique characteristics. These segments may yield different prices and incur different costs as customers demand more or less of different product/services.

Pricing of product/services is crucial to business success, in terms of increasing the perceived value so as to maximize the margin between price and cost and to increase volume and market share without eroding profits. Pricing strategies may be aimed at *penetration* – achieving long-term market share – or *skimming* – maximizing short-term profits from a limited market.

A focus on customer relationship management entails taking a longer-term view than product/service profitability and emphasizes the profits that can be derived from a satisfied customer base. Doyle (1998) describes loyal customers as assets, quoting research that tried to measure the value of a loyal customer. Doyle says, 'If managers know the cost of losing a customer, they can evaluate the likely pay-off of investments designed to keep customers happy' (pp. 51–2). Doyle explained that the cost of winning new customers is high, loyal customers tend to buy more regularly, spend more and are often willing to pay premium prices. This is an element of the business goodwill, part of the 'intellectual capital' that is not reported in financial statements (see Chapter 7).

A further element of marketing is the distribution channel to be used. This may range from the company's own salesforce to retail outlets, direct marketing and the number of intermediaries between the product/service provider and the ultimate customer.

Marketing texts typically introduce marketing strategy as a combination of the 4 Ps of product, price, place and promotion. The marketing strategy for a business will encompass decisions about product/service mix, customer mix, market segmentation, value and cost drivers, pricing and distribution channel. Each element of marketing strategy implies an understanding of accounting, which can help to answer questions such as:

■ What is the volume of product/services that we need to sell to maintain profitability?
■ What alternative approaches to pricing can we adopt?
■ What is our customer, product/service and distribution channel profitability in each of our market segments?

This chapter is concerned with answering these questions. Although information on competitors, customers and suppliers is likely to be limited, strategic management accounting (see Chapter 4) can apply the same tools and techniques in the pursuit of competitive advantage.

COST BEHAVIOUR

Marketing decisions cannot be made in isolation from knowledge of the costs of the business and the impact that marketing strategy has on operations and on business profitability. Profitability for marketing decisions is the difference between *revenue* – the income earned from the sale of product/services – and cost. As we saw in Chapter 3, it is the notion of cost that is problematic.

For many business decisions, it is helpful to distinguish between how costs behave, i.e. whether they are fixed or variable. **Fixed costs** are those that do not change with increases in business activity (such as rent). This is not to say that fixed costs never change (obviously rents do increase in accordance with the terms of a lease) but there is no connection (except sometimes in large retail sites) between cost and the volume of activity. By contrast, **variable costs** do increase/decrease in proportion to an increase/decrease in business activity, so that as a business produces more units of a good or service, the business incurs proportionately more costs.

For example, advertising is a fixed cost because there is no relationship between spending on advertising and generating revenue (although we may wish there was). However, sales commission is a variable cost because the more a business sells, the more commission it pays out.

A simple example shows the impact of fixed and variable cost behaviour on total and average cost. XYZ Limited has the capacity to produce between 10,000 and 30,000 units of a product each period. Its fixed costs are £200,000. Variable costs are £10 per unit. The example is shown in Table 10.1.

In this example, even if the business produces no units, costs are still £200,000 because fixed costs are independent of volume. Total costs increase as the business incurs variable costs of £10 for each unit produced. However, the average cost declines with the increase in volume because the fixed cost is spread over more units.

Not all costs are quite so easy to separate between fixed and variable. Some costs are semi-fixed, while others are semi-variable. **Semi-fixed costs** (also called step fixed costs)

Table 10.1   Cost behaviour – fixed and variable costs

Activity (number of units sold)	Fixed costs (£200,000)	Variable costs (£10 per unit)	Total cost (£)	Average cost (per unit)
10,000	200,000	100,000	300,000	£30.00
15,000	200,000	150,000	350,000	£23.33
20,000	200,000	200,000	400,000	£20.00
25,000	200,000	250,000	450,000	£18.00
30,000	200,000	300,000	500,000	£16.67

are constant within a particular level of activity, but can increase when activity reaches a critical level. This can happen, for example, with changes from a single-shift to a two-shift operation, which requires not only additional variable costs but additional fixed costs (e.g. extra supervision). **Semi-variable costs** have both fixed and variable components. A simple example is a telephone bill, which will have a fixed component (rental) and a variable component (calls). Maintenance of motor vehicles can be both time based (the fixed component) and mileage based (the variable component).

This example introduces the notion of marginal cost. The **marginal cost** is the cost of producing one extra unit. In the above example, to increase volume from 10,000 to 15,000 units incurs a marginal cost of £50,000 (which in this case is 5,000 additional units at a variable cost of £10 each). However, marginal costs may include a fixed-cost element (in the case of semi-fixed costs).

The notion of cost is therefore quite difficult. Is the cost in the above example the average cost or the marginal cost? If it is the average cost, what level of activity is chosen to determine that average, given fluctuating volumes of sales from period to period?

COST–VOLUME–PROFIT ANALYSIS

A method for understanding the relationship between revenue, cost and sales volume is cost–volume–profit analysis, or CVP. CVP is concerned with understanding the relationship between changes in activity (the number of units sold) and changes in selling prices and costs (both fixed and variable). Typical questions that CVP may help with are:

■ What is the likely effect on profits of changes in selling price or the volume of activity?
■ If we incur additional costs, what changes should we make to our selling price or to the volume that we need to sell?

CVP is used by accountants in a relatively simplistic manner. While most businesses will sell a wide range of product/services at many different prices (e.g. quantity discounts), accountants assume a constant product/service mix and average selling prices per unit. The assumption is that these relationships are linear, rather than the curvilinear models preferred by economists that reflect economies and diseconomies of scale. The accountant limits this problem by recognizing the relevant range. The **relevant range** is the volume of activity within which the business expects to be operating over the short-term planning horizon, typically the current or next accounting period, and the business will usually have experience of operating at this level of output. Within the relevant range, the accountant's model and the economist's model are similar.

Profit can be shown as the difference between revenue and costs (both fixed and variable). This relationship can be shown in the following formula:

net profit = revenue − (fixed costs + variable costs)

net profit = (units sold × selling price)

− [fixed costs + (units sold × unit variable cost)]

In mathematical terms, this is:

$$N = Pu − (F + Bu)$$

where:

N = net profit
u = number of units sold
P = selling price per unit
F = total fixed costs
B = variable cost per unit

Using the example of XYZ Limited, a selling price of £25 for 20,000 units would yield a net profit of:

N = (£25 × 20,000) − [£200,000 + (£10 × 20,000)]
N = £500,000 − £400,000
N = £100,000

CVP permits sensitivity analysis. **Sensitivity analysis** is an approach to understanding how changes in one variable (e.g. price) affect other variables (e.g. volume). This is important, because revenues and costs cannot be predicted with certainty and there is always a range of possible outcomes, i.e. different mixes of price, volume and cost.

Using sensitivity analysis, a business may ask questions such as: What is the selling price (P) required for a profit (N) of £150,000 on sales of 25,000 units? To calculate this, we enter the data we know in the formula and solve for the missing figure (in this case price):

£150,000 = £P × 25,000 − [£200,000 + (£10 × 25,000)]
£150,000 = £25,000P − £450,000

$$P = \frac{£600,000}{25,000} \text{ per unit}$$

P = £24 per unit

The **breakeven point** is the point at which total costs equal total revenue, that is where there is neither a profit nor a loss. How many units have to be sold for the business to break even? This question can be answered by using simple algebra to solve the above equation for u (the number of units) where N (net profit) is 0, as follows:

$$0 = Pu - (F + Bu)$$
$$0 = 20u - (200,000 + 10u)$$
$$u = \frac{200,000}{10}$$
$$u = 20,000$$

However, a simpler formula for breakeven is:

$$\text{breakeven sales (in units)} = \frac{\text{fixed costs}}{\text{selling price per unit} - \text{variable cost per unit}}$$
$$= \frac{fl200,000}{20 - 10}$$
$$= 20,000 \text{ units}$$

Note that £10 is the *unit contribution*, i.e. the difference between the selling price and the variable cost per unit. The unit contribution can also be expressed as a percentage of sales of 0.5 or 50% (£10/£20), which applies to any level of sales as the ratio of contribution (£10) to selling price (£20) remains constant within the relevant range.

$$\text{breakeven sales (in fls)} = \frac{\text{fixed costs}}{\text{unit contribution as a \% of sales}}$$
$$= \frac{fl200,000}{0.5}$$
$$= fl400,000$$

This is equivalent to the breakeven units of 20,000 at £20 selling price per unit.

Businesses establish profit targets, and a variation on the above calculations is to calculate the number of units that need to be sold to generate a target net profit.

$$\text{sales (in units) for profit of } fl150,000 = \frac{\text{fixed costs} + \text{target profit}}{\text{selling price per unit} - \text{variable cost per unit}}$$
$$= \frac{fl200,000 + fl150,000}{20 - 10}$$
$$= 35,000 \text{ units}$$

$$\text{sales (in fls) for profit of } fl150,000 = \frac{\text{fixed costs} + \text{target profit}}{\text{unit contribution as a \% of sales}}$$
$$= \frac{fl200,000 + fl150,000}{0.5}$$
$$= fl700,000$$

This is equivalent to the sales in units of 35,000 at £20 selling price per unit. However, if the business has a maximum capacity of 25,000 units, the limit of its relevant

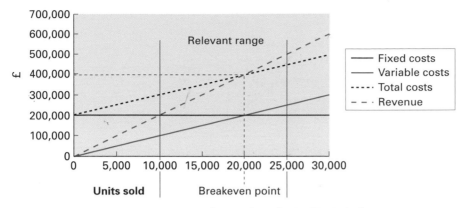

Figure 10.1 Breakeven chart for XYZ Limited

range, this profitability may not be achievable and the cost structure of the business reflected in the CVP relationship would have to be revised.

CVP can be understood through a graphical representation. Using the same data, the CVP graph is shown in Figure 10.1. In this CVP diagram, the vertical axis represents money (both revenue and cost) and the horizontal axis represents volume (the number of units sold). Fixed costs are seen to be constant, as increases in volume do not influence total fixed cost within the relevant range. Variable costs are nil at zero level of activity and increase in proportion to that activity. Total costs are the sum of variable and fixed costs. They begin above zero because, even with zero level of activity, fixed costs are still incurred. Total revenue starts at nil and increases with the volume sold.

As fixed costs remain constant, profit per unit will vary at different levels of activity. The point at which the total cost line intersects the total revenue line is the breakeven point.

The breakeven point is shown by the dotted black line and can be read as the revenue required (£400,000) to sell a given volume (20,000 units) at a selling price of £20 per unit. The area of profit is found to the right of the breakeven point, between total revenue and total cost. The area of loss is found to the left of the breakeven point, between total cost and total revenue. Note, however, that outside the relevant range (shown in the diagram as between 10,000 and 25,000 units) cost behaviour may be different and so the CVP diagram may have to be redrawn. The breakeven chart shows the margin of safety. The *margin of safety* is a measure of the difference between the anticipated and breakeven levels of activity. It is expressed as a percentage:

$$\text{margin of safety (\%)} = \frac{\text{expected sales} - \text{breakeven sales}}{\text{expected sales}} \times 100$$

Using the same example, the margin of safety assuming anticipated sales of 25,000 units is:

$$\frac{25{,}000 - 20{,}000}{25{,}000} \times 100 = 20\%$$

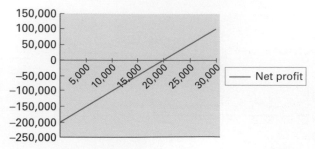

Figure 10.2   Profit–volume graph for XYZ Limited

The lower the margin of safety, the higher the risk, as sales do not have to fall much before reaching the breakeven point. Conversely, there is less risk where businesses operate with higher margins of safety.

Whereas the breakeven graph shows the breakeven point, the *profit–volume graph* shows the profit or loss at different levels of activity. For the same example, the profit–volume graph is shown in Figure 10.2.

At any level of output the net profit (or loss) can be seen. This example shows the breakeven point of 20,000 units and the small margin of safety to the anticipated sales level of 25,000 units, compared with the risk of substantial loss following from any level of activity below 20,000 units.

Despite the advantages presented by CVP analysis, there are some significant limitations arising from the assumptions made:

■   Volume is the only factor that causes prices and variable costs to alter (in practice, production efficiencies, product/service mix, price levels etc. all influence costs and revenues).

■   There is a single product/service or a product/service mix that remains constant (in practice, product/service mix can vary significantly and different product/services may have different cost structures, prices and contributions).

■   Costs can be accurately divided into fixed and variable elements (although in practice many costs are semi-variable and semi-fixed).

■   Fixed costs do not change (although in practice they vary with the range of items produced and with product complexity, as we will see in Chapter 13).

■   Total costs and revenues are linear (while this is likely within the relevant range, increases in volume may still lead to lower unit prices or economies of scale and curvilinear costs and revenues may be more accurate).

■   The CVP analysis applies only to the relevant range (although decisions may be made in the current period to move outside this range).

■   The analysis applies only to the short term and cannot reliably be used in the longer term.

Despite its limitations, CVP analysis is a useful tool in making decisions about pricing and volume, based on an understanding of the cost structure of the business. How, then, do firms make decisions about what price to charge?

ALTERNATIVE APPROACHES TO PRICING

Accounting information can be used for pricing in various marketing strategies:

■ Cost-plus pricing.
■ Target rate of return pricing.
■ Optimum selling price.
■ Special pricing decisions.
■ Transfer pricing.

COST-PLUS PRICING

Accounting information may be used in pricing decisions, particularly where the firm is a market leader or *price-maker*. In these cases, firms may adopt **cost-plus pricing**, in which a margin is added to the total product/service cost in order to determine the selling price. In many organizations, however, prices are set by market leaders and competition requires that prices follow the market (i.e. the firms are *price-takers*). Nevertheless, even in those cases an understanding of cost helps in making management decisions about what product/services to produce, how many to make and whether the price that exists in the market warrants the business risk involved in any decision to sell in that market. An understanding of the firm's marketing strategy is therefore essential in using cost information for pricing decisions.

In the long term, the prices that a business charges must cover all of its costs. If it is unable to do so, it will make losses and may not survive. For every product/service the full cost must be calculated, to which the desired profit margin is added. **Full cost** includes an allocation to each product/service of all the costs of the business, including producing and delivering a good or service, and all its marketing, selling, finance and administration costs. The calculation of full cost is covered in Chapter 13, but it is taken as given for the purposes of this chapter.

Using the CVP example provided earlier in this chapter, the average cost was £20 assuming a level of activity of 20,000 units. The cost-plus pricing formula may be applied as a *mark-up* on any element of cost. For example, a mark-up of 25% would result in a selling price of £25.

cost + mark-up on cost = selling price

£20 + (25% of £20) = £25

The profit margin is the profit as a percentage of the selling price. Using the same example, the profit *margin* of £5 is 20% of the selling price of £25. A **mark-up** is the percentage added to cost for profit, whereas the **margin** is the percentage of the selling price that is represented by profit.

The actual mark-up used may be based on a ratio (see Chapter 7) such as return on sales (as in the above example), which is likely to be arbitrary or as a target return on investment.

TARGET RATE OF RETURN PRICING

Target rate of return pricing estimates the (fixed and working) capital investment required for the business and the need to generate an adequate return on that investment to satisfy shareholders.

For example, if the investment required is £1,000,000 and the company wants a 12% return on investment, the desired profit is £120,000 (£1,000,000 @ 12%). Assuming a volume of 20,000 units, each unit would need to generate a profit of £6 (£120,000/20,000 units). If the total cost was £20, the selling price would be £26. This represents a 30% mark-up on cost and a 23.1% margin on selling price. Target rate of return pricing is likely to lead to pricing decisions that are more closely linked to shareholder value than adding an arbitrary margin to total cost.

OPTIMUM SELLING PRICE

While cost-plus pricing is useful, it ignores the relationship between price and demand in a competitive business environment. The sensitivity of demand to changes in price is reflected in the *price elasticity of demand*. *Elastic demand* exists when a price increase leads to a fall in demand as customers place little value in the product or switch to substitutes. *Inelastic demand* exists where small price increases/decreases cause only a small change in demand because customers value the product or because no substitute is available.

The **optimum selling price** is the point at which profit is maximized. To ascertain the optimum selling price, a business must understand cost behaviour in terms of variable or fixed and have some ability, via market research, to predict likely changes in volume as prices increase or decrease.

Using the example earlier in this chapter, XYZ Limited is able to estimate the likely increase in demand as the selling price falls. For each level of activity we can calculate the revenue, variable costs and total contribution. The figures are shown in Table 10.2.

An approach that seeks to maximize sales revenue will result in a strategy that seeks to sell 25,000 units at £25 each, with total revenue being £625,000. However,

Table 10.2   XYZ Limited – contribution at different activity levels

Selling price per unit	Volume expected at given selling price (units)	Revenue (selling price × volume) (£)	Variable costs (@ £10 per unit)	Contribution (revenue – variable costs) (£)
40	10,000	400,000	100,000	300,000
35	15,000	525,000	150,000	375,000
30	20,000	600,000	200,000	400,000
25	25,000	625,000	250,000	375,000
20	30,000	600,000	300,000	300,000

taking account of the price/volume relationship and costs (which were estimated as £10 variable cost per unit) shows that the business will *maximize its contribution* towards fixed costs and profit at £400,000 with an optimum selling price of £30. This is even though the number of units sold will be less at 25,000 with total revenue of £600,000.

The highest contribution will always be the highest profit as the fixed costs (£200,000) will be unchanged at each level of activity within the relevant range (note that the price of £20 leading to 30,000 units is outside the relevant range). Although businesses seek to increase sales revenue, they wish to *maximize* contribution and therefore profitability. This issue is often the cause of conflict between marketing and finance staff in organizations.

SPECIAL PRICING DECISIONS

Special pricing decisions are those outside the main market. These are usually one-time orders at a price below that usually sold in the market. In the long term, all the costs of the business must be covered by the selling price if the business is to be profitable. However, in the short term, spare capacity may lead to decisions to accept orders from customers at less than the full cost. As fixed costs remain the same irrespective of volume, provided that the selling price covers the variable costs it makes a positive contribution to recovering some of the fixed costs of the business and therefore to a greater profit (or lower loss).

Using the figures from the previous example, the business may have adopted a marketing strategy to sell at a price of £30, but only 17,000 units have been sold. The business profitability will be:

		£'000
Revenue	17,000 @ £30	510
Variable costs	17,000 @ £10	170
Contribution		340
Fixed costs		200
Net profit		140

Accepting an order of 3,000 units at £12 will increase profits by £6,000 (3,000 at a selling price of £12 less variable costs of £10) because fixed costs will remain unchanged. The business profitability will then be:

		£'000
Revenue	17,000 @ £30	510
	3,000 @ £12	36
		546
Variable costs	20,000 @ £10	200
Contribution		346
Fixed costs		200
Net profit		146

Consequently, provided that the business can sell at a price that at least covers variable costs, in the short term the business will be better off. This argument does not follow through into the long term, over which the business must cover all its costs in order to be profitable. However, a business will also minimize its losses by selling at a price that covers variable costs but not full costs. If in the above example volume falls below the breakeven point:

		£'000
Revenue	8,000 @ £30	240
Variable costs	8,000 @ £10	80
Contribution		160
Fixed costs		200
Net loss		40

If an order of 3,000 units at £12 is accepted, the loss will be reduced by £6,000:

		£'000
Revenue	8,000 @ £30	240
	3,000 @ £12	36
		276
Variable costs	11,000 @ £10	110
Contribution		166
Fixed costs		200
Net loss		34

However, consideration needs to be given to the long-term marketing implications of accepting orders at less than normal selling price:

1 The future selling price may be affected by accepting a special order, if competitors adopt similar pricing tactics.

2 Customers who receive or become aware of a special selling price may expect a similar low price in the future.

3 Accepting this order may prevent the firm from accepting a more profitable order at a higher price if one subsequently comes along.

4 It is assumed that the business has spare capacity that has no alternative use.

5 It is assumed that fixed costs are unavoidable in the short term.

TRANSFER PRICING

One special pricing decision is that concerned with the price at which goods or services are sold between business units in the same company, rather than the arm's-length price at which sales may be made to external customers. Transfer prices may be based on:

■ the market price to external customers, including a normal profit margin;

■ the market price to external customers, but including a lower profit margin;

■ the total cost of producing the goods or services, including fixed and variable costs but excluding any profit margin;

■ the marginal cost of producing the goods or services, i.e. including only variable costs, with or without a profit margin;

■ a negotiated price.

An important issue in establishing a transfer price is the motivational effect that this may have on managers of both the buying and selling business units, who may prefer to buy and sell on the open market. However, in the increasingly globalized business world, manufacturing, assembly and selling operations may take place in different countries. In these cases, transfer prices are often set to ensure that reported profits are earned in countries where lower corporation tax is payable to maximize the after-tax earnings of the multinational corporation. Transfer pricing is discussed in more detail in Chapter 15.

SEGMENTAL PROFITABILITY

As well as being price-makers or price-takers, businesses also adopt *market-skimming* or *market-penetration* strategies at different phases of the product/service lifecycle (see Chapter 11). A common marketing strategy is *differential pricing*, where prices vary between each market segment.

Where products/services are sold in different market segments at different prices, the price can be considered in different ways:

■ A minimum short-term price taking into account only marginal, i.e. usually variable, costs.

■ A minimum long-term price that covers the full product/service cost.

■ A target long-term price that takes into account the return on investment necessary to increase shareholder value.

Table 10.3   Profitability of business segments for an accounting practice

	Business (accounting services)	Business (tax only)	Personal	Total
Revenue	120,000	50,000	30,000	200,000
Variable costs	50,000	22,000	18,000	90,000
Contribution	70,000	28,000	12,000	110,000
Avoidable fixed costs for administrative support	20,000	10,000	5,000	35,000
Contribution to overhead	50,000	18,000	7,000	75,000
Unavoidable fixed business expenses (rent, partner salaries etc.) allocated as a percentage of revenue	60%	25%	15%	
Profit	20,000	5,500	(500)	25,000

Market segments may be defined geographically, by customer or by customer groups, by product/service or by product/service groups, or by different distribution channels. In any of these cases, decisions may be made about expanding or contracting in different segments based on the relative profitability of those segments. These are important decisions, but the methods by which costs are allocated over each segment must be understood before informed decision-making can take place.

As we will see in Chapter 13, major assumptions are involved in how costs are allocated within a business. However, for the purposes of the present chapter, we will separate fixed costs into unavoidable business-wide costs and avoidable segment-specific costs. **Unavoidable costs** are allocated by an often arbitrary method to each business unit or market segment, although these costs are only able to be influenced at the corporate level. Avoidable costs are identifiable with and are able to be influenced by decisions made at the business unit level.

As this chapter has already shown, provided that the selling price exceeds variable costs, there is a contribution from the sales of products/services towards covering fixed costs and towards profitability. This position is confused when financial reports include an allocation of unavoidable business-wide costs and those reports need to be analysed more carefully.

An example is an accounting practice that prepares tax returns on behalf of clients. The clients are grouped into three market segments: business (where the practice also carries out accounting services); business (where the practice only completes the tax return); and personal returns. The practice thinks that personal returns may be unprofitable and a partner has produced the data in Table 10.3.

As the example in Table 10.3 shows, despite the loss made by the personal tax returns market segment, these clients contribute £7,000 in the period towards the unavoidable overhead. If this segment were discontinued, the profit of the practice would fall by £7,000 to £18,000. This is because, even though the fixed costs for administrative support would be saved if the segment were discontinued, the whole of the unavoidable costs of £50,000 would continue. The following case study illustrates segmental profitability.

Case Study 10.1:   Retail Stores PLC – the loss-making division

Retail Stores has three segments, producing the results in Table 10.4. The contribution as a percentage of sales, assuming a constant sales mix, is 70.6% (£600,000/£850,000). The company's breakeven point in sales is calculated as:

$$\frac{\text{fixed costs}}{\text{unit contribution as a \% of sales}} \quad \frac{280,000 + 255,000}{0.706} = \frac{535,000}{0.706}$$

or £758,000.

Current sales of £850,000 represent a margin of safety of:

$$\frac{\text{expected sales} - \text{breakeven sales}}{\text{expected sales}} \times 100 = \frac{£850,000 - £758,000}{£850,000}$$

or 10.8%.

Management is considering dropping the Toys segment due to its reported loss after deducting avoidable segment-specific fixed costs and unavoidable business wide costs, which are allocated as a percentage of sales revenue. However, an understanding of cost behaviour helps to identify that each segment is making a positive contribution to business-wide costs after deducting the segment-specific fixed costs, as the modification to the reported profits in Table 10.5 demonstrates.

Based on the figures in Table 10.5, despite the Toys segment making a loss, it makes a positive contribution of £30,000 to allocated business-wide costs. If the Toys segment was discontinued, total profit would fall by £30,000, as Table 10.6 shows.

This is because the loss of the contribution by the Toys segment to business-wide costs and profits amounts to £30,000 (after deducting avoidable segment-specific fixed costs). The business-wide costs of £255,000 are reallocated over the two remaining business segments in proportion to sales revenue, which in turn makes the Electrical segment appear only marginally profitable.

If the Toys division were discontinued, the impact would be to reduce costs by £60,000 and a new, higher contribution as a percentage of sales results (£510,000/£700,000 = 72.9%, up from 70.6%). Consequently, Retail Stores' breakeven point in sales

Table 10.4   Retail Stores PLC – analysis of trading results

	Clothing	Electrical	Toys	Total
Sales	400,000	300,000	150,000	850,000
Variable costs	25%	30%	40%	
	100,000	90,000	60,000	250,000
Contribution	300,000	210,000	90,000	600,000
Segment-specific fixed costs	120,000	100,000	60,000	280,000
Allocated busines-wide costs (as a % of sales revenue)	120,000	90,000	45,000	255,000
Profit/(loss)	60,000	20,000	(15,000)	65,000

Table 10.5 Retail Stores PLC – contribution by business segment

	Clothing	Electrical	Toys	Total
Sales	400,000	300,000	150,000	850,000
Variable costs	25%	30%	40%	
	100,000	90,000	60,000	250,000
Contribution	300,000	210,000	90,000	600,000
Segment-specific fixed costs	120,000	100,000	60,000	280,000
Segment contribution to business wide costs and profits	180,000	110,000	30,000	320,000
Allocated business-wide costs (as a % of sales revenue)	120,000	90,000	45,000	255,000
Profit/(loss)	60,000	20,000	(15,000)	65,000

Table 10.6 Retail Stores PLC – effect of closure of business segment

	Clothing	Electrical	Toys	Total
Sales	400,000	300,000		700,000
Variable costs	25%	30%		
	100,000	90,000		190,000
Contribution	300,000	210,000		510,000
Segment-specific fixed costs	120,000	100,000		220,000
Segment contribution to business-wide costs and profits	180,000	110,000		290,000
Allocated business-wide costs (as a % of sales revenue)	146,000	109,000		255,000
Profit/(loss)	34,000	1,000		35,000

can be revised to:

$$\frac{\text{fixed costs}}{\text{unit contribution as a \% of sales}} = \frac{220{,}000 + 255{,}000}{0.729} = \frac{475{,}000}{0.729}$$

or £652,000.

Current sales of £700,000 represent a margin of safety of 6.8%, a fall of 4% from the three-division breakeven calculation. This is calculated by:

$$\frac{\text{expected sales} - \text{breakeven sales}}{\text{expected sales}} \times 100 = \frac{£700{,}000 - £652{,}000}{£700{,}000}$$

Segmental profitability is the result of avoidable variable costs and fixed costs that are segment-specific and an allocation of unavoidable business-wide fixed costs. It is important to differentiate these costs in decision-making. We will return to the cost allocation problem in Chapter 13.

The following case study shows how an understanding of financial information can assist more directly in carrying out the marketing function.

Case Study 10.2: SuperTech – using accounting information to win sales

One of Global Enterprises' target customers is SuperTech, a high-technology company involved in making semiconductors for advanced manufacturing capabilities. SuperTech has grown rapidly and its sales are £35 million per annum. Variable costs consume about 60% of sales and fixed selling, distribution and administrative expenses are about £10 million, leaving a profit of £4 million. The challenge facing SuperTech is to continue to grow while maintaining profitability. It plans to achieve this by continuing to re-engineer its production processes to reduce the lead time between order and delivery and improve the yield from its production by improving quality.

Global sees SuperTech as a major customer for its services. However, it operates in a highly price-competitive industry. Global is unwilling to reduce its pricing because it has a premium brand image and believes that it should be able to use its customer knowledge, including published financial information, to increase sales and justify the prices being charged. Global believes that its services can contribute to SuperTech's strategy of reducing lead time and improving yield.

Global has been able to ascertain the following information from the published accounts of SuperTech:

■ Its cost of sales last year was £21.6 million and its inventory was £17.5 million. This is because the equipment made by SuperTech is highly technical and requires long production lead times.

■ Employment-related costs for the 250 employees were £8 million, 25% of the total business costs of £31 million.

■ The company has borrowings of £14.5 million, its gearing being 90%, and interest costs last year were £787,000.

We need to make a number of assumptions about the business, but these are acceptable in order to estimate the kind of savings that Global's services might obtain for SuperTech.

We can calculate that the company's cost of production, assuming 240 working days per year, as £90,000 per day (£21.6 million/240). Given the low number of employees and the knowledge that many of these are employed in non-production roles, the vast majority (over 80%) of production costs are believed to be material costs. Using the inventory days ratio (see Chapter 7), we can calculate that the year-end inventory holding is 194 days (£17.5 million/£90,000), equivalent to 81% of working days (194/240).

Global's services will increase the production costs because of its premium pricing, and expects the price differential to be £250,000 per annum. However, Global's services will generate savings for SuperTech. First, the service will reduce the lead time in manufacture by 10 days. The company's interest cost of £787,000 is 5.4% of its borrowings of £14.5 million. This is a very rough estimate as borrowings increased during the year and the company most likely had different interest rates in operation. However, it is useful as a guide. If Global's services can reduce SuperTech's lead time by 10 days, that will reduce the level of inventory by £900,000 (£90,000 per day × 10), which can be used to reduce debt, resulting in an interest saving of £48,600 (£900,000 @ 5.4%).

Second, Global also believes that its services will increase the yield from existing production because of the higher quality achieved. Global estimates that this yield improvement will lower the cost of sales from 60% to 59%. This 1% saving on sales of £35 million is equivalent to £350,000 per annum.

Global's business proposal (which of course needs to demonstrate how these gains can be achieved from a technical perspective) can contain the following financial justification:

	per annum
Savings:	
Interest savings on reduced lead time	£48,600
Yield improvements	£350,000
Total savings	£398,600
Additional cost of Global's services	£250,000
Net saving per annum	£148,600

This is equivalent to an increase of 3.7% in the net profit (after interest) to SuperTech.

CONCLUSION

This chapter has introduced various cost concepts, including cost behaviour, cost–volume–profit analysis, alternative approaches to pricing and understanding segmental profitability. While marketing is critical to business success, so is the fulfilment of the promises made by marketing, which is the subject of the next chapter.

After you have read this chapter, you should:

■ Revise your understanding of the accounting terms. The Glossary in Part IV is a helpful aid.
■ Practice the Questions for this chapter and then check your answers against the solutions. Questions for each chapter are in Appendix 1. The solutions are in Appendix 2.

REFERENCES

Doyle, P. (1998). *Marketing Management and Strategy.* (2nd edn). London: Prentice Hall Europe.

Porter, M. E. (1980). *Competitive Strategy: Techniques for Analyzing Industries and Competitors.* New York, NY: Free Press.

Porter, M. E. (1985). *Competitive Advantage: Creating and Sustaining Superior Performance.* New York, NY: Free Press.

11

OPERATING DECISIONS

This chapter introduces the operations function through the value chain and contrasts the different operating decisions faced by manufacturing and service businesses. Operational decisions are considered, in particular capacity utilization, the cost of spare capacity and the product/service mix under capacity constraints. Relevant costs are considered in relation to the make versus buy decision, equipment replacement and the relevant cost of materials. Other costing approaches such as lifecycle, target and kaizen costing and the cost of quality are also introduced.

THE OPERATIONS FUNCTION

Operations is the function that produces the goods or services to satisfy demand from customers. This function, interpreted broadly, includes all aspects of purchasing, manufacturing, distribution and logistics, whatever those may be called in particular industries. While purchasing and logistics may be common to all industries, manufacturing will only be relevant to a manufacturing business. There will also be different emphases such as distribution for a retail business and the separation of 'front office' (or customer-facing) functions from 'back office' (or support) functions for a financial institution.

Irrespective of whether the business is in manufacturing, retailing or services, we can consider *operations* as the all-encompassing processes that *produce* the goods or services that satisfy customer demand. In simple terms, operations is concerned with the conversion process between resources (materials, facilities and equipment, people etc.) and the products/services that are sold to customers. There are four aspects of the operations function: quality, speed, dependability and flexibility (Slack *et al.*, 1995). Each of these has cost implications and the lower the cost of producing goods and services, the lower can be the price to the customer. Lower prices tend to increase volume, leading to economies of scale such that profits should increase (as we saw in Chapter 10).

A useful analytical tool for understanding the conversion process is the *value chain* developed by Porter (1985) and shown in Figure 11.1. According to Porter every business is:

> a collection of activities that are performed to design, produce, market, deliver, and support its product ... A firm's value chain and the way it performs individual activities are a reflection of its history, its strategy, its approach to implementing its strategy, and the underlying economics of the activities themselves. (Porter, 1985, p. 36)

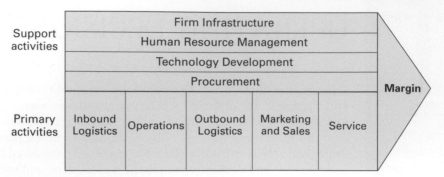

Figure 11.1   Porter's value chain
Reprinted from Porter, M. E. (1985). *Competitive Advantage: Creating and Sustaining Superior Performance.*
New York, NY: Free Press.

Porter separated these activities into primary and secondary activities.

This approach has similarities to the business process re-engineering approach of Hammer and Champy (1993, p. 32). Their emphasis on processes was on 'a collection of activities that takes one or more kinds of input and creates an output that is of value to the customer' (p. 35).

Porter argued that costs should be assigned to the value chain but that accounting systems can get in the way of analysing those costs. Accounting systems categorize costs through line items (see Chapter 3) such as salaries and wages, rental, electricity etc. rather than in terms of value activities that are technologically and strategically distinct. This 'may obscure the underlying activities a firm performs' (Porter, 1985).

Porter developed the notion of cost drivers, which he defined as the structural factors that influence the cost of an activity and are 'more or less' under the control of the business. He proposed that the cost drivers of each value activity be analysed to enable comparisons with competitor value chains. This would result in the relative cost position of the business being improved by better control of the cost drivers or by reconfiguring the value chain, while maintaining a differentiated product. This is an approach that is supported by strategic management accounting (see Chapter 4).

The value chain as a collection of inter-related business processes is a useful concept to understand businesses that produce either goods or services.

MANAGING OPERATIONS – MANUFACTURING

A distinguishing feature between the sale of goods and services is the need for inventory or stock in the sale of goods. Inventory enables the timing difference between production capacity and customer demand to be smoothed. This is of course not possible in the supply of services.

Manufacturing firms purchase **raw materials** (unprocessed goods) and undertake the *conversion process* through the application of labour, machinery and know-how to manufacture **finished goods**. The finished goods are then available to be sold to customers. There are actually three types of inventory in this example: raw materials, finished goods and work-in-progress. **Work-in-progress** consists of goods that have begun but have not yet completed the conversion process.

There are different types of manufacturing and it is important to differentiate the production of the following:

■ *Custom:* Unique, custom products produced singly, e.g. a building.
■ *Batch:* A quantity of the same goods produced at the same time (often called a production run), e.g. textbooks.
■ *Continuous:* Products produced in a continuous production process, e.g. oil and chemicals.

For custom and batch manufacture, costs are collected through a **job costing** system that accumulates the cost of raw materials as they are issued to each job (either a custom product or a batch of products) and the cost of time spent by different categories of labour. In a manufacturing business the materials are identified by a **bill of materials**, a list of all the components that go to make up the completed project, and a **routing**, a list of the labour or machine processing steps and times for the conversion process. To each of these costs overhead is allocated to cover the manufacturing costs that are not included in either the bill of materials or the routing (this will be explained in Chapter 13).

The bill of materials and routing contain standard quantities of material and time. Standard quantities are the expected quantities, based on past and current experience and planned improvements in product design, purchasing and methods of production. **Standard costs** are the standard quantities multiplied by the current and anticipated purchase prices for materials and the labour rates of pay. The standard cost is therefore a budget cost for a product or batch. As actual costs are not known for some time after the end of the accounting period, standard costs are generally used for decision-making. Standard costs are usually expressed *per unit*.

The manufacturing process and its relationship to accounting can be seen in Figure 11.2. When a custom product is completed, the accumulated cost of materials, labour and overhead is the cost of that custom product. For a batch the total job cost is divided by the number of units produced (e.g. the number of copies of the textbook) to give a cost per unit (cost per textbook). The actual cost per unit can be compared to the budget or standard cost per unit. Any variation needs to be investigated and corrective action taken (this is the feedback cycle described in Chapter 4, to which we return in Chapter 18).

A simple example is the job cost for the printing of 5,000 copies of a textbook. The costing system shows:

Materials (paper, ink etc.)	£12,000
Labour for printing	£20,000
Overhead allocated	£10,000
Total job cost	£42,000
Cost per textbook (£42,000/5,000 copies)	£8.40

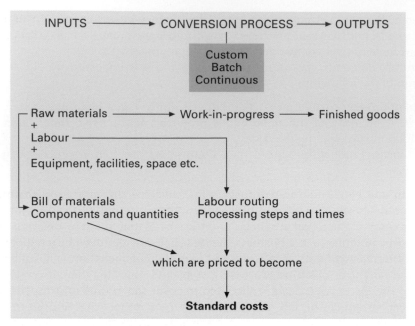

Figure 11.2   The manufacturing process and its relationship to accounting

For continuous manufacture a **process costing** system is used, under which costs are collected over a period of time, together with a measure of the volume of production. At the end of the accounting period, the total costs are divided by the volume produced to give a cost per unit of volume. For example, if the cost of producing a chemical in the month of November is £1,200,000 and 400,000 litres have been produced in the same period, the cost per litre is £3.00 (£1,200,000/400,000 litres). Again, there will be a comparison between the standard cost per unit and the actual cost per unit.

The distinction between custom and batch is not always clear. Some products are produced on an assembly line as a batch of similar units but with some customization, since technology allows each unit to be unique. For example, motor vehicles are assembled as 'batches of one', since technology facilitates the sequencing of different specifications for each vehicle along a common production line. Within the same model, different colours, transmissions (manual or automatic), steering (right-hand or left-hand drive) etc. can all be accommodated. Any manufacturing operation involves a number of sequential activities that need to be scheduled so that materials arrive at the appropriate time at the correct stage of production and labour is available to carry out the required process. Organizations that aim to have material arrive in production without holding buffer stocks are said to operate a just-in-time (or JIT) manufacturing system.

Most manufacturing processes require an element of *set-up* or *make-ready* time, during which equipment settings are made to meet the specifications of the next production run (a custom product or batch). These settings may be made by manual labour or by computer through CNC (computer numerical control) technology. As Chapter 1 described, investments in computer and robotics technology have changed the shape of the manufacturing industry. These investments involve substantial costs that need to be justified by an increased volume of production or by efficiencies that reduce production costs (we discuss this in Chapter 14).

MANAGING OPERATIONS – SERVICES

Fitzgerald *et al.* (1991) emphasized the importance of the growing service sector and identified four key differences between products and services: intangibility, hetero-gcneity, simultaneity and perishability. Services are *intangible* rather than physical and are often delivered in a 'bundle' such that customers may value different aspects of the service. Services involving high labour content are *heterogeneous*, i.e. the consistency of the service may vary significantly. The production and consumption of services are *simultaneous* so that services cannot be inspected before they are delivered. Services are also *perishable*, so that unlike physical goods, there can be no stock of services that have been provided but remain unsold.

Fitzgerald *et al.* also identified three different service types. *Professional services* are 'front office', people based, involving discretion and the customization of services to meet customer needs in which the process is more important than the service itself. Examples given by Fitzgerald *et al.* include professional firms such as solicitors, auditors and management consultants. *Mass services* involve limited contact time by staff and little customization, with services equipment based and product oriented with an emphasis on the 'back office' and little autonomy. Examples here are rail transport, airports and mass retailing. The third type of service is the *service shop*, a mixture of the other two extremes with emphasis on front and back office, people and equipment and product and process. Examples of service shops are banking and hotels.

Fitzgerald *et al.* emphasized how cost traceability differed between each of these service types. Their research found that many service companies did not try to cost individual services accurately either for price-setting or profitability analysis, except for the time-recording practices of professional service firms. In mass services and service shops there were:

> multiple, heterogeneous and joint, inseparable services, compounded by the fact that individual customers may consume different mixes of services and may take different routes through the service process. (p. 24)

In these two categories of services, costs were controlled not by collecting the costs of each service but through responsibility centres (which is covered in more detail in Chapter 15).

Slack *et al.* (1995) contrasted types of service provision with types of manufacturing and used a matrix of low volume/high variety and high volume/low variety to compare professional service with customized or batch manufacturing, mass service with continuous manufacture, and service shop with a batch-type process. Slack *et al.* noted that this product-process matrix led to decisions about the design of the operations function, while deviating from these broad groups had implications for both flexibility and cost.

In describing operations, we will use the term *production* to refer to both goods and services and use *manufacturing* where raw materials are converted into finished goods.

Accounting information has an important part to play in operational decisions. Typical questions that may arise include:

■   What is the cost of spare capacity?
■   What product/service mix should be produced where there are capacity constraints?
■   What are the costs that are relevant for operational decisions?

ACCOUNTING FOR THE COST OF SPARE CAPACITY

Production resources (material, facilities and equipment, and people) allocated to the process of supplying goods and services provide a capacity. The utilization of that capacity is a crucial performance driver for businesses, as the investment in capacity often involves substantial outlays of funds that need to be recovered by utilizing that capacity fully in the production of products/services. Capacity may also be a limitation for the production and distribution of goods and services where market demand exceeds capacity.

A weakness of traditional accounting is that it equates the cost of *using* resources with the cost of *supplying* resources. Activity-based costing (which is described further in Chapters 13 and 16) has as a central focus the identification and elimination of unused capacity. According to Kaplan and Cooper (1998), there are two ways in which unused capacity can be eliminated:

1   Reducing the supply of resources that perform an activity, i.e. spending reductions that reduce capacity.
2   Increasing the quantity of activities for the resources, i.e. revenue increases through greater utilization of existing capacity.

Activity-based costing identifies the difference between the cost of resources supplied and the cost of resources used as the cost of the unused capacity:

cost of resources supplied – cost of resources used = cost of unused capacity

An example illustrates this.

Ten staff, each costing £30,000 per year, deliver banking services where the cost driver (the cause of the activity) is the number of banking transactions. Assuming that each member of staff can process 2,000 transactions per annum, the cost of resources supplied is £300,000 (10 × £30,000) and the capacity number of transactions is 20,000 (10 × 2,000). The standard cost per transaction would be £15 (£300,000/ 20,000 transactions).

If in fact 18,000 transactions were carried out in the year, the cost of resources used would be £270,000 (18,000 @ £15) and the cost of unused capacity would be

£30,000 (2,000 @ £15, or £300,000 resources supplied – £270,000 resources used). If the cost of resources used is equated with the cost of resources supplied, the actual transaction cost becomes £16.67 (£300,000/18,000 transactions) and the cost of unused capacity is not identified. This is a weakness of traditional accounting systems.

Although there can be no carry forward of an 'inventory' of unused capacity in a service delivery function, management information is more meaningful if the standard cost is maintained at £15 and the cost of spare capacity is identified separately. Management action can then be taken to reduce the cost of spare capacity to zero, either by increasing the volume of business or reducing the capacity (i.e. the number of staff).

CAPACITY UTILIZATION AND PRODUCT MIX

Where demand exceeds the capacity of the business to produce goods or deliver services as a result of scarce resources (whether that is space, equipment, materials or staff), the scarce resource is the limiting factor. A business will want to maximize its profitability by selecting the optimum product/service mix. The product/service mix is the mix of products or services sold by the business, each of which may have different selling prices and costs. It is therefore necessary, where demand exceeds capacity, to rank the products/services with the highest contributions, per unit of the limiting factor (i.e. the scarce resource).

For example, Beaufort Accessories makes three parts (F, G and H) for a motor vehicle, each with different selling prices and variable costs and requiring a different number of machining hours. These are shown in Table 11.1. However, Beaufort has an overall capacity limitation of 10,000 machine hours.

The first step is to identify the ranking of the products by calculating the contribution per unit of the limiting factor (machine hours in this case) for each product. This is shown in Table 11.2.

Although both Part G and Part H have higher contributions per unit, the contribution per machine hour (the unit of limited capacity) is higher for Part F. Profitability will be maximized by using the limited capacity to produce as many Part Fs as can be

Table 11.1   Beaufort Accessories cost information

	Part F	Part G	Part H
Selling price per unit	£150	£200	£225
Variable material cost per unit	£50	£80	£40
Variable labour cost per unit	£50	£60	£125
Contribution per unit	£50	£60	£60
Machine hours per unit	2	4	5
Estimated sales demand (units)	2,000	2,000	2,000
Required machine hours based on estimated demand	4,000	8,000	10,000

Table 11.2 Beaufort Accessories – product ranking based on contribution

	Part F	Part G	Part H
Contribution per unit	£50	£60	£60
Machine hours per unit	2	4	5
Contribution per machine hour	£25	£15	£12
Ranking (preference)	1	2	3

sold, followed by Part Gs. Based on this ranking, the available production capacity can be allocated as follows:

Production	Contribution
2,000 of Part F @ 2 hours = 4,000 hours. Based on the capacity limitation of 10,000 hours, there are 6,000 hours remaining, so Beaufort can produce 3/4 of the demand for Part G (6,000 hours available/8,000 hours to meet demand) equivalent to 1,500 units of Part G (3/4 of 2,000 units).	2,000 @ £50 per unit = £100,000
1,500 of Part G @ 4 hours = 6,000 hours	1,500 @ £60 per unit = £90,000
Maximum contribution	£190,000
There is no available capacity for Part H	

THEORY OF CONSTRAINTS

A different approach to limited capacity was developed by Goldratt and Cox (1986), who focused on the existence of bottlenecks in production and the need to maximize volume through the bottleneck (throughput). Goldratt and Cox developed the Theory of Constraints (ToC), under which only three aspects of performance are important: throughput contribution, operating expense and inventory. **Throughput contribution** is defined as sales revenue less the cost of materials:

throughput contribution = sales − cost of materials

Goldratt and Cox considered all other costs as fixed and independent of customers and products, so operating expenses included all costs except materials. They emphasized the importance of maximizing throughput while holding constant or reducing operating expenses and inventory. Goldratt and Cox also recognized that there is little point in maximizing non-bottleneck resources if this leads to an inability to produce at the bottlenecks.

Applying the Theory of Constraints to the Beaufort Accessories example and assuming that machine hours are the bottleneck resource, Table 11.3 shows the

Table 11.3 Beaufort Accessories – product ranking based on throughput

	Part F	Part G	Part H
Selling price per unit	£150	£200	£225
Variable material cost per unit	£50	£80	£40
Throughput contribution per unit	£100	£120	£185
Machine hours per unit	2	4	5
Return per machine hour	£50	£30	£37
Ranking (preference)	1	3	2

throughput ranking. Under the Theory of Constraints, Part F retains the highest ranking but Part H has a higher return per unit of the bottleneck resource than Part G after deducting only the variable cost of materials. This is a different ranking to the previous method, which used the contribution after deducting *all* variable costs. The difference is due to the treatment of variable costs other than materials.

Strategic management accounting (see Chapter 4) can assist a business by applying these concepts to competitors in order to gain a better understanding of how those competitors are utilizing their capacity. Understanding their irrelative strengths and weaknesses can result in gaining competitive advantage in the market.

OPERATING DECISIONS: RELEVANT COSTS

Operating decisions imply an understanding of costs, but not necessarily those costs that are defined by accountants. We have already seen in Chapter 10 the distinction between avoidable and unavoidable costs. This brings us to the notion of relevant costs. **Relevant costs** are those costs that are relevant to a particular decision. Relevant costs are the *future, incremental cash flows* that result from a decision. Relevant costs specifically do not include sunk costs, i.e. costs that have been incurred in the past, as nothing we can do can change those earlier decisions. Relevant costs are avoidable costs because, by taking a particular decision, we can avoid the cost. Unavoidable costs are not relevant because, irrespective of what our decision is, we will still incur the cost. Relevant costs may, however, be opportunity costs. An **opportunity cost** is not a cost that is paid out in cash. It is the loss of a future cash flow that takes place as a result of making a particular decision.

MAKE VERSUS BUY?

A concern with subcontracting or outsourcing has dominated business in recent years as the cost of providing goods and services in-house is increasingly compared to the cost of purchasing goods on the open market. The make versus buy decision should be based on which alternative is less costly on a relevant cost basis, that is taking into account only future, incremental cash flows.

Table 11.4   Relevant costs – make versus buy

	Cost to make	Cost to buy
Stationery	5,000	
10,000 @ £0.50		
Labour	20,000	
10,000 @ £2		
Share of depreciation costs	10,000	10,000
Outsourcing cost		20,000
Total relevant cost	£35,000	£30,000

Table 11.5   Relevant costs – make versus buy, simplified

	Relevant cost to make	Relevant cost to buy
Stationery	5,000	
10,000 @ £0.50		
Labour	20,000	
10,000 @ £2		
Outsourcing cost		20,000
Total relevant cost	£25,000	£20,000

For example, the costs of in-house production of a computer processing service that averages 10,000 transactions per month are calculated as £25,000 per month. This comprises £0.50 per transaction for stationery and £2 per transaction for labour. In addition, there is a £10,000 charge from head office as the share of the depreciation charge for equipment. An independent computer bureau has tendered a fixed price of £20,000 per month.

Based on this information, stationery and labour costs are variable costs that are both avoidable if processing is outsourced. The depreciation charge is likely to be a fixed cost to the business irrespective of the outsourcing decision. It is therefore unavoidable. The fixed outsourcing cost will only be incurred if outsourcing takes place. The relevant costs for each alternative can be compared as shown in Table 11.4. The £10,000 share of depreciation costs is not relevant as it is unavoidable. The relevant costs for this decision are therefore those shown in Table 11.5.

Based on relevant costs, there would be a £5,000 per month saving by outsourcing the computer processing service.

EQUIPMENT REPLACEMENT

A further example of the use of relevant costs is in the decision to replace plant and equipment. Once again, the concern is with future incremental cash flows, not with historical or sunk costs or with non-cash expenses such as depreciation.

Table 11.6 Relevant costs – equipment replacement

	Retain old kitchen	Buy new kitchen
Purchase price of new kitchen		−£150,000
Trade-in value of old machine		+£25,000
Operating costs		
£40,000 p.a. × 5 years	−£200,000	
£30,000 p.a. × 5 years		−£150,000
Additional income from dining of		+£125,000
£25,000 p.a. × 5 years		
Total relevant cost	−£200,000	−£150,000

Mammoth Hotel Company replaced its kitchen one year ago at a cost of £120,000. The kitchen was to be depreciated over five years, although it will still be operational after that time. The hotel manager wishes to expand the dining facility and needs a larger kitchen with additional capacity. A new kitchen will cost £150,000, but the kitchen equipment supplier is prepared to offer £25,000 as a trade-in for the old kitchen. The new kitchen will ensure that the dining facility earns additional income of £25,000 for each of the next five years.

The existing kitchen incurs operating costs of £40,000 per year. Due to labour saving technology, operating costs, even with additional dining, will fall to £30,000 per year if the new kitchen is bought. These figures are shown in Table 11.6. On a relevant cost basis, the difference between retaining the old kitchen and buying the new kitchen is a saving of £50,000 cash flow over five years. On this basis, it makes sense to buy the new kitchen.

The original kitchen cost has been written down to £96,000 (cost of £120,000 less one year's depreciation at 20% or £24,000). The original capital cost is a sunk cost and is therefore irrelevant to a future decision. The loss on sale of £71,000 (£96,000 written down value – £25,000 trade-in) will affect the hotel's reported profit, but it is not a future incremental cash flow and is therefore irrelevant to the decision.

However, there is a tension between a decision based on future incremental cash flows and the reported financial position that will show a significant (non-cash) financial loss in the year in which the old kitchen is written off. The political aspects of such a decision were discussed in Chapter 5. Other aspects of capital expenditure decisions are explained in Chapter 14.

RELEVANT COST OF MATERIALS

As the definition of relevant cost is the future incremental cash flow, it follows that the relevant cost of direct materials is not the historical (or sunk) cost but the replacement price of the materials. Therefore it is irrelevant whether or not those materials are held in inventory, unless such materials have only scrap value or an alternative use, in

Table 11.7   Material requirements

Material	Total kg required	Kg in stock	Original purchase price per kg	Scrap value per kg	Current purchase price per kg
A	750	0	–	–	6.00
B	1,000	600	3.50	2.50	5.00
C	500	400	3.00	2.50	4.00
D	300	500	4.00	6.00	9.00

Table 11.8   Relevant cost of materials

Material		Relevant cost
A	750 @ £6 (replacement price)	4,500
B	1,000 @ £5 (replacement price)	5,000
C	400 @ £2.50 (opportunity cost of scrap value)	1,000
	100 @ £4 (replacement price)	400
D	300 @ £6 (opportunity cost of scrap value)	1,800
	or	
	300 @ £8 (substitute for material E)	2,400
Total relevant material cost		13,300
Proceeds of sale		16,000
Incremental gain		2,700

which case the relevant cost is the opportunity cost of the forgone alternative. The cost of using materials can be summarized as follows:

■ If the material is purchased specifically the relevant cost is the purchase price.
■ If the material is already in stock and is used regularly, the relevant cost is the purchase price (i.e. the replacement price).
■ If the material is already in stock but is surplus as a result of previous overbuying, the relevant cost is the opportunity cost, which may be its scrap value or its value in any alternative use.

Stanford Potteries Ltd has been approached by a customer who wants to place a special order and is willing to pay £16,000. The order requires the materials shown in Table 11.7.

Material A would have to be purchased specifically for this order. Material B is used regularly and any inventory used for this order would have to be replaced. Material C is surplus to requirements and has no alternative use. Material D is also surplus to requirements but can be used as a substitute for material E. Material E, although not required for this order, is in regular use and currently costs £8.00 per kg, but is not in stock. The relevant material costs are shown in Table 11.8.

As a result of the above, Stanford Potteries would accept the special order because the additional income exceeds the relevant cost of materials. In the case of A, the material is purchased at the current purchase price. For B, even though some inventory is held at a lower cost price, it is used regularly and has to be replaced at the current purchase price. For C, the 400 kg in inventory have no other value than scrap, which is the opportunity cost of using it in this order. The 100 kg of C not in inventory have to be purchased at the current replacement price. For D, the opportunity cost is either the scrap value or the saving made by using material D as a substitute for material E. As the substitution value is higher, this is what Stanford would do in the absence of this particular order. Therefore, the opportunity cost of D is the loss of the ability to substitute for material E.

Relevant costs are a useful tool in helping to make operational decisions. However, there are other approaches to costing that are also valuable.

OTHER COSTING APPROACHES

Lifecycle costing

All products and services go through a typical lifecycle, from introduction, through growth and maturity to decline. The lifecycle is represented in Figure 11.3.

Over time, sales volume increases, then plateaus and eventually declines. Management accounting has traditionally focused on the period after product design and development, when the product/service is in production for sale to customers. However, the product design phase involves substantial costs that may not be taken into account in product/service costing. These costs may have been capitalized (see Chapters 3 and 6) or treated as an expense in earlier years. Similarly, when products/services are discontinued, the costs of discontinuance are rarely identified as part of the product/service cost.

Lifecycle costing estimates and accumulates the costs of a product/service over its entire lifecycle, from inception to abandonment. This helps to determine whether the profits generated during the production phase cover all the lifecycle costs. This information helps managers make decisions about future product/service development and the need for cost control during the development phase.

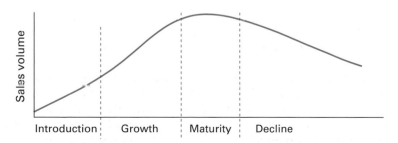

Figure 11.3 Typical product/service lifecycle

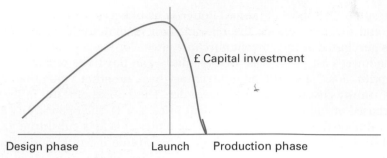

Figure 11.4 Investment decisions

The design and development phase can determine up to 80% of costs in many advanced technology industries. This is because decisions about the production process and the technology investment required to support production are made long before the product/services are actually produced. This is shown in Figure 11.4.

Consequently, efforts to reduce costs during the production phase are unlikely to be successful when the costs are committed or locked in as a result of technology and process decisions made during the design phase.

Target costing

Target costing is concerned with managing whole-of-life costs *during the design phase*. It has four stages:

1 Determining the target price that customers will be prepared to pay for the product/service.
2 Deducting a target profit margin to determine the target cost, which becomes the cost to which the product/service should be engineered.
3 Estimating the actual cost of the product/service based on the current design.
4 Investigating ways of reducing the estimated cost to the target cost.

target price − target profit margin = target cost

The technique was developed in the Japanese automotive industry and is customer oriented. Its aim was to build a product at a cost that could be recovered over the product lifecycle through a price that customers would be willing to pay to obtain the benefits (which in turn drive the product cost).

Target costing is equally applicable to a service. The design of an Internet banking service involves substantial up-front investment, the benefits of which must be recoverable in the selling price over the expected lifecycle of the service.

Using a simple example, a new product is expected to achieve a desired volume and market share at a price of £1,000, from which the manufacturer wants a 20% margin, leaving a target cost of £800. Current estimates suggest the cost as £900. An investigation seeks to find which elements of design, manufacture or purchasing contribute to the costs and how those costs can be reduced, or whether features can be eliminated that cannot be justified in the target price. This is an iterative process, but an essential one if the lifecycle costs of the product/service are to be managed and recovered in the (target) selling price. Importantly, this process of estimating costs over the product/service lifecycle and establishing a target selling price takes place *before* decisions are finalized about product/service design and the production process to be used.

The investigation of cost reduction is a *cost-to-function* analysis that examines the relationship between how much cost is spent on the primary functions of the product/service compared with secondary functions. This is consistent with the value chain approach described earlier in this chapter. Such an investigation is usually a team effort involving designers, purchasing, production/manufacturing, marketing and costing staff. The target cost is rarely achieved from the beginning of the manufacturing phase. Japanese manufacturers tend to take a long-term perspective on business and aim to achieve the target cost during the lifecycle of the product.

Kaizen costing

Kaizen is a Japanese term – literally 'tightening' – for making continuous, incremental improvements to the production process. While target costing is applied during the design phase, kaizen costing is applied during the production phase of the lifecycle when large innovations may not be possible. Target costing focuses on the product/service. Kaizen focuses on the production process, seeking efficiencies in production, purchasing and distribution.

Like target costing, kaizen establishes a desired cost-reduction target and relies on teamwork and employee empowerment to improve processes and reduce costs. This is because employees are assumed to have more expertise in the production process than managers. Frequently, cost-reduction targets are set and producers work collaboratively with suppliers who often have cost-reduction targets passed on to them.

TOTAL QUALITY MANAGEMENT

One aspect of operational management that deserves particular attention is total quality management and the cost of quality. *Total quality management (TQM)* encompasses design, purchasing, operations, distribution, marketing and administration (see for example Slack *et al.* (1995) for a fuller description).

TQM involves comprehensive measurement systems, often developed from statistical process control (SPC). *Continuous improvement* is perhaps the latest form of total quality management. This is a systematic approach to quality management that focuses on customers, re-engineers business processes and ensures that all employees are committed to quality. Standardization of processes ensures consistency, which may be documented in a quality management system such as ISO 9000. Continuous improvement goes beyond processes to encompass employee remuneration strategies, management information systems and budgetary systems.

The *Six Sigma* approach, developed by Motorola, is a measure of standard deviation, that is how tightly clustered observations are around a mean (the average). Six Sigma aims to improve quality by removing defects and the causes of defects. Balanced Scorecard-type measures (see Chapter 4) are often used in Six Sigma, which is well developed as a management tool in high-technology manufacturing organizations. It is part of a larger performance measurement model called DMAIC, an acronym for Define, Measure, Analyse, Improve and Control.

A holistic approach is taken by the *Business Excellence* model of the European Foundation for Quality Management (EFQM; see also Chapter 4). The EFQM model is a self-assessment tool to aid continuous improvement based on nine criteria, five of which are enablers and four results. Each is scored in order to demonstrate improvement over time, although a criticism of the model is the subjectivity of the scoring system (further information is available from the EFQM website at *www.efqm.org*).

Not only is non-financial performance measurement crucial in TQM, but accounting has a significant role to play because of its ability to record and report the cost of quality and how cost influences, and is influenced by, continuous improvement in production processes.

Cost of quality

Recognizing the cost of quality is important in terms of continuous improvement processes. The Chartered Institute of Management Accountants define the cost of quality as the difference between the actual costs of production, selling and after-sales service and the costs that would be incurred if there were no failures during production or usage of product/services. There are two broad categories of the cost of quality: conformance costs and non-conformance costs.

Conformance costs are those costs incurred to achieve the specified standard of quality and include prevention costs such as quality measurement and review, supplier review and quality training etc. (i.e. the procedures required by an ISO 9000 quality management system). Costs of conformance also include the costs of inspection or testing to ensure that products or services actually meet the quality standard.

The costs of *non-conformance* include the cost of internal and external failure. Internal failure is where a fault is identified by the business before the product/service reaches the customer, typically evidenced by the cost of waste or rework. The cost of external failure is identified after the product/service is in the hands of the customer. Typical costs are warranty claims, discounts and replacement costs.

Identifying the cost of quality is important to the continuous improvement process, as substantial improvements to business performance can be achieved by investing in conformance and so avoiding the much larger costs usually associated with non-conformance.

Two case studies illustrate the main concepts identified in this chapter.

Case Study 11.1:   Quality Printing Company – pricing for capacity utilization

Quality Printing Company (QPC) is a listed PLC, a manufacturer of high-quality, multi-colour printed brochures and stationery. Historically, orders were for long-run, high-volume printing, but over recent years the sales mix has changed to shorter runs of greater variety. This was reflected in a larger number of orders but a lower average order size. Expenses have increased throughout the business in order to process the larger number of orders. The result was an increase in sales but a decline in profitability. By the latest year, QPC had virtually no spare production capacity to increase its sales but needed to improve profitability. The trend in business performance is shown in Table 11.9.

An analysis of these figures shows that while sales have increased steadily, profit has declined as a result of a lower gross margin (materials and other costs have increased as a percentage of sales). QPC noticed that the change in sales mix had led not only to a higher material content, and therefore to more working capital, but also to higher costs in manufacturing, selling and administration, since employment had increased to support the larger number of smaller order sizes. An analysis of the data in Table 11.9 is shown in Table 11.10.

A throughput contribution approach that calculates the sales less cost of materials and relates this to the production capacity utilization shows how the contribution per hour of capacity has declined. This is shown in Table 11.11.

Table 11.9   Quality Printing Company – business performance trends

	Last year	One year ago	Two years ago
Sales	2,255,000	2,125,000	2,000,000
Variable production costs:			
Materials	1,260,000	1,105,000	980,000
Labour	250,000	225,000	205,000
Other production costs	328,000	312,000	295,000
	1,838,000	1,642,000	1,480,000
Contribution	417,000	483,000	520,000
Fixed selling and administration expenses	325,000	285,000	250,000
Net profit	92,000	198,000	270,000
Production capacity utilization (hours)	12,100	11,200	10,500

Table 11.10   Quality Printing Company – analysis of business performance

	Last year	One year ago	Two years ago
Sales growth	6.1%	6.3%	
Net profit as a % of sales	4.1%	9.3%	13.5%
Gross margin as a % of sales	18.5%	22.7%	26.0%
Materials as a % of sales	55.9%	52.0%	49.0%
Labour and other costs as a % of sales	25.6%	25.3%	25.0%
Fixed selling and administration expenses as a % of sales	14.4%	13.4%	12.5%

Table 11.11 Quality Printing Company throughput contribution

	Last year	One year ago	Two years ago
Throughput contribution	995,000	1,020,000	1,020,000
No. production hours	12,100	11,200	10,500
Throughput contribution per hour	£82	£91	£97

As a result of the above analysis, QPC initiated a pricing strategy that emphasized the throughput contribution per hour in pricing decisions. Target contributions were set in order to force price increases and alter the sales mix to restore profitability.

Unfortunately, the change had no time to take effect as QPC was taken over by a larger printing company. The larger company was aware of QPC's situation, perhaps having applied strategic management accounting techniques to its knowledge of its smaller competitor.

Case Study 11.2:   Vehicle Parts Co. – the effect of equipment replacement on costs and prices

Vehicle Parts Co. (VPC) is a privately owned manufacturer of components and a Tier 1 supplier to several major motor vehicle assemblers. VPC has a long history and substantial machinery that was designed for long-run, high-volume parts. The nature of the machinery meant that long set-up times were needed to make the machines ready for the small production runs. The old equipment kept breaking down and quality was poor. As a result of these problems, about 35% of VPC's production was delivered late. Consequently, there was a gradual loss of production volume as customers sought more reliable suppliers. Demand was unlikely to increase in the short term because of delivery performance. However, as the current machinery had been fully written off, the company incurred no depreciation expense. As a result, its reported profits were quite high.

The market now demands more flexibility with more short runs of parts to meet the assemblers' just-in-time (JIT) requirements. New computer-numerically controlled (CNC) equipment was bought in order to satisfy customer demand and provide the ability to grow sales volume. While the new CNC equipment substantially reduced set-up times, the significant depreciation charge increased the product cost and made the manufactured parts less profitable. The marketing manager believed that the depreciation cost should be discounted as otherwise the business would lose sales by retaining the existing mark-up on cost. VPC's accountant argued that depreciation is a cost that must be included in the cost of the product and prepared the summary in Table 11.12.

If the capital investment was not made, volume would decline as a result of quality and delivery performance. If existing prices were maintained, reported profitability would decline by £200,000 p.a. (the depreciation cost). If prices were increased to cover the depreciation cost, volume would fall further and profitability would decline.

There was little choice but to make the capital investment if the business was to survive. On a target costing basis, unless volume increased there was little likelihood of an adequate return on investment being achieved. VPC believed that, under a lifecycle approach, volume would increase and returns would be generated once quality and delivery performance improved with the new equipment. On a relevant cost basis, once

Table 11.12 Vehicle Parts Co.

	Existing machine	New CNC machine
Original cost	250,000	1,000,000
Depreciation at 20% p.a.	fully written off	200,00
Available hours (2 shifts)	1,920	1,920
Set-up time	35%	5%
Running time	65%	95%
Available running hours	1,248	1,824
Hours per part	0.5	0.35
Production capacity (number of parts)	2,496	5,211
Market capacity		2,500
Depreciation cost per part	0	80
Material cost per part	75	75
Labour and other costs per part	30	20
Total cost per part	105	175
Mark-up 50%	53	88
Selling price	158	263
Maximum selling price		158
Effective markdown on cost		−10%

the capital investment decision had been made, depreciation could be ignored as it did not incur any future, incremental cash flow. This case is a good example of how accounting makes visible certain aspects of organizations and changes the way managers view events, i.e. that events were socially constructed by accounting, a concept that was introduced in Chapter 5.

CONCLUSION

Operations decisions are critical in satisfying customer demand. Optimizing production capacity for products or services using relevant costs for decision-making and under-standing the long-term impact of production design and continuous improvement are both necessary to improve business performance. These techniques can be applied to other organizations in the value chain (suppliers and customers) and to competitors in order to improve competitive advantage.

After you have read this chapter, you should:

■ Revise your understanding of the accounting terms. The Glossary in Part IV is a helpful aid.
■ Practice the Questions for this chapter and then check your answers against the solutions. Questions for each chapter are in Appendix 1. The solutions are in Appendix 2.

■ Read Case Study 2. This will help you to interpret accounting information. Try to write an answer. The Case Studies are in Appendix 3 and suggested solutions are in Appendix 4.

REFERENCES

Fitzgerald, L., Johnston, R., Brignall, S., Silvestro, R. and Voss, C. (1991). *Performance Measurement in Service Businesses*. London: Chartered Institute of Management Accountants.

Goldratt, E. M. and Cox, J. (1986). *The Goal: A Process of Ongoing Improvement*. (Revd edn). Croton-on-Hudson, NY: North River Press.

Hammer, M. and Champy, J. (1993). *Reengineering the Corporation: A Manifesto for Business Revolution*. London: Nicholas Brealey Publishing.

Kaplan, R. S. and Cooper, R. (1998). *Cost and Effect: Using Integrated Cost Systems to Drive Profitability and Performance*. Boston, MA: Harvard Business School Press.

Porter, M. E. (1985). *Competitive Advantage: Creating and Sustaining Superior Performance*. New York, NY: Free Press.

Slack, N., Chambers, S., Harland, C., Harrison, A. and Johnston, R. (1995). *Operations Management*. London: Pitman Publishing.

12 HUMAN RESOURCE DECISIONS

This chapter explains the components of labour costs and how those costs are applied to the production of goods or services. The relevant cost of labour for decision-making purposes is explained. This chapter also introduces the notion of activity-based costs.

According to Armstrong (1995a, p. 28), 'personnel management is essentially about the management of people in a way that improves organizational effectiveness'. Personnel management – or human resources as it is more commonly called – is a function concerned with job design; recruitment, training and motivation; performance appraisal; industrial relations, employee participation and team work; remuneration; redundancy; health and safety; and employment policies and practices. It is through human resources, that is people, that the production of goods and services takes place. Historically, as Chapter 1 suggested, employment costs were a large element of the cost of manufacture. Even with the shift to service industries, people costs have tended to decline in proportion to total costs, a consequence of computer technology.

Armstrong (1995b) argued that the tighter grip of accountants on business management and the diffusion of management accounting techniques were forces with which human resource managers had to contend. This was particularly the case where the human resource (HR) function was being increasingly devolved to divisionalized business units under line management control. Line management is in turn increasingly accountable for achieving corporate targets.

Many non-accounting readers ask why the balance sheet of a business does not show the value of its human assets (what the HR literature refers to as *human resource accounting*). The knowledge, skills and abilities of people are a key resource in satisfying markets through the provision of goods and services. But people are not *owned* by a business. They are recruited, trained and developed, then motivated to accomplish tasks for which they are appraised and rewarded. People may leave the business for personal reasons or be made redundant when there is a business downturn. The value of people to the business is in the application of their knowledge, skills and abilities towards the provision of goods and services. The limitations of accounting in relation to the organizational stock of knowledge, that is intellectual capital, was described in Chapter 7.

In accounting terms, people are treated as *labour*, a resource that is consumed – therefore an expense rather than an asset – either *directly* in producing goods or services or *indirectly* as a business overhead. This distinction between *direct* and *indirect labour* is an important concept that is considered in more detail in Chapter 13.

THE COST OF LABOUR

The cost of labour can be considered either over the short term or long term. In the short term, the cost of labour is the total expense incurred in relation to that resource, which may, for direct labour, also be calculated as the *cost per unit of production*, for either goods or services. The cost of labour is the salary or wage cost paid through the payroll, plus the oncost. The **labour oncost** consists of the nonsalary or wage costs that follow from the payment of salaries or wages. The most obvious of these are National Insurance contributions and pension contributions made by the business. These oncosts can be expressed as a percentage of salary. The *total employment cost* may include other forms of remuneration such as bonuses, profit shares and non-cash remuneration such as share options, expense allowances, business-provided motor vehicles and so on.

A less visible but important element of the cost of labour is the period during which employees are paid but do not work, covering public holidays, annual leave, sick leave etc. A second element of the cost of labour is the time when people are at work but are unproductive, such as when they are on refreshment or toilet breaks, socializing, during equipment downtimes etc. These unproductive times all increase the cost of labour in relation to the volume of production. The actual at-work and productive time is an important calculation in determining the production capacity of the business (see Chapter 11).

The following example shows how the total employment cost may be calculated for an individual:

	£	
Salary		30,000
Oncosts:		
National insurance 10%	3,000	
Pension contribution 4%	1,200	4,200
		34,200
Bonus paid as share options		1,000
Total salary cost		35,200
Non-salary benefits:		
Cost of motor vehicle	4,000	
Expense allowance	500	4,500
Total employment cost		39,700

Assuming a five-day week and twenty days' annual leave, five days' sick leave and eight public holidays per annum, the actual days at work (the production capacity) can be calculated as:

Working days 52 × 5		260
Less:		
Annual leave	20	
Sick leave	5	
Public holidays	8	33
Actual days at work		227

The total employment cost per working day for this employee is therefore £174.89 (£39,700/227 days). Assuming that the employee works eight hours per day and the employee is productive for 80% of the time at work, then the cost per hour worked is £27.33 (£174.89/(8 × 80%)).

The employee, taking home £30,000 for a 40-hour week, may consider their cost as £14.42 per hour (£30,000/52/40). This example shows the total employment cost and the effect of the paid but unproductive time on this cost, which almost doubles (what is £14.42 per hour to the employee is £27.33 per hour to the employer). The cost per unit of production can be expressed either as the (total employment) cost per (productive) hour worked, in this case a *labour cost per hour* of £27.33, or as a cost per unit of production. If an employee during their productive hours completes four units of a product, the *direct labour cost per unit of production* is £6.83 (£27.33/4). If a service employee processes five transactions per hour, the *direct labour cost per unit of production* (a transaction is still a unit of production) is £5.47 (£27.33/5). An employee who is not involved in production but carries out a support role is classified as an *indirect labour cost*. This is referred to as a business *overhead* (see Chapter 13).

The calculation of the cost of labour is shown in Table 12.1.

In the longer term, a business may want to take a broader view of the total cost of employment. As Chapter 11 showed in relation to the product development phase of the lifecycle, many costs are incurred before a product/service comes to market. The same is true of employees, who must be recruited and trained before they can be productive. A longer-term approach to the total cost of employment may include these

Table 12.1 The cost of labour

Cost	Time
Salaries and wages + oncosts (pensions, National Insurance etc.) + non-salary benefits (motor vehicles, expenses etc.) — total employment cost	Working days − annual leave, sick leave, public holidays, etc. = actual days at work × at work hours × productivity = actual hours worked

$$\frac{\text{total employment cost}}{\text{actual hours worked}} = \text{labour cost per hour}$$

costs as additional costs of employment. In relation to short term and long term, the issue arises as to whether the cost of labour is a fixed or variable cost, following the distinction made in Chapter 10.

Accountants have historically considered labour that is consumed in producing goods or services, i.e. direct labour, as a variable cost. This is because it is expressed as a cost per unit of production, which, in total, increases or decreases in line with business activity. However, changing legislation, the influence of trade unions and business HR policies have meant that in the very short term, all labour takes on the appearance of a fixed cost. The consultation process for redundancy takes time, and legislation such as Transfer of Undertakings Protection of Employment (TUPE) secures the employment rights of labour that is transferred between organizations, a fairly common occurrence as a consequence of outsourcing arrangements. Consequently, reflecting the underlying practicality, many businesses now account for direct labour as a fixed cost.

RELEVANT COST OF LABOUR

The distinction between fixed and variable costs is not sufficient for the purpose of making decisions about labour in the very short term as, in that short term, labour will still be paid irrespective of whether people are busy or occupied. Therefore, in the short term, a business bidding for a special order may only take into account the *relevant* costs. As was seen in Chapter 11, the relevant cost is the cost that will be affected by a particular decision to do (or not to do) something. As decision-making is not concerned with the past, historical (or *sunk*) costs are irrelevant. The relevant cost is the future, incremental cash flow that will result from making a particular decision. This may be an additional cash payment or an *opportunity cost*, i.e. the loss from the opportunity forgone. For example, in the case of full capacity, the relevant cost could be the additional labour costs (e.g. overtime) that may have to be incurred, or the opportunity cost following from the inability to sell products/services (e.g. both the loss of income from a particular order and the wider potential loss of customer goodwill).

Costs that are the same irrespective of the alternative chosen are irrelevant for the purposes of a particular decision, as there is no financial benefit or loss as a result of either choice. The costs that are relevant may change over time and with changing circumstances. This is particularly so with the cost of labour.

Where there is spare capacity, with surplus labour that will be paid whether a particular decision is taken or not, the labour cost is irrelevant to the decision. Where there is casual labour or use of overtime and the decision causes the cost to increase (or decrease), the labour cost is relevant. Where labour is scarce and there is full capacity, so that labour has to be diverted from alternative work involving an opportunity cost, the opportunity loss is relevant.

For example, Brown & Co. is a small management consulting firm that has been offered a market research project for a client. The estimated workloads and labour costs for the project are:

	Hours	Hourly labour cost
Partners	120	£60
Managers	350	£45
Support staff	150	£20

There is at present a shortage of work for partners, but this is a temporary situation. Managers are fully utilized and if they are used on this project, other clients will have to be turned away, which will involve the loss of revenue of £100 per hour. Other staff can be hired and fired on a temporary basis. Fixed costs are £100,000 per annum.

The relevant cost of labour to be used when considering this project can be calculated by considering the future, incremental cash flows:

Partners	120 hours – irrelevant as unavoidable surplus labour	Nil
Managers	350 hours @ £100 – this is the opportunity cost of the lost revenue from clients who are turned away	£35,000
Support staff	150 hours @ £20 cost	3,000
Relevant cost of labour		£38,000

The fixed/variable cost approach would have identified the cost of labour as:

	Hours	Hourly labour cost	Total labour cost
Partners	120	£60	£7,200
Managers	350	£45	£15,750
Support staff	150	£20	£3,000
Variable cost of labour			£25,950

The relevant cost approach identifies the future, incremental cash flows associated with acceptance of the order. This ignores the cost of partners as there is no future, incremental cash flow. The cost of managers is the opportunity cost – the lost revenue from the work to be turned away. The support staff cost is due to the need to employ more temporary staff. Fixed costs are irrelevant as they are unaffected by this project.

Chapter 11 introduced outsourcing as a business strategy that has been in favour to reduce the cost of labour and increase capacity utilization. The example given for the make versus buy decision in Chapter 11 related to an in-house computer processing service in which the relevant costs are shown in Table 12.2.

In the above example, it was implicit that TUPE required the cost of labour to be transferred to the external company, as labour ceased to be a relevant cost under the outsourcing option. However, if the labour were not transferred to the external company but retained in the organization, it could become a relevant cost and the financial calculation of the outsourcing decision may be different, depending on the

Table 12.2   Make versus buy – relevant costs

	Relevant cost to make	Relevant cost to buy
Stationery 10,000 @ £0.50	5,000	
Labour 10,000 @ £2	20,000	
Outsourcing cost		20,000
Total relevant cost	£25,000	£20,000

Table 12.3   Make versus buy – relevant costs

	Relevant cost to make	Relevant cost to buy
Stationery 10,000 @ £0.50	5.000	
Outsourcing cost		20,000
Total relevant cost	£5,000	£20,000

alternative use of the labour. The relevant costs for each alternative would then be those shown in Table 12.3.

Note in the example in Table 12.3 that labour is no longer a relevant cost, as it is incurred irrespective of the decision to outsource. In this case it would be more costly to outsource the service unless the underutilized labour could be directed at tasks that generated a contribution of at least £15,000. This example shows how it is important in any calculation of relevant costs to be sure about which costs are avoidable and which costs are unavoidable.

Unfortunately, one of the first business responses to a downturn in profits is to make staff redundant. Although the redundancy payments will be recognized as a cost, there is a substantial social cost, not reflected in the financial reports of a business. The social effects will be borne by the redundant employee, while the financial burden of unemployment benefits may be borne by the taxpayer (see Chapter 5 for a discussion). This short-term concern with reducing labour cost often ignores the potential for cost improvement that can arise from a better understanding of business processes.

BUSINESS PROCESSES AND ACTIVITY-BASED COSTS

Activity-based costing (or ABC) was introduced in Chapter 11 in relation to the cost of unused capacity. ABC developed from the work of Cooper and Kaplan (Cooper and Kaplan, 1988; Cooper, 1990; Cooper and Kaplan, 1992), who argued that many resource demands are not proportional to volume but arise from the diversity and complexity of the product and customer mix. ABC systems estimate the costs of resources used to perform activities for various outputs and directly link the cost of performing activities to the products/services and customers for which those activities are performed.

ABC achieves this through the concept of the cost driver, which is the most significant determinant of the cost of an activity. The cost driver seeks to determine cause-and-effect relationships for costs, and measures the demand for activities by each product or service. ABC is described more fully in Kaplan and Cooper (1998) and is covered in more detail in Chapter 13.

A parallel concern has been with *business process re-engineering (BPR)*, a term coined by Hammer and Champy (1993) and which they defined as:

> the fundamental rethinking and radical design of business processes to achieve dramatic improvements in critical, contemporary measures of performance, such as cost, quality, service, and speed. (p. 32)

The recognition by both ABC and BPR is that business processes flow through the organization (i.e. horizontally) and are not confined to hierarchical departments (i.e. vertically). This is not a dissimilar concept to Porter's value chain (see Chapter 11), where activities do not follow the route of the typical business organization chart. However, accounting reports are typically structured in accordance with the organizational chart, either on a functional basis (marketing, operations, finance etc.) or on a divisionalized basis (by product/service, geographic unit etc., as described in Chapter 2). The lack of cost information in relation to business processes is a limitation of traditional accounting systems.

Two examples, one from manufacturing and one from financial services, help to understand the importance of BPR and ABC as tools that can aid in human resource decision-making.

Example 1: manufacturing

Purchasing in a manufacturing business is a *process* that is not confined to a centralized purchasing department. The process begins with the identification of the need to order raw materials. A requisition may be raised in a production department, is approved and is submitted to a purchasing department that will have an approved list of suppliers and negotiated prices. A purchase order will be created and sent to the supplier. The process continues when the goods are received in the store, signed for and placed in a storage area. The paperwork is sent to the accounting department where the supplier's delivery note, the purchase order and the goods receipt record are matched to await the supplier invoice. The invoice prices and quantities are checked and a cheque will be issued.

In this example, purchasing is a cross-functional process that affects the personnel in many departments. However, a traditional accounting system arranged around hierarchical departments and line items (e.g. salaries) will not recognize the *total* cost of the purchasing process. Building on the principles of BPR, an ABC accounting system will collect and report the total process cost. This can lead to improved management decisions.

In the motor vehicle industry, an understanding of cost drivers has led to the recognition that the number of suppliers and the number of parts had to be rationalized. It has also led to the adoption of designs that more frequently use common parts between different models (a recognition of the importance of the product design phase, see Chapter 11). This is a more sophisticated method of driving down purchasing costs than the conventional approach of reducing the personnel headcount while leaving business processes unchanged, resulting in an increased workload for the remaining personnel.

Example 2: financial services

Serving customers in a bank involves many different personnel in many different departments. A customer service employee may open an account and arrange cheque books and bank cards. The teller will process deposits. A loans officer will take the details of loan applications. These are 'front office' or customer-facing personnel. In the 'back office', cheques will be processed by data-entry operators, the production of cheque books and bank cards will take place, customer funds will be invested, statements printed and so on.

For most of these services (the exception is the loan, where a separate charge may be made) a single bank charge covers the bank's administration costs. Some banks no longer charge fees to non-business customers as their costs are absorbed against the interest earned by the bank on their customers' bank balances (less any, usually smaller, interest payment to the customer).

Given this complexity, banks need to understand the profitability of different branch locations and different types of customers (market segments, see Chapter 10). In order to do this, an activity-based approach can be used. The cost drivers for each major activity can be identified, e.g. the number of new customers (for account-opening costs); the number of cheque and deposit transactions (for the teller and data-entry costs); the number (or value) of loans (for loan-processing costs); and the number of accounts (for account-maintenance costs). The number of transactions for each branch and type of customer multiplied by the direct labour cost per transaction (see earlier in this chapter) can then be compared with the income earned from bank charges and interest.

In banking, understanding these costs has led to the introduction of automatic teller machines (ATMs) to reduce the cost of front-office staff who previously cashed cheques in the bank branch. ATMs increased bank profitability as many employees were made redundant, although more recently there has been an attempt (impeded by the competition authorities) to impose charges for the use of ATMs by customers.

The following case studies show the impact of an activity-based approach to labour costs and capacity utilization.

Case Study 12.1:   The Database Management Company – labour costs and unused capacity

The Database Management Company (DMC) is a call centre within a multinational company that has built a sophisticated database to hold consumer buying preferences. DMC contracts with large retail organizations to provide information on request and charges a fixed monthly fee plus a fee for each transaction (request for information). DMC estimates transaction volume based on past experience and recruits employees accordingly, to ensure that it is able to satisfy its customers' demands without delay.

Employees are on a mix of permanent and temporary contracts. Labour costs are separated into variable (transaction-processing costs, which can be directly attributable to specific contracts) and fixed elements (administration and supervision). DMC also incurs fixed costs, the main items being for building occupancy (a charge made by the parent company based on floor area occupied) and the lease of computer equipment. As these costs follow staffing levels that relate to specific contracts, they can be allocated with a reasonable degree of accuracy.

DMC's budget (based on anticipated activity levels and standard costs) is shown in Table 12.4. As a result of declining retail sales the demand for transactions has fallen, but because of uncertainty in DMC about how long this downturn will last, it has only been able to reduce its variable labour cost by ending the contracts of a small number of temporary staff. DMC's actual results for the same period are shown in Table 12.5.

How can the poor performance compared with budget be interpreted?

DMC's income has fallen across the board because of the reduced number of transactions on all its contracts. Because it has been unable to alter its variable labour cost significantly in the short term, the contribution towards fixed costs and profits has fallen. Therefore, although the business treats these costs as variable, in practice they are fixed costs, especially in the short term. The fixed salary and non-salary costs are constant despite

Table 12.4   DMC budget

(in f'000)	Contract 1	Contract 2	Contract 3	Total
Budgeted numer of transactions	10,000	15,000	25,000	50,000
Fee per transaction	£1.00	£0.85	£0.70	
Budgeted transaction income	10,000	12,750	17,500	40,250
Fixed monthly fee	5,000	7,500	12,000	24,500
Total budgeted income	15,000	20,250	29,500	64,750
Variable labour costs	4,000	6,000	9,000	19,000
Contribution	11,000	14,250	20,500	45,750
Fixed labour costs	3,000	2,000	2,000	7,000
Occupancy costs	5,000	6,000	12,000	23,000
Computer costs	2,500	3,500	5,000	11,000
Budgeted net profit	500	2,750	1,500	4,750

Table 12.5 DMC actual results

(In £'000)	Contract 1	Contract 2	Contract 3	Total
Actual number of transactions	9,000	10,500	22,000	41,500
Fee per transaction	£1.00	£0.85	£0.70	
Actual transaction income	9,000	8,925	15,400	33,325
Fixed monthly fee	5,000	7,500	12,000	24,500
Actual income	14,000	16,425	27,400	57,825
Variable labour costs	3,750	5,000	8,000	16,750
Contribution	10,250	11,425	19,400	41,075
Fixed labour costs	3,000	2,000	2,000	7,000
Occupancy costs	5,000	6,000	12,000	23,000
Computer costs	2,500	3,500	5,000	11,000
Actual net profit/(-loss)	−250	−75	400	75

the fall in transaction volume and so profitability has been eroded. DMC cannot alter its floor space allocation from the parent company or its computer lease costs despite having spare capacity.

What information can be provided to help in making a decision about cost reductions?

Calculating the variance (or difference) between the budget and actual income and variable costs shows how the difference between budget and actual profit of £4,675 (£4,750 − £75) is represented by a fall in income of £6,925 offset by a reduction in variable labour costs of £2,250 (all figures are in £'000). This is shown in Table 12.6.

Calculating the cost of unused capacity identifies the profit decline more clearly, as can be seen in Table 12.7.

Of the gap between budget and actual profit, £3,280 is accounted for by the cost of unused capacity in variable labour. This gap has been offset to some extent by the reduction in variable labour costs of £2,250. There remains the capability to reduce variable costs to meet the actual transaction volume, as Table 12.8 shows.

What conclusions can be drawn from this information?

It is clear that DMC has either to increase its income or reduce its costs in order to reach its profitability targets. The company has a significant cost of unused capacity. However, it can only reduce this unused capacity based on sound market evidence or else it may be

Table 12.6 DMC loss of contribution

	Contract 1	Contract 2	Contract 3	Total
Income reduction from budget	1,000	3,825	2,100	6,925
Variable labour costs reduction	250	1,000	1,000	2,250
Contribution reduction	750	2,825	1,100	4,675

Table 12.7 DMC cost of unused capacity

	Contract 1	Contract 2	Contract 3	Total
Budgeted variable labour costs	4,000	6,000	9,000	19,000
Budgeted number of transactions	10,000	15,000	25,000	50,000
Budgeted cost per transaction	£0.40	£0.40	£0.36	
Actual number of transactions	9,000	10,500	22,000	41,500
Budgeted cost per transaction	£0.40	£0.40	£0.36	
Standard variable labour cost[1]	3,600	4,200	7,920	15,720
Cost of unused capacity (budget variable labour cost less standard variable labour cost)	400	1,800	1,080	3,280

Note [1] The actual number of transactions multiplied by the budgeted variable labour cost per transaction.

Table 12.8 DMC variable costs

	Contract 1	Contract 2	Contract 3	Total
Actual variable labour costs	3,750	5,000	8,000	16,750
Standard variable labour costs	3,600	4,200	7,920	15,720
Difference	150	800	80	1,030

constraining its ability to provide services to its customers in future, which may in turn result in a greater loss of income. DMC needs to renegotiate its prices and volumes with its customers.

Case study 12.2: Trojan Sales – the cost of losing a customer

Trojan Sales is a business employing a number of sales representatives, each costing the business £40,000 per annum, a figure that includes salary, oncosts and motor vehicle running costs. Sales representatives also earn a commission of 1% on the orders placed by their customers. On average, each sales representative looks after 100 customers (one driver of activity) and each year, customers place an average of five orders, with an average order size of £2,500. Therefore, each representative generates sales of:

$$100 \times 5 \times £2,500 = £1,250,000$$

and earns commission of 1%, amounting to £12,500.

However, Trojan suffers from a loss to competitors of about 10% of its customer base each year. Consequently, only about 70% of each sales representative's time is spent with existing customers, the other 30% being spent on winning replacement customers, with each representative needing to find 10 new customers each year (a second driver of activity). The business wants to undertake a campaign to prevent the loss of customers and has asked for a calculation of the cost of each lost customer.

A first step is to calculate the cost of the different functions carried out by each sales representative:

employment cost of £40,000

$$\frac{\times 70\% \text{ of time}}{100 \text{ existing customers}} = £280 \text{ per customer (account maintenance)}$$

employment cost of £40,000

$$\frac{\times 30\% \text{ of time}}{10 \text{ new customers}} = £1,200 \text{ per new customer}$$

The cash cost of winning a new customer is £1,200. However, the opportunity cost provides a more meaningful cost. If there were no lost business and sales representatives could spend all of their time with existing customers, each representative could look after 142 customers (100 customers × 100%/70%) in the same time.

If each of the 142 customers placed the average five orders with an average order size of £2,500, each representative could generate income of £1,775,000 and earn commission of £17,750. The opportunity cost is the loss of the opportunity by the company to generate the extra income of £525,000 (£1,775,000 − £1,250,000) and the opportunity cost to the representative personally of £5,250 (commission of £17,750 − £12,500).

Each customer lost costs Trojan £1,200 in time taken by sales representatives to find a replacement customer. However, on an opportunity cost basis, each lost customer potentially costs the company £52,500 in lost sales and the sales representative £525 in lost commission. For this kind of reason, businesses sometimes adopt a strategy of splitting their salesforce into those representatives who are good at new account prospecting and those who are better at account maintenance.

CONCLUSION

This chapter has calculated the cost of labour and developed relevant costs to include labour. It has introduced the concept of activity-based costing as a method by which the cost of business processes can be measured in order to improve business decision-making.

After you have read this chapter, you should:

■ Revise your understanding of the accounting terms. The Glossary in Part IV is a helpful aid.
■ Practice the Questions for this chapter and then check your answers against the solutions. Questions for each chapter are in Appendix 1. The solutions are in Appendix 2.
■ Read Case Studies 3 and 4. This will help you to interpret accounting information. Try to write an answer. The Case Studies are in Appendix 3 and suggested solutions are in Appendix 4.

REFERENCES

Armstrong, M. (1995a). *A Handbook of Personnel Management Practice.* (5th edn). London: Kogan Page.

Armstrong, P. (1995b). Accountancy and HRM. In J. Storey (ed.), *Human Resource Management: A Critical Text,* London: International Thomson Business Press.

Cooper, R. (1990). Cost classifications in unit-based and activity-based manufacturing cost systems. *Journal of Cost Management,* Fall, 4–14.

Cooper, R. and Kaplan, R. S. (1988). Measure costs right: make the right decisions. *Harvard Business Review,* Sept–Oct, 96–103.

Cooper, R. and Kaplan, R. S. (1992). Activity-based systems: measuring the costs of resource usage. *Accounting Horizons,* **6**(3), 1–13.

Hammer, M. and Champy, J. (1993). *Reengineering the Corporation: A Manifesto for Business Revolution.* London: Nicholas Brealey Publishing.

Kaplan, R. S. and Cooper, R. (1998). *Cost and Effect: Using Integrated Cost Systems to Drive Profitability and Performance.* Boston, MA: Harvard Business School Press.

13

ACCOUNTING DECISIONS

This chapter explains how accountants classify costs and determine the costs of products/services through differentiating product and period costs, and direct and indirect costs. The chapter emphasizes the overhead allocation problem: how indirect costs are allocated over products/services. In doing so, it contrasts absorption with activity-based costing. The chapter concludes with an overview of contingency theory, Japanese approaches to management accounting and the behavioural consequences of accounting choices.

COST CLASSIFICATION

Product and period costs

The first categorization of costs made by accountants is between period and product. Period costs relate to the accounting period (year, month). Product costs relate to the cost of goods (or services) produced. This distinction is particularly important to the link between management accounting and financial accounting, because the calculation of profit is based on the separation of product and period costs. However, the value given to inventory is based only on product costs, a requirement of accounting standards (see later in this chapter).

Although Chapters 10, 11 and 12 introduced the concept of the contribution (sales less variable costs), as we saw in Chapter 6 there are two types of profit: gross profit and net profit:

$$\textbf{gross profit} = \textbf{sales} - \textbf{cost of sales}$$

The cost of sales is the product (or service) cost. It is either:

- the cost of providing a service; or
- the cost of buying goods sold by a retailer; or
- the cost of raw materials and production costs for a product manufacturer.

$$\textbf{net (or operating) profit} = \textbf{gross profit} - \textbf{expenses}$$

Expenses are the period costs, as they relate more to a period of time than to the production of product/services. These will include all the other (selling, administration, finance etc.) costs of the business, i.e. those not directly concerned with buying, making or providing goods or services, but supporting that activity.

To calculate the cost of sales, we need to take into account the change in inventory, to ensure that we match the income from the sale of goods with the cost of the goods sold. As we saw in Chapter 6, *inventory* (*or stock*) is the value of goods purchased or manufactured that have not yet been sold. Therefore:

cost of sales = opening stock + purchases − closing stock

for a retailer, or:

cost of sales = opening stock + cost of production − closing stock

for a manufacturer. For a service provider, there can be no inventory of services provided but not sold, as the production and consumption of services take place simultaneously, so:

cost of sales = cost of providing the services that are sold

Financial statements produced for external purposes, as we saw in Chapter 6, show merely the value of sales, cost of sales, gross profit, expenses and net profit. For management accounting purposes, however, a greater level of detail is shown. A simple example is:

Sales		1,000,000
Less: cost of sales		
Opening stock	250,000	
Plus purchases (or cost of production)	300,000	
	———	
Stock available for sale	550,000	
Less closing stock	200,000	
	———	
Cost of sales		350,000
		———
Gross profit		650,000
Less period costs		400,000
		———
Operating profit		250,000

Direct and indirect costs

Accounting systems typically record costs in terms of line items. As we saw in Chapter 3, line items reflect the structure of an accounting system around accounts for each type of expense, such as materials, salaries, rent, advertising etc. Production costs (the cost of producing goods or services) may be classed as direct or indirect. Direct costs are readily traceable to particular product/services. Indirect costs are necessary to produce a product/service, but are not able to be readily traced to particular products/services. Indirect costs are often referred to as overheads. Any cost may be either direct or indirect, depending on its traceability to particular products/services. Because of their traceability, direct costs are generally considered variable costs because costs increase or decrease with the volume of production. However, as we saw in Chapter 12, direct labour is sometimes treated as a fixed cost. Indirect costs may be variable (e.g. electricity) or fixed (e.g. rent).

Direct materials are traceable to particular products through *material issue* documents. For a manufacturer, direct material costs will include the materials bought and used in the manufacture of each unit of product. They will clearly be identifiable from a *bill of materials*: a detailed list of all the components used in production. There may be other materials of little value that are used in production, such as screws, adhesives, cleaning materials etc., which do not appear on the bill of materials because they have little value and the cost of recording their use would be higher than the value achieved. These are still costs of production, but because they are not traced to particular products they are *indirect material* costs.

While the cost of materials will usually only apply to a retail or manufacturing business, the cost of labour will apply across all business sectors. *Direct labour* is traceable to particular products or services via a *time-recording* system. It is the labour directly involved in the conversion process of raw materials to finished goods (see Chapter 11). Direct labour will be clearly identifiable from an instruction list or *routing*, a detailed list of all the steps required to produce a good or service. In a service business, direct labour will comprise those employees providing the service that is sold. In a call centre, for example, the cost of those employees making and receiving calls is a direct cost. Other labour costs will be incurred that do not appear on the routing, such as supervision, quality control, health and safety, cleaning, maintenance etc. These are still costs of production, but because they are not traced to particular products, they are *indirect labour* costs.

Other costs are incurred that may be direct or indirect. For example, in a manufacturing business, the depreciation of machines (a fixed cost) used to make products may be a direct cost if each machine is used for a single product or an indirect cost if the machine is used to make many products. The electricity used in production (a variable cost) may be a direct cost if it is metered to particular products or indirect if it applies to a range of products. A royalty paid per unit of a product/service produced or sold will be a direct cost. The cost of rental of premises, typically relating to the whole business, will be an indirect cost.

Prime cost is an umbrella term to refer to the total of all direct costs. **Production overhead** is the total of all indirect material and labour costs and other indirect costs, i.e. all production costs other than direct costs. This distinction applies equally to the production of goods and services.

However, not all costs in an organization are production costs. Some, as we have seen, relate to the period rather than the product. These other costs (such as marketing, sales, distribution, finance, administration etc.) are not included in production overhead. These other costs are classed generally as overheads, but in the case of period costs they are **non-production overheads**.

Distinguishing between production and non-production costs and between materials, labour and overhead costs as direct or indirect is *contingent* on the type of product/service and the particular production process used in the organization. Contingency theory is described later in this chapter. There are no strict rules, as the classification of costs depends on the circumstances of each business and the decisions

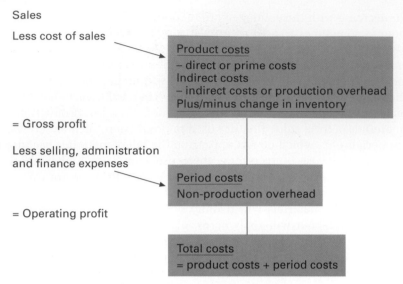

Figure 13.1   Cost classification

made by the accountants in that business. Consequently, unlike financial accounting, there is far greater variety between businesses – even in the same industry – in how costs are treated for management accounting purposes.

Figure 13.1 shows the relationship between these different types of costs.

CALCULATING PRODUCT/SERVICE COSTS

We saw in Chapter 10 the important distinction between fixed and variable costs and how the calculation of contribution (sales less variable costs) was important for short-term decision-making. However, we also saw that in the longer term, all the costs of a business must be recovered if it is to be profitable. To assist with pricing and other decisions, accountants calculate the full or absorbed cost of product/services.

As direct costs by definition are traceable, this element of product/service cost is usually quite accurate. However indirect costs, which by their nature cannot be traced to products/services, must in some way be *allocated* over products/services in order to calculate the full cost. Overhead allocation is the process of spreading production overhead (i.e. those overheads that cannot be traced directly to products/services) equitably over the volume of production. The overhead allocation problem can be seen in Figure 13.2.

The *overhead allocation problem* is a significant issue, as most businesses produce a range of products/services using multiple production processes. The most common form of overhead allocation employed by accountants has been to allocate overhead costs to products/services in proportion to direct labour. However, this may not accurately reflect the resources consumed in production. For example, some processes

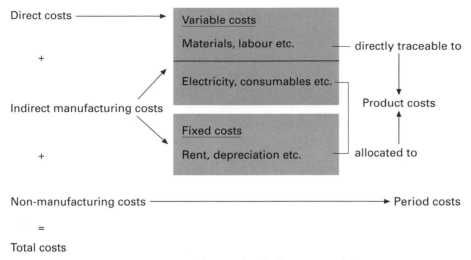

Figure 13.2 The overhead allocation problem

may be resource intensive in terms of space, machinery, people or working capital. Some processes may be labour intensive while others use differing degrees of technology. The cost of labour, due to specialization and market forces, may also vary between different processes. Further, the extent to which these processes consume the (production and non-production) overheads of the firm can be quite different. The allocation problem can lead to overheads being arbitrarily allocated across different products/ services, which can lead to misleading information about product/service profitability. As production overheads are a component of the valuation of inventory (because they are part of the cost of sales), different methods of overhead allocation can also influence inventory valuation and hence reported profitability. An increase or decrease in inventory valuation will move profits between different accounting periods.

SHIFTS IN MANAGEMENT ACCOUNTING THINKING

In their book *Relevance Lost: The Rise and Fall of Management Accounting*, Johnson and Kaplan (1987) emphasized the limitations of traditional management accounting systems that failed to provide accurate product costs:

> Costs are distributed to products by simplistic and arbitrary measures, usually direct-labor based, that do not represent the demands made by each product on the firm's resources ... the methods systematically bias and distort costs of individual products ... [and] usually lead to enormous cross subsidies across products. (p. 2)

Management accounting, according to Johnson and Kaplan (1987), failed to keep pace with new technology and became subservient to the needs of external financial reporting, as costs were allocated by accountants between the valuation of inventory and the cost of goods sold. Johnson and Kaplan claimed that '[m]any accountants and managers have come to believe that inventory cost figures give an accurate guide to product costs, which they do not' (p. 145). They argued that:

> as product life cycles shorten and as more costs must be incurred before production begins ... directly traceable product costs become a much lower fraction of total costs, traditional financial measures such as periodic earnings and accounting ROI become less useful measures of corporate performance. (p. 16)

Johnson and Kaplan claimed that the goal of a good product cost system:

> should be to make more obvious, more transparent, how costs currently considered to be fixed or sunk actually do vary with decisions made about product output, product mix and product diversity. (p. 235)

Johnson and Kaplan also argued against the focus on short-term reported profits and instead for short-term non-financial performance measures that were consistent with the firm's strategy and technologies (these were described in Chapter 4).

In their latest book, Kaplan and Cooper (1998) describe how activity-based cost (ABC) systems:

> emerged in the mid-1980s to meet the need for accurate information about the cost of resource demands by individual products, services, customers and channels. ABC systems enabled indirect and support expenses to be driven, first to activities and processes, and then to products, services, and customers. The systems gave managers a clearer picture of the economics of their operations. (p. 3)

ABC systems were introduced in Chapters 11 and 12 and are further developed in the next section of this chapter.

Kaplan and Cooper (1998) argued that cost systems perform three primary functions:

1　Valuation of inventory and measurement of the cost of goods sold for financial reporting.
2　Estimation of the costs of activities, products, services and customers.
3　Provision of feedback to managers about process efficiency.

Leading companies, according to Kaplan and Cooper (1998), use their enhanced cost systems to:

■ design products and services that meet customer expectations and can be produced at a profit;
■ identify where improvements in quality, efficiency and speed are needed;
■ assist front-line employees in their learning and continuous improvement;
■ guide product mix and investment decisions;

Table 13.1 Alternative methods of overhead allocation

Variable costing	Absorption costing	Activity-based costing
Allocates only variable costs as product costs	Allocates all fixed and variable production costs as product costs.	Allocates all costs to products/services that can be allocated by cost drivers.
All fixed costs are treated as period costs.	All non-production costs are treated as period costs.	The distinction between production and non-production costs is not important.
	Accumulate costs in cost centres and measure activity in each cost centre.	Accumulate costs in activity cost pools and measure the drivers of activities for each cost pool.
	Budgeted overhead $$\text{rate} = \frac{\text{cost centre costs}}{\text{unit of activity}}$$ (e.g. labour hours)	Cost driver $$\text{rate} = \frac{\text{activity cost pool}}{\text{activity volume}}$$ (e.g. purchase orders)
	Calculate product/service cost for each cost centre as unit of activity (e.g. labour hours) × budgeted overhead rate and add for all cost centres to give total product/service cost.	Calculate product/service cost for each cost pool as activity volume × cost driver rate and add for all pools to give total product/service cost.

■ choose among alternative suppliers;
■ negotiate price, quality, delivery and service with customers;
■ structure efficient and effective distribution and service processes to targeted market segments.

There are two methods of overhead allocation: absorption costing (the traditional method) and activity-based costing. These are compared in the next section, together with variable costing, a method that does not allocate overheads at all.

Table 13.1 shows a comparison between the three methods.

ALTERNATIVE METHODS OF OVERHEAD ALLOCATION

Variable costing

We have already seen (in Chapters 10, 11 and 12) the separation of fixed from variable costs. A method of costing that does not allocate fixed production overheads to products/services is variable (or marginal) costing. Under **variable costing**, the product cost only includes variable production costs. Fixed production costs are treated as period costs and charged to the Profit and Loss account. This method avoids much of the overhead allocation problem, as most production overheads tend to be fixed rather than variable in nature.

However, variable costing does not comply with IAS2, the International Financial Reporting Standard (IFRS) on inventories. IAS2 requires that the cost of stock should:

> comprise that expenditure which has been incurred in the normal course of business in bringing the product or service to its present location and condition. Such costs will include all related production overheads.

The effect of IAS2 is to require companies to account – for financial reporting purposes – on an absorption costing basis, as 'all related production overheads' include both fixed and variable production costs.

ABSORPTION COSTING

Absorption costing is a system in which all (fixed and variable) production overhead costs are charged to product/services using an *allocation base* (a measure of activity or volume such as labour hours, machine hours, or the number of units produced etc.). The allocation base used in absorption costing is often regarded as arbitrary. Under absorption costing, a *budgeted overhead rate* can be calculated as either:

■   a business-wide rate, or
■   a cost centre overhead rate.

A *business-wide budgeted overhead rate* is calculated by dividing the production overheads for the total business by some measure of activity. Overhead rates can also be calculated for each cost centre separately. A *cost centre* is a location within the organization to which costs are assigned (it may be a department or a group of activities within a department, see Chapter 2). A *cost centre budgeted overhead rate* is a result of determining the overheads that are charged to each cost centre and the activity of that cost centre. It is preferable to calculate a separate overhead rate for each cost centre, as the costs and activity of each may be quite different.

The overhead charged to each cost centre must then be recovered as a rate based on the principal unit of activity within a cost centre, typically direct labour hours, machine hours or the number of units produced. We therefore calculate a *direct labour hour rate* or a *machine hour rate* or a *rate per unit produced* for each production cost centre, or for the business as a whole.

Under both methods, the budgeted overhead rate is:

$$\frac{\textbf{estimated overhead expenditure for the period}}{\textbf{estimated activity for the period}}$$

For example, a business with budgeted overhead expenditure of £100,000 and an activity level of 4,000 direct labour hours would have a business-wide budgeted overhead rate of £25 per hour (£100,000/4,000). Most businesses are able to identify their overhead costs and activity to individual cost centre levels and determine cost centre overhead rates. This can be achieved using a three-stage process:

1 Identify indirect costs with particular cost centres. In many cases, although costs cannot be traced to products/services, they can be traced to particular cost centres. Accounting systems will separately record costs incurred by each cost centre. For example, supervision costs may be traceable to each cost centre. Certain consumables may only be used in particular cost centres. Each cost centre may order goods and services and be charged for those goods and services separately.

2 Analyse each line item of expenditure that cannot be traced to particular cost centres and determine a suitable method of allocating each cost across the cost centres. There are no rules for the methods of allocation, which are contingent on the circumstances of the business and the choices made by accountants. However, common methods of allocating indirect costs include:

Expense	Allocation basis
Management salaries	Number of employees in each cost centre
Premises cost	Floor area occupied by each cost centre
Electricity	Machine hours used in each cost centre
Depreciation on equipment	Asset value in each cost centre

3 Identify those cost centres that are part of the production process and those service cost centres that provide support to production cost centres. Allocate the total costs incurred by service cost centres to the production cost centres using a reasonable method of allocation. Common methods of allocating service cost centres include:

Service cost centre	Allocation basis
Maintenance	Timesheet allocation of hours spent in each production cost centre
Canteen	Number of employees in each cost centre
Scheduling	Number of production orders

An example of cost allocation between departments is shown below. Using the previous example and the same overhead costs of £200,000, suitable methods of allocation have been identified over five departments (stages 1 and 2) as follows:

Expense item	Method of allocation
Indirect wages	From payroll
Factory rental	Floor area
Depreciation on equipment	Asset value
Electricity	Machine hours

Table 13.2 Overhead allocations

Expense	Total cost	Dept 1	Dept 2	Dept 3	Canteen	Scheduling	Allocation calculation
Indirect wages	£36,000	£18,000	£9,000	£2,000	£2,000	£5,000	from payroll
Factory rental	£23,000						
Area (sqm)	10,000	5,000	2,500	1,500	500	500	£2.30/sqm
Allocation		£11,500	£5,750	£3,450	£1,150	£1,150	
Depreciation	£14,000						
Asset value	140,000	40,000	60,000	30,000	7,000	3,000	
Allocation		£4,000	£6,000	£3,000	£700	£300	10% of asset value
Electricity	£27,000						
Machine hours	9,000	3,000	2,000	4,000			
Allocation		£9,000	£6,000	£12,000			£3 per machine hour
Total	£100,000	£42,500	£26,750	£20,450	£3,850	£6,450	
Reallocate service cost centres							
Canteen							
No. employees	60	20	25	15			
Allocation		£1,283	£1,604	£963	−£3,850		£64.16/ employee
scheduling							
No. production orders	250	100	70	80			
Allocation		£2,580	£1,806	£2,064		−£6,450	£25.80/order
Total cost	£100,000	£46,363	£30,160	£23,477	£0	£0	

Of the five departments, two are service departments. Their costs can be allocated as follows (stage 3):

Service cost centre	Method of allocation
Canteen	Number of employees
Scheduling	Number of production orders

Table 13.2 shows the figures produced to support the allocation process.

Once the costs have been allocated, a reasonable measure of activity is determined for each cost centre. While this is often direct labour hours (the most common measure of capacity), the unit of activity can be different for each cost centre (e.g. machine hours, material volume, number of units produced etc. For non-manufacturing businesses the unit of activity may be hotel rooms, airline seats, consultancy hours etc.) Using the above example and given the number of labour hours in each cost centre, we can now calculate a cost centre overhead rate, i.e. a budgeted overhead rate for each cost centre, as shown in Table 13.3.

Table 13.3 Cost centre budget overhead rate

	Total cost	Dept 1	Dept 2	Dept 3
Total cost	£100,000	£46,363	£30,160	£23,477
Direct labour hours	4,000	2,000	750	1,250
Hourly rate	£25.00	£23.18	£40.21	£18.78

Table 13.4 Overhead allocation to products based on cost centre budget overhead rate

	Total cost	Dept 1	Dept 2	Dept 3
Hourly rate	£25.00	£23.18	£40.21	£18.78
Product A: direct labour hours		2	5	3
Overhead allocation	£303.77	£46.36	£201.07	£56.34
Product B: direct labour hours		5	1	4
Overhead allocation	£231.25	£115.91	£40.21	£75.13

The most simplistic form of overhead allocation uses a single overhead rate for the whole business. As we previously calculated, the *business-wide budgeted overhead* rate is £25.00 *per direct labour hour* (£100,000/4,000). This rate would apply irrespective of whether the hours were worked in stages of production that had high or low machine utilization, different levels of skill, different pay rates or required different degrees of support.

Under the *cost centre budgeted overhead rate*, the rate per direct labour hour varies from a low of £18.78 for Dept 3 to a high of £40.21 for Dept 2. This reflects the different cost structure and capacity of each cost centre.

Consider an example of two products, each requiring 10 machine hours. The extent to which each product requires different labour hours in each of the three departments will lead to quite different overhead allocations.

Assume that product A requires 2 hours in Dept 1, 5 hours in Dept 2 and 3 hours in Dept 3. The overhead allocation would be £303.77. If product B requires 5, 1 and 4 hours respectively in each department, the overhead allocation would be £231.25, as Table 13.4 shows. By contrast, the overhead allocation to both products (each of which requires 10 hours of production time) using a business-wide rate would be £250 (10 @ £25).

The total cost of a product comprises the prime cost (the total of direct costs) and the overhead allocation. Whether a business-wide or cost centre overhead allocation rate is used, the prime cost is unchanged. Assuming that the costs per unit for our two example products are:

	Product A	Product B
Direct materials	110	150
Direct labour	75	90
Prime cost	185	240

The allocation of overhead based on cost centre rates (rounded to the nearest £) would be:

	Product A	Product B
Overhead allocation	304	231
Full (or absorbed) cost	489	471

As can be seen in the above example, the overhead allocation as a percentage of total cost can be very high. This is not unusual in business, particularly in those organizations that have invested heavily in technology or (except for professional services; see Chapter 11) in service businesses, where direct costs are a small proportion of total business costs.

The cost centre rate is more accurate than the business-wide rate because it does attempt to differentiate between the different cost structures of cost centres. However, the three-stage method of allocating costs between cost centres and then allocating those costs to products/services using a single activity measure can be quite arbitrary. The absorption method of allocating overhead costs to products/services has received substantial criticism because of the arbitrary way in which overheads are allocated. Most businesses use allocation bases such as direct labour hours, machine hours or production units, because that data is readily available. The implicit assumption of absorption costing is that the allocation base chosen is a reflection of why business overheads are incurred. For example, if the allocation base is direct labour or machine hours, the assumption of absorption costing is that overhead costs are incurred in proportion to direct labour or machine hours. This is unlikely to be the case in most businesses as many overheads are caused by the range and complexity of product/services.

ACTIVITY-BASED COSTING

As we saw in Chapter 12, **activity-based costing** (or ABC) is an attempt to identify a more accurate method of allocating overheads to product/services. ABC uses *cost pools* to accumulate the cost of significant business activities and then assigns the costs from the cost pools to products based on *cost drivers*, which measure each product's demand for activities.

Cost pools accumulate the cost of business processes, irrespective of the organizational structure of the business. The costs that correspond to the formal organization structure may still be accumulated for financial reporting purposes through a number of cost centres, but this will not be the method used for product costing. For example, the purchasing process can take place in many different departments. A stores-person or computer operator may identify the need to restock a product. This will often lead to a purchase requisition, which must be approved by a manager before being passed to the purchasing department. Purchasing staff will have negotiated with suppliers in relation to quality, price and delivery and will generally have approved suppliers and terms. A purchase order will be raised. The supplier will deliver the goods against the purchase order and the goods will be received into the store. The paperwork (a delivery note from the supplier and a goods received note) will be passed to the accounting department to be matched to the supplier invoice and a cheque will be produced and posted. This business process cuts across several departments. ABC collects the costs in all departments for the purchasing *process* in a cost pool.

A cost driver is then identified. The **cost driver** is the most significant cause of the activity. In the purchasing example, the causes of costs are often recognized as the number of suppliers and/or the number of purchase orders. Cost drivers enable the cost of activities to be assigned from cost pools to cost objects. Rates are calculated for each cost driver and overhead costs are applied to product/services on the basis of the cost driver rates.

There are no rules about what cost pools and cost drivers should be used, as this will be contingent on the circumstances of each business and the choices made by its accountants. Examples of cost pools and drivers are:

Cost pool	Cost driver
Purchasing	No. of purchase orders
Material handling	No. of set-ups (i.e. batches)
Scheduling	No. of production orders
Machining	Machine hours (i.e. not labour hours)

For example, a rate will be calculated for each cost driver (e.g. purchase order, set-up) and assigned to each product based on how many purchase orders and setups the product has consumed. The more purchase orders and set-ups a product requires, the higher will be the overhead cost applied to it. ABC does not mean that direct labour hours or machine hours or the number of units produced are ignored. Where these are the significant cause of activities for particular cost pools, they are used as the cost drivers for those cost pools.

Using the same example as for absorption costing, assume for our two products that there are two cost pools: purchasing and scheduling. The driver for purchasing is the number of purchase orders and the driver for scheduling is the number of production orders. Costs are collected by the accounting system into cost pools and the measurement of cost drivers takes place, identifying how many activities are required for each product. The cost per activity is the cost pool divided by the cost drivers, as shown in Table 13.5.

We can then calculate the overhead cost per product/service by dividing the total cost pool by the quantity of products/services produced. This is shown in Table 13.6.

The prime cost (the total of direct costs) is not affected by the method of overhead allocation. The total cost of each product using ABC for overhead allocation is shown

Table 13.5 Overhead accumulated in cost pools and allocated by cost drivers

Cost pool and driver	Total cost	Product A	Product B
Purchasing	£40,000		
−no. or purchase orders	4,000	3,000	1,000
	(£10 each)	£30,000	£10,000
Scheduling	£60,000		
−no. of production orders	100	75	25
	(£600 each)	£45,000	£15,000
Total overhead	£100,000	£75,000	£25,000

Table 13.6 Overhead per product based on ABC

	Product A	Product B
Total overhead	£75,000	£25,000
Quantity produced	150	250
Per product (/100)	£500	£100

Table 13.7 Product costing under ABC

	Direct materials	Direct labour	Manufacturing overhead	Total cost per table
Product A	£110	£75	£500	£685
Product B	£150	£50	£100	£300

Table 13.8 Comparison of product costs under absorption costing and activity-based costing

	Product A	Product B
Total cost using absorption costing	£489	£471
Total cost using activity-based costing	£685	£300

in Table 13.7. Table 13.8 compares the cost of each product calculated using absorption costing with that using ABC.

Although this is an extreme example, significant differences can result from the adoption of an activity-based approach to overhead allocation. In this example, overheads allocated using direct labour hours under absorption costing do not reflect the actual causes for overheads being incurred. Product A not only uses more purchasing and production order activity (the drivers of overheads), but also has a lower volume. Reflecting the cause of overheads in overhead allocations more fairly represents the cost of each product. Under absorption costing, Product B was subsidizing Product A. Cross-subsidization can be hidden where a business sells a mixture of high-volume and low-volume products/services.

The distinction between fixed and variable costs and between production overhead and non-production overhead that applies to absorption costing is not so important under ABC. Costs under an ABC approach are identified as follows:

- *Unit-level activities*: These are performed each time a unit is produced, e.g. direct labour, direct materials and variable manufacturing costs such as electricity. These activities consume resources in proportion to the number of units produced. If we are producing books, then the cost of paper, ink and binding, and the labour of printers, are unit-level activities. If we produce twice as many books, unit-level activities will be doubled.
- *Batch-related activities*: These are performed each time a batch of goods is produced, e.g. a machine set-up. The cost of these activities varies with the number of batches, but is fixed irrespective of the number of units produced within the batch. Using our book example, the cost of making the printing machines ready, e.g. washing up, changing the ink, changing the paper etc., is fixed irrespective of how many books are printed in that batch, but variable on the number of batches that are printed.
- *Product-sustaining activities*: These enable the production and sale of multiple products/services, e.g. maintaining product specifications, after-sales support, product design and development. The cost of these activities increases with the number of products, irrespective of the number of batches or the number of units produced. For each differently titled book published, there is a cost incurred in dealing with the author, obtaining copyright approval, typesetting the text etc. However many batches of the book are printed, these costs are fixed. Nevertheless, the cost is variable depending on the number of books that are published. Similarly, *customer-sustaining activities* support individual customers or groups of customers, e.g. different costs may apply to supporting retail, that is end-user, customers compared with resellers. In the book example, particular costs are associated with promoting a textbook to academics in the hope that it will be set as required reading. Fiction books may be promoted through advertising and in-store displays.
- *Facility-sustaining activities*: These support the whole business and are common to all products/services. Examples of these costs include senior management and administrative staff, premises costs etc. Under ABC these costs are fixed and unavoidable and irrelevant for most business decisions, being unrelated to the number of products, customers, batches or units produced.

Because costs are assigned to cost pools rather than cost centres under ABC, and as business processes cross through many cost centres, the distinction between production and non-production overhead also breaks down under ABC. While the distinction is still important for stock valuation (as IAS2 requires the inclusion of production overheads), this distinction is not necessary for management decision-making. The more (production and non-production) overheads that are able to be allocated accurately to product/services, the more accurate will be the information for decision-making about relevant costs, pricing and product/service profitability.

The ABC method is preferred because the allocation of costs is based on *cause-and-effect* relationships, while the absorption costing system is based on an *arbitrary* allocation of overhead costs. However, ABC can be costly to implement because of the need to analyse business processes in detail, to collect costs in cost pools as well as cost centres, and to identify cost drivers and measure the extent to which individual products/services consume resources.

Survey research by Drury and Tayles (2000) suggested that 27% of companies reported using ABC, although this was affected by business size and sector, being especially evident in larger organizations and the financial and service sectors. However, the extent to which organizations use ABC for decision-making rather than stock valuation has not been fully explored.

Why, then, do different organizations adopt different methods of management accounting? One explanation is provided by contingency theory.

CONTINGENCY THEORY

The central argument of contingency theory is that there is no control system (which, as described in Chapter 4, includes accounting systems) that is appropriate to all organizations. Fisher (1995) contrasts contingency with situation-specific and universalist models. The situation-specific approach argues that each control system is developed as a result of the unique characteristics of each organization. The universalist approach is that there is an optimal control system design that applies at least to some extent across different circumstances and organizations. The contingency approach is situated between these two extremes, in which the appropriateness of the control system depends on the particular circumstances faced by the business. However, generalizations in control systems design can be made for different classes of business circumstances.

Fisher (1995) reviewed various contingency studies and found that the following variables have been considered in research studies as affecting control systems design:

■ *External environment*: whether uncertain or certain; static or dynamic; simple or complex.
■ *Competitive strategy*: whether low cost or differentiated (e.g. Porter, see Chapter 10) and the stage of the product lifecycle (see Chapter 11).
■ *Technology*: the type of production technology (see Chapter 11).
■ *Industry and business variables*: size, diversification and structure (see Chapter 15).
■ *Knowledge and observability of outcomes and behaviour*: the transformation process between inputs and outputs (see Chapter 4).

Otley (1980) argued that a simple linear explanation was inadequate. The linear explanation assumed that contingent variables affected organizational design, which in turn determined the type of accounting/control system in use and led to organizational effectiveness. Otley emphasized the importance of other controls outside accounting, how many factors other than control system design influenced organizational performance and that organizational effectiveness is itself difficult to measure. He argued that the contingent variables were outside the control of the organization, and those that could be influenced were part of a *package* of organizational controls including personnel selection, promotion and reward systems. Otley also argued that there were intervening variables that, together with the contingent variables, influenced organizational effectiveness, which was measured in relation to organizational objectives. Otley believed that an organization 'adapts to the contingencies it faces by arranging the factors it can control into an appropriate configuration that it hopes will lead to effective performance' (p. 421).

In Chapters 1 and 2, the comment by Clark (1923) that there were 'different costs for different purposes' can be seen as an early understanding of the application of the contingency approach. Clark further commented that 'there is no one correct usage, usage being governed by the varying needs of varying business situations and problems'. This reflected the need to use cost information in different ways depending on the circumstances, which has been the focus of Chapters 10 to 12.

INTERNATIONAL COMPARISONS

Alexander and Nobes (2001) described various approaches to categorizing international differences in accounting, including:

■ legal systems;
■ commercially driven, government-driven or professional regulation;
■ strength of equity markets.

Alexander and Nobes argued that legal systems, tax systems and the strength of the accountancy profession all influence the development of accounting, but the main explanation for the most important international differences in financial reporting is the financing system (such as the size and spread of corporate shareholding).

There have been efforts to harmonize financial reporting within the European Union (see Chapter 8). Through the International Accounting Standards Committee (IASC) there are moves towards harmonization, to a large extent following US practices. This is likely to be a continuing trend given the globalization of capital markets. Whether there will be any effect of harmonization on management accounting practices is as yet unknown.

In understanding management accounting, practising managers and students of accounting receive little exposure to management accounting practices outside the UK and US. It is important to contrast the UK/US approach with other practices, particularly those in Japan. These practices are different because they are predicated on different assumptions, particularly the different emphases on long-term strategies for growth versus short-term strategies for shareholders. There are historical, cultural, political, legal and economic influences underlying the development of different management accounting techniques in that country, to take a single example.

MANAGEMENT ACCOUNTING IN JAPAN

Japan has a strong history of *keiretsu*, the interlocking shareholdings of industrial conglomerates and banks, with overlapping board memberships. This has, at least in part, influenced long-term strategy because of the absence of strong stock market pressures for short-term performance, as is the case in the UK and US.

Demirag (1995) studied three Japanese multinationals with manufacturing subsidiaries in the UK, two in consumer electronics and one in motor vehicles. The companies had strongly decentralized divisional profit responsibilities with autonomous plants focused on target results. A complex matrix structure resulted in reporting to general management in the UK as well as to functional and product management in Japan. The company's basic philosophy was that the design team was responsible for profit. Continuous processes were in place to monitor and reduce production costs.

According to Demirag (1995), Japanese companies exhibited a strategic planning style of management control rather than an emphasis on financial control. The strategic planning systems were bureaucratic, although business units gave top management the information necessary to formulate and implement plans. As Japanese managers move frequently between plants and divisions, they have a better understanding of communication and co-ordination than their British counterparts. Japanese managers put the interest of the organization above their own divisions. There is less attention to accounting and management control than to smooth production and quality products. Performance targets were set in the context of strategy but were flexible, with results expected in the longer term.

Manufacturing and sales were independent of each other, each having its own profit responsibility, the underlying principle being that each side of the business drives the other to be more effective and efficient. Although traditionally manufacturing had the greatest negotiating power, this did lead to a failure of market information reaching top decision-makers in Japan. There was a top-down approach to capital investment decisions, with managers taking a strategic and company-wide perspective that reduced the importance of financial decisions, with ROI not being seen as a particularly useful measure.

Pressures to meet short-term financial targets were not allowed to detract from long-term progress. In performance measurement, much more emphasis was placed on design, production and marketing than on financial control, although profit was increasing in importance. Although fixed and variable costs were used, the main emphasis was on market-driven product costing, i.e. target costing, on the assumption that if market share increased the cost per unit would reduce, which would enable prices to be reduced and so prevent competition. Overhead allocation was not important, but there was a focus on how the allocation techniques used encouraged employees to reduce costs.

Hiromoto (1991) described Japanese management accounting practices and the central principle that accounting policies should be subservient to corporate strategy, not independent of it. Japanese companies use accounting systems more to motivate employees to act in accordance with long-term manufacturing strategies. Japanese management accounting does not stress optimizing within existing constraints, but encourages employees to make continual improvements by tightening operations.

Hiromoto describes the example of Hitachi, which used direct labour hours as the overhead allocation base as this 'creates the desired strong pro-automation incentives throughout the organization' (p. 68). By contrast, another Hitachi factory uses the number of parts as the allocation base in order to influence product engineering to drive reductions in the number of parts. Standard costs are not used in Japan as they are in the West. A market-driven target costing approach 'emphasizes doing what it takes to achieve a desired performance level under market conditions . . . how efficiently it must be able to build it for maximum marketplace success' (Hiromoto, 1991, p. 70). Overall, Japanese accounting policies are subservient to strategy.

Williams *et al.* (1995) reported similar findings to Demirag and, taking a critical perspective, asserted:

> In Japanese firms financial calculations are integrated into productive and market calculations; the result is a three-dimensional view which denies the universal representational privilege of financial numbers. Furthermore the integration of different kinds of calculation broadens out the definition of performance and identifies new points of intervention in a way which undermines the privilege of financial guidance techniques; in Japanese firms the main practical emphasis is on productive and market intervention rather than orthodox financial control. (p. 228)

In Japan, production engineering knowledge has an equal or higher status to accounting knowledge, with the result that, for example in Toyota, the 'visible benefits' of lower inventory in the financial statements was outweighed by the invisible production benefits, 'especially the ability to run mixed model lines in a small batch factory' (Williams *et al.*, 1995, p. 233).

Currie (1995) undertook a comparative study of costing and investment appraisal for the evaluation of advanced manufacturing technology (AMT). Research identified that Japanese managers were uninterested in new management accounting techniques such as activity-based costing, since knowledge that some products were more expensive to produce than others was not important to product strategy decisions. On the contrary, expensive products were likely to have strategic value to the company.

Japanese companies emphasize costing in the pre-manufacturing phase through target and lifecycle costing (see Chapter 11). In investment decisions, Japanese managers stress the qualitative benefits of AMT such as quality control, scrap, rework, service costs, space saving etc. These are difficult to quantify. ROI measures are considered unhelpful because the focus on short-term returns overestimates the cost of capital and results in discounted cash flow hurdles (see Chapter 14) being too high. Japanese companies did, however, use simple payback calculations with targets of between two and five years.

BEHAVIOURAL IMPLICATIONS OF MANAGEMENT ACCOUNTING

Hopper *et al.* (2001) traced the rise of behavioural and organizational accounting research from 1975. In the UK, a paradigm shift occurred that did not happen in the US (where agency theory – see Chapter 6 – has been the dominant research approach). In the UK, contingency theory and neo-human relations approaches were abandoned for more sociological and political approaches that drew from European social theory and were influenced by Scandinavian case-based research.

Burchell *et al.* (1980) argued:

> What is accounted for can shape organizational participants' views of what is important, with the categories of dominant economic discourse and organizational functioning that are implicit within the accounting framework helping to create a particular conception of organizational reality. (p. 5)

Similarly, Miller (1994) argued that accounting was a social and institutional practice. Accounting is not a neutral device that merely reports 'facts' but a set of practices that affects the type of world in which we live, the way in which we understand the choices able to be made by individuals and organizations, and the way in which we manage activities. Miller argued that 'to calculate and record the costs of an activity is to alter the way in which it can be thought about and acted upon' (p. 2).

Cooper *et al.* (1981) reflected that accounting systems are a significant component of power in organizations:

> Internal accounting systems by what they measure, how they measure and who they report to can effectively delimit the kind of issues addressed and the ways in which they are addressed. (p. 182)

Various published research studies have adopted an interpretive or critical perspective in understanding the link between accounting systems, organizational change and the behaviour of people in organizations as a result of culture and power (see Chapter 5 for the theoretical framework of these subjects).

The interpretive perspective has provided a number of interesting studies. The study of an area of the National Coal Board by Berry *et al.* (1985) emphasized a dominant operational culture and the extent to which accounting reports were 'ignored, trivialised and/or misunderstood' (p. 16). The accounting system was:

> consistent with the values of the dominant managerial culture, and being malleable and ambiguous it reflected and helped coping with the uncertainties inherent with the physical task of coal extraction and its socioeconomic environment. (p. 22)

Dent (1991) carried out a longitudinal field study of accounting change in EuroRail (which is one of the readings in this book), in which organizations were portrayed as cultures, i.e. systems of knowledge, belief and values. Prior to the study the dominant culture was engineering and production, in which accounting was incidental. This was displaced by economic and accounting concerns that constructed the railway as a profit-seeking enterprise. New accounts:

> were coupled to organizational activities to reconstitute interpretations of organizational endeavour. Accounting actively shaped the dominant meanings given to organizational life ... [in which a] new set of symbols, rituals and language emerged. (p. 708)

Dent traced the introduction of a revised corporate planning system, the amendment of capital expenditure approval procedures and the revision of budgeting systems, each of which gave power to business managers, and described how accounting played a role 'in constructing specific knowledges' (p. 727).

Roberts (1990) studied the acquisition and subsequent management of ELB Ltd by Conglom Inc. Following acquisition, 'the dominance of a production culture was instantly supplanted by the dominance of a purely financial logic' and the sale of the European operations to a competitor 'signalled the dominance of corporate financial concerns over long term market concerns' (p. 123), although this was reinforced by share options, bonuses and managers' fear of exclusion. Accounting information was:

> able to present an external image of 'success' ... and hence conceals the possibility of the damaging strategic consequences for individual business units of Conglom's exclusive preoccupation with financial returns. (p. 124)

In adopting a critical perspective, Miller and O'Leary (1987) described the construction of theories of standard costing in the period 1900–30, which they viewed as 'an important calculative practice which is part of a much wider modern apparatus of power' aimed at 'the construction of the individual person as a more manageable and efficient entity' (p. 235). The contribution of standard costing was to show how 'the life of the person comes to be viewed in relation to standards and norms of behaviour' (p. 262).

Laughlin (1996) played on 'principal and agent' theory to question the legitimacy of the principal's economic right to define the activities of the agent. He coined 'higher principals' to refer to the values held, particularly in the caring professions (education, health and social services), which could, he argued, overrule the rights of economic principals. These higher principals could be derived from religion, professional bodies or personal conscience. Broadbent and Laughlin (1998) studied schools and GP (medical) practices and identified financial reforms as 'an unwelcome intrusion into the definition of professional activities' (p. 404), which lead to resistance in the creation of 'informal and formal "absorption" processes to counteract and "mute" the changes' (p. 405).

Similarly, Covaleski et al. (1998) studied the 'Big Six' accounting firms, where management by objectives and mentoring were used as techniques of control, revealing that the 'discourse of professional autonomy' fuelled resistance to these changes.

Finally, the limitations of formal accounting have been identified in academic research. For example, Preston (1986) explained how 'the process of informing was fundamentally different to the formal or official documented information systems' (p. 523). In Preston's study, managers arranged to inform each other, predominantly through interaction, observation and keeping personal records but to a lesser extent through meetings. It was through these interactions that managers found out what was going on. They found 'the official documented information to be untimely, lacking in detail and sometimes inaccurate' (p. 535).

The overhead allocation problem is illustrated in the next case study.

Case Study 13.1: Quality Bank – the overhead allocation problem

Quality Bank has three branches and a head office. Table 13.9 shows how the accounting system, based on absorption costing, has calculated the costs for each branch. Direct costs of £104,000 are traceable based on staff working in each location. Overhead costs of £400,000 for the bank have been allocated as a percentage of the direct labour cost.

The bank used its internal staff to study the effects of introducing an activity-based costing system. Table 13.10 shows the cost pools and cost drivers that were identified.

The bank calculated costs for each cost driver as shown in Table 13.11. It then

Table 13.9 Quality Bank – direct costs and allocated overheads by branch

	Total	Branch A	Branch B	Branch C	Total branch	HO	Total
Direct labour cost (£)		14,000	11,000	9,000	34,000	70,000	104,000
Overheads	£400,000						
Allocated as % of direct labour	384.6%	53,846	42,308	34,615	130,769	269,231	400,000
Total costs		67,846	53,308	43,615	164,769	339,231	504,000

Table 13.10 Quality Bank – cost pools and drivers

Cost pools	£	Cost driver
Branch costs	120,000	No. of branch transactions
Computer system costs	180,000	No. of total transactions
Telecommunications costs	60,000	No. of customers
Credit checking costs	40,000	No. of new accounts
	400,000	

Table 13.11 Quality Bank – costs per driver

	Branch costs	Computer system	Telecomms	Credit checking	Total
Overheads (£)	120,000	180,000	60,000	40,000	400,000
No. transactions	16,000	38,000	10,000	1,500	
Overhead per transaction	£7.50	£4.74	£6.00	£26.67	
Per	Branch trans.	Total trans.	Customer	New account	

Table 13.12 Quality Bank – transaction volumes by branch

	Branch A	Branch B	Branch C	Total branch	HO	Total
No. of new accounts	350	100	50	500		500
No. of new loan accounts	600	300	100	1,000		1,000
Total no. new accounts	950	400	150	1,500	0	1,500
No. transactions – cashiers	3,000	1,500	500	5,000	.	5,000
No. transactions – loans	1,500	2,000	500	4,000	4,000	
No. transactions – ATM	3,000	3,000	1,000	7,000		7,000
No. transactions – HO					22,000	22,000
Total no. transactions	7,500	6,500	2,000	16,000	22,000	38,000
No. customers					10,000	10,000

Table 13.13 Quality Bank – cost analysis using ABC

	Total	Branch A	Branch B	Branch C	Total branch	HO	Total
New accounts	£26.67	25,333	10,667	4,000	40,000	0	40,000
Branch transactions	£7.50	56,250	48,750	15,000	120,000		120,000
Total transactions	£4.74	35,526	30,789	9,474	75,789	104,211	180,000
No. of customers	£6.00					60,000	60,000
Overhead allocation (£)		117,110	90,206	28,474	235,789	164,211	400,000
Direct labour (£)		14,000	11,000	9,000	34,000	70,000	104,000
Total (ABC)		131,110	101,206	37,474	269,789	234,211	504,000

Table 13.14 Quality Bank – comparison of costs under absorption and activity-based costing

	Branch A	Branch B	Branch C	Total branch	HO	Total
Absorption costing	67,846	53,308	43,615	164,769	339,231	504,000
Activity-based costing	131,110	101,206	37,474	269,789	234,211	504,000

analysed the transaction volume for each of its branches and head office. These figures are shown in Table 13.12.

The bank was then able to apply the cost per cost driver against the actual transaction volume for each branch and head office. This resulted in the cost analysis shown in Table 13.13. A comparison of the costs allocated to each branch under absorption and activity-based costing is shown in Table 13.14.

The ABC approach revealed that many of the costs charged to head office under absorption costing should be charged to branches based on transaction volumes. This had a significant impact on the measurement of branch profitability and the profitability of different business segments (e.g. new accounts, lending, ATM transactions etc.).

Applying different perspectives to management accounting: costs

In Chapters 4 and 5, we considered rational-economic, interpretive and critical per-spectives that help to provide multiple views about the world in which we live. Chapters 10 through 13 have introduced many aspects of costs and how management accounting techniques are used in planning, decision-making and control in relation to marketing, operations, human resource and accounting.

Implicit in most of what is contained in these four chapters is an acceptance of the rational-economic paradigm described in Chapter 4. The notion of shareholder value and the importance of profit have dictated acceptable approaches to calculating costs, at least for financial reporting purposes to shareholders. In financial reporting, regula-tion and audit generally prevents (except in creative accounting) any but a single interpretation, the rational-economic one. However, as we have seen through notions like relevant cost, different interpretations are possible. The interpretive perspective applied to management accounting accepts that different understandings exist. So, there are alternative approaches to pricing (Chapter 10) in which different solutions are possible, yet all are correct if based on different assumptions. Different methods of judging the best use of capacity are also possible (Chapter 11). Relevant costs are an entirely different approach to traditional historical costing (Chapters 11 and 12) while variable, absorption and activity-based costing are very different interpretations about the treatment of overhead costs (this chapter). The critical paradigm privileges one or other treatment in each of these examples as a result, not necessarily of rational choice, but of the power of the dominant management group which can influence the techniques adopted.

CONCLUSION

In Chapters 10, 11 and 12, various accounting techniques were identified that can be used by non-financial managers as part of the decision-making process. With the shift in most western economies to service industries and high-technology manufacture, overheads have increased as a proportion of total business costs. This chapter has shown the importance to decision-making of the methods used by accountants to allocate overheads to products/services. Understanding the methods used, and their limitations, is essential if informed decisions are to be made by non-financial managers.

This chapter has also shown that we need to consider the underlying assumptions behind the management accounting techniques that are in use. Other countries adopt different approaches and we have something to learn from the success or failure of those practices. We also need to consider the behavioural consequences of the choices made in relation to accounting systems.

After you have read this chapter, you should:

■ Revise your understanding of the accounting terms. The Glossary in Part IV is a helpful aid.
■ Practise the Questions for this chapter and then check your answers against the

solutions. Questions for each chapter are in Appendix 1. The solutions are in Appendix 2.

■ Read Case Study 5. This will help you to interpret accounting information. Try to write an answer. The Case Studies are in Appendix 3 and suggested solutions are in Appendix 4.

■ Read and think about Reading A. The Readings are in Part IV of this book.

REFERENCES

Alexander, D. and Nobes, C. (2001). *Financial Accounting: An International Introduction.* Harlow: Financial Times/Prentice Hall.

Berry, A. J., Capps, T., Cooper, D., Ferguson, P., Hopper, T. and Lowe, E. A. (1985). Management control in an area of the NCB: Rationales of accounting practices in a public enterprise. *Accounting, Organizations and Society,* **10**(1), 3–28.

Broadbent, J. and Laughlin, R. (1998). Resisting the 'new public management': Absorption and absorbing groups in schools and GP practices in the UK. *Accounting, Auditing and Accountability Journal,* **11**(4), 403–35.

Burchell, S., Clubb, C., Hopwood, A. and Hughes, J. (1980). The roles of accounting in organizations and society. *Accounting, Organizations and Society,* **5**(1), 5–27.

Clark, J. M. (1923). *Studies in the Economics of Overhead Costs.* Chicago, IL: University of Chicago Press.

Cooper, D. J., Hayes, D. and Wolf, F. (1981). Accounting in organized anarchies: Understanding and designing accounting systems in ambiguous situations. *Accounting, Organizations and Society,* **6**(3), 175–91.

Covaleski, M. A., Dirsmith, M. W., Heian, J. B. and Samuel, S. (1998). The calculated and the avowed: Techniques of discipline and struggles over identity in big six public accounting firms. *Administrative Science Quarterly,* **43**, 293–327.

Currie, W. (1995). A comparative analysis of management accounting in Japan, USA/UK and west Germany. In D. Ashton, T. Hopper and R. W. Scapens (eds), *Issues in Management Accounting* (2nd edn), London: Prentice Hall.

Demirag, I. S. (1995). Management control systems of Japanese companies operating in the united kingdom. In A. J. Berry, J. Broadbent and D. Otley (eds), *Management Control: Theories, Issues and Practices,* Basingstoke: Macmillan.

Dent, J. F. (1991). Accounting and organizational cultures: A field study of the emergence of a new organizational reality. *Accounting, Organizations and Society,* **16**(8), 705–32.

Drury, C. and Tayles, M. (2000). *Cost System Design and Profitability Analysis in UK Companies,* London: Chartered Institute of Management Accountants.

Fisher, J. (1995). Contingency-based research on management control systems: Categorization by level of complexity. *Journal of Accounting Literature,* **14**, 24–53.

Hiromoto, T. (1991). Another Hidden Edge – Japanese Management Accounting, *Getting Numbers You Can Trust: The New Accounting.* Boston, MA: Harvard Business Review Paperback.

Hopper, T., Otley, D. and Scapens, B. (2001). British management accounting research: Whence and whither: Opinions and recollections. *British Accounting Review,* **33**, 263–91.

Johnson, H. T. and Kaplan, R. S. (1987). *Relevance Lost: The Rise and Fall of Management Accounting.* Boston, MA: Harvard Business School Press.

Kaplan, R. S. and Cooper, R. (1998). *Cost and Effect: Using Integrated Cost Systems to Drive Profitability and Performance.* Boston, MA: Harvard Business School Press.

Laughlin, R. (1996). Principals and higher principals: Accounting for accountability in the caring professions. In R. Munro and J. Mouritsen (eds), *Accountability: Power, Ethos and the Technologies of Managing*, London: International Thomson Business Press.

Miller, P. (1994). Accounting as social and institutional practice: An introduction. In A. G. Hopwood and P. Miller (eds), *Accounting as Social and Institutional Practice*, Cambridge: Cambridge University Press.

Miller, P. and O'Leary, T. (1987). Accounting and the construction of the governable person. *Accounting, Organizations and Society*, **12**(3), 235–65.

Otley, D. (1980). The contingency theory of management accounting: Achievement and prognosis. *Accounting, Organizations and Society*, **5**(4), 413–28.

Preston, A. (1986). Interactions and arrangements in the process of informing. *Accounting, Organizations and Society*, **11**(6), 521–40.

Roberts, J. (1990). Strategy and accounting in a U.K. conglomerate. *Accounting, Organizations and Society*, **15**(1/2), 107–26.

Williams, K., Haslam, C., Williams, J., Abe, M., Aida, T. and Mitsui, I. (1995). Management accounting: The western problematic against the Japanese application. In A. J. Berry, J. Broadbent and D. Otley (eds), *Management Control: Theories, Issues and Practices*, Basingstoke: Macmillan.

14 STRATEGIC INVESTMENT DECISIONS

We introduced strategy in Chapter 2 to explain its link with achieving shareholder value. In this chapter we are more concerned with strategy implementation through capital investment decisions and the tools used to evaluate those decisions.

STRATEGY

Ansoff (1988) provided a typical description of strategy formulation: objectives and goals were established; then an internal appraisal of strengths and weaknesses and an external appraisal of opportunities and threats led to strategic decisions such as diversification or the formulation of competitive strategy. He established a hierarchy of objectives that were centred on performance measures such as return on investment (see Chapter 7, later in this chapter and Chapter 15).

A contrasting approach was developed by Quinn (1980), which he called *logical incrementalism*. Quinn argued against formal planning systems, which he believed had become 'costly paper-shuffling exercises', observing that 'most major strategic decisions seemed to be made outside the formal planning structure' (p. 2). Quinn further argued that:

> the real strategy tends to evolve as internal decisions and external events flow together to create a new, widely shared consensus for action among key members of the top management team. (p. 15)

Logical incrementalism is similar to work by Mintzberg and Waters (1985), which defined strategy as a pattern in a stream of decisions. Mintzberg and Waters separated the *intended* from the *realized* strategy, arguing that *deliberate* strategies provided only a partial explanation, as some intended strategies were unable to be realized while other strategies *emerged* over time.

The difficulty for businesses in the twenty-first century is that they must continually adapt to technological and market change, making long-term strategy problematic. However, to give the external appearance of being well managed they need to develop strategies, even if only to legitimize what senior managers are doing. Nevertheless, strategy can be crucial in enabling a business to be proactive in increasingly competitive and turbulent business conditions. The absence of strategy can lead to reactivity and a steady erosion of market share.

As we saw in Chapter 10, Porter (1980) developed his 'five forces' model for analysing an industry. This focused on the effects of rivalry among existing firms, the threat of new entrants, the bargaining power of suppliers and customers, and the threat of substitute products and services. Porter also identified three 'generic strategies' for competitive advantage: cost leadership, differentiation and focus. Cost leadership requires efficiency, tight cost control and the avoidance of unprofitable work, with low cost a defence against competition. Differentiation can be achieved through, for example, brand image, technology or a unique distribution channel. These factors insulate against price competition because of brand loyalty and lower customer sensitivity to pricing differences. Focus emphasizes servicing a particular market segment (whether customer, territory or product/service) better than competitors who may be competing more broadly. In his second book, Porter (1985) introduced the 'value chain' as a tool to help create and sustain competitive advantage (see Chapter 11).

However, the formulation of strategy is frequently divorced from the annual budgeting cycle (see Chapter 16), as organizations produce strategic planning documents separately from the annual budget based on last year plus or minus a percentage in order to achieve short-term financial targets. Consequently, the issue of translating strategy formulation into implementation is problematic unless resource allocations follow strategy.

In their most recent addition to the strategy literature, Kaplan and Norton (2001) built on the success of their *Balanced Scorecard* approach (see Chapter 4) to emphasize the 'strategy-focused organization' that links financial performance with non-financial measures. Non-financial measures in the Balanced Scorecard measure how well the organization is meeting the targets established in its strategy. Kaplan and Norton use 'strategy maps' to identify cause-effect relationships, although these should be modified over time as a result of experience gained within organizations. They also argued that budgetary allocations and incentives need to be consistent with strategy, while reflecting the importance of continual learning and improvement.

One of the most important elements of strategy implementation is capital investment decision-making, because investment decisions provide the physical and human infrastructure through which businesses produce and sell goods and services. This is the topic of this chapter.

INVESTMENT APPRAISAL

Capital investment or capital expenditure (often abbreviated as 'cap ex') means spending money now in the hope of getting it back later through future cash flows. The process of evaluating or appraising potential investments is to:

- generate ideas based on opportunities or identifying solutions to problems;
- research all relevant information;
- consider possible alternatives;
- evaluate the financial consequences of each alternative;

- assess non-financial aspects of each alternative;
- decide to proceed;
- determine an implementation plan and implement the proposal;
- control implementation by monitoring actual results compared to plan.

There are three main types of investment:

- new facilities for new product/services;
- expanding capacity to meet demand;
- replacing assets in order to reduce production costs or improve quality or service.

These are inextricably linked to the implementation of business strategy.
  Most investment appraisals consider decisions such as:

- whether or not to invest;
- whether to invest in one project or one piece of equipment rather than another;
- whether to invest now or at a later time.

There are three main methods of evaluating investments:

1   Accounting rate of return.
2   Payback.
3   Discounted cash flow.

While the first is concerned with profits, the second and third are concerned with cash flows from a project. For any project, investment appraisal requires an estimation of future incremental cash flows, i.e. the additional cash flow (net of income less expenses) that will result from the investment, as well as the cash outflow for the initial investment. Depreciation is, of course, an expense in arriving at profit that does not involve any cash flow (see Chapter 6). Cash flow is usually considered to be more important than accounting profit in investment appraisal because it is cash flow that drives shareholder value (see Chapter 2).
  It is important to note the following:

1   The financing decision is treated separately to the investment decision. Hence, even though there may be no initial cash outflow for the investment (because it may be wholly financed), all investment appraisal techniques assume an initial cash outflow. If a decision is made to proceed, then the organization is faced with a separate decision about how best to finance the investment.
2   The outflows are not just additional operating costs, as any new investment that generates sales growth is also likely to have an impact on working capital, since inventory, debtors and creditors are also likely to increase (see Chapters 6 and 7).
3   Income tax is treated as a cash outflow as it is a consequence of the cash inflows from the new investment. As we consider each method, let us assume three alternative investments. Table 14.1 shows the estimated cash flows.

Table 14.1   Cash flows for investment alternatives

Year	Project 1	Project 2	Project 3
0 initial investment	−100,000	−125,000	−200,000
1 inflows	25,000	35,000	60,000
2 inflows	25,000	35,000	60,000
3 inflows	25,000	35,000	80,000
4 inflows	25,000	35,000	30,000
5 inflows	25,000	35,000	30,000

For simplicity, we assume that each of the cash flows occurs at the end of each year. Year 0 represents the beginning of the project when the initial funds are paid out. If we add up the cash flows in the above example, Project 1 returns £125,000 (5 @ £25,000), Project 2 returns £175,000 (5 @ £35,000) and Project 3 returns £260,000 (2 @ £60,000 + £80,000 + 2 @ £30,000), although the initial investment in each is different.

ACCOUNTING RATE OF RETURN

The accounting rate of return (ARR) is the profit generated as a percentage of the investment. This is equivalent to the return on investment (ROI) that was introduced in Chapter 7. The investment value for ARR is the depreciated value each year. The depreciated value each year, assuming a life of five years with no residual value at the end of that time, is shown in Table 14.2. The accounting rate of return varies annually, as Table 14.3 shows for Project 1.

For the whole investment period, the accounting rate of return is the average annual return divided by the average investment. The average annual return is the total profit divided by the number of years. As we assume that depreciation is spread equally throughout the life of the asset, the average investment is half the initial investment, i.e. half-way through its life.

$$\frac{\textbf{total profits/no. of years}}{\textbf{initial investment/2}}$$

Table 14.2   Depreciated value of alternative investments

End of year	Project 1	Project 2	Project 3
1	80,000	100,000	160,000
2	60,000	75,000	120,000
3	40,000	50,000	80,000
4	20,000	25,000	40,000
5	0	0	0

Table 14.3 ARR/ROI for Project 1

Year	Cash flow	Depreciation	Profit	Investment	ROI
1	25,000	20,000	5,000	80,000	6.25%
2	25,000	20,000	5,000	60,000	8.3%
3	25,000	20,000	5,000	40,000	12.5%
4	25,000	20,000	5,000	20,000	25%
5	25,000	20,000	5,000	0	

Table 14.4 ARR/ROI for Project 2

Year	Cash flow	Depreciation	Profit	Investment	ROI
1	35,000	25,000	10,000	100,000	10%
2	35,000	25,000	10,000	75,000	13.3%
3	35,000	25,000	10,000	50,000	20%
4	35,000	25,000	10,000	25,000	40%
5	35,000	25,000	10,000	0	

The average ROI for Project 1 is:

$$\frac{25,000/5}{100,000/2} = \frac{5,000}{50,000} = 10\%$$

The accounting rate of return for Project 2 is shown in Table 14.4.
The average ROI for Project 2 is:

$$\frac{50,000/5}{125,000/2} = \frac{10,000}{62,500} = 16\%$$

The accounting rate of return for Project 3 is shown in Table 14.5.
The average ROI for Project 3 is:

$$\frac{10,000/5}{200,000/2} = \frac{2,000}{100,000} = 2\%$$

Table 14.5 ARR/ROI for Project 3

Year	Cash flow	Depreciation	Profit	Investment	ROI
1	60,000	40,000	20,000	160,000	13%
2	60,000	40,000	20,000	120,000	17%
3	80,000	40,000	40,000	80,000	50%
4	30,000	40,000	−10,000	40,000	−25%
5	30,000	40,000	−10,000	0	

Project 3 in particular has substantial fluctuations in ROI from year to year. Using this method, Project 2 shows the highest return. However, it does not take into account either the scale of the investment required or the timing of the cash flows.

PAYBACK

This second method calculates how many years it will take – in cash terms – to recover the initial investment, on the assumption that the shorter the payback period, the better the investment. Based on the cash flows for each project:

■   Project 1 takes four years to recover its £100,000 investment (4 @ £25,000).
■   Project 2 has recovered £105,000 by the end of the third year (3 @ £35,000) and will take less than seven months (20/35 = .57 of 12 months) to recover its £125,000 investment. The payback is therefore 3.57 years.
■   Project 3 recovers its investment of £200,000 by the end of the third year (£60,000 + £60,000 + £80,000).

Based on the payback method, Project 3 is preferred (followed by Projects 2 and 1) as it has the fastest payback. However, the payback method ignores the size of the investment and any cash flows that take place after the investment has been recovered.

Neither the accounting rate of return nor the payback method considers the *time value of money*, i.e. that £100 is worth more now than in a year's time, because it can be invested now at a rate of interest that will increase its value. For example, £100 invested today at 10% interest is equivalent to £110 in a year's time. Conversely, receiving £100 in a year's time is not worth £100 today. Assuming the same rate of interest it is worth only £91, because the £91, invested at 10%, will be equivalent to £100 in a year's time.

The time value of money needs to be recognized in investment appraisals in order to compare investment alternatives with different cash flows over different time periods. The third method of investment appraisal therefore involves **discounted cash flow** (DCF), i.e. it discounts the future cash flows to present values using a discount rate (or interest rate) that is usually the firm's cost of capital (the risk-adjusted cost of borrowing for the investment).

There are two discounted cash flow techniques: net present value and internal rate of return.

DISCOUNTED CASH FLOW

Net present value

The **net present value** (NPV) method discounts future cash flows to their present value and compares the *present value of future cash flows* to the initial capital investment.

Table 14.6 NPV for Project 1

Year	Project 1 cash flows	Discount factor (10%)	Present value of cash flows
1	25,000	.909	22,725
2	25,000	.826	20,650
3	25,000	.751	18.775
4	25,000	.683	17,075
5	25,000	.621	15,525
Total			94,750
Less: Initial investment			100,000
Net present value			−5,250

present value (PV) of cash flows = cash flow

× discount factor (based on number of years

in the future and the cost of capital)

net present value (NPV) = present value of future cash flows

− initial capital investment

The discount rates to be applied are based on the company's cost of capital. The cost of capital (see Chapter 2) represents the weighted average of the cost of debt and equity and takes into account the riskiness of a project. As the cost of borrowing has been taken into account, an investment makes sense if the NPV is positive. The discount rate can be obtained from net present value tables (see Appendix to this chapter for an example). More commonly, spreadsheet software (e.g. Excel or Lotus) is used as this contains an NPV function.

Table 14.7 NPV for Project 1

Year	Project 2 cash flows	Discount factor (10%)	Present value of cash flows
1	35,000	.909	31,815
2	35,000	.826	28,910
3	35,000	.751	26,285
4	35,000	.683	23,905
Total			132,650
Less: Initial investment			125,000
Net present value			7,650

Table 14.8   NPV for Project 3

Year	Project 3 cash flows	Discount factor (10%)	Present value of cash flows
1	60,000	.909	54,540
2	60,000	.826	49,560
3	80,000	.751	60,080
4	30,000	.621	18,630
Total			203,300
Less: Initial investment			200,000
Net present value			3,300

Using the same example, the NPV for Project 1 is shown in Table 14.6. As the net present value is negative, Project 1 should not be accepted since the present value of future cash flows does not cover the initial investment.

The NPV for Project 2 is shown in Table 14.7. Project 2 can be accepted because it has a positive net present value. However, we need to compare this with Project 3 to see if that alternative yields a higher net present value. The NPV for Project 3 is shown in Table 14.8.

Despite the faster payback for Project 3, the application of the net present value technique to the timing of the cash flows reveals that the net present value of Project 3 is lower than that for Project 2, and therefore Project 2 – which also showed the highest accounting rate of return – is the recommended investment. However, using the NPV method it is difficult to determine how much better Project 2 (with an NPV of £7,650) is than Project 3 (with an NPV of £3,300) because each has a different initial investment.

One way of ranking projects with different NPVs is cash value added (CVA) or profitability index, which is a ratio of the NPV to the initial capital investment:

$$\text{cash value added} = \frac{\text{NPV}}{\text{initial capital investment}}$$

In the above example, Project 2 returns a CVA of 6.12% (7,650/125,000) while Project 3 returns a CVA of 1.165% (3,300/200,000). Companies may have a target CVA, such that, for example, to be approved a project must have a CVA of 10% (i.e. the NPV is at least 10% of the initial capital investment).

The second DCF technique is the internal rate of return.

Internal rate of return

The internal rate of return (IRR) method determines, by trial and error, the discount rate that produces a net present value of zero. This involves repeated calculations from the discount tables on a trial-and-error basis using different discount rates until an NPV of 0 is reached. The discount rate may need to be interpolated between whole numbers. Spreadsheet software also contains an IRR function. The IRR for each project, using the spreadsheet function, is:

Project 1   7.9%
Project 2   12.4%
Project 3   10.7%

This is a more informative presentation of the comparison because it presents the cash flows as an effective interest rate. The project with the highest internal rate of return would be preferred, provided that the rate exceeds the cost of capital (i.e. the borrowing cost).

Comparison of techniques

While the accounting rate of return method provides an average return on investment and a business may select the highest return, it ignores the timing of cash flows. Sometimes where there are high short-term ROIs, managers may prefer those investments even though the longer-term impact is detrimental to the organization. This is because managers may be evaluated and rewarded on their short-term performance (see Chapter 15). Payback measures the number of years it will take to recover the capital investment and while this takes timing into account, it ignores cash flows after the payback period. Both methods ignore the time value of money.

Discounted cash flow techniques take account of the time value of money and discount future cash flows to their present value. This is a more reliable method of investment appraisal. Discounted cash flow is similar to the method of calculating shareholder value proposed by Rappaport and described in Chapter 2.

However, for investment evaluation, while all projects with a positive net present value are beneficial, a business will usually select the project with the highest net present value, or in other words the highest internal rate of return, sometimes using the initial cash investment (CVA) or the cost of capital (IRR) as a benchmark for the return.

Because of rapid change in markets and increased demands for shareholder value, the use of discounted cash flow techniques has declined in many businesses. Boards of directors typically set quite high 'hurdle' rates for investing in new assets. These are commonly in terms of payback periods of two to four years or ROI rates of 25–50%. This approach reduces the importance of discounted cash flow techniques.

However, for larger investments where returns are expected over many years, discounted cash flow techniques are still important. Investments in buildings, major items of plant, mining exploration and so on etc. commonly use NPV and IRR as methods of capital investment appraisal.

The following case study provides an example of investment appraisal.

Case Study 14.1:   Goliath Co. – investment evaluation

Goliath Co. is considering investing in a project involving an initial cash outlay for an asset of £200,000. The asset is depreciated over five years at 20% p.a. Goliath's cost of capital is 10%. The cash flows from the project are expected to be as follows:

Year	Inflow	Outflow
1	75,000	30,000
2	90,000	40,000
3	100,000	45,000
4	100,000	50,000
5	75,000	40,000

The company wishes to consider the return on investment (each year and average), payback and net present value as methods of evaluating the proposal.

The depreciation expense is £40,000 per year. Net cash flows and profits are as follows:

Year	Inflow	Outflow	Net cash flow	Depreciation	Profit
1	75,000	30,000	45,000	40,000	5,000
2	90,000	40,000	50,000	40,000	10,000
3	100,000	45,000	55,000	40,000	15,000
4	100,000	50,000	50,000	40,000	10,000
5	75,000	40,000	35,000	40,000	−5,000

Return on investment:

	1	2	3	4	5
Investment	160	120	80	40	0
Profit	5	10	15	10	−5
ROI	3.125%	8.33%	18.75%	25%	−

Over the five years:

Profit £35/5 = £7   Investment £200/2 = £100
ROI 7/100 = 7%

Cumulative cash flows are:

Year	Cash flow	Cumulative
1	45	45
2	50	95
3	55	150
4	50	200

The payback period is the end of year 4 when £200,000 of cash flows has been recovered.
Net present value of the cash flows:

Year	Cash flow	Factor	Present value
1	45,000	.9091	40,910
2	50,000	.8264	41,320
3	55,000	.7513	41,321
4	50,000	.6830	34,150
5	35,000	.6209	21,731

Present value of net cash flows	179,432
Cash outflow	−200,000
Net present value	−20,568

Table 14.9   NPV for Goliath Co.

A	B Year 0	C Year 1	D Year 2	E Year 3	F Year 4	G Year 5
Cash flows		45,000	50,000	55,000	50,000	35,000
Present value	179,437					
Initial investment	−200,000	= +NPV (10%, C36:G36)				
NPV	−20,563					

Using the spreadsheet NPV function, the answer is calculated in Table 14.9 (the difference is due to rounding).

Although the ROI is 7% and the payback is four years, the discounted cash flow shows that the net present value is negative. Therefore the project should be rejected, as the returns are insufficient to recover the company's cost of capital.

CONCLUSION: A CRITICAL PERSPECTIVE

In this chapter we have introduced strategy and the role of investment appraisal in capital investment decisions. In particular, we have described the main methods of capital investment appraisal. Often, however, decisions are made subjectively and then justified after the event by the application of financial techniques. This is particularly so for emergent strategy, described earlier in this chapter. Despite the usefulness of these techniques, the assumption has been that future cash flows can be predicted with some accuracy. This is, however, one of the main difficulties in accounting, as we will see in Chapter 16.

Shank (1996) used a case study to show how the conventional NPV approach was limited in high-technology situations as it did not capture the 'richness' of the investment evaluation problem. Shank saw NPV more as a constraint than a decision tool because it was driven by how the investment proposal was framed. Shank argued that a strategic cost management approach (see Chapter 4 for a description of strategic management accounting) could apply value chain analysis, cost driver analysis and competitive advantage analysis to achieve a better fit between investment decisions and business strategy implementation.

After you have read this chapter, you should:

■ Revise your understanding of the accounting terms. The Glossary in Part IV is a helpful aid.
■ Practice the Questions for this chapter and then check your answers against the solutions. Questions for each chapter are in Appendix 1. The solutions are in Appendix 2.

REFERENCES

Ansoff, H. I. (1988). *The New Corporate Strategy*. New York, NY: John Wiley & Sons.

Kaplan, R. S. and Norton, D. P. (2001). *The Strategy-Focused Organization: How Balanced Scorecard Companies Thrive in the New Business Environment*. Boston, MA: Harvard Business School Press.

Mintzberg, H. and Waters, J. A. (1985). Of strategies, deliberate and emergent. *Strategic Management Journal*, **6**, 257–72.

Porter, M. E. (1980). *Competitive Strategy: Techniques for Analyzing Industries and Competitors*. New York, NY: Free Press.

Porter, M. E. (1985). *Competitive Advantage: Creating and Sustaining Superior Performance*. New York, NY: Free Press.

Quinn, J. B. (1980). *Strategies for Change: Logical Incrementalism*. Homewood, IL: Irwin.

Shank, J. K. (1996). Analysing technology investments – from NPV to strategic cost management (SCM). *Management Accounting Research*, **7**, 185–97.

APPENDIX: PRESENT VALUE FACTORS

Table 14.10 gives the present value of a single payment received in years in the future discounted at an interest rate of x% per annum. For example, with a discount rate of 6% a single payment of £100 in five years' time has a present value of £74.73 (£100 × .7473).

Table 14.10 Present value factors

Years	1%	2%	3%	4%	5%	6%	7%	8%	9%	10%	11%	12%	13%	14%	15%	16%	17%	18%	19%	20%
1	0.9901	0.9804	0.9709	0.9615	0.9524	0.9434	0.9346	0.9259	0.9174	0.9091	0.9009	0.8929	0.8850	0.8772	0.8696	0.8621	0.8547	0.8475	0.8403	0.8333
2	0.9803	0.9612	0.9426	0.9246	0.9070	0.8900	0.8734	0.8573	0.8417	0.8264	0.8116	0.7972	0.7831	0.7695	0.7561	0.7432	0.7305	0.7182	0.7062	0.6944
3	0.9706	0.9423	0.9151	0.8890	0.8638	0.8396	0.8163	0.7938	0.7722	0.7513	0.7312	0.7118	0.6931	0.6750	0.6575	0.6407	0.6244	0.6086	0.5934	0.5787
4	0.9610	0.9238	0.8885	0.8548	0.8227	0.7921	0.7629	0.7350	0.7084	0.6830	0.6587	0.6355	0.6133	0.5921	0.5718	0.5523	0.5337	0.5158	0.4987	0.4823
5	0.9515	0.9057	0.8626	0.8219	0.7835	0.7473	0.7130	0.6806	0.6499	0.6209	0.5935	0.5674	0.5428	0.5194	0.4972	0.4761	0.4561	0.4371	0.4190	0.4019
6	0.9420	0.8880	0.8375	0.7903	0.7462	0.7050	0.6663	0.6302	0.5963	0.5645	0.5346	0.5066	0.4803	0.4556	0.4323	0.4104	0.3898	0.3704	0.3521	0.3349
7	0.9327	0.8706	0.8131	0.7599	0.7107	0.6651	0.6227	0.5835	0.5470	0.5132	0.4817	0.4523	0.4251	0.3996	0.3759	0.3538	0.3332	0.3139	0.2959	0.2791
8	0.9235	0.8535	0.7894	0.7307	0.6768	0.6274	0.5820	0.5403	0.5019	0.4665	0.4339	0.4039	0.3762	0.3506	0.3269	0.3050	0.2848	0.2660	0.2487	0.2326
9	0.9143	0.8368	0.7664	0.7026	0.6446	0.5919	0.5439	0.5002	0.4604	0.4241	0.3909	0.3606	0.3329	0.3075	0.2843	0.2630	0.2434	0.2255	0.2090	0.1938
10	0.9053	0.8203	0.7441	0.6756	0.6139	0.5584	0.5083	0.4632	0.4224	0.3855	0.3522	0.3220	0.2946	0.2697	0.2472	0.2267	0.2080	0.1911	0.1756	0.1615
11	0.8963	0.8043	0.7224	0.6496	0.5847	0.5268	0.4751	0.4289	0.3875	0.3505	0.3173	0.2875	0.2607	0.2366	0.2149	0.1954	0.1778	0.1619	0.1476	0.1346
12	0.8874	0.7885	0.7014	0.6246	0.5568	0.4970	0.4440	0.3971	0.3555	0.3186	0.2858	0.2567	0.2307	0.2076	0.1869	0.1685	0.1520	0.1372	0.1240	0.1122
13	0.8787	0.7730	0.6810	0.6006	0.5303	0.4688	0.4150	0.3677	0.3262	0.2897	0.2575	0.2292	0.2042	0.1821	0.1625	0.1452	0.1299	0.1163	0.1042	0.0935
14	0.8700	0.7579	0.6611	0.5775	0.5051	0.4423	0.3878	0.3405	0.2992	0.2633	0.2320	0.2046	0.1807	0.1597	0.1413	0.1252	0.1110	0.0985	0.0876	0.0779
15	0.8613	0.7430	0.6419	0.5553	0.4810	0.4173	0.3624	0.3152	0.2745	0.2394	0.2090	0.1827	0.1599	0.1401	0.1229	0.1079	0.0949	0.0835	0.0736	0.0649
16	0.8528	0.7284	0.6232	0.5339	0.4581	0.3936	0.3387	0.2919	0.2519	0.2176	0.1883	0.1631	0.1415	0.1229	0.1069	0.0930	0.0811	0.0708	0.0618	0.0541
17	0.8444	0.7142	0.6050	0.5134	0.4363	0.3714	0.3166	0.2703	0.2311	0.1978	0.1696	0.1456	0.1252	0.1078	0.0929	0.0802	0.0693	0.0600	0.0520	0.0451
18	0.8360	0.7002	0.5874	0.4936	0.4155	0.3503	0.2959	0.2502	0.2120	0.1799	0.1528	0.1300	0.1108	0.0946	0.0808	0.0691	0.0592	0.0508	0.0437	0.0376
19	0.8277	0.6864	0.5703	0.4746	0.3957	0.3305	0.2765	0.2317	0.1945	0.1635	0.1377	0.1161	0.0981	0.0829	0.0703	0.0596	0.0506	0.0431	0.0367	0.0313
20	0.8195	0.6730	0.5537	0.4564	0.3769	0.3118	0.2584	0.2145	0.1784	0.1486	0.1240	0.1037	0.0868	0.0728	0.0611	0.0514	0.0433	0.0365	0.0308	0.0261
21	0.8114	0.6598	0.5375	0.4388	0.3589	0.2942	0.2415	0.1987	0.1637	0.1351	0.1117	0.0926	0.0768	0.0638	0.0531	0.0443	0.0370	0.0309	0.0259	0.0217
22	0.8034	0.6468	0.5219	0.4220	0.3418	0.2775	0.2257	0.1839	0.1502	0.1228	0.1007	0.0826	0.0680	0.0560	0.0462	0.0382	0.0316	0.0262	0.0218	0.0181
23	0.7954	0.6342	0.5067	0.4057	0.3256	0.2618	0.2109	0.1703	0.1378	0.1117	0.0907	0.0738	0.0601	0.0491	0.0402	0.0329	0.0270	0.0222	0.0183	0.0151
24	0.7876	0.6217	0.4919	0.3901	0.3101	0.2470	0.1971	0.1577	0.1264	0.1015	0.0817	0.0659	0.0532	0.0431	0.0349	0.0284	0.0231	0.0188	0.0154	0.0126
25	0.7798	0.6095	0.4776	0.3751	0.2953	0.2330	0.1842	0.1460	0.1160	0.0923	0.0736	0.0588	0.0471	0.0378	0.0304	0.0245	0.0197	0.0160	0.0129	0.0105
26	0.7720	0.5976	0.4637	0.3607	0.2812	0.2198	0.1722	0.1352	0.1064	0.0839	0.0663	0.0525	0.0417	0.0331	0.0264	0.0211	0.0169	0.0135	0.0109	0.0087
27	0.7644	0.5859	0.4502	0.3468	0.2678	0.2074	0.1609	0.1252	0.0976	0.0763	0.0597	0.0469	0.0369	0.0291	0.0230	0.0182	0.0144	0.0115	0.0091	0.0073
28	0.7568	0.5744	0.4371	0.3335	0.2551	0.1956	0.1504	0.1159	0.0895	0.0693	0.0538	0.0419	0.0326	0.0255	0.0200	0.0157	0.0123	0.0097	0.0077	0.0061
29	0.7493	0.5631	0.4243	0.3207	0.2429	0.1846	0.1406	0.1073	0.0822	0.0630	0.0485	0.0374	0.0289	0.0224	0.0174	0.0135	0.0105	0.0082	0.0064	0.0051
30	0.7419	0.5521	0.4120	0.3083	0.2314	0.1741	0.1314	0.0994	0.0754	0.0573	0.0437	0.0334	0.0256	0.0196	0.0151	0.0116	0.0090	0.0070	0.0054	0.0042
35	0.7059	0.5000	0.3554	0.2534	0.1813	0.1301	0.0937	0.0676	0.0490	0.0356	0.0259	0.0189	0.0139	0.0102	0.0075	0.0055	0.0041	0.0030	0.0023	0.0017
40	0.6717	0.4529	0.3066	0.2083	0.1420	0.0972	0.0668	0.0460	0.0318	0.0221	0.0154	0.0107	0.0075	0.0053	0.0037	0.0026	0.0019	0.0013	0.0010	0.0007
45	0.6391	0.4102	0.2644	0.1712	0.1113	0.0727	0.0476	0.0313	0.0207	0.0137	0.0091	0.0061	0.0041	0.0027	0.0019	0.0013	0.0009	0.0006	0.0004	0.0003
50	0.6080	0.3715	0.2281	0.1407	0.0872	0.0543	0.0339	0.0213	0.0134	0.0085	0.0054	0.0035	0.0022	0.0014	0.0009	0.0006	0.0004	0.0003	0.0002	0.0001

15

PERFORMANCE EVALUATION OF BUSINESS UNITS

This chapter describes the methods by which the performance of divisions and their managers is evaluated. It builds on the foundation established in Chapter 2, which explained how divisionalized business structures have evolved to implement business strategy. We also consider controllability and the transfer pricing problem and introduce the theory of transaction cost economics. This chapter suggests that some techniques may provide an appearance rather than the reality of 'rational' decision-making.

THE DECENTRALIZED ORGANIZATION AND DIVISIONAL PERFORMANCE MEASUREMENT

The evaluation of new capital expenditure proposals is a key element in allocating resources by the whole organization (see Chapter 14). However, a further aspect of strategy implementation is improving and maintaining divisional performance.

Businesses may be organized in a centralized or decentralized manner. The centralized business is one in which most decisions are made at a head office level, even though the business may be spread over a number of market segments and geographically diverse locations. *Decentralization* implies the devolution of authority to make decisions. *Divisionalization* adds to decentralization the concept of delegated profit responsibility (Solomons, 1965). We introduced the notion of divisional structures and responsibility centres in Chapter 2.

Divisionalization makes it easier for a company to diversify, while retaining overall strategic direction and control. Performance improvement is encouraged by assigning individual responsibility for divisional performance, typically linked to executive remuneration (bonuses, profit-sharing, share options etc.).

Shareholder value is the criterion for overall business success, but divisional performance is the criterion for divisional success. However, divisional performance measurement has also moved beyond financial measures to incorporate the drivers of financial results, i.e. non-financial performance measures (see Chapter 4).

Solomons (1965) highlighted three purposes for financial reporting at a divisional level:

1   To guide divisional managers in making decisions.
2   To guide top management in making decisions.
3   To enable top management to appraise the performance of divisional management.

The decentralization of businesses has removed the centrality of the head office with its functional structure (marketing, operations, distribution, finance etc.). Instead, many support functions are now devolved to business units, which may be called subsidiaries (if they are legally distinct entities), divisions, departments etc. For simplicity, we will use the term divisionalization although the same principle applies to any business unit. This divisionalization allows managers to have autonomy over certain aspects of the business, but those managers are then accountable for the performance of their business units. Divisionalized business units may be:

- *Cost centres* – where managers are responsible for controlling costs within budget limits. Managers are evaluated on their performance compared to budget by keeping costs within budget constraints.
- *Profit centres* – where managers are responsible for sales performance, achieving gross margins and controlling expenses, i.e. for the 'bottom-line' profit performance of the business unit. Managers are evaluated on their performance compared to budget in achieving or exceeding their profit target.
- *Investment centres* – where managers have profit responsibility but also influence the amount of capital invested in their business units. Managers are evaluated based on a measure of the return on investment made by the investment centre.

Budgets and performance against budget are the subjects of Chapters 16 and 17. Evaluating divisional performance in comparison to a strategic investment is the subject of this chapter.

Solomons (1965) identified the difficulties involved in measuring managerial performance. Absolute profit is not a good measure because it does not consider the investment in the business and how long-term profits can be affected by short-term decisions such as reducing research, maintenance and advertising expenditure. These decisions will improve reported profits in the current year, but will usually have a detrimental long-term impact. The performance of divisions and their managers can be evaluated using two methods: either return on investment or residual income.

RETURN ON INVESTMENT

The relative success of managers can be judged by the **return on investment** (or ROI, which was introduced in Chapter 7). This is the rate of return achieved on the capital employed and was a method developed by the DuPont Powder Company early in the twentieth century. Using ROI, managerial and divisional success is judged according to the rate of return on the investment. However, a problem with this approach is whether a high rate of return on a small capital investment is better or worse than a lower return on a larger capital. For example:

	Div A	Div B
Capital invested	£1,000,000	£2,000,000
Operating profit	£200,000	£300,000
Return on investment	20%	15%

Division B makes a higher profit in absolute terms but a lower return on the capital invested in the business. Solomons (1965) also argued that a decision cannot be made about relative performance unless we know the cost of capital.

RESIDUAL INCOME

A different approach to evaluating performance is residual income, which takes into account the cost of capital. **Residual income (or RI)** is the profit remaining after deducting the notional cost of capital from the investment in the division. The RI approach was developed by the General Electric Company and more recently has been compared with Economic Value Added (EVA, see Chapter 2), as both methods deduct a notional cost of capital from the reported profit. Using the above example:

	Div A	Div B
Capital invested	£1,000,000	£2,000,000
Operating profit	£200,000	£300,000
less cost of capital at 17.5%	£175,000	£350,000
Residual income	£25,000	−£50,000

As the cost of capital is 17.5% in the above example, Division A makes a satisfactory return but Division B does not. Division B is eroding shareholder value while Division A is creating it.

The aim of managers should be to maximize the residual income from the capital investments in their divisions. However, Solomons (1965) emphasizes that the RI approach assumes that managers have the power to influence the amount of capital investment. Solomons argued that an RI target is preferred to a maximization objective because it takes into account the differential investments in divisions, i.e. that a larger division will almost certainly produce – or should produce – a higher residual income. Johnson and Kaplan (1987) believe that the residual income approach:

> overcame one of the dysfunctional aspects of the ROI measure in which managers could increase their reported ROI by rejecting investments that yielded returns in excess of their firm's (or division's) cost of capital, but that were below their current average ROI. (p. 165)

One of the main problems in evaluating divisional performance is the extent to which managers can exercise control over investments and costs charged to their responsibility centres.

CONTROLLABILITY

The principle of controllability, according to Merchant (1987, p. 316), is that 'individuals should be held accountable only for results they can control' (p. 336).

One of the limitations of operating profit as a measure of divisional performance is the inclusion of costs over which the divisional manager has no control. The need for the company as a whole to make a profit demands that corporate costs be allocated to divisions so that these costs can be recovered in the prices charged. The problem arises when a division's profit is not sufficient to cover the head office charge (we introduced this concept in relation to segmentation in Chapter 10). Solomons (1965) argued that so long as corporate expenses are independent of divisional activity, allocating corporate costs is irrelevant because a positive contribution by divisions will cover at least some of those costs.

Solomons separated these components in the divisional profit report, a simplified version of which is shown below:

Sales		£££
Less Variable cost of goods sold	£££	
Other variable expenses	£££	£££
Contribution margin		£££
Less Controllable divisional overhead		£££
Controllable profit		£££
Less Non-controllable overhead		£££
Operating profit		£££

While the business as a whole may consider the operating profit to be the most important figure, performance evaluation of the manager can only be carried out based on the controllable profit. The **controllable profit** is the profit after deducting expenses that can be controlled by the divisional manager, but ignoring those expenses that are outside the divisional manager's control. What is controllable or non-controllable will depend on the circumstances of each organization. Solomons argued that the most suitable figure for appraising divisional managers was the *controllable residual income before taxes*. Using this method, the controllable profit is reduced by the corporate cost of capital. For decisions in relation to a division's performance, the relevant figure is the *net residual income after taxes*.

One of the problems with both the ROI and RI measures of divisional performance is the calculation of the capital investment in the division: should it be total (i.e. capital employed) or net assets (allowing for gearing)? Should it include fixed or current assets, or both? Should assets be valued at cost or net book value? Should the book value be at the beginning or end of the period? Solomons (1965) argued that it was the amount of capital put into the business, rather than what could be taken out, that was relevant. The investment value, according to Solomons, should be total assets less controllable liabilities, with fixed assets valued at cost using the value at the beginning of the period. ROI calculations therefore relate controllable operating profit as a percentage of controllable investment. An RI approach would measure net residual income plus actual interest expense (because the notional cost of capital has been deducted in calculating RI) against the total investment in the division.

The following case study provides an example of divisional performance measurement using ROI and RI techniques.

Case Study 15.1: Majestic Services – divisional performance measurement

Majestic Services has two divisions, both of which have bid for £1 million for projects that will generate significant cost savings. Majestic has a cost of capital of 15% and can only invest in one of the projects.

The current performance of each division is as follows:

	Division A	Division B
Current investment	£4 million	£20 million
Profit	£1 million	£2 million

Each division has estimated the additional controllable profit that will be generated from the £1 million investment. A estimates £200,000 and B estimates £130,000.

Each division also has an asset of which they would like to dispose. A's asset currently makes a return on investment (ROI) of 19%, while B's asset makes an ROI of 12%. The business wishes to use ROI and residual income techniques to determine in which of the £1 million projects Majestic should invest, and whether either of the division's identified assets should be disposed of.

Using ROI, the two divisions can be compared as in Table 15.1. While Division B is the larger division and generates a higher profit in absolute terms, Division A achieves a higher return on investment.

Again using ROI, the impact of the additional investment can be seen in Table 15.2. Using ROI, Division A may not want its project to be approved as the ROI of 20% is less

Table 15.1 ROI on original investment

	A	B
Current investment	£4 million	£20 million
Current profit	£1 million	£2 million
ROI	25%	10%

Table 15.2 ROI on additional investment

	A	B
Additional investment	£1 million	£1 million
Additional contribution	£200,000	£130,000
ROI on additional investment	20%	13%

Table 15.3   RI on original investment

	A	B
Current investment	£4 million	£20 million
Current profit	£1,000,000	£2,000,000
Cost of capital @ 15%	£600,000	£3,000,000
Residual income (profit − cost of capital)	£400,000	−£1,000,000

Table 15.4   RI on additional investment

	A	B
Additional investment	£1 million	£1 million
Additonal contribution	£200,000	£130,000
Less cost of capital @ 15%	£150,000	£150,000
Residual income	£50,000	−£20,000

than the current ROI of 25%. The impact of the new investment would be to reduce the divisional ROI to 24% (£1.2 million/£5 million). However, Division B would want its project to be approved as the ROI of 13% is higher than the current ROI of 10%. The effect would be to increase Division B's ROI slightly to 10.14% (£2.13 million/£21 million). However, the divisional preference for B's investment over A, because of the rewards attached to increasing ROI, are dysfunctional to Majestic. The corporate view of Majestic would be to invest £1 million in Division A's project because the ROI to the business as a whole would be 20% rather than 13%.

The disposal of the asset can be considered even without knowing its value. If Division A currently obtains a 25% ROI, disposing of an asset with a return of only 19% will increase its average ROI. Division B would wish to retain its asset because it generates an ROI of 12% and disposal would reduce its average ROI to below the current 10%. Given a choice of retaining only one, Majestic would prefer to retain Division A's asset as it has a higher ROI.

The difficulty with ROI as a measure of performance is that it ignores both the difference in size between the two divisions and Majestic's cost of capital. These issues are addressed by the residual income method.

Using residual income (RI), the divisional performance can be compared as in Table 15.3. In this case, we can see that Division A is contributing to shareholder value as it generates a positive RI, while Division B is eroding its shareholder value because the profit it generates is less than the cost of capital on the investment.

Using RI, the impact of the additional investment is shown in Table 15.4. Under the residual income approach, Division A's project would be accepted (positive RI) while Division B's would be rejected (negative RI).

Similarly for the asset disposal, Division A's asset would be retained (ROI of 19% exceeds cost of capital of 15%), while Division B's asset would be disposed of (ROI of 12% is less than cost of capital of 15%).

The main problem facing Majestic is that the larger of the two divisions (both in terms of investment and profits) is generating a negative residual income and consequently eroding shareholder value.

A further problem associated with measuring divisional performance is that of transfer pricing, which was introduced in Chapter 10.

TRANSFER PRICING

When decentralized business units conduct business with each other, an important question is what price to charge for in-company transactions, as this affects the profitability of each business unit. However, transfer prices that are suitable for evaluating divisional performance may lead to divisions acting contrary to the corporate interest (Solomons, 1965).

For example, consider a company with two divisions. Division A can produce 10,000 units for a total cost of £100,000, but additional production costs are £5 per unit. Division A sells its output to Division B at £13 per unit in order to show a satisfactory profit. Division B carries out further processing on the product. It can convert 10,000 units for a total cost of £300,000, but additional production costs are £15 per unit. The prices B can charge to customers will depend on the quantity it wants to sell. Market estimates of selling prices at different volumes (net of variable selling costs) are:

Volume	Price
10,000 units	£50 per unit
12,000 units	£46 per unit
15,000 units	£39 per unit

The financial results for each division at each level of activity are shown in Table 15.5. Division A sees an increase in profit as volume increases and will want to increase production volume to 15,000 units. However, Division B sees a steady erosion of divisional profitability as volume increases and will seek to keep production limited to 10,000 units, at which point its maximum profit is £70,000. The company's overall profitability increases between 10,000 and 12,000 units, but then falls when volume increases to 15,000 units. From a whole-company perspective, therefore, volume should be maintained at 12,000 units to maximize profits at £112,000. However, neither division will be satisfied with this result, as both will see it as disadvantaging them in terms of divisional profits, against which divisional managers are evaluated.

For Division A, variable costs over 10,000 units are £5, but its transfer price is £13, so additional units contribute £8 each to divisional profitability. A's average costs reduce as volume increases, as Table 15.6 shows.

However for Division B, its variable costs over 10,000 units are £28 (transfer price of £13 plus conversion costs of £15). The reduction in average costs of £2.50 per unit is more than offset by the fall in selling price (net of variable selling costs), as Table 15.7 shows.

Table 15.5   Divisional financial results

Activity	10,000	12,000	15,000
Division A			
10,000 units	100,000	100,000	100,000
2,000 units @ £5		10,000	
5,000 units @ £5			25,000
Total cost	100,000	110,000	125,000
Transfer price @ £13	130,000	156,000	195,000
Division profit	30,000	46,000	70,000
Division B			
Transfer from Division A	130,000	156,000	195,000
Conversion cost			
10,000 units	300,000	300,000	300,000
2,000 units @ £15			75,000
Total cost	430,000	486,000	570,000
Selling price @	50	46	39
Sales revenue	500,000	552,000	585,000
Division profit	70,000	66,000	15,000
Company			
Sales revenue	500,000	552,000	585,000
Division A cost	−100,000	−110,000	−125,000
Division B cost	−300,000	−330,000	−375,000
Company profit	100,000	112,000	85,000

Table 15.6   Division A costs

	10,000	12,000	15,000
Division A total costs	100,000	110,000	125,000
Average per unit	10.000	9.17	8.33

Table 15.7   Division B costs

	10,000	12,000	15,000
Division B total costs	430,000	486,000	570,000
Average per unit	43.000	40.50	38.00
Reduction in average cost per unit		2.50	2.50
Reduction in selling price		4.00	7.00

There are several methods by which transfer prices between divisions can be established:

■ *Market price*: Where products/services can be sold on the outside market, the market price is used. This is the easiest way to ensure that divisional decisions are compatible with corporate profit maximization. However, if there is no external market, particularly for an intermediate product – i.e. one that requires additional processing before it can be sold – this method cannot be used.

■ *Marginal cost*: The transfer price is the additional (variable) cost incurred. In the above example, the transfer price would be £5, but Division A would have little motivation to produce additional volume if only incremental costs were covered.

■ *Full cost*: This method would recover both fixed and variable costs. This has the same overhead allocation problem as identified in Chapter 13 and would have the same motivational problems as for the marginal cost transfer price.

■ *Cost-plus*: This method provides a profit to each division, but has the problem identified in this example of leading to different management decisions in each division and at corporate level.

■ *Negotiated prices*: This may take into account market conditions, marginal costs and the need to motivate managers in each division. It tends to be the most practical solution to align the interests of divisions with the whole organization and to share the profits equitably between each division. In using this method, care must be taken to consider differential capital investments between divisions, so that both are treated equitably in terms of ROI or RI criteria.

In practice, many organizations adopt negotiated prices in order to avoid demotivating effects on different business units. In some Japanese companies it is common to leave the profit with the manufacturing division, placing the onus on the marketing division to achieve better market prices.

TRANSACTION COST ECONOMICS

A useful theoretical framework for understanding divisionalization and the transfer pricing problem is the transactions cost approach of Oliver Williamson (1975), which is concerned with the study of the economics of internal organization. Transaction cost economics seeks to explain why separate activities that require co-ordination occur within the organization's hierarchy (i.e. within the corporate structure), while others take place through exchanges outside the organization in the wider market (i.e. between arm's-length buyers and sellers).

The work of business historians such as Chandler (1962) reflects a transaction cost approach in explanations of the growth of huge corporations such as General Motors, in which hierarchies were developed as alternatives to market transactions. It is important to note that transactions take place within organizations, not just between them. For managers using accounting information, attention is focused on the transaction costs associated with different resource-allocation decisions and whether markets or hierarchies are more cost effective.

Transactions are more than exchanges of goods, services and money. They incur costs over and above the price for the commodity bought or sold, such as costs associated with negotiation, monitoring, administration, insurance etc. They also involve time commitments and obligations, and are associated with legal, moral and power conditions. Understanding these costs may reveal that it is more economic to carry out an activity in-house than to accept a market price that appears less costly but may incur 'transaction' costs that are hidden in overhead costs.

Under transaction cost economics, attention focuses on the transaction costs involved in allocating resources within the organization, and determining when the costs associated with one mode of organizing transactions (e.g. markets) would be reduced by shifting those transactions to an alternative arrangement (e.g. the internal hierarchy of an organization). The high costs of market-related transactions can be avoided by specifying the rules for co-operative behaviour within the organization.

The markets and hierarchies perspective considers the vertical integration of production and the decision about whether organizations should make or buy. Both bounded rationality and opportunistic behaviour are assumed in this perspective (see Chapter 6 for a discussion of this in relation to agency theory) and transaction costs are affected by asset specificity, when an investment is made for a specific rather than a general purpose. Transaction costs are also affected by uncertainty and the frequency with which transactions take place.

Seal (1995) provided the example of a make versus buy decision for a component. In management accounting, a unit cost comparison would take place. (Relevant costs for make versus buy decisions were described in Chapter 11.) A transaction cost approach would consider whether the production of the component required investment in specialized equipment or training, a problem of asset specificity. This approach raises the problem that an external contract may be difficult to draw up and enforce because the small number of organizations bargaining may be hindered by opportunistic behaviour. It may therefore be cheaper to produce in-house due to contractual problems.

Williamson (1975) argued that the desire to minimize transaction costs resulting from bounded rationality leads to transactions being kept within the organization, favouring the organizational hierarchy over markets. Markets are favoured where there are a large number of trading partners, which minimizes the risk of opportunistic behaviour.

Recurring, complex and uncertain exchanges that involve substantial investment may be more efficiently undertaken when internal organization replaces market transactions. The efficiency of a transaction that takes place within the organization depends on how the behaviour of managers is governed or constrained, how economic activities are subdivided and how the management accounting system is structured.

However, decision-makers may themselves indulge in opportunistic behaviour that causes the benefits of internal transactions to be reduced. Therefore, the management accounting system can be used to ensure that these internal transactions are conducted efficiently.

Rather than reflecting a concern with utility maximization (the assumption of agency theory), the transaction cost framework is more concerned with bounded rationality. While an agency perspective ignores the power of owners and also that of employees, who can withdraw their labour, transaction cost theory gives recognition to power in the hierarchy that is used to co-ordinate production.

CONCLUSION: A CRITICAL PERSPECTIVE

In this chapter we have described the divisionalized organization and how divisional performance can be evaluated. We have discussed the controllability principle and the transfer pricing problem.

The divisional form is a preferred organizational structure because it allows devolved responsibility while linking performance to organizational goals through measures such as ROI and RI that are meaningful at different organizational levels, particularly when these support shareholder value methods such as the link between RI and EVA.

However, research by Merchant (1987) concluded that the controllability principle was not found in practice and that managers should be evaluated 'using all information that gives insight into their action choices'.

Managers are often critical that the corporate head office fails to distinguish adequately between controllable and non-controllable overhead. The point has already been made in Chapter 2 that determining a risk-adjusted cost of capital can be a subjective exercise.

Relationships between business units frequently cause friction, particularly in some organizations where the number of business units has been increased to a level that is difficult to manage. Transaction cost economics, a rational markets/hierarchies approach like agency theory described in Chapter 6, provides a useful though limited perspective. For example, Child (1972) concluded:

> When incorporating strategic choice in a theory of organization, one is recognizing the operation of an essentially political process in which constraints and opportunities are functions of the power exercised by decision-makers in the light of ideological values. (p. 16)

The political process inherent in transfer pricing between divisions is also evidenced in many multinational corporations, where transfer pricing is more concerned with how to shift profits between countries so as to minimize income taxes on profits and maximize after-tax profits to increase shareholder value. While this is undoubtedly in the interests of individual companies and does need the approval of taxation authorities, it still raises issues of the ethics of transfer pricing when multinationals minimize their profits and taxation in relatively high-tax countries such as the UK.

After you have read this chapter, you should:

- Revise your understanding of the accounting terms. The Glossary in Part IV is a helpful aid.
- Practice the Questions for this chapter and then check your answers against the solutions. Questions for each chapter are in Appendix 1. The solutions are in Appendix 2.
- Read Case Study 6. This will help you to interpret accounting information. Try to write an answer. The Case Studies are in Appendix 3 and suggested solutions are in Appendix 4.
- Read and think about Reading D. The Readings are in Part IV of this book.

REFERENCES

Chandler, A. D. J. (1962). *Strategy and Structure: Chapters in the History of the American Industrial Enterprise*. Cambridge, MA: Harvard University Press.

Child, J. (1972). Organizational structure, environment and performance: The role of strategic choice. *Sociology*, **6**, 1–22.

Johnson, H. T. and Kaplan, R. S. (1987). *Relevance Lost: The Rise and Fall of Management Accounting*. Boston, MA: Harvard Business School Press.

Merchant, K. A. (1987). How and why firms disregard the controllability principle. In W. J. Bruns and R. S. Kaplan (eds), *Accounting and Management: Field Study Perspectives*, Boston, MA: Harvard Business School Press.

Seal, W. (1995). Economics and control. In A. J. Berry, J. Broadbent and D. Otley (eds), *Management Control: Theories, Issues and Practices*, London: Macmillan.

Solomons, D. (1965). *Divisional Performance: Measurement and Control*. Homewood, IL: Richard D. Irwin.

Williamson, O. E. (1975). *Markets and Hierarchies: Analysis and Antitrust Implications. A Study in the Economics of Internal Organization*. New York, NY: Free Press.

16 BUDGETING

Anthony and Govindarajan (2000) described budgets as 'an important tool for effective short-term planning and control' (p. 360). They saw strategic planning (see Chapter 14) as being focused on several years, contrasted to budgeting that focuses on a single year. Strategic planning:

> precedes budgeting and provides the framework within which the annual budget is developed. A budget is, in a sense, a one-year slice of the organization's strategic plan. (p. 361)

Anthony and Govindarajan also differentiated the strategic plan from the budget, on the basis that strategy is concerned with product lines while budgets are concerned with responsibility centres. This is an important distinction, as although there is no reason that profit reports for products/services cannot be produced (they tend to stop at the contribution margin level, perhaps because of the overhead allocation problem described in Chapter 13), traditional management accounting reports are produced for responsibility centres and used for divisional performance evaluation, as described in Chapter 15.

WHAT IS BUDGETING?

A budget is a plan expressed in monetary terms covering a future time period (typically a year broken down into months). Budgets are based on a defined level of activity, either expected sales revenue (if market demand is the limiting factor) or capacity (if that is the limiting factor). While budgets are typically produced annually, rolling budgets add additional months to the end of the period so that there is always a 12-month budget for the business. Alternatively, budgets may be re-forecast part way through a year, e.g. quarterly or six-monthly, to take into account changes since the last budget cycle (hence the common distinction made by organizations between budget and forecast. A forecast usually refers to a revised estimate, or a budgetary update, part-way through the budget period.)

Budgeting provides the ability to:

- implement strategy by allocating resources in line with strategic goals;
- co-ordinate activities and assist in communication between different parts of the organization;
- motivate managers to achieve targets;
- provide a means to control activities; and
- evaluate managerial performance.

In establishing the budget allocation to specific profit centres, cost centres or departments, there are four main methods of budgeting: incremental, priority based, zero based and activity based.

Incremental budgets take the previous year's budget as a base and add (or subtract) a percentage to give this year's budget. The assumption is that the historical budget allocation reflected organizational priorities and was rooted in some meaningful justification developed in the past.

Priority-based budgets allocate funds in line with strategy. If priorities change in line with the organization's strategic focus, then budget allocations would follow those priorities, irrespective of the historical allocation. A public-sector version of the priority-based budget is the **planning, programming and budgeting system (PPBS)** that was developed by the US space programme. Under PPBS, budgets are allocated to projects or programmes rather than to responsibility centres. Priority-based budgets may be responsibility centre based, but will typically be associated with particular projects or programmes. The intention of PPBS and priority-based budgeting systems is to compare costs more readily with benefits by identifying the resources used to obtain desired outcomes. An amalgam of incremental and priority-based budgets is *priority-based incremental budgeting*. Here, the budget-holder is asked what incremental (or decremental) activities or results would follow if budgets increased (or decreased). This method has the advantage of comparing changes in resources with the resulting costs and benefits.

Zero-based budgeting identifies the costs that are necessary to implement agreed strategies and achieve goals, as if the budget-holder were beginning with a new organizational unit, without any prior history. This method has the advantage of regularly reviewing all the activities that are carried out to see if they are still required, but has the disadvantage of the cost and time needed for such reviews. It is also very difficult to develop a budget while ignoring current resource allocations.

Activity-based budgeting is associated with activity-based costing (ABC, see Chapter 13). ABC identifies *activities* that consume resources and uses the concept of *cost drivers* (essentially the cause of costs) to allocate costs to products or services according to how much of the resources of the firm they consume. Activity-based budgeting (ABB) follows the same process to develop budgets based on the expected activities and cost drivers to meet sales (or capacity) projections.

Whichever method of budgeting is used, there are two approaches that can be applied. Budgets may be top down or bottom up. *Top-down budgets* begin with the sales forecast and, using the volume of sales, predict inventory levels, staffing and production times within capacity limitations. These are based on bills of materials, labour routings and standard costs. For services, the top-down budget is based largely on capacity utilization and staffing levels needed to meet expected demand. In both cases, senior management establishes spending limits within which departments allocate costs to specific line items (salaries, travel, office expenses etc.). Senior managers set the revenue targets and spending limits that they believe are necessary to achieve profits that will satisfy shareholders. *Bottom-up budgets* are developed by the managers of each department based on current spending and agreed plans, which are then aggregated to the corporate total.

Top-down budgets can ignore the problems experienced by operational managers.

However, boards of directors often have a clear idea of the sales growth and profit requirement that will satisfy stock market conditions. By contrast, the result of the bottom-up budget may be inadequate in terms of 'bottom-line' profitability or unachievable as a result of either capacity limitations elsewhere in the business or market demand. Therefore, the underlying factors may need to be modified. Consequently, most budgets are the result of a combination of top-down and bottom-up processes. By adopting both methods, budget-holders are given the opportunity to bid for resources (in competition with other budget-holders) within the constraints of the shareholder value focus of the business.

THE BUDGETING PROCESS

Budgets are based on standard costs (see Chapter 11) for a defined level of sales demand or production activity. The typical budget cycle – the period each year over which budgets are prepared – will follow the sequence:

1 Identify business objectives.
2 Forecast economic and industry conditions, including competition.
3 Develop detailed sales budgets by market sectors, geographic territories, major customers and product groups.
4 Prepare production budgets (materials, labour and overhead) by responsibility centre managers in order to produce the goods or services needed to satisfy the sales forecast and maintain agreed levels of inventory.
5 Prepare non-production budgets by cost centre.
6 Prepare capital expenditure budgets.
7 Prepare cash forecasts and identify financing requirements.
8 Prepare master budget (profit and loss, balance sheet and cash flow).
9 Obtain board approval of profitability and financing targets.

Good practice in budgeting at the level of each responsibility centre involves looking at the causes of costs and the business processes in use. Bidding for funds for capital expenditure or to fund new initiatives or projects is an important part of budgeting because of the need to question past practice and continually seek improvement. The process of budgeting is largely based on making informed judgements about:

■ how business-wide strategies will affect the responsibility centre;
■ the level of demand placed on the business unit and the expected level of activity to satisfy (internal or external) customers;
■ the technology and processes used in the business unit to achieve desired productivity levels, based on past experience and anticipated improvements;
■ any new initiatives or projects that are planned and require resources;
■ the headcount and historic spending by the business unit.

In preparing a budget it is important to carry out a thorough investigation of current performance, i.e. to get behind the numbers. For example, as many costs (particularly in service industries) follow headcount (as we saw in Chapter 12), it is essential that salary and related costs are accurately estimated, and the impact of recruitment, resignation and training is taken into account in cost and productivity calculations.

The complexity of the budget will depend on a number of factors, such as:

■   knowledge of past performance;
■   understanding of market trends, seasonal factors, competition etc.;
■   whether the business is a price leader or price follower (see Chapter 10);
■   understanding the drivers of business costs;
■   the control that managers are able to exercise over expenses.

How well these factors can be understood and modelled using a spreadsheet will depend on the knowledge, skills and time available to the business. Typically, budgets either at the corporate or responsibility centre level will contain a number of subjective judgements of likely future events, customer demand and a number of simplifying assumptions about product/service mix, average prices, cost inflation etc.

Once the budget is agreed in total, the budget needs to be allocated over each month. This is commonly based on working days or takes into account seasonal fluctuations etc. This is a process of profiling or time-phasing the budget. Profiling is important because the process of budgetary control (see Chapter 17) relies on an accurate estimation of when revenue will be earned and when costs will be incurred.

Table 16.1 is a simplified example of a budget for a small hotel. It shows some statistics that the Superior Hotel has used for its budget for next year. Both last year's and the current year's figures are shown. For ease of presentation, the budget year has been divided into four quarters and some simplifying assumptions have been made. The hotel capacity is limited to the number of rooms, but in common with the industry rarely achieves full occupancy, although there are substantial variations both during the week and at peak times. The main income driver is the number of rooms occupied, the price able to be charged (which can vary significantly depending on the number of vacant rooms) and the average spend per head on dining, the bar and business services.

The statistical information, together with estimations of direct costs (food and drink) and expenses, is based on historical experience and expected cost increases. The budget for the year for the Superior Hotel, based on these assumptions, is shown in Table 16.2.

A budget for a retailer will require an estimation, separate from the sales forecast, of the level of inventory to be held. This results in a purchasing budget. Similarly, a budget for a manufacturing business will involve developing a production budget (materials, labour and overhead) by cost centre in order to produce the goods or services needed to satisfy the sales forecast and maintain agreed levels of inventory.

The first problem to consider is stock, which is shown in the following example.

Table 16.1 Service budget example: Superior Hotel – budget statistics

Superior Hotel BUDGET STATISTICS	Explanation	Last year	Current year	Qtr1 Jan–Mar	Qtr 2 Apr–June	Qtr 3 Jul–Sep	Qtr 4 Oct–Dec	Next year
Number of bedrooms		80	80	80	80	80	80	
Days per year (per quarter)		365	365	90	91	92	92	365
Rooms available – 365 days/year	No. days × no. rooms	29,200	29,200	7,200	7,280	7,360	7,360	29,200
Average occupancy rate (7-day basis)	Historical	50%	50%	40%	45%	55%	60%	
Average no. rooms occupied	No. rooms × occup. rate	14,600	14,600	2,880	3,276	4,048	4,416	14,620
Average room rate	Historical/planned	£65.00	£70.00	£70.00	£72.00	£75.00	£75.00	
Average spend on dining per room	Historical/planned	£25.00	£25.00	£25.00	£25.00	£25.00	£25.00	
Average spend on bar per room	Historical/planned	£5.00	£5.00	£5.00	£5.00	£5.00	£5.00	
Average spend on business services per room	Historical/planned	£2.00	£2.00	£2.00	£2.00	£2.00	£2.00	

Table 16.2 Service budget example: Superior Hotel budget

SUPERIOR HOTEL BUDGET INCOME	Explanation	Last year	Current year	Qtr 1 Jan–Mar	Qtr 2 Apr–June	Qtr 3 Jul–Sep	Qtr 4 Oct–Dec	Next year
Rooms	No. of rooms × average spend	949,000	1,022,000	201,600	235,872	303,600	331,200	1,072.272
Dining	No. of rooms × average spend	365,000	365,000	72,000	81,900	101,200	110,400	365,500
Bar	No. of rooms × average spend	73,000	73,000	14,400	16,380	20,240	22,080	73,100
Business services	No. of rooms × average spend	29,200	29,200	5,760	6,552	8,096	8,832	29,240
Total income		1,416,200	1,489,200	293,760	340,704	433,136	472,512	1,540,112
EXPENDITURE Direct costs								
Food cost of sales	35% of dining income	127,750	127,750	25,200	28,665	35,420	38,640	127,925
Liquor cost of sales	40% of bar income	29,200	29,200	5,760	6,552	8,096	8,832	29,240
Total cost of sales		156,950	156,950	30,960	35,217	43,516	47,472	157,165
Salaries and wages								
Hotel staff	increases 3% p.a.	212,000	218,360	56,228	56,228	56,228	56,228	224,911
Dining staff	increases 3% p.a.	75,000	77,250	19,892	19,892	19,892	19,892	79,568
Office staff	increases 4% p.a.	35,000	36,400	9,464	9,464	9,464	9,464	37,856
Management	increases 5% p.a.	50,000	52,500	13,781	13,781	13,781	13,781	55,125
Fuel, light and water	Historical/estimate	12,000	14,000	4,000	4,000	4,000	4,000	16,000
Laundry	Historical/estimate	8,000	9,000	2,500	2,500	2,500	2,500	10,000
Cleaning	Historical/estimate	6,000	7,000	2,000	2,000	2,000	2,000	8,000
Repairs and maintenance	Historical/estimate	12,000	20,000	4,000	4,000	4,000	4,000	16,000
Advertising and promotion	Historical/estimate	10,000	12,000	3,000	3,000	3,000	3,000	12,000
Telephones	Historical/estimate	4,000	5,000	1,500	1,500	1,500	1,500	6,000
Consumables	Historical/estimate	5,000	5,000	1,500	1,500	1,500	1,500	6,000
Other expenses	Historical/estimate	6,000	7,000	2,000	2,000	2,000	2,000	8,000
Total expenditure		591,950	620,460	150,825	155,082	163,381	167,337	636,624
Net profit before interest		824,250	868,740	142,935	185,622	269,755	305,175	903,488

RETAIL BUDGET EXAMPLE: SPORTS STORES CO-OPERATIVE LTD

Sports Stores Co-operative (SSC) is a large retail store selling a range of sportswear. Its anticipated sales levels and expenses for each of the next six months are shown in Table 16.3.

Although there are several hundred different items of stock and the product mix does fluctuate due to seasonal factors, SSC is only able to budget based on an average sales mix and applies an average cost of sales of 40%. SSC carries six weeks' inventory, i.e. sufficient stock to cover six weeks' sales (at cost price). At the end of each month, therefore, the stock held by SSC will equal all of next month's cost of sales, plus half of the following month's cost of sales. This is shown in Table 16.4.

In Table 16.4, for example, the inventory required at the end of February (£48,000) is the cost of sales for March (£34,000) plus half the cost of sales for April (£14,000). In order to budget for the inventory for May and June, SSC needs to estimate its sales for July and August. As this is the peak selling time, the sales are estimated at £90,000 and £85,000 respectively. The cost of sales (based on 40%) is therefore £36,000 for July and £34,000 for August. Using these figures, the inventory required at the end of June (£53,000) is equal to the cost of sales for July (£36,000) and half the cost of sales for August (£17,000).

SSC also needs to know its inventory on 1 January, which is £45,000. Purchases can be calculated as:

inventory required at end of month – inventory at beginning of month

= increase (or decrease) in inventory

plus the cost of sales for the current month (which need to be replaced)

Table 16.3 Sports Stores Co-operative sales and expenses estimate

	Jan	Feb	Mar	Apr	May	Jun	Total
Sales (in £'000)	75	80	85	70	65	90	465
Average cost of sales 40%	30	32	34	28	26	36	186
Gross profit	45	48	51	42	39	54	279
Less: expenses							
Salaries	10	10	10	8	7	10	55
Rent	15	15	15	15	15	15	90
Insurance	1	1	1	1	1	1	6
Depreciation on shop fittings	2	2	2	2	2	2	12
Advertising and promotion	8	8	8	9	9	8	50
Electricity, telephone etc.	5	5	5	5	5	5	30
Total expenses	41	41	41	40	39	41	243
Net profit	4	7	10	2	0	13	36

Table 16.4   Sports Stores Co-operative inventory calculation

In £'000s	Jan	Feb	Mar	Apr	May	Jun
Inventory required at end of month	49	48	41	44	54	53
Inventory at beginning of month	45	49	48	41	44	54
Increase/Decrease in inventory	4	−1	−7	3	10	−1
Sales during month (at cost)	30	32	34	28	26	36
Total purchases	34	31	27	31	36	35

Table 16.5   Sports Stores Co-operative closing stock

	Jan	Feb	Mar	Apr	May	Jun
Opening stock	45	49	48	41	44	54
Plus purchases	34	31	·27	31	36	35
Less cost of sales	−30	−32	−34	−28	−26	−36
Closing stock	49	48	41	44	54	53

Table 16.4 shows the calculation of total purchases. However, it can also be shown in the Profit and Loss report format introduced in previous chapters. This format is shown in Table 16.5.

The second example is the construction of the production budget for a manufacturing business.

MANUFACTURING BUDGET EXAMPLE: TELCON MANUFACTURING

Telcon is a manufacturer. Its budget is shown in Table 16.6.

Telcon estimates its sales for July and August as 1,400 units per month. Its production budget is based on needing to maintain one month's stock of finished goods, i.e. the cost of sales for the following month. Its finished goods inventory at the beginning of January is 1,000 units. Table 16.7 shows that the production required of £56,250 is greater than the cost of sales of £53,250 because of the need to produce an additional 400 units at a variable cost of £7.50, i.e. an increase in inventory of £3,000.

However, in order to produce the finished goods, Telcon must also ensure that it has purchased sufficient raw materials. Once again, it wishes to have one month's stock of raw materials (2 kg of the materials are required for each unit of finished goods). There are 2,000 units of raw materials at the beginning of January. Table 16.8 shows the materials purchases budget.

Table 16.6   Telecon Manufacturing budget

in £'000s	Jan	Feb	Mar	Apr	May	Jun	Total
Sales units	1,000	1,100	1,200	1,200	1,300	1,300	7,100
Expected selling price	£10	£10	£10	£10	£10	£11	
Revenue	10,000	11,000	12,000	12,000	13,000	14,300	72,300
Cost of sales							
Direct materials							
@ £4 (2 kg @ £2)	4,000	4,400	4,800	4,800	5,200	5,200	28,400
Direct labour							
@ £2.50	2,500	2,750	3,000	3,000	3,250	3,250	17,750
Variable overhead							
@ £1	1,000	1,100	1,200	1,200	1,300	1,300	7,100
Variable costs	7,500	8,250	9,000	9,000	9,750	9,750	53,250
Contribution margin	2,500	2,750	3,000	3,000	3,250	4,550	19,050
Fixed costs (in total)	1,500	1,500	1,500	1,500	1,500	1,500	9,000
Net profit	1,000	1,250	1,500	1,500	1,750	3,050	10,050

Table 16.7   Production budget

	Jan	Feb	Mar	Apr	May	Jun	Total
Variable costs per unit	£7.50	£7.50	£7.50	£7.50	£7.50	£7.50	£7.50
Inventory units at end of month	1,100	1,200	1,200	1,300	1,300	1,400	
Inventory units at beginning of month	1,000	1,100	1,200	1,200	1,300	1,300	
Increase in inventory	100	100	0	100	0	100	
Production required							
Units sold	1,000	1,100	1,200	1,200	1,300	1,300	
Increase in inventory	100	100	0	100	0	100	
Total units to be produced	1,100	1,200	1,200	1,300	1,300	1,400	
Production units @ variable cost	8,250	9,000	9,000	9,750	9,750	10,500	56,250
Of which:							
Materials @ £4	4,400	4,800	4,800	5,200	5,200	5,600	30,000
Labour @ £2.50	2,750	3,000	3,000	3,250	3,250	3,500	18,750
Variable overhead @ £1	1,100	1,200	1,200	1,300	1,300	1,400	7,500

Table 16.8   Telcon Manufacturing materials budget

	Jan	Feb	Mar	Apr	May	Jun	Total
Total units to be produced	1,100	1,200	1,200	1,300	1,300	1,400	
Total kg of materials (units × 2 kg)	2,200	2,400	2,400	2,600	2,600	2,800	
Inventory units at end of month	2,400	2,400	2,600	2,600	2,800	2,800	
Inventory units at beginning of month	2,000	2,400	2,400	2,600	2,600	2,800	
Increase in inventory	400	0	200	0	200	0	
Materials required							
Kg used in production	2,200	2,400	2,400	2,600	2,600	2,800	
Increase in inventory	400	0	200	0	200	0	
Total kg to be purchased	2,600	2,400	2,600	2,600	2,800	2,800	
Purchase cost @ £2/kg	5,200	4,800	5,200	5,200	5,600	5,600	31,600

The purchases budget of £31,600 is more than the materials usage of £30,000 from the production budget because an additional 800 kg of materials is bought at £2 per kg (i.e. £1,600), due to the need to increase raw materials inventory.

CASH FORECASTING

Once a profit budget has been constructed, it is important to understand the impact on cash flow. The purpose of the cash forecast is to ensure that sufficient cash is available to meet the level of activity planned by the sales and production budgets and to meet all the other cash inflows and outflows of the business. Cash surpluses and deficiencies need to be identified in advance to ensure effective business financing decisions, e.g. raising short-term finance or investing short-term surplus funds.

There is a substantial difference between profits and cash forecasts (for a detailed explanation see Chapter 6) because of:

■ the timing difference between when income is earned and when it is received (i.e. debtors);
■ increases or decreases in inventory for both raw materials and finished goods;
■ the timing difference between when expenses are incurred and when they are paid (i.e. creditors);
■ non-cash expenses (e.g. depreciation);
■ capital expenditure;
■ income tax;
■ dividends;
■ new loans and loan repayments.

CASH FORECASTING EXAMPLE: RETAIL NEWS GROUP

Retail News is a store selling newspapers, magazines, books, confectionery etc. Its budget for six months has been prepared and is shown in Table 16.9.

Retail News makes half of its sales in cash and half on credit to business customers, who typically pay their account in the month following sale. Credit sales in December to customers who will pay during January amount to £3,500. Retail News' sales receipts budget is shown in Table 16.10.

Retail New's debtors have increased by £1,000 from £3,500 to £4,500, since 50% of the sales in June (£9,000) will not be received until July.

As in the previous examples, we also need to determine the purchases budget for Retail News, which needs stock equal to one month's sales (at cost price) at the end of each month. The stock at the beginning of January is £4,500.

The sales and cost of sales estimated for July are £12,000 and £4,800 respectively. The purchases budget is shown in Table 16.11.

Table 16.9   Retail News Group budget

	Jan	Feb	Mar	Apr	May	Jun	Total
Sales	10,000	12,000	15,000	12,000	11,000	9,000	69,000
Cost of sales (40%)	4,000	4,800	6,000	4,800	4,400	3,600	27,600
Gross profit	6,000	7,200	9,000	7,200	6,600	5,400	41,400
Less expenses							
Salaries and wages	2,000	2,000	2,000	2,200	2,200	2,200	12,600
Selling and distribution expenses (7.5%)	750	900	1,125	900	825	675	5,175
Rent	1,000	1,000	1,000	1,000	1,000	1,000	6,000
Electricity, telephone etc.	500	500	500	500	500	500	3,000
Insurance	500	500	500	500	500	500	3,000
Depreciation	500	500	500	500	500	500	3,000
Total expenses	5,250	5,400	5,625	5,600	5,525	5,375	32,775
Net profit	750	1,800	3,375	1,600	1,075	25	8,625

Table 16.10   Retail News Group sales receipts budget

	Jan	Feb	Mar	Apr	May	Jun	Total
50% of sales received in cash	5,000	6,000	7,500	6,000	5,500	4,500	34,500
50% of sales on credit – 30-day terms	3,500	5,000	6,000	7,500	6,000	5,500	33,500
Total receipts	8,500	11,000	13,500	13,500	11,500	10,000	68,000

Table 16.11   Retail News Group purchase budget

	Jan	Feb	Mar	Apr	May	Jun	Total
Inventory at end of month	4,800	6,000	4,800	4,400	3,600	4,800	
Inventory at beginning of month	4,500	4,800	6,000	4,800	4,400	3,600	
Increase/Decrease in inventory	300	1,200	−1,200	−400	−800	1,200	
Sales during month (at cost)	4,000	4,800	6,000	4,800	4,400	3,600	
Total purchases	4,300	6,000	4,800	4,400	3,600	4,800	27,900

Table 16.12   Retail News Group creditors' payments budget

	Jan	Feb	Mar	Apr	May	Jun	Total
Payment on 60-day terms	3,800	3,500	4,300	6,000	4,800	4,400	26,800

Purchases are £27,900 compared with a cost of sales of £27,600, because inventory has increased by £300 (from £4,500 to £4,800). However, purchases are on credit and Retail News has arranged with its suppliers to pay on 60-day terms. Therefore, for example, purchases in January will be paid for in March. Retail News will pay for its November purchases in January (£3,800) and its December purchases in February (£3,500). The creditor payments budget is shown in Table 16.12.

Retail News creditors have increased by £1,100 from £7,300 (£3,800 for November and £3,500 for December) to £8,400 (£3,600 for May and £4,800 for June).

We can now construct the cash forecast for Retail News using the sales receipts budget and creditor payments budget. We also need to identify the timing of cash flows for all expenses. In this case, we determine that salaries and wages, selling and distribution costs and rent are all paid monthly, as those expenses are incurred. Electricity and telephone are paid quarterly in arrears in March and June. The annual insurance premium of £6,000 is paid in January. As we know, depreciation is not an expense that involves a cash flow.

However, the business also has a number of other cash payments that do not affect profit. These 'below-the-line' payments are:

■   capital expenditure of £2,500 committed in March;
■   income tax of £5,000 due in April;
■   £3,000 of dividends due to be paid in June;
■   a loan repayment of £1,000 due in February.

The opening bank balance of Retail News is £2,500. The cash forecast in Table 16.13 shows the total cash position.

In summary, the bank balance has reduced from an asset of £2,500 to a liability (bank overdraft) of £575 due to a net cash outflow of £3,075. The main issue here is

Table 16.13 Retail News Group cash forecast

	Jan	Feb	Mar	Apr	May	Jun	Total
Sales receipts	8,500	11,000	13,500	13,500	11,500	10,000	68,000
Creditors' payments	3,800	3,500	4,300	6,000	4,800	4,400	26,800
Salaries and wages	2,000	2,000	2,000	2,200	2,200	2,200	12,600
Selling and distribution expenses	750	900	1,125	900	825	675	5,175
Rent	1,000	1,000	1,000	1,000	1,000	1,000	6,000
Electricity, telephone etc.		1,500				1,500	3,000
Insurance	6,000						6,000
Total payments	13,550	7,400	9,925	10,100	8,825	9,775	59,575
Trading cash flow	−5,050	3,600	3,575	3,400	2,675	225	8,425
Capital expenditure			2,500				2,500
Income tax paid				5,000			5,000
Dividends paid						3,000	3,000
Loan repayments		1,000					1,000
Net cash flow	−5,050	2,600	1,075	−1,600	2,675	−2,775	−3,075
Opening bank balance	2,500	−2,550	50	1,125	−475	2,500	
Closing bank balance	−2,550	50	1,125	−475	2,200	−575	

that, in anticipation of the overdrawn position of the bank account in January, April and June, Retail News needs to make arrangements with its bankers to extend its facility.

One last thing remains, which is for Retail News to reconcile the profit with the cash flow and the movement in working capital over the budget period. This is shown in Table 16.14.

THEORETICAL PERSPECTIVES ON BUDGETING

Although the tools of budgeting and cash forecasting are well developed and made easier by the wide use of spreadsheet software, the difficulty of budgeting is in predicting the volume of sales for the business, especially the sales mix between different products or services and the timing of income and expenses.

Buckley and McKenna (1972) emphasized the importance of participation in the budget process; frequent communications and information flow throughout the organization; inclusion of the budget in decisions about salary, bonuses and career promotion; and clear communication by accountants to non-accountants as elements of 'good budgeting practice'. However, Buckley and McKenna also recognized the behavioural

Table 16.14 Retail News Group profit and cash flow reconciliation

Net profit		£8,625
Plus non-cash expense		3,000
Depreciation		
		11,625
Less increase in working capital –		
Debtors	1,000	
Inventory	300	
Insurance prepayment	3,000	
	4,300	
Less increase in creditors	1,100	
Net increase		3,200
Net cash flow from operating activities		8,425
Other outflows of cash –		
Capital expenditure	2,500	
Income tax	5,000	
Dividend	3,000	
Loan repayment	1,000	11,500
Decrease in cash		3,075

effects of budgeting, such as the impact of setting difficult budget targets and the introduction of bias.

Lowe and Shaw (1968) carried out research into sales budgeting in a retail chain, in which annual budgeting was an 'internal market by which resources are allocated' (p. 304) and in which managers had to co-operate and compete. Lowe and Shaw identified three sources of forecasting error: unpredicted changes in the environment; inaccurate assessment of the effects of predicted changes; and forecasting bias.

Lowe and Shaw examined the sources of bias: the reward system; the influence of recent practice and norms; and the insecurity of managers, arguing that bias may be a common phenomenon as in 'the desire to please superiors in a competitive managerial hierarchy' (p. 312). They also explained counterbias as 'the attempt by other managers to eliminate that part of a forecast which stems from the personal interest of the forecaster' (p. 312).

However, there are also problems with aggregation of divisional budgets into a corporate budget. Berry and Otley (1975) explored the estimation of budget figures made by individuals at one hierarchical level in an organization, and the coupling of these estimates to those made at a higher level to show the resulting bias in estimating that takes place. Otley and Berry (1979) argued that quite mild deviations from 'expectation budgets' at the unit level can produce severe distortions when budgets are aggregated to the organizational level.

An interpretive or critical perspective is appropriate for a study of budgeting, in particular because budgets are one of the main sources of power in organizations, as a result of the influence of accountants over budgetary allocations. Czarniawska-Joerges and Jacobsson (1989) depicted budgets as:

> a symbolic performance rather than a decision-making process; a means of conversation rather than a means of control; and an expression of values rather than an instrument for action . . . Budgeting is seen as a ritual of reason; budgets are presented according to and conforming with prevailing norms of rationality. Budgeting is also a language of consensus; there are several mechanisms in budgetary processes for reducing the level and amount of conflict. (pp. 29–30)

Covaleski and Dirsmith (1988) described the budgetary process between a state university and its state government and argued that budgeting systems help to represent vested interests in political processes and maintain existing power relationships. Other aspects of power relate to shifts in the dominant coalition within organizations. Covaleski *et al.* (1993) presented a case study of the introduction of diagnostic-related costing in hospitals in which case-mix accounting systems 'appear also to determine power by redistributing that power from physician to administrator' (p. 73).

In a UK university, Ezzamel (1994) studied the budgeting system and how it was involved in power relations at two levels. First, it provided a vehicle through which the proposed reallocation of funds was translated, communicated and given initial visibility. Second, it provided a basis for much of the discourse that took place between the various constituencies.

Preston *et al.* (1992) described the process of management budgeting in the UK hospital system, showing how budgeting was 'fabricated' – put together in a fragile manner – and, in the process of its design and implementation, new possibilities for decision-making and definitions of responsibility emerged. Preston *et al.* emphasized how people:

> attempt to enmesh accounting innovations within the functioning of organizations and the processes by which new patterns of language, meaning and significance emerge through the fabrication of accounting and budgeting systems. (p. 562)

They concluded:

> [r]esistance and scepticism occurs from the outset and is a central element in the fabrication process . . . resistance not only impedes and constrains the process, but also shapes it in specific ways designed to overcome the scepticism. (p. 589)

A final word in relation to budgeting concerns risk. Collier and Berry (2002) identified risk as being managed in four different domains: financial, operational, political and personal. These were the result of the unique circumstances, history and technology in different organizations that had led to different ideas about risk. These domains of risk revealed how participants in the budgeting process influenced the content of the budget through their unique perspectives.

The research distinguished the content of budgets from the process of budgeting. It contrasted three types of budget. In the risk-modelled process, there is an explicit use of formal probability models to assess the effect of different consequences over a range of different assumptions. In the risk-considered process, informal sensitivity (or what-if) analysis is used to produce (for example) high, medium and low consequences of different assumptions. The risk excluded budget manages risk outside the budget process, and the budget relies on a single expectation of performance. Collier and Berry found that little risk modelling may be used in practice, and that the consideration of risk during the budgeting process influenced the content of budgets that were largely risk excluded.

Case Study 16.1:   Svenska Handelsbanken – is budgeting necessary?

Jan Wallander is an executive director of Handelsbanken. He was appointed to the role when the bank, the largest commercial bank in Sweden, faced a crisis. Although at the time Swedish banks did not use budgets, Handelsbanken had started to install a sophisticated budgeting system.

Wallander (1999) was very critical of budgeting. For example:

You can make forecasts very complicated by putting a lot of variables into them and using sophisticated techniques for evaluating the time series you have observed and used in your work. However, if you see through all this technical paraphernalia you will find that there are a few basic assumptions which determine the outcome of the forecast. (p. 408)

The accuracy of the budget therefore depends on how accurate the assumptions are. Wallander argued that there are two reasons to abandon budgeting:

1   If there is economic stability and the business will continue as usual, we use previous experience in order to budget. Wallander argued that we do not need an intricate budgeting system in this case, because people will continue working as they presently are. Even when conditions are not normal, the expectation is that they will return to normal.

2   If events arise that challenge economic stability then budgets will not reflect this, because, Wallander says, 'we have no ability to foresee something of which we have no previous experience' (p. 411).

He concluded that traditional budgeting is 'an outmoded way of controlling and steering a company. It is a cumbersome way of reaching conclusions which are either commonplace or wrong' (p. 419).

However, Wallander did not reject planning outright. He argued that it is important to have an 'economic model' that establishes the basic relationships in the company, such as the ability to plan production. He commented, 'This type of planning is something that is going on all the year round and has nothing to do with the annual budget' (p. 416).

Handelsbanken has an information system that is focused on the information needed to influence actual behaviour. It incorporates both financial and 'Balanced Scorecard' measures at the profit centre level, and performance is benchmarked externally and internally. The bank rewards its staff through a profit-sharing scheme.

> Despite its abandonment of budgeting, Handelsbanken remains a very successful bank. Wallander concluded: abandoning budgeting, which was an essential part of the changes, had no adverse effect on the performance of the bank compared to other banks, which all installed budgeting systems during the period. (p. 407)

After you have read this chapter, you should:

■ Revise your understanding of the accounting terms. The Glossary in Part IV is a helpful aid.
■ Practice the Questions for this chapter and then check your answers against the solutions. Questions for each chapter are in Appendix 1. The solutions are in Appendix 2.
■ Read Case Study 7. This will help you to interpret accounting information. Try to write an answer. The Case Studies are in Appendix 3 and suggested solutions are in Appendix 4.

CONCLUSION

In this chapter we have linked budgeting to the strategy process. We described various approaches to budgeting and the mechanics of the budgeting cycle. Through a series of examples we explored budgeting for a service, retail and manufacturing organization. We also introduced cash forecasting and the reconciliation between profit and cash flow.

The chapter concluded with a snapshot of theoretical perspectives on budgeting that contrast the rational-economic view of budgets with the subjectivity of budgets as a consequence of bias and aggregation, and the power that underlies the budgeting process. We also questioned whether risk is really reflected in the content of the budget document and whether budgets have any value at all.

The assumptions behind the production of budgets are important for planning purposes, but crucial when managers are held accountable for achieving budget targets. This is the process of budgetary control, which is the subject of Chapter 17.

REFERENCES

Anthony, R. N. and Govindarajan, V. (2000). *Management Control Systems*. (10th international edn). New York, NY: McGraw-Hill Irwin.

Berry, A. J. and Otley, D. T. (1975). The aggregation of estimates in hierarchical organizations. *Journal of Management Studies*, May, 175–93.

Buckley, A. and McKenna, E. (1972). Budgetary control and business behaviour. *Accounting and Business Research*, Spring, 137–50.

Collier, P. M. and Berry, A. J. (2002). Risk in the process of budgeting. *Management Accounting Research*, **13**, 273–97.

Covaleski, M. A. and Dirsmith, M. W. (1988). The use of budgetary symbols in the political arena: an historically informed field study. *Accounting, Organizations and Society*, **13**(1), 1–24.

Covaleski, M. A., Dirsmith, M. W. and Michelman, J. E. (1993). An institutional theory perspective on the DRG framework, case-mix accounting systems and health-care organizations. *Accounting, Organizations and Society*, **18**(1), 65–80.

Czarniawska-Joerges, B. and Jacobsson, B. (1989). Budget in a cold climate. *Accounting, Organizations and Society*, **14**(1/2), 29–39.

Ezzamel, M. (1994). Organizational change and accounting: Understanding the budgeting system in its organizational context. *Organization Studies*, **15**(2), 213–40.

Lowe, E. A. and Shaw, R. W. (1968). An analysis of managerial biasing: Evidence from a company's budgeting process. *Journal of Management Studies*, October, 304–15.

Otley, D. and Berry, A. (1979). Risk distribution in the budgetary process. *Accounting and Business Research*, **9**(36), 325–7.

Preston, A. M., Cooper, D. J. and Coombs, R. W. (1992). Fabricating budgets: A study of the production of management budgeting in the National Health Service. *Accounting, Organizations and Society*, **17**(6), 561–93.

Wallander, J. (1999). Budgeting – an unnecessary evil. *Scandinavian Journal of Management*, **15**, 405–21.

For a useful critique of budgeting, see the 'Beyond Budgeting Round Table' website at **www.beyondbudgeting.org**

17

BUDGETARY CONTROL

In this chapter, we describe the budgetary control that takes place in organizations through the techniques of flexible budgets and variance analysis. However, we caution against variance analysis in circumstances where this could conflict with more broadly based improvement strategies within the business. The chapter also considers how cost control can be exercised in practice.

WHAT IS BUDGETARY CONTROL?

Budgetary control is concerned with ensuring that actual financial results are in line with targets. An important part of this *feedback process* (see Chapter 4) is investigating variations between actual results and budgeted results and taking appropriate corrective action.

Budgetary control provides a yardstick for comparison and isolates problems by focusing on variances, which provide an early warning to managers. Buckley and McKenna (1972) argued:

> The sinews of the budgeting process ... are the influencing of management behaviour by setting agreed performance standards, the evaluation of results and feedback to management in anticipation of corrective action where necessary. (p. 137)

Budgetary control is typically exercised at the level of each responsibility centre. Management reports show, for each line item, the budget expenditure, usually for both the current accounting period and the year to date. The report will also show the actual income and expenditure and a variance.

A typical actual versus budget financial report is shown in Table 17.1. There are two types of variance:

- A favourable variance occurs where income exceeds budget and/or expenses are lower than budget.
- An adverse variance occurs where income is less than budget and/or expenses are greater than budget.

It is important to look both at the current period, which in the above example shows an underspend of £6,500 (budget of £80,000 less actual spending of £73,500), and the year to date, which shows an overspend of £1,000. The weakness of traditional management reports for budgetary control is that the business may not be comparing like with like. For

Table 17.1   Actual v. budget financial report

	Budget for this period	Actual for this period	Budget for the year to date	Actual for the year to date	Variance
Materials	40,000	45,000	100,000	96,000	4,000 Fav
Labour	21,000	19,000	30,000	32,000	2,000 Adv
Energy	9,000	7,000	40,000	38,000	2,000 Fav
Other costs	10,000	2,500	50,000	55,000	5,000 Adv
Total	80,000	73,500	220,000	221,000	1,000 Adv

example, if the business volume is lower than budgeted, then it follows that any variable costs should (in total) be lower than budgeted. Conversely, if business volume is higher than budget, variable costs should (in total) be higher than budget. In many management reports, the distinction between variable and fixed costs (see Chapter 10) is not made and it becomes very difficult to compare costs incurred at one level of activity with budgeted costs at a different level of activity and to make judgements about managerial performance.

FLEXIBLE BUDGETING

Flexible budgets provide a better basis for investigating variances than the original budget, because the volume of production may differ from that planned. If the actual activity level is different to that budgeted, comparing revenue and/or costs at different (actual and budget) levels of activity will produce meaningless figures. A flexible budget is a budget that is *flexed*, that is standard costs per unit are applied to the actual level of business activity. It makes little sense to compare the budgeted costs of producing (say) 40,000 units with the costs incurred in producing 35,000 units. Variance analysis is then carried out between the flexed budget costs and actual costs.

Flexible budgets take into account variations in the volume of activity. Using the above example, costs are budgeted at £2 per unit for 40,000 units but actual costs are £2.10 for 35,000 units. A standard actual versus budget report will show:

Budget	Actual	Variance
£80,000	£73,500	£6,500 Favourable
40,000 @ £2	35,000 @ £2.10	

The favourable variance disguises the fact that fewer units were produced. A flexible budget adjusts the original budget to the actual level of activity. The variance under a flexed budget would then show:

Original budget	Flexed budget	Actual	Variance
£80,000	£70,000	£73,500	£3,500 Adverse
40,000 @ £2	35,000 @ £2	35,000 @ £2.10	

This is a more meaningful comparison, because the manager responsible for cost control has spent more per unit and should not have this responsibility negated by the effect of a reduced volume, which may have been outside that manager's control. Separately, the adverse effect of the volume variance – the difference between the original and flexed budgets – is shown as 5,000 units @ £2 or £10,000. This may be controllable by a different manager. As can be seen by comparing the two styles of presentation, there is still a £6,500 favourable variance, but the flexed budget identifies the two separate components of this variance:

■ £10,000 favourable variance (in terms of cost) because of the reduction in volume from 40,000 to 35,000 units at £2 each. This is offset by
■ £3,500 adverse variance because the 35,000 units produced each cost 10p more than the standard cost.

VARIANCE ANALYSIS

An important part of the feedback process (see Chapter 4) is variance analysis. **Variance analysis** involves comparing actual performance against plan, investigating the causes of the variance and taking corrective action to ensure that targets are achieved. Variance analysis needs to be carried out for each responsibility centre, product/service and for each line item.

The steps involved in variance analysis are:

1 Ascertain the budget and phasing (see Chapter 16) for each period.
2 Report the actual spending.
3 Determine the variance between budget and actual (and determine whether it is either favourable or adverse).
4 Investigate why the variance occurred.
5 Take corrective action.

Not only adverse variances need to be investigated. Favourable variances provide a learning opportunity that can be repeated.

The questions that need to be asked as part of variance analysis are:

■ Is the variance significant?
■ Is it early or late in the year?
■ Is it likely to be repeated?
■ Can it be explained (and understood)?
■ Is it controllable?

Only significant variations need to be investigated. However, what is significant can be interpreted differently by different people. Which is more significant, for example, a 5% variation on £10,000 (£500) or a 25% variation on £1,000 (£250)? The significance of the variation may be either an absolute amount or a percentage.

A variance later in the year will be more difficult to correct, so variances should be detected for corrective action as soon as they occur. Similarly, a one-off variance requires a single corrective action, but a variance that will continue requires more drastic action. A variance that can be understood can be corrected, but if the causes of the variance are not understood or are outside the manager's control, it may be difficult to correct and control in the future.

Explanations need to be sought in relation to different types of variance:

■   sales variances: price and quantity of product/services sold;
■   material variances: price and quantity of materials used;
■   labour variances: wage rate and efficiency;
■   overhead variances: spending and efficiency.

The following case study provides an example of variance analysis.

VARIANCE ANALYSIS EXAMPLE: WOOD'S FURNITURE CO.

Wood's Furniture has produced a budget versus actual report, which is shown in Table 17.2. The difference between budget and actual is an adverse variance of

Table 17.2   Budget v. actual report

	Budget	Actual	Variance
Sales units	10,000	9,000	
Selling price			
Revenue	1,700,000	1,575,000	125,000
Variable costs			
Materials			
Plastic	30,000	26,600	3,400
Metal	20,000	21,000	1,000
Wood	30,000	26,600	3,400
Labour			
Skilled	900,000	838,750	61,250
Semi-skilled	225,000	195,000	30,000
Variable overhead	300,000	283,250	16,750
Total variable costs	1,505,000	1,391,200	113,800
Contribution	195,000	183,800	11,200
Fixed costs	125,000	130,000	−5,000
Net profit	70,000	53,800	16,200

Table 17.3 Flexible budget

	Original budget	Flexed budget	Actual	Variance
Sales units	10,000	9,000	9,000	
Selling price				
Revenue	1,700,000	1,530,000	1,575,000	−45,000
Variable costs				
Materials				
Plastic	30,000	27,000	26,600	400
Metal	20,000	18,000	21,000	−3,000
Wood	30,000	27,000	26,600	400
Labour				
Skilled	900,000	810,000	838,750	−28,750
Semi-skilled	225,000	202,500	195,000	7,500
Variable overhead	300,000	270,000	283,250	−13,250
Total variable costs	1,505,000	1,354,500	1,391,200	−36,700
Contribution	195,000	175,500	183,800	−8,300
Fixed costs	125,000	125,000	130,000	−5,000
Net profit	70,000	50,500	53,800	−3,300

£16,200. However, the firm's accountant has produced a flexed budget to assist in carrying out a more meaningful variance analysis. This is shown in Table 17.3.

The flexed budget shows a favourable variance of £3,300 compared to the flexed budget. In order to undertake a detailed variance analysis, we need some additional information, which the accountant has produced in Table 17.4.

Sales variance

The sales variance is used to evaluate the performance of the sales team. There are two sales variances for which the sales department is responsible:

■ The sales price variance is the difference between the actual price and the standard price for the actual quantity sold.
■ The sales quantity variance is the difference between the budget and actual quantity at the standard margin (i.e. the difference between the budget price and the standard variable costs), because it would be inappropriate to hold sales managers accountable for production efficiencies and inefficiencies.

The sales price variance is the difference between the flexed budget and the actual sales revenue, i.e. £45,000. This is calculated in Table 17.5. The variance is favourable because the business has sold 9,000 units at an additional £5 each.

Table 17.4 Variance report

	Std cost per unit	Original budget	Std cost per unit	Flexed budget	Usage qty	Act cost per unit	Actual	Variance
Sales unit		10,000		9,000			9,000	
Selling price	£170		£170			£175		
Revenue		£1,700,000		£1,530,000			£1,575,000	−£45,000
Variable costs								
Materials								
Plastic		30,000	2 @ £1.50	27,000	19,000	£1.40	26,600	400
Metal		20,000	1 @ £2	18,000	10,000	£2.10	21,000	−3,000
Wood			4 @ £0.75					
Labour								
skilled		900,000	6 @ £15	810,000	55,000	£15.25	838,750	−28,750
Semi-skilled		225,000	3 @ £7.50	202,500	26,000	£7.50	195,000	7,500
Variable overhead		300,000	6 @ £5	270,000	55,000	£5.15	283,250	−13,250
Total variable costs	£150.50	1,505,000	£150.50	1,354,500		£154.58	1,391,200	−36,700
Contribution	£19.50	195,000	£19.50	175,500		£20.42	183,800	−8,300
Fixed costs		125,000		125,000			130,000	−5,000
Net profit		70,000		50,500			53,800	−3,300

Table 17.5 Sales price variance

Actual quantity	9,000	
@ actual price	£175	£1,575,000
	————	
Actual quantity	9,000	
@ standard price	£170	£1,530,000
	————	
Favourable price variance		£45,000

Table 17.6 Sales quantity variance

Budget quantity	10,000	
– Actual quantity	9,000	1,000
	————	
@ standard margin	£19.50	
Unfavourable quantity variance		£19,500

The sales quantity variance is the difference between the original budget profit of £70,000 and the flexed budget profit of £50,500 – an unfavourable variance of £19,500. This is calculated in Table 17.6. The variance is unfavourable because 1,000 units budgeted have not been sold and the standard margin for each of those units was £19.50 (selling price of £170 less variable costs of £150.50), resulting in a lost contribution of £19,500.

It is important to note that the sales mix can affect the quantity and price variances significantly. Therefore, a sales variance analysis should reflect the budget and actual sales mix.

We have now accounted for the variance between the original budget and the flexed budget (i.e. due to volume of units sold) and between the revenue in the flexed budget and the actual (i.e. due to the difference in selling price). We now have to look at the variances between the costs in the flexed budget and the actual costs incurred.

Cost variances

Each cost variance – for materials, labour and overhead – can be split into two types, a price variance and a usage variance. This is because each type of variance may be the responsibility of a different manager. Price variances occur because the cost per unit of resources is higher or lower than the standard cost. Usage variances occur because the actual quantity of labour or materials used is higher or lower than the routing or bill of materials (these concepts were covered in Chapter 11). The relationship between price and usage variances is shown in Figure 17.1.

Figure 17.1   Price and usage variances

Materials variance

The total materials variance is £2,200 unfavourable, as shown in Table 17.7. However, we need to consider the price and usage variances for each type of material, because the reasons for the variance and the corrective action may be different for each.

Materials usage variance

Using the above formula we can calculate the usage variance for each of the three materials. This is shown in Table 17.8. In each case, while holding the (standard) price constant, there has been a higher than expected usage of materials. This is an efficiency variance, which may be the result of:

- poor productivity;
- out-of-date bill of materials;
- poor quality materials.

Materials price variance

Using the formula, the price variance for each of the three materials is shown in Table 17.9. While holding the (actual) quantity constant, we can see the effect of price

Table 17.7   Materials variance

	Std cost per unit	Original budget	Std cost per unit	Flexed budget	Usage qty	Act cost per unit	Actual	Variance
Plastic	2 @ £1.50	30,000	2 @ £1.50	27,000	19,000	1.4	26,600	400
Metal	1 @ £2	20,000	1 @ £2	18,000	10,000	2.1	21,000	−3,000
	4 @ £0.75		4 @ £0.75					
Wood		30,000		27,000	38,000	0.7	26,600	400
		80,000		72,000			74,200	−2,200

Table 17.8 Materials usage variance

	Plastic	
Standard quantity	9,000 × 2	
Standard price	@ £1.50	27,000
Actual quantity	19,000	
Standard price	@ £1.50	28,500
Adverse variance		−1,500
	Metal	
Standard quantity	9,000 × 1	
Standard price	@ £2.00	18,000
Actual quantity	10,000	
Standard price	@ £2.00	20,000
Adverse variance		−2,000
	Wood	
Standard quantity	9,000 × 4	
Standard price	@ £0.75	27,000
Actual quantity	38,000	
Standard price	@ £0.75	28,500
Adverse variance		−1,500
Total usage variance – adverse		−5,000

fluctuations. Both plastic and wood have been bought below the standard price, while metal has cost more than standard. These variances may be the result of:

■ changes in supplier prices not yet reflected in the bill of materials;
■ poor purchasing.

In total, the materials variance is £2,200. We can see that of the three materials, metal contributes the greatest variance – an adverse £3,000 (£2,000 usage and £1,000 price), which needs to be investigated as a matter of priority – while there may be a trade-off between the price and usage variances for plastic and wood, as sometimes quality and price can conflict with each other. The total materials variance is shown in Table 17.10.

Similarly, we need to analyse the usage and price variances for both skilled and semi-skilled labour.

Labour variance

The total labour variance is an unfavourable £21,250, as shown in Table 17.11.

Table 17.9   Materials price variance

	Plastic	
Actual quantity	19,000	
Standard price	@ £1.50	28,500
Actual quantity	19,000	
Actual price	@ £1.40	26,600
Favourable variance		1,900
	Metal	
Actual quantity	10,000	
Standard price	@ £2.00	20,000
Actual quantity	10,000	
Actual price	@ £2.10	21,000
Adverse variance		−1,000
	Wood	
Actual quantity	38,000	
Standard price	@ £0.75	28,500
Actual quantity	38,000	
Actual price	@ £0.70	26,600
Favourable variance		1,900
Total price variance – favourable		2,800

Table 17.10   Total materials variance

Usage – adverse	−5,000
Price – favourable	2,800
Total – adverse	−2,200
Plastic	400
Metal	−3,000
Wood	400
	−2,200

Similarly, we need to look at the usage variance (which is a productivity or efficiency measure) and the price variance (which is a wage rate variance) for each of the two types of labour.

Labour efficiency variance

Using the same formula, the efficiency variance for labour is shown in Table 17.12. The adverse variance is a result of 1,000 additional hours being worked for skilled labour

Table 17.11 Labour variance

	Std cost per unit	Original budget	Std cost per unit	Flexed budget	Usage qty	Act cost per unit	Actual	Variance
Skilled	6 @ £15	900,000	6 @ £15	810,000	55,000	£15.25	838,750	−28,750
Semi-skilled	3 @ £7.50	225,000	3 @ £7.50	202,500	26,000	£7.50	195,000	7,500
		1,125,000		1,012,500			1,033,750	−21,250

Table 17.12 Labour efficiency variance

	Skilled	
Standard quantity	9,000 × 6	
Standard price	@ £15.00	810,000
Actual quantity	55,000	
Standard price	@15.00	825,000
Adverse variance		−15,000
	Unskilled	
Standard quantity	9,000 × 3	
Standard price	@ £7.50	202,500
Actual quantity	26,000	
Standard price	@ £7.50	195,000
Favourable variance		7,500
Total efficiency variance – adverse		−7,500

and 1,000 hours less being worked by unskilled labour. This may have been the result of:

■ poor-quality material that required greater skill to work;
■ the lack of unskilled labour that was replaced by skilled labour;
■ poor production planning.

Labour rate variance

The labour rate variance is shown in Table 17.13. Skilled labour costs an additional 25p for each hour worked, while unskilled labour was paid the standard rate. This may be the result of:

■ unplanned overtime payments;
■ a negotiated wage increase that has not been included in the labour routing.

Table 17.13   Labour rate variance

	Skilled	
Actual quantity	55,000	
Standard price	@ £15.00	825,000
Actual quantity	55,000	
Actual price	@ £15.25	838,750
Adverse variance		−13,750
	Unskilled	
Actual quantity	26,000	
Standard price	@ £7.50	195,000
Actual quantity	26,000	
Actual price	@ £7.50	195,000
Favourable variance		0
Total rate variance – adverse		−13,750

Table 17.14   Total labour variance

Efficiency – adverse	−7,500
Rate – adverse	−13,750
Total – adverse	−21,250
Skilled	−28,750
Unskilled	7,500
	−21,250

The total labour variance is an unfavourable £21,250. This is a combination of efficiency and rate variances, but it is all in relation to skilled labour. The total labour variance is shown in Table 17.14.

Variable production costs also need to be analysed.

Variable overhead variance

The overhead variance is an adverse variation of £13,250, as shown in Table 17.15.

There are two types of overhead variance, the efficiency variance and the spending variance.

The overhead efficiency variance is £5,000 adverse, as shown in Table 17.16. The variance has occurred because an extra 1,000 hours have been worked. The efficiency variance is typically related to production hours and often follows from variances in

Table 17.15 Variable overhead variance

	Std cost per unit	Original budget	Std cost per unit	Flexed budget	Usage qty	Act cost per unit	Actual	Variance
Variable overhead	6 @ £5	300,000	6@ £5	270,000	55,000	5.15	283,250	−13,250

Table 17.16 Overhead efficiency variance

Standard quantity	9,000 × 6	
Standard price	@ £5.00	270,000
Actual quantity	55,000	
Standard price	@ £5.00	275,000
Adverse efficiency variance		−5,000

Table 17.17 Overhead spending variance

Actual quantity	55,000	
Standard price	@ £5	275,000
Actual quantity	55,000	
Actual price	@ £5.15	283,250
Adverse spending variance		−8,250

labour (see Chapter 13). The reason may be that as more hours have been worked this has consumed more variable costs, e.g. the more machines running, the more electricity may be consumed.

The overhead spending variance is £8,250 adverse. This is shown in Table 17.17. This variance is due to extra spending for each hour worked. The reason for this variance may be a higher cost per hour, e.g. the rate per kilowatt used paid to the utility provider may have increased.

The total variable overhead variance is an adverse £13,250, which is a combination of both efficiency and rate variances. The total variable overhead variance is shown in Table 17.18.

Fixed cost variance

The fixed cost variance is straightforward. As changes in quantity cannot influence fixed costs (which by definition are constant over different levels of production), the

Table 17.18   Total variable overhead variance

Efficiency – adverse	−5,000
Spending – adverse	−8,250
Total – adverse	−13,250

variation must be the result of a spending variance. In this case the variance is an adverse £5,000, because costs of £130,000 exceed the budget cost of £125,000.

RECONCILING THE VARIANCES

The difference between the original budget profit of £70,000 and the actual result of £53,800 can now be reconciled, as in Table 17.19.

While the example used here is a manufacturing example, variance analysis is equally applicable to service businesses, although there will, of course, be no need for a materials price variance. Differences in the volume of activity, sales variances, labour variances and overhead variances will constitute the difference between actual and budgeted profit.

Once variances have been identified, managers need to investigate the reasons that each occurred and take corrective action. This is part of the management control cycle – the feedback loop – described in Chapter 4.

CRITICISM OF VARIANCE ANALYSIS

Standard costing, flexible budgeting and variance analysis can be criticized as tools of management, because these methods emphasize variable costs in a manufacturing environment. While labour costs are typically a low proportion of manufacturing cost, material costs are typically high and variance analysis has a role to play in many manufacturing organizations.

However, even in manufacturing the introduction of new management techniques such as just-in-time is often not reflected in the design of the management accounting system. *Just-in-time (JIT)* aims to improve productivity and eliminate waste by obtaining manufacturing components in the right quality, at the right time and place to meet the demands of the manufacturing cycle. It requires close co-operation within the supply chain and is generally associated with continuous manufacturing processes with low inventory holdings, a result of eliminating buffer inventories – considered waste – between the different stages of manufacture. Many of these costs are hidden in a traditional cost accounting system. Variance analysis has less emphasis in a JIT environment because price variations are only one component of total cost. Variance analysis does not account, for example, for higher or lower investments in inventory. Purchasing managers should therefore consider the *total cost of ownership* rather than the initial purchase price.

Table 17.19 Reconciliation

Original budgeted net profit			70,000
Sales variances			
Favourable price variance		45,000	
Unfavourable quantity variance	See note	−19,500	25,000
Materials variances			
Total usage variance – adverse		−5,000	
Total price variance – favourable		2,800	−2,200
Labour variances			
Total efficiency variance – adverse		−7,500	
Total rate variance – adverse		−13,750	−21,250
Overhead variances			
Adverse efficiency variance		−5,000	
Adverse spending variance		−8,250	−13,250
Fixed cost spending variance			−5,000
Total variances			−16,200
Actual net profit			53,800

Note The difference between the original budget and the flexed budget is £19,500 adverse (the quantity variance). The difference between the flexed budget and the actual is £3,300 favourable. Together, the adverse variance is £16,200. However, it is important to remember that the individual variances for each type of material and labour need to be investigated and corrected as the total material, labour and overhead variances of £41,700 adverse are 'disguised' by the favourable price variance of £45,000.

In the non-manufacturing sector, overheads form the dominant part of the cost of producing a service and so price and usage variance analysis has a limited role to play. However, organizations can use variance analysis in a number of ways to support their business strategy, most commonly by investigating the reasons for variations between budget and actual costs, even if those costs are independent of volume. These variations may identify poor budgeting practice, lack of cost control or variations in the usage or price of resources that may be outside a manager's control.

We have already described approaches to total quality management (TQM) and continuous improvement in Chapter 11 and the implications of these processes for cost management. It is important to recognize that reducing variances based on standard costs can be an overly restrictive approach in a TQM or continuous improvement environment. This is because there will be a tendency to aim at the more obvious cost reductions (cheaper labour and materials) rather than issues of quality, reliability, on-time delivery, flexibility etc. in purchased goods and services. It will also tend to emphasize following standard work instructions rather than encouraging employees to adopt an innovative approach to re-engineering processes.

Using a case study of the Portables division of Tektronix, Turney and Anderson (1989) found that accounting systems were obsolete, reporting information that was no longer used, but that the role of accounting changed 'from being a watchdog to being a change facilitator' (p. 41). They described how:

> the accounting function has failed to adapt to a new competitive environment that requires continuous improvement in the design, manufacturing, and marketing of a product. (p. 37)

The traditional focus for cost collection was labour, material and overhead for a work order, but shifted to the output of a production line based on standard costs. This moved improvement from individual worker performance to overall process effectiveness. Variance reports were replaced by a system of stopping production when a defect was found. Overhead was 'bloated' due to:

> the enormous complexity of the production process . . . long production runs tended to produce large inventories of the wrong product . . . [in which the] additional cost of unique components was not fully reflected in the standard cost of the product. (p. 44)

and

> the low-volume and tailored products consumed significantly more support services per unit than did the high-volume, mainline products. (p. 45)

Turney and Anderson described how Tektronix Portables introduced new measures of continuous improvement and a new method of overhead allocation that 'shifts product cost from products with high-volume common parts to those with low-volume unique parts' (p. 46) that 'has influenced product design decisions, encouraging a simpler product that is less costly and easier to manufacture' (p. 47).

Variance analysis is therefore a tool that can be used in certain circumstances, but is not one that should be used without consideration of the wider impact on improvement strategies being implemented by the business. Nevertheless, neither accountants nor non-financial managers should overlook the importance of cost control.

COST CONTROL

Cost control is a process of either reducing costs while maintaining the same levels of productivity, or maintaining costs while increasing levels of productivity through economies of scale or efficiencies in producing goods or services. For this reason cost control is more accurately considered as *cost improvement*. Cost improvement needs to be exercised by all budget holders in order to ensure that limited resources are effectively utilized and budgets are not over-spent. This is best achieved by understanding the causes of costs – the cost drivers.

For example, the cost of purchasing as an activity can be traced to the number of suppliers and the number of purchase orders that are required for different activities. The more suppliers and purchase orders (the drivers), the higher will be the cost of purchasing. Cost control over the administration of purchasing can be exercised by reducing the number of suppliers and/or reducing the number of purchase orders. This is an example of the application of activity-based costing, described in Chapter 13.

Cost control can also be exercised by undertaking a review of horizontal business processes, i.e. crossing organizational boundaries, rather than within the conventional hierarchical structure displayed on an organization chart. Such a review aims to find out what activities people are carrying out, why they are carrying out those activities, whether they need to be carried out at all, and whether there is a more efficient method of achieving the desired output. This is called business process re-engineering (BPR, see Chapter 12).

Understanding cost drivers and reviewing business processes can be used as tools to help in controlling costs such as:

■ projects: why are they being undertaken?
■ salaries and overtime: what tasks are people performing, and why and how are they performing those tasks?
■ travel: what causes people to travel to other locations and by what methods?
■ IT and telecommunication costs: what data is being processed and why?
■ stationery: what is being used and why?

The questions that can be asked in relation to most costs are: What is being done? Why is it being done? When is it being done?

Where is it being done? How is it being done? We have already mentioned both activity-based costing (ABC, Chapter 13) and activity-based budgeting (ABB, Chapter 16). Kaplan and Cooper (1998) defined activity-based management (ABM) as:

the entire set of actions that can be taken, on a better informed basis, with activity-based cost information. With ABM, the organization accomplishes its outcomes with fewer demands on organizational resources. (p. 137)

Kaplan and Cooper differentiated *operational* and *strategic* ABM. The former is concerned with doing things right: increasing efficiency, lowering costs and enhancing asset utilization. Strategic ABM is about doing the right things, by attempting to alter the demand for activities to increase profitability.

Strategic ABM can be used in relation to product mix and pricing decisions. It works by shifting the mix of activities from unprofitable applications to profitable ones. The demand for activities is a result of decisions about products, services and customers. Costing was the first application of activity-based management. It attempted to remove the distortions caused by traditional methods of overhead allocation based on direct labour. ABC assigned overhead costs to products/services based on the cost drivers of activities and the resources consumed by those activities for individual products.

Product-related actions can reduce the resources required to produce existing products/ services. Pricing and product substitution decisions can shift the mix from difficult-to-produce items to simple-to-produce ones. Redesign, process improvement, focused production facilities and new technology can enable the same products or services to be produced with fewer resources.

Strategic ABM extends the domain of analysis beyond production costs to marketing, selling and administrative expenses, reflecting the belief that the demand for resources arises not only from products/services but from customers, distribution and delivery channels. Cost information can be used to modify a firm's relationships with its customers, transforming unprofitable customers into profitable ones through negotiations on price, product mix, delivery and payment arrangements.

Similarly, strategic ABM can be pushed further back along the value chain (see Chapter 11) to suppliers, designers and developers. Managing supplier relationships can lower the costs of purchased materials. ABM can also inform product/service design and development decisions, which can result in a lowering of production costs for new products/services *before* they reach the production stage.

APPLYING DIFFERENT PERSPECTIVES TO MANAGEMENT ACCOUNTING: BUDGETS

In Chapters 4 and 5, we considered rational-economic, interpretive and critical perspectives that help to provide multiple views about the world in which we live. Chapters 14 through 17 have introduced many aspects of how management accounting techniques are used in planning, decision-making and control in relation to investments, business unit evaluation, budgeting and budgetary control.

Implicit in most of what is contained in these four chapters is an acceptance of the rational-economic paradigm described in Chapter 4. Profit-oriented businesses make investment decisions to maximize profits (Chapter 14), monitor the performance of different business segments (Chapter 15), budget for future profits (Chapter 16) and use variance analysis for control in order to take appropriate corrective action. These are rational-economic choices.

However, numbers often reinforce subjective decisions and accounting choices are not so straight forward. The interpretive perspective is useful here. For example, different views exist about the choice of investment evaluation method (accounting return, payback and discounted cash flow in Chapter 14), each of which gives different answers and can result in a different interpretation. There are divergent views about whether divisional performance should be assessed on return on investment or residual income criteria (Chapter 15) and again, different interpretations of performance are possible. Budgeting is itself an estimate of future activity (Chapter 16) and a wide range of different estimates are possible.

Equally, we have seen that the critical perspective can also apply. Power determines particular choices of approach. The discounted cash flow technique for example (Chapter 14) can be biased in practice by the use of cash flows that support the proposers view that an investment should be approved. Evaluation criteria can be altered by boards of directors to raise or lower hurdle rates. The choice of transfer pricing technique (Chapter 15) will depend on the relative power of buying and selling divisions within an organization and top-management influence over the selection of price.

The power of accounting departments over every segment of the business due to accountants' control of the budget process exists in every business. The adoption (or non-adoption) of variance analysis or particular cost control techniques (Chapter 17) also is a source of significant power (which may be in the hands of other departments as well as accounting).

CONCLUSION

In this chapter, we have described budgetary control through flexible budgets, variance analysis and cost control. There are, however, concerns about how well these techniques are able to contribute to organizational effectiveness in practice.

In his landmark study, Hopwood (1973) found that despite the sophistication of management accounting systems, they failed to contribute to achieving effective operations. Although managers:

> made extensive use of the accounting information, they did so in a rigid manner, either attributing too much validity to the information or being unaware of its intended purposes, with the result that again, despite the thought and consideration which went into the design and operation of the system, its final value was questionable. (p. 185)

Hopwood differentiated three styles of evaluation of budget information. The budget-constrained manager is evaluated based on the ability to meet the budget continually on a short-term basis. The profit-conscious manager is evaluated on the basis of the ability to increase the general effectiveness of operations to meet long-term objectives. In the non-accounting style, accounting information plays little part in the evaluation of a manager's performance.

A manager who adopts a budget-constrained style takes budget information at face value, has a short time horizon, considering each month's variances in isolation rather than the trend or the long-term implications. An unfavourable budget variance is an indicator of poor management performance, even though the standards used by the accounting system may be faulty.

By contrast, managers adopting a profit-conscious style realize that accounting information is not a constraint, and that variances are a meaningful guide to action, even though they may be misleading. The profit-conscious manager is more likely to experiment and innovate even though cost may exceed budget in the short term.

A survey by Armstrong *et al.* (1996) found that accounting controls were not as evident in business units and that 'whether or not to use any or all of the apparatus of management accounting is a managerial choice largely devoid of consequences' (p. 20).

Samuelson (1986) argued that 'senior management often articulate one role for the budget but budgetees then perceive that another very different role may be intended'

(p. 35). Samuelson contrasted the 'role articulated' by management for budgetary control (planning), which may be different to the 'real role' and the 'role intended' by managers (responsibility).

After you have read this chapter, you should:

■ Revise your understanding of the accounting terms. The Glossary in Part IV is a helpful aid.

■ Practice the Questions for this chapter and then check your answers against the solutions. Questions for each chapter are in Appendix 1. The solutions are in Appendix 2.

■ Read Case Study 8. This will help you to interpret accounting information. Try to write an answer. The Case Studies are in Appendix 3 and suggested solutions are in Appendix 4.

REFERENCES

Armstrong, P., Marginson, P., Edwards, P. and Purcell, J. (1996). Budgetary control and the labour force: Findings from a survey of large British companies. *Management Accounting Research*, **7**(1), 1–24.

Buckley, A. and McKenna, E. (1972). Budgetary control and business behaviour. *Accounting and Business Research*, 137–50.

Hopwood, A. G. (1973). *An Accounting System and Managerial Behaviour*. London: Saxon House.

Kaplan, R. S. and Cooper, R. (1998). *Cost and Effect: Using Integrated Cost Systems to Drive Profitability and Performance*. Boston, MA: Harvard Business School Press.

Samuelson, L. A. (1986). Discrepancies between the roles of budgeting. *Accounting, Organizations and Society*, **11**(1), 35–45.

Turney, P. B. B. and Anderson, B. (1989). Accounting for continuous improvement. *Sloan Management Review*, Winter, 37–47.

PART IV

SUPPORTING INFORMATION

In Part IV, Chapter 18 suggests an approach to research in accounting, provides some concluding comments and suggestions for further reading.

Four readings are included in Chapter 19 that cover the spectrum of the accounting academic literature and support the most important concepts in the book.

Each reading has a series of questions that the reader is encouraged to think about and discuss with others. This part also contains an extensive glossary of the accounting terms used in this book.

18

RESEARCH IN MANAGEMENT ACCOUNTING, CONCLUSIONS AND FURTHER READING

RESEARCH AND THEORY IN MANAGEMENT ACCOUNTING

Theory is an explanation of what is observed in practice. The development of theory from practice is the result of a process of research. Practice informs theory, which in turn, via various forms of publication and education, can influence the spread of practice between organizations and countries.

Otley (2001) argued that management accounting research 'has, in a number of respects, lost touch with management accounting practices' (p. 255), having concentrated too much on accounting and not enough on management. Otley reinforced earlier arguments that management accounting had become 'irrelevant to contemporary organizations, but worse that it was often actually counter-productive to good management decision-making' (p. 243) and that we need to 'put the management back into management accounting' (p. 259).

Hopper *et al.* (2001) argued that there have been few British scholars who have achieved innovation in practice, either because of 'the anti-intellectualism of British managers and accountants ... or the marginal role of academics in British policy making' (p. 285).

Both issues are important, because an understanding of accounting tools and techniques without an understanding of theory has the same problems as theories divorced from business practice. An understanding of the underlying assumptions of accounting and the limitations of the tools and techniques of accounting is essential. If we ignore those assumptions and limitations, we are likely to make decisions on the basis of numbers that do not adequately reflect any underlying business reality.

Theory has been integrated with practical examples in this book to reflect the importance of taking an interpretive and critical perspective on financial reports. Theory is not developed by academics in ivory towers divorced from practical business situations. It is developed from research, which typically takes one of two forms:

■ a quantitative study of a large number of business organizations that yields a large database that can be analysed statistically in order to produce generalizations about accounting practice;

■ a qualitative study of a single organization or a small number of organizations through case studies comprising interviews, observation and documentary research that aims to explain accounting practice in the context in which it is situated.

Both methods are valuable in helping to understand accounting practice. The reader is encouraged to look at some of the literature referred to in the chapters throughout this book in order to understand the context of accounting in organizations.

Hopper *et al.* (2001) traced the development of accounting research through four approaches:

■ conventional teaching emphasizing the needs of the professional accounting bodies;
■ the application of economics and management science;
■ history and public-sector accounting;
■ behavioural and organizational approaches.

The first approach is that traditionally taken by students of accounting. The second approach relies heavily on econometric and mathematical models, which are outside the scope of this book. This book has taken the view that managers who use accounting information do not need as thorough an understanding of how to prepare accounting information, but rather that they should take a more interpretive and critical perspective. This implies a concern with the behavioural and organizational approach, rooted in organizational history and the unique circumstance of each organization.

Power (1991) described his own experience of a professional accounting education and argued that 'the lived reality of accounting education shows that it does not serve the functional ends that are claimed for it' (p. 347). He described:

the institutionalization of a form of discourse in which critical and reflective practices are regarded as 'waffle' . . . of a cynicism and irony among students towards the entire examination process . . . and the public game that they are required to play. (p. 350)

Power (1991) concluded that this 'may be dysfunctional for the profession itself and for the goal of producing flexible and critical experts' (p. 351).

Research in management accounting tends to fall into two distinct categories:

■ The normative view – what ought to happen – that there is one best way of doing accounting, that accounting information is economically rational and serves an instrumental purpose in making decisions in the pursuit of shareholder value. The

normative view has been evident in this book through the presentation of accounting tools and techniques in each chapter.

■ The interpretive and critical view – what does happen – the explanation of how
accounting systems develop and are used in particular organizational settings.
This view recognizes that people do not necessarily make decisions based on
economically rational reasons but have limited information, limited cognitive
ability and are influenced by organizational structures and systems (including, but
not limited to, accounting systems) and by organizational power and culture. The
interpretive and critical view has been evident in the theories and case studies
presented in the book.

This second – interpretive and critical – view is descriptive or qualitative rather than
statistical or quantitative. This is a necessary approach to explain the practice of
accounting in both its organizational setting and the wider social context in which it
exists. This second view has tended to be developed through case study research.

For example, Kaplan (1986) argued for empirical studies of management accounting systems in their organizational contexts, by 'observing skilled practitioners in
actual organizations' (p. 441). Kaplan described empirical research methods, especially
case or field studies that communicate the 'deep, rich slices of organizational life'
(p. 445) and are 'the only mechanism by which management accounting can become
a scientific field of inquiry' (p. 448).

Spicer (1992) argued that case study research is appropriate when 'why?' or 'how?'
questions are asked about contemporary events. He classified two types of case study
research: descriptive and/or exploratory, and informing and/or explanatory, arguing
that:

> the case method, when used for explanatory purposes, relies on analytical not
> statistical generalization. The objective of explanatory case research is not to draw
> inferences to some larger population based on sample evidence, but rather to
> generalize back to theory. (p. 12)

Hopper et al. (2001) emphasized the rise of behavioural and organizational accounting
research from 1975. In the UK, a paradigm shift occurred that did not happen in the
US (where agency theory remains the dominant research approach), as contingency
theory and neo-human relations approaches were abandoned for more sociological
and political approaches that drew from European social theory and were influenced
by Scandinavian case-based research. Under Thatcherism:

> accounting data and the consulting arms of accounting firms had been central to
> economic and policy debates, involving privatization, industrial restructuring,
> reform of the public sector, and worries about de-industrialization ... it appeared
> apparent that accounting had to be studied in its broader social, political and
> institutional context. (Hopper et al., 2001, p. 276)

Humphrey and Scapens (1996) argued for the capacity of explanatory case studies 'to move away from managerialist notions of accounting and to provide more challenging reflections on the nature of accounting knowledge and practice' (p. 87) and to its 'intricacies, complexities and inconsistencies' (p. 90).

One problem that has arisen in academic research is the variety of theories used to explain practice, which Humphrey and Scapens (1996) believe excessively dominate the analysis of case study evidence. Similarly, Hopper *et al.* (2001) argued that 'the research thrust may lie in attempting to integrate and consolidate the variety of theories and methodologies which have emerged in recent years, rather than seeking to add yet more' (p. 283).

For example, case study researchers are:

becoming aware of the need to study accounting change from the perspective of global competition ... there is a need to re-incorporate economics into social theory, and case study based research. (p. 284)

This book has attempted to integrate both views, i.e. to understand the tools and techniques of accounting as though they were rational, while also introducing alternative ways of seeing accounting. It is hoped that it may also encourage readers to undertake research into accounting, either in an academic environment or in their own business organizations, in order to challenge conventional wisdom and better understand the context in which accounting is practised and the consequences of the use of accounting information for decision-making.

In their introduction to a special issue of *Management Accounting Research* devoted to management accounting change, Burns and Vaivio (2001) noted that many firms have experienced significant change in their organizational design (structures and processes), competitive environment and information technologies. There is a need for management accounting change, despite the relatively recent (in the last 20 years) introduction of activity-based costing and the Balanced Scorecard. Information technology in particular is driving the routine financial accounting functions into centralized head offices or is being outsourced. However, management accounting is increasingly decentralized to business units, where it becomes the responsibility of functional and business unit managers. These operating managers are more and more responsible for setting and achieving budget targets. As the role of non-accounting managers is being extended to encompass (management) accounting functions, the role of the professional accountant is also changing to a business consultant, advisory or change management role, often with responsibilities outside the traditional accounting one.

One of the reasons for this changed role for accountants is that they do understand the numbers, both financial and non-financial. The challenge for non-accounting managers is to understand the numbers sufficiently well to be able to contribute to the formulation and implementation of business strategy. Those who do not understand, or who do not want to understand, the numbers are likely to be increasingly marginalized in their organizations.

CONCLUSION: REVISITING THE RATIONALE

In the preface to this book, its rationale was described as being practitioner centric rather than accounting centric. In this, the subtitle of the book – *Interpreting accounting information for decision-making* – identifies its aim as not only to describe the tools and techniques used by accountants, but to help managers understand that these tools and techniques exist, to know when to apply them and to appreciate their underlying assumptions and limitations. It is more important for the non-accounting manager to be able to use accounting than to be able to do accounting. Hence, in the Appendices to this book a number of questions and case studies are provided to assist readers in testing themselves as to whether or not they understand the concepts and can draw the appropriate interpretations and critique. The concepts are also illustrated by four key readings from the accounting literature in the next chapter.

The aim of the book has been to present both the tools and techniques and the interpretive and critical perspective in an accessible language to the non-accountant. Every effort has been made to define terms clearly when they are first used and to cross-reference topics to the main chapters in which they are covered. A glossary in this part describes all the terms used in one place, while the comprehensive index should make it easy for readers to find the information they need.

REFERENCES

Burns, J. and Vaivio, J. (2001). Management accounting change. *Management Accounting Research*, **12**, 389–402.

Hopper, T., Otley, D. and Scapens, B. (2001). British management accounting research: Whence and whither: Opinions and recollections. *British Accounting Review*, **33**, 263–91.

Humphrey, C. and Scapens, R. W. (1996). Theories and case studies of organizational and accounting practices: Limitation or liberation? *Accounting, Auditing and Accountability Journal*, **9**(4), 86–106.

Kaplan, R. S. (1986). The role for empirical research in management accounting. *Accounting, Organizations and Society*, **11**(4/5), 429–52.

Otley, D. (2001). Extending the boundaries of management accounting research: Developing systems for performance management. *British Accounting Review*, **33**, 243–61.

Power, M. K. (1991). Educating accountants: Towards a critical ethnography. *Accounting, Organizations and Society*, **16**(4), 333–53.

Spicer, B. II. (1992). The resurgence of cost and management accounting: A review of some recent developments in practice, theories and case research methods. *Management Accounting Research*, **3**, 1–37.

FURTHER READING

One of the aims of this book has been to encourage readers to access the research-based academic literature of accounting, in particular in relation to the broader social, historical and contextual influences on accounting; the organizational and behavioural consequences of accounting information; and the assumptions and limitations underlying the tools and techniques used by accountants.

For those who wish to read further, whether as part of their preparation for academic research at postgraduate level or as part of their personal pursuit of greater knowledge, we identify some recommended additional reading.

Books

Alvesson, M. and Willmott, H. (eds) (1992). *Critical Management Studies.* London: Sage Publications.

Ashton, D., Hopper, T. and Scapens, R. W. (eds) (1995). *Issues in Management Accounting* (2nd edn). London: Prentice Hall.

Berry, A. J., Broadbent, J. and Otley, D. (eds) (2005). *Management Control: Theories, Issues and Performance.* 2nd edition. London: Palgrave Macmillan.

Chapman, C. S. (ed) (2005). *Controlling Strategy: Management, Accounting, and Performance Measurement.* Oxford: Oxford University Press.

Emmanuel, C., Otley, D. and Merchant, K. (eds) (1992). *Readings in Accounting for Management Control.* London: Chapman & Hall.

Emmanuel, C., Otley, D. and Merchant, K. (1990). *Accounting for Management Control.* (2nd edn). London: Chapman & Hall.

Gowthorpe, C. and Blake, J. (eds) (1998). *Ethical Issues in Accounting.* London: Routledge.

Hope, J. and Fraser, R. (2003). *Beyond Budgeting: How Managers Can Break Free from the Annual Performance Trap.* Boston, Mass.: Harvard Business School Press.

Hopwood, A. G. and Miller, P. (1994). *Accounting as Social and Institutional Practice.* Cambridge: Cambridge University Press.

Johnson, H. T. and Kaplan, R. S. (1987). *Relevance Lost: The Rise and Fall of Management Accounting.* Boston, MA: Harvard Business School Press.

Jones, T. C. (1995). *Accounting and the Enterprise: A Social Analysis.* London: Routledge.

Kaplan, R. S. and Cooper, R. (1998). *Cost and Effect: Using Integrated Cost Systems to Drive Profitability and Performance.* Boston, MA: Harvard Business School Press.

Kaplan, R. S. and Norton, D. P. (2001). *The Strategy-Focused Organization: How Balanced Scorecard Companies Thrive in the New Business Environment.* Boston, MA: Harvard Business School Press.

Macintosh, N. B. (1994). *Management Accounting and Control Systems: An Organizational and Behavioral Approach.* Chichester: John Wiley & Sons.

Munro, R. and Mouritsen, J. (eds) (1996). *Accountability: Power, Ethos and the Technologies of Managing.* London: Internation Thomson Business Press.

Puxty, A. G. (1993). *The Social and Organizational Context of Management Accounting.* London: Academic Press.

Ryan, B., Scapens, R. W. and Theobald, M. (1992). *Research Method and Methodology in Finance and Accounting.* London: Academic Press.

Scapens, R. W. (1991). *Management Accounting: A Review of Recent Developments.* (2nd edn). London: Macmillan.

Scott, W. R. (1998). *Organizations: Rational, Natural, and Open Systems.* (4th edn). Prentice Hall International, Inc.

Articles published in the following journals

■ *Accounting, Auditing and Accountability Journal*
■ *Accounting, Organizations and Society*
■ *British Accounting Review*

- *Critical Perspectives in Accounting*
- *Financial Accountability and Management* (public sector)
- *Journal of Management Accounting Research* (US)
- *Management Accounting Research* (UK)

These articles are generally available on-line for students through university libraries.

19 INTRODUCTION TO THE READINGS

A rationale for this book was to provide a theoretical underpinning to accounting, drawn from accounting research, to assist in interpretation and critical questioning. This underpinning provides a critical perspective on the most common accounting techniques and describes the social and organizational context in which accounting exists. This context influences accounting but is also influenced by accounting, as the way we see the world – even if only our small organizational part of the world – is significantly influenced by the ways in which accounting portrays and represents that world.

In this part of the book, we reproduce four readings from the academic literature to present four different yet complementary perspectives on accounting in organizations. Each reading has several questions that the reader should think about and try to answer in order to help understand the concepts.

The article by Cooper and Kaplan is a classic, explaining clearly how traditional management accounting techniques have distorted management information and the decisions made by managers. The authors criticize the distinction between variable and fixed costs, the limitations of marginal costing and the arbitrary methods by which overhead costs are allocated to products. The activity-based approach recommended by Cooper and Kaplan treats all costs as variable, although only some vary with volume.

Covaleski, Dirsmith and Samuel's paper describes the contribution of contingency theory, and interpretive perspectives using organizational and sociological theories (including institutional theory) and critical perspectives. The authors call for 'paradigmatic pluralism', not as competing perspectives but as 'alternative ways of understanding the multiple roles played by management accounting in organizations and society' (p. 24).

Otley, Berry and Broadbent's paper reviews the development of the management control literature in the context of organization theories and argues for the expansion of management control beyond accounting. The authors use a framework of open/closed systems and rational/natural systems to contrast each of these four perspectives and give examples of research in each. They conclude that management control research needs to recognize the environment in which organizations exist. While the definition of management control is 'managerialist in focus ... this should not preclude a critical stance and thus a broader choice of theoretical approaches' (p. S42).

Dent's case study of EuroRail is a highly regarded field study of accounting change in which organizations are portrayed as cultures, i.e. systems of knowledge, belief and values. Prior to the study, the dominant culture in EuroRail was engineering and production, but this culture was displaced by economic and accounting concerns that constructed the railway as a profit-seeking enterprise. Dent traced the introduction of a revised corporate planning system, the amendment of capital expenditure approval procedures and the revision of budgeting systems, each of which gave power to business managers. Dent describes how accounting played a role 'in constructing specific knowledges' (p. 727).

Taken together, these readings provide a practical critique of traditional costing methods, several theoretical perspectives from which accounting can be viewed and a field study of how accounting changed the reality in one organization.

READING A

Cooper, R. and Kaplan, R. S. (1988). How cost accounting distorts product costs. *Management Accounting* (April), 20–27. Reproduced by permission of Copyright Clearance Center, Inc.

Questions

1   What are the criticisms that Cooper and Kaplan make about variable costs and why do they claim that marginal costing has failed?
2   Cooper and Kaplan argue that fixed cost allocations are faulty and that the 'cost of complexity' requires a more comprehensive breakdown of costs. How do they propose that such a breakdown takes place?
3   How can the product cost system proposed by Cooper and Kaplan be strategically valuable to an organization that adopts it?

Further reading

Brignall, S. (1997). A contingent rationale for cost system design in services. *Management Accounting Research*, **8**, 325–46.

Kaplan, R. S. (1994). Management accounting (1984–1994): Development of new practice and theory. *Management Accounting Research*, **5**, 247–60.

Kaplan, R. S. and Cooper, R. (1998). *Cost and Effect: Using Integrated Cost Systems to Drive Profitability and Performance*. Boston, MA: Harvard Business School Press.

Mitchell, F. (1994). A commentary on the applications of activity-based costing. *Management Accounting Research*, **5**, 261–77.

Turney, P. B. B. and Anderson, B. (1989). Accounting for continuous improvement. *Sloan Management Review*, Winter, 37–47.

HOW COST ACCOUNTING DISTORTS PRODUCT COSTS

The traditional cost system that defines variable costs as varying in the short-term with production will misclassify these costs as fixed.

by Robin Cooper and Robert S. Kaplan

In order to make sensible decisions concerning the products they market, managers need to know what their products cost. Product design, new product introduction decisions, and the amount of effort expended on trying to market a given product or product line will be influenced by the anticipated cost and profitability of the product. Conversely, if product profitability appears to drop, the question of discontinuance will be raised. Product costs also can play an important role in setting prices, particularly for customized products with low sales volumes and without readily available market prices.

The cumulative effect of decisions on product design, introduction, support, discontinuance, and pricing helps define a firm's strategy. If the product cost information is distorted, the firm can follow an inappropriate and unprofitable strategy. For example, the low-cost producer often achieves competitive advantage by servicing a broad range of customers. This strategy will be successful if the economies of scale exceed the additional costs, the diseconomies of scope, caused by producing and servicing a more diverse product line. If the cost system does not correctly attribute the additional costs to the products that cause them, then the firm might end up competing in segments where the scope-related costs exceed the benefits from larger scale production.

Similarly, a differentiated producer achieves competitive advantage by meeting specialized customers' needs with products whose costs of differentiation are lower than the price premiums charged for special features and services. If the cost system fails to measure differentiation costs properly, then the firm might choose to compete in segments that are actually unprofitable.

FULL VS. VARIABLE COST

Despite the importance of cost information, disagreement still exists about whether product costs should be measured by full or by variable cost. In a full-cost system, fixed production costs are allocated to products so that reported product costs measure total manufacturing costs. In a variable cost system, the fixed costs are not allocated and product costs reflect only the marginal cost of manufacturing.

Academic accountants, supported by economists, have argued strongly that variable costs are the relevant ones for product decisions. They have demonstrated, using increasingly complex models, that setting marginal revenues equal to marginal costs will produce the highest profit. In contrast, accountants in practice continue to report full costs in their cost accounting systems.

The definition of variable cost used by academic accountants assumes that product decisions have a short-time horizon, typically a month or a quarter. Costs are variable only if they vary directly with monthly or quarterly changes in production volume. Such a definition is appropriate if the volume of production of all products can be changed at will and there is no way to change simultaneously the level of fixed costs.

In practice, managers reject this short-term perspective because the decision to offer a product creates a long-term commitment to manufacture, market, and support that product. Given this perspective, short-term variable cost is an inadequate measure of product cost.

While full cost is meant to be a surrogate for long-run manufacturing costs, in nearly all of the companies we visited, management was not convinced that their full-cost systems were adequate for its product-related decisions. In particular, management did not believe their systems accurately reflected the costs of resources consumed to manufacture products. But they were also unwilling to adopt a variable-cost approach.

Of the more than 20 firms we visited and documented, Mayers Tap, Rockford, and Schrader Bellows provided particularly useful insights on how product costs were systematically distorted.[1] These companies had several significant common characteristics.

They all produced a large number of distinct products in a single facility. The products formed several distinct product lines and were sold through diverse marketing channels. The range in demand volume for products within a product line was high, with sales of high-volume products between 100 and 1,000 times greater than sales of low-volume products. As a consequence, products were manufactured and shipped in highly varied lot sizes. While our findings are based upon these three companies, the same effects were observed at several other sites.

In all three companies, product costs played an important role in the decisions that surrounded the introduction, pricing, and discontinuance of products. Reported product costs also appeared to play a significant role in determining how much effort should be assigned to marketing and selling products.

Typically, the individual responsible for introducing new products also was responsible for setting prices. Cost-plus pricing to achieve a desired level of gross margin predominantly was used for the special products, though substantial modifications to the resulting estimated prices occurred when direct competition existed. Such competition was common for high-volume products but rarely occurred for the low-volume items. Frequently, no obvious market prices existed for low-volume products because they had been designed to meet a particular customer's needs.

ACCURACY OF PRODUCT COSTS

Managers in all three firms expressed serious concerns about the accuracy of their product-costing systems.

For example, Rockford attempted to obtain much higher margins for its low-volume products to compensate, on an ad hoc basis, for the gross underestimates of costs that it believed the cost system produced for these products. But management was not able to justify its decisions on cutoff points to identify low-volume products or the magnitude of the ad hoc margin increases. Further, Rockford's management believed that its faulty cost system explained the ability of small firms to compete effectively against it for high-volume business. These small firms, with no apparent economic or technological advantage, were winning high-volume business with prices that were at or below Rockford's reported costs. And the small firms seemed to be prospering at these prices.

At Schrader Bellows, production managers believed that certain products were not earning their keep because they were so difficult to produce. But the cost system reported that these products were among the most profitable in the line. The managers also were convinced that they could make certain products as efficiently as anybody else. Yet competitors were consistently pricing comparable products considerably lower. Management suspected that the cost system contributed to this problem.

At Mayers Tap, the financial accounting profits were always much lower than those predicted by the cost system, but no one could explain the discrepancy. Also, the senior managers were concerned by their failure to predict which bids they would win or lose. Mayers Tap often won bids that had been overpriced because it did not really want the business, and lost bids it had deliberately underpriced in order to get the business.

TWO-STAGE COST ALLOCATION SYSTEM

The cost systems of all companies we visited had many common characteristics. Most important was the use of a two-stage cost allocation system: in the first stage, costs were assigned to cost pools (often called cost centers), and in the second stage, costs were allocated from the cost pools to the products.

The companies used many different allocation bases in the first stage to allocate costs from plant overhead accounts to cost centers. Despite the variation in allocation bases in the first stage, however, all companies used direct labor hours in the second stage to allocate overhead from the cost pools to the products. Direct labor hours was used in the second allocation stage even when the production process was highly automated so that burden rates exceeded 1,000%. Figure 19.1 illustrates a typical two-stage allocation process.

Of the three companies we examined in detail, only one had a cost accounting system capable of reporting variable product costs. Variable cost was identified at the budgeting stage in one other site, but this information was not subsequently used for product costing. The inability of the cost system to report variable cost was a common feature of many of the systems we observed. Reporting variable product costs was the exception, not the rule.

Firms used only one cost system even though costs were collected and allocated for several purposes, including product costing, operational control, and inventory

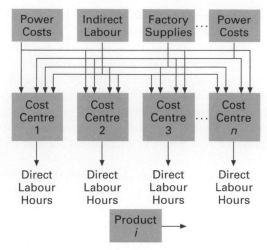

Figure 19.1 The two-stage progress

valuation. The cost systems seemed to be designed primarily to perform the inventory valuation function for financial reporting because they had serious deficiencies for operational control (too delayed and too aggregate) and for product costing (too aggregate).

THE FAILURE OF MARGINAL COSTING

The extensive use of fixed-cost allocations in all the companies we investigated contrasts sharply with a 65-year history of academics advocating marginal costing for product decisions. If the marginal-cost concept had been adopted by companies' management, then we would have expected to see product-costing systems that explicitly reported variable-cost information. Instead, we observed cost systems that reported variable as well as full costs in only a small minority of companies.

The traditional academic recommendation for marginal costing may have made sense when variable costs (labor, material, and some overhead) were a relatively high proportion of total manufactured cost and when product diversity was sufficiently small that there was not wide variation in the demands made by different products on the firm's production and marketing resources. But these conditions are no longer typical of many of today's organizations. Increasingly, overhead (most of it considered 'fixed') is becoming a larger share of total manufacturing costs. In addition, the plants we examined are being asked to produce an increasing variety of products that make quite different demands on equipment and support departments. Thus, even if direct or marginal costing were once a useful recommendation to management, direct costing, even if correctly implemented, is not likely a solution – and may perhaps be a major problem – for product costing in the contemporary manufacturing environment.

THE FAILURE OF FIXED-COST ALLOCATIONS

While we consistently observed managers avoiding the use of variable or marginal costs for their product-related decisions, we observed also their discomfort with the full-cost allocations produced by their existing cost systems. We believe that we have identified the two major sources for the discomfort.

The first problem arises from the use of direct labor hours in the second allocation stage to assign costs from cost centers to products. This procedure may have been adequate many decades ago when direct labor was the principal value-adding activity in the material conversion process. But as firms introduce more automated machinery, direct labor is increasingly engaged in setup and supervisory functions (rather than actually performing the work on the product) and no longer represents a reasonable surrogate for resource demands by product.

In many of the plants we visited, labor's main tasks are to load the machines and to act as troubleshooters. Labor frequently works on several different products at the same time so that it becomes impossible to assign labor hours intelligently to products. Some of the companies we visited had responded to this situation by beginning experiments using machine hours instead of labor hours to allocate costs from cost pools to products (for the second stage of the allocation process). Other companies, particularly those adopting just-in-time or continuous-flow production processes, were moving to material dollars as the basis for distributing costs from pools to products. Material dollars provide a less expensive method for cost allocation than machine hours because, as with labor hours, material dollars are collected by the existing cost system, A move to a machine-hour basis would require the collection of new data for many of these companies.

Shifting from labor hours to machine hours or material dollars provides some relief from the problem of using unrealistic bases for attributing costs to products. In fact, some companies have been experimenting with using all three allocation bases simultaneously: labor hours for those costs that vary with the number of labor hours worked (e.g., supervision – if the amount of labor in a product is high, the amount of supervision related to that product also is likely to be high), machine hours for those costs that vary with the number of hours the machine is running (e.g., power – the longer the machine is running the more power that is consumed by that product), and material dollars for those costs that vary with the value of material in the product (e.g., material handling – the higher the value of the material in the product, the greater the material-handling costs associated with those products are likely to be).

Using multiple allocation bases allows a finer attribution of costs to the products responsible for the incurrence of those costs. In particular, it allows for product diversity where the direct labor, machine hours, and material dollars consumed in the manufacture of different products are not directly proportional to each other.

For reported product costs to be correct, however, the allocation bases used must be capable of accounting for all aspects of product diversity. Such an accounting is not always possible even using all three volume-related allocation bases we described. As the number of product items manufactured increases, so does the number of direct labor hours, machine hours, and material dollars consumed. The designer of the cost system, in adopting these bases, assumes that all allocated costs have the same behavior; namely that they increase in direct relationship to the volume of product items manufactured. But there are many costs that vary with the diversity and complexity of products, not by the number of units produced.

THE COST OF COMPLEXITY

The complexity costs of a full-line producer can be illustrated as follows. Consider two identical plants. One plant produces 1,000,000 units of product A. The second plant produces 100,000 units of product A and 900,000 units of 199 similar products. (The similar products have sales volumes that vary from 100 to 100,000 units.)

The first plant has a simple production environment and requires limited manufacturing-support facilities. Few setups, expediting, and scheduling activities are required.

The other plant presents a much more complex production-management environment. Its 200 products have to be scheduled through the plant, requiring frequent setups, inventory movements, purchases, receipts, and inspections. To handle this complexity, the support departments must be larger and more sophisticated.

The traditional cost accounting system plays an important role in obfuscating the underlying relationship between the range of products produced and the size of the support departments. First, the costs of most support departments are classified as fixed, making it difficult to realize that these costs are systematically varying. Second, the use of volume-related allocation bases makes it difficult to recognize how these support-department costs vary.

Support-department costs must vary with something because they have been among the fastest growing in the overall cost structure of manufactured products. As the example demonstrates, support-department costs vary not with the volume of product items manufactured, rather they vary with the range of items produced (i.e., the complexity of the production process). The traditional definition of variable cost, with its monthly or quarterly perspective, views such costs as fixed because complexity-related costs do not vary significantly in such a short time frame. Across an extended period of time, however, the increasing complexity of the production process places additional demands on support departments, and their costs eventually and inevitably rise.

The output of a support department consists of the activities its personnel perform. These include such activities as setups, inspections, material handling, and scheduling. The output of the departments can be represented by the number of distinct activities that are performed or the number of transactions handled. Because most of the output of these departments consists of human activities, however, output can increase quite significantly before an immediate deterioration in the quality of service is detected. Eventually, the maximum output of the department is reached and additional personnel are requested. The request typically comes some time after the initial increase in diversity and output. Thus, support departments, while varying with the diversity of the demanded output, grow intermittently. The practice of annually budgeting the size of the departments further hides the underlying relationship between the mix and volume of demand and the size of the department. The support departments often are constrained to grow only when budgeted to do so.

Support-department costs are perhaps best described as 'discretionary' because they are budgeted and authorized each year. The questions we must address are: What determines the level of these discretionary fixed costs? Why, if these costs are not affected by the quantity of production, are there eight people in a support department and not one? What generates the work, if not physical quantities of inputs or outputs, that requires large support-department staffs? We believe the answers to these questions on the origins of discretionary overhead costs (i.e., what drives these costs) can be found by analyzing the activities or transactions demanded when producing a full and diverse line of products.

TRANSACTION COSTING

Low-volume products create more transactions per unit manufactured than their high-volume counterparts. The per unit share of these costs should, therefore, be higher for the low-volume products. But when volume-related bases are used exclusively to allocate support-department costs, high-volume and low-volume products receive similar transaction-related costs. When only volume-related bases are used for second-stage allocations, high-volume products receive an excessively high fraction of support-department costs and, therefore, subsidize the low-volume products.

As the range between low-volume and high-volume products increases, the degree of cross-subsidization rises. Support departments expand to cope with the additional complexity of more products, leading to increased overhead charges. The reported product cost of all products consequently increases. The high-volume products appear more expensive to produce than previously, even though they are not responsible for the additional costs. The costs triggered by the introduction of new, low-volume products are systematically shifted to high-volume products that may be placing relatively few demands on the plant's support departments.

Many of the transactions that generate work for production-support departments can be proxied by the number of setups. For example, the movement of material in the plant often occurs at the commencement or completion of a production run. Similarly, the majority of the time spent on parts inspection occurs just after a setup or change-over. Thus, while the support departments are engaged in a broad array of activities, a considerable portion of their costs may be attributed to the number of setups.

Not all of the support-department costs are related (or relatable) to the number of setups. The cost of setup personnel relates more to the quantity of setup hours than to the actual number of setups. The number of inspections of incoming material can be directly related to the number of material receipts, as would be the time spent moving the received material into inventory. The number of outgoing shipments can be used to predict the activity level of the finished-goods and shipping departments. The assignment of all these support costs with a transactions-based approach reinforces the effect of the setup-related costs because the low-sales-volume items tend to trigger more small incoming and outgoing shipments.

Table 19.1   Comparison of reported product costs at Schrader Bellows

Product	Sales volume	Existing cost system		Transaction-based system		Percent of change	
		Unit cost[a]	Unit gross margin	Unit cost[a]	Unit gross margin	Unit cost	Unit gross margin
1	43,562	7.85	5.52	7.17	6.19	(8.7)	12.3
2	500	8.74	3.76	15.45	(2.95)	76.8	(178.5)
3	53	12.15	10.89	82.49	(59.45)	578.9	(645.9)
4	2,079	13.63	4.91	24.51	(5.97)	79.8	(221.6)
5	5,670	12.40	7.95	19.99	0.36	61.3	(93.4)
6	11,169	8.04	5.49	7.96	5.57	(1.0)	1.5
7	423	8.47	3.74	6.93	5.28	(18.2)	41.2

[a] The sum of total cost (sales volume × unit cost) for all seven products is different under the two systems because the seven products only represent a small fraction of total production.

Schrader Bellows had recently performed a 'strategic cost analysis' that significantly increased the number of bases used to allocate costs to the products; many second-stage allocations used transactions costs to assign support-department costs to products. In particular, the number of setups allocated a sizable percentage of support-department costs to products.

The effect of changing these second-stage allocations from a direct labor to a transaction basis was dramatic. While the support-department costs accounted for about 50% of overhead (or about 25% of total costs), the change in the reported product costs ranged from about minus 10% to plus 1,000%. The significant change in the reported product costs for the low-volume items was due to the substantial cost of the support departments and the low batch size over which the transaction cost was spread.

Table 19.1 shows the magnitude of the shift in reported product costs for seven representative products. The existing cost system reported gross margins that varied from 26% to 47%, while the strategic analysis showed gross margins that ranged from −258% to +46%. The trends in the two sets of reported product profitabilities were clear: the existing direct-labor-based system had identified the low-volume products as the most profitable, while the strategic cost analysis indicated exactly the reverse.

There are three important messages in the table and in the company's findings in general.

■ Traditional systems that assign costs to products using a single volume-related base seriously distort product costs.
■ The distortion is systematic. Low-volume products are under-costed, and high-volume products are over-costed.
■ Accurate product costs cannot, in general, be achieved by cost systems that rely only on volume-related bases (even multiple bases such as machine hours and material quantities) for second-stage allocations. A different type of allocation base must be used for overhead costs that vary with the number of transactions performed, as opposed to the volume of product produced.

The shift to transaction-related allocation bases is a more fundamental change to the philosophy of cost-systems design than is at first realized. In a traditional cost system that uses volume-related bases, the costing element is always the product. It is the product that consumes direct labor hours, machine hours, or material dollars. Therefore, it is the product that gets costed.

In a transaction-related system, costs are assigned to the units that caused the transaction to be originated. For example, if the transaction is a setup, then the costing element will be the production lot because each production lot requires a single setup. The same is true for purchasing activities, inspections, scheduling, and material movements. The costing element is no longer the product but those elements the transaction affects.

In the transaction-related costing system, the unit cost of a product is determined by dividing the cost of a transaction by the number of units in the costing element. For example, when the costing element is a production lot, the unit cost of a product is determined by dividing the production lot cost by the number of units in the production lot.

This change in the costing element is not trivial. In the Schrader Bellows strategic cost analysis (see table 1), product seven appears to violate the strong inverse relationship between profits and production-lot size for the other six products. A more detailed analysis of the seven products, however, showed that product seven was assembled with components also used to produce two high-volume products (numbers one and six) and that it was the production-lot size of the components that was the dominant cost driver, not the assembly-lot size, or the shipping-lot size.

In a traditional cost system, the value of commonality of parts is hidden. Low-volume components appear to cost only slightly more than their high-volume counterparts. There is no incentive to design products with common parts. The shift to transaction-related costing identifies the much lower costs that derive from designing products with common (or fewer) parts and the much higher costs generated when large numbers of unique parts are specified for low-volume products. In recognition of this phenomenon, more companies are experimenting with assigning material-related overhead on the basis of the total number of different parts used, and not on the physical or dollar volume of materials used.

LONG-TERM VARIABLE COST

The volume-unrelated support-department costs, unlike traditional variable costs, do not vary with short-term changes in activity levels. Traditional variable costs vary in the short run with production fluctuations because they represent cost elements that require no managerial actions to change the level of expenditure.

In contrast, any amount of decrease in overhead costs associated with reducing diversity and complexity in the factory will take many months to realize and will require specific managerial actions. The number of personnel in support departments will have to be reduced, machines may have to be sold off, and some supervisors will become redundant. Actions to accomplish these overhead cost reductions will lag, by months, the complexity-reducing actions in the product line and in the process technology. But this long-term cost response mirrors the way overhead costs were first built up in the factory – as more products with specialized designs were added to the product line, the organization simply muddled through with existing personnel. It was only over time that overworked support departments requested and received additional personnel to handle the increased number of transactions that had been thrust upon them.

The personnel in the support departments are often highly skilled and possess a high degree of firm-specific knowledge. Management is loathe to lay them off when changes in market conditions temporarily reduce the level of production complexity. Consequently, when the workload of these departments drops, surplus capacity exists.

The long-term perspective management had adopted toward its products often made it difficult to use the surplus capacity. When it was used, it was not to make products never to be produced again, but rather to produce inventory of products that were known to disrupt production (typically the very low-volume items) or to produce, under short-term contract, products for other companies. We did not observe or hear about a situation in which this capacity was used to introduce a product that had only a short life expectancy. Some companies justified the acceptance of special orders or incremental business because they 'knew' that the income from this business more than covered their variable or incremental costs. They failed to realize that the long-term consequence from accepting such incremental business was a steady rise in the costs of their support departments.

WHEN PRODUCT COSTS ARE NOT KNOWN

The magnitude of the errors in reported product costs and the nature of their bias make it difficult for full-line producers to enact sensible strategies. The existing cost systems clearly identify the low-volume products as the most profitable and the high-volume ones as the least profitable. Focused competitors, on the other hand, will not suffer from the same handicap. Their cost systems, while equally poorly designed, will report more accurate product costs because they are not distorted as much by lot-size diversity.

With access to more accurate product cost data, a focused competitor can sell the high-volume products at a lower price. The full-line producer is then apparently faced with very low margins on these products and is naturally tempted to deemphasize this business and concentrate on apparently higher-profit, low-volume specialty business. This shift from high-volume to low-volume products, however, does not produce the anticipated higher profitability. The firm, believing in its cost system, chases illusory profits.

The firm has been victimized by diseconomies of scope. In trying to obtain the benefits of economy of scale by expanding its product offerings to better utilize its fixed or capacity resources, the firm does not see the high diseconomies it has introduced by creating a far more complex production environment. The cost accounting system fails to reveal this diseconomy of scope.

A COMPREHENSIVE COST SYSTEM

One message comes through overwhelmingly in our experiences with the three firms, and with the many others we talked and worked with. Almost all product-related decisions – introduction, pricing, and discontinuance – are long-term. Management accounting thinking (and teaching) during the past half-century has concentrated on information for making short-run incremental decisions based on variable, incremental, or relevant costs. It has missed the most important aspect of product decisions. Invariably, the time period for measuring 'variable,' 'incremental,' or 'relevant' costs has been about a month (the time period corresponding to the cycle of the firm's internal financial reporting system). While academics admonish that notions of fixed and variable are meaningful only with respect to a particular time period, they immediately discard this warning and teach from the perspective of one-month decision horizons.

This short-term focus for product costing has led all the companies we visited to view a large and growing proportion of their total manufacturing costs as 'fixed.' In fact, however, what they call 'fixed' costs have been the most variable and rapidly increasing costs. This paradox has seemingly eluded most accounting practitioners and scholars. Two fundamental changes in our thinking about cost behavior must be introduced.

First, the allocation of costs from the cost pools to the products should be achieved using bases that reflect cost drivers. Because many overhead costs are driven by the complexity of production, not the volume of production, nonvolume-related bases are required. Second, many of these overhead costs are somewhat discretionary. While they vary with changes in the complexity of the production process, these changes are intermittent. A traditional cost system that defines variable costs as varying in the short term with production volume will misclassify these costs as fixed.

The misclassification also arises from an inadequate understanding of the actual cost drivers for most overhead costs. Many overhead costs vary with transactions: transactions to order, schedule, receive, inspect, and pay for shipments; to move, track, and count inventory; to schedule production work; to set up machines; to perform quality assurance; to implement engineering change orders; and to expedite and ship orders. The cost of these transactions is largely independent of the size of the order being handled; the cost does not vary with the amount of inputs or outputs. It does vary, however, with the need for the transaction itself. If the firm introduces more products, if it needs to expedite more orders, or if it needs to inspect more components, then it will need larger overhead departments to perform these additional transactions.

SUMMARY

Product costs are almost all variable costs. Some of the sources of variability relate to physical volume of items produced. These costs will vary with units produced, or in a varied, multiproduct environment, with surrogate measures such as labor hours, machine hours, material dollars and quantities, or elapsed time of production. Other costs, however, particularly those arising from overhead support and marketing departments, vary with the diversity and complexity in the product line. The variability of these costs is best explained by the incidence of transactions to initiate the next stage in the production, logistics, or distribution process.

A comprehensive product cost system, incorporating the long-term variable costs of manufacturing and marketing each product or product line, should provide a much better basis for managerial decisions on pricing, introducing, discontinuing, and reengineering product lines. The cost system may even become strategically important for running the business and creating sustainable competitive advantages for the firm.

THE IMPORTANCE OF FIELD RESEARCH

The accompanying article, coauthored with Robin Cooper, is excerpted from *Accounting & Management: Field Study Perspectives* (Boston, Mass., Harvard Business School Press, 1987) William J. Bruns, Jr. and Robert S. Kaplan (eds.). The book contains 13 field studies on management accounting innovations presented at a colloquium at the Harvard Business School in June 1986 by leading academic researchers from the U.S. and Western Europe. The colloquium represents the largest single collection of field research studies on management accounting practices in organizations.

The HBS colloquium had two principal objectives. First, the authors were to understand and document the management accounting practices of actual organizations. Some of the organizations would be captured in a process of transition: attempting, and occasionally succeeding to modify their systems to measure, motivate and evaluate operating performance. Other organizations were studied just to understand the system of measurement and control that had evolved in their particular environment.

A second, and even more important, objective of the colloquium was to begin the process by which field research methods in management accounting could be established as a legitimate method of inquiry. Academic researchers in accounting have extensive experience with deductive, model-building, analytic research with the design and analysis of controlled experiments, usually in a laboratory setting; and with the empirical analysis of large data bases. This experience has yielded research guidance and criteria that, while not always explicit, nevertheless are widely shared and permit research to be conducted and evaluated.

At a time when so many organizations are reexamining the adequacy of their management accounting systems it is especially important that university-based researchers spend more time working directly with innovating organizations. We are pleased that MANAGEMENT ACCOUNTING, through publication of this article, is helping to publicize the existence of the field studies performed to date.

The experiences described in the accompanying article, as well as in the other papers in the colloquium volume, indicate a very different role for management accounting systems in organizations than is currently taught in most of our business schools and accounting departments. We believe that present and future field research and case writing will lead to major changes in management accounting courses. To facilitate the needed changes in curriculum and research, however, requires extensive cooperation between university faculty and practicing management accountants. As noted by observers at the Harvard colloquium:

> There is a tremendous store of knowledge about management accounting practices and ideas out there in real companies. Academicians as a whole are far too ignorant of that knowledge. When academics begin to see the relevance of this data base, perhaps generations of students will become more aware of its richness. Such awareness must precede any real progress on prescribing good management accounting for any given situation.
>
> To observe is also to discover. The authors have observed interesting phenomena. We do not know how prevalent these phenomena are or under what conditions they exist or do not exist. But the studies suggest possible relationships, causes, effects, and even dynamic process in the sense that Yogi Berra must have had in mind when he said, 'Sometimes you can observe a lot just by watching.'

With the research support and cooperation of the members of the National Association of Accountants, many university professors are looking forward to watching and also describing the changes now under way so that academics can begin to develop theories, teach, and finally prescribe about the new opportunities for management accounting.

Robert S. Kaplan

ENDNOTES

1   Mayers Tap (disguised name) is described in Harvard Business School, case series 9-185-111. Schrader-Bellows is described in HBS Case Series 9-186-272.

Robin Cooper is an associate professor of business administration at the Harvard Business School and a fellow of the Institute of Chartered Accountants in England and Wales. He writes a column, 'Cost Management Principles and Concepts,' in the Journal of Cost Management *and has produced research on activity-based costing for the CAM-1 Cost Management System Project. Robert S. Kaplan is the Arthur Lowes Dickinson Professor of Accounting at the Harvard Business School and a professor of industrial administration at Carnegie-Mellon University. Currently, Professor Kaplan serves on the Executive Committee of the CAM-1 Cost Management System Project, the Manufacturing Studies Board of the National Research Council, and the Financial Accounting Standards Advisory Committee.*

READING B

Otley, D. T., Broadbent, J. and Berry, A. J. (1995). Research in management control: An overview of its development. *British Journal of Management*, **6**, Special Issue, S31–S44.

Questions

1 What is the distinction made by Otley *et al.* between management control and financial control?
2 What is the contribution of systems theory to an understanding of management control?
3 How does Scott's distinction between open and closed, rational and natural models help to categorize the accounting literature, and why is any such categorization important?
4 Why does an emphasis on accounting limit an understanding of the broader importance of management control?
5 What contribution can non-financial performance management make to our understanding of management control within organizations?

Further reading

Berry, A. J., Broadbent, J. and Otley, D. (eds). (1995). *Management Control: Theories, Issues and Practices*. London: Macmillan.

Fitzgerald, L., Johnston, R., Brignall, S., Silvestro, R. and Voss, C. (1991). *Performance Measurement in Service Businesses*. London: Chartered Institute of Management Accountants.

Hopper, T., Otley, D. and Scapens, B. (2001). British management accounting research: Whence and whither: Opinions and recollections. *British Accounting Review*, **33**, 263–91.

Humphrey, C. and Scapens, R. W. (1996). Theories and case studies of organizational and accounting practices: Limitation or liberation? *Accounting, Auditing and Accountability Journal*, **9**(4), 86–106.

Kaplan, R. S. and Norton, D. P. (2001). *The Strategy-Focused Organization: How Balanced Scorecard Companies Thrive in the New Business Environment*. Boston, MA: Harvard Business School Press.

Macintosh, N. B. (1994). *Management Accounting and Control Systems: An Organizational and Behavioral Approach*. Chichester: John Wiley & Sons.

Otley, D. (1999). Performance management: A framework for management control systems research. *Management Accounting Research*, **10**, 363–82.

Otley, D. (2001). Extending the boundaries of management accounting research: Developing systems for performance management. *British Accounting Review*, **33**, 243–61.

Scott, W. R. (1998). *Organizations: Rational, Natural, and Open Systems*. (4th edn). Upper Saddle River, NJ: Prentice Hall International, Inc.

RESEARCH IN MANAGEMENT CONTROL: AN OVERVIEW OF ITS DEVELOPMENT

David Otley*, Jane Broadbent† and Anthony Berry‡

*Lancaster University Management School, †Department of Accounting and Financial Management, University of Essex, ‡Manchester Business School

SUMMARY

This paper builds on a series of earlier reviews of the management control literature (Giglioni and Bedeian, 1974; Hofstede, 1968; Merchant and Simons, 1986; Parker, 1986) and considers the development of the management control literature in the context of organizational theories. Early themes which have provided the roots for the development of the subject area are explored as is more recent work which has evolved both as a continuation and a reaction against them, with Scott's (1981) framework being used to organize this literature. It is argued that one of the unintended consequences of the influential work of Robert Anthony (1965) has been a restriction of the subject to an accounting-based framework and that this focus needs to be broadened. The review points to the potential of the subject as a integrating theme for the practice and research of management and some themes for future research are suggested.

INTRODUCTION

This paper reviews the development of research in management control, building upon other reviews both to examine the roots of the subject from the turn of the century and to demonstrate the depth and breadth of the subject. Four previous reviews form the foundation for our overview.

Giglioni and Bedeian (1974) review the contribution of the general management and organizational theory literature for the period 1900–1972, drawing out several different strands to conclude that

'even though control theory has not achieved the level of sophistication of some other management functions, it has developed to a point that affords the executive ample opportunity to maintain the operations of his firm under check.'

Parker (1986) argues that accounting control developments lagged developments in the management literature, and criticizes accounting models for offering only an imperfect reflection of management models of control. Hofstede (1968) offers an early survey of the behavioural approach to budgetary control. He explores how the role of budgets has been viewed in accounting theory, in motivation theory, and from the perspective of systems theory. Finally, the brief overview of research into control in complex organizations by Merchant and Simons (1986) takes a broad view of what constitutes control, as does the present paper. It differs, however, in also paying attention to agency theory literature and psychologist research both omitted from consideration here.[1]

It will be argued that one of the unintended consequences of Anthony's (1965) seminal work is that management control has primarily been developed in an accounting-based framework which has been unnecessarily restrictive. Although radical theorists have studied control processes more extensively, their attention has been focused much more on the exercise of power and its consequences than on the role of control systems as a means of organizational survival. This is an important area, but one which is outside the remit set for this review which is in closer alignment with Mills (1970) who argued for the place of management control as a central management discipline. He suggested that it was a more appropriate integrating discipline for general management courses than the tradition of using business policy or corporate strategy courses. 'Control' is itself a highly ambiguous term as evidenced by the difficulty of translating it into many European languages and the list of '57 varieties' in its connotations given by Rathe (1960). Given this diversity some attention will be paid to matters of definition and the establishment of appropriate boundaries for this review.

Anthony's (1965) classic definition of management control was

'the process by which managers assure that resources are obtained and used effectively and efficiently in the accomplishment of the organization's objectives.'

He saw management control as being sandwiched between the processes of strategic planning and operational control; these processes being super-imposed upon an organizational hierarchy to indicate the respective managerial levels at which they operate.

Strategic planning is concerned with setting goals and objectives for the whole organization over the long term. By contrast, operational control is concerned with the activity of ensuring that immediate tasks are carried out. Management control is the process that links the two. Global goals are broken down into sub-goals for parts of the organization; statements of future intent are given more substantive content; long-term goals are solidified into shorter term goals. The process of management control is designed to ensure that the day-to-day tasks performed by all participants in the organization come together in a coordinated set of actions which lead to overall goal specification and attainment. This can be seen primarily as the planning and

---

[1] The authors recognize that this provides a narrow focus for the review, but space restraints preclude the possibility of providing a more comprehensive survey. Our choice has been, therefore, to restrict the survey to one which focuses on the literature which sees management control as a practical activity of managers. See pages S32–S33 for a discussion of the boundaries of our survey.

coordination function of management control. The other side of the management control coin is its monitoring and feedback function. Regular observations and reports on actual achievement are used to ensure that planned actions are indeed achieving desired results.

It may be argued that Anthony's approach is too restrictive in that it assumes away important problems (*see* Lowe and Puxty, 1989 for further discussion of these issues). The first problem is concerned with problems of defining strategies, goals and objectives. Such procedures are typically complex and ill-defined, with strategies being produced as much by accident as by design. It is clear that Anthony was aware of the problems of ambiguity and uncertainty when he located these issues in the domain of strategy, but he then avoided their further consideration. The second problem concerns the methods used to control the production (or service delivery) processes, which are highly dependent upon the specific technology in use and which are widely divergent. Anthony conveniently relegates these issues to the realm of operational control. Finally, his textbooks concentrate upon planning and control through accounting rationales and contain little or no discussion of social-psychological or behavioural issues, despite his highlighting the importance of the latter. Anthony's approach can, thus, be seen as a preliminary ground-clearing exercise, whereby he limits the extent of the problem he sets out to study. In a complex field this was probably a very sensible first step, however, it greatly narrowed the scope of the topic.

A broader view of management control is suggested by Lowe (1971) in a more comprehensive definition:

'A system of organizational information seeking and gathering, accountability and feedback designed to ensure that the enterprise adapts to changes in its substantive environment and that the work behaviour of its employees is measured by reference to a set of operational sub-goals (which conform with overall objectives) so that the discrepancy between the two can be reconciled and corrected for.'

This stresses the role of a management control system (MCS) as a broad set of control mechanisms designed to assist organizations to regulate themselves, whereas Anthony's definition is more specific and limited to a narrower sub-set of control activities. Machin (1983) continues this line of thought in his critical review of management control systems as a specialist subject of academic study. He explores each of the terms 'management', 'control' and 'system', defining a research focus:

'Those formal, systematically developed, organization-wide, data-handling systems which are designed to facilitate management control which "is the process by which managers assure that resources are obtained and used effectively and efficiently in the accomplishment of the organization's objectives."'

Machin notes that such a definition has the merit of leaving scope for academics to disagree violently whilst still perceiving themselves to be studying the same thing! Further, Machin argues that research in MCSs, led, as it was, by qualified accountants, made the research questions

'virtually immune from philosophical analysis',

a critique also reflected in Hofstede's (1978) criticism of the

'poverty of management control philosophy',

– the narrow, accounting focus which had become so prevalent.

Such diverse opinions leave a number of issues to be clarified. First, is the meaning of the term 'control'. In this review we will include within the definition of control both the ideas of informational feedback and the implementation of corrective actions. Equally, we explicitly exclude the exercise of power for its own sake, restricting ourselves to those activities undertaken by managers which have the intention of furthering organizational objectives (at least, insofar as perceived by managers). We are, thus, primarily concerned with the exercise of legitimate authority rather than power. This is no doubt a controversial position, but gives the review a clear managerial focus.

There is also a distinction to be drawn between management control and financial control, which is of some importance given the accounting domination of the subject in recent years. Financial control is clearly concerned with the management of the finance function within organizations. As such it is one business function amongst many, and comprises but one facet of the wider practice of management control. On the other hand, management control can be defined as a general management function concerned with the achievement of overall organizational aims and objectives. Financial information is thus used in practice to serve two interrelated functions. First, it is clearly used in a financial control role, where its function is to monitor financial flows; that is, it is concerned with looking after the money. Second, it is also often used as a surrogate measure for other aspects of organizational performance. That is, management control is concerned with looking after the overall business with money being used as a convenient measure of a variety of other more complex dimensions, not as an end in itself.

Having set some boundaries, the next section of the paper will provide a brief account of the main themes that have formed the starting point for the development of the field. Whilst well known, these roots cannot be ignored as their influence is reflected in work which continues today. There follows a review of the literature that has evolved over the last 20 years both as a continuation of and as a reaction against those roots, using a heuristic map provided by Scott (1981). Finally, we will suggest possible themes for future development.

THE STARTING POINTS

The roots of management control issues lie in early managerial thought. The significance of the work of Weber, Durkheim and Pareto upon the development managerial thought is well rehearsed. Less well known, but providing an excellent example of the classical management theorists, is the contribution of Mary Parker Follett, described by Parker (1986) as providing almost all of the ideas of modern control theory. Follett saw that the manager controlled not single elements but complex interrelationships and argued that the basis for control lay in self-regulating, self-directing individuals and groups who recognized common interests and objectives. It may be that Follett was an idealist in her search for unity in organizations for she sought a control that was

'fact control' not 'man control', and 'correlated control' rather than 'superimposed control'.

Further she saw coordination as the reciprocal relating of all factors in a setting that involved direct contact of all people concerned. The application of these

'fundamental principles of organisation'

was the control activity itself, for the whole point of her principles was to ensure predictable performance for the organization.

Scientific management, another important root of management control, is frequently associated with the work of F.W. Taylor (Miller and O'Leary, 1987), although there were earlier contributors to this movement. For example, Babbage (1832) was concerned with improving manufacture and systems and analysed operations, the skills involved, the expense of each process and suggested paths for improvement. In 1874 Fink (see Wren, 1994) developed a cost accounting system that used information flows, classification of costs and statistical control devices; innovations which led directly to 20th century processes of management control.

What seems to characterize these theorists is an attention to real problems, a scientific approach which centred upon understanding and conceptual analysis, and a wish to solve problems. Their contribution to management control lay in their attention to authority and accountability, an awareness of the need for analytical and budgetary models for control, forging the link between cost and operational activities, and the separation of cost accounting from financial accounting, with the former being a precursor of management accounting and control. However, these practical theorists may have pursued rationality of economic action and the search for universal solutions too far, although their ideas are still current and form the basis for much work in the field, many being echoed in the work of Robert Anthony. The ideas of the common purpose of social organizations along with a concern for the relationship between effectiveness and efficiency foreshadow the concept of autopoeis (the view that systems can have a 'life of their own') developed by cyberneticians. These will be examined in the next section.

EVOLUTION OF THE MANAGEMENT CONTROL LITERATURE

As previously noted, Parker (1986) argued that developments in accounting control have followed and lagged developments in management theory. Developments in management control seem to have followed a similar pattern, so we use the schema suggested by Scott (1981) for categorizing developments in organization theory as a framework for organizing this part of our review. We would argue that systems thinking has had an important influence on the development of MCSs and Scott's schema is based on a systems approach, so it is to this we now turn.

Cybernetics and systems theory

Organizational theory in general and management control research in particular have been influenced considerably by cybernetics (the science of communication and control (Weiner, 1948)). These insights have been extended in the holistic standpoint taken by general systems theory and the 'soft systems' approach (Checkland, 1981). Its central contribution has been in the systemic approach it adopts, causing attention to be paid to the overall control of the organization, in contrast to the systematic approach dominant in accounting control, which has often assumed that the multiplication of 'controls' will lead inexorably to overall 'control', a view roundly routed by Drucker (1964). Cybernetics and systems theory have developed in such an interlinked manner that it is difficult to draw a meaningful dividing line between them (for a fuller survey see Otley, 1983), although a simple distinction would be to suggest that cybernetics is concerned with closed systems, whereas systems theory specifically involves a more open perspective.

The major contribution of cybernetics has been in the study of systems in which complexity is paramount (Ashby, 1956); it attempts to explain the behaviour of complex systems primarily in terms of relatively simple feedback mechanisms (Wisdom, 1956). There have been a number of attempts to apply cybernetic concepts to the issue of management control, but these have all been of a theoretical nature, albeit based on general empirical observation. The process of generating feedback information is fundamental to management accounting on which much management control practice rests, although this is not usually elaborated in any very insightful manner. However, Otley and Berry (1980) developed Tocher's (1970) control model and applied it to organizational control. They maintain that effective control depends upon the existence of an adequate means of predicting the consequences of alternative control actions. In most organizations such predictive models reside in the minds of line managers, rather than in any more formal form, and they argue that improvements in control practice need to focus on improving such models. It is also argued that feedforward (anticipatory) controls are likely to be of more importance than feedback (reactive) controls. This echoes previous comments by authors such as Ashby (1956), who points to the biological advantages in controlling not by error but by what gives rise to error, and Amey (1979) who stresses the importance of anticipatory control mechanisms in business enterprises.

Arguably the most insightful use of cybernetic ideas applied to management practice is also one of the earliest. Vickers (1965, 1967) applied many cybernetic ideas to management practice during the 1950s. Although developed in a primarily closed systems context, he also started to explore the issue of regulating institutions from a societal perspective. This is also a major theme of Stafford Beer, most comprehensively in his 1972 book *Brain of the Firm*. Here he uses the human nervous system as an analogy for the control mechanisms that need to be adopted at various levels in the control of an organization. However, Beer's major contribution lies in his attempt to tackle issues of the overall societal and political context within which more detailed organizational forms and controls emerge. This is a theme which is picked up, albeit in a very different form, by the radical theorists of the 1980s and 1990s. The standard concepts of the cybernetic literature do not have such a straightforward application to the issue of organizational control as some presentations of them tend to imply. However, they do provide a language in which any of the central issues of management control may be expressed.

Further progress comes from the use of general systems theory which stresses the importance of *emergent* properties of systems, that is, properties which are characteristic of the level of complexity being studied and which do not have meaning at lower levels; such properties are possessed by the system but not by its parts. Systems thinking is thus primarily a tool for dealing with high levels of complexity, particularly with reference to systems which display adaptive and apparently goal-seeking behaviour (Lilienfeld, 1978). Some useful conceptual distinctions are drawn by Lowe and McInnes (1971) who attempt to apply a systems approach to the design of MCSs. An important extension to the realm of so-called 'soft' systems (i.e. systems which include human beings, where objectives are vague and ambiguous, decision-making processes ill-defined, and where, at best, only qualitative measures of performance exist) has been made by the Checkland school at Lancaster (Checkland, 1981; Wilson, 1984).

One of the central issues with which the 'soft' systems methodology has to cope is the imputation of objectives to the system. In many ways this methodology reflects the *verstehen* (or insight) tradition of thought in sociology, where great stress is laid upon the accuracy and honesty of observation, the sensitivity and perception of the observer, and on the imaginative interpretations of observations. Although the soft systems approach has had considerable success in producing solutions to real problems, it does not appear to have contributed to the development of the theory of control in the normal academic sense. It is very much an applied problem-solving methodology in its present form rather than a research method designed to yield generalizable explanations, although it undoubtedly has further potential in this area. This raises the issue of the nature and type of theories that can be expected in such a complex area of human and social behaviour.

A framework to map developments in management control research

Scott (1981) analysed the development of organization theory using two dimensions. First, he saw a transition from closed to open systems models of organization, reflecting the influence of systems ideas. Prior to 1960 most theorists tended to assume that organizations could be understood apart from their environments, and that most important processes and events were internal to the organization. After that date it was increasingly recognized that organizations were highly interdependent with their environments, and that boundaries are both permeable and variable. Second, he distinguished between rational and natural systems models. The rational systems model assumes that organizations are purposefully designed for the pursuit of explicit objectives, whereas the natural systems model emphasizes the importance of unplanned and spontaneous processes, with organically emerging informal structures supplementing or subduing rationally designed frameworks. The distinction between rational and natural systems is applicable to both sides of the closed-open system divide, resulting in the definition of the four approaches.

We use these categories to summarize work in MCSs, although we recognize that such categorization is not necessarily 'neat'. Organizations can be viewed as being *both* rational and natural (Thompson, 1967; Boland and Pondy, 1983); they are often intentionally designed to achieve specific purposes, yet also display emergent properties. It can be argued that each successive theoretical development provides an additional perspective which is helpful in understanding organizational processes, and which is likely to be additional and complementary to those which have preceded it. However, it is also recognized that this is a controversial statement that would not be accepted by some of those adopting a post-modernist viewpoint.

The Closed Rational Perspective   This work is characterized by being both universal in orientation and systematic in approach, scientific management being a typical example. In the management control literature we find a continuing emphasis on rational solutions, implicitly assuming a closed systems model of organization, which are universalistic in nature. Indeed, this can also be seen in much of the modern popular management literature, where a universal 'how-to-do-it' approach continues to find a ready market.

From a research point of view, there is much work which has sought to identify the 'one best way' to operate a control system. An excellent example of this approach applied to budgetary control is that conducted by Hofstede (1968). He sought to reconcile the US findings that budgets were extensively used in performance evaluation and control, but were associated with negative feelings on the part of many managers and dysfunctional consequences to the organization, with the European experience that budgets were seen positively but were little used. Multiple perspectives are brought to bear, including systems theory, although this draws primarily on cybernetics. His conclusions list several pages of recommendations as to how budgets could be used effectively without engendering negative consequences, and indicate an implicit universalistic orientation. Similarly, the well known text co-authored by Anthony and a host of collaborators (see for example, Anthony *et al.*, 1984) also clearly falls into the closed rational mode with its heavy emphasis on accounting controls.

The Closed Natural Perspective   The closed natural approach is centred around an increasing interest in the behavioural consequences of control systems operation. This was perhaps first introduced to the control literature by Argyris (1952) in his article entitled 'The Impact of Budgets on People', an emphasis reversed neatly almost 20 years later by Schiff and Lewin (1970) in their article 'The Impact of People on Budgets'. Lowe and Shaw (1968) discussed the tendency of managers to bias budgetary estimates that were subsequently used for control purposes. Buckley and McKenna (1972) were able to publish a review article summarizing current knowledge on the connection between budgetary control and managerial behaviour in the early 1970s.

Mintzberg followed his 1973 study of the nature of managerial activity with a 1975 study of the impediments to the use of management information, which dealt with many of the behavioural issues in the operation of control systems. There was thus a growing awareness of the human consequences of control systems use and operation beginning to emerge in the early 1970s, perhaps lagging some 20 years behind the equivalent human relations movement in the organization theory literature.

A behavioural perspective on the theme of managerial performance evaluation also began to emerge at this time. Hopwood (1972, 1974a) identified the different styles that managers could adopt in their use of accounting information and studied their impact on individual behaviour and (implicitly) organizational performance. Rhaman and McCosh (1976) sought to explain why different uses of accounting control information were observed, and concluded that both individual characteristics and organizational climate were significant factors. A study by Otley (1978) yielded almost exactly contrary results to those of Hopwood (1972) because the research site had significant differences; the conflicting findings could be reconciled only by adopting a contingent approach, a task that was more thoroughly undertaken by Hirst (1981).

The idea that systems used to evaluate performance are affected by the information supplied by those being evaluated has led to the concept of information inductance (Prakash and Rappaport, 1977; Dirsmith and Jablonsky, 1979). This generalized the observations of information bias and manipulation reported previously as just one manifestation of a more general phenomenon. Such work was extended by Birnberg *et al.* (1983) into a unified contingent framework, based on the ideas of Thompson (1967), Perrow (1970) and Ouchi (1979).

Despite the categorization of organizational contingency theorists into the open systems box by Scott (1981), the early contingent work in accounting-based control systems has a clear closed systems flavour. It was only in the late 1970s that the open systems ideas in contingency theory, which followed primarily from the use of environment as a contingent variable, began to be reflected in the management control literature. This parallels developments in Organization Theory (OT), for it is arguable that early contingent work by writers such as Woodward (1958, 1965) concentrated on internal factors such as technology, and did not adopt an open systems approach until later. Thus, texts in the management control area, such as Emmanuel *et al.* (1985, 1990), Merchant (1985), and Johnson and Gill (1993) which recognized the behavioural aspects of MCSs as well as adopting some tenets of the contingency framework, tend to lie along the boundary of the closed natural category and the open rational approach.

The Open Rational Perspective   As in OT, the emergence of an open systems perspective was accompanied by a return to more rational approaches and a relative neglect of the natural (albeit) closed approaches of the preceding years. The recognition of the external environment, key to the open systems approach, had never been strong in the early MCS literature. However, in the early 1970s there was a movement towards an open systems perspective, if only from a theoretical standpoint, an approach well illustrated by the collection of readings in the monograph *New Perspectives in Management Control* (Lowe and Machin, 1983). This approach was most cogently led by Lowe (1971) in an article which clearly recognizes the coalition of stakeholders involved in an enterprise (a concept used by Scott (1981) as an exemplar of an open systems approach) and the need for adaptation to the external environment. It is further clarified in Lowe and McInnes' (1971) article which adds the concept of resolution level. At the same time Beer (1972) was developing his own, somewhat idiosyncratic, approach and moving beyond cybernetics into more general systems analysis drawing heavily on neurophysiological ideas.

More significant, empirically, was the development of the contingency theory of management accounting control systems (summarized by Otley, 1980). Although several contingent variables were shown to be significant (e.g. technology, environment, organizational structure, size, corporate strategy), it was the impact of the external environment in general, and of external uncertainty in particular, that most clearly indicated the adoption of an open systems perspective. It is this distinction that marks the divergence of the study of management accounting systems, which have steadfastly retained their internal orientation (despite valiant attempts by a few proponents of so-called 'strategic management accounting' (Simmonds, 1981; Bromwich, 1990), and the study of the wider area of management control systems. Within management accounting, contingency theory waned in the early 1980s, to be replaced by various critical approaches in Europe, and to continue down a universalistic track in the US with the burgeoning popularity of activity-based costing under the leadership of Kaplan (1983) in particular. The wider study of control systems picked up on the neglected variable of corporate strategy at this point, which led to a small but significant stream of work most notably by Govindarajan and Gupta (1985) and Simons (1987, 1990, 1991, 1995).

The Open Natural Perspective   There are two developments which can be seen to mark a movement into this final perspective, which are illustrated by the collection of papers published in the monograph *Critical Perspectives in Management Control* (Chua *et al.*, 1989). First, there is a recognition that contingent variables are not to be seen as deterministic drivers of control systems design. In particular, the environment is not to be seen only as a factor to be adapted to, but also something which can itself be manipulated and managed. Second, there is the recognition of the political nature of organizational activity. However, although radical theorists have clearly been concerned with the exercise of power in and around organizations, it is not clear that they have contributed greatly to the study of control in its adaptive sense, nevertheless they have clearly indicated the complex political environment within which control systems have to function (see, for example, Ezzamel and Watson, 1993; Hogler and Hunt, 1993). This touches on the theme of legitimacy at various levels of resolution and addresses the question of how legitimacy becomes established and how it works through to different hierarchical levels in organizations. Examples of such work include research examining the reforms of the NHS using a post-modern perspective (Preston, 1992; Preston *et al.*, 1992) and that, taking a critical theory approach, of Laughlin and Broadbent (1993) who examined the impact of attempts to control particular organizations through the medium of the law. In a more general sense the discontinuities of history and the diverse roots of control systems are brought out by Miller and O'Leary (1987). Other work in this field has taken a more interpretive or anthropological approach, examining the role of values or culture in determining the extent to which it is possible to control organizational members. Ansari and Bell (1991) illustrate the effect of national culture; Broadbent (1992) and Dent (1991) focus in different ways on the impact of organizational cultures.

Overview

This retrospective review of the roots of management control provides the opportunity to reflect on its overall nature before moving forward to consider the prospects for the subject. It is clear that there is a wide range of research into the functioning of MCSs, even when its focus is narrowed to the more managerialist approach which we have adopted. A rough categorization of MCSs research work since 1965 set into this framework is given in Table 19.2 and allows some reflection on the basic assumptions which underlie the work that has been undertaken.

As mentioned earlier, whilst the framework developed by Scott provides a means by which to structure this review, it is important to note that every paper reviewed does not fit tidily into such a sequence. Further, it is clear that while practical theorists and scholars have developed ideas in new sectors of the diagram, this has not led to the abandonment of work in earlier sectors. The scientific management tradition is alive and well in areas such as operational research and in the consultancy world (e.g. in business process reengineering). The diversity of research approaches available is illustrated in the contents of the text *Managerial Control, Theories Issues and Practices* (Berry *et al.*, 1995) as well as the special issue of the *British Journal of Management* on MCSs published in 1993 (September, Vol. 4, No. 3). Both these publications (plus the edited collections by Lowe and Machin, 1983 and Chua *et al.*, 1989) have been spawned by the activities of the Management Control Association, a group of UK academics, which has sought for the past 20 years to promote wide-ranging research in the field. The latest review of nearly 20 research approaches is by Macintosh (1994), which unusually develops the issues through a selection of methodological approaches.

The predominant ontological stance is realist, stemming from the original concentration of the practical theorists on what they saw as real problems in practice. The

Table 19.2 Representative papers from four perspectives

Closed system models		Open system models	
Rational models	Natural models	Rational models	Natural models
Classical management theory	*Behavioural approaches*	*Systems and contingent approaches*	*Radical perspectives*
Classical theorists	Argyris (1952)	Ouchi (1979)	Chua *et al.* (1989)
Woodward (1958, 1965, 1970)	Hopwood (1972, 1974a, 1974b)	Beer (1972)	Ansari and Bell (1991)
Burns and Stalker (1961)	Vickers (1965, 1967)	Lowe and Machin (1983)	Dent (1991)
Drucker (1964)	Otley and Berry (1980)	Lowe and McInnes (1971)	Laughlin and Broadbent (1993)
Simon *et al.* (1954)		Otley (1980)	

primary epistemological stance of these control theorists is positivist and functionalist. Functionalist approaches have been severely criticized (e.g. Burrell and Morgan, 1979) as being part of the sociology (and perhaps the economy) of preservation, and thus antithetical to radical change. In the sense that management control is concerned with forms of stability this might be so, but the pursuit of efficiency has led to radical, and often unwelcome, change for many people, and control techniques have been used to promote quite radical social changes. Whilst some of the more radical theorists have examined this issue it, perhaps, remains somewhat under researched. Laughlin and Lowe (1990) using the framework of Burrell and Morgan (1979) along with Scott's framework to review accounting research and demonstrate the diversity of approaches available argued that only the open systems approaches were beginning to move away from the functionalist orientation. Given our argument as to the paucity of open systems research, similar claims can be made for the need to extend the theoretical and methodological boundaries of management control research.[2]

The review shows that accounting still acts as an important element of management control. Whilst there have been developments in control in associated areas (such as Management Information Systems (MIS), human relations, operations research) these disciplines have been less inclined to see themselves as offering themselves as vehicles for integration of the diversity of organizational life than has accounting. Accounting is still seen as a pre-eminent technology by which to integrate diverse activities from strategy to operations and with which to render accountability. There is a sense in which the reduction of values to accounting measurements can contribute to management control sliding into the merely technical. Such a tendency is reinforced by the very constructs of the management information system and of information management which accounting uses. The ubiquity of computers, data capture, high-speed software, electronic data interchange and open access has changed the speed of data flow without yet having had great impact on either management control research or practice. Yet the topic of management control holds the promise of providing a powerful integrating idea to provide a very practical focus to concepts developed in other disciplines if it is not wholly accounting focused. Mills' (1970) thoughts about the role of management control as an integrative teaching device also appear to apply with some force to its role as an integrative research framework for an important part of management studies. With this in mind we move to the final section.

THEMES FOR FUTURE DEVELOPMENT

Here, we suggest some lines of enquiry which we believe it would be fruitful to pursue in developing research in management control. These are our own views, and we acknowledge we come to these issues from our own particular history and perspectives, thus running the risk of being both biased and incomplete. However, we believe they cover a wide-ranging agenda of important issues from both a practical and theoretical

---

[2] Agency theory research, not included in this review, would not be immune from this comment.

perspective. This prospective part of the paper flows from the retrospective review and is in two sub-sections. The first sub-section considers that the nature of the current environment and the needs this engenders are significantly different from those that determined and yet developed the earlier control approaches. The second sub-section considers the possibilities which could be available in the context of a broadening of the theoretical and methodological approaches adopted in research in the area.

THE ENVIRONMENT OF CONTROL

The development of earlier MCSs theory took place in the context of large, hierarchically structured organizations. It centred upon accounting controls and developed measures of divisional performance, such as return on investment and residual income. It considered the issues raised in utilizing accounting performance measures to control large, diversified companies, in particular the construction of quasi-independent responsibility centres using systems of cost allocation and transfer pricing. The central theme was to produce measures of controllable performance against which managers could be held accountable, yet the empirical evidence (Merchant, 1987; Otley, 1990) suggests that the 'controllability principle' was more often honoured only in its breach. It can also be argued (see Otley, 1994) that changes in the business and social environment have led to the replacement of large integrated organizations by smaller and more focused organizational units, which require appropriate control mechanisms to be developed. Several features of the business environment seem to point towards a change in emphasis. A key trend is in the impact of uncertainty. It is a moot point whether uncertainty has increased, but it is true that the rate of change in both the commercial and governmental environment is rapid, requiring considerable adaptation on the part of organizations. Change appears to be affecting a much broader range of the population, whether it be technological, social or political change. The process of adaptation can no longer be left to a few senior managers who develop organizational strategies to be enacted by others; rather the process of change has become embedded in normal operating practices, and involves a wider range of organizational participants.

One consequence of this rapid rate of change has been encapsulated in ideas of global competition and 'world class' companies. As the rate of change increases, organizations need to devote more of their resources to adaptation and correspondingly less to managing current operations efficiently. One method of adaptation is planning, but this requires the prediction of the consequences of change, which is becoming more difficult; an alternative response is to develop the flexibility to adapt to the consequences of change as they become apparent. The 'management of change' remains an important managerial skill, but it should no longer be seen as a discrete event bounded by periods of stability; rather we are concerned with management in a context of continual change. This requires continual adaptation, a note which is reflected in the current popular terminology of 'continuous improvement'.

A second feature has been a movement towards reducing the size of business units, certainly in terms of the number of people employed. In part, this has been driven by technological change, but there has also often been a strategic choice to encourage units to concentrate on their 'core' business and to avoid being distracted by irrelevant side issues. In turn, this has led to 'non-core' activities being outsourced, a process which can be most reliably undertaken in the context of long-term alliances. Such a trend is emphasized by just-in-time production and the processes of 'market testing' which have been imposed upon the public sector in the UK. The number of middle managers is being reduced and the range of responsibilities of those who remain is being increased. The split between strategic planning, management control and operational control, which was always tendentious has now become untenable, and a much closer integration between those functions has developed.

The boundaries of the organization and the boundaries of the control function are not necessarily co-terminus. Within the organization, ideas of 'business process re-engineering' have reinforced the need to devise control mechanisms that are horizontal (i.e. which follow the product or service through its production process until its delivery to the customer) rather than solely vertical (i.e. which follow the organizational hierarchy within organizational functions). As production processes are increasingly spread across legal boundaries (and often across national boundaries) new processes for the control of such embedded operations are needed (Berry, 1994). That is, control systems need to be devised which coordinate the total production and delivery process regardless of whether these processes are contained within a single (vertically integrated) organization or spread across a considerable number of (quasi-independent) organizations.

Traditional approaches to management control have been valuable in defining an important topic of study, but they have been predicated on a model of organizational functioning which has become increasingly outdated. This has resulted in the study of control systems becoming over narrow by remaining focused primarily upon accounting control mechanisms which are vertical rather than horizontal in their orientation. Contemporary organizations display flexibility, adaptation and continuous learning, both within and across organizational boundaries, but such characteristics are not encouraged by traditional systems. There is considerable anecdotal evidence to suggest that organizational practices are beginning to reflect these needs, so a key task for MCSs researchers is to observe and codify these developments.

In this type of changing environment the logic of systems theory could be argued to be of some importance in emphasizing issues such as the importance of environment and the holism of the organization. Although MCSs theory often makes references to the concepts of cybernetics, and sometimes to those of general systems theory, such approaches rarely inform empirical research work. Perhaps the most important contribution these disciplines can make is to broaden the horizons of management control researchers to include an appreciation of the overall context within which their work is located. The issues of the appropriate level of analysis, the definition of systems boundaries and the nature of systems goals deserve much more thorough attention. Even more importantly, the idea of control in an open system facing a complex and uncertain environment is also central for the design of effective systems to assist organizations to survive.

Current issues

Our suggestions here are seen partly as an attempt to raise important issues which appear under-researched at present and partly to promote the use of broader theoretical and methodological perspectives. Our argument is that the closed and functionalist perspective which still predominates needs to be extended.

We see the environment of control as changing, we also see it as of central importance and it is this to which we first turn. Although there have been attempts to broaden the scope of what is perceived as part of a control system (notably by Hopwood, 1974b, Merchant, 1985, and Lowe and Machin, 1983), a narrow financially biased perspective still dominates much of the control literature. The management literature has relatively recently emphasized ideas such as the balanced scorecard (predated by many years in France by the 'tableau de bord') where non-financial measures (e.g. customer, operations and innovation perspectives) are placed alongside traditional financial measures (Kaplan and Norton, 1992). The range of what is included as a management control is being extended with studies of performance-related pay, operational and process controls, and the whole issue of the management of corporate culture. However, studies of the overall practice of control, integrating the whole range of such functional controls, within particular organizations are still scarce. It should be clearly recognized that such attempts raise considerable methodological problems, of both a practical and theoretical nature. From a practical point of view, there is the issue of the extent to which a single researcher (or even a small team) can come to grips with such a wide range of practices in a sensible timescale. Such work would seem to be necessarily case study based, which raises issues of generalizability.

More fundamentally, it raises epistemological issues regarding the nature of theory in this field (Otley and Berry, 1994). It may well be that applied problem-solving methodologies are all that can be expected at high levels of resolution such as those necessary when observing practice within single organizations. Nevertheless, it is also our belief that the insight such attempts would provide would form an important basis for subsequent theoretical development. Another potentially fruitful approach is that of 'middle range thinking', as proposed by Laughlin (1995), which is both rooted in the critical tradition and strikes a balance between the notions of reality and subjectivity. This type of theory involves the use of skeletal frameworks which are then 'fleshed out' with empirical details of particular situations.

The recognition of the importance of the environment raises another important issue, the relationships across the boundary of what has traditionally been seen as the firm. Most of the management control literature has concentrated its attention at the level of the firm (or sub-units within it). There has been comparatively little exploration of control from a more macro or societal perspective. Although these issues have been addressed to some extent by the radical theorists, the 'micro' and the 'macro' have been seen as distinct areas. Despite the quite radical changes that have occurred in the UK environment over the past 15 years (not least due to the Thatcher government) the general issue has not been well explored in the control (as distinct from the economic) literature. In particular, the role of competition as a control mechanism is under-researched. Further, such institutional arrangements affect the legitimacy of different methods of control within organizations, such as the appropriate boundaries for managerial action and the role of consultation and participation amongst the workforce and these issues need fuller exploration. This also raises the issue of what have been called embedded organizations. We have already alluded to the fact that control systems increasingly operate across both the legal boundaries of firms and national boundaries. The needs of managing business processes in an extended supply and distribution chain that crosses many organizational boundaries raise challenging control issues. These have been explored to some extent in both the operations management and management information systems literature, and have surfaced in the popular management literature under the banner of 'business process re-engineering', but have yet to receive proper attention from an overall control framework. The open systems framework appears to be especially appropriate in this area.

We have also found very little research addressing the problems of control in multinational and international organizations, in either the public or private sector. This is an issue that seems to have been given much more attention in the fields of strategy and marketing, than in control. Undoubtedly a complex field, issues as disparate as the impact of differing legal and institutional structures, financial and exchange control constraints, and the varied impact of national and corporate cultures all seem worthy of attention.

Wider fields also need to be addressed. The advent of environmental management and the attention now paid to 'green' issues has yet to impact on the control literature. However, the developing understanding of both human ecology (including issues of demography, population, ethnicity and religion) and physical ecology suggests that wider considerations need to be brought into the conceptualization of the problems of regulation and control of, and within, organizations. Clearly, these considerations raise new ethical issues for both control theorists and practitioners.

Gender issues in management control have received scant attention, despite an emerging set of questions about the extent to which there are 'feminine' and 'masculine' styles of managing. It may be that the language of management control needs reframing to encompass a wider range of possibilities. There is some support in the popular management literature for styles associated with the feminine gender stereotype, such as empowerment, group or mutual accountabilities and upward appraisal. The whole concept of the learning organization suggests approaches to management which are more supportive than directive in their orientation. Numbers of women in the workforce continue to increase, although the 'glass ceiling' still exists. The implications of these changes on MCSs remains to be researched.

CONCLUSIONS

This paper extends previous reviews of the area of management control and provides some suggestions for further research. Our suggestions stem from the belief that the practice and researching of management control needs to recognize the environment in which organizations exist and to loosen the boundaries around the area of concern. We are also anxious to promote more critical research. Undoubtedly some of the narrowness of the research in the topic which we have highlighted is the result of our choice of definition of management control which remains rather managerialist in its focus. It is clear that the field of management control is of relevance to the practice of management but this should not preclude a critical stance and thus a broader choice of theoretical approaches.

The area is also under-researched, which might be explained by the nature of the methodologies required for its study and their unpopularity over the last 25 years especially in the US. This indicates a significant opportunity for contributions, offering a broader set of methodological stances, to be made in an important and developing field. In conclusion, we hope that this paper might play a small part in defining and developing management control as a coherent field of study within the management disciplines.

REFERENCES

Amey, L. R. (1979). *Budget Planning and Control Systems*. Pitman, London.

Ansari, S. and J. Bell (1991). 'Symbolism, Collectivism and Rationality in Organizational Control', *Accounting, Auditing and Accountability Journal*, pp. 4–27.

Anthony, R. N. (1965). Planning and Control Systems: A Framework for Analysis. Division of Research, Harvard Business School, Boston.

Anthony, R. N., J. Dearden and N. M. Bedford (1984). *Management Control Systems*. Irwin, Homewood, IL.

Argyris, C. (1952). The Impact of Budgets on People. The Controllership Foundation, Ithaca, NY.

Ashby, W. R. (1956). *An Introduction to Cybernetics*. Chapman and Hall, London.

Babbage, C. (1832). *On the Economy of Machinery and Manufacturers*. Charles Knight, London.

Beer, S. (1972). *Brain of the Firm*. Allen Lane, Harmondsworth, Middlesex.

Berry, A. J. (1994). 'Spanning Traditional Boundaries: Organization and Control of Embedded Operations', *Leadership and Organisational Development Journal*, pp. 4–10.

Berry, A. J., J. Broadbent and D. T. Otley (eds) (1995). *Managerial Control: Theories, Issues and Practices*. Macmillan, London.

Birnberg, J. G., L. Turopolec and S. M. Young (1983). 'The Organizational Context of Accounting', *Accounting, Organizations and Society*, pp. 111–129.

Boland, R. J. Jnr. and L. R. Pondy (1983). 'Accounting in Organizations: A Union of Rational and Natural Perspectives', *Accounting, Organizations and Society*, pp. 223–234.

Broadbent, J. (1992). 'Change in Organisations: A Case Study of the Use of Accounting Information in the NHS', *British Accounting Review*, pp. 343–367.

Bromwich, M. (1990). 'The Case for Strategic Management Accounting: The Role of Accounting Information for Strategy in Competitive Markets', *Accounting, Organizations and Society*, pp. 27–46.

Buckley, A. and E. McKenna (1972). 'Budgetary Control and Business Behaviour', *Accounting and Business Research*, pp. 137–150.

Burns, T. and G. M. Stalker (1961). *The Management of Innovation*. Tavistock, London.

Burrell, G. and G. Morgan (1979). *Sociological Paradigms and Organizational Analysis*, Heinemann, London.

Checkland, P. B. (1981). *Systems Thinking, Systems Practice*. Wiley, Chichester.

Chua, W. F., T. Lowe and T. Puxty (1989). *Critical Perspectives in Management Control*. Macmillan, London.

Dent, J. F. (1991). 'Accounting and Organizational Cultures: A Field Study of the Emergence of a New Organizational Reality', *Accounting, Organizations and Society*, pp. 705–732.

Dirsmith, M. W. and S. F. Jablonsky (1979). 'MBO, Political Rationality and Information Inductance', *Accounting, Organizations and Society*, pp. 39–52.

Drucker, P. (1964). 'Control, Controls and Management'. In: C. P. Bonini, R. K. Jaedieke and H. M. Wagner, *Management Controls: New Directions in Basic Research*, McGraw-Hill, Maidenhead.

Emmanuel, C. R. and D. T. Otley (1985). *Accounting for Management Control*. Van Nostrand Reinhold, Wokingham.

Emmanuel, C. R., D. T. Otley and K. Merchant (1990). *Accounting, for Management Control* (2nd edition). Chapman and Hall, London.

Ezzamel, M. and R. Watson (1993). 'Organizational Form, Ownership Structure and Corporate Performance: A Contextual Empirical Analysis of UK Companies', *British Journal of Management*, pp. 161–176.

Giglioni, G. B. and A. B. Bedeian (1974). 'A Conspectus of Management Control Theory: 1900–1972', *Academy of Management Journal*, pp. 292–305.

Govindarajan, V. and A. K. Gupta (1985). 'Linking Control Systems to Business Unit Strategy: Impact on Performance', *Accounting, Organizations and Society*, pp. 51–66.

Hirst, M. K. (1981). 'Accounting Information and the Evaluation of Subordinate Performance: A Situational Approach', *Accounting Review*, pp. 771–784.

Hofstede, G. H. (1968). *The Game of Budget Control*. Tavistock, London.

Hofstede, G. H. (1978). 'The Poverty of Management Control Philosophy', *Academy of Management Review*, July.

Hogler, R. L. and H. G. Hunt (1993). 'Accounting and Conceptions of Control in the American Corporation', *British Journal of Management*, pp. 177–190.

Hopwood, A. G. (1972). 'An Empirical Study of the Role of Accounting Data in Performance Evaluation', Supplement to *Journal of Accounting Research*, pp. 156–193.

Hopwood, A. G. (1974a). 'Leadership Climate and the Use of Accounting Data in Performance Appraisal', *Accounting Review*, pp. 485–495.

Hopwood, A. G. (1974b). *Accounting and Human Behaviour*. Prentice-Hall.

Johnson, P. and J. Gill (1993). *Management Control and Organizational Behaviour*. Paul Chapman, London.

Kaplan, R. S. (1983). 'Measuring Manufacturing Performance: A New Challenge for Management Accountants', *Accounting Review*, **LVIII**, pp. 686–705.

Kaplan, R. S. and D. P. Norton (1992). 'The Balanced Scorecard – Measures that Drive Performance', *Harvard Business Review*, Jan/Feb, pp. 71–79.

Laughlin, R. C. (1995). 'Empirical Research in Accounting: A Case for Middle Range Thinking', *Accounting, Auditing and Accountability*, pp. 63–87.

Laughlin, R. C. and J. Broadbent (1993). 'Accounting and Law: Partners in the Juridification of the Public Sector in the UK?', *Critical Perspectives on Accounting*, pp. 337–368.

Laughlin and Lowe (1990). 'A Critical Analysis of Accounting Thought: Prognosis and Prospects for Understanding and Changing Accounting Systems Design'. In: D. J. Cooper, and T. M. Hopper (eds), *Critical Accounts*, Macmillan, London, pp. 15–43.

Lilienfeld, R. (1978). *The Rise of Systems Theory: An Ideological Analysis*. Wiley, New York.

Lowe, E. A. (1971). 'On the Idea of a Management Control System: Integrating Accounting and Management Control', *Journal of Management Studies*, pp. 1–12.

Lowe, E. A. and J. L. J. Machin (eds) (1983). *New Perspectives in Management Control*. Macmillan, London.

Lowe, E. A. and J. M. McInnes (1971). 'Control in Socio-Economic Organizations: A Rationale for the Design of Management Control Systems (Section 1)', *Journal of Management Studies*, pp. 213–227.

Lowe, E. A. and R. W. Shaw (1968). 'An Analysis of Managerial Biasing: Evidence from a Company's Budgeting Process', *Journal of Management Studies*, pp. 304–315.

Machin, J. L. J. (1983). 'Management control systems: whence and whither?' pp. 22–42. In: E. A. Lowe and J. L. J. Machin (eds), *New Perspectives in Management Control*. Macmillan, London.

Macintosh, N. B. (1994). *Management Accounting and Control Systems, An Organizational and Behavioural Approach*. John Wiley and Sons, Chichester.

Merchant, K. A. (1985). *Control in Business Organizations*. Pitman, Boston.

Merchant, K. A. (1987). 'How and Why Firms Disregard the Controllability Principle'. In: W. J. Bruns and R. Kaplan (eds), *Accounting and Management: Field Study Perspectives*. Harvard Business School Press, Boston.

Merchant, K. A. and R. Simons (1986). 'Research and Control in Complex Organizations: An Overview', *Journal of Accounting Literature*, pp. 183–203.

Miller, P. and T. O'Leary (1987). 'Accounting and the Construction of the Governable Person', *Accounting, Organizations and Society*, pp. 235–266.

Mills, A. E. (1970). 'Management Controls and Integration at the Conceptual Level', *Journal of Management Studies*, pp. 364–375.

Mintzberg, H. (1973). *The Nature of Managerial Work*. Harper and Row, London.

Mintzberg, H. (1975). 'The Managers Job: Folklore and Fact', *Harvard Business Review*, pp. 49–61.

Otley, D. T. (1978). 'Budget Use and Managerial Performance', *Journal of Accounting Research*, pp. 122–149.

Otley, D. T. (1980). 'The Contingency Theory of Management Accounting: Achievement and Prognosis', *Accounting, Organizations and Society*, pp. 413–428.

Otley, D. T. (1983). 'Concepts of Control: The Contribution of Cybernetics and Systems Theory to Management Control'. In: E. A. Lowe and J. L. J. Machin (eds), *New Perspectives in Management Control*. Macmillan, London.

Otley, D. T. (1990). 'Issues in Accountability and Control: Some Observations from a Study of Colliery Accountability in the British Coal Corporation', *Management Accounting Research*, pp. 91–165.

Otley, D. T. (1994). 'Management Control in Contemporary Organizations: Towards A Wider Framework', *Management Accounting Research*, pp. 289–299.

Otley, D. T. and A. J. Berry (1980). 'Control, Organization and Accounting', *Accounting, Organizations and Society*, pp. 231–244.

Otley, D. T. and A. J. Berry (1994). 'Case Study Research in Management Accounting and Control', *Management Accounting Research*, pp. 45–65.

Ouchi, W. G. (1979). 'A Conceptual Framework for the Design of Organizational Control Systems', *Management Science*, pp. 833–848.

Parker, L. D. (1986). *Developing Control Concepts in the 20th Century*. Garland, New York.

Perrow, C. (1970). *Organizational Analysis: A Sociological View*. Wadsworth, Belmont, California.

Prakash, P. and A. Rappaport (1977). 'Information Inductance and its Significance for Accounting', *Accounting, Organizations and Society*, pp. 29–38.

Preston, A. M. (1992). 'The Birth of Clinical Accounting: A Study of the Emergence and Transformation of Discourses on Costs and Practices of Accounting in US Hospitals', *Accounting, Organizations and Society*, pp. 63–100.

Preston, A. M., D. J. Cooper and R. W. Coombs (1992), 'Fabricating Budgets: A Study of the Production of Management Budgeting in the NHS', *Accounting, Organizations and Society*, pp. 561–594.

Rathe, A. W. (1960). 'Management Controls in Business'. In: D. G. Malcolm and A. J. Rowe, *Management Control Systems*, Wiley, New York.

Rhaman, M. and A. M. McCosh (1976). 'The Influence of Organizational and Personal Factors on the Use of Accounting Information: An Empirical Study', *Accounting, Organizations and Society*, pp. 339–355.

Scott, W. R. (1981). 'Developments in Organization Theory: 1960–1980', *American Behavioral Scientist*, pp. 407–422.

Simmonds, K. (1981). 'Strategic Management Accounting', *Management Accounting*, 59(4), pp. 26–29.

Simon, H. A., G. Kozmetsky, H. Guetzkow and G. Tyndall (1954). *Centralization vs. Decentralization in the Controller's Department*. Reprinted by Scholar's Book Co., Houston (1978).

Simons, R. (1987). 'Accounting Control Systems and Business Strategy: An Empirical Analysis', *Accounting, Organizations and Society*, pp. 357–374.

Simons, R. (1990). 'The Role of Management Control Systems in Creating Competitive Advantage: New Perspectives', *Accounting, Organizations and Society*, pp. 127–143.

Simons, R. (1991). 'Strategic Orientation and Top Management Attention to Control Systems', *Strategic Management Journal*, pp. 49–62.

Simons, R. (1995). *Levers of Control*. Harvard Business School Press.

Thompson, J. D. (1967). *Organizations in Action*. McGraw-Hill, Maidenhead.

Tocher, K. D. (1970). 'Control', *Operational Research Quarterly*, pp. 159–180.

Vickers, G. (1965). *The Art of Judgement: A Study of Policy-Making*. Chapman and Hall, London.

Vickers, G. (1967). *Towards a Sociology of Management*. Chapman and Hall, London.

Weiner, N. (1948). *Cybernetics*. MIT Press. Cambridge, MA.

Wilson, B. (1984). *Systems: Concepts, Methodologies and Applications*. Wiley, Chichester.

Wisdom, J. O. (1956). 'The Hypothesis of Cybernetics', *Yearbook for the Advancement of General Systems Theory*, Vol. 1.

Woodward, J. (1958). *Management and Technology*. HMSO, London.

Woodward, J. (1965). *Industrial Organization: Theory and Practice*. Oxford University Press, London.

Woodward, J. and J. Rackham (1970). *Industrial Organization: Behaviour and Control*. Oxford University Press, London.

Wren, P. A. (1994). *The Evolution of Management Thought* (4th edition). Wiley, Chichester.

READING C

Covaleski, M. A., Dirsmith, M. W. and Samuel, S. (1996). Managerial accounting research: The contributions of organizational and sociological theories. *Journal of Management Accounting Research*, 8, 1–35. Reproduced by permission of American Accounting Association.

Questions

1 Contrast contingency theory, interpretive and critical perspectives in terms of how each perspective can inform an understanding of management accounting. What are the strengths and weaknesses of each paradigm?
2 What is the advantage of the 'paradigmatic pluralism' that Covaleski *et al.* promote?
3 In undertaking management accounting research in an organizational setting, how would you determine the methods of enquiry that you would adopt?

Further reading

Boland, J. R. J. and Pondy, L. R. (1983). Accounting in organizations: A union of natural and rational perspectives. *Accounting, Organizations and Society*, **8**(2/3), 223–34.

Hopper, T. and Powell, A. (1985). Making sense of research into the organizational and social aspects of management accounting: A review of its underlying assumptions. *Journal of Management Studies*, **22**(5), 429–65.

Lowe, T. and Puxty, T. (1989). The problems of a paradigm: A critique of the prevailing orthodoxy in management control. In: W. F. Chua, T. Lowe and T. Puxty (eds), *Critical Perspectives in Management Control*, London: Macmillan.

Neimark, M. and Tinker, T. (1986). The social construction of management control systems. *Accounting, Organizations and Society*, **11**(4/5), 369–95.

Otley, D. (1989). A strategy for the development of theories in management control. In: W. F. Chua, T. Lowe and T. Puxty (eds), *Critical Perspectives in Management Control*, London: Macmillan.

MANAGERIAL ACCOUNTING RESEARCH: THE CONTRIBUTIONS OF ORGANIZATIONAL AND SOCIOLOGICAL THEORIES

Mark A. Covaleski
University of Wisconsin-Madison

Mark W. Dirsmith
Pennsylvania State University

Sajay Samuel
Bucknell University

ABSTRACT

Organizational and sociological theories explicitly recognize the centrality of issues of social control and coordination in organizations, thus providing intellectual approaches from which to study managerial accounting as important aspects of the manner in which organizations and society function. This paper examines various organizational and sociological perspectives which have provided meaningful contributions to our understanding of managerial accounting. The credibility of both the theoretical and methodological traditions which typically underpin these alternative organizational and sociological perspectives is then discussed. Finally, this paper considers the unique insights which organizational and sociological theories offer in contrast to more traditional managerial accounting research perspectives for understanding the multiple roles of management accounting in contemporary organizations.

Managerial accounting research, which has adapted organizational or sociological theories to examine the development, maintenance and change in managerial accounting practices, explicitly recognizes the centrality of issues of social control and coordination in organizations, thus providing intellectual approaches from which to study managerial accounting as problematic aspects of the organizational and social context. The purpose of our paper is to provide a critique of the organizational and

We wish to thank Anthony Hopwood (Oxford University), John Meyer (Stanford University), Mike Shields (University of Memphis), and S. Mark Young (University of Southern California) for their many useful suggestions.

sociological theoretical traditions which have been used in managerial accounting research in order to facilitate understanding, and perhaps influence usage, by accounting scholars adopting more traditional research perspectives. In our effort to provide a sweeping critique of organizational and sociological perspectives, rather than a detailed and nuanced treatment of this stream of management accounting research from these theoretical perspectives, there are points of omission, under-representation, and compression of the multitude of views within these theoretical traditions. And yet, it is precisely through such a broad treatment that we hope to reveal the distinctiveness of these organizational and sociological research traditions which exhibit a cluster of tendencies that distinguish it from the more familiar research traditions which draw on neoclassical economics and contemporary social and organizational psychology.[3]

The paper is organized into four sections. The first section addresses the contributions which contingency theory has had in situating managerial accounting in the control processes and structures of organizations. Contingency theory (Thompson 1967; Perrow 1967; Lawrence and Lorsch 1969) represents a rich blend of organizational theory – i.e., it has roots in the organizational decision-making perspectives of the 1950s (Simon 1957; March and Simon 1958) – and sociological functionalist perspectives of organizations – i.e., it has roots in the sociological concerns about organizational structure of the 1960s (Burns and Stalker 1961; Woodward 1965; Aiken and Hage 1966; Hickson 1966). Contingency theory took the insights on such critical organizational processes as decision-making and control as depicted in the literature on organizational decision-making and combined these with sociological functionalist concerns regarding the impact of such structural factors as environment, size, technology, etc., on organizational behavior. Important to both the decision-making perspective of organizations and the sociological concerns for organizational structure are issues of organizational control and coordination. This explicit concern for issues of coordination and control, in turn, has provided important contributions to managerial accounting research in our understanding of such issues as the design of information and control systems, budgeting and strategic planning.

The second major section of this paper deals with the various organizational and sociological theories which concern themselves with the social construction and spread of rationality and, in turn, the manner in which this rationality impacts the

---

[3] Our focus on managerial accounting research motivated by organizational and sociological theories precludes this paper from addressing managerial accounting research generated from other theoretical traditions (economic, psychological, historical); nor does our paper address some excellent descriptive and applied work in managerial accounting. Here our approach complements such recent work as that of Young and Selto (1991) whose primary concern was to review the managerial accounting literature by topic, i.e., strategic cost accounting, product life cycle cost management, flexible manufacturing systems, etc., while embracing a variety of theoretical and non-theoretical work, albeit with less of an explicit focus on critiquing the theoretical traditions. McMann and Nanni (1996) took the same approach as Young and Selto (1991), however with a more specific focus on one topic – Japanese managerial accounting. This explicit focus allowed them to provide more insight on such critical subtopics as continuous improvement, quality, target costing, etc. – with the research once again cutting across theoretical and non-theoretical traditions, as well as across research methods.

power and politics in organizational functioning (Weber 1947). These organizational and sociological theories – often referred to as interpretive perspectives – also draw from the organizational decision-making perspective (Simon 1957; March and Simon 1958), thus sharing intellectual heritage with contingency theory. We also see, however, the influence of more interpretive sociological traditions beginning with the work of Weber (1947) and his concerns for the 'politics of rationality,' as well as the work of Berger and Luckmann (1967) (see also Garfinkel 1967) and their work on the social construction (the development of cognitive processes) and the manner which subjective meaning becomes objective facts. Specifically, we examine the relevance of interpretive perspectives by considering a number of organizational and social theories including institutional theory (Meyer and Rowan 1977; DiMaggio and Powell 1983), resource dependency theories (Pfeffer 1981), political perspectives (Edelman 1977; Wildavsky 1964), and the sociology of professions (Abbott 1988; Freidson 1986).

The third section of this paper examines the critical organizational and sociological perspectives which provide an even more direct explanation of power and politics. Perhaps the most important attribute of critical perspectives is its attention to issues of conflict, domination and power – an attention motivated by a theoretical backdrop of capitalist social relations, and premised upon an irreducible conflict between capital and labor which ensures perpetual antagonistic relations between the classes. Despite theoretical differences within critical perspectives regarding the manner and form in which to conceptualize power, a common attribute is that they eschew a consensus view of society. These critical perspectives argue that functionalist and interpretive views of power stipulate that individual interests mesh into a harmony at the societal level which contrasts with the critical perspectives' focus on presumed perpetual antagonistic relations between the classes. More specifically, whether through general equilibrium in economics (e.g., the functionalist concern for market value) or the public good in politics (the interpretive concerns for the negotiation and bargaining), the social interest is assumed to emerge from the interaction of individual interests. In sharp contrast, critical perspectives deal explicitly with the role that accounting plays in relation to issues of conflict, domination and power as defined by the presumed irreducible conflict between capital and labor (Cooper and Sherer 1984). Here we will confine our attention to two major research strands of the many critical perspectives that have illuminated our understanding of managerial accounting: labor process theory which is concerned with the extraction of surplus from laborers (e.g., Hopper *et al.* 1987; Hopper and Armstrong 1991), and the Foucaultian perspective which is concerned with the methods by which the actions of individuals are made visible and susceptible to discipline and control, thereby rendering the individual to be governed (e.g., Miller and O'Leary 1987; Walsh and Stewart 1993).

The fourth section of the paper offers concluding remarks in which we consider the relationship among the three dominant organizational and sociological perspectives considered in this paper, as well as their relationship to more orthodox, neoclassical, and social and organizational psychology perspectives of managerial accounting with a focus on the issue as to whether these various perspectives can be meaningfully blended, or whether a 'champion' perspective may emerge. This section also addresses issues pertaining to assessing the credibility of the field-based research methods commonly (but not necessarily) utilized in these alternative theoretical traditions.[4] Finally, this section considers the unique contributions that the different organizational and sociological theories may make beyond those offered by more traditional approaches.

CONTINGENCY THEORY

Contingency theory has provided considerable inspiration to managerial accounting researchers through an elaboration of the basic theme that 'tight' control systems should be used in centralized organizations faced with simple technology and stable task environments; 'loose' control systems should be used in decentralized organizations, presumably faced with dynamic, complex task environments. Furthermore, a given means of control such as embedded in managerial accounting information can only be understood through reference to other control approaches used in organizations as well as their organizational/task environment context. For example, budgets may take on important meaning both for planning and control purposes for work processes or product lines which are more routine, standardized and predictable. However, in situations where the processes or product lines are less routine, less standardized and less predictable, the budgets may be generated but are subject to much revision and are of little use as a control benchmark (Swieringa and Moncur 1975). Contingency theory is essentially a theoretical perspective of organizational behavior that emphasizes how contingent factors such as technology and the task environment affected the design and functioning of organizations. For example, Thompson's (1967) *Organizations in Action* attempted to link task environment and technological contingencies to various organizational arrangements, focusing particularly on the different mechanisms of coordination which were appropriate for more complex, dynamic technologies and task environmental conditions. Perrow's (1967) theory of technology focused on the congruence between different types of technologies and organizational arrangements, emphasizing that more flexible, loosely-structured arrangements were more appropriate for organizations with non-routine technologies, while just the opposite type of organizational arrangements were more likely to fit routine technologies. Lawrence and Lorsch's (1969) *Organizations and Environment* developed, in a related manner the fit between organizational arrangements, including mechanisms of social control and coordination, and environments of organizations.

The sociological tradition embedded in contingency theory developed during the 1960s through various 'structural' approaches to organizational studies (Woodward 1965; Aiken and Hage 1966; Hage and Aiken 1967; Blau 1970, 1973; Hickson

---

[4] Our paper is primarily organized along theoretical traditions, thus cutting across methodological approaches including fieldwork, surveys, lab experiments, etc., without a particular intent to critique the use of these various methods. In this sense, our paper complements the recent work of Keating (1995) who examined management accounting research in terms of methodology – focusing exclusively on case research in managerial accounting with the intent of providing an in-depth review of case research as a methodology – without a particular concern to critique the theoretical traditions which motivate these research studies.

1966; Child 1972; Pugh *et al.* 1968). These studies suggested that organizations' structures are contingent upon contextual factors which have been variously defined to include technology (Woodward 1965), dimensions of task environment (Burns and Stalker 1961), and organizational size (Pugh *et al.* 1969; Blau 1970). These contextual factors are hypothesized to influence dimensions of structure including the degree of formalization, specialization, differentiation and bureaucratization. Discussions of social control and coordination were sometimes elicited to explain some of the observed relationships among structural properties, but, by and large, were not of a central importance.

Not all functionalist theories of organizations developed during this period presented such static images of organizations. Contingency frameworks, for example, drew directly from these sociological functionalist theories of organization structure, while also using March and Simon's (1958) organizational decision-making perspective. March and Simon (1958) developed a complex macro-perspective of organizations that viewed them as flexible, loosely-coupled systems in which human choice and voluntarism, and hence unpredictability, were major characteristics. The very essence of this decision-making perspective held that decision-makers in organizations are unlikely in most circumstances to have the information they need and want, and therefore, that many if not most decisions are made under conditions of uncertainty. In short, the primary concern of the organizational decision-making perspective is for the treatment of the problematic 'boundedly rational' person which, in turn, is the core legacy passed onto contingency theory as it seeks to provide insight as to this boundedly rational decision-maker in relation to the various contingent contextual factors (technology, environment, etc.) as suggested by the sociological structural perspectives.

March and Simon's (1958) depiction of the organizational decision-maker under such conditions of uncertainty was influenced by an earlier organizational theory tradition: the 'human relations' approach to organizational analysis as developed in the work of Mayo (1933) and more concretely articulated by Barnard's (1938) seminal work, *The Functions of the Executive*. Perhaps the fundamental insight of this human relations approach in terms of its contribution to the organizational decision-making of March and Simon (1958), and eventually the contingency theory perspective, was that social and psychological attitudes were significant factors to be considered in the design of production processes and its related control systems. The human relations approach, in turn, extended the early scientific management work of Frederick W. Taylor was concerned with the rationalization of work in order to maximize efficiency and productivity and, hence, profits. Scientific management ushered in the monitoring of the individual worker, but ultimately contributed to the monitoring of work units within organizations as well. The fascinating issue which the human relations perspective brought forth (as compared to earlier scientific management work) and pervades through contingency theory was the depiction of corporations existing in a tentative equilibrium which is inherently fragile, short lived and ever subject to a complex of personal, social, physical and biological destructive forces (Miller and O'Leary 1989). As Miller and O'Leary (1989) argued, it was axiomatic for the human relations perspective that all organizations are founded on self-interest and a contractual principle; this is the core reason that they are so fragile. This characterization of the organizations founded on self-interest and contractual principles becomes a major thrust of the organizational decision-making perspective as articulated in the work of March and Simon (1958) but also in the related work of Simon (1957) and the later work of Cyert and March (1963) and March and Olsen (1976).

In summary, March and Simon (1958) and the organizational decision-making perspective started with an image of human behavior and individual decision-making that was considerably more complex than the human relations perspective that had preceded them, but nonetheless, reflected a common concern for the managing of the organization. In turn, contingency theory blended the insights on human behavior and individual decision-making as depicted in March and Simon's (1958) organizational decision-making perspective with the sociological functionalist concerns regarding the impact of such structural factors as environment, size, technology, etc., on organizational behavior. Important in this lineage of work were issues of organizational control and coordination which are so germane to managerial accounting research.

Traditional management accounting research which has been based in the contingency literature (as well as its predecessors – organizational decision-making, human relations and scientific management) suggests that managerial accounting information should reflect and promote rationality in decision-making. Accordingly, management accounting information used by managers serve as quantitative expressions of organizational goals and are used to support rational decision-making (Ijiri 1965). The prescriptive character of managerial accounting information espoused by this traditional school of thought is essentially internal and downward and also prescriptive in character (Anthony 1965), thus reflecting the strong scientific management heritage, albeit later becoming more complex when sociological and psychological as well as structural factors are brought in.[5]

Among the earliest managerial accounting research which adopted a contingency perspective was Hofstede's (1967) classic field work which found that economic, technological and sociological considerations have a significant impact on the way budgeting systems function, concluding that managers used budgetary information in

---

[5] Caplan (1971, 13) identifies scientific management as providing the basis for the 'Traditional Management Accounting of the Firm' where the accounting system is assumed to be neutral and rational as it serves as '. . . a control device which permits management to identify and correct undesirable performance.' In contrast, entitling the human relations tradition as 'The Modern Organizational Theory Model,' Caplan (1971, 43) defined management accounting issues coming from this perspective as being concerned with social and psychological factors as stated in his terms, '. . . the interaction of the accounting technique of the individual to be controlled.' Both of these functionalist perspectives are precursors to contingency theory and reflect work in managerial accounting research much earlier than contingency theory. For example, the human relations tradition is the intellectual basis for the classic work of Argyris (1952) who found that budgetee participation in the budgetary process tends to foster fuller and more robust control over budgetees. He suggested that genuine participation in the budget process as a remedy to negative budget attitudes at lower levels (also see Hopwood (1973) as to the importance of budgetary participation in the behavioral attitudes of employees). Through this initial work of Argyris (1952) accounting researchers have adapted this human relations approach and have been concerned with modifying and assessing the effects of budgetary participation. This research tradition advocated bringing managers into the budgetary process with the objective of exercising fuller and more robust control

difficult economic environments to pressure workers; but in more lucrative environments, the budget was used more in a problem solving mode. Golembiewski (1964) was also among the earliest to explicitly examine various aspects of organizational structure in relationship to the use of budgets. In this tradition, Hayes (1977) investigated the appropriateness of management accounting systems for measuring the effectiveness of different departments in large industrial organizations, finding that contingency factors proved to be the major predictors of effectiveness for production departments. Extending this theme, Hirst (1981, 1983) examined external control factors such as environmental uncertainty and their impact on the reliance on accounting measures of performance. In applying contingency theories to control systems design, some researchers have sought to uncover direct relationships between these contextual factors and organizations' accounting and information systems (Khandwalla 1972). Technology also was specifically introduced as a major explanatory variable of an effective accounting information system by Daft and MacIntosh (1981). Others have articulated more subtle relationships between contextual factors, structural characteristics, and control system design (Gordon and Miller 1976; Waterhouse and Tiessen 1978). For example, Gordon and Miller (1976) hypothesized that accounting information systems could be designed to cope with environmental uncertainty by incorporating more nonfinancial data, increasing reporting frequency, and tailoring systems to local needs (see also MacIntosh 1981; Ansari 1977). Dent's (1987) focus was on the design of formal control systems in complex organizations, being concerned with the question of appropriate contingency principles underlying the design of such systems.

More recently, accounting researchers have sought to extend contingency arguments to embrace relationships between firms' strategies and the design of their control systems (see Govindarajan and Gupta 1985; Merchant 1985; Simons 1987). For example, Kaplan (1983) reasoned that managerial accounting has served business inadequately; it has become overly simplistic, structured and misdirected. He urged a

---

over them (Stedry 1960; Becker and Green 1962). Further extensions of this human relations research tradition which eventually led into contingency theory included Schiff and Lewin's (1970) analysis of the budget process, which identified the dysfunctional aspects of participative budgeting in terms of using it to create organizational slack. Swieringa and Moncur's (1975) study found self-assurance and assertiveness to be the most important predictors of how managers achieve their budget and how influential they are in the budgeting process. Otley (1978) studied the use of financial control systems in a coal mining firm and observed that consideration on the part of the immediate superior may be a moderating factor. Otley's (1978, 143) findings suggested that a non-considerate, non-supportive leadership style combined with high emphasis on budget performance, was primarily 'punitive in its ethos and may have a net result that is counterproductive.' Finally, Brownell (1981, 1982) also examined the influence of personality as a moderating factor in the budgetary participation process. In summary of the human relations tradition, research pertaining to managerial accounting suggests that personality traits, participative budgeting patterns, and other psychological and sociological factors are important issues to consider in the design of information systems (Milani 1975; Collins 1978). This managerial accounting research tradition eventually included consideration of the structural factors espoused in contingency theory.

close scrutiny of organizational activity of successful organizations so that the managerial accounting systems adopted accurately reflect the complex conditions confronting contemporary organizations. Merchant (1981, 1984, 1985) found contingent relationships between corporate context (size, product diversity and extent of decentralization) and the uses of budgeting information. Govindarajan (1984, 1988) found environmental uncertainty to be a major explanatory variable regarding the appropriateness of accounting data in evaluating the performance of business units. Govindarajan and Gupta (1985) extended the concern for contingency relationships between organizational control mechanisms and variables such as technology, environment and size, by exploring the utility of relating these contingency relationships to strategy, where the utility of a particular incentive bonus system is contingent upon the strategy of the focal strategic bonus unit. The work of Shank (1989) and Simons (1987) also are important research efforts which mobilized contingency principles in the examination of the use of managerial accounting systems and information in a strategic manner.

Reflecting concerns for the role of managerial accounting information in contemporary organizations, the work of McNair and Mosconi (1988) and McNair et al. (1989) also reflects an implicit contingency tradition, finding that changes in technologies are accompanied by changes in performance management systems. Furthermore, McNair's group (McNair and Mosconi 1988; McNair et al. 1989) found that actual costs have begun to replace standards in JIT environments because of the ability to trace costs more easily and because of the more simplified manufacturing process. On this point, Foster and Gupta (1990) provided a cross sectional comparison of manufacturing plants in an electronics firm, arguing that contingency variables (size and complexity of cost drivers) affect manufacturing overhead. Patell's (1987) longitudinal study of JIT implementation and changes in cost accounting procedures also highlighted the importance of contingency structural factors in the coordination problems of many new manufacturing operations with regards to information for control and evaluation. The impact of structural factors is also apparent in the work of Banker et al. (1991) who found that firms that have implemented JIT or other teamwork programs are more likely to provide manufacturing performance information to shop-floor workers. A contingency theme underlies Young's (1992) work which raises the intriguing issue that power shifting can occur within the organization as a result of the implementation of JIT. Here it is argued that workers are given much more power under JIT than management may realize (i.e., a workers' strike could cripple them) because of the tight coupling that takes place (see Wilkinson and Oliver 1989). Finally, Selto et al. (1995) provided a rather comprehensive contingency perspective of the adaptation of JIT manufacturing and a total quality control system (JIT/TQC system) when they considered JIT in relationship to classical contingency theory constructs, organizational structure, context and control to get some sense of the fit of these organizational variables and the JIT system. Drawing from Drazin and Van de Ven's (1985) review of the extensive contingency literature, Selto et al. (1995) found contingency theory to have intuitive appeal in understanding broad issues of management controls, but also argued that the extensive interaction of variables as well as continuous changes in organizations would make it difficult to apply contingency theory.

The influence of contingency theory and its precursor theoretical traditions on managerial accounting research, however, have been criticized for presenting a deterministic, ahistorical view of organizations which provides limited insight as to the mediating processes of organizations. Among the earlier critiques of the application of contingency theory in managerial accounting, Otley (1980) observed that reliance tended to be placed on a relatively few number of very general variables, task environment and structure, which, in turn, were used to explain organization structure and design of managerial accounting systems. He argued that these variables tended to be ill-defined and measured, and were not comparable across earlier accounting studies, thus yielding fragmented results. Further, the proposal that the link between accounting systems design and organizational effectiveness was far from proven, Otley (1980) concluded that there remained a need to imbed accounting systems in the overall package of organizational control approaches, to develop more nuanced expressions of organizational effectiveness, and in general to move to a more complex expression of the contingency framework. Also, he observed that many of the issues relating to the development of accounting systems, and the relationships with the organization's differentiated environment, were political as opposed to technical in nature, and urged the application of a field study approach to examine these issues.

INTERPRETIVE PERSPECTIVES

By focusing on the management of complex relational networks and the exercise of coordination and control, contingency theory has adhered to the strong influence of the classical sociological functionalist perspectives (Durkheim 1938) at the cost of neglecting alternative sociological theories such as expressed in the work of Weber (1947, 1958, 1964) whose primary concern was with the source of formal structure: the legitimacy of rationalized formal structures. In contingency theory, legitimacy is given; assertions about bureaucratization such as the role of managerial accounting practices and information systems rest on the assumptions of norms of rationality. When such norms do play causal roles in theories of bureaucratization, it is because they are thought to be built into modern societies and organizations as very general values, which are thought to facilitate formal organization. But norms of rationality are not simply general values. They exist in much more specific and powerful ways in the rules, understandings and meanings attached to institutionalized social structures. The causal importance of such institutions has been neglected. According to Meyer and Rowan (1977, 343):

> Formal structures are not only the result of their relational network in the social organization ... [t]he elements of rationalized formal structure are also deeply ingrained in, and reflect, widespread understandings of social reality. ... Such elements of formal structure are manifestations of powerful institutional rules which function as highly rationalized myths that are binding on particular organizations.

Strands of this Weberian sociological tradition are embedded in March and Simon's (1958) organizational decision-making model which provides a key contribution in its focus on the routine, taken-for-granted aspects of organizational life. Traces of a cognitive orientation in Weber's theory of bureaucracy – his emphasis on the role of calculable rules in reducing uncertainty and rationalizing power relations – are apparent in the richness of March and Simon's (1958) decision-making model where they urged a focus on understanding the initiation and preservation of power relationships on two fronts: (1) the power to set premises and define the norms and standards that shape and channel behavior; and (2) the power to delimit appropriate models of bureaucratic structure and policy that go unquestioned for years. Weber's concern was to understand the dominance of organizations and their forms of rationality upon society's technical, economic and political forms of life. Weber reasoned that rationalization is concerned not only with the long-term process of social structure transformation, but simultaneously and more importantly, the perpetuation of existing power relations concealed in the advancement of rational imperatives. Thus, the critical issue is the politics of rationality itself.

This concern for the power and politics of rationality is inherent in other interpretive sociological work such as Berger and Luckmann's (1967). *The Social Construction of Reality*, in which they reasoned that the central question for sociological theory is: How is it possible that subjective meanings become objective facts? Berger and Luckmann's (1967) argument is that social order is based fundamentally on a shared social reality which, in turn, is a human construction, being created in social interaction. The process by which actions become repeated over time and are assigned similar meanings by self and others is defined as institutionalization. Further, Berger and Luckmann (1967) emphasized the importance of employing an historical approach, arguing that it is impossible to understand an institution adequately without an understanding of the historical processes in which it was produced. The result is the paradox 'that man is capable of producing a world that he then experiences as something other than a human product' (Berger and Luckmann 1967, 61). Similarly, Garfinkel (1967) developed an approach to social investigation, ethnomethodology, which shifted the image of cognition from a rational, discursive, quasiscientific process to one that operates largely beneath the level of consciousness, a routine and conventional practical reason governed by rules that are recognized only when they are breached. To this he added a perspective on interaction that casts doubts on the importance of normative or cognitive consensus. Here Garfinkel (1967) argued that action is largely scripted and justified, after the fact, by reference to a stock of culturally available legitimating accounts. Interpretive perspectives, and their underlying concerns pertaining to the cognitive decision-making issues of the organizational decision-making model, the Weberian concern for the politics of rationality, and the ethnomethodological concerns for the construction of social reality, have perhaps been most forcefully developed within institutional theory. Following Selznick's (1957, 17) definition '. . . to institutionalize is to infuse with value beyond the technical requirements of the task at hand,' the general theme of the institutional perspective is that an organization's survival requires it to conform to social norms of acceptable behavior as much as to achieve levels of production efficiency. Among the sociologists whose work reflected the Weberian tradition, Selznick (1957) viewed organizational structure as an adaptive vehicle shaped in reaction to the characteristics and commitments of participants as well as to influences and constraints from the external environment. Institutionalization refers to this adaptive process: the processes by which societal expectations of appropriate organizational form and behavior come to take on rule-like status in social thought and action. In particular, institutional theory extends beyond the focus of contingency theory on an organization's task environment, which has received much attention in managerial accounting research, to instead focus on its institutional environment. According to Scott (1987, 507):

> Until the introduction of institutional conceptualizations, organizations were viewed as being shaped largely by their technologies, their transactions, or the power-dependency relations growing out of such interdependencies. Environments were conceived of as task environments ... While such views are not wrong, they are clearly incomplete. Institutional theorists have directed attention to the importance of symbolic aspects of organizations and their environments. They reflect and advance a growing awareness that no organization is just a technical system and that many organizations are not primarily technical systems. All social systems, hence all organizations, exist in an institutional environment that defines and delimits social reality.

The general theme of the institutional perspective is that an organization's survival requires it to conform to social norms of acceptable behavior as much as to achieve high levels of production efficiency. Thus, many aspects of an organization's formal structure, policies and procedures serve to demonstrate a conformity with institutionalized rules, thereby legitimizing it, to assist in gaining society's continued support (Meyer and Rowan 1977; Scott 1987; DiMaggio and Powell 1983, 1991). Meyer and Rowan (1977) proposed that such externally legitimated, formal assessment criteria as managerial accounting information play a heightened though ritualistic role in a variety of settings as organizations grope to find, conform to, and demonstrate for their internal and external constituents some form of rationality in order to gain legitimacy. Thus, rather than merely representing some notion of an objective reality, managerial accounting may serve as a ceremonial means for symbolically demonstrating an organization's commitment to a rational course of action. Here accountants gain their power by the responsible development and application of generally legitimated categories. Similarly, Zucker (1977) argued that the rationalization in formal control systems is an important part of a network of political and power relations which are built into the fabric of social life, a process of transforming the moral into the merely factual.

Covaleski and Dirsmith (1988a, 1988b) adopted an institutional perspective to examine the manner in which societal expectations of acceptable budgetary practices are articulated, enforced and modified during a period of organizational decline. They examined a large university system's budgeting process both through extensive archival documents and through in-depth interview with budgetary actors (see also Covaleski and Dirsmith 1983, 1986 for work pertaining to health care settings). Covaleski and Dirsmith (1988a, 1988b) followed a university budget category through periods of ascent, transformation and decline, describing the process of how a university challenged and rejected a traditional institutionalized budgetary framework for allocating state funding when this framework became inconsistent with the university's goals and interests. Self-interest is foremost in the minds of the various parties who propose, oppose, co-opt and contest the budget category. Covaleski and Dirsmith (1988a, 1988b) show how conflicting interests get couched in the common and legitimate language of budgeting, thus concluding that the budgetary process is an important manner in which societal expectations are reproduced.

Ansari and Euske (1987) also drew from institutional theory to examine the role of accounting information in the public sector, identifying this role in terms of documenting institutional compliance, i.e., seeking external legitimation or masking underlying sociopolitical reality. Ansari and Euske (1987) examined the manner in which cost information is used in the Department of Defense, finding disparity between the formally stated objective of the system to improve organization efficiency, and the lack of accounting system use for this purpose. The authors drew from an institutional perspective to explain the use of accounting information in the Department of Defense, in the light of this agency having ambiguous missions that foster rationalizing uses of accounting information.

Mezias (1990) examined the financial reporting practices of the Fortune 200 and concluded that the institutional model adds significant explanatory power over and above the models that currently dominate the applied economics literature. Recognizing the institutional work that has been done pertaining to the accounting practices of not-for-profit organizations, Mezias (1990) studied relationships between institutional variables and the financial reporting practices used by for-profit organizations. Mezias and Scarselletta (1994) extended this work by examining the decision process of a public policy task force that plays a role in establishing financial reporting standards to determine the affects of the kinds of decisions made. Drawing upon institutional theory, this study modeled the decision process as an organized anarchy embedded in a larger institutional context of accounting.

In summary, Carruthers (1995) argued that institutionalism views accounting practices as one of a larger set of features that can legitimize organizations through the construction of an appearance of rationality and efficiency. As Carruthers (1995, 326) stated, 'Accounts are the quintessential rationalized myth, and it is surprising that new institutionalists have not devoted more time to studying them.' Perhaps the single most important contribution of institutional theorists to the study of organizations is their reconceptualization of the environments of organizations. Earlier organizational and sociological models had emphasized technical facets. Meyer and Rowan's (1977) work, however, called attention to a neglected facet of environments: institutional beliefs, rules and roles – symbolic elements capable of affecting organizational forms independent of resource flows and technical requirements. They emphasized (drawing from Berger and Luckmann 1967; Garfinkel 1967) that shared cognitive systems, although created in interaction by humans, come to be viewed as objectified and external structures defining social reality. This is an ethnomethodological view of human action as shaped by conventions, built up by participants in the course of interactions to the point that much behavior takes on a taken-for-granted quality. The more institutionalized the cognitive categories and belief systems, the more human actions are defined by a widening sphere of taken-for-granted routines (Weber 1947).

Reflecting a theme similar to institutional theory, resource dependency theorists argue that organizations are limited by a variety of external pressures (Pfeffer and Salancik 1978; Pfeffer 1981), that environments are collectivities and interconnected, and that organizations must be responsive to external demands and expectations in order to survive. Resource dependency theorists also suggest that organizations attempt to obtain stability and legitimacy, and that organizational stability is achieved through the exercise of power or control for purposes of achieving a predictable inflow of vital resources and reducing environmental uncertainty (Oliver 1991). In this tradition, Weick (1976) stated that the chief responsibilities of organizational administrators are to provide a common language from which to reaffirm and solidify ties with outsiders through symbol management, consistent articulation of a common vision, and interpretation of diverse actions in terms of common themes. In like manner, Burns (1986) observed that such 'rule systems' as formal control systems, rather than being neutral or merely technical in nature, constitute power resources that actors use in advocating organizational structural forms which serve their own interests. On this theme, Boland and Pondy's (1983, 1986) accounting studies highlight the ceremonial, seemingly irrational, aspects of resource allocation activities where, for example, they found that in a university case, the budget provided a context for state agencies to exercise their legitimate authority in allocating funds to particular priorities. At the same time the underlying flexibility was such that funds could be diverted from one program to another at will. In short, resource dependency theorists also have placed a strong emphasis on the role of political language, particularly in budgeting processes.

Generally, the resource dependency tradition has recognized that budgeting is closely linked with power, self-interest and political advocacy in contemporary organizations (Pfeffer and Salancik 1974, 1978; Salancik and Pfeffer 1974; Rose 1977; Pfeffer 1981; Schick 1985). More specifically, self-interest and internal power and politics, actively expressed, for example, through budgeting systems, have been found to play heightened roles during periods of organizational decline in terms of resource allocation decisions made within organizations, possibly so that the organization maintains some semblance of subunit harmony (Hackman 1985; Hills and Mahoney 1978; Gray and Ariss 1985). In addition, not only do organizations appear to use budgeting in a political mode to allocate resources internally, but the visibility of these internal budgetary allocations to external constituents also appears to influence the generation of resources (Hackman 1985). This dual role of budgeting in generating and allocating resources suggests an expanded linkage between the values of external constituents and the internal resource needs and uses of an individual organization, most particularly in times of financial stress.

Cyert and March (1963) have defined budgets as both the substance and result of political bargaining processes that are useful for legitimizing and maintaining systems of power and control within organizations. Similarly, Pfeffer (1981) argued that a particularly effective way of influencing resource allocation decisions is to do it as unobtrusively as possible, such as through the apparently objective mechanism of the budgetary process which tends to legitimate subjective and political decision-making processes (see also Pfeffer and Salancik 1974, 1978). Here, according to Hopwood (1974), the trivial, dull, seemingly objective nature of accounting enables it to be used in taking the debatable out of the realm of open debate and into the realm of calculation. Consequently, these theorists considered managerial accounting information such as budgeting as a socially constructed phenomenon rather than a technically rational function driven by and serving the internal operations of organizations. Moreover, these perspectives recognized that once implemented, what a budgeting system accounts for shapes organizational members' views of what is important and, more radically, what constitutes reality. Budgeting, then, has been implicated in the construction of social reality rather than being the passive mirror of a technical reality. On this point, Pfeffer (1981, 184) concluded:

> [t]he task of political language and symbolic activity is to rationalize and justify decisions that are largely a result of power and influence, in order to make these results acceptable and legitimate in the organization.

Regarding the political perspective of budgeting, Wildavsky (1964, 1975, 1979) long argued that budgeting systems achieve many purposes beyond control, that they are at once forms and sources of power, and that they serve both the guardians of scarce resources and the advocates of budgetary units. Wildavsky also reasoned that inherently conflictual organizations may use budgets in establishing and maintaining existing power relations as opposed to serving decision-making and problem solving directly in a technically rational manner. Instead, he argued, decision-making and problem solving are served by the sometimes asymmetrical political confrontation between budgeters and budgetees. Wildavsky concluded that the political nature of budgeting may well be inherent in complex organizational life, and is not an aberrant defect in budgetary practice. Resource allocation, he suggests, is not the consequence of dispassionate analysis, but emerges through a subtle role of advocates and guardians. Building on Wildavsky's analysis, Jonsson (1982) sought to capture some of the implicit political dynamics by following the way in which the budgetary process unfolded over three years in a Swedish municipality in a time of financial stringency.

Edelman's (1977) broader political view and his concern for probing the consent of the governed in American politics also reflects concern for the significance of power and language. He argued that power relationships are seen as being reflected in daily life through the use of language, myths and symbolic displays directed at maintaining the status quo. Viewed as a form of language, quantitative data is selectively deployed by the state not to reflect underlying economic conditions, but to create public values, acquiescence and support. As Edelman (1977, 58) observed:

> Language is always an intrinsic part of some particular social situation; it is never an independent instrument or simply a tool for description. By naively perceiving it as a tool, we mask its profound part in creating social relationships and in evoking the roles and the selves of those involved in the relationships.

Consent of the governed, then, comes about not from the conscious acceptance of rules of procedure, but as acquiescence to and taking for granted an accepted language, thus at once creating and supporting a hierarchical relationship between the governed and the state. Always cloaked in the appearance of objectivity and neutrality, this language is ultimately directed toward establishing and maintaining hierarchies of authority and status (Clegg 1987). This acceptable discourse, such as accounting information, is always an intrinsic part of some particular social situation; it is never an independent instrument or simply a tool to be assessed for such attributes as its representational faithfulness. On this point, Scott (1987, 509) emphasized that:

> Outcomes will ... be strongly shaped by the agents' differential ability to lay successful claim to the normative and cognitive facets of the political processes: those identified by such concepts as authority, legitimacy, and sovereignty.

Finally, Abbott's (1988) work on professions can be meaningfully integrated into the concern of interpretive perspectives. Here Abbott has observed both that the professions seek to legitimize themselves to society by attaching their expertise to the widely held values of rationality, efficiency and science, and that a key characteristic lies in the use of power both externally to preserve an abstract system of knowledge and, more importantly, internally in terms of hierarchical stratification and differentiation (see also Sarfatti-Larson 1977). Joining Abbott in recognizing the importance of power, Freidson (1986) alluded to a decoupling between the administrative or formalized and structurally oriented component of professional bureaucracies and the practitioner component comprised of those possessing and using internalized values and norms. Objectivity, having a close association with scientific endeavor, encodes expertise in an organizational structure and away from individuals (Freidson 1986; Abbott 1988). Both authors pointed to the necessity of conducting research at the micro-level of everyday practitioner experience, where self-interest may come into play, in order to understand professional endeavor. Abbott (1988) lamented that insufficient attention has been directed at studying professionals, not as freestanding autonomous agents, but as members of organizations, particularly for professions arising out of a commercial enterprise such as accounting. Abbott's (1988, 226–235) findings suggest that in the early twentieth century, U.S. engineers battled accountants for professional jurisdiction over the growing volume of quantitative work associated with corporations; a battle won by the accountants who won control and established a professional monopoly (Loft 1986; see also Armstrong 1985).

In summary, interpretive perspectives of managerial accounting and organizations take issue with the assumption of an objective reality, arguing that the implementation of such apparently rational, bureaucratic mechanisms as managerial accounting systems is one manner in which the social world flows through organizations and changes them. These theorists have begun to see managerial accounting practices and information as socially constructed phenomena with the full implications of the power and politics of social construction rather than as a technically rational function driven by and serving the internal operations of organizations. Furthermore, these interpretive perspectives recognize that once managerial accounting practices and information are implemented, what it accounts for shapes organizational members' views of what is important and, more radically, what constitutes reality. Managerial accounting, then, is seen as being implicated in the social construction of reality rather than as being passively reflective of the reality as depicted in contingency theory and its predecessors.

Although the thrust of the interpretive perspectives in general and institutional theory in particular have received a growing amount of empirical support, a number of useful criticisms of them have been offered. DiMaggio (1988), for example, suggested that an apparent paradox resides in the two senses in which theorists have used the term 'institutionalization.' Institutionalization as an *outcome* places societal expectations and organizational structures and practices beyond the reach of power and self-interest; expectations of acceptable practice merely exist and are taken for granted (Perrow 1985; Powell 1985). By contrast, institutionalization as a *process* may be profoundly political and reflects the relative power of organized interests (see also Tolbert 1988; DiMaggio and Powell 1991). Within this concern for institutionalization as a process, the major problem in institutionalized settings can be defined in terms of finding some mechanism that can be mobilized by interested actors to change an overly stable social system (DiMaggio 1988), or in terms of finding some process wherein social order is produced in a system where organizations are constantly eroding (Zucker 1988). Regarding power and group interest, DiMaggio (1988) has observed that institutional and interest-based explanations of organizational practices are not necessarily antagonistic to one another, but combined, may yield a more comprehensive theoretical apparatus for gaining insight into the social dynamics of organizations. He concluded that allusions to power and group interests tend to be smuggled into the institutional perspective rather than provide the focus of a sustained theoretical analysis.

CRITICAL PERSPECTIVES

Since the early 1980s an increasing number of researchers have begun to adopt diverse critical perspectives to explore and investigate the roles of accounting practices in society. These critical perspectives in accounting research are marked by a great deal of intellectual ferment evident in the different theoretical approaches and methodologies deployed and the wide range of topics and issues addressed. Accordingly, in the light of such heterogeneity and the constraints of space, our intent is to provide a flavor of these alternative accounting research agendas without claiming to be exhaustive.[6]

Classifying these heterogeneous theoretical stances as 'critical perspectives,' in contrast to the functionalist and interpretative traditions explored above, can be justified by their singular attention to the interrelation between accounting and issues of conflict, domination and power. Despite the theoretical differences within the different strands of the critical perspectives regarding the manner and form in which

---

[6] For a more in-depth treatment of alternative research agendas in accounting, consult for example, Critical Accounts by David Cooper and Trevor Hopper (1990), *Sociological Perspectives on Modern Accounting* by Robin Rosenlender (1992), *The Social and Organizational Context of Management Accounting* by Anthony Puxty (1993), and *Accounting as a Social and Institutional Practice* by Anthony Hopwood and Peter Miller (1994).

to conceptualize power, they all avoid a consensus view of society that is the hallmark of both the functional and interpretive perspectives.

It may be argued that power, in both the functional and interpretive perspectives, is formulated as if it were a possession belonging to someone which he or she exercises for individual gain and further, that this power is diffused over society in a manner as to preclude the sustained and systematic negation of any individuals' preferences (Alford and Friedland 1985). In sharp contrast, this individualist basis of power and ultimately consensus view of society is eschewed by the critical perspectives which attempt to deal explicitly with conflict, domination and power (Cooper and Sherer 1984). For example, rather than treating various managerial accounting practices as a response to transaction costs considerations as in Johnson and Kaplan (1987) or agency cost considerations as in Christensen (1983), they are treated as modes by which the extraction of labor from laborers is made possible (Hopper and Armstrong 1991) and as methods by which the actions of individuals are made visible and susceptible to greater discipline and control (Hoskins and Macve 1988, Miller and O'Leary 1987). Accordingly, class conflict, the hegemony of elites, and the power of experts and professionals are some of the elements that the critical perspectives systematically foreground (not all such analyses incorporate all of these emphases) in their attempt to understand accounting practices.

Despite the theoretical richness within the critical perspectives, we will confine our attention to two major research strands that have illuminated our understanding of managerial accounting. First, we will consider the labor process perspective which draws from the Marxist tradition and then we will examine the Foucaultian perspective which, as the name suggests, draws from the work of Michel Foucault. While both of these alternatives are critical in orientation, there are significant differences in the kinds of insights they offer and consequently, we will first describe their relevant theoretical infrastructure and then, tease out from extant accounting studies their implications for our understanding of managerial accounting.

The labor process perspective

> It thus becomes essential for the capitalist that control over the labor process pass from the hands of the worker into his own. The transition presents itself in history as the *progressive alienation of the process of production* from the worker; to the capitalist, it presents itself as the problem of *management*. (Braverman 1974, 58, emphasis in original)

Harry Braverman, in the much acclaimed *Labor and Monopoly Capitalism: The Degradation of Work in the Twentieth Century*, offered a resounding critique of conventional understandings of work processes in capitalist economic systems. Drawing from the pioneering work of Karl Marx, Braverman asserted the primacy of the social relations of production for any attempt to understand the manner and modes in which goods and services are created in the capitalist economy. Specifically, Braverman (1974, 52) following Marx, suggested that the *differentia specifica* of capitalist economies was 'the purchase and sale of labor power.' Understanding the historical novelty of this feature is crucial, for this defining aspect of modern economies which we take for granted is, as a general phenomenon, unknown to prior epochs of human history. Capitalist economies are accordingly differentiated from prior epochs by the social relation embedded within the employment relation. Employment relations in contrast to, say, self-employment as the general form by which modern people earn their livelihood is an extremely recent phenomenon, and requires that workers sell their labor power to capitalists; for a wage. This historical reduction of persons to hired hands deprive them of their connectedness to the production process. Treated as a commodity, labor consequently 'has no material interest in doing more that securing the highest wages and best conditions for the minimum of sacrifice' (Hopper *et al.* 1987, 445).[7]

Wage labor, or hired labor, is treated within capitalist economies as a cost of production – as any other input factor of production – which need, *from the capitalist's point of view*, to be both minimized and optimized. The minimization of labor costs is 'rational' since it avoids the dependence on a factor of production that, unlike other factors, can rebel against its own use. Similarly, optimizing the use of labor is 'rational' since, as with any other factor of production, the efficient use of resources is the precondition for profits. Consequently, and built into the capitalist relations of production are the pressures to not only supplant labor by machinery but also to control the labor process – how labor power is deployed, the actual mode of work – in all its aspects, in the interest of capital accumulation. It is this pressure that motivates the capitalist to gain control over the labor process and make the latter 'the responsibility of the capitalist' (Braverman 1974, 57). However, treating human beings as just another factor of production sets the stage for the exploitation and expropriation of labor by capital. Accordingly, there is an irreducible conflict between capital and labor ensuring perpetually antagonistic relations between the classes. It is on this backdrop of capitalist social relations that the labor process perspective on cost and managerial accounting is fleshed out (see also Edwards 1979; Burawoy 1979; Noble 1977; Clawson 1980).

Hopper *et al.* (1987) introduced the labor process perspective to accounting by contrasting this perspective from both functional and interpretative understandings of managerial accounting. Their central argument was that management accounting cannot be properly understood, except in the light of the social relations of production. They argued that to view organizations as united by a common purpose is to fictionalize what is, in fact, a site of irreconcilable conflict. Such organization goals as the maximization of the net present value of future cash flows transforms what is the goal of one

---

[7] According to Braverman (1974, 53) 'In the United States, perhaps four-fifths of the population was self-employed in the early part of the nineteenth century ... by 1970 only about one-tenth of the population was self-employed.' Laborers in having to sell their labor power as a commodity, are now alienated from the fruits of their labor. This is the significance of the *labor theory of value* which asserts that the value of goods and services originate from and thus belong to those who make them. Moreover, since workers can produce far more per unit time than is necessary to keep them alive, this surplus value created is the source and object of capitalist strategies to make more profits. Accordingly, profits come from extracting as much labor from the purchased labor power, and then expropriating the surplus value so generated.

sectional interest into the overriding goal of all, thus obscuring the class-based distributional conflicts inherent in all capitalist organizations.

Accordingly, labor process theorists deny that management accounting is a neutral tool serving the general interests of efficiency and emphasize its role in legitimizing partisan interests, in contributing to the control and domination of labor, and in reinforcing the dominant mode of production, i.e., capitalist production, albeit in a contested terrain. Moreover, management accounting also is capable of showing up the ambiguous position of managers within capitalist firms. Where on the one hand, they are 'materially privileged' agents of the capitalists' class and must accordingly serve the interests of the latter, they are on the other hand, wage labor and to that extent interested in 'securing their own employment, and in fighting for an improved share of available resources' (Hopper *et al.* 1987, 450–451). Thus, managers are at once 'both agents and victims of control' such that phenomena such as budget games and divisional budgeting slack must not be seen as the consequence of some 'individual pathology' but rather as the 'deep effects of exploitative and oppressive social structures' that are embedded and presupposed in the capitalist system of production.

While Hopper *et al.* (1987) offered a programmatic introduction to the labor process perspective and distinguish it from the more functionalist and interpretive traditions, a later paper by Hopper and Armstrong (1991) presented a historically rooted reflection on the development of management and cost accounting since the middle of the nineteenth century, in part by challenging the very popular reading of the history of cost and managerial accounting given by Johnson and Kaplan (1987) (see also Johnson 1972, 1981, 1983). Deploying a transactions-cost approach, Johnson and Kaplan (1987) argued for understanding the emergence and prevalence of cost accounting as techniques which contributed to increasing operational efficiencies, and for ROI and budgets as techniques which reduced the costs of managing large vertically integrated bureaucracies as opposed to securing market-based coordination. In contrast, Hopper and Armstrong (1991) challenged this interpretation by linking the presence and even subsequent absence of cost and managerial accounting practices to the changing forms of control over the labor process that are in turn linked to different phases of capitalism.

Accordingly, Hopper and Armstrong (1991) suggested that for the early factory organizations of the mid-nineteenth century (they especially consider Lyman Mills which was also the focus for Johnson and Kaplan (1987)), increases in profits were secured primarily from extending the number of hours worked without significantly changing the wages and from applying a closer degree of control over the labor process. Such 'innovations' as the 'stretch-out (an increase in the number of machines supervised by each operator), the speed-up (an increase in the operating speed of machines),' and 'a premium bonus system' for overseers to enforce productivity, were monitored and achieved by accounting records, while such labor practices as firing workers for trade union activity and disciplining dormitory behavior of workers by the 'moral police' ensured a relatively docile labor force which was the precondition for managerial action that is based on cost accounting information (Hopper and Armstrong 1991, 414–415). Hence, they argued that some of the accounting and cost information was not used for making the production process more efficient but rather used to intensify the extraction of labor from the labor force.

Moreover, the decline of internal contracts (outsourcing products and skilled labor) during the late nineteenth century was based on appropriating the profits made by subcontractors, though it involved increased costs for the companies (from replacing contractors with college trained executive who lacked knowledge of production processes). Where previously 'companies kept no records of the hours worked by the contractors' employees, or of how much and on what basis they were paid,' by paying workers directly, companies began to keep a host of new records including 'work records' (Hopper and Armstrong 1991, 416). Consequently, the creation of these new records, which also 'laid the foundation for the later development of standard costing systems' had 'nothing to do with the efficiency of the conversion process ... but was a means of redistributing [the] profits ... made by the contractors to the companies' (Hopper and Armstrong 1991, 417). Furthermore, these records not only transferred 'financial knowledge from the worker to the factor owner' but also fostered the 'imposition of an additional system of activity surveillance' (Hopper and Armstrong 1991, 417). Again, they argued that accounting records are hardly neutral but are deeply intertwined with the expropriation of profits, the intensification of the labor process and the surveillance of worker activities.

Regarding the late nineteenth and the early twentieth century, Hopper and Armstrong (1991) said that such developments as standard costing, ROI measures, and budgets cannot be understood except in the context of the correlative destruction of craft labor. Management accounting was one element in the development of a vast paper bureaucracy (measured by the increase in record-keeping and the swelling ranks of white-collar employees) by which the production process should be replicated, monitored and controlled. In the continual attempt to control the labor process, owners, and by now also managers, sought to redesign, fragment and simplify the labor process 'so that skill levels were reduced and the mental aspects of production incorporated into management' (Hopper and Armstrong 1991, 419).

The labor process perspective has illuminated not only historical issues but also has been successfully applied to contemporary times. For example, Knights and Collinson (1987) found that British workers in one factory were unable to contest management's accounting reports, even when these reports led to worker layoffs. They suggested that accounting has inherent characteristics which make it difficult for workers to challenge these numbers, thus accounting information is not contested by labor on the grounds that its cultural values of 'objectivity' and 'hard facts' mirror the 'masculine values' on the shop floor. Similarly, Oakes and Covaleski (1994) examined organized labor's involvement with accounting-based incentive plans, and the role this involvement played in labor-management relations. This study involved case studies of profit-sharing plans implemented at three firms, Parker Pen, Kaiser Steel, and American Motors, in the 1950s and early 1960s, suggesting that 'accounting takes on characteristics or is constructed in ways that make it more or less likely that it will be contested at certain periods of time' (Oakes and Covaleski 1994, 595). Bougen *et al.* (1990) (see also Bougen 1989) documented the appearance and disappearance of accounting in British coal industry labor debates. Their study showed the partisan nature of the disclosure of financial reports to trade unions, the contested and sometimes self-defeating results of such disclosures, and of the many alternative managerial mechanisms (joint consultations committees and profit-sharing schemes) that attempt to gain cooperation by persuasion and cooperation.

In summary, labor process theory is consistent with the other organizational sociological perspectives such as contingency theory and interpretive work in the sense that it embeds management accounting in a wider context than more orthodox approaches. However, labor-process theory departs from these alternative approaches by focusing on the structural antagonism between classes inherent in capitalist societies. Also consistent with other organizational and sociological perspectives, labor-process theory offers a relatively non-technical understanding of management accounting in that management accounting appears within the context of a class-divided society to aid economic expropriation. Finally, the labor-process perspective moves towards considering accounting as a social practice rather than merely a technique, arguing that political events and ideologies, status, class, trust and technological changes impel people to act in certain ways, all potentially impinging on the roles served by management accounting.

The Foucaultian Perspective

Michel Foucault (1926–1984) was both a philosopher and historian who used history to raise philosophical questions.[8] A central motif that runs through his work and one which has also been productive for accounting scholarship is perhaps best described in his own words: '... the goal of my work during the last twenty years ... has been to create a history of the different modes by which, in our culture, human beings are made subjects' (Foucault 1983, 208). To begin to unpack this seemingly innocuous statement let us consider the key word here – 'subject' – in both the meanings that it admits: 'subject to someone else by control and dependence, and tied to his own identity by a conscience or self-knowledge. Both meanings suggest a form of power which subjugates and makes subject to' (Foucault 1983, 212). While the first meaning is a relatively familiar one (hierarchical employment relations, prisoner-guard, parent-child etc.), the second hints at the radical and innovative nature of Foucault's thought. What is equally significant regarding the exercise of this power, is the interrelation between power and knowledge which Foucault signifies by the slash in the term 'Power/Knowledge.' Foucault argued that to properly grasp the conditions for the emergence of the 'human sciences' – all those 'sciences' that are concerned with describing, explaining, understanding, predicting and controlling human behavior – one must understand its complicity with the historically unprecedented presence of a widespread and general control of human beings. Foucault (1979, 191) argued that the 'birth of the sciences of man' probably lies in the various written techniques (of notation, registration, columnar and tabular presentation, of measurement, classification etc.) by which individuals are turned into a 'case.' Transforming a

---

[8] A solid entry into the work and thought of Michel Foucault is the Paul Rabinow, ed. (1984) *Foucault Reader*. The introductory essay is an especially good and clear statement while the selection of readings is representative.

human being into a 'case' (patient, student, prisoner, worker) simultaneously homogenizes (by classifying as one within a series) and individualizes (by measuring the individual differences). Implicit in such classification and measurement is the presence of normalizing judgments wherein the measurement of individual differences are made in regard to deviations from a norm (for example, students grades, standard cost, time and motion studies, budgets, benchmarks). According to Foucault, it was only by the late eighteenth century that this manner of describing, or more precisely, writing up individuals as cases became widespread and general. It furthermore represented a reversal of historic proportions, as stated by Foucault (1979, 191):

> For a long time ordinary individuality – the everyday individuality of everybody – remained below the threshold of description. To be looked at, observed, described in detail, followed from day to day by an uninterrupted writing was a privilege. . . . The disciplinary methods reversed this relation, lowered the threshold of describable individuality and made of this description a means of control and a method of domination.

Power, in this light, is not negative or repressive but rather positive and productive, because 'it produces reality; it produces domains of objects and rituals of truth. The individual and the knowledge gained of him belongs to this production' (Foucault 1979, 194). Accordingly, for Foucault (1990, 98), power and knowledge are constitutive of, but not identical, to each other, since 'between techniques of knowledge and strategies of power, there is no exteriority, even if they have specific roles and are linked together on the basis of their difference.' The scientific disciplines which generate our knowledge of human beings is thus also complicit in their disciplining, or as Foucault (1979, 222) suggested, 'The "Enlightenment," which discovered the liberties, also invented the disciplines.'

Foucault's work has, as already been stated, sparked much attention in the critical accounting tradition. In a recent paper, Walsh and Stewart (1993) explored the history of managerial accounting practices from a rigorously Foucaultian perspective. In comparing 'two assemblages of people making things,' one from the 1700s and the other from the 1800s, they find support for one of Foucault's most provocative theses. By asserting that 'the individual' was the result of disciplinary mechanisms, Foucault also is implying that prior to the late eighteenth century individuals could not be known and therefore controlled since they lay below the threshold of description. Accordingly, what we consider axiomatic in managerial accounting – namely the linking of accounting calculations and measures to the work of individuals and groups – must not have been prevalent prior to the late eighteenth century. Indeed, this is precisely what Walsh and Stewart (1993) find when they compare the New Mills Woolen Manufactory (1681–1703) with the New Lanark Cotton Factory (1800–1812). Some features which characterized the manufactory of the late seventeenth century include: master-servant relationships between the managers and workers; customary rather than market driven rates of profit, calculations of selling prices and wages; use of the pillory and the prison as threats of retribution to workers for pilferage or shortages in piece work; bookkeeping as a 'physical memory of the real proceedings of each day and each week to be certified by the masters' (Walsh and Stewart 1993, 786).

While Walsh and Stewart (1993) focused on the early days of the factory system to provide some solid evidence and support for Foucault's thesis, Miller and O'Leary (1994) studied another time period to examine the rising popularity of standard costing and budgetary practices in the U.S. during the turn of the century. Again, using a Foucaultian perspective, they illuminated dimensions of that much studied period that have hitherto escaped attention. Miller and O'Leary (1994, 99) argued that such accounting practices as standard costing and budgeting should be understood 'as a technology of government,' where the latter is understood as 'the ensemble of rationalities and technologies' by which 'authorities attempt to act on the conduct of others, to shape their beliefs and behavior in directions deemed desirable.' Accordingly, the widespread emergence of standard costing and budgetary techniques by the 1930s in both the U.K. and the U.S. are seen as indicative of a new modality in the governance of economic life. This emergence was linked not only to the scientific management movement associated with Taylor and the spread of industrial psychology but also to the concern with national efficiency in the U.K. and the 'efficiency craze' in the U.S. The term efficiency was deployed in a wide range of contexts from individual performance on the factory floor to articulation the social responsibilities of the state in correcting the ills of society, and subsumed under itself a host of financial and nonfinancial techniques. Linkages were also forged between the scientific management of industrial enterprises and the rational and orderly planning of society as a whole. A host of such social sciences as public administration, engineering, and sociology as well as a slew of such experts as accountants, urban planners and economists sought to 'normalize and govern populations of individuals' (Miller and O'Leary 1994, 111). It is this new modality of governing economic life that forms a context that is both constitutive of and constituted by the standard costing and budgetary practices of the early twentieth century.

To date, within accounting as well as organizational theory, a majority of work applying what has been termed Foucault's archeological and genealogical perspectives have had an historical perspective. However, the application of Foucault's insights into the functioning of modern societies is not limited to forays into the past. More pertinently, his work proves to be of continuing value as it is being profitably used to illuminate certain aspects of the contemporary uses and redefinitions of accounting. For example, Preston (1992, 64) studied the relative emergence of Diagnostic Related Groups (DRGs) as an 'accounting technology based upon principles of cost control rather than cost reimbursement.' Using a longitudinal study Preston (1992, 97) showed how this practice of reimbursement cannot be exclusively related to 'a logic of economic incentives and rational economic behavior.' Rather, a shifting complex of events, including Medicare and Medicaid, the private structure of American health care, the power of professional associations, changing public attitudes towards health care, is seen as being part of this transformation of accounting practices. Accordingly, Preston, following Foucault, revealed the emergence of DRGs as being implicated in a wider and more general transformation in the 'politics of health' which involves not only economic factors but more decisively, social and cultural ones as well. On this same issue of contemporary application of Foucault's work, Rose (1991) argued for an interrelation between the mode of liberal democratic governance and the technology of quantification, numeracy and statistics. Rose (1991, 691) stated that 'numbers have an unmistakable power in modern political culture' evident from opinion pools to the federal budget and the national income statistics. The role of accounting in this Foucaultian view, is that accounting, along with other various calculations, form the basis for democratic politics whose singular characteristic is 'arms-length' management from a distance.

Consistent with the underpinnings of critical perspectives, the Foucaultian view situates management accounting in a wider political and social context. Specifically, in the Foucaultian approach, management accounting is considered as part of a larger historical trend through which people at large were subjected to a variety of disciplinary techniques. Whereas in labor-process theory, management accounting appears within the context of a class-divided society to aid economic expropriation, the Foucaultian tradition reveals management accounting as an element of a general historical process by which people are made calculable and governable. The Foucaultian view also considers management accounting as a social practice rather than a technique by examining the intricacies and richness in such social relations that are embedded in social patterns of interaction as language, discipline and intimacy, all cultural norms and forces which potentially impinge on the roles and nature of management accounting.

CLOSING DISCUSSION

It is important to note our interpretation of the relationship among the alternative managerial and sociological theories considered, as well as their relationship to more traditional perspectives of managerial accounting: can these various perspectives be compared and contrasted or possibly blended, and a 'champion' paradigm isolated? In exploring the structure of more general scientific revolutions, Kuhn (1970) reasoned that because of fundamentally different philosophical presumptions, it is impossible to employ the tenets of one paradigm to assist those subscribing to a second paradigm to transition to understand the first paradigm. But rather, the 'leap' from one paradigm to another must be based on faith in order to fully appreciate what a particular paradigm may offer for understanding our existence. In this spirit, and more closely concerned with organizational analysis, Morgan (1980) (see also Burrell and Morgan 1979; in accounting see Dirsmith *et al.* 1985) theorized that different paradigms both address different sorts of problems and, where paradigms address common problems, portray them in fundamentally different ways and thereby offer differing insights into their nature. Thus, what is called for is not a blending of paradigms nor the isolation of a particular paradigm as champion, but rather paradigmatic pluralism as a way of enhancing our understanding of issues in the social sciences. Consequently, we offer the various paradigms not as competing perspectives but in some sense as alternative ways of understanding the multiple roles played by management accounting in organizations and society.

Extending this theme and drawing upon Churchman's (1971) characterization of influencing systems, Mitroff and Mason (1982) offered a useful way to understand the properties of more orthodox research approaches and one which calls for a plurality of theories used in a dialectic fashion. The argument of Mitroff and Mason (1982) also highlights fundamental differences in the types of problems which may be addressed. Within the traditional approach to management accounting research, one seeks regularity, consistency or consensus by two means. In the first, one seeks patterns in specific sets of empirical data in a purely inductive mode. 'Consensus' of data is in essence a guarantor of faithfully representing a concrete reality. Any lack of regularity or consensus in the data (e.g., low r^2) serves to question the validity of the pattern isolated or theory used. One seeks improved understanding by refining the model's specification. In the second approach, one seeks internal consistency in a postulational system wherein reality *is* the axiomatic structure. In a deductively driven system, only the lack of internal consistency or conflict in the propositional network can cause one to abandon it in favor of a competing network.

The rational frame of reference importantly assumes that the phenomena under investigation are either well specified and well known, or able to be well known through some preliminary fieldwork (Keating 1995), or further refinement of the model or propositional network, and hence, are eminently structurable. However, because of its reliance on a set of fixed concrete data or variables expressed in a fixed postulational structure, it is limited in its abilities to preserve or reflect anomalies and uniqueness in phenomena and to capture the essence of ill structured problems. Its use is, therefore, relegated to examining well structured though perhaps technically complex problems. Paradoxically, because of their very comprehensiveness, these traditional perspectives tend to suppress conflict, anomaly and uniqueness. By contrast, a more interpretive or critical view emphasizes the use of multiple conceptual views of ill structured, anomalous phenomena on the presumption that reality is too ill structured to be meaningfully represented by any set of data or propositional network, no matter how comprehensive they may appear.

The use of alternative research theories also has resulted in alternative research methods of forms of inquiry. The general literature which describes the use of qualitative, naturalistic methods in field research is growing in volume and stature. From this literature, it is possible to outline various criteria of 'good' research which are provisionally consistent with the knowledge claims advanced by its theoretical perspective discussed in the paper (Morgan (1983) sounds a useful warning note in such matters). However, we avoid detailed treatment of such philosophical issues as epistemology, or such methodological issues as falsification, or indeed of research methods. These and related matters have been adequately dealt with in both the philosophy of science and accounting literatures.[9]

---

[9] Notable in this regard was the paper by Tinker *et al.* (1982). Others addressing the philosophical underpinnings of different accounting research include Christenson (1983), Chua (1986) and Hopper and Powell (1985). For statements by philosophers on the philosophy of science, consult Bernstein (1978), for those by organizational theorists see Burrell and Morgan (1979).

Denzin and Lincoln (1983) offer a useful discussion regarding criteria to consider for alternative methods of research inquiry. The first criteria is credibility which relates to the believability of the observations and interpretations to both the academic community and participants in the study. This criteria is addressed through such techniques as prolonged engagement at the organizational context studied which provides research scope, and persistent observations which concerns penetration into the context studied to identify relationships, forces, etc., which have salience in under- standing the lived experiences of organizational members. Representative adequacy also is important to credibility which entails having sufficient notes, transcripts, audio or video recordings to enable different researchers to examine field observations and form similar though not necessarily identical interpretations.

The second criteria is transferability, or the ability of the interpretations of one organizational context to be transferred to another. Given the primary focus on the context or substantive domain and the lived experience of its members, interpretive and critical field members would typically emphasize the importance of providing thick description in the research text, presenting vibrant, exact interview quotes, archival abstracts, etc., that provide both scope and depth in understanding the context. This thick description, in turn, influences theoretical perspectives being provisionally used to interpret the organizational context. It is this informed theory, not the observations, that may be transferred to begin providing another organizational context.

The third and fourth criteria are dependability and conformability. The former concerns developing reliable interpretations, but interpretations that simultaneously recast the state of its organization studied (i.e., its stability) and the process by which the organization is changing (i.e., its instability); in turn the field worker concedes instrumental unreliability, albeit a constructive unreliability. The latter criterion relates to the field observations themselves, can observations be corroborated by another investigator or another method? On this theme, Van Maanen (1995), has observed that the accounts rendered by field researchers employing qualitative, naturalistic methods may be described as 'impressionist takes,' using the analogy of impressionist art wherein the viewer of a piece of art sees both the subject being painted *and* the artist.

It is also important to note what may be gained by management accounting scholars beyond a more general appreciation of the technical, social and interest-based forces which may flow through and influence management accounting, and how management accounting, by embodying and reproducing these forces, may come to influence its own historical, socio-political context. Christenson (1983) argues that what may be derived is not the first-order concern of somehow modifying management accounting as a set of somewhat disembodied practices to somehow more faithfully represent an objective, albeit complex reality and thereby solve the technical problems of running an organization. But rather, what can be gained is a second-order focus of serving the problem solver, i.e., helping them recognize the multiple realities they confront and live, and the multiple meanings attached to and served by management accounting.

One of the principle tendencies exhibited by alternative research theories and related methods which distinguish them from the more familiar approaches is that of embedding management accounting in a wider social context than usual. Accounting research inspired by contemporary social and organizational psychology and neo-classical economics largely examines the roles and nature of management accounting from the perspective of the individual decision-maker or information processor within the organization. The alternative streams of research discussed here, in contrast, typically approach the study of managerial accounting from an inter-organizational and sociological perspective.

To illustrate the broader orientation, Selto *et al.*'s (1995) field study of a Fortune 500 firm examines the adaptation of JIT manufacturing and a total quality control system (JIT/TQC system) in relationship to classical contingency theory constructs – organizational structure, context and control – to ascertain the fit of these organizational variables and the JIT system. An interpretive perspective, such as institutional theory, might relate the adaption of the JIT/TQC system to even larger societal values of rationality while perhaps sacrificing on the robustness of insight provided by contingency theory regarding the impact of organizational-level variables. Here the theoretical and empirical focus would be more on probing the firm's broader field of relations, such as mimicking the structure of dominant firms in the industry, or responding to the coercion of the government, or adapting the norms of professional associations, expressed in terms of a more widespread JIT/TQC movement. Finally, critical perspectives would advance their theoretical frame of reference by characterizing the JIT/TQC efforts in this firm as related to the structural antagonism between classes inherent in capitalist societies (labor process perspective), or as part of a larger historical trend through which people at large were subjected to a variety of disciplinary techniques rendering the minute details of their behavior more visible (the Foucaultian approach). With the critical perspective's theoretical and empirical point of departure being at the broadest social and historical level (i.e., parts of larger historical trends of structural antagonism or disciplinary techniques) the more immediate organizational influences (contingency theory) or organizational fields (interpretive perspectives) become more tangential to the research focus. In summary, despite the differences between the theoretical points of departure and related demands for empirical inquiry pertaining to the contingency, interpretive, and critical perspectives, these approaches to management accounting provide multiple understandings of management accounting that are not offered by more narrowly focused analysis which centers around individual preference and cognitive functions.

A second aspect that distinguishes the management accounting research which draws on organizational and sociological traditions is its tendency to offer a relatively non-technical understanding of management accounting. For example, it is usual to suppose that management accounting is an information system that can be designed to influence decisions and to so gain control over behavior. Here, accounting is a tool that not only signals certain states of the world, but also works as an instrument by which certain outcomes are made more probable. This instrumental and consequently asocial, ahistorical and apolitical view of accounting contrasts with that gained from the various alternative research streams. Again, referring to the contributions of Selto *et al.*'s (1995) contingency perspective driven field work, such management accounting practices as JIT/TQC systems are seen to be invested with the social aspects of worker empowerment, workgroup performance, and relations within and between workgroups, operators and supervisors. By modifying the system, aided by management accounting, the fit may be enhanced and performance consequently improved. An interpretive perspective of management accounting would particularly probe the issue as to whether JIT/TQC systems are as much a symbol demonstrating efficiency and rationality to be displayed for external consumption as they are an instrument for achieving efficiencies, thus focusing their theoretical and empirical efforts to inform our understanding of the symbolic nature of JIT/TQC. Critical perspectives, in turn, might mobilize their empirical efforts around their respective theoretical motivations to examine JIT/TQC systems within the context of a class-divided society to aid economic expropriation of workers' surplus, or, in the Foucaultian tradition, to examine JIT/TQC systems as artifacts of a general historical mechanism by which people are made calculable and manageable.

Accordingly, alternative streams of research, to varying degrees, move towards considering accounting as a social practice rather than a technique. To treat accounting as a 'practice' instead of a 'technique' is to embed accounting within the web of human actions which are, in turn, constitutive of social relations. The intricacies and richness of social relations that are suffused by such aspects of sociality as symbols, myths, language, status, class, trust and intimacy, comprises the backdrop for the organizationally and sociologically informed studies of accounting. More specifically, management accounting research rooted in the contemporary social and organizational psychology and neo-classical economics usually examines management accounting procedures and techniques with the intent to improve its efficacy. In general, these traditional approaches are problem driven and directed towards improving and refining the instrument that is management accounting to better serve exogenously given organizational goals and thus somewhat narrow in focus. Designing better costing procedures, incentive contracts, information systems to account for processing biases, and so on, are examples of the problem-driven nature of mainstream management accounting research.

In contrast, the research drawing on organizational and sociological theories, to different degrees, situate management accounting practice within the context of social life in general. The problem-driven focus is less apparent since, in part, the very ways in which problems come to be defined as problems needing solutions, or indeed how particular calculative techniques come to be called 'accounting,' comprise the subject for analysis. From this perspective, managerial accounting practices are not techniques that can be abstracted from the general milieu of social life but rather one strand in the complex weave that makes up the social fabric. Political events and ideologies, cultural norms and forces, social patterns of interaction and societal presuppositions, technological changes and subjective meanings that impel people to act in certain ways, all potentially impinge on the roles and nature of management accounting. It is in this manner that a different light is shed on the role and nature of management accounting practices by the research which draws from organizational and sociological theories.

REFERENCES

Abbott, A. (1988). *The System of Professions*. Chicago: University of Chicago Press.

Aiken, M., and J. Hage (1966). Organizational alienation. *American Sociological Review*, **31**: 497–507.

Alford, R., and R. Friedland (1985). *Powers of Theory*. Cambridge: Cambridge University Press.

Ansari, S. L. (1977). An integrated approach to control systems design. *Accounting, Organizations and Society*, **2**: 101–112.

———, and K. J. Euske (1987). Rational, rationalizing and reifying uses of accounting data in organizations. *Accounting, Organizations and Society*, **12**: 549–570.

Anthony, R. (1965). *Planning and Control Systems: A Framework for Analysis*. Boston, MA: Harvard University Press.

Argyris, C. (1952). *The Impact of Budgets on People*. New York: Controllership Foundation.

Armstrong, P. (1985). Changing management control strategies: the role of competition between accountancy and other organizational professions. *Accounting, Organizations and Society*, **10**: 129–148.

Banker, R. D., S. M. Datar, and L. Kemerer (1991). A model to evaluate variables impacting the productivity of software maintenance. *Management Science*, 1–18.

Barnard, C. (1938). *The Functions of the Executive*. Boston: Harvard University Press.

Becker, S., and D. Green (1962). Budgeting and employee behavior. *Journal of Business* (October): 392–402.

Berger, P. L., and T. Luckmann (1967). *The Social Construction of Reality*. New York: Doubleday.

Bernstein, R. (1978). *The Restructuring of Social and Political Theory*. Philadelphia: University of Pennsylvania Press.

Blau, P. M. (1970). A formal theory of differentiation in organizations. *American Sociological Review*, **35**: 201–218.

——— (1973). *The Organization of Academic Work*. New York: John Wiley.

Boland, R. J., and L. R. Pondy (1983). Accounting in organizations: A union of natural and rational perspectives. *Accounting, Organizations and Society*, **8**: 223–234.

———, and ——— (1986). The micro-dynamics of a budget cutting process: Modes, models and structure. *Accounting, Organizations and Society*, **11**: 403–422.

Bougen, P. D. (1989). The emergence, roles and consequences of an accounting-industrial relations interaction. *Accounting, Organizations and Society*, **14**: 203–234.

———, S. G. Ogden, and Q. Outram (1990). The appearance and disappearance of accounting: wage determination in the U.K. Coal industry. *Accounting, Organizations and Society*, **15**: 149–170.

Braverman, H. (1974). *Labor and Monopoly Capital*. New York: Monthly Review Press.

Brownell, P. (1981). Participation in budgeting, locus of control and organizational effectiveness. *The Accounting Review*, **56**: 844–860.

——— (1982). The role of accounting data in performance evaluation, budgetary participation, and organizational effectiveness. *Journal of Accounting Research*, 12–27.

Burawoy, M. (1979). *Manufacturing Consent*. Chicago: University of Chicago Press.

Burns, T. R. (1986). Actors, transactions and social structures. In: *Sociology: From Crisis to Science?*, edited by V. Hemmelstrand, 8–37. London: Sage.

———, and G. M. Stalker (1961). *The Management of Innovation*. Tavistock.

Burrell, G., and G. Morgan (1979). *Sociological Paradigms and Organizational Analysis*. Heinemann.

Caplan, E. H. (1971). *Management Accounting and Behavioral Science*. Reading, MA: Addison-Wesley.

Carruthers, B. G. (1995). Accounting, ambiguity, and the new institutionalism. *Accounting, Organizations and Society*, **20**: 313–328.

Child, J. (1972). Organization structure and strategies of control: A replication of the Ashton Study. *Administrative Science Quarterly*, **17**: 163–177.

Christensen, J. (1983). The determination of performance standards and participation. *Journal of Accounting Research*, **20**: 589–603.

Christenson, C. (1983). The methodology of positive accounting. *The Accounting Review*, 58 (January): 1–22.

Chua, W. F. (1986). Radical developments in accounting thought. *The Accounting Review*, **61**(4): 601–632.

Churchman, C. W. (1971). *The Design of Inquiry Systems*. New York: Basic Books.

Clawson, D. (1980). *Bureaucracy and the Labor Process: The Transformation of U.S. Industry, 1860–1920*. New York: Monthly Review Press.

Clegg, S. (1987). The language of power and the power of language. *Organization Studies*, **8**: 61–70.

Collins, F. (1978). The interaction of budget characteristics and personality variables with budgetary response attitudes. *The Accounting Review*, **53**: 324–335.

Cooper, D., and T. Hopper (1990). Critical studies in accounting. *Accounting, Organizations and Society*, **12**: 407–414.

———, and M. Sherer (1984). The value of corporate accounting reports: Arguments for a political economy of accounting. *Accounting, Organizations and Society*, **9**: 407–414.

Covaleski, M. A., and M. W. Dirsmith (1983). Budgeting as a means for control and loose coupling. *Accounting, Organizations and Society*, **8**: 323–340.

———, and ——— (1986). The budgetary process of power and politics. *Accounting, Organizations and Society*, **11**: 193–214.

———, and ——— (1988a). The use of budgetary symbols in the political arena: An historically informed field study. *Accounting, Organizations and Society*, **13**: 1–24.

———, and ——— (1988b). An institutional perspective on the rise, social transformation, and fall of a university budget category. *Administrative Science Quarterly*, **33**: 562–587.

Cyert, R. N., and J. G. March (1963). *A Behavioral Theory of the Firm*. Englewood Cliffs, NJ: Prentice Hall.

Daft, R. L., and N. B. MacIntosh (1981). A tentative exploration into the amount and equivocality of information processing in organizational work units. *Administrative Science Quarterly*, **26**: 207–224.

Dent, J. F. (1987). Tensions in the design of formal control systems: A field study in a computer company. In: *Accounting and Management Field Study Perspectives*, edited by W. J. Bruns and R. S. Kaplan, 119–145. Harvard.

Denzin, N., and Y. Lincoln (1983). *Beyond Method: Strategies for Social Research*. London: Sage.

DiMaggio, P. J. (1988). Interest and agency in institutional theory. In: *Institutional Patterns and Organizations: Culture and Environment*, edited by L. G. Zucker, 3–22. Cambridge, MA: Ballinger Publishing Company.

———, and W. W. Powell (1983). The iron cage revisited: institutional isomorphism and collective rationality in organizational field. *American Sociological Review*, **48**: 147–160.

———, and ——— (1991). Introduction to the new institutionalism in organizational analysis. In: *The New Institutionalism in Organizational Analysis*, edited by W. W. Powell and P. J. DiMaggio, 1–38. Chicago: University of Chicago Press.

Dirsmith, M., M. Covaleski, and J. McAllister (1985). Of paradigms and metaphors in auditing thought. *Contemporary Accounting Research*, **2**: 46–68.

Drazin, R., and A. Van de Ven (1985). Alternative forms of fit in contingency theory. *Administrative Science Quarterly*, **30**: 514–539.

Durkheim, E. (1938). *The Rules of Sociological Method*. Glencoe, IL: Free Press.

Edelman, J. M. (1977). *Political Language: Words that Succeed and Policies that Fail*. New York: Academic Press.

Edwards, R. (1979). *Contested Terrain*. New York: Basic Books.

Foster, G., and M. Gupta (1990). Manufacturing overhead cost driver analysis. *Journal of Accounting and Economics*, 309–337.

Foucault, M. (1979). *Discipline and Punish: The Birth of the Prison*. New York: Vintage Books.

——— (1983). The subject and power. In: *Power/Knowledge: Selected Interviews and Other Writing: 1972–1977*, edited by C. Gordon, 78–108. New York: Pantheon Books.

——— (1990). *The History of Sexuality, Vol. 1: An Introduction*, trans. by R. Hurley. New York: Vintage Books.

Freidson, E. (1986). *Professional Powers: A Study of the Institutionalization of Formal Knowledge*. Chicago: University of Chicago Press.

Garfinkel, H. (1967). *Studies in Methodology*. Prentice Hall.

Golembiewski, R. T. (1964). Accountancy as a function of organization theory. *The Accounting Review*, **39**: 333–341.

Gordon, L. A., and D. Miller (1976). A contingency framework for the design of accounting information systems. *Accounting, Organizations and Society*, **1**: 59–70.

Govindarajan, V. J. (1984). Appropriateness of accounting data in performance evaluation: An empirical examination of environmental uncertainty as an intervening variable. *Accounting, Organizations and Society*, **9**: 125–136.

——— (1988). A contingency approach to strategy implementation at the business level: Integrating administrative mechanisms with strategy. *Academy of Management Journal*, 828–853.

———, and A. K. Gupta (1985). Linking control systems to business unit strategy: Impact on performance. *Accounting, Organizations and Society*, **10**: 51–66.

Gray, B., and S. S. Ariss (1985). Politics and strategic change across organizational life. *Academy of Management Review*, **10**: 707–723.

Hackman, J. D. (1985). Power and centrality in the allocation of resources in colleges and universities. *Administrative Science Quarterly*, **30**: 61–77.

Hage, J., and M. Aiken (1967). Relationship of centralization to other structural properties. *Administrative Science Quarterly*, **12**: 79–92.

Hayes, D. (1977). The contingency theory of management accounting. *The Accounting Review*, **52**: 22–39.

Hickson, D. (1966). A convergence in organization theory. *Administrative Science Quarterly*, **11**: 225–237.

Hills, F. S., and T. Mahoney (1978). University budgets and organizational decision-making. *Administrative Science Quarterly*, **23**: 61–77.

Hirst, M. K. (1981). Accounting information and the evaluation of subordinate performance: A situational approach. *The Accounting Review*, **56**: 771 784.

——— (1983). Reliance on accounting performance measures, task uncertainty, and dysfunctional behavior: some extensions. *Journal of Accounting Research*, **20**: 596–605.

Hofstede, G. (1967). *The Game of Budget Control*. London: Tavistock.

Hopper, T., and P. Armstrong (1991). Cost accounting, controlling labor and the rise of conglomerates. *Accounting, Organizations and Society*, **16**: 408–438.

———, and A. Powell (1985). Making sense of research into the organizational and social aspects of management accounting: A review of its underlying assumptions. *Journal of Management Studies*, **22**: 429–465.

———, J. Storey, and H. Willmott (1987). Accounting for accounting: Towards the development of a dialectical view. *Accounting, Organizations and Society*, **12**: 437–456.

Hopwood, A. (1973), *An Accounting System and Managerial Behavior*. Saxon House.

——— (1974). *Accounting and Human Behavior*. London: Haymarket.

———, and P. Miller (1994). *Accounting as a Social and Institutional Practice*. Cambridge: Cambridge University Press.

Hoskins, K., and R. Macve (1988). The genesis of accountability: The West Point connections. *Accounting, Organizations and Society*, **13**: 37–73.

Ijiri, Y. (1965). *Management Goals and Accounting for Control*. New York: North Holland.

Johnson, H. T. (1972). Early cost accounting for internal management control: Lyman Mills in the late 1850s. *Business History Review*: 466–474.

——— (1981). Toward a new understanding of nineteenth century cost accounting. *The Accounting Review*, **56**: 510–518.

——— (1983). The search for gain in markets and firms: A review of the historical emergence of management accounting systems. *Accounting, Organizations and Society*, **8**: 139–146.

———, and R. S. Kaplan (1987). *Relevance Lost: The Rise and Fall of Management Accounting*. Boston: Harvard Business School Press.

Jonsson, S. (1982). Budgetary behavior in local government – A case study over 3 years. *Accounting, Organizations and Society*, **7**: 287–304.

Kaplan, R. S. (1983). Measuring manufacturing performance: A new challenge for managerial accounting research. *The Accounting Review*, **58**: 686–705.

Keating, P. J. (1995). A framework for classifying and evaluating the theoretical contribution of case research in management accounting. *Journal of Management Accounting Research*, **7**: 66–86.

Khandwalla, P. (1972). The effect of different types of competition on the use of management controls. *Journal of Accounting Research*, **9**: 276–295.

Knights, D., and D. Collinson (1987). Disciplining the shopfloor: A comparison of the disciplinary effects of managerial psychology and financial accounting. *Accounting, Organizations and Society*, **12**: 457–477.

Kuhn, T. (1970). *The Structure of Scientific Revolutions*. Chicago: University of Chicago Press.

Lawrence, P. R., and J. W. Lorsch (1969). *Organizations and Environment*. Homewood, IL: Irwin.

Loft, A. (1986). Towards a critical understanding of accounting: A case of cost accounting in the U.K., 1914–1925. *Accounting, Organizations and Society*, **11**: 137–169.

MacIntosh, N. (1981). A contextual model for information systems. *Accounting, Organizations and Society*, **6**: 39–52.

March, J., and J. P. Olsen (1976). *Ambiguity and Choice in Organizations*. Oslo: Universitiete Forlaget.

———, and H. A. Simon (1958). *Organizations*. New York: Wiley.

Mayo, E. (1933). *Human Problems of an Industrial Civilization*. New York: Macmillan.

McMann, P., and A. J. Nanni, Jr. (1996). Means versus ends: A review of the literature on Japanese management accounting. *Journal of Management Accounting Research* (forthcoming).

McNair, C. J. and W. Mosconi (1989). *Beyond the Bottom Line*. New York: Dow Jones-Irwin.

———, ———, and T. Norris (1988). *Meeting the Technology Challenge: Cost Accounting in a JIT Environment*. Montvale, NJ: National Association of Accountants.

Merchant, K. A. (1981). The design of the corporate budgeting system: Influences on managerial behavior and performance. *The Accounting Review*, **56**: 813–829.

——— (1984). Influences on departmental budgeting: An empirical examination of a contingency model. *Accounting, Organizations and Society*, **9**: 291–307.

——— (1985). Organizational controls and discretionary program decision-making: A field study. *Accounting, Organizations and Society*, **10**: 67–86.

Meyer, J. W., and B. Rowan (1977). Institutional organizations: Formal structures as myth and ceremony. *American Journal of Sociology*, **80**: 340–363.

Mezias, S. J. (1990). An institutional model of organizational practice: Financial reporting at the Fortune 200. *Administrative Science Quarterly*, **35**: 431–457.

———, and M. Scarselletta (1994). Resolving financial reporting problems: An institutional analysis of the process. *Administrative Science Quarterly*, **39**: 654–678.

Milani, K. (1975). The relationship of participation in budget setting to industrial supervisor performance and attitudes: A field study. *The Accounting Review*, **50**: 274–284.

Miller, P. (1994). Governing the calculable person. In: *Accounting as a Social and Institutional Practice*, edited by A. Hopwood and P. Miller, 98–115. Cambridge: Cambridge University Press.

———, and T. O'Leary (1987). Accounting and the construction of the governable person. *Accounting, Organizations and Society*, **12**: 235–265.

———, and ——— (1989). Hierarchies and American ideals, 1900–1940. *Academy of Management Review*, **14**: 250–265.

Mitroff, I., and R. Mason (1982). Business policy and metaphysics: some philosophical considerations. *Academy of Management Review*, **7**: 361–371.

Morgan, G. (1980). Paradigms, metaphors and puzzle solving in organizational theory. *Administrative Science Quarterly*, **25**: 605–622.

——— (1983). *Beyond Method: Strategies for Social Research*. London: Sage.

Noble, D. (1977). *American by Design*. London: Oxford University Press.

Oakes, L. S., and M. A. Covaleski (1994). A historical examination of the use of accounting-based incentive plans in the structuring of labor-management relations. *Accounting, Organizations and Society*, **19**: 579–599.

Oliver, C. (1991). Strategic responses to institutional processes. *Academy of Management Review*, **16**: 145–179.

Otley, D. (1978). Budget use and managerial behavior. *Journal of Accounting Research*, **15**: 122–149.

——— (1980). The contingency theory of management accounting: Achievement and prognosis. *Accounting, Organizations and Society*, **5**: 413–428.

Patell, J. M. (1987). Cost accounting process controls and product design: A case study of the H-P personal office computer division. *The Accounting Review*, **63**: 808–839.

Perrow, C. (1967). A framework for comparative organizational analysis. *American Sociological Review*, **32**: 194–208.

——— (1985). Review essay: Overboard with myths and symbols. *American Journal of Sociology*, **91**: 194–208.

Pfeffer, J. (1981). *Power in Organizations*. Marshfield, MA: Pitman.

———, and G. R. Salancik (1974). Organizational decision-making as a political process: The case of a university budget. *Administrative Science Quarterly*, **19**: 135–151.

———, and ——— (1978). *The External Control of Organizations: A Resource Dependence Perspective*. New York: Harper & Row.

Powell, W. W. (1985). The institutionalization of rational organizations. *Contemporary Sociology*, **14**: 151–155.

Preston, A. (1992). The birth of clinical accounting: A study of the emergence and transformation of discourse on costs and practices of accounting in U.S. hospitals. *Accounting, Organizations and Society*, **17**: 63–100.

Pugh, D. S., D. J. Hickson, and C. R. Hinnings (1969). The context of organization structures. *Administrative Science Quarterly*, **14**: 91–114.

———, ———, ———, and C. Turner (1968). Dimensions of organization structure. *Administrative Science Quarterly*, **13**: 65–105.

Puxty, A. (1993). *The Social and Organizational Context of Managerial Accounting*. New York: Academic Press.

Rabinow, P. (1984). *The Foucault Reader*. Pantheon Press.

Rose, N. (1991). Governing by the numbers: Figuring out democracy. *Accounting, Organizations and Society*, **16**: 673–692.

Rose, R. (1977). Implementation and cooperation: The record of MBO. *Public Administrative Review*, 64–71.

Rosenlender, R. (1992). *Sociological Perspective in Modern Accounting*. Englewood Cliffs, NJ: Prentice Hall.

Salancik, G. R., and J. Pfeffer (1974). The base and use of power in organizational decision making: the case of a university. *Administrative Science Quarterly*, **19**: 453–473.

Sarfatti-Larson, M. (1977). *The Rise of Professionalism*. Berkley: University of California Press.

Schick, A. G. (1985). University budgeting: Administrative perspective, budget structure, and budget process. *Academy of Management Review*, **19**: 794–802.

Schiff, M., and A. Y. Lewin (1970). The impact of people on budgets. *The Accounting Review*, **45**: 259–268.

Scott, W. R. (1987). The adolescence of institutional theory. *Administrative Science Quarterly*, **32**: 493–511.

Selto, F. H., C. J. Renner, and S. M. Young (1995). Assessing the organizational fit of a just-in-time manufacturing system: Testing selection, interaction and systems models of contingency theory. *Accounting, Organizations and Society*, **20**: 665–684.

Selznick, P. (1957). Foundations of the theory of organizations. *American Sociological Review*, **12**: 25–35.

Shank, J. K. (1989). Strategic cost management: New wine, or just new bottles. *Journal of Management Accounting Research*, **1**: 47–65.

Simon, H. A. (1957). *Administrative Behavior*. Glencoe, IL: The Free Press.

Simons, R. (1987). Accounting control systems and business strategy. *Accounting, Organizations and Society*, **12**: 357–374.

Stedry, A. (1960). *Budget Control and Cost Behavior*. Englewood Cliffs, NJ: Prentice Hall.

Swieringa, R., and R. Moncur (1975). *Some Effects of Participative Budgeting on Managerial Behavior*. National Association of Accountants.

Thompson, J. D. (1967). *Organizations in Action*. New York: McGraw-Hill.

Tinker, A., B. Merino, and M. Neimark (1982). The normative origins of positive theories: Ideology and accounting thought. *Accounting, Organizations and Society*, **7**: 167–200.

Tolbert, P. (1988). Institutional sources of organizational culture in major law firms. In: *Institutional Patterns and Organizations: Culture and Environment*, edited by L. Zucker, 101–113. Cambridge, MA: Ballinger Publishing Company.

Van Maanen, J. (1995). The end of innocence: The ethnography of ethnography. In: *Representation in Ethnography*, edited by J. Van Maanen, 1–35. London: Sage.

Walsh, E., and R. Stewart (1993). Accounting and the construction of institutions: The case of a factory. *Accounting, Organizations and Society*, **18**: 783–800.

Waterhouse, J. H., and P. A. Tiessen (1978). A contingency framework for management accounting systems research. *Accounting, Organizations and Society*, **3**: 65–76.

Weber, M. (1947). *The Theory of Social and Economic Organizations*. Glencoe, IL: Free Press.

——— (1958). *From Max Weber*. Glencoe, IL: Free Press.

——— (1964). *Basic Concepts in Sociology*. New York: Citidal Press.

Weick, K. (1976). Education organizations as loosely coupled systems. *Administrative Science Quarterly*, **24**: 1–19.

Wildavsky, A. B. (1964). *The Politics of the Budgetary Process*. Boston, MA: Little Brown.

——— (1975). *Budgeting: A Comparative Theory of Budgeting Processes*. Boston, MA: Little Brown.

——— (1979). *Speaking Truth to Power: The Art and Craft of Policy Analysis*. Boston, MA: Little Brown.

Wilkinson, B., and N. Oliver (1989). Power, control and the Kanban. *Journal of Management Studies*, **26**: 47–58.

Woodward, J. (1965). *Industrial Organizations: Theory and Practice*. London: Oxford University Press.

Young, S. M. (1992). A framework for research on successful adoption and performance of Japanese manufacturing practices in the United States. *Academy of Management Review*, **17**: 677–700.

———, and F. Selto (1991). New manufacturing practices and cost management: A review of the literature and direction for research. *Journal of Accounting Literature*, **10**: 265–298.

Zucker, L. (1977). The role of institutionalization in cultural persistence. *American Sociological Review*, **42**: 725–743.

——— (1988). Where do institutional patterns come from? Organizational actors as social systems. In: *Institutional Patterns and Organizations: Culture and Environment*, edited by L. Zucker, 23–52. Cambridge, MA: Ballinger Publishing Company.

READING D

Reprinted from *Accounting, Organizations and Society*, Vol 16, No 8, J. F. Dent, Accounting and organizational cultures: A field study of the emergence of a new organizational reality, pp. 705–32, Copyright 1991, with permission from Elsevier Science.

Questions

1   How does Dent define culture in his study of EuroRail?
2   What was the research method used by Dent in this study? Why do you think he chose this particular method?
3   How does the transition from a 'railway' to a 'business' culture take place in Dent's study? What was the role of accounting in this transition? What meaning did accounting have to each of the two cultures?
4   How does accounting help to construct a particular knowledge?

Further reading

Allaire, Y. and Firsirotu, M. E. (1984). Theories of organizational culture. *Organization Studies*, **5**(3), 193–226.

Atkinson, A. A. and Shaffir, W. (1998). Standards for field research in management accounting. *Journal of Management Accounting Research*, **10**, 41–68.

Deal, T. E. and Kennedy, A. A. (1982). *Corporate Cultures*. Reading, MA: Addison-Wesley.

Humphrey, C. and Scapens, R. W. (1996). Theories and case studies of organizational and accounting practices: Limitation or liberation? *Accounting, Auditing and Accountability Journal*, **9**(4), 86–106.

Langfield-Smith, K. (1995). Organisational culture and control. In A. J. Berry, J. Broadbent and D. Otley (eds), *Management Control: Theories, Issues and Practices*, London: Macmillan.

Otley, D. T. and Berry, A. J. (1994). Case study research in management accounting and control. *Management Accounting Research*, **5**, 45–65.

Pettigrew, A. M. (1979). On studying organizational cultures. *Administrative Science Quarterly*, **24**, 570–81.

Scapens, R. W. (1990). Researching management accounting practice: The role of case study methods. *British Accounting Review*, **22**, 259–81.

Smircich, L. (1983). Concepts of culture and organizational analysis. *Administrative Science Quarterly*, **28**, 339–58.

Smith, C., Whipp, R. and Willmott, H. (1988). Case-study research in accounting: Methodological breakthrough or ideological weapon? *Advances in Public Interest Accounting*, **2**, 95–120.

ACCOUNTING AND ORGANIZATIONAL CULTURES: A FIELD STUDY OF THE EMERGENCE OF A NEW ORGANIZATIONAL REALITY*

Jeremy F. Dent
London School of Economics and Political Science

ABSTRACT

Organizations have long been known to have cultural properties. A more recent innovation is the study of organizations as cultures: systems of knowledge, beliefs and values in which action and artifact are vested with expressive qualities. We know little about the way in which accounting is implicated in organizations' cultures. This paper reports a longitudinal field study of organizational change, tracing out the way in which new accounting practices were implicated in an emergent reconstruction of the organization's culture.

The train arrived at Capital City Terminus at 12.10. It was on time despite a delay on the line. Walking up the platform, I saw the train driver leaning out of his cab. He must have driven the train fast to recover the time: the windscreens were spattered with dead insects. He exchanged some words with men dressed in smart overalls. Muttering a few words into 'walkie-talkies', they jumped down onto the track to check the engine. Men driving small electric trucks towing streams of trailers with logos on the side collected parcels and mail bags from the guard's van. Others set about replenishing water and food supplies in the train. At the barrier, a man wearing a smile and a dark uniform with red piping on the seams checked my ticket.

Moving on, the concourse was bright and airy, concealed lighting illuminating the white tiled floor. People were milling about. Soft music was playing on the tannoy. Large electronic

---

* This research was generously supported by the Chartered Institute of Management Accountants. Earlier versions of the paper were presented at the AAA Annual Convention, New York, 1986, the EAA Annual Congress, London, 1987, and the EIASM Workshop on Strategy, Accounting & Control, Venice, 1990. Ken Euske, Anthony Hopwood, Keith Hoskins, Kenneth Merchant, Peter Miller and two anonymous reviewers provided helpful comments.

screens indicated arrival and departure times. There were colourful boutiques displaying ties, handkerchiefs, socks and bags, and cafés where people were drinking coffee and eating croissants. What a change, I thought, from just a short time ago, when the station was dark and grimy, and a grumpy employee had greeted my question about departure times with a crude response.

At the new executive offices across the street I tangled with the revolving glass and stainless steel door. In the foyer, a manicured receptionist called upstairs to say I'd arrived. The security guard, at least I presumed he was a security guard (his appearance was quite like a ticket inspector, but his commanding presence was more like a policeman), showed me to the lift. He deftly pressed the fourth floor button, removing himself before the doors closed. After a few moments the lift doors opened onto what appeared to be open-plan office space, but in fact comprised zones of compartmentalized activity separated by cleverly positioned shoulder-height cabinets and screens. A person came up to me: 'Mr Charles will be here in a minute', he said; 'he's at a retirement do'. The man looked busy; his tie was loose, the top button of his shirt was undone, he must have left his jacket on his chair. He was courteous: 'his secretary just popped out for a few minutes, but she told me to expect you. Why don't you wait in his office?'

Walking through the office space, I could see over the cabinets. The arrangements were utilitarian. Some people were stabbing at computer keyboards, others were studying documents, others were writing or working out sums on calculators. There were piles of print-out everywhere.

We entered Mr Charles' office through his secretary's room. From the large windows there was a fine view into, and over, the station. I could see trains arriving and leaving. I followed one right into the hills across the city. The office was softly furnished. At one end, there was a large desk, at the other a couple of sofas; opposite the windows there were bookshelves and a cabinet. The lighting was bright but unobtrusive. There wasn't a computer in sight. My guide and I made small talk – incidental conversation about the comforts of the new building and the air conditioning. Conscious that his work was pressing and not wishing to detain him, I told him not to worry about me. Eventually he made to leave. 'Ah! Mr General Manager', I heard him say before he had even left the secretary's office. 'Your visitor has arrived'. 'Thanks John', came the reply. Mr Charles, the General Manager, entered the room. 'Good to see you again, Mr Charles', I said to him as we exchanged greetings.

Settling down in one of the sofas he said to me 'I am glad you could come. I think you will find this afternoon's meeting interesting. We're deeply embroiled in cost allocations. Intercity are holding Freight to ransom'. After my query, he continued: 'At night, we push freight up the main line routes. Intercity don't use them at night. You don't want the speed then; after all you can't expect passengers to get off the train at 2 or 3 in the morning. Sleeper trains make their separate way on roundabout routes. Intercity say the wear and tear caused by freight trains, and they are very heavy, means they need to increase the engineering specification of the track. As it's an Intercity track, they pick up the cost; and they want Freight to pay. They're holding them to ransom. Freight have responded by running their trains slower. This reduces the damage to the track. They don't go very fast anyway, so I mean SLOW. Now Intercity say they can't get back on the track when they want it in the morning. They have threatened not to let Freight use the track unless they pay. Its going to be an interesting meeting. Would you like a drink before we have lunch?'

Going to the cabinet, he poured two glasses of mineral water . . .

Organizations have long been known to have distinct cultural properties (cf. Weber, 1947; Parsons, 1951). They create and sustain particular work customs. They establish norms for proper and improper behaviour and performance. They propagate stories and myths, and are replete with rituals (Van Maanen & Barley, 1984; Martin et al., 1983). Communities in organizations have particular codes of communication: behaviour, language, dress, presentation, design, architecture, ceremony . . . The operation of work technologies in organizations is not a purely technical-rational affair. Rather it is embedded in a cultural system of ideas (beliefs, knowledges) and sentiments (values), in which actions and artifacts are vested with symbolic qualities of meaning. The appreciation of organizational dynamics requires a sensitivity to local frames of significance and interpretation.

Accounting practices are a common feature of most work organizations. Planning and budgeting activities, systems of hierarchical accountability, performance appraisal procedures, budgetary controls and remuneration arrangements, all rely to a greater or lesser extent on accounting practices. Inevitably, therefore, accounting is likely to be implicated in organizations' cultural systems. But how, and in what way? Drawing on the insights of Meyer & Rowan (1977), Pfeffer & Salancik (1978), DiMaggio & Powell (1983), Scott (1987), Zucker (1988) and others, one theme in the literature appeals to accounting's potential significance in the context of wider societal values and beliefs. Put crudely, organizations depend on a flow of resources for survival; society has beliefs in the efficacy of 'rational' management practices; organizations which adopt such practices are more likely to be rewarded. Thus, recent empirically grounded studies (Berry *et al.*, 1985; Ansari & Euske, 1987; Covaleski & Dirsmith, 1988) have cast accounting as a culturally expressive symbol of rationality, particularly oriented towards powerful external constituencies, moderating environmental control. In this view, following especially Meyer & Rowan's (1977) discussion, accounting is often seen to be neutral in its effects within the organization. It is kept at arm's length, symbolically construed as necessary but irrelevant, and, as it were, not taken seriously. It is purposefully uncoupled from organizations' core technological activities.

All knowledges and practices can be reflexive, however. Accounting can reflect back on those institutions which adopt it. Hopwood (1987), Hines (1988), Miller & O'Leary (1987) and others have argued for its constitutive role in the construction of organizational life. Finely crafted notions of costliness, efficiency, profitability, earnings-per-share and so forth, actively construct particular definitions of reality which privilege the financial and economic sphere. Rather than being kept at arm's length, uncoupled from organizations' core technological activities, these can permeate into organizational settings, leading to the creation of particular agendas (in the sense of objectives and priorities and the means for their achievement), stylized definitions of success and failure, the characterization of heroic performance and the mobilization of particular dynamics of change. This suggests the possibility of a more intimate involvement of accounting in organizational cultures.

In fact, evidence in the field suggests that accounting practices are not uniformly implicated in organizational activities (Goold & Campbell, 1987; Miles & Snow, 1978). In some organizations, accounting is centrally involved in work rituals: financial achievement is celebrated; budgets are massaged, pored over, and matter. In others, accounting is incidental, perhaps existing as a practice, but with no particular significance. Similarly, entrepreneurial risk taking is sometimes valued for its own sake. Dynamic, decisive, action-oriented men and women who innovate are heroes, almost irrespective of the financial consequences. In other organizations, risk taking is valued only if successful in financial terms. Arguably, the multi-faceted interplay of accounting with organizations' cultural and technical systems is under-researched. More empirically grounded research is needed to ascertain the way in which accounting is drawn upon by actors within organizations in the creation and maintenance of cultures.

Responding, with others, to appeals for field studies (e.g. Bruns & Kaplan, 1987) and for the study of accounting in its organizational and social context (e.g. Hopwood, 1978, 1983; Dent, 1986), this paper reports a longitudinal study undertaken in one organization to research this issue. The organization is a railway company. The study focuses on its senior management élite: a group of approximately 120 people including head office executives, senior line management and people in senior staff positions (i.e. finance and engineering). Prior to the study, the dominant culture within this management group was well established, and centred on engineering and production concerns. Accounting was incidental in this culture: it was necessary in the technical-rational sense of ensuring that revenues were accounted for and suppliers were paid, but it was not incorporated into the culture among the senior management élite in any significant way. Rituals, symbols and language celebrated the primacy of the engineering and production orientation. During the course of the study, a new culture emerged. The previously dominant orientation was displaced by a new preoccupation with economic and accounting concerns. New accounts were crafted. Gradually, through action and interaction, they were coupled to organizational activities to reconstitute interpretations of organizational endeavour. Accounting actively shaped the dominant meanings given to organizational life, ultimately obtaining a remarkable significance in the senior management culture. A new set of symbols, rituals and language emerged to celebrate an economic rationale for organized activity. This paper carefully traces the events and interactions through which accounting was endowed with significance.

The paper is written from a cultural perspective, but in a very real sense the study is also concerned with power and influence in the organization. A new culture can be a major source of power, particularly if it gains ascendancy to become dominant, for it effectively alters the legitimacy of accepted criteria for action.

The next section of the paper outlines the cultural approach adopted in the subsequent analysis. The following section explains the method employed in the study. Two sections then document the study itself. Thereafter, some implications for accounting and culture are drawn out. Finally, there is a concluding comment.

CULTURE

In recent years, a prolific literature has emerged to offer a wide array of perceptual, symbolic and processual characterizations of organization (e.g. Hedberg *et al.*, 1976;

Jonsson & Lundin, 1977; Hedberg & Jonsson, 1978; Pondy, 1978; Weick, 1979; Ranson *et al.*, 1980; Argyris & Schon, 1981; Pfeffer, 1981; Starbuck, 1982; Pondy *et al.*, 1983; Brunsson, 1985; Greenwood & Hinings, 1988). As a result, we are now used to conceptualizing organizations as bodies of thought, variously described as myths, causal schema, theories-of-action, interpretive schemes, ideologies, paradigms and so forth. The concept of culture, drawn from anthropology and ethnography, has entered the organizational literature as a framework for extending this ideational understanding of organizations[10] (Pettigrew, 1979; Smircich, 1983a; Allaire & Firsirotu, 1984; Van Maanen & Barley, 1984; Meek, 1988).

Culture is an elusive concept.[11] Here, drawing on Geertz' (1973, 1983) interpretive anthropology, it is defined to be the broad constellation of interpretive structures through which action and events are rendered meaningful in a community. Balinese cockfights, a sheep raid in Morocco, funeral rites in Java – or nearer home, the graduation ceremony, the distinguished lecture series, the publication of papers in prestigious journals – all have singular meanings in their respective communities (as does all social action). Culture is the 'ordered clusters of significance' (Geertz, 1973, p. 363), the shared 'webs of significance' (p. 5) through which people appreciate the meaningfulness of their experience, and are guided to action. Culture, as an ideational system, is produced and reproduced through action and interaction. But it is not just lodged in people's minds. Culture is public, the product of minds, between minds. Culturally significant events give public expression to the ideational system.

The appreciation of organizations as cultures brings the interpretive, experiential aspects of their activities to the foreground of analysis, emphasizing their expressive qualities[12] (Van Maanen, 1979, 1988; Feldman, 1986). Looking at the railway, for example, the train is not seen as cold technology; the concourse is not just glass and marble; 'Mr General Manager' is not an anybody; cost allocations are not mere calculations: everything is expressive. Local knowledge, beliefs and values vest them with symbolic qualities of meaning. The train may be vested with a sacred quality (or not,

---

[10] Cultural ideas are not new to organizational research. They surface in many classic descriptive studies of organizational behaviour (e.g. Roethlisberger & Dickson, 1939; Whyte, 1948, [1943] 1955; Selznick, 1949; Gouldner, 1954; Blau, 1955; Roy, 1954, 1960; Goffman, 1959; Hughes, 1958; Dalton, 1959; Buroway, 1979). Only in the late 1970s, however, did organizational culture emerge as an explicit theme.

[11] In cultural anthropology, culture is used in different ways. The broad idea of culture as a 'total way of life' of a community, developed by classical anthropologists (e.g. Radcliffe-Brown, 1952; Malinowski, 1922; Evans Pritchard, 1937, 1940), is continued by Harris (1979), among others. More commonly, culture is used to denote a system of ideas, a position associated in different ways with Goodenough (1971), Levi Strauss (1963, [1962] 1966) and Geertz (1973, 1983). Allaire & Firsirotu (1984) trace implications of these different perspectives on culture for organizational research. Wuthnow & Witten (1988) discuss the use of culture in contemporary sociology, see also Wuthnow *et al.* (1984).

[12] With Meek (1988), Feldman (1986) and others, I wish to distance myself from the current vogue of 'pop-culture' literature on the management of meaning, which is ill-informed in the anthropological tradition: e.g. Ouchi (1981), Peters & Waterman (1982), Deal & Kennedy (1982), Kilmann *et al.* (1985). No one has a monopoly of meanings (Smircich, 1983b). See Barley *et al.* (1988) for an interesting discussion of the contaminating effects of this literature.

as the case may be) quite beyond its technical properties; beliefs about the skills required to operate a railway and appropriate forms of organizing may endow the General Manager with special status and privilege (or not). Cultural analysis attempts to uncover these meanings and to trace the underlying thematic relationships. The objective is interpretation and 'thick description': the production of rich contextually laden accounts conveying the symbolic content of social action.

Meaning systems may differ within organizations, of course. The train, the framing of the routing problem as a cost allocation issue and so on are likely to be interpreted differently by different groups. Within the overarching concept of an organization as a culture, it is sensible to recognize the possibility and likelihood of distinct subcultures existing among managerial teams, occupational groups, members of different social classes and so on; many of which may transcend organizational boundaries (Van Maanen & Barley, 1984). As a limiting case, these subcultures may be isomorphic; more commonly, they may only partially overlap.[13] Also, some maybe dominant-cultures and others counter-cultures (Martin & Siehl, 1983), perhaps partially un-coupled from each other (Berry *et al.*, 1985), or co-existing in an 'uneasy symbiosis' (Martin & Siehl, 1983), or in contest with each other for dominance (Gregory, 1983; Riley, 1983; Pettigrew, 1985; Feldman, 1986). Moreover, cultures in organizations are not independent of their social context. They are interpenetrated by wider systems of thought, interacting with other organizations and social institutions, both importing and exporting values, beliefs and knowledge.

Accounting is likely to be differentially implicated in these subcultures in organiza-tions. Accounting systems, and information systems more generally, inevitably offer highly stylized views of the world. Any representation is partial, an interpretation through a particular framing of reality, rendering some aspects of events important and others unimportant; counter-interpretations are possible (Hedberg & Jonsson, 1978). Accounting systems embody particular assumptions about organization, ration-ality, authority, time and so forth. These may be more or less consonant with local subcultures in organizations (cf. Markus & Pfeffer, 1983). For example, to senior managers in some organizations accounting may symbolize efficiency, calculative rationality, order and so forth: 'the name of the game is profit'. This may motivate the development of sophisticated accounting systems measuring economic performance this way and that. To others (nearer the ground?), accounting may symbolize confusion or irrelevance: 'no one understands the business'; 'when all else fails they resort to the

---

[13] Geertz' (1973, pp. 407–408) analogy is relevant here: 'Systems need not be exhaustively connected . . . They may be densely interconnected or poorly . . . the problem of cultural analysis is as much a matter of determining independencies as interconnections, gulfs as well as bridges. The appropriate image . . . of cultural organisation, is . . . the octopus, whose tentacles are in large part separately integrated, neurally quite poorly connected with one another and with what in an octopus passes for a brain, and yet who nonetheless manages to get around and to preserve himself, for a while anyway, as a viable if somewhat ungainly entity'. He goes on: 'Culture moves like an octopus too – not all at once in a smoothly coordinated synergy of parts, a massive coaction of the whole, but by disjointed movements of this part, then that, and now the other which somehow cumulate to directional change'.

numbers' (see Jones & Lakin, 1978, chapter 11, for a graphic example). Similarly, meanings may differ across occupational groups. Commercial managers may appreciate accounting rather differently to engineers, for example.

It is useful to think of societal cultures as emergent, unfolding through time[14] (Geertz, 1973; Douglas, 1966), and similarly with organizational cultures (Pettigrew, 1985; Feldman, 1986). That is not to say that given cultures do not survive for long periods, or that changes may be proactively managed: organizational cultures probably have inertial tendencies (cf. Miller & Friesen, 1984), perhaps sometimes not even incorporating changes in wider patterns of social thought[15] (cf. Burns & Stalker's, 1961, pathological responses in mechanistic firms). Rather, the implication is that culture is not programmed or static. The processes of cultural change in organizations are poorly understood, however. Perhaps cultural change is a political process: subcultures competing with one another for legitimacy and dominance (Pettigrew, 1985). Perhaps cultural change is akin to the diffusion of organizational forms, whole fields of organizations rapidly adopting knowledge innovations in leading firms (cf. Fligstein, 1990). Perhaps in a Kuhnian sense, cultural change is precipitated by crisis: the adoption of new cultural knowledge only being possible when faith is undermined, for example by the failure of strategies for subsistence. Maybe new cultures are autonomously crafted in organizations (cf. 'groping' towards 'solutions-in-principle' and their subsequent elaboration: Mintzberg, 1978; Jonsson & Lundin, 1977); or perhaps they are already there, 'lying around' in counter-cultures, waiting to be discovered by others (cf. Cohen *et al.*, 1972); alternatively, cultures may be imported from the environment through new actors (cf. Starbuck & Hedberg, 1977).

Clearly, there are multiple modes and possibilities for cultural change. However, the point of importance for this paper is the conceptualization of cultural change as the uncoupling of organizational action from one culture and its recoupling to another (cf. Greenwood & Hinings, 1988; Hedberg, 1981). It is a process of fundamental reinterpretation of organizational activities. Things cease to be what they were and become what they were not: a new reality, if you will. In the railway, for example, the sacred train could turn into cold steel, or the priest-like general manager could become an anybody. Moreover, this process of uncoupling and recoupling is unlikely to be sudden, but emergent: the gradual disintegration of one coupling and the crystallization of another. This crystallization may be around an idea not fully understood, a kind of ill-articulated new knowledge, perhaps imported from the environment. In the railway, this idea was a new accounting.

---

[14] Douglas (1966, p. 5) states: '. . . we think of ourselves as passively receiving our native language, and discount responsibility for shifts it undergoes in our life time. The anthropologist falls into the same trap if he thinks of a culture he is studying as a long established pattern of values'.
[15] There is a link here to the cultural adaptation literature (Harris, 1979), but it is not developed in this paper; cf. Lawrence & Lorsch ([1967] 1969), Aldrich (1979).

RESEARCH METHOD

Arm's length analysis is clearly inappropriate for cultural analysis of the kind described here. Instead, it calls for closer engagement in the research setting and 'interpretive' methodology (Geertz, 1973; Burrell & Morgan, 1979; Denzin, 1983). Necessarily, this precludes the imposition of exteriorized accounts, and radical critique. In part, the goal is 'to grasp the native's point of view, his relation to life, to realise his vision of his world' (Malinowski, 1922, p. 25); in part it is to reflect on the processes through which that vision comes to be and is sustained.[16]

This kind of research is necessarily qualitative. Data consist of descriptions and accounts provided by participants in the research site, together with the *researcher's observations* on activities and interactions and the context in which they take place. Data must be collected over an extended period of time so that processes can be recorded. The researcher, in general, does not seek to test a prior hypothesis. Rather, he or she seeks to theorize through the data in an inductive manner. Analysis of the data is itself an emergent process.

The researcher seeks gradually to develop an empathy with the data, to understand what they tell of participants' realities and the process through which they unfold. The researcher must constantly construct alternative interpretations ('readings': Levi Strauss, quoted in Turner, 1983) until he or she is satisfied that the representation is a faithful account. Interpretations must be grounded in context and consistent with the chronological ordering of events and interactions. Finally, research results must be presented in such a way that the reader can independently judge their credibility, as far as is possible.[17]

The study reported here was conducted over a period of two years, with follow up visits one year and two years later. It involved ongoing iterations between data collection and analysis. Access to the organization was gained through various channels and contacts. The researcher was given freedom to interview anyone he wished. At no point in the data collection process did the researcher express opinions, save where it was necessary to prompt interviewees. Data were collected from staff within the organization in several ways. The first source was a series of unstructured interviews. Approximately 30 managers were interviewed, sometimes twice or more times at the researcher's request. These included head office executives and their advisors or assistants, senior line management and people in senior staff positions (finance and engineering). Interviews averaged one and a half hours in length, and were spread

---

[16] For Geertz (1983, p. 58): 'The trick is not to get yourself into some inner correspondence of spirit with your informants . . . The trick is to figure out what they think they are up to'. While one may attempt to move towards an 'experience near' understanding in the field, however, the presentation of an ethnography inevitably will recast these understandings through the 'experience far' theoretical categories of the reader. Crapanzano (1986) argues that this claim to 'native view' interpretations is illusory: 'There is only the constructed understanding of the constructed native's constructed point of view' (p. 74). See also Marcus & Fischer (1986) for contemporary critique.

[17] The anthropological literature is brimming with reflexive discussion of ethnographic writing styles. See Geertz (1988), Marcus & Cushman (1982), Clifford & Marcus (1986), also Van Maanen (1988).

over the period of the research. They were tape-recorded and transcribed. Secondly, access was granted to various internal meetings. Debates were observed and dialogue noted. Activities in these meetings were subsequently written up in abbreviated form. Thirdly, data were collected through casual conversations and by simply 'being around'.

As the project progressed, the data were repeatedly analysed. At first, it seemed that there was a real probability of drowning in the data. Transcripts and notes were accumulating rapidly, and the material appeared to be incoherent. This is apparently a common feature of the initial stages of cultural research (Smircich, 1983b). But different ways of making sense of it all were explored and gradually a pattern began to emerge. At each stage emerging appreciations were checked against the next round of data in an attempt to confirm the researcher's understanding of the situation. This continued until such time as the subsequent data became predictable.

It may be useful to indicate the precise way in which the data were found to give a coherent picture. Ultimately, the analysis hinged on three dimensions: role (function), and level of hierarchy of the subject, and time. Firstly, the data were categorized according to content and underlying values. Opinions, sentiments, interpretations, confusions and so forth in each interview transcript were noted. This was done without reference to the identity of the person who had been interviewed. The data collected at any one time seemed to fall naturally into distinct constellations or clusters (in the sense that groups of people expressed similar views). Attaching identity to the data, it transpired that these constellations corresponded broadly to interviewees' roles and positions in the hierarchy. Among those performing similar roles (functions) at a similar level in the hierarchy, there was a marked similarity of perspective. Perspectives differed, however, across roles and at different levels of the hierarchy. These data were set up on a two-dimensional space with role on one axis and hierarchy on the other.

This exercise was repeated on data collected at different times, and found to give similar results, in the sense that the data again fell into role-hierarchy clusters. The specific content of the data differed over time, however. So, the two-dimensional spaces were set out in chronological order. In effect, a third dimension was added to the space, representing elapsed time. Studying the content of the data as one moved through time, it transpired that the opinions, sentiments and interpretations of each group were in fact evolving in a systematic way. In this three-dimensional space was a story of unfolding meanings in the organization.

This was indicative of the existence of different cultures in the organization, and some systematic underlying trajectory in the emergence of those cultures. In fact, during the data collection process, it became clear that new interviewees' views were predictable, given a knowledge of (a) the role (function) of the participant, (b) his or her position in the hierarchy, and (c) the time of the interview.

At this point, the data were analysed from a different perspective. Specifically, the level of analysis shifted from content to process. The data were re-examined to see if the process through which the new meanings were emerging was observable. Some key turning points were obvious in the data. There was a series of events and interactions through which the emergence of the new meaning structure could be traced.

These are documented in following sections. Finally, the findings of the research project were noted and informally discussed with various participants.[18]

THE ORGANIZATION: AN OVERVIEW

The research was undertaken in a major railway company. The company is referred to here as ER[19] ('Euro Rail'). It is, and has been for some while, in public sector ownership. It is large by any standards, employing approximately 160,000 people. It has a distinguished history.

History and traditions

ER has its origins in the great private-sector railway companies set up in the middle decades of the last century. These each built and operated a main line out of the capital city, i.e. radial routes and associated branch lines.[20] The companies are legendary. They raised capital to fund their projects on an unprecedented scale. Their railways were built by world-famous engineers who pioneered emerging industrial technology, designing magnificent steam locomotives and tracks and bridges which the world admired. The railways were, and are, a visible celebration of Victorian accomplishment.

These companies enjoyed a monopoly in the nation's transport well into this century. They had good relationships with successive governments. They paid consistent dividends and their shares were blue-chip stocks. This monopoly position and government patronage, coupled with a remarkable continuity in the underlying nature of their operations, rendered them highly bureaucratic: rules and procedures were well defined, there were clear chains of command and formalized systems for managing operations.[21] Their managements were conservative, cultivating a belief in the uniqueness of railway management and the wisdom of practices built up over many decades.

---

[18] There were several fascinating aspects of this last stage in the field. One was that many managers had simply forgotten what had happened, or at least had retrospectively reconstructed it. In particular, some seemed to forget how tentative their initiatives had been, the anguish and stress of trying to imagine a new future, the tense moments at the heights of political intrigue and the sheer uncertainty of the outcomes. They read the past through the present. Geertz' (1973, p. 19) notion, drawn from Ricoeur, of the ethnographer '. . . tracing the curve of social discourse; fixing it in inspectable form . . . He turns it from a passing event which exists only in its own moment of occurrence, into an account, which . . . can be reconsulted', is particularly pertinent here. Secondly, my intervention at this stage actually constructed a past (and hence a present) for participants; in other words, the theory developed here on the constitutive potential of accounting may be a general theory of accounts.

[19] The company's name has been disguised.

[20] This is an oversimplification, for in fact there were then a multitude of local regional railway companies in addition. It was only in the 1920s that government inspired mergers led to their consolidation around the major routes.

[21] This was not unique to ER. See Chandler (1965), Crozier (1964) and Gourvish (1986).

Importantly, though, while established as commercial concerns and earning their founders a handsome return,[22] these companies also embraced a spirit of public service, for the railway network provided a transport infrastructure much needed for the pursuit of trade and manufacturing, and for social mobility. This notion of public service was significant in the managements' interpretations of the railways: they took the rough with the smooth. They were run by 'railway men': engineers and operators who took pride in the professional management of the railway and its public service.

The railway companies were nationalized in the late 1940s. In many respects, this was of limited significance. The nationalized railway consolidated the old management structure: it was organized by region, each representing one of the radial routes out of the capital city; and each still managed by a General Manager (the same title as before). An Executive Committee was established to oversee policy decisions and to interface with government. This committee comprised the regional General Managers together with the Chief Executive of ER and various engineering chiefs.[23] Management practices of the former railways survived intact. Furthermore, nationalization re-inforced the public service orientation, for this was the era of the Welfare State. Public-sector ownership established the railway as a social service. Its prime purpose was to provide a transport infrastructure. Profitability was secondary.

This interpretation of the railway remained dominant among senior managers for thirty years or more. Post-nationalization governments, faced with deficits and huge in-vestment sums required for modernization, frequently sought to contain the costs of maintaining this infrastructure. Following a fundamental review in the 1960s many branch lines were closed. Later, during the 1970s, the government imposed investment ceilings and set out expectations for the maximum level of its support. But, although now tempered with a concern for thrift and the avoidance of waste, old traditions endured. Financial deficits continued. ER remained a bureaucratic organization with a heritage of railway engineering and public service. The railways were still run for prac-tical purposes by regional General Managers, each one of these standing in a direct line of descent from a founding pioneer. They occupied the same grand offices. There were portraits of previous incumbents on their walls. They were, very consciously, carrying on a tradition of professional railway management.

This was the reality of the dominant 'railway culture'. The railway was a public service. The purpose of the railway was to run trains. In so doing profitability was secondary. The accepted professional concerns were to do with railway engineering

---

[22] In this connection, Bryer's (1991) account of the differential returns to investors in Britain's railways is interesting.

[23] Committee structures were continually revised and amended during the post-nationalization period. My terminology anticipates the structure in place in the early 1980s, at the start of this research. Broadly speaking, this structure is not unrepresentative of early patterns, for the representation of interests in railway management committees was constant throughout this period. The railway companies were also diversified into related businesses, however, e.g. engineer-ing, shipping, harbours, property and hotels, which were also represented in the management structure. These other businesses are not discussed here. They only accounted for about 25% of headcount and turnover, and the railway operations remained the dominant managerial concern. For the record, they were gradually privatized during and after the period of this research.

and the logistical problems of operating trains. And although the 'golden age' of steam had passed, new electrical and electronic technologies still offered scope for railway people to further their engineering heritage.[24]

The emergence of the economic perspective

In a profound sense, nationalization thirty years before had created a relationship of dependence for the railways, a dependence on government for sustenance. In the early 1980s the implications of this became clear. Government policy became stringent. Social aims ceased to be a legitimate criterion for support. Government sought to impose harsh economic disciplines in all areas of public and private endeavour. Declaring a determination to 'take on' the public services in particular, it orchestrated a campaign challenging the competence of public-sector management. For the railway, government 'expectations' were translated into more specific financial 'objectives'. These were progressively tightened. Investment funds were withheld. Reporting escalating losses, ER found itself in a malign, resource constrained environment.

We need, for a moment, to backtrack. Apparently, in the late 1970s, the Chief Executive of the railway had set up a strategy think-tank to improve long-term planning.[25] Embryonic ideas developed there, and subsequently nurtured by a small group of executives, were now rolled out for more general consideration. Senior managers, by this time fully appreciative of the real hostility of government and the precarious position of the railway, fastened onto the ideas as a solution to the current problems. The organization, through the Executive Committee, created new management positions. For the first time, 'Business Managers' were appointed. For analytical purposes (only), railway operations were broken down into market sectors: for example, long distance passenger traffic, short distance passenger traffic, freight, parcels and postal traffic. Business Managers were assigned responsibility for developing strategies to enhance financial performance in each sector – in effect to manage the 'bottom line(s)'.

These people were appointed outside the main line-management hierarchy of the railway. They were long-range planning people in staff positions at the Head Office, with no formal control or authority over railway operations. In fact, their initial responsibilities were thought to be confined to the identification of market-related initiatives. The Business Managers reported to the Chief Executive and joined the Executive Committee. But the regional management hierarchies remained intact. Regional General Managers, carrying on the old traditions, continued to run the railway.

---

[24] A notorious example of this was the development of an advanced passenger train in the late 1970s. Powered by a gas turbine, it employed a revolutionary suspension technology, the whole train tilting as it went round corners. In trials, the prototypes proved unreliable, and made passengers sick. The project was shelved in the subsequent 'business regime' of the 1980s. A prototype was sent to a railway museum.

[25] I am indebted to independent archival research for this information. In the railway folklore these events are shrouded in the mystery of (recent) time. This pattern of events is not unique: see Gourvish (1990) for comparable accounts.

The appointment of Business Managers was to have far reaching consequences, however, for it introduced a new 'business' culture, a counter-culture. They brought a different interpretation of reality. For them the railway was a business, its purpose was to make profit. Engineering and logistical operations were essentially a means for extracting revenues from customers. Professional management was about making the railway profitable.

Business Managers were appointed without staff or support at the margins of the organization. But during the course of the study, they gained influence at the expense of the regional General Managers. They persuaded many around them of their idea of a business railway. Gradually, people converted to the 'business culture'. Others left the organization. The nature of dialogue and debate changed. Appeals to the old traditions of railway excellence and public service were repudiated. New kinds of policy decisions emerged, motivated by the business logic. Operational activities out in the regions began to be informed by the new rationale.

Now, the old world view, the preoccupation with engineering and logistics, the belief in the railway as a social service, the railway culture, has been substantially displaced by the business perspective, the belief that railways should be instrumental in making profit and managed to that end. The counter-culture has emerged to become the dominant-culture among the senior management. Traditions established over longer than a century were quickly overthrown.

TRACING THE DYNAMICS OF CHANGE

The story is one of evolving interpretations, meanings and perceived possibilities. No one in the organization foresaw the outcome at the start, not even the Business Managers. At first, their 'business culture' was vague and indistinct, a kind of abstract generality. But as events unfolded, it became more specific. Possibilities for coupling their business reality to organizational action were perceived. Gradually, as people elaborated the new logic for organized activity, momentum was created. Capturing the emergent nature of these developments, one senior manager described the experience as 'a voyage of discovery and development'.

This section traces the dynamics of change. Firstly, it considers the context surrounding the appointment of Business Managers. Then it outlines the crafting of new accounting systems. Subsequently, it traces the process through which the new accounting was coupled to organizational activities and endowed with meaning. Finally, it gives an account of the regional General Managers' perspective in these events. The section is interspersed with representative comments from managers in the organization.

People and context

The context of the Business Managers' appointments in ER is important in appreciating the trajectory of events. The railway was under acute threat. The competence of public-sector management was openly under challenge. The railway was charged with being 'old fashioned'. Governmental pressures for profitability were onerous, and sanctions were being applied. These threats were clearly appreciated by senior management. The railway has always prided itself on being modern in its technological activities. The charge of being 'old-fashioned' in its management practice was deeply challenging. Moreover, there was some recognition that the old traditions were not, in themselves, proving sufficient to manage the threats away, and needed to be supplemented in some way. The skills the Business Managers brought, marketing, long-term planning, 'bottom line' management, had an image of modernity, enabling the railway to throw off the charge of being 'old-fashioned', and were thought to be a useful supplementation of the railway traditions. Moreover, they were thought to be unintrusive, a 'grafting-on' to the old traditions. The Business Managers had no operational authority. They were 'back office' planning people. Their roles were defined through a remote accounting construct, the 'bottom line', outside the prevailing mainstream understanding of railway activities. In bringing new knowledge to bear to cope with environmental pressures, they were not expected to disrupt the railway or existing patterns of authority. Senior managers commented:

> Everything has its time. You've got to realize the environment of the (transport) industry. We're now in the most competitive environment the railway has ever faced. And there were clear objectives emerging from the Government. These things made people think differently. . . . It's all in the market place in the end, and how to exploit the market place. The traditional railway wasn't sensitive to the market place (Senior Executive).

> We were weak in marketing and business issues generally. The government targets were stiff. We needed those skills (General Manager).

Equally important are the personalities and backgrounds of the Business Managers. While they had all at some time worked in or with the railway, practically all had also worked outside. Thus, while they understood the railway culture and could talk railway talk, they also appreciated what they saw as wider business practice: 'managing for profit'. Furthermore, the semen became evangelists, hungry people with a mission. They developed a zeal to convert the railway from a social service to a business enterprise.

In addition, the nature of their appointments was rather unusual (at least for a mechanistic organization). There were no briefs or manuals. Ultimate intentions were not articulated. Business Managers were just told to see what they could do.

> We introduced it in an evolutionary way. We said: 'Let's appoint Business Managers and then let it evolve. Be patient and let it evolve' (Senior Executive).

> When the Chief Executive introduced the Business Managers he didn't have any idea how to take the concept forward. I think he deliberately chose people who would win the day, and left them to get on with it. It was up to each of us to build our influence. The regional General Managers had great centres of power: buildings

and armies of people. They were the Gods on high, the last remnants of the Railway Companies. He wanted to stand back from it all, and see what would happen (Business Manager).

They had, at best, a vague job description, one which they could legitimately expand.

Subsequent events were not independent of changes in the social and political climate during the decade. It was one dominated by economic liberalism: deregulation in many spheres of activity, privatization of state owned enterprises, and a sea change in attitudes towards the public services and the Welfare State. These substantive effects were to come later, but there was already a clear 'idealization' by government of private sector management practices, and a belief that they could be introduced in the public sector. (Industrialists were rationalizing 'old fashioned' work routines in the Civil Service, for example.) There was also a stated political agenda to subject the public services to 'market disciplines' wherever possible.

Evolutionary change and organizational acclimatization

The railway has long traditions and consensually accepted preoccupations. At first, the Business Managers could only see limited opportunities for coupling their concept to day-to-day activities. But as events unfolded, tentative new possibilities were perceived. Stage-by-stage, as if in episodes, their abstract notion of the business railway became more concrete.

The railway is a very formal organization. People in it describe the management process in bureaucratic analogies, talking of 'chains-of-command' and 'good old soldiers falling into line'. In meetings, people are often referred to through their official titles. There is much deference to authority. The Business Managers recognized the significance of this formal management style in their quest to convert the railway. In fact they worked through it. As their ideas evolved, in each episode they sought first to persuade the Chief Executive and his advisors. These people were likely to be the most sympathetic to their economic rhetoric, for they interfaced with government and felt the external pressures most immediately. Carefully negotiating in principle a course of action, often after much private and closed debate, then, sure of their support, the Business Managers set out to convert a wider group.

Each episode involved a fairly small incremental step. None, in isolation, was especially threatening or difficult to accommodate in the old railway culture. Indeed, at first, even those who ultimately stood to lose influence and status appreciated the blending of the business perspective into the railway culture. As the organization became acclimatized to each change, however, as each episode had a chance to 'soak', so new possibilities were perceived. Repeatedly, new episodes were enacted.

Commenting on the way in which they operated, a Business Manager reflected:

In the early days, there was nothing in writing, except that we had a responsibility for improving the bottom line. There were no organization charts. This made life difficult. It was all about relationships. We had to persuade everyone around us . . .

As we did so, our ideas evolved. We became increasingly aware of the potential of the Businesses.

Senior Executives recalled:

> Our ideas were constrained because we were . . . well I was going to say traditional railwaymen. We were coloured by the views of the complexity of running a railway. No one foresaw the present state as a possibility. Our minds were opened.

> It takes time to change an organization like the railways and to change attitudes. There's 150 years' history. You don't overturn that lightly. Nor would you want to, or the railways would cease to operate . . . The Business Managers recognized that. First, they convinced a small group, then gradually widened that group until everyone was aboard . . .

> They operated in stages . . . Incremental changes were easier to sell. It was easier to build commitment and minimize opposition from those who stood to lose . . . They took each stage to the limit.

Creating an alternative account

For the Business Managers the purpose of the railway was to make a profit. The significance of customers was revenues; the significance of operations, that is, trains, infrastructure and staff, was cost. Upon their appointment, however, there was no account of the railway's activities in each market sector consistent with their reality. While profit or loss was measured for the organization as a whole, and was used in dealings with government, no such measures existed for component parts of the railway.[26]

In fact, during the 1970s, primarily for analytical purposes (rather than for responsibility accounting), the railway had moved towards a system of contribution accounting, matching directly traceable costs to revenues for various market segments.[27] Common costs were not allocated to the segments. The railway is a remarkably integrated activity, with common staff, infrastructure and, to some extent, train-related activities, so these unallocated costs were very substantial. Senior accounting executives had long argued, both privately and publicly, that allocation was neither possible nor meaningful. Fundamental to the Business Managers' appointments, however, was not just a profit-contribution responsibility, but a 'bottom line' responsibility, and this called for the allocation of common costs. In a definite way, this 'bottom line' responsi-

---

[26] Under existing systems, costs were accounted for by region, corresponding to the physical location of the operational activities concerned. The regions were thus essentially cost centres. Revenue responsibility was more diffuse, for passengers and freight were frequently transported across two or more regions. In fact it was not as simple as this, but in practical terms, the railway network alone was a huge profit centre.

[27] These did not precisely correspond to the present market sectors, but provided a basis on which to build the subsequent measures.

bility had a normative symbolism – private sector managers were concerned with the 'bottom line'. But there was a more practical logic: this was to ensure that one or other of the Business Managers would be responsible for all costs, and motivated, as events unfolded, to ask questions about the necessity and consequences of incurring cost. A Senior Executive commented:

> You appoint a Business Manager and say: 'We believe this is freight'. The first thing he says is: 'What's mine? What are the boundaries of my business?' Then he pursues questions such as: 'How are costs being allocated to me? I want to know more about it. Let me analyse and fillet all the cost you are suggesting is mine' . . . Then he asks: 'How do these costs relate to my revenues'.

An individual within the accounting department was appointed to develop profit or loss measures by business sector. This person was in rather an invidious position. Given senior finance officials' former public repudiation of the possibility of developing these measures, he had to tread carefully. He later recalled:

> At first I was not convinced that it was either sensible or feasible. There's a whole history of avoiding cost allocations in the railway. But if the Business Managers were to take responsibility, they needed different Management Accounting. I was persuaded of this new way to run the railway. I wanted Finance to play a fundamental part in supporting it.

> When I was appointed I spent several months bouncing ideas off walls – walls not people – because finance people didn't believe you could or should develop the information they needed.

He became involved in intensive discussions with the Business Managers, and with representatives of the Chief Executive's office. Different ways of apportioning costs were discussed, and a firm of accountants consulted. The guiding principle was 'cost exhaustion' – all costs incurred by the railway had somehow to be attributed to one or more of the businesses.

The precise details of the method of arriving at the profit or loss for each business are unimportant here. It suffices to say that it was founded on principles reflecting the primacy of use of resources, and that the development of computer systems to operationalize the principle in full took some while. The significant point is that these measures were introduced, manually at first, and that they were fundamental to the emergence of the new culture.

Business Managers were appointed without any operational authority. Their positions were an abstract economic construct. They were made meaningful through the new accounting constructs. Moreover, the accounting measures provided a means through which they could later couple debate on operational and physical concerns to an economic calculus. Reflecting on the penetration of the new account of organizational activities, one Business Manager observed:

> It's my impression that the engineers, and after all we are an engineering company, had no real understanding of what they were doing in terms of the 'bottom line' . . . Now the engineers know what a 'bottom line' specification really is and they can respond to it.

One regional General Manager commented:

> I always behaved with the 'bottom line' in mind. But the Business Managers took it further. They challenge to a much greater extent. Making the railway profitable is the real meaning of the Business.

And another:

> I didn't realize the extent to which budgets would be challenged, and challenged so vehemently.

Coupling railway activities to the new account

At the head of the railway is the office of Chief Executive. Attached to this are various staff functions – Finance, Engineering Directorates and so forth. Reporting to the Chief Executive in a line-management relationship are the General Managers of the regions. Underneath these are the railway operations. Overlaid on this management structure are formal planning and decision-making systems of various kinds.

The Business Managers were appointed in staff positions outside the formal line-management structure of the railway organization. They wished to explore their reality with others. But, there was, at first, no formal context for them to interact with others. Neither did they have the formal status they perceived necessary to influence others. In a sequence of moves, they sought, first, to institutionalize their status, and then to secure bases for participating in an increasing range of dialogue and debate.

Securing status. First they lobbied the Chief Executive and his advisors for a change in reporting relationships. If he was serious about the idea of marketing and business planning in the railway, they argued, then they had to have comparable status to the regional General Managers. After some considerable debate, a new management structure was introduced. The Chief Executive appointed two Joint Managing Directors, one taking a responsibility for the regions – the operations side of the railway, the regional General Managers; the other taking a responsibility for planning and marketing – in effect, the Business Managers. In a symbolic sense, although not at first in practice, this gave the Business Managers parity with the regional General Managers. It also stood for the Chief Executive's acknowledgement of the legitimacy of the 'business' reality, the reality of the railways being managed for profit. Commenting on the significance of this, one Business Manager observed:

The General Managers used to report directly to the Chief Executive. The joint Managing Directors gave us parity.

Creating contexts for interaction. Later, in subsequent episodes, they lobbied for successive changes in the formal planning and decision-making systems. Changes, they argued at each juncture, were necessary to provide a balance to the overbearing influence of the regional General Managers and engineers. Over the period of the study, three changes were forthcoming. Each change secured opened up possibilities for perceiving the potential of the next. Firstly, the corporate planning system was revised. This dealt with longer-term matters. Formerly, regional General Managers prepared plans and presented them to the Executive Committee for ratification. The change gave Business Managers a formal input into the preparation of plans. In fact, the planning process became 'business-led', with these managers setting financial and other objectives for the regions, the regions being required to identify actions to achieve those objectives. Next, capital expenditure approval procedures were amended. Formerly, regional General Managers and engineering chiefs had significant autonomy in the approval of capital expenditures. The new system required expenditure proposals to be underwritten by one or more Business Managers, and effectively gave them a right to veto if they thought the proposals were uneconomic. Finally, budgeting systems were revised. Budgets emanating from each region were analysed by market sector. Business Managers became involved in their review.

The significance of these changes is that, in the context of ER's formal management style, formal systems and procedures imply rights to participate in and influence decisions and actions. The Business Managers' participation in the operation of these systems gave them a context to interact with others and question the rationale underlying railway decisions. In meetings, they could be seen translating operational and engineering concerns into the new profit calculus, feeding their financial vocabulary back into the stream of discourse. Appealing to the 'ideal' of the profit-conscious customer-oriented private sector manager, they challenged and sometimes ridiculed beliefs.

Thus, participation in the planning procedures enabled them to reinterpret longer-run engineering and operational initiatives in business terms: what does it mean for the customer? Will it improve journey times and punctuality? What implications does it raise in terms of costs and revenues? Their sponsorship of capital investments enabled them to ask: will it improve train reliability, eliminating the need for back up resources? Can the businesses afford it? What are the investment options? The redesign of the budgeting system gave them opportunities to challenge the cost effectiveness and profit implications of operational issues like train routing, train scheduling and the programming of maintenance.

Moving from the remote concerns of long-term planning, through capital investments, to immediate issues of train scheduling and maintenance programming, they recast management debate into a language of the 'bottom line'. Others began to take up their vocabulary. Railway matters gradually came to be discussed as financial matters. Furthermore, planning and budgeting activities began to assume a new significance. Formerly, they were introverted acts of cost containment. Now they came to symbolize the search for profit-maximizing opportunities.

Commenting on the importance of these changes in formal systems, a Business Manager observed:

> We had responsibility for improving the profitability of the railway. But it wasn't clear who was in control – I think there was some diffidence in spelling that out with the utmost clarity. We lobbied to get control of the planning process. Clarity has emerged, now that we have taken responsibility for planning and budgeting. That's become our power base.

Over time, these changes cumulatively extended the opportunity for Business Managers to interact with engineers and operators far beyond their original remit. Through this interaction, their ideas became more specific. But they were still located in the Head Office. Accordingly, in a later episode, they set about extending their influence into the regional organizations. They appealed to the Chief Executive for the appointment of individuals to represent their interests within the regions. These Regional Business Managers, once appointed, carried the economic perspective deep into the regional organizations, carving underneath the regional General Managers and giving Business Managers a direct line of influence to operational activities. One commented:

> People in the regions are used to doing things without asking. They find themselves subject to our scrutiny. I can take things up in a big way, if necessary, and howl for their blood.

And commenting on their influence, an operations manager in the regions observed:

> Five years ago it would have been revolutionary to challenge what an engineer wanted to spend money on. Now it happens frequently.

Consolidating the emerging reality through symbolic events. Through interaction in meetings and elsewhere, many in the organization began to understand the Business Managers' emerging reality. Most also found it appealing. The continual attacks on the competence of public sector managers had worn morale down. To be business-like was 'good', it gave them pride, and made the railway modern. Increasingly people came to share the normative symbolism of the 'bottom line'. But to a large extent this was uncoupled from their concrete day-to-day activities. Meaningful symbols relating to everyday tasks, events and recollections through which people could connect the business reality to their ongoing decisions and actions, were absent.

As the situation unfolded, this changed, however. In parallel with the formal changes, a sequence of important events was enacted. The Business Managers staged 'contests' with the regional General Managers, forcing collisions between the railway culture and the business culture. As before, they worked through the bureaucratic structure of the railway. Focusing, in each episode, on a specific issue demonstrative of their concerns, they sought first to persuade the Chief Executive and his advisors. Once sure of this group's support they set out to convert a wider group. Finally, they forced the issue for resolution. Again, each issue resolved opened up the possibility of the next. Three events stand out. They are reported in sequence.

The first concerned the disposition of locomotives and rolling stock. Over a period of time, one regional General Manager had been successful in acquiring resources to invest in high speed trains for passenger transport. These he zealously guarded against suggestions from other regional General Managers that they should be more widely dispersed on the railway network. The relevant Business Manager's analysis suggested that this situation was uneconomic. Profit could be improved by relocating some of these train sets to other regions. This Business Manager lobbied the Chief Executive and his advisors to have the location decision determined by economic criteria. This was supported and the trains were moved. Commenting on this event, the relevant Business Manager observed:

> Regional prejudices had stopped the movement of high speed trains to the areas where they could earn the most money. The General Managers were barons. You just didn't go into their territory. It was a sort of unwritten law. I got those trains moved early on, it was one of the first things I did.

A second event concerned capital investments. In this case, a major track was being upgraded to take faster trains. According to engineering precedent, it was usual to renew signalling equipment at the same time. The Business Manager's analysis indicated that this was neither necessary nor economic. Again, the Chief Executive was lobbied. The signalling was not renewed. As the Business Manager observed:

> The main line was being electrified at significant expense. When wires are being strung over the track, it is customary to renew signalling equipment at the same time.

> We can't afford it. Anyway, the existing signalling will last another 15 years. All we needed to do was immunize the signals for electrification. The General Manager and his engineers were horrified. 'This isn't the way to run a railway', they said. 'It's a cash flow decision'.

A third decision concerned the scheduling of trains. Note that this is getting down to operational and logistical detail, by any standards the province of professional railway operators. Traditionally, train schedules had been set to maximize operational convenience. For the sake of passenger convenience, a Business Manager wanted to alter the schedule on a route. This intervention was bitterly resented by the regional General Managers. Even in this case, the Business Manager's judgement was supported by the Chief Executive.

> Traditionally, timetables have been set for operational convenience. I was dissatisfied and wanted to change the frequency of trains on the route.

> The General Manager was determined not to have it. I took it to the Chief Executive. I said to the General Manager half an hour before the meeting: 'I've got to win, and will win, the writing's on the wall whether you like or not. I like you, why are

you putting your head in a noose? Why don't you back off?'. But he didn't (Business Manager).

All these events came to have a significance way beyond the decisions themselves. Each stood for a whole class of decisions, signifying the primacy of the business reality in relation to those kinds of decisions. The high speed train issue redefined all decisions concerning the location of locomotives and rolling stock as economic decisions. The signalling decision redefined all investment decisions as economic decisions. The scheduling decision established the economic nature of detailed operational issues.

These events coupled the business culture to concrete railway activities. They were widely celebrated in the organization, both in public documents and in internal discussions, and are recalled in explanations of the emergence of the business rationale for railway management. Cumulatively, they embrace almost all aspects of the railway. People used them to attribute a new meaning to their everyday activities.

Not all decisions went in the Business Managers' favour, though. Secure in their conversion of the majority of the senior management élite, the Business Managers sought to explore their new reality with those within the organization. As already noted, representatives were appointed in regional offices: Regional Business Managers. At first, these individuals reported formally to the regional General Managers, and were on their payroll. The Business Managers wanted to pay their salaries from their own budgets to avoid them having divided loyalties. Regional General Managers found this unacceptable.

Apparently the Business Managers acted too soon; they lost. But the momentum they had already established was too great and they came back to win support some weeks later. A Business Manager explained:

> There was a famous breakfast meeting where I soundly lost. The organization was not ready. But of course, one rises again. Later, we were on firmer ground. I raised the matter again, and I won the votes of everyone.

In the regions, a similar process of change seems to be being enacted. These individuals appear to be following a similar strategy, gaining contexts for interaction, persuading others of their views, and staging contests. The 'bottom line' for each business is now decomposed into subsidiary 'bottom line' accounts. In regional meetings, these managers reinterpret dialogue and debate through the subsidiary accounts. A sequence of new symbolic events is being enacted in each region. Commenting on his experiences, one Regional Business Manager observed:

> At first we had to stand out there in front battling on our own. But now it's like a tide coming in. Nobody can actually fight the tide. I'm coming in on a surfboard really.

The picture then, is one of sequencing, momentum and cumulation. The Business Managers started on their mission with a vague concept of a business railway. They secured increasing contexts for interaction. Their ideas gradually became more concrete and they persuaded others around them. In an episodic manner, moving from the general to the particular, they secured changes to reporting relationships and systems. Each episode was punctuated by a key event. These events became symbols of the business culture, endowing railway activities with a new meaning, and provided a basis for continual and cumulative reinterpretations of railway operations.

Of course, there was tension. These decisions challenged the status of the regional General Managers and others who still subscribed to old beliefs. There was resentment and hostility. But the Business Managers let each step 'soak' so the organization could acclimatize, before embarking on the next episode, and a majority of the senior management gradually converted to the 'business culture'. Appealing to another metaphor, a Senior Executive commented:

> We've lit a bonfire and it's burning like mad.

The Regional General Managers' perspective

Regional General Managers were steeped in tradition. They were the descendants of the railway pioneers, the bastions of the railway culture. The business culture struck at their values and beliefs. When asked why and how they had let these things happen, they responded:

> It wasn't obvious at the time. The Business Managers were planners. We didn't expect the railway operations to change (General Manager).

One quoted from a memo he had written to his staff immediately after the Executive Committee meeting which had approved the principle of the Business Managers' appointment:

> The respective roles of Headquarters and the Regions will not change . . . Policies, as now will evolve from discussions. The Regions will participate . . .

In fact, from the General Managers' perspective, the story is one of initial seduction, followed by surprise and ambivalence, defection and resignation. They were aware of external pressures for financial performance. Some thought it was a whim, and would pass. But most perceived a need for a business perspective, and supported the creation of the Business Managers' positions in the Executive Committee. When the Business Managers were appointed, most welcomed their influence. At an early stage, one General Manager commented:

> This is good for us. I'm quite pleased at the way the culture is changing. You talk around now and nobody is in any doubt that the railway is business-led.

And another, commenting on the decision to relocate the high speed trains:

> Why do we have fancy train sets? It's not for General Managers to play trains. It's to make the businesses more profitable.[28]

One joined the Senior Executives, representing the Business Managers. According to his critics, he is reputed to have seen 'which way the wind was blowing', but he himself described it thus:

> Initially I was opposed. But I saw the logic of the changes. I was converted.

Thus, most found the abstract normative symbolism of the 'bottom line' appealing. They thought it 'good' to be more business-like. They aspired to 'private sector practice'. Few perceived the underlying momentum of events or their potential significance. Acting out the new rationale, they thought they need have no fear for the railway traditions. In fact, sitting in their grand offices with portraits and plaques around their walls and other symbols of former grandeur, it was inconceivable to them that the railway traditions could be undermined by anything.

As the significance of the economic reality emerged through subsequent events, however, the situation became less congenial for them. It threatened their pride as professional railway operators. Commenting on the resignalling decision noted earlier, a General Manager said:

> We'll have to do it all again in 15 years' time. It's not a sensible long-term decision.

Furthermore, the appointment of Regional Business Managers within their own organizations undermined their authority.

At this point, they protested vigorously. This prompted a report from the centre discussing the relationship between Businesses and the Regions. The report placated them with the soothing idea of Business Managers and regional General Managers as equals in a team-based organization. Nevertheless, the business perspective continued to impinge on operational matters.

Many General Managers became unhappy. They thought the emerging decisions unprofessional, and feared for the quality of the railway. By this time, however, their appeals fell on deaf ears. Most others among the senior management élite had converted to the business culture. The General Managers were characterized as reactionary, protective and old-fashioned.

Towards the end of the study, most of them left the organization or took 'early retirement'. One stayed in office a while longer. Shortly before his retirement he had this to say:

> With the benefit of hindsight, I think the Chief Executive was right in allowing it through . . . But it's gone too far . . .

---

[28] This General Manager claimed that he had repeatedly requested some of these train sets himself.

While I've been in office, through good engineering management, I've just about managed to get rid of all the speed restrictions on the main line. Business Managers are taking a maintenance holiday [i.e. neglecting maintenance]. In five years someone will be faced with exactly the situation I inherited.

Former regional General Managers have been replaced with sympathetic men. They repudiate the old traditions. They are proud to subscribe to the business culture. A newly appointed General Manager had this to say:

I personally feel that this new approach is right. I support the businesses. I see it as my job to influence my current staff to accept the business managers.

Far from being equals in a team, the regional General Managers are seen to be subservient to Business Managers. 'Business managers set policy and standards; regions implement'. Career patterns have changed. To become a regional General Manager was the ultimate aspiration for a railway-man; by the end of the field research it was to become a Business Manager. There was open discussion of removing the regional General Managers from the Railway Executive.

ACCOUNTING AND CULTURE

Initially, there was a dominant 'railway' culture. The Business Managers brought a counter 'business' culture. This cascaded across the senior management élite to become dominant. The Business Managers had an abstract idea of a business railway. New accounts were crafted representing the railway as a series of businesses. The Business Managers gained contexts to interact with others. In these contexts, they recast dialogue and debate from a railway language of operations and engineering to their business language of markets and profit. Gradually the idea of a business railway became more specific. Moving from remote concerns to immediate issues, they persuaded others of their interpretations. There were contests over the definition of specific activities. The outcomes became symbols through which people attributed new meaning to railway operations. Momentum built up behind the business culture. People converted, others left. For senior managers, the abstract idea became a tangible, energizing reality, a source of pride. Now the railway culture is repudiated.

A broad range of theories can be brought to bear to interpret the pattern of these events. Fundamental to this account is the notion of culture as a system of ideas: beliefs, knowledges and values in which action and artifacts are vested with expressive qualities (Geertz, 1973, 1983); and the idea that organizations have distinctive cultures (Pettigrew, 1979). This is exemplified in the contrasting 'railway' and 'business' cultures described. Associated with this is the conceptualization of organizational change as a process of uncoupling and recoupling (cf. Greenwood & Hinings, 1988): exemplified in the railway by the uncoupling of activities from the railway culture and their recoupling to the business culture.[29] We can also see a theory of inertia in operation, change being precipitated by crisis (cf. Starbuck & Hedberg, 1977; Jonsson & Lundin, 1977; Mintzberg, 1978; Miller & Friesen, 1984). The railway culture was remarkably resilient over many previous decades, despite several attacks; real threats only being perceived when the severity of the current onslaught on the public services became apparent. There are also traces of the 'garbage can' (Cohen *et al.*, 1972; March & Olsen, 1976): the Business Management idea was developed independently of the crisis, only subsequently coupled to the threats facing the organization.

Continuing, change was emergent (March & Olsen, 1976; Pettigrew, 1985). This was not a controlled process, relying on plans and rational analyses engineered by those standing outside, untainted as it were; the whole management group was bound up in the creation of the business culture. The process unfolded through tentative initiatives, buffeted by the timing of events, the ambition and (relative) political skills of the 'champions' (Kanter, 1983) and other actors involved, and their failures and successes. Nor were the vagaries of chance unimportant[30] (Pettigrew, 1985). Moreover, we see changes in systems (planning, capital investment, budgeting) interpenetrating the emergence and elaboration of the business culture.

It also is possible to appeal to the insights of institutional theory (Meyer & Rowan, 1977; DiMaggio & Powell, 1983; Scott, 1987; Zucker, 1988). Government, the railway's key environmental constituency, was intolerant of (what it saw as) managerial incompetence. The Business Management initiative could be interpreted as a symbol of the railway becoming more modern and business-like: the 'bottom line' idea standing for the railway adopting private sector practices. Such solutions may have real and unintended internal consequences, however. One was the Business Managers amassing power and influence at the expense of the General Managers. Although a theoretically impoverished theory in this context, there is some link here with the strategic contingencies' perspective of intraorganizational power (Hickson *et al.*, 1971; Hinings *et al.*, 1974). Subsequent to the appointment of the Business Managers, the railway managed to persuade government to make funds available, on a one-off basis, for a major electrification project (giving rise to the signalling controversy discussed earlier). Apparently, approval was forthcoming as a result of the 'rigorous business case' orchestrated by the relevant Business Manager.

The purpose here is not to discuss these theories further, however. It is to develop a cultural appreciation of accounting. The study shows that accounting was implicated

---

[29] This characterization, of course, emphasizes change; and there is also a sense in which there is continuity. The railway still runs trains, it still provides a transport infrastructure (of sorts), and it is still a very mechanistic bureaucracy. Nevertheless, managers in the organization currently emphasize change, and there is a sense in which linkages with the past have been ruptured, for the railway, as I will explain, is interpreted quite differently.

[30] In ER, subsequent to the events described, there was an unfortunate accident in which one crowded commuter train collided into the back of another. A formal inquiry found that basic supervision of electrical rewiring in a signalling scheme had been neglected, attributing blame, in part, to ER's pursuit of profit. It is interesting to speculate how outcomes might have differed had this accident happened two years before.

differently in the two cultures described. At this point, it is appropriate to explicate its linkages to underlying knowledge, values and beliefs.

A cultural system incorporates, among other things, knowledge about environments, and strategies for extracting subsistence from them. This knowledge is quite different in the two cultures. In the railway culture it revolved around the public service idea, later coupled to notions of thrift. Essentially, the knowledge was this: if the organization provided the nation with a transport infrastructure (without undue waste), then sustenance would be forthcoming from government. This knowledge is not unique to the railway culture. The expectation that low-cost, generally available services will be rewarded by the state is common to many public service organizations in Europe, for example the health and education services. Given this knowledge, accounting was incidental in the railway culture: it was necessary to ensure that revenues were accounted for and suppliers paid, and perhaps to contain waste, but that was the limit of its significance in the structures of meaning. The purpose of the railway was to run trains; operating the railway would be rewarded by government. In this knowledge, the train, therefore, was endowed with a special significance.

The business culture, revolving around the 'bottom line', incorporates a quite different knowledge. Rather obviously, in view of events in ER, the bottom line constructs the notion of the railway as a profit-seeking enterprise. This is not just a matter of 'cost efficiency', however, although that is important. More importantly, in ER it constructs the idea of looking to product markets, rather than to government, for sustenance. There is nothing somehow uniquely 'public service' about the railway network in this construction. Rail transport is a product (or service), to be bought and sold like any other; in fact it is a series of products: intercity travel, freight, suburban commuting, etc. Revenues from these products, rather than government support, must cover costs; and, critically, revenues are earned in the market place. Survival depends on extracting resources from these markets, perhaps in competition with other firms. Hence the new-found concern for competition with other means of transport (road, air, buses), expressed by railway managers early in the account above, a concern which in the railway culture would have been probably inconsequential.[31] Given this knowledge, accounting activities become hugely significant. The search for profit opportunities, and the elimination of non-profit-making activities, is a quest for survival. It is now the customer, not the train, which has special importance.

No culture is completely coherent, of course. Each has ambiguities and contradictions. In ER, residues of the past create tensions. One is the partial incompatibility of the business culture with the restrictions placed on it by state ownership. ER is not allowed to borrow in financial markets to fund investment, for example, and as government funds are tight, this means investments necessary for competitive purposes cannot always be made. It also has statutory obligations to keep certain branch lines open, even if they are unprofitable. Here it still looks to government for support

---

[31] A Business Manager's comment on market research is also interesting in this respect: 'The single most important question we ask is: "Are you more likely or less likely to travel on the railway as a result of your most recent journey?" ' This question would have been substantially irrelevant in the railway culture.

(although a government conceptualized as a customer). Nevertheless, the underlying knowledge systems are quite different, and constitute different realities.

This shift in knowledge which accounting helps to construct, the shift from looking to the state for subsistence to looking to markets, is fundamental, and it interpenetrates the operation and management of ER's core technology with pervasive effects. For a start, it changes the appropriate form of organization. In the old knowledge, the prime task was the operation of trains. The meaningful management structure was one which facilitated operations. The physical facilities of the railway are geographically laid out along the radial routes of the old prenationalization companies. Thus the appropriate management organization was around these routes, i.e. the regional management structures. The regional General Managers and engineers, because of their acknowledged expertise in operating trains, were afforded substantial status and influence.

Now, in the new knowledge, this is 'mere' production, subservient to markets. The prime task is serving markets. The meaningful form of management organization is one which reflects and confronts markets. Since the long distance intercity travel market is not confined to one main line, for example, or the freight market confined to one region, the regional and business forms of organization do not map perfectly onto one another. Hence the reorientation of management structures and systems around the Business Managers, and their subsequent elaboration through the Business Manager's subordinates located in the regions. Of course, there is still an operational task to be performed: trains, tracks, maintenance and so forth. But in this new knowledge it is Business Managers, with supposed expertise in markets and extracting resources from them, who attract status and influence.

The changing knowledge also redefines the appropriate form of action. In the old knowledge, that of the celebration of the train, there were norms that made things intrinsically necessary. 'Of course' professional railwaymen renewed signalling equipment when they electrified the track, for example; it was inconceivable not to do so. The train needs to be taken care of and nurtured. The interest in thrift, the avoidance of waste, also meant the elimination of activities not strictly necessary for the operation of trains: training staff to smile at customers, for example. In the new knowledge, activities are neither intrinsically necessary, nor intrinsically wasteful. Rather they are judged for their consequences in the market. Through the 'bottom line', activities become desirable to the extent that they add more 'value' than they cost. This is not simply cost minimization: the avoidance of unnecessary gold-plating. The 'bottom line engineering specification', mentioned earlier, means designing for the market, as it were: adding comfort, reliability, speed, customer service where its returns outweigh its cost. Attractive concourse design is not wasteful extravagance, it is reinterpreted as a 'good' thing which brings in custom.

Action is also judged against a different concept of time. In the old knowledge, time was practically infinite. The railways were built to last for decades, for centuries. The nation would always need a transport infrastructure. Professional standards were oriented towards doing a long-lasting thorough job. Government would reward the railway for maintaining the viability of the network into the future. In the new knowledge, the concept of time is much shorter. Survival is a day-to-day affair. Markets are ephemeral. Don't spend money now on activities that you can put off until the future. Take 'maintenance holidays' where you can: deterioration of the infra-structure can be remedied later.

The point being made here is that accounting can play a significant role in constructing specific knowledges. Accounting systems embody particular assumptions about rationality, organization, authority, time and so forth. If these permeate into underlying values, knowledges and beliefs they can have very real consequences. Above we see accounting coming in to the organization to construct a new theory of subsistence, which in turn implies particular modes of organizing, patterns of influence and authority, criteria for action and a new concept of time.

The cultural knowledge described here was not discovered completely formed. Nor was it coupled to the railway's management structures (or to action) in an instant. Rather the meaning of the bottom line gradually crystallized around the initial accounts, and the coupling had to be actively crafted. The business culture unfolded in episodes: bursts of exhausting creativity, each building on what had previously been accomplished, and punctuated by a concluding event; followed by a pause for consolidation, recovery and imagination before the next. Successive episodes moved from the abstract realm to the particular; from long-term issues to immediate issues. In each, senior management struggled to reconceptualize a class of activities; then it was uncoupled, or perhaps one should say wrenched, from the railway culture and re-coupled to the business culture. Again and again these episodes continued, until cumulatively practically all classes of railway activity were redefined. Later, in the regions, a similar process of episodic uncoupling and recoupling was enacted. In the process, linkages to the railway culture were only bit-by-bit ruptured.

The general point arising is that organizations have different classes of activity. Cultural change is not simply uncoupling and recoupling, or even reconceptualization. Each class of activity may need to be separately uncoupled and recoupled. During the process, different classes of activity may be informed by different rationales and knowledge. In ER, this led to a strange schizophrenia in the organization (and difficulties in making sense of the data), in which some activities were railway-culture issues, and some business-culture issues. It also led to strange disjunctures between the interpretive schemes brought to bear in the head office and in the regions. Only towards the end of the research did this schizophrenia begin to be resolved.

This process, however, needs to be enveloped in an awareness of the conditions for its possibility, conditions for the emergence of the particular culture described. In some ways, perhaps, the business culture in ER may be seen to be inevitable. Today, the belief in markets (as an optimal form of organization) seems to be firmly entrenched in Anglo-American political cultures, and in those of some continental-European states. Governmental pressures, inevitably, in this view, led to investment in financial calculation and the construction of the railway as a business enterprise. Support for this 'theory of inevitability' might be sought by retrospective application of the present political determination to privatize ER, or at least some of its businesses.

As Fligstein (1990) notes, in a rather different critique, such an interpretation relies on understandings of the present to construct appreciations of the past: interpreting the past through the present, rather than the present through the past. ER had a remarkably strong heritage which survived previous attacks. In the early 1980s, its privatization was not just undiscussed, it was inconceivable. Arguably, the business culture in ER, the reconstruction of the railway through the 'bottom line(s)' as a series of businesses, actually created preconditions for the discussion of privatization, not vice versa.

For sure, the early 1980s witnessed the beginnings of the sea change in attitudes towards the public services that swept across the political culture later in the decade. Through influential right-wing think-tanks the idea of subjecting public services to an entrepreneurial principle was then emerging, later to be manifested in the 'rolling back' of the public sector through the privatization of many public utilities and attempts to introduce market mechanisms in others. Associated with this was the emerging idea of the 'dependence' culture, and its repudiation; to be replaced by an 'enterprise' culture. Individuals, and organizations, were expected to take a responsibility for their own destiny.

However, the initiative for business management in ER, conceived in the late 1970s, preceded these political developments, and appears to have been a substantially autonomous development in a separate arena: as one of the initiators in the senior management group explained, it was 'the product of thinking railwaymen'. Explicating this claim would require careful analysis of historical materials beyond the scope of this paper. But such evidence as is available supports the view that the initiative was developed largely independently of political ideas, its private sector leanings probably owing more to the advice of a few business consultants than to any political agenda. Certainly it was not government-inspired; indeed government was initially sceptical, only later endorsing the ideas (and applying them to its own ends).

That said, the initiative was congruent with the ideas emerging outside, and its subsequent elaboration into the business culture undoubtedly owes much to their development. Even here, though, due importance must be attached to the specific circumstances within the organization. Public sector management was under challenge, morale was low. Many in the senior management group were receptive to the new ideas. Business Management was seen as a home-grown solution to governmental attack. It expressed some kind of empowerment, a potential freedom from the yoke of government restriction, and an opportunity for managers to show their entrepreneurial capabilities.

CONCLUDING COMMENT

The purpose of this paper is to articulate a cultural analysis of accounting in organizations. The appreciation of organizations as cultures provides a rich insight into organizational life, drawing out the expressive qualities of action and artifact. Cultural knowledge in organizations vests organizational activities with symbolic meanings; so also it vests accounting with symbolic meaning. A cultural analysis of accounting seeks to uncover these particular meanings, and to locate them in underlying local knowledges, values and beliefs.

The paper has sought to apply this cultural perspective in an empirical setting. Through a field study of organizational change, it showed how accounting can be vested with different meanings in local cultures. And it showed how accounting can enter into organizational settings to constitute cultural knowledge in particular ways, creating particular rationalities for organizational action; and in turn how this can lead to new patterns of organization, of authority and influence, new concepts of time and legitimate action. The study also traced the emergent, episodic process through which cultural knowledge was constituted in this organization, and coupled to organizational activities.

The study certainly flashes out the constitutive potential of accounting proposed by Hopwood (1987), Hines (1988) and others. However, the specific findings of the field study – the reorientation of a strategy for subsistence from government to markets, and its subsequent elaboration; and the process through which this realization was accomplished – are not offered as a general proposition on the cultural significance of accounting. Accounting systems are implicated in organizational cultures in different, possibly unique ways. The cultural knowledge constructed in this organization is but one possibility; there are many others. In this, as in other fields, 'the road to the grand abstractions of science winds through a thicket of singular facts' (Geertz, 1973, p. 145).

Rather, the purpose of the field study is to explicate a mode of theorizing linkages between accounting and culture. The mode of theorizing is interpretive, getting underneath surface descriptions to understand the significance of accounting in local settings; and it is reflective, in the sense that the theorist reflects on that significance in the context of the underlying ideational system. Applying this mode of analysis in different settings would contribute hugely to our emergent appreciation of the way in which accounting is used in organizations, usefully supplementing the more quantitative approaches to research pursued by contingency theorists, for example. It may be particularly valuable also in the development of comparative theories of the use of accounting in different social contexts. We know, for example, that accounting systems within organizations in different countries are often not that dissimilar to Anglo-American designs; it seems, however, that they may be used quite differently. The mode of theorizing advanced here would enable us to address this issue in a productive way.

Finally, while the paper has deliberately refrained from casting judgements on the developments described in the organization studied, it is probably worth acknowledging that there is widespread criticism of 'bottom line' orientations such as those described here, particularly for their construction of time. Far from creating an underlying competitiveness in organizations, the preoccupation with the 'bottom line' is seen to discourage technological innovation and investments in operational capability (e.g. Hayes & Abernathy, 1980; Johnson & Kaplan, 1987). ER, it seems, has adopted this vocabulary just as those organizations that have it are being exhorted to move towards longer-term, more strategic appreciations of time. In the railway, assets have long lives and the lead-time on capital investment is also long. To some extent the maintenance of the infrastructure is inevitably compromised by its new culture. Quite possibly with innovations in transport, the railway network will be an irrelevance in 50 years' time; on the other hand, it may not be. The green lobby, in particular, might argue that it is sensible to keep options open in a way that at present may not be possible.

Postscript

The process of change in ER continues. The regional management structure is today being dissolved. The operational side of the railway is currently being reorganized and assimilated into the Businesses. The crafted accounts representing the railway as a series of businesses have now permeated through management structures and systems to operations on the ground. The railway quite literally has become its businesses. There are no longer any regional General Managers, no vestiges of the railway culture . . . or are there? High up on a building above one of the main-line termini, out of sight except to observant motorists on a nearby flyover, there is a residue of the past: a large illuminated logo – the logo of a pre-nationalization railway.

BIBLIOGRAPHY

Aldrich, H. E., *Organizations & Environments* (Englewood Cliffs, NJ: Prentice Hall, 1979).

Allaire, Y. & Firsirotu, M. E., Theories of Organizational Culture, *Organizational Studies* (1984) pp. 51–64.

Ansari, S. & Euske, K. J., Rational, Rationalizing and Reifying Uses of *Accounting Data in Organizations, Accounting, Organizations and Society* (1987) pp. 549–570.

Argyris, C. & Schon, D. A., *Organizational Learning* (Reading, MA: Addison-Wesley, 1981).

Barley, S. R., Meyer, G. W. & Gash, D. C., Cultures of Culture: Academics, Practitioners and the Pragmatics of Normative Control, *Administrative Science Quarterly* (March 1988) pp. 24–60.

Berry, A., Capps, T., Cooper, D., Fergusson, P., Hopper, T. & Lowe, A., Management Control in an Area of the National Coal Board, *Accounting, Organizations and Society* (1985) pp. 3–28.

Blau, P. M., *The Dynamics of Bureaucracy: A Study of Interpersonal Relationships in Two Government Agencies* (Chicago, IL: University of Chicago Press, 1955).

Bruns, W. & Kaplan, R. S. (eds), *Accounting and Management: A Field Study Perspective* (Cambridge, MA: Harvard Business School Press, 1987).

Brunsson, N., *The Irrational Organization* (New York: Wiley, 1985).

Bryer, R. A., Accounting for the Railway Mania of 1845 – A Great Railway Swindle?, *Accounting, Organizations and Society* (1991) pp. 439–486.

Burns, T. & Stalker, G. M., *The Management of Innovation* (London: Tavistock Press, 1961).

Buroway, M., *Manufacturing Consent* (Chicago, IL: University of Chicago Press, 1979).

Burrell, G. & Morgan, G., *Sociological Paradigms and Organizational Analysis* (London: Heineman, 1979).

Chandler, A. D., *The Railroads* (New York: Harcourt, Brace & World, 1965).

Clifford, J. & Marcus, G. E. (eds), *Writing Culture* (Berkeley, CA: University of California Press, 1986).

Cohen, M. D., March, J. G. & Olsen, J. P., A Garbage Can Model of Organizational Choice, *Administrative Science Quarterly* (March 1972) pp. 1–25.

Covaleski, M. & Dirsmith, M., The Use of Budgetary Symbols in the Political Arena: An Historically Informed Field Study, *Accounting, Organizations and Society* (1988) pp. 1–24.

Crapanzano, V., Hermes Dilemma: The Masking of Subversion in Ethnographic Description, in Clifford, J. & Marcus, G. E. (eds), *Writing Culture* (Berkeley, CA: University of California Press, 1986) pp. 51–76.

Crozier, M., *The Bureaucratic Phenomenon* (London: Tavistock, 1964).

Dalton, M., *Men Who Manage* (New York: Wiley, 1959).

Deal, T. E. & Kennedy, A. A., *Corporate Culture: The Rites and Rituals of Corporate Life* (Reading, MA: Addison-Wesley, 1982).

Dent, J. F., Organizational Research in Accounting: Perspectives, Issues and a Commentary, in Hopwood, A. G. & Bromwich, M., *Research and Current Issues in Management Accounting* (London: Pitman, 1986).

Denzin, N. K., Interpretive Interactionism, in Morgan, G. (ed), *Beyond Method* (Beverly Hills, CA: Sage, 1983) pp. 129–146.

DiMaggio, P. J. & Powell, W. W., The Iron Cage Revisited: Institutional Isomorphism and Collective Rationality in Organizational Fields, *American Sociological Review* (April 1983) pp. 147–160.

Douglas, M., *Purity and Danger: An Analysis of Concepts of Pollution and Taboo* (London: Routledge & Kegan Paul, 1966).

Evans Pritchard, E. E., *Witchcraft, Oracles and Magic among the Azande* (Oxford: Oxford University Press, 1937).

Evans Pritchard, E. E., *The Nuer* (Oxford: Oxford University Press, 1940).

Feldman, S. P., Management in Context: An Essay on the Relevance of Culture to the Understanding of Organizational Change, *Journal of Management Studies* (November 1986) pp. 587–607.

Fligstein, N., *The Transformation of Corporate Control* (Cambridge, MA: Harvard University Press, 1990).

Geertz, C., *The Interpretation of Cultures* (New York: Basic Books, 1973).

Geertz, C., *Local Knowledge* (New York: Basic Books, 1983).

Geertz, C., *Works and Lives: The Anthropologist as Author* (Cambridge: Polity Press, 1988).

Goffman, E., *The Presentation of Self in Everyday Life* (New York: Doubleday, 1959).

Goodenough, W. H., *Culture, Language and Society* (Reading, MA: Addison-Wesley, 1971).

Goold, M. & Campbell, A., *Strategies and Styles* (Oxford: Blackwell, 1987).

Gouldner, A. W., *Patterns of Industrial Bureaucracy* (New York: Free Press, 1954).

Gourvish, T. R., *British Railways 1948–73: A Business History* (Cambridge University Press, 1986).

Gourvish, T. R., *British Rail's 'Business Led' Organization, 1977–90: Government–Industry Relations in Britain's Public Sector, Business History Review* (1990) pp. 109–149.

Greenwood, R. & Hinings, C. R., Organization Design Types, Tracks and the Dynamics of Strategic Change, *Organization Studies* (1988) pp. 293–316.

Gregory, K. L., Native-View Paradigms: Multiple Cultures & Culture Conflicts in Organizations, *Administrative Science Quarterly* (September 1983) pp. 359–377.

Harris, M., *Cultural Materialism: the Struggle for a Science of Culture* (New York: Random House, 1979).

Hayes, R. & Abernathy, S. J., Managing Our Way to Economic Decline, *Harvard Business Review* (July–August 1980) pp. 67–77.

Hedberg, B. L. T., How Organizations Learn and Unlearn, in Nystrom, P. C. & Starbuck, W. H. (eds), *Handbook of Organization Design: Volume 1* (Oxford: Oxford University Press, 1981).

Hedberg, G. & Jonsson, S., Designing Semi-confusing Information Systems for Organizations in Changing Environments, *Accounting, Organizations and Society* (1978) pp. 47–65.

Hedberg, B., Nystrom, P. C. & Starbuck, W. H., Camping on See Saws: Prescriptions for a Self-Designing Organization, *Administrative Science Quarterly* (March 1976) pp. 41–65.

Hickson, D. J., Hinings, C. R., Lee, C. A., Schneck, R. E. & Pennings, J. M., A Strategic Contingencies' Theory of Intra Organizational Power, *Administrative Science Quarterly* (June 1971) pp. 216–229.

Hines, R., Financial Accounting: In Communicating Reality, We Construct Reality, *Accounting, Organizations and Society* (1988) pp. 251–261.

Hinings, C. R., Hickson, D. J., Pennings, J. M. & Schneck, R. E., Structural Conditions of Intra Organizational Power, *Administrative Science Quarterly* (March 1974) pp. 22–44.

Hopwood, A. G., Towards an Organizational Perspective for the Study of Accounting and Information Systems, *Accounting, Organizations and Society* (1978) pp. 3–13.

Hopwood, A. G., On Trying to Study Accounting in the Contexts in which it Operates, *Accounting, Organizations and Society* (1983) pp. 287–305.

Hopwood, A. G., The Archaeology of Accounting Systems, *Accounting, Organizations and Society* (1987) pp. 207–234.

Hughes, E. C., *Men and their Work* (Glencoe, IL: Free Press, 1958).

Johnson, H. T. & Kaplan, R. S., *Relevance Lost: The Rise and Fall of Management Accounting* (Cambridge, MA: Harvard, 1987).

Jones, P. R. & Lakin, C., *The Carpet Makers* (Maidenhead: McGraw-Hill, 1978).

Jonsson, S. & Lundin, R. A., Myths and Wishful Thinking as Management Tools, in Nystrom, P. C. & Starbuck, W. H. (eds), *Prescriptive Models of Organization*, pp. 157–170 (Amsterdam: North-Holland, 1977).

Kanter, R., *The Change Masters: Corporate Entrepreneurs at Work* (New York: Simon & Schuster, 1983).

Kilmann, R. H., Saxton, M. J. & Serpa, R. (eds), *Gaining Control of the Corporate Culture* (San Francisco: Jossey Bass, 1985).

Lawrence, P. R. & Lorsch, J. W., *Organization and Environment: Managing Differentiation and Integration* (IL: Irwin, [1967] 1969).

Levi Strauss, C., *Structural Anthropology* (New York: Basic Books, 1963).

Levi Strauss, C., *The Savage Mind* (Chicago, IL: University of Chicago Press, [1962] 1966).

Malinowski, B., *Argonauts of the Western Pacific* (London: Routledge & Kegan Paul, 1922).

March, J. G. & Olsen, J. P., *Ambiguity and Choice in Organizations* (Oslo: Universitetforlaget, 1976).

Marcus, G. E. & Cushman, R., Ethnographies as Texts, *Annual Review of Anthropology* (1982) pp. 25–69.

Marcus, G. E. & Fischer, M. M. J., *Anthropology as Cultural Critique* (Chicago, IL: University of Chicago Press, 1986).

Markus, M. L. & Pfeffer, J., Power and the Design and Implementation of Accounting and Control Systems, *Accounting, Organizations and Society* (1983) pp. 205–218.

Martin, J., Fieldman, M. S., Hatch, M. J. & Sitkin, S. M., The Uniqueness Paradox in Organizational Stories, *Administrative Science Quarterly* (September 1983) pp. 438–453.

Martin, J. & Siehl, C., Organizational Culture and Counterculture: An Uneasy Symbiosis. *Organizational Dynamics* (Autumn 1983) pp. 52–64.

Meek, V. L., Organizational Culture: Origins and Weaknesses, *Organization Studios* (1988) pp. 453–473.

Meyer, J. W. & Rowan, B., Institutionalized Organizations: Formal Structure as Myth and Ceremony, *American Journal of Sociology* (1977) pp. 340–363.

Miles, R. E. & Snow, C. C., *Organizational Strategy, Structures and Process* (New York: McGraw-Hill, 1978).

Miller, D. & Friesen, P. H., *Organizations: A Quantum View* (Englewood Cliffs, NJ: Prentice Hall, 1984).

Miller, P. & O'Leary, T., The Construction of the Governable Person, *Accounting, Organizations and Society* (1987) pp. 235–265.

Mintzberg, H., Patterns in Strategy Formulation, *Management Science* (May 1978) pp. 934–948.

Ouchi, W., *Theory Z: How American Business Can Meet the Japanese Challenge* (Reading, MA: Addison-Wesley, 1981).

Parsons, T., *The Social System* (New York: Free Press, 1951).

Peters, T. J. & Waterman, R. A., *In Search of Excellence: Lessons from America's Best Run Companies* (New York: Harper & Row, 1982).

Pettigrew, A., On Studying Organizational Cultures, *Administrative Science Quarterly* (December 1979) pp. 570–581.

Pettigrew, A., *The Awakening Giant, Continuity and Change in ICI* (Oxford: Blackwell, 1985).

Pfeffer, J., Management as Symbolic Action: The Creation and Maintenance of Organizational Paradigms, in Cummings, I. L. & Staw, B. M. (eds), *Research in Organizational Behavior*, pp. 1–52 (Greenwich, CT: JAI Press, 1981).

Pfeffer, J. & Salancik, G. R., *The External Control of Organizations* (New York: Harper & Row, 1978).

Pondy, L. R., Leadership is a Language Game, in McCall, M. W. & Lombardo, M. M. (eds), *Leadership: Where Else Can We Go?* (Durham, NC: Duke University Press, 1978).

Pondy, L. R., Frost, P. J., Morgan, G. & Dandridge, T. C. (eds), *Organizational Symbolism* (Greenwich, CT: JAI Press, 1983).

Radcliffe-Brown, A. R., *Structure and Function in Primitive Society* (Oxford: Oxford University Press, 1952).

Ranson, S., Hinings, R. & Greenwood, R., The Structuring of Organizational Structures, *Administrative Science Quarterly* (March 1980) pp. 1–17.

Riley, P., A Structurationist Account of Political Culture, *Administrative Science Quarterly* (September 1983) pp. 414–437.

Roethlisberger, F. J. & Dickson, W. J., *Management and the Worker* (Cambridge, MA: Harvard University Press, 1939).

Roy, D., Efficiency and 'the Fix': Informal Intergroup Relations in a Piecework Machine Shop, *American Journal of Sociology* (November 1954) pp. 255–266.

Roy, D., Banana Time: Job Satisfaction and Informal Interactions, *Human Organization* (Winter 1960) pp. 158–168.

Scott, W. R., The Adolescence of Institutional Theory, *Administrative Science Quarterly* (December 1987) pp. 493–511.

Selznick, P., *TVA and the Grass Roots* (Berkeley, CA: University of California Press, 1949).

Smircich, L., Concepts of Culture and Organizational Analysis, *Administrative Science Quarterly* (September 1983a) pp. 339–358.

Smircich, L., Studying Organizations as Cultures, in Morgan, G. (ed.), *Beyond Method*, pp. 160–172 (Beverley Hills, CA: Sage, 1983b).

Starbuck, W. H., Congealing Oil: Inventing Ideologies to Justify Acting Ideologies Out, *Journal of Management Studies* (January 1982) pp. 3–27.

Starbuck, W. H. & Hedberg, B., Saving an Organization from a Stagnating Environment, in Thorelli, H. B. (ed.), *Strategy + Structure = Performance*, pp. 249–258 (Bloomington, IN: Indiana University Press, 1977).

Turner, S., Studying Organization Through Levi Strauss' Structuralism, in Morgan, G. (ed.), *Beyond Method*, pp. 189–201 (Beverley Hills, CA: Sage, 1983).

Van Maanen, J., The Fact of Fiction in Organizational Ethnography, *Administrative Science Quarterly* (December 1979) pp. 539–550.

Van Maanen, J., *Tales of the Field* (Chicago, IL: University of Chicago Press, 1988).

Van Maanen, J. & Barley, S. R., Occupational Communities: Culture and Control in Organizations, in Cummings, L. L. & Staw, B. M. (eds), *Research in Organizational Behavior*, pp. 287–365 (Greenwich, CT: JAI Press, 1984).

Weber, M., *The Theory of Social and Economic Organization* (New York: Collier-Macmillan, 1947).

Weick, K. E., *The Social Psychology of Organizing*, 2nd edn (Reading, MA: Addison-Wesley, 1979).

Whyte, W. F., *Human Relations in the Restaurant Industry* (New York: McGraw-Hill, 1948).

Whyte, W. F., *Street Corner Society* (Chicago, IL: University of Chicago Press, [1943] 1955).

Wuthnow, R., Hunter, J. D., Bergesen, A. & Kurzweil, E., *Cultural Analysis* (London: Routledge & Kegan Paul, 1984).

Wuthnow, R. & Witten, M., New Directions in the Study of Culture, *Annual Review of Sociology* (1988) pp. 49–67.

Zucker, L. G. (ed.), *Institutional Patterns and Organizations* (Cambridge, MA: Ballinger, 1988).

GLOSSARY OF ACCOUNTING TERMS

Absorption costing A method of costing in which all fixed and variable production costs are charged to products or services using an allocation base.

Account An explanation or report in financial terms about the transactions of an organization.

Accountability The process of satisfying stakeholders in the organization that managers have acted in the best interests of the stakeholders, a result of the stewardship function of managers, which takes place through accounting.

Accounting A collection of systems and processes used to record, report and interpret business transactions.

Accounting equation The representation of the double-entry system of accounting such that assets are equal to liabilities plus capital.

Accounting period The period of time for which financial statements are produced – see also Financial year.

Accounting rate of return (ARR) A method of investment appraisal that measures the profit generated as a percentage of the investment – see Return on investment.

Accounting standards See International Financial Reporting Standards (IFRS).

Accounting system A set of accounts that summarize the transactions of a business that have been recorded on source documents.

Accounts 'Buckets' within the ledger, part of the accounting system. Each account contains similar transactions (line items) that are used for the production of financial statements. Or commonly used as an abbreviation for financial statements.

Accrual An expense for profit purposes even though no payment has been made.

Accruals accounting A method of accounting in which profit is calculated as the difference between income *when it is earned* and expenses *when they are incurred*.

Activity-based budgeting   A method of budgeting that develops budgets based on expected activities and cost drivers – see also Activity-based costing.

Activity-based costing   A method of costing that uses cost pools to accumulate the cost of significant business activities and then assigns the costs from the cost pools to products or services based on cost drivers.

Activity-based management (ABM)   The ability to take actions based on activity-based cost information, in order to accomplish objectives with fewer demands on resources – see also Activity-based costing.

Allocation base   A measure of activity or volume such as labour hours, machine hours or volume of production used to apportion overheads to products and services.

Amortization   See Depreciation, but usually in relation to assets attached to leased property.

Annual Report   The report required by the Stock Exchange for all listed companies, containing the company's financial statements, chairman's, statutory and audit reports.

Assets   Things that the business owns. A resource controlled by an entity as a result of past events and from which future economic benefits are expected to flow to the entity. An entity acquires assets to produce goods or services capable of satisfying customer needs. Physical form is not essential.

Audit   A periodic examination of the accounting records of a company carried out by an independent auditor to ensure that those records have been properly maintained and that the financial statements which are drawn up from those records give a true and fair view.

Avoidable costs   Costs that are identifiable with and able to be influenced by decisions made at the business unit (e.g. division) level.

Balanced Scorecard   A system of non-financial performance measurement that links innovation, customer and process measures to financial performance.

Balance Sheet   A financial statement showing the financial position of a business – its assets, liabilities and capital – at the end of an accounting period.

Bank   Money in a bank cheque account, the difference between receipts and payments.

Bank overdraft   Money owed to the bank in a cheque account where payments exceed receipts.

Batch   A group of similar products produced together.

Bill of materials   A listing of all the materials and quantities that go to make up a completed product.

Breakeven point   The point at which total costs equal total revenue, i.e. where there is neither a profit nor a loss.

Budget A plan expressed in monetary terms covering a future period of time and based on a defined level of activity.

Budget cycle The annual period over which budgets are prepared.

Budgetary control The process of ensuring that actual financial results are in line with targets – see Variance analysis.

Capacity The maximum volume of products or services that can be produced given limitations of space, people, equipment or financial resources.

Capacity utilization The proportion of capacity that is able to be utilized to fulfil customer demand for products or services.

Capital The shareholders' investment in the business; the difference between the assets and liabilities of a business.

Capital employed The total of debt and equity, i.e. the total funds in the business.

Capitalize To make a payment that might otherwise be an expense (in the Income Statement or Profit and Loss account) an asset (in the Balance Sheet).

Capital market The market in which investors buy and sell shares of companies, normally associated with a Stock Exchange.

Cash accounting A method of accounting in which profit is calculated as the difference between income *when it is received* and expenses *when they are paid*.

Cash cost The amount of cash expended.

Cash Flow statement A financial report that shows the movement in cash for a business during an accounting period.

Cash value added (CVA) A method of investment appraisal that calculates the ratio of the net present value of an investment to the initial capital investment.

Combined Code on Corporate Governance A set of principles for corporate governance.

Contribution The difference between the selling price and variable costs, which can be expressed either per unit or in total.

Controllable profit The profit made by a division after deducting only those expenses that can be controlled by the divisional manager and ignoring those expenses that are outside the divisional manager's control.

Cost A resource sacrificed or forgone to achieve a specific objective (Horngren *et al.*), defined typically in monetary terms.

Cost behaviour The idea that fixed costs and variable costs react differently to changes in the volume of products/services produced.

Cost centre A division or unit of an organization that is responsible for controlling costs.

Cost control   The process of either reducing costs while maintaining the same level of productivity or maintaining costs while increasing productivity.

Cost driver   The most significant cause of the cost of an activity, a measure of the demand for an activity by each product/service enabling the cost of activities to be assigned from cost pools to products/services.

Cost object   Anything for which a measurement of cost is required – inputs, processes, outputs or responsibility centres.

Cost of capital   The costs incurred by an organization to fund all its investments, comprising the risk-adjusted cost of equity and debt weighted by the mix of equity and debt.

Cost of goods sold   See Cost of sales.

Cost of manufacture   The cost of goods manufactured for subsequent sale.

Cost of quality   The difference between the actual costs of production, selling and service and the costs that would be incurred if there were no failures during production or usage of products or services.

Cost of sales   The manufacture or purchase price of goods sold in a period or the cost of providing a service.

Cost-plus pricing   A method of pricing in which a mark-up is added to the total product/service cost.

Cost pool   The costs of (cross-functional) business processes, irrespective of the organizational structure of the business.

Cost-volume-profit analysis (CVP)   A method for understanding the relationship between revenue, cost and sales volume.

Credit   Buying or selling goods or services now with the intention of payment following at some time in the future (as opposed to buying or selling goods or services for cash).

Creditors   Purchases of goods or services from suppliers on credit to whom the debt is not yet paid. Or a term used in the Balance Sheet to denote current liabilities.

Current assets   Amounts receivable by the business within a period of 12 months, including bank, debtors, inventory and prepayments.

Current liabilities   Amounts due and payable by the business within a period of 12 months, e.g. bank overdraft, creditors and accruals.

Debt   Borrowings from financiers.

Debtors   Sales to customers who have bought goods or services on credit but who have not yet paid their debt.

Depreciation   An expense that spreads the cost of an asset over its useful life.

Direct costs   Costs that are readily traceable to particular products or services.

Discounted cash flow (DCF) A method of investment appraisal that discounts future cash flows to present value using a discount rate, which is the risk-adjusted cost of capital.

Dividend The payment of after-tax profits to shareholders as their share of the profits of the business for an accounting period.

Double entry The system of recording business transactions in two accounts.

Earnings before interest and taxes (EBIT) The operating profit before deducting interest and tax.

Earnings before interest, taxes, depreciation and amortization (EBITDA) The operating profit before deducting interest, tax, depreciation and amortization.

Economic Value Added^{TM} **(EVA)** Operating profit, adjusted to remove distortions caused by certain accounting rules, less a charge to cover the cost of capital invested in the business.

Elements The broad classes of transactions according to their economic characteristics: assets, liabilities, equity, income, and expenses.

Equity Funds raised from shareholders. The residual interest in the assets of the entity after deducting all its liabilities. See also Shareholders' funds.

Expenses The costs incurred in buying, making or producing goods and services.

Feedback The retrospective process of measuring performance, comparing it with plan and taking corrective action.

Feedforward The process of determining prospectively whether strategies are likely to achieve the target results that are consistent with organizational goals.

Financial accounting The production of financial statements, primarily for those interested parties who are external to the business.

Financial statements A Balance Sheet, Income Statement, statement showing changes in equity (i.e. shareholders' funds), Cash Flow statement, explanatory policies and explanatory notes.

Financial year The accounting period adopted by a business for the production of its financial statements.

Finished goods Inventory that is ready for sale, either having been purchased as such or the result of a conversion from raw materials through a manufacturing process.

Fixed assets Things that the business owns and are part of the business infrastructure – fixed assets may be tangible or intangible. See also Non-current assets.

Fixed costs Costs that do not change with increases or decreases in the volume of goods or services produced, within the relevant range.

Flexible budget A method of budgetary control that flexes, i.e. adjusts the original budget by applying standard prices and costs per unit to the actual production volume.

Forecast   A revised budget estimate or update, part-way through a budget period.

Full cost   The cost of a product/service that includes an allocation of all the (production and non-production) costs of the business.

Framework for the Preparation and Presentation of Financial Statements   Part of the International Financial Reporting Standards (IFRS) that sets out the concepts underlying the preparation and presentation of financial statements for external users, including the objective of financial statements, the qualitative characteristics that determine decision usefulness, the definition, recognition and measurement of the elements from which financial statements are constructed, and capital maintenance.

Gains   A form of income not in the ordinary course of business, such as income from the disposal of non-current assets or revaluations of investments.

Gearing   A measure of the extent of long-term debt in comparison with shareholders' funds.

Goodwill   Goodwill arises where a company buys a business and pays more than the fair value of the tangible assets. Goodwill is an intangible asset and represents the value of brands, customer lists, location, reputation, etc. and is reflected in the expectation of future profits.

Governance   Corporate governance is the system by which companies are directed and controlled by boards of directors.

Gross margin   Gross profit, expressed as a percentage of sales.

Gross profit   The difference between the price at which goods or services are sold and the cost of sales.

Income   The revenue generated from the sale of goods or services. Increases in economic benefits.

Income Statement   A financial statement measuring the profit or loss of a business – income less expenses – for an accounting period. Previously known as a Profit and Loss account.

Incremental budget   A budget that takes the previous year as a base and adds (or deducts) a percentage to arrive at the budget for the current year.

Indirect costs   Costs that are necessary to produce a product/service but are not readily traceable to particular products or services – see Overhead.

Intangible fixed assets   Non-physical assets, e.g. customer goodwill or intellectual property (patents and trademarks).

Interest   The cost of money, received on investments or paid on borrowings.

Internal control   The whole system of internal controls, financial and otherwise, established in order to provide reasonable assurance of effective and efficient operation; internal financial control; and compliance with laws and regulations.

Internal rate of return (IRR)   A discounted cash flow technique used for investment appraisal that calculates the effective cost of capital that produces a net present value of zero from a series of future cash flows and an initial capital investment.

International Financial Reporting Standards (IFRS) Standards that set out recognition, measurement, presentation and disclosure requirements dealing with transactions and events that are important in general purpose financial statements.

Inventory   Goods bought or manufactured for resale but as yet unsold, comprising raw materials, work-in-progress and finished goods.

Investment centre   A division or unit of an organization that is responsible for achieving an adequate return on the capital invested in the division or unit.

Job costing   A method of accounting that accumulates the costs of a product/service that is produced either customized to meet a customer's specification or in a batch of identical product/services.

Kaizen   A method of costing that involves making continual, incremental improvements to the production process during the manufacturing phase of the product/service lifecycle, typically involving setting targets for cost reduction.

Labour oncost   The non-salary or wage costs that follow from the payment of salaries or wages, e.g. National Insurance and pension contributions.

Leasing   A method of finance for equipment used by business organizations, in which a business needing equipment (the lessee) 'rents' that equipment from a financial institution (the lessor) which in turn pays the supplier for the equipment. The lessee pays a fixed monthly sum over a number of years to the lessor in payment of the debt.

Ledger   A collection of all the different accounts of the business that summarize the transactions of the business.

Liabilities   Debts that the business owns. A present obligation of the entity arising from past events, the settlement of which is expected to result in an outflow from the entity of resources embodying economic benefits.

Lifecycle costing   An approach to costing that estimates and accumulates the costs of a product/service over its entire lifecycle, i.e. from inception to abandonment.

Limiting factor   The production resource that, as a result of scarce resources, limits the production of goods or services, i.e. a bottleneck.

Line item   Generic types of assets, liabilities, income or expense that are common to all businesses and used as the basis of financial reporting, e.g. rent, salaries, advertising etc.

Liquidity   A measure of the ability of a business to pay its debts as they fall due – see also working capital.

Long-term liabilities   Amounts owing after more than one year.

Losses   A form of expense not arising from the ordinary course of business, such as those resulting from disasters such as fire and flood and following the disposal of non-current assets or losses following from changes in foreign exchange rates.

Make-ready   See Set-up.

Management accounting   The production of financial and non-financial information used in planning for the future; making decisions about products, services, prices and what costs to incur; and ensuring that plans are implemented and achieved.

Margin   The amount added to a lower figure to reach a higher figure, expressed as a percentage of the higher figure, e.g. the margin that profit represents as a percentage of selling price.

Marginal cost   The cost of producing one extra unit.

Margin of safety   A measure of the difference between the anticipated and breakeven levels of activity.

Mark-up   The amount added to a lower figure to reach a higher figure, expressed as a percentage of the lower figure, e.g. cost is marked up by a percentage to cover the desired profit to determine a selling price.

Matching   See Accruals accounting.

Net present value (NPV   A discounted cash flow technique used for investment appraisal that calculates the present value of future cash flows and deducts the initial capital investment.

Net profit   See operating profit.

Non-current assets   Things that the business owns and are part of the business infrastructure – non-current assets may be tangible or intangible. See also Fixed assets.

Non-production overhead   A general term referring to period costs, such as selling, administration and financial expenses.

Operating and Financial Review (OFR)   Part of the Annual Report. A report by directors to shareholders which discusses and analyses the business's performance and the factors underlying its results and financial position, in order to assist users to assess for themselves the future potential of the business.

Operating margin   Operating profit, expressed as a percentage of sales.

Operating profit   The profit made by the business for an accounting period, equal to gross profit less selling, finance, administration etc. expenses, but before deducting interest or taxation.

Opportunity cost   The lost opportunity of not doing something, which may be financial or non-financial, e.g. time.

Optimum selling price   The price at which profit is maximized, which takes into account the cost behaviour of fixed and variable costs and the relationship between price and demand for a product/service.

Overhead   Any cost other than a direct cost – may refer to an indirect production cost and/or to a non-production expense.

Overhead allocation   The process of spreading production overhead equitably over the volume of production of goods or services.

Overhead rate   The rate (often expressed per hour) applied to the time taken to produce a product/service, used to allocate production overheads to particular products/services based on the time taken. May be calculated on a business-wide or cost centre basis.

Payback   A method of investment appraisal that calculates the number of years taken for the cash flows from an investment to cover the initial capital outlay.

Period costs   The costs that relate to a period of time.

Planning, programming and budgeting system (PPBS)   A method of budgeting in which budgets are allocated to projects or programmes rather than to responsibility centres.

Prepayment   A payment made in advance of when it is treated as an expense for profit purposes.

Prime cost   The total of all direct costs.

Priority-based budget   A budget that allocates funds in line with strategies.

Process costing   A method of costing for continuous manufacture in which costs for an accounting period are compared with production for the same period to determine a cost per unit produced.

Product cost   The cost of goods or services produced.

Product market   A business's investment in technology, people and materials in order to make, buy and sell products or services to customers.

Product/service mix   See Sales mix.

Production overhead   A general term referring to indirect costs.

Profiling   A method of budgeting that takes into account seasonal fluctuations and estimates of when revenues will be earned and costs will be incurred over each month in the budget period.

Profit   The difference between income and expenses.

Profit and Loss account   See Income Statement – a financial statement measuring the profit or loss of a business – income less expenses – for an accounting period.

Profit before interest and taxes (PBIT)   See EBIT.

Profit centre   A division or unit of an organization that is responsible for achieving profit targets.

Profitability index   See Cash value added.

Provision Estimates of possible future liabilities that may arise, but where there is uncertainty as to timing or the amount of money.

Ratio analysis A method of analysing financial reports to interpret trends and make comparisons by using ratios – two numbers, with one generally expressed as a percentage of the other.

Raw materials Unprocessed goods bought for manufacture, part of inventory.

Recognition The process of incorporating in the Balance Sheet or Income Statement in words and with a monetary amount, an item that meets the definition of an element – see Element.

Relevant cost The cost that is relevant to a particular decision – future, incremental cash flows.

Relevant range The upper and lower levels of activity within which the business expects to be operating within the short-term planning horizon (the budget period).

Residual income (RI) The profit remaining after deducting from profit a notional cost of capital on the investment in a business or division of a business.

Responsibility centre A division or unit of an organization for which a manager is held responsible – may be a cost centre, profit centre or investment centre.

Retained profits The amount of profit after deducting interest, taxation and dividends that is retained by the business.

Return on capital employed (ROCE) The operating profit before interest and tax as a percentage of the total shareholders' funds plus the long-term debt of the business.

Return on investment (ROI) The net profit after tax as a percentage of the share-holders' investment in the business.

Revenue A form of income that arises in the ordinary course of business. Typically income earned from the sale of goods and services, including fees, interest, dividends, royalties and rent.

Rolling budgets A method of budgeting in which as each month passes, an additional budget month is added such that there is always a 12-month budget.

Routing A list of all the labour or machining processes and times required to convert raw materials into finished goods or to deliver a service.

Sales mix The mix of product/services offered by the business, each of which may be aimed at different customers, with each product/service having different prices and costs.

Semi-fixed costs Costs that are constant within a defined level of activity but that can increase or decrease when activity reaches upper and lower levels.

Semi-variable costs Costs that have both fixed and variable components.

Sensitivity analysis An approach to understanding how changes in one variable of cost-volume-profit analysis are affected by changes in the other variables.

Set-up The time required to make ready a machine or process for production, e.g. changing equipment settings.

Shareholders' funds The capital invested in a business by the shareholders, including retained profits. See also Equity.

Shareholder value Increasing the value of the business to its shareholders, achieved through a combination of dividend and capital growth in the value of the shares.

Shareholder value analysis The process of increasing shareholder value through new or redesigned product/services, cost management, performance management systems and improved decision-making.

Source document The document that records a transaction and forms the basis for recording in a business's accounting system.

Standard costs A budget cost for materials and labour used for decision-making, usually expressed as a per unit cost that is applied to standard quantities from a bill of materials and to standard times from a routing.

Stock See Inventory.

Strategic management accounting (SMA) The provision and analysis of management accounting data about a business and its competitors, which is of use in the development and monitoring of strategy (Simmonds).

Sunk costs Costs that have been incurred in the past.

Tangible fixed assets Physical assets that can be seen and touched, e.g. buildings, machinery, vehicles, computers etc.

Target costing A method of costing that is concerned with managing whole-of-life costs of a product/service during the product design phase – the difference between target price (to achieve market share) and the target profit margin.

Target rate of return pricing A method of pricing that estimates the desired return on investment to be achieved from the fixed and working capital investment and includes that return in the price of a product/service.

Throughput contribution Sales revenue less the cost of materials.

Transaction The financial description of a business event.

Transfer price The price at which goods or services are bought and sold within divisions of the same organization, as opposed to an arm's-length price at which sales may be made to an external customer.

True and fair view A judgement made by directors and auditors about the content and presentation of financial statements.

Turnover The business income or sales of goods and services.

Unavoidable cost A cost that cannot be influenced at the business unit level but is controllable at the corporate level.

Value added tax (VAT) A form of indirect taxation, levied on the sale of most goods and services.

Value-based management (VBM) A variety of approaches (see Chapter 2) that emphasize increasing shareholder value as the primary goal of every business.

Variable cost A cost that increases or decreases in proportion with increases or decreases in the volume of production of goods or services.

Variable costing A method of costing in which only variable production costs are treated as product costs and in which all fixed (production and non-production) costs are treated as period costs.

Variance analysis A method of budgetary control that compares actual performance against plan, investigates the causes of the variance and takes corrective action to ensure that targets are achieved.

Weighted average cost of capital See cost of capital.

Working capital Current assets less current liabilities. Money that revolves in the business as part of the process of buying, making and selling goods and services, particularly in relation to debtors, creditors, inventory and bank.

Work-in-progress Goods or services that have commenced the production process but are incomplete and unable to be sold.

Zero-based budgeting A method of budgeting that ignores historical budgetary allocations and identifies the costs that are necessary to implement agreed strategies.

PART V

APPENDICES: QUESTIONS AND CASE STUDIES

One of the problems that most students of accounting face is being able to tackle calculation problems. The 'fear of numbers' is quite common with postgraduate students and practicing managers. Students often look back to find a similar 'model question' and then try to repeat the calculation, simply replacing the numbers. This is not good practice as it does not help the student to think about the concepts involved. Each problem is different, and this mirrors day-to-day business decisions. Solving these problems is about applying the underlying concepts. The questions in the Appendices to this book require the reader to perform calculations. These are contained in Appendix 1 with the solutions in Appendix 2. This is a good way of learning about the techniques. In attempting to solve these problems, you need to think about

- What the business problem is;
- The information that is provided to solve the problem;
- The most appropriate technique to apply to the problem; and
- How to apply the technique to solve the problem.

The Case Studies in Appendix 3 already have calculations as these would most likely have already been produced by an accountant in business organizations. What is required to answer these questions is to apply your understanding of the techniques employed by accountants and critically analyse the information given (some of which contains questionable assumptions) so that you can

- Interpret the financial information;
- Identify the underlying assumptions used; and
- Make suggestions to management to overcome any problems you have identified.

The Case Studies are also provided with suggested solutions (Appendix 4) so that students can self-test themselves.

APPENDIX 1: QUESTIONS

The questions are arranged by the chapter that contains the relevant tools and techniques, so that readers can check their understanding after they have read each chapter. The questions rely on knowledge gained from a reading of that chapter and knowledge gained from the previous chapters. Attempting these questions will help the reader to understand how accountants produce information needed by non-accounting managers. An understanding of accounting tools and techniques is important in using the results of these tools and techniques for decision-making.

Appendix 2 contains answers for all the questions.

QUESTIONS FOR CHAPTER 6

6.1 Kazam Services begins the month with capital of £200,000 and the following assets and liabilities:

Assets	Liabilities
Fixed assets £500,000	Bank overdraft £35,000
Debtors £125,000	Creditors £90,000
	Long-term loan £300,000

The following transactions took place in the accounting records of the business during the last month:

Take out long-term loan for new building £150,000.
Receive £45,000 from debtors.
Pay £30,000 to creditors.
Invoice customers for £70,000 for services carried out.
Pay salaries £15,000.
Pay various office expenses £5,000.

In addition, depreciation of £20,000 is to be provided for the period.

- Produce a schedule of transactions under appropriate headings for each account.
- Total each account and produce an Income Statement and Balance Sheet.

6.2 Vibro PLC has fixed assets of £250,000, current assets of £125,000, long-term debt of £125,000 and creditors payable within 12 months of £75,000.

- What is the working capital?
- What is the capital employed in the company?
- What is the shareholders' capital?

6.3 XYZ Ltd's Income Statement shows the following:

	2001	2000
Sales	1,250,000	1,175,000
Cost of sales	787,000	715,000
Selling and admin. expenses	324,000	323,000

Based on these figures, which of the following statements is true?

a   Sales, cost of sales and expenses have all increased, therefore profit, gross margin and operating margin have all increased.

b   The operating profit has increased due to sales growth, higher gross margins and similar expenses.

c   Although the operating profit has decreased, the operating margin has increased as a result of sales growth and an increase in gross profit.

d   The operating profit has decreased due to lower gross margins and higher expenses, despite sales growth.

e   Although the operating profit has increased, the operating margin has decreased as a result of a reduction in the gross margin and higher expenses, despite sales growth.

6.4 National Retail Stores has identified the following data from its accounting records for the year ended 31 December: sales £1,100,000; purchases £650,000; expenses £275,000. It had an opening stock of £150,000 and a closing stock of £200,000.
Calculate the:

- gross profit; and
- operating profit.

6.5 What is the impact of the following prepayment, accrual and provision transactions on profit, the Balance Sheet and cash flow?

a   A business has 24 motor vehicles that it leases in return for a monthly payment, excluding insurance. The company's financial year is 1 April/31 March, but the annual insurance premium of £400 per vehicle for the calendar year January–December is due for payment on 31 December.

b   A business budgets for energy costs of £6,000 per annum over its financial year 1 January/31 December. Bills for usage are sent each quarter on the last days of each of February, May, August and November. Historically, 70% of the annual energy cost is spent during the autumn and winter (September–February).

c   A business with a financial year of 1 April/31 March purchases a new computer network server for £12,000 on 30 June. The business depreciates computer hardware at the rate of 20% of cost per annum, beginning the month following purchase.

6.6   NOP plc has recently acquired a business, for which it paid £12 million. The assets of the business comprise:

Plant & Equipment	£7,000,000
Debtors	£1,500,000
Inventory	£2,300,000
Creditors	£500,000

The Directors decide to amortise any goodwill over a period of 10 years. Calculate the goodwill in the Balance Sheet (ignoring any impairment) at the end of the first year after the business was purchased.

6.7   PUH Limited leases all of its assets. In its Balance Sheet, PUH shows a current liability of £750,000 and a long-term debt of £1,640,000 for lease commitments. What type of expenses will a user of PUH's financial statements expect to see in the Income Statement?

6.8   A business sells a non-current asset for less than its Balance Sheet value. Under IFRS, how will the difference between the asset value in the Balance Sheet and the amount received on the sale of the asset be disclosed in the Income Statement?

6.9   A business sells a non-current asset for more than its Balance Sheet value. Under IFRS, how will the difference between the asset value in the Balance Sheet and the amount received on the sale of the asset be disclosed in the Income Statement?

6.10   A manufacturing business has invoiced customers £5,875,000 including value added tax (VAT) of 17.5%. What sales value will be shown in the Income Statement?

QUESTIONS FOR CHAPTER 7

7.1   Following are the accounts for Drayton Ltd (Tables A1.1 and A1.2). Calculate the following ratios for Drayton for both 2001 and 2000:

■   Return on shareholders' investment (ROI).
■   Return on capital employed (ROCE).
■   Operating profit/sales.

Table A1.1 Drayton Ltd Income Statement for the year ended 31 December

In £mill	2001	2000
Turnover	141.1	138.4
Net operating costs	−113.9	−108.9
Operating profit	27.2	29.5
Non-operating income	1.4	1.3
Interest payable	−7.5	−8.8
Profit before tax	21.1	22.0
Tax on profit	−7.3	−5.7
Profit after tax	13.8	16.3
Dividends	−8.0	−8.0
Retained profit	5.8	8.3

Table A1.2 Balance Sheet as at 31 December

in £mill	2001	2000
Fixed assets		
Tangible assets	266.7	265.3
Current assets		
Stock	5.3	5.8
Trade debtors	15.7	20.9
Other debtors and prepayments	2.4	2.0
Bank	4.9	6.3
	28.3	35.0
Creditors falling due within one year	−66.8	−27.6
Net current assets (− liabilities)	−38.5	7.4
Total assets less current liabilities	228.2	272.7
Creditors falling due after one year	−96.7	−146.1
Net assets	131.5	126.6
Capital and reserves		
Share capital	81.9	82.8
Profit and Loss account	49.6	43.8
Shareholders' funds	131.5	126.6

- Sales growth.
- Gearing.
- Asset turnover.

Draw some conclusions from the change in the ratios over the two years.

7.2 Jupiter Services has produced some financial ratios for the past two years. Use the ratios that have already been calculated to draw some conclusions about Jupiter's:

- profitability;
- liquidity;
- gearing;
- efficiency.

	Current year	Previous year
Return on (shareholders') investment (ROI)		
$\dfrac{\text{net profit after tax}}{\text{shareholders' funds}}$	$\dfrac{193.4}{2,610.1} = 7.4\%$	$\dfrac{251.9}{2,547.0} = 9.9\%$
Return on capital employed (ROCE)		
$\dfrac{\text{net profit before interest and tax}}{\text{shareholders' funds+long-term debt}}$	$\dfrac{367.3}{2,610.1 + 1,770} = 8.4\%$	$\dfrac{394.7}{2,547 + 1,537.7} = 9.7\%$
Net profit/sales		
$\dfrac{\text{net profit before interest and tax}}{\text{sales}}$	$\dfrac{367.3}{1,681.6} = 21.8\%$	$\dfrac{394.7}{1,566.6} = 25.2\%$
Working capital		
$\dfrac{\text{current assets}}{\text{current liabilities}}$	$\dfrac{613.3}{1,444} = 42.5\%$	$\dfrac{475.3}{1,089.2} = 43.6\%$
Gearing ratio		
$\dfrac{\text{long-term debt}}{\text{shareholders' funds+long-term debt}}$	$\dfrac{1,770}{2,610.1 + 1,770} = 40.4\%$	$\dfrac{1,537.7}{2,547 + 1,537.7} = 37.6\%$
Interest cover		
$\dfrac{\text{profit before interest and tax}}{\text{interest payable}}$	$\dfrac{367.3}{161.1} = 2.28$	$\dfrac{394.7}{120.7} = 3.27$
Debtors' collections		
$\dfrac{\text{debtors}}{\text{average daily sales}}$	$\dfrac{414.7}{1,681.6/365 = 4.607} = 90$	$\dfrac{353.8}{1,566.6/365 = 4.292} = 82.4$
Asset turnover		
$\dfrac{\text{sales}}{\text{total assets}}$	$\dfrac{1,681.6}{5,304.5 + 613.3} = 28.4\%$	$\dfrac{1,566.6}{4,794.6 + 475.3} = 29.7\%$

7.3 Jones and Brown Retail Stationery sells its products to other businesses. It has provided the following information:

Sales	£1,200,000
Cost of sales	£450,000
Inventory at end of year	£200,000
Debtors at end of year	£200,000
Creditors at end of year	£100,000

Using 250 days as the number of days the business is open, calculate:

- the days' sales outstanding;
- the stock turnover; and
- the days' purchases outstanding.

7.4 The five-year financial statements of RST plc show the following sales figures:

	2005	2004	2003	2002	2001
Sales (in £million)	155	144	132	130	120

Calculate the sales growth figures for each year.

7.5 RST's Income Statement for 2005 shows:

	£mill
Sales	155
Cost of sales	45
Gross profit	110
Selling, administration expenses	65
Operating profit before interest and taxes	45
Interest	10
Profit before tax	35
Income tax	7
Profit after tax	28

Calculate the overhead to sales ratio.

QUESTIONS FOR CHAPTER 10

10.1 Plastic Emoluments has a relevant range between 100,000 and 200,000 units, fixed costs are £645,000 and variable costs are £7 per unit. Calculate the average costs at a production volume of each of 100,000, 150,000 and 200,000 units.

10.2 Hilltop Solutions has a planned level of activity of 150,000 units, fixed costs are £300,000 and variable costs are £7 per unit. The actual production volume is 140,000 units.
   Identify the:

   ■ standard cost per unit;
   ■ actual cost per unit;
   ■ marginal cost per unit.

10.3 Corporate Document Service incurs variable costs of £7 every time a document is processed. The business providing the service has fixed costs of £100,000 per month. The selling price for each service is £25.

   ■ By how much does the average cost change between processing 10,000 and 20,000 documents?
   ■ Does the marginal cost change in the same way?
   ■ Explain why the average cost changes.

10.4 The Cook Co. has two divisions, Eastern and Western. The divisions have the following revenue and expenses:

	Eastern £	Western £
Sales	550,000	500,000
Variable costs	275,000	200,000
Divisional fixed costs	180,000	150,000
Allocated corporate costs	170,000	135,000

The management of Cook is considering the closure of the Eastern division sales office. If the Eastern division were closed, the fixed costs associated with this division could be avoided but allocated corporate costs would continue.
   Given this data:

   ■ Calculate the effect on Cook Co.'s operating profit before and after the closure.
   ■ Should the Eastern division be closed?

10.5   Jacobean Creek PLC has provided the following data for last year:

Sales	5,000 units
Sales price	£80 per unit
Variable cost	£55 per unit
Fixed cost	£25,000

For the current year, Jacobean Creek believes that although sales volume will remain constant, the contribution margin per unit can be increased by 20% and total fixed cost can be reduced by 10%.

■   Calculate the operating profit for last year and the current year.
■   What is the increase in profit between the two years?

10.6   Relay Co. makes batons. It can make 300,000 batons a year at a variable cost of £750,000 and a fixed cost of £450,000. Relay predicts that next year it will sell 240,000 batons at the normal price of £5 per baton. In addition, a special order has been placed for 60,000 batons to be sold at a 40% discount. What will be Relay Co.'s total operating profit if the special order were accepted in addition to the planned sales at full price?

10.7   Yorkstar plans for a profit of £40,000 and expects to sell 20,000 units. Variable cost is £8 per unit and total fixed costs are £100,000. Calculate the selling price per unit.

10.8   Jasper's IT consultancy has fixed costs of £450,000 per annum. There are 10,000 hours billed on average per annum. If variable costs are £35 per hour, calculate the breakeven charge rate per hour.

10.9   Hong Long Ltd has a product that is sold for £75, variable costs are £30 and fixed costs are £1,000 per month. Calculate how many products need to be sold to obtain a profit of £10,000 per annum.

10.10 John Richards PLC has a cost per unit of £10 and an annual volume of sales of 18,000 units. If a £200,000 investment is required and the target rate of return is 12%, calculate the target mark-up per unit.

10.11 Victory Sales Co. predicts its selling price to be £20 per unit. Estimated costs are direct materials £8 per unit, direct labour £5 per unit and fixed overhead £7,000. Calculate the number of units to be sold to generate a profit of £5,000.

10.12 Luffer Enterprises estimates the following demand for its services at different selling prices. All demand is within Luffer's relevant range. Variable costs are £15 per unit and fixed costs are £10,000.

Price (£)	Quantity
26	1,075
27	1,000
28	925
29	850
30	775

Calculate the level of sales that will generate the highest profit.

10.13 Godfrey Consultancy adopts a cost-plus pricing system for its services and applies a target rate of return of 25% on an investment of £750,000. Its labour costs are £25 per hour and other variable costs are £4 per hour. The consultancy anticipates charging 20,000 hours per year to clients and has fixed overheads of £250,000. Calculate Godfrey's target selling price per hour.

10.14 The marketing department of Giggo Hotels has estimated the number of hotel rooms (it has 120) that could be sold at different price levels. This information is shown below:

Number of rooms sold	Price per room per night (£)
120	90
100	105
80	135
60	155
50	175

Giggo Hotels has estimated its variable costs at £25 per room per night. Calculate the occupancy rate that Giggo will need in order to maximize its profits.

QUESTIONS FOR CHAPTER 11

11.1 The following data relate to activity and costs for two recent months:

	November	December
Activity level in units	5,000	10,000
	£	£
Variable costs	10,000	?
Fixed costs	30,000	?
Semi-variable costs	20,000	?
Total costs	60,000	75,000

Assuming that both activity levels are within the relevant range, calculate for December the:

■ variable costs;
■ fixed costs;
■ semi-variable costs.

11.2 Maxitank makes two products. Its costs are:

	Product R	Product S
Selling price	12	20
Direct materials	4	11
Direct labour hours	2	4
Machine hours	4	3

Maxitank's sales are limited by the machine capacity of the factory. Which of the two products should be produced first in order to maximize the profits generated from the limited capacity?

11.3 Goldfish Enterprises' costs for selling 15,000 hours of consultancy services are £345,000 and costs for 7,000 hours are £185,000. The company wishes to estimate its fixed and variable costs.

■ What are the fixed and variable costs for Goldfish?
■ What is the principal assumption behind your calculation?

11.4 Midlands Refrigeration estimates the costs per unit of a product as:

Direct materials   40 kg @ £2.50 per kg
Direct labour   7 hours machining @ £12 per hour
                     4 hours finishing @ £7 per hour
Variable production overhead @ £5 per direct labour hour
Fixed production overhead of £1,000,000 based on a production volume of 12,500 units.

Calculate the:

■ variable production cost;
■ total production cost.

11.5 Harrison Products' capacity is 20,000 units a year. A summary of operating results for last year is:

Sales (12,000 units @ £100)	£1,200,000
Variable costs	588,000
Contribution margin	612,000
Fixed costs	245,000
Net operating income	£367,000

A foreign distributor has offered to buy a guaranteed 8,000 units at £95 per unit next year. Harrison expects its regular sales next year to be 15,000 units.

If Harrison accepts this offer and forgoes some of its expected sales to ensure that it does not exceed capacity, what would be the total operating profit next year assuming that total fixed costs increase by £100,000?

11.6 Global Conglomerates has a new product that requires 150 kg of material Y876, which is in constant use within the firm. There are 100 kg in stock that cost £11.00/kg. The replacement value is £12.50/kg and the scrap value is £2.00/ kg. Calculate the relevant cost of the material to be used in the new product.

11.7 Magnificent Products makes three products, each requiring two machine hours per unit to produce. The following information has been provided by the Sales Dept in relation to each product:

	Macro	Mezzo	Micro
Budgeted sales units	10,000	7,500	5,000
Selling price per unit	£12	£16	£18
Variable costs per unit	£6	£7	£4

If the company has a limited production capacity, preventing all its budgeted sales from being produced, how should Magnificent rank its products for manufacture in order to maximize profitability?

11.8 CarParts has a new automotive product that is in the final stages of design. Marketing expects to achieve the desired market share and volume at a price of £29 per unit and the manufacturer expects a 25% margin on the selling price. Current designs have been calculated to result in a production cost of £22.50 per unit.

Calculate the reduction required to meet the target cost per unit.

11.9 Buena Manufacturing has sales of £850,000. It used materials of £450,000, direct labour of £175,000 and incurred other variable manufacturing expenses of £30,000. The business also incurred fixed manufacturing expenses of £65,000 and selling and administrative expenses of £40,000. Its opening stock of finished goods was £120,000 and its closing stock had reduced by £25,000.

Calculate each of the:

■ cost of production;
■ cost of sales;
■ contribution margin; and
■ operating profit.

QUESTIONS FOR CHAPTER 12

12.1   Grant & McKenzie is a firm of financial advisers that needs to calculate an hourly rate to charge customers for its services.

The average salary cost for its advisers is £40,000. National Insurance is 11% and the firm pays a pension contribution of 6%. Each adviser has four weeks' annual holiday and there are 10 days per annum when the firm closes for bank holidays and Christmas. Each adviser is expected to do chargeable work for clients of 25 hours per week, the remainder of the time being administrative work.

Calculate an hourly rate (to the nearest hour) to cover the cost of each financial adviser.

12.2   Local Bank does not know how much of its cheque-processing costs are fixed and how much are variable. However, total costs have been estimated at £750,000 for processing of 1,000,000 transactions and £850,000 for processing of 1,200,000 transactions.

■   What are the variable costs per transaction?
■   What are the fixed costs?

12.3   Cardinal Co. needs 20,000 units of a certain part to use in one of its products. The following information is available.

Cost to Cardinal to make each part:

Direct materials	£4
Direct labour	16
Variable manufacturing overhead	8
Fixed manufacturing overhead	10
Total	38

The cost to buy the part from the Oriole Co. is £36. If Cardinal buys the part from Oriole instead of making it, Cardinal would have no use for the spare capacity. Additionally, 60% of the fixed manufacturing overheads would continue regardless of what decision is made. Cardinal decides that direct labour is an avoidable cost for the purposes of this decision.

Decide whether to make or buy the 20,000 parts, by comparing the relevant costs.

12.4   Cirrus Company has calculated that the cost to make a component is made up of direct materials £120, direct labour £60, variable overhead £30 and fixed overhead of £25. Another company has offered to make the component for £140.

If the company has spare capacity and wishes to retain its skilled labour force, should it make or buy the component?

12.5 Bromide Partners provides three services: accounting, audit and tax. The total business overheads of £650,000 have been divided into two cost pools. The cost pools are:

Partners	£200,000
Juniors	£450,000

Partner hours are a measure of complexity and junior hours define the duration of the work. The hours spent by each type of staff are:

	Accounting	Audit	Tax	Total
Partner hours	150	250	400	800
Junior hours	1,200	2,800	1,000	5,000

Calculate the total activity-based cost of providing audit services.

12.6 Bendix Ltd is considering the alternatives of either purchasing component VX-1 from an outside supplier or producing the component itself. Production costs to Bendix are estimated at:

Direct labour	£200
Direct materials	600
Variable overheads	100
Fixed overheads	300
Total	£1,200

An outside supplier, Cosmo PLC, has quoted a price of £1,000 for each VX-1 for an order of 100 of these components. However, if Bendix accepts the quote from Cosmo, the company will need to give three months' notice of redundancy to staff.

■ Calculate the relevant costs of the alternative choices (show your workings) and make a recommendation to management as to which choice to accept.
■ How would your recommendation differ if Bendix employees were on temporary contracts with no notice period?
■ Explain the significance of a stock valuation of £1,300 for the VX-1 at the end of the last accounting period.

12.7 Victory Products Ltd manufactures high-technology products for the computer industry. Victory's accountant has produced a profit report showing the profitability of each of its three main customers for last year (Table A1.3).

Table A1.3 Victory Products profit report

	Franklin Industries	Engineering Partners	Zeta PLC	Other customers	Total
Sales	1,000,000	1,500,000	2,000,000	1,500,000	6,000,000
Cost of materials	250,000	600,000	750,000	750,000	2,350,000
Cost of labour	300,000	200,000	300,000	75,000	875,000
Gross profit	450,000	700,000	950,000	675,000	2,775,000
Corporate overheads: allocated as 30% of sales	300,000	450,000	600,000	450,000	
Rental					250,000
Depreciation					350,000
Non-production salaries					600,000
Selling expenses					350,000
Administration					250,000
Operating profit	150,000	250,000	350,000	225,000	975,000

Victory is operating at almost full capacity, but wishes to improve its profitability further. The accountant has reported that, based on the above figures, Franklin Industries is the least profitable customer and has recommended that prices be increased. If this is not possible, the accountant has suggested that Victory discontinues selling to Franklin and seeks more profitable business from Engineering Partners and Zeta.

Labour is the most significant limitation on capacity. It is highly specialized and is difficult to replace. Consequently, Victory does all it can to keep its workforce even where there are seasonal downturns in business. The company charges £100 per hour for all labour, which is readily transferable between each of the customer products.

You have been asked to comment on the accountant's recommendations.

QUESTIONS FOR CHAPTER 13

13.1 Intelco, a professional services firm, has overheads of £500,000. It operates three divisions and an accountant's estimate of the overhead allocation per division is 50% for Division 1, 30% for Division 2 and 20% for Division 3. The divisions respectively bill 4,000, 2,000 and 3,000 hours. Calculate the:

■ blanket (organization-wide) overhead recovery rate; and the
■ cost centre overhead recovery rate for each division.

13.2 BCF Ltd manufactures a product known as a Grunge. Direct material and labour costs for each Grunge are £300 and £150 respectively. To produce a Grunge requires 20 hours, comprising 10 hours in machining, 7 hours in assembly and 3 hours in finishing. Information for each department is:

	Machining	Assembly	Finishing
Overhead costs (£)	120,000	80,000	30,000
Labour hours	20,000	10,000	10,000

Calculate the cost of producing a Grunge using a departmental overhead recovery rate.

13.3 Engineering Products PLC produces Product GH1, which incurs costs of £150 for direct materials and £75 for direct labour. The company has estimated its production overhead and direct labour hours for a period as:

	Dept A	Dept B	Dept C
Overheads £	150,000	200,000	125,000
Direct labour hours	5,000	10,000	5,000

Product GH1 is produced using 10 hours in Dept A, 12 hours in Dept B and 5 hours in Dept C.

Calculate the total cost of each GH1 using:

■ a plant-wide overhead recovery rate; and
■ cost centre overhead recovery rates.

13.4 Haridan Co. uses activity-based costing. The company has two products, A and B. The annual production and sales of Product A are 8,000 units and of product B 6,000 units. There are three activity cost pools, with estimated total cost and expected activity as follows:

Activity Cost pool	Estimated cost	Expected activity		
		Product A	Product B	Total
Activity 1	£20,000	100	400	500
Activity 2	£37,000	800	200	1,000
Activity 3	£91,200	800	3,000	3,800

Calculate the cost per unit of Product A and Product B under activity-based costing.

13.5 Cooper's Components uses an activity-based costing system for its product costing. For the last quarter, the following data relates to costs, output volume and cost drivers:

Overhead Costs	£
Machinery	172,000
Set-ups	66,000
Materials handling	45,000
Total	283,000

Product	A	B	C
Production and sales	4,000 units	3,000 units	2,000 units
Number of production runs	12	5	8
Number of stores orders	12	6	4

	per unit	per unit	per unit
Direct costs	£25	£35	£15
Machine hours	5	2	3
Direct labour hours	4	2	4

a   If set-up costs are driven by the number of production runs, what is the set-up cost per unit traced to product A?

b   If materials handling costs are driven by the number of stores orders, what is the materials handling cost per unit traced to product B?

13.6   Elandem PLC produces 20,000 units of Product L and 20,000 units of Product M. Under activity-based costing, £120,000 of costs are purchasing related. If 240 purchase orders are produced each period, and the number of orders used by each product is:

	Product L	Product M
No. of orders	80	160

■   calculate the per-unit activity-based cost of purchasing for Products L and M;

■   calculate the overhead recovery for purchasing costs if those costs were recovered over the number of units of the product produced.

13.7   Heated Tools Ltd uses activity-based costing. It has identified three cost pools and their drivers as follows:

	Purchasing	Quality control	Despatch
Cost pool	£60,000	£40,000	£30,000
Driver	12,000	4,000	2,000
	Purchase orders	Stores issues	Deliveries

Product Hekla uses £100 of direct materials and £75 of direct labour. In addition, each Hekla has been identified as using five purchase orders, eight stores issues and two deliveries. Calculate the total cost of each Hekla.

13.8   Samuelson uses activity-based costing. The company manufactures two products, X and Y. The annual production and sales of Product X are 3,000 units and of Product Y 2,000 units. There are three activity cost pools, with estimated total cost and expected activity as follows:

Cost pool	Estimated cost	Expected activity		
		X	Y	Total
Activity 1	£12,000	300	500	800
Activity 2	£15,000	100	400	500
Activity 3	£32,000	400	1200	1600
Total costs	£59,000			

a   Calculate the overhead cost per unit of Product X and Y under activity based costing.

b   Samuelson wishes to contrast its overhead allocation with that under the traditional costing method it previously used. Samuelson charged its overheads of £59,000 to products in proportion to machine hours. Each unit of X and Y consumed five machine hours in production. Calculate the overhead cost per unit of Product X and Y under the traditional method of overhead allocation.

13.9   Brixton Industries PLC makes three products: Widgets, Gadgets and Helios. The following budget information relates to Brixton for next year (Table A1.4).

Table A1.4   Brixton Industries budget information.

	Widgets	Gadgets	Helios
Sales and production (units)	50,000	40,000	30,000
Selling price (£ per unit)	45	95	73
Direct labour and materials (£ per unit)	32	84	65
Machine hours per unit in machining dept	2	5	4
Direct labour hours per unit in assembly dept	7	3	2

Overheads allocated and apportioned to production departments (including service cost centres) were to be recovered in product costs as follows:

Machining department at £1.20 per machine hour.
Assembly department at £0.825 per direct labour hour.

However, you have determined that the overheads could be reanalysed into cost pools as in Table A1.5.

Table A1.5   Brixton Industries activity cost pools and drivers

Cost pool	£ Cost	Cost driver	Quantity
Machining services	357,000	Machine hours	420,000
Assembly services	318,000	Direct labour hours	530,000
Set-up costs	26,000	Set-ups	520
Order processing	156,000	Customer orders	32,000
Purchasing	84,000	Supplier orders	11,200

You have also been provided with the following estimates for the period (Table A1.6).

Table A1.6 Brixton Industries estimates

	Widgets	Gadgets	Helios
Number of set-ups	120	200	200
Customer orders	8,000	8,000	16,000
Supplier orders	3,000	4,000	4,200

■ Prepare and present a profit calculation showing the profitability of each product using traditional absorption costing.
■ Prepare and present a profit calculation showing the profitability of each product using activity-based costing.
■ Explain the differences between the product profitability using absorption and activity-based costing.

13.10 Klingon Holdings has prepared a marketing study that shows the following demand and average price for each of its services for the following period:

	A	B	C
Volume	150,000	200,000	350,000
Estimated selling price per unit	£50	£35	£25
The variable costs for each of these services is:	£20	£17	£14

Fixed expenses have been budgeted as £6,900,000.
Using the above information:

■ Calculate the contribution per unit of volume (and in total) for each service. Which is the preferred service? Why? What should the business strategy be?
■ Determine the absorption (full) cost per unit for the three services using three different methods of allocating overheads.
■ How do the results of these different methods compare?
■ Assuming a constant mix of the services sold, calculate the breakeven point for the business.

QUESTIONS FOR CHAPTER 14

14.1 The Whitton Co. has an opportunity to buy a computer now for £18,000 that will yield annual net cash inflows of £10,000 for the next three years, after which its resale value would be zero. Whitton's cost of capital is 16%.

■ Calculate the net present value of the cash flows for the computer using spreadsheet formula.
■ What is the IRR?

14.2 SmallCo is considering the following project, whose cost of capital is 12% per annum:

Year	0	1	2	3
	£	£	£	£
Cash flows of project	(2,000)	1,000	800	700

Calculate the NPV of the project.

14.3 Goliath Hotel projects the cash flows for three alternative investment projects (in £'000) as:

Project	Year 0	1	2	3	4	5
A	−350	100	200	100	100	140
B	−350	40	100	210	260	160
C	−350	200	150	240	40	0

Depreciation is £70,000 per annum. For each project, calculate the:

■ payback period;
■ accounting rate of return (average);
■ net present value (assuming a cost of capital of 9%); and
■ comment on which (if any) project should be accepted.

14.4 Freddie PLC has £5million to invest this year. Three projects are available, and all are divisible, i.e. part of a project may be accepted and the cash flow returns will be pro-rata. Details of the projects are:

Project	1	2	3
Cash outlay (£M)	3.0	2.0	1.5
NPV (£M)	1.7	1.1	1.0

What is the ranking of the projects that should be accepted?

14.5 Tropic Investments is considering a project involving an initial cash outlay for an asset of £200,000. The asset is depreciated over five years at 20% p.a. (based on the value of the investment at the beginning of each year). The cash flows from the project are expected to be:

	Inflow	Outflow
Year 1	75,000	30,000
Year 2	90,000	40,000
Year 3	100,000	45,000
Year 4	100,000	50,000
Year 5	75,000	40,000

- What is the payback period?
- What is the return on investment (each year and average)?
- Assuming a cost of capital of 10% and ignoring inflation, what is the net present value of the cash flows? (Use the tables rather than a spreadsheet to answer this question.)
- Should the project be accepted?

QUESTIONS FOR CHAPTER 15

15.1 Jakobs Ladder has capital employed of £10 million and currently earns an ROI of 15% per annum. It can make an additional investment of £2 million for a five-year life. The average net profit from this investment would be 14% of the original investment. The division's cost of capital is 12%.

Calculate the residual income before and after the investment.

15.2 China Group has a division with capital employed of £10 million that currently earns an ROI of 15% per annum. It can make an additional investment of £2 million for a five-year life with no scrap value. The average net profit from this investment would be £280,000 per annum after depreciation. The division's cost of capital is 9%.

Calculate the ROI and residual income for the:

- original investment;
- additional investment; and
- total new level of investment.

15.3 Brummy PLC consists of several investment centres. Green Division has a controllable investment of £750,000 and profits are expected to be £150,000 this year. An investment opportunity is offered to Green that will yield a profit of £15,000 from an additional investment of £100,000. Brummy accepts projects if the ROI exceeds the cost of capital, which is 12%.

- Calculate Green's ROI currently, for the additional investment and after the investment.
- How will Green and Brummy view this investment opportunity?
- Calculate the effect of the new investment opportunity on Green's residual income.

15.4 Anston Industries is the manufacturing division of a large multinational. The divisional general manager is about to purchase new equipment for the manufacture of a new product. He can buy either the Compax or the Newpax equipment, each of which has the same capacity and an expected life of four years. Each type of equipment has different capital costs and expected cash flows, as follows:

	Compax	Newpax
Initial capital investment	6,400,000	5,200,000
Net cash inflows (before tax)		
Year 1	2,400,000	2,600,000
Year 2	2,400,000	2,200,000
Year 3	2,400,000	1,500,000
Year 4	2,400,000	1,000,000
Net present value (@ 16% p.a.)	£315,634	£189,615

The equipment will be installed and paid for at the end of the current year (Year 0) and the cash flows accrue at the end of each year. There is no scrap value for either piece of equipment. In calculating divisional returns, divisional assets are valued at net book value at the beginning of each year.

The multinational expects each division to achieve a minimum return before tax of 16%. Anston is just managing to achieve that target. Anything less than a 16% return would make the divisional general manager ineligible for his profit-sharing bonus.

■ Prepare return on investment (ROI) and residual income (RI) calculations for the Compax and the Newpax for each year.
■ Suggest which equipment is preferred under each method.
■ Compare this with the NPV calculation.

15.5 Magna Products PLC has three divisions, A, B and C. The current investments in and net profits earned by each division are as follows:

Division A
   Investment   £1,000,000
   Net profit   £75,000

Division B
   Investment   £1,500,000
   Net profit   £90,000

Division C
   Investment   £2,000,000
   Net profit   £150,000

Each division has put forward to the parent board a capital expenditure proposal for £500,000. Each division expects to produce net profits of £40,000 from that investment. Magna's cost of capital is 7% p.a.

Use ROI and RI calculations to:

- evaluate the current performance of each division; and
- evaluate which proposal the board should approve if finance limits the decision to a single proposal.

QUESTIONS FOR CHAPTER 16

16.1 April Co. receives payment from debtors for credit sales as follows:

- 30% in the month of sale.
- 60% in the month following sale.
- 8% in the second month following the sale.
- 2% become bad debts and are never collected.

The following sales are expected:

January	£100,000
February	£120,000
March	£110,000

- Calculate how much will be received in March.
- What is the value of debtors at the end of March?

16.2 Creassos Ltd was formed in July 2000 with £20,000 of capital. £7,500 of this was used to purchase equipment. The owner budgeted for the following:

	Sales	Receipts from debtors	Purchases	Payments to creditors	Wages	Other
July	20,000	–	8,000	5,000	3,000	2,000
Aug	30,000	20,000	15,000	10,000	4,000	2,000
Sept	40,000	30,000	20,000	20,000	5,000	3,000

Wages and other expenses are paid in cash. In addition to the above, depreciation is £2,400 per annum. No inventory is held by the company.

- Calculate the profit for each of the three months from July to September and in total.
- Calculate the cash balance at the end of each month.
- Prepare a Balance Sheet at the end of September.

16.3 Highjinks Corporation's sales department has estimated revenue of £2,250,000 for your division. 60% of this will be achieved in the first half year and 40% in the remaining half year. Variable operating costs are typically 40% of revenue and fixed operating costs are expected to be £35,000 per month for the first six months and £40,000 per month thereafter.

The selling expense recharged from the sales department is £15,000 per month for the first half year, thereafter £12,000. Salaries are £25,000 per month, depreciation is £5,000 per month and rates £8,000 per month. Light, heat and power are expected to cost £3,000 per month for the first half year, falling to £2,000 thereafter.

■ Construct a budget for the year based on the above figures.
■ What can you say about the rate of gross profit?

16.4 Griffin Metals Co. has provided the following data.
Anticipated volumes (assume production equals sales each quarter):

Quarter 1   100,000 tonnes
Quarter 2   110,000 tonnes
Quarter 3   105,000 tonnes
Quarter 4   120,000 tonnes

The selling price is expected to be £300 per tonne for the first six months and £310 per tonne thereafter. Variable costs per tonne are predicted as £120 in the first quarter, £125 in the second and third quarters, and £130 in the fourth quarter.

Fixed costs (in £'000 per quarter) are estimated as follows:

Salaries and wages	£3,000 for the first half year, increasing by 10% for the second half year
Maintenance	£1,500
Rates	£400
Insurance	£120
Electricity	£1,000
Depreciation	£5,400
Other costs	£2,500 in the first and fourth quarters, £1,800 in the second and third quarters
Interest	£600
Capital expenditure	£6,500 in the first quarter, £2,000 in the second quarter, £1,000 in the third quarter and £9,000 in the fourth quarter
Dividend payment	£10,000 in the third quarter
Debt repayments	£1,000 in the first quarter, £5,000 in the second quarter, £4,000 in the third quarter and £3,000 in the fourth quarter

Griffin has asked you to produce a profit budget and a cash forecast for the year (in four quarters) using the above data.

16.5 Mega Stores is a chain of 125 retail outlets selling clothing under the strong Mega brand. Its sales have increased from £185 million to £586 million over the last five years. The company's gross profit is currently 83% of sales, giving it a little more than 20% mark-up on the cost of goods and retail store running costs. Corporate overhead is £19 million and the operating profit is £81 million.

Mega Stores' finance director has produced a budget, which has been approved by the board of directors, to increase sales by 35% next year and to improve operating profit margin to 15% of sales. Corporate overheads will be contained at £22 million.

The strategy determined by the marketing director is to continue expanding its sales by winning market share from competitors and by increasing the volume of sales to existing customers. It aims to increase its direct mailing of catalogues to customers and its television advertising. The company also intends to open new stores to extend its geographic coverage.

Mega Stores also plans to improve its cost effectiveness by continuing its investments in major regional warehouses and distribution facilities servicing its national network of stores, together with upgrading its information systems to reduce inventory and delivery lead times to its retail network.

You have been asked to produce a report for the senior management team identifying the financial information that is required to support the business strategy. You are also asked to identify any non-financial issues arising from the strategy.

QUESTIONS FOR CHAPTER 17

17.1 Conrad Corporation has a budget to produce 2,000 units at a variable cost of £3 per unit, but actual production is 1,800 units with an actual cost of £3.20 per unit.

Calculate the variance based on a flexible budget and determine whether it is favourable or adverse.

17.2 Calculate the material price variance for Cracker Barrel based on the following information:

	Standard	Actual
Quantity purchased (units)	5,000	5,200
Price per unit	£3.10	£3.05

17.3 Gargantua PLC has produced the following budget and actual information (Table A1.7).

Table A1.7 Gargantua budget and actual

	Budget	Actual
Sales units	10,000	11,000
Price per unit	£37.10	£36
Direct materials		
Magna – per unit	4 kg @ £1.50/kg	46,500 kg – cost £67,425
Carta – per unit	1 kg @ £5/kg	11,500 kg – cost £58,650
Labour – per unit	2.5 hours @ £7	26,400 – cost £187,440
Fixed costs	75,000	68,000

a   Prepare a traditional budget versus actual report using the above figures.
b   Prepare a flexible budget for Gargantua.
c   Calculate all sales and cost price and efficiency variances.
d   Reconcile the original budget and actual profit figures using the variance analysis.

APPENDIX 2: SOLUTIONS TO QUESTIONS

6.1   Kazam Services' accounting records are shown in Table A2.1 (overleaf).

Kazam Services

Income Statement

Income	70,000		
Less expenses	40,000		
Operating profit	30,000		

Balance Sheet

Fixed assets	650,000		
Less depreciation	20,000		630,000
Debtors		150,000	
Less creditors:			
Bank overdraft	40,000		
Creditors	60,000	100,000	
Net current assets			50,000
Total assets less current liabilities			680,000
Long-term loans			450,000
Net assets			230,000
Capital			200,000
Income Statement			30,000
			230,000

Table A2.1

	Fixed assets	Debtors	Bank	Creditors	Long-term loan	Capital	Income	Expenses
Opening balance	+500,000	+125,000	−35,000	+90,000	+300,000	+200,000		
Takes out loan for new building	+150,000				+150,000			
Receive from debtors		−45,000	+45,000					
Pays creditors			−30,000	−30,000				
Invoice for services		+70,000					+70,000	
Pay salaries			−15,000					+15,000
Pay office expenses			−5,000					+5,000
Depreciation	−20,000							+20,000
	630,000	150,000	−40,000	60,000	450,000	200,000	70,000	40,000
Profit transferred						+30,000	30,000	
						230,000		

Note + indicates the account increases.
  − indicates the account decreases.
  The bank account is a liability (withdrawals exceed deposits) and is shown here as a minus to distinguish it from an asset.

6.2   See Table A2.2.

Table A2.2

Fixed assets		250,000
Current assets	125,000	
– Creditors	−75,000	
Working capital		50,000
Capital employed		300,000
– Long-term debt		−125,000
Shareholders' capital		175,000

6.3   **Answer e**
Although the operating profit has increased (from £137,000 to £139,000), the operating margin has decreased (from 11.6% to 11.1%) as a result of a reduction in the gross margin (from 39% to 37%) and higher expenses (from £323,000 to £324,000), despite sales growth (of 6.4%). See Table A2.3.

Table A2.3

	2001	2000
Sales	1,250,000	1,175,000
Sales growth	6.4%	
Cost of sales	787,000	715,000
Gross profit	463,000	460,000
Gross margin	37%	39%
Selling and admin. expenses	324,000	323,000
Operating profit	139,000	137,000
Operating margin	11.1%	11.6%

6.4   See Table A2.4 (overleaf).

6.5   a   **Prepayment**
The annual payment is 24 × £400 = £9,600 (this is £800/mth). The prepayment at 31 March is 9/12 (Apr–Dec) @ £800 = £7,200.

Profit is reduced by £2,400 (expense: 3 mths @ £800).
Asset in the Balance Sheet is increased by £7,200 (prepayment is an asset: 9 mths @ £800).
Cash flow is reduced by £9,600 (payment 31 December).

NB: The effect of the prepayment of £7,200 is to carry forward the expense to the next financial year.

Table A2.4

Sales		1,100,000
Less cost of sales		
Opening stock	150,000	
Purchases	650,000	
	800,000	
– Closing stock	200,000	
Cost of sales		600,000
Gross profit		500,000
– Expenses		275,000
Operating profit		225,000

b   Accrual

The simple solution is to divide £6,000 by 12 months and charge £500/mth to profit. However, this ignores seasonal fluctuations and cash flow differences from quarter to quarter.

The quarterly bills have been paid during the year, but the last quarterly bill was in November. Therefore the business is missing one month's expense (i.e. December). To determine the amount we need to calculate the seasonal charges:

£6,000 × 70% = £4,200 for September–February/6 = £700/mth.
£6,000 × 30% = £1,800 for March–August/6 = £300/mth.
Accrue for one month (December) = £700.

Profit reduced by £700 (expense). This is the profit adjustment. In total, expenses are £6000 for the year.
Balance Sheet reduced by £700 (accrual is a creditor).
Cash flow has no impact (no money yet paid).

NB: The effect of the accrual is to reduce by £700 the expense impact of the expected bill for three months of £2,100, which will be received in February. This leaves £1,400 as the expense (£700 for each of January and February).

c   Depreciation

Depreciation is 20% of £12,000 = £2,400 p.a. or £200/mth. As depreciation is charged from the next month, it needs to be provided for the period July–March. For that period, depreciation is £200 × 9 = £1,800.

Profit reduced by £1,800 (depreciation expense).

Balance Sheet increased by £12,000 (new asset) and reduced by £1,800 (depreciation), leaving a net value of £10,200.
Cash flow reduced by £12,000 (payment for new system).

NB: The Balance Sheet value of the asset will be reduced by £2,400 p.a. until the asset is written down to a nil value, or sold or disposed of.

6.6   Net assets are

Plant & Equipment	£7,000,000
Debtors	£1,500,000
Inventory	£2,300,000
	£10,800,000
Creditors	£500,000
	£10,300,000
Purchase price	£12,000,000
Goodwill	£1,700,000
Amortisation over 10 years:	
£170,000 per annum	£170,000
Net goodwill in Balance Sheet at	
End of first year	£1,530,000

6.7   **Depreciation and interest**
Payments made to the lessor are apportioned between the interest cost which is treated as an expense in the Income Statement and a reduction of the liability in the Balance Sheet. The asset is depreciated in the Income Statement and reduces the Balance Sheet asset value as though it was owned.

6.8   As a loss

6.9   As a gain

Note re 6.8 and 6.9: Revenue arises in the ordinary course of business (e.g. sales, fees, interest, dividends, royalties and rent). Gains represent other items such as income from the disposal of non-current assets or revaluations of investments. Expenses arise in the ordinary course of business (e.g. salaries, advertising, etc.) as well as losses. Losses represent other items such as those resulting from disasters such as fire and flood and following the disposal of non-current assets or losses following from changes in foreign exchange rates.

6.10   Gross sales are £5,875,000. VAT is 17.5%, therefore net sales are £5,875,000/ 1.175 giving net sales in the Income Statement of £5,000,000

SOLUTIONS FOR CHAPTER 7

7.1

	2001	2000

Return on (shareholders')
investment (ROI)

$\dfrac{\text{net profit after tax}}{\text{shareholders' funds}}$ $\dfrac{13.8}{131.5} = 10.5\%$ $\dfrac{16.3}{126.6} = 12.9\%$

Return on capital employed (ROCE)

$\dfrac{\text{profits before interest and tax}}{\text{shareholders' funds} + \text{long-term debt}}$ $\dfrac{27.2}{131.5 + 96.7 = 228.2} = 11.9\%$ $\dfrac{29.5}{126.6 + 146.1 = 272.7} = 10.8\%$

Operating profit/sales

$\dfrac{\text{profit before interest and tax}}{\text{sales}}$ $\dfrac{27.2}{141.1} = 19.3\%$ $\dfrac{29.5}{138.4} = 21.3\%$

Sales growth

$\dfrac{\text{sales year 2} - \text{sales year 1}}{\text{sales year 1}}$ $\dfrac{141.1 - 138.4 = 2.7}{138.4} = 1.95\%$

Expense growth

$\dfrac{\text{expenses year 2} - \text{expenses year 1}}{\text{expenses year 1}}$ $\dfrac{113.9 - 108.9 = 5}{108.9} = +4.6\%$

Gearing ratio

$\dfrac{\text{long-term debt}}{\text{shareholders' funds} + \text{long-term debt}}$ $\dfrac{96.7}{131.5 + 96.7 = 228.2} = 42.3\%$ $\dfrac{146.1}{126.6 + 146.1 = 272.7} = 53.5\%$

Asset turnover

$\dfrac{\text{sales}}{\text{total assets}}$ $\dfrac{141.1}{266.7 + 28.3 = 295} = 47.8\%$ $\dfrac{138.4}{265.3 + 35 = 300.3} = 46.1\%$

ROI has reduced while ROCE has increased. There has been a very small sales growth (less than 2%, i.e. less than the rate of inflation) but expenses have increased by 4.6%. Consequently, operating profit has fallen, as has profit as a percentage of sales. The fall in profits and the increase in shareholders' funds and capital employed have resulted in the decline in ROI but not ROCE as long-term debt has fallen. Gearing has also fallen as a result of a large reduction in long-term debt. Asset turnover has improved marginally.

Although two years is too short a period to draw any meaningful trends, we can say that Drayton needs to increase its sales and/or contain its expenses.

7.2   Conclusions include:

- Profit has declined on each of the measures.
- Liquidity: Working capital has deteriorated and debtors are taking longer to pay their accounts.
- Gearing: Long-term debt has increased in proportion to shareholders' funds and there is less profit to pay a higher amount of interest.
- Assets are being used less efficiently to generate sales.

Overall, Jupiter's performance on all four criteria has been worse in the current year.

7.3 Debtors/average daily sales

$$\frac{200,000}{1,200,000/250} \quad \frac{200,000}{4,800} \quad \text{41.7 day's sales outstanding}$$

Stock turnover

Cost of sales/stock $\quad \dfrac{450,000}{200,000} \quad$ 2.25 times p.a. or every 100 days (250/2.5).

Creditors/average daily purchases

$$\frac{100,000}{450,000/250} \quad \frac{100,000}{1,800} \quad \text{55.5 days' purchases outstanding}$$

7.4

	2005	2004	2003	2002	2001
Sales (in £million)	155	144	132	130	120
Sales growth	$\dfrac{155-144}{144}$	$\dfrac{144-132}{1132}$	$\dfrac{132-130}{130}$	$\dfrac{130-120}{120}$	
	7.6%	9.1%	1.5%	8.3%	

7.5 Overheads are £65 million. Sales are £155 million. The overhead/sales ratio is 65/155 or 41.9%

SOLUTIONS FOR CHAPTER 10

10.1 See Table A2.5.

Table A2.5

Units	Fixed	Variable @ £7	Total	Average
100,000	645,000	700,000	1,345,000	£13.45
150,000	645,000	1,050,000	1,695,000	£11.30
200,000	645,000	1,400,000	2,045,000	£10.22

10.2

Volume	Variable	Fixed	Total	Standard	Average	Marginal
150,000	1,050	300	1,350	9.00		7.00
140,000	980	300	1,280		9.14	

The standard cost per unit is £9.00 at the budgeted level of activity.

The actual cost per unit is £9.14 – this is the actual average production cost per unit.

The marginal cost per unit is £7.00 – this is the variable cost per unit.

10.3

Volume	Variable	Fixed	Total	Avg cost/unit
10,000	70,000	100,000	170,000	£17
20,000	140,000	100,000	240,000	£12

The average cost reduces by £5 from £17 to £12. This is because the fixed costs of £100,000 are spread over 20,000 documents (£5 per document) rather than 10,000 documents (£10 per document).

The marginal cost is £7, i.e. the variable cost. It does not change per unit irrespective of volume within the relevant range.

The costs per unit at each activity level are:

	10,000	20,000
Variable costs	£7	£7
Fixed costs	£10	£5
Average cost	£17	£12

10.4 Current position:

	Eastern £	Western £	Total £
Sales	550,000	500,000	1,050,000
Variable costs	275,000	200,000	475,000
Direct fixed costs	180,000	150,000	330,000
Contribution to corporate costs	95,000	150,000	245,000
Allocated corporate costs	170,000	135,000	305,000
Operating profit	(75,000)	15,000	(60,000)

After closure of Eastern division:

	Eastern £	Western £	Total £
Sales	–	500,000	1,050,000
Variable costs	–	200,000	200,000
Direct fixed costs	–	150,000	150,000
Allocated corporate costs	–	305,000	305,000
Operating profit		(155,000)	(155,000)

The Eastern division should not be closed. It currently contributes £95,000 towards corporate costs. If the division were closed, the corporate costs would remain unchanged and the current loss of £60,000 would increase to £155,000.

10.5

	Last year		Current year
Sales price	80		
Variable cost	55		
Contribution margin	25	+20% (£5)	30
Units	5,000		5,000
Contribution	125,000		150,000
− Fixed costs	25,000	−10% (£2,500)	22,500
Operating profit	100,000		127,500

Contribution margin is £25 (£80 − £55) + 20% = £5 × 5,000 units = +£25,000
Fixed costs   £25,000 × 10% =   +£2,500

Increase in profit is   £27,500

10.6 Variable costs are £750,000/300,000 batons = £2.50/baton. As the selling price is £5/baton, the normal contribution/baton = £2.50 (£5 − £2.50).
     If 240,000 batons are sold at the normal price:

Contribution = 240,000 @ £2.50	£600,000
− Fixed costs	450,000
Operating profit	£150,000

If 60,000 batons are sold at a 40% discount:

Sales = 60% of £5 = £3/baton, and contribution is 50p (£3 − variable
   costs £2.50)

Contribution = 60,000 @ 50p/baton	£30,000
Total operating profit	£180,000

10.7 Profit = selling price per unit × number of units − (VC/unit × no. units + fixed costs) therefore, £40,000 = SP × 20,000 − ((£8 × 20,000) + £100k)

$$\text{Selling price} = \frac{£40,000 + £160,000 + £100,000}{20,000 \text{ units}} = £300,000/20,000 \text{ units} = £15$$

10.8 Breakeven is:

$$\frac{(10,000 \times 35) + 450,000 + 0}{10,000} = \frac{800,000}{10,000} = £80$$

Or:

Profit = price × no. of units − (fixed costs + variable costs × no. of units)
$0 = 10,000P - (450,000 + 35 \times 10,000)$
$0 = 10,000P - (450,000 + 350,000)$
$0 = 10,000P - 800,000$
$800,000 = 10,000P$
$P = 800,000/10,000 = 80$

Proof
$10,000 \times (80 - 35) = 10,000 \times 45 = 450,000 - 450,000 = 0$

10.9 Contribution per unit is $75 - 30 = 45$
Fixed costs are $1,000 \times 12 = 12,000$

$$\text{Breakeven} = \frac{12,000 + 10,000}{45} = 489 \text{ p.a.}$$

10.10

$$\frac{200,000 \times 12\%}{18,000 \text{ units}} = \frac{£24,000}{18,000} = £1.33 \text{ per unit}$$

10.11

Selling price		20
Direct materials	8	
Direct labour	5	13
Contribution margin		7

10.12 See Table A2.6.

Table A2.6

Price	VC	Contribution p.a.	Quantity	Total contribution
26	15	11	1,075	11,825
27	15	12	1,000	12,000
28	15	13	925	12,025
29	15	14	850	11,900
30	15	15	775	11,625

The maximum contribution is at a selling price of £28. Note that this is not necessarily the highest sales revenue. The highest contribution will also be the highest profit because the same amount of fixed costs are deducted from each level of activity (within the relevant range).

10.13

Direct labour costs	25.00
Variable costs	4.00
Fixed costs £250,000/20,000	12.50
Target return (750,000 * 25%)/20,000	9.38
	———
Price	50.88

10.14 See Table A2.7.

Table A2.7

Number of rooms sold	Price per room per night	Revenue	Variable costs @ £25	Contribution
120	90	10,800	3,000	£7,800
100	105	10,500	2,500	£8,000
80	135	10,800	2,000	£8,800
60	155	9,300	1,500	£7,800
50	175	8,750	1,250	£7,500

Contribution maximized at £135 (80 rooms). This is an occupancy rate of 67% (80/120).

SOLUTIONS FOR CHAPTER 11

11.1 Variable costs are £2 per unit (£10,000/5,000), for December 10,000 @ £2 = £20,000.

Fixed costs do not change with activity, for December £30,000.

As total costs are £75,000, semi-variable costs for December are £25,000 (£75,000 − £20,000 − £30,000).

11.2

	Product R	Product S
Selling price	12	20
Direct materials	4	11
Throughput contribution	8	9
Machine hours	4	3
Return per machine hour	£2	£3
Ranking	2	1

Product S generates more throughput contribution per machine hour (the limiting factor). Labour hours are irrelevant.

11.3

	Hours	Cost £
	15,000	345,000
	7,000	185,000
Increase	8,000	160,000

The increase in hours sold of 8,000 has generated a higher cost of £160,000. This cost must be a variable cost as, by definition, fixed costs do not vary with the volume of activity. Therefore variable costs are £160,000/8,000 or £20 per hour.

At the 15,000 level of activity, 15,000 @ £20 = £300,000. Therefore fixed costs are £45,000 (£345,000 − 300,000).

At the 7,000 level of activity, 7,000 @ £20 = £140,000. Therefore fixed costs are £45,000 (£185,000 − £140,000).

However, this only applies in the relevant range, as outside the relevant range the cost structure of fixed and variable costs may alter.

11.4

Direct materials	40 @ 2.50		100
Direct labour	7 @ £12	84	
	4 @ £7	28	112
	11		212
Variable overhead	11 @ £5 =		55
Variable production cost			267
Fixed production overhead £1,000,000/12,500			80
Total production cost			347

11.5 Production will be 8,000 units special order plus 12,000 units regular sales to give a maximum production capacity of 20,000 units.

Variable costs are £49 per unit (£588,000/12,000 units).
Fixed costs are £345,000 (£245,000 + £100,000).

Sales 12,000 units at £100	£1,200,000
Sales 8,000 @ £95	760,000
Total	£1,960,000
Variable costs 20,000 @ £49	980,000
Contribution margin	980,000
Fixed costs	345,000
Operating profit	£635,000

11.6 As the material is in regular use and has to be replaced, it is irrelevant that some is already in stock as the relevant cost – the future, incremental cash flow (in this case the replacement cost) – is 150 kg @ £12.50, a total of £1,875. The scrap value is not relevant.

11.7

	Macro	Mezzo	Micro
Contribution per unit	£6	£9	£14
Machine hours	2	2	2
Contribution per hour	£3	£4.50	£7
Ranking	3	2	1

Therefore the ranking should be to maximize production of Micro, followed by Mezzo, and finally Macro.

11.8

Target price	£29.00
Less 25%	7.25
Target cost	21.75
Production cost	22.50
Reduction per unit	0.75

11.9 See Table A2.8.

Table A2.8

Sales		850,000
Less cost of production		
Materials	450,000	
Labour	175,000	
Variable manufacturing expense	30,000	
Cost of production	655,000	
Opening stock	120,000	
	775,000	
– Closing stock	95,000	
Cost of sales		680,000
Contribution margin		170,000
– Fixed manufacturing expenses		65,000
– Selling and administrative expenses		40,000
Operating profit		65,000

SOLUTIONS FOR CHAPTER 12

12.1

Salary	40,000
National Insurance 11%	4,400
Pension 6%	2,400
Total employment cost	46,800

Working weeks per person
$52 - 4 - 2 = 46$

Cost per week 46,800/46	£1,017
Chargeable hours per week	25
Hourly rate (£1,017/25)	£40.68 or £41 to the nearest hour

12.2

	Volume	Cost
	1,200,000	£850,000
	1,000,000	£750,000
Increase	200,000	£100,000

Variable cost = £100,000/200,000 = £0.50
1,200,000 @ £0.50 = £600,000. Therefore, fixed costs are £250,000 (i.e., £850,000 − £600,000)

12.3 Direct materials and variable costs are relevant costs as they are only incurred if manufacture takes place. Direct labour is avoidable, i.e. it will only be incurred if Cardinal makes the part. As 60% of the fixed costs will continue regardless of the decision, only 40% of the fixed cost is relevant for the decision. Therefore, relevant costs of in-house manufacture:

Direct material	£4
Direct labour	16
Variable costs	8
Fixed costs (40% of £10)	4
Total	32 × 20,000 units = £640,000

Relevant costs of outsourcing to Oriole are:

Purchase cost	36 × 20,000 units = £720,000

Consequently, based on relevant costs, it is cheaper to manufacture the part in-house.

Note: the fixed manufacturing overhead of £10 per unit is an arithmetic calculation of total fixed costs divided by the number of units produced. This does not mean that the cost is a variable cost, just because it is expressed as a cost per unit.

12.4 The manufactured cost is £235 (120 + 60 + 30 + 25). The relevant costs are direct materials £120 and variable overhead £30, a total of £150. Direct labour and fixed costs are not relevant. Direct labour cannot be avoided as the business has spare capacity and wishes to retain its skilled employees. As the cost of purchasing the component is £140, on a relevant cost basis Cirrus should buy the component rather than make it.

12.5

Partners' cost   £200,000
Total hours 800 =   £250 per hour
Juniors' cost   £450,000
Total hours 5,000 = £90 per hour

See Table A2.9.

Table A2.9

	Accounting	Audit	Tax	Total
Partner hours	150	250	400	800
@ £250	37,500	62,500	100,000	200,000
Junior hours	1200	2800	1000	5,000
@ £90	108,000	252,000	90,000	450,000
Total	145,500	314,500	190,000	650,000

Audit services cost £314,500.

12.6 The comparison of costs under each alternative is shown in Table A2.10.

Table A2.10

	Manufacture 100	Purchase 100
Direct labour 100 @ £200	20,000	20,000
Direct material 100 @ £600	60,000	
Variable overhead 100 @ £100	10,000	
Fixed overheads 100 @ £300	30,000	30,000
Supplier price 100 @ £1,000		100,000
Total	£120,000	£150,000

Direct labour and fixed overheads are irrelevant in making a choice between alternatives.

Direct materials and variable overheads will not be incurred if the components are purchased, and are therefore relevant costs. Relevant costs are therefore as in Table A2.11.

Table A2.11

	Manufacture 100	Purchase 100
Direct material	60,000	
Variable overhead	10,000	
Supplier price		100,000
Total	70,000	100,000

If employees were on a temporary contract, labour cost would be avoidable and therefore the comparison of costs would be as in Table A2.12.

Table A2.12

	Manufacture 100	Purchase 100
Direct labour 100 @ £200	20,000	
Direct material 100 @ £600	60,000	
Variable overhead 100 @ £100	10,000	
Fixed overheads 100 @ £300	30,000	30,000
Supplier price 100 @ £1,000		100,000
Total	£120,000	£130,000

Fixed overheads are irrelevant in making a choice between alternatives. Direct labour, materials and variable overheads will not be incurred if the components are purchased, and are therefore relevant costs.

Relevant costs are therefore as in Table A2.13.

Table A2.13

	Manufacture 100	Purchase 100
Direct labour	20,000	
Direct material	60,000	
Variable overhead	10,000	
Supplier price		100,000
Total	90,000	100,000

Costs based on stock valuation are not relevant, as we are concerned with future costs only.

12.7 An alternative format for these figures is as in Table A2.14.

Table A2.14

	Franklin Industries	Engineering Partners	Zeta PLC	Other customers	Total (average)
Sales	1,000,000	1,500,000	2,000,000	1,500,000	6,000,000
Cost of materials	250,000	600,000	750,000	750,000	2,350,000
Contribution	750,000	900,000	1,250,000	750,000	3,650,000
Cost of labour	300,000	200,000	300,000	75,000	875,000
%	75%	60%	62.5%	50%	(60.8%)
Gross profit	450,000	700,000	950,000	675,000	2,775,000
%	45%	46.7%	47.5%	45%	(46.25%)
No. of hours (labour/£100)	3,000	2,000	3,000	750	8,750
Contribution per labour hour	£250	£450	£417	£1,000	(£417)

This format shows the contribution, which based on the contribution after deducting material is in fact highest for Franklin. However, calculating the contribution per labour hour (by dividing the contribution by the number of hours, i.e. labour cost divided by £120 per hour) verifies the lower contribution by Franklin per unit of the limiting factor, i.e. labour capacity. This is reflected in the rate of gross profit being the lowest of the three main customers.

The issues that arise from these figures are:

1 Labour is in effect a fixed cost given the circumstances of the business and its allocation to different products is questionable, other than in terms of determining the most profitable utilization of the limited capacity.

2 Can the high labour cost for Franklin be reduced by mechanization given that Franklin contributes almost 17% of total sales (£1,000,000/£6,000,000) with the highest contribution margin of 75%?

3 While Engineering Partners and Zeta are the most profitable customers in the accountant's report, the revised format shows the highest contribution per labour hour from the 'other' customer segment. Zeta, which on the accountant's figures appears more profitable than Engineering Partners, is using the revised format, less profitable per labour hour.

4 Do the corporate overheads, presently allocated arbitrarily in proportion to sales volume (30% of sales), accurately reflect the different cost structure of each segment of the business in terms of space utilization (rent), capital investment in production processes (depreciation), non-production salaries,

selling and administration expenses? An activity-based approach may lead to more meaningful allocation of costs and a different decision as to the profitability of different business segments.

SOLUTIONS FOR CHAPTER 13

13.1 See Table A2.15.

Table A2.15

Division	1	2	3	Total
Overheads	50%	30%	20%	
	250,000	150,000	100,000	500,000
Hours	4,000	2,000	3,000	9,000
Hourly rate	£62.50	£75	£33.33	£55.55

13.2

	Machining	Assembly	Finishing	Total
Overhead costs	120,000	80,000	30,000	230,000
Labour hours	20,000	10,000	10,000	40,000
Hourly rate	£6	£8	£3	£5.75

Costing:

Material		300	
Labour		150	
Overhead	10 @ £6	60	
	7 @ £8	56	
	3 @ £3	9	125
		—	—
Total			575

13.3

	Dept A	Dept B	Dept C	Total
Overheads £	150,000	200,000	125,000	475,000
Direct labour hours	5,000	10,000	5,000	20,000
Overhead per hour	£30	£20	£25	£23.75
Hours for GH1	10	12	5	27
Overhead	300	240	125	£641.25

Overhead using cost centre rate = £665 (£300 + £240 + £125)
Using plant-wide rate:

Direct materials	£150
Direct labour	£75
Overhead	£641
Total	£866

Using cost centre rate:

Direct materials	£150
Direct labour	£75
Overhead	£665 (£300 + £240 + £125)
Total	£890

13.4

Cost pool	Estimated cost	Expected activity Product A	Product B	Total	Rate £/activity
Activity 1	£20,000	100	400	500	40.00
Activity 2	£37,000	800	200	1,000	37.00
Activity 3	£91,200	800	3,000	3,800	24.00

Product A:

		Total	per unit (/8,000)
Activity 1:	£40.00 × 100	£4,000	£0.50
Activity 2:	£37.00 × 800	£29,600	£3.70
Activity 3:	£24.00 × 800	£19,200	£2.40
			£6.60

Product B:

		Total	per unit (/6,000)
Activity 1:	£40.00 × 400	£16,000	£2.67
Activity 2:	£37.00 × 200	£7,400	£1.23
Activity 3:	£24.00 × 3,000	£72,000	£12.00
			£15.90

13.5 (a) Set-up costs £66,000
Production runs 12 + 5 + 8 = 25
Cost per set-up £66,000/25 = £2,640
Product A has 12 runs @ £2,640 = £31,680
And 4,000 units are produced
Cost per set-up per unit is £31,680/4,000 = £7.92

(b) Materials handling costs £45,000
Stores orders 12 + 6 + 4 = 22
Cost per store order £45,000/22 = £2,045
Product B has 6 stores orders @ £2,045 = £12,270
And 3,000 units are produced
Cost per stores order per unit is £12,270/3,000 = £4.09

13.6

Purchasing cost	£120,000
No. purchase orders	240

Cost per purchase order	£500
L uses 80 @ £500	£40,000
For 20,000 units =	£2 per unit
M uses 160 @ £500	£80,000
For 20,000 units =	£4 per unit

If £120,000 of costs were recovered over the number of units produced (20,000 + 20,000 = 40,000), the purchasing cost per unit would be £3 (£120,000/40,000 units) for both L and M.

13.7

	Purchasing	Quality control	Despatch
Total cost	£60,000	£40,000	£30,000
Driver	12,000	4,000	2,000
Cost/driver	£5	£10	£15
Hekla uses	5	8	2
Overhead	£25	£80	£30

Total overhead	£25 + 80 + 30 = £135
Direct materials	£100
Direct labour	£75
Total cost	£310

13.8 (a)

		Expected activity			
Cost pool	Estimated cost	X	Y	Total	Cost/activity
Activity 1	£12,000	300	500	800	12,000/750 = £15
Activity 2	£15,000	100	400	500	15,000/500 = £30
Activity 3	£32,000	400	1,200	1,600	32,000/1,600 = £20

X			Y		
	300 @ 15 =	4,500		500 @ 15 =	7,500
	100 @ 30 =	3,000		400 @ 30 =	12,000
	400 @ 20 =	8,000		1,200 @ 20 =	24,000
		15,500			43,500
Units		3,000			2,000
Overhead cost per unit £5.17					£21.75

(b)

	X	Y	
Units	3,000	2,000	
Machine hours	5	5	
Total machine hours	15,000	10,000	25,000
Hourly rate £59,000/25,000 = £2.36 per hour			
Overhead cost	5 @ 2.36	5 @ 2.36	
Overhead cost per unit	£11.80	£11.80	

13.9   Traditional absorption costing

Machining overheads:

Widgets	50,000 × 2 @ £1.20	120,000
Gadgets	40,000 × 5 × £1.20	240,000
Helios	30,000 × 4 @ £1.20	144,000

Assembly overheads:

Widgets	50,000 × 7 @ £0.825	288,750
Gadgets	40,000 × 3 × £0.825	99,000
Helios	30,000 × 2 @ £0.825	49,500

See Table A2.16.

Table A2.16

	Widgets	Gadgets	Helios
Sales volume	50,000	40,000	30,000
Selling price	45	95	73
Direct labour and materials	32	84	65
Contribution per unit	13	11	8
Total contribution	650,000	440,000	240,000
Machining overheads	120,000	240,000	144,000
Assembly overheads	288,750	99,000	49,500
Profit	241,250	101,000	46,500

Total profit £388,750.

Activity-based costing

See Tables A2.17 and A2.18.

Total £389,000.

The total overhead and therefore the total profit is the same under both methods of overhead allocation (the difference is due to rounding). Each method has simply allocated the total overheads in different ways. The activity-based approach charges overheads to products based on the activities that are carried out in producing each product. This demonstrates, for example, that the Helios

Table A2.17

	Machining	Assembly	Set-ups	Order processing	Purchasing
Cost pool	357,000	318,000	26,000	156,000	84,000
Cost drivers	420,000	530,000	520	32,000	11,200
Rate	£0.85 per m/c hour	£0.60 per direct labour hour	£50 per set-up	£4.875 per cust. order	£7.50 per supp. order

Table A2.18

	Widgets	Gadgets	Helios
Sales volume	50,000	40,000	30,000
Total contribution	650,000	440,000	240,000
Machining @ £0.85	85,000	170,000	102,000
Assembly @ £0.60	210,000	72,000	36,000
Set-up @ £50	6,000	10,000	10,000
Order processing @ £4.875	39,000	39,000	78,000
Purchasing @ £7.50	22,500	30,000	31,500
Profit/(loss)	287,500	119,000	(17,500)

is actually making a loss as its high overheads compared with its low volume are not being recovered in the selling price. Under traditional absorption costing, the Helios is being subsidized by the other two products.

13.10 See Table A2.19.

Table A2.19

	A	B	C	Total
No. units	150,000	200,000	350,000	
Selling price	£50	£35	£25	
Variable costs	£20	£17	£14	
Contribution per unit	£30	£18	£11	
Sales revenue	7,500,000	7,000,000	8,750,000	23,250,000
Variable costs	3,000,000	3,400,000	4,900,000	11,300,000
Contribution (total)	4,500,000	3,600,000	3,850,000	11,950,000
Fixed expenses				6,900,000
Operating profit				5,050,000

Preferred services
Based on volume of production (Production Dept preference?):

C, B, A

Based on sales revenue (Sales Dept preference?):

C, A, B

Based on contribution per unit of volume:

A, B, C

Based on total contribution (Accounting Dept preference?):

A, C, B

Strategy should be to shift sales mix as far as possible to Product A (highest contribution per unit).

Absorption of overhead
See Table A2.20.

Table A2.20

	A	B	C	Total
Absorption costs based on sales value	7,500,000	7,000,000	8,750,000	23,250,000
	32.2%	30.1%	37.7%	
Variable costs	3,000,000	3,400,000	4,900,000	11,300,000
Fixed expenses	2,221,800	2,076,900	2,601,300	6,900,000
Total costs	5,221,800	5,476,900	7,501,300	18,200,000
Cost per unit of volume	£34.81	£27.38	£21.43	
Absorption costs based on volume	150,000	200,000	350,000	700,000
	21.4%	28.6%	50%	
Variable costs	3,000,000	3,400,000	4,900,000	11,300,000
Fixed expenses	1,476,000	1,973,400	3,450,000	6,900,000
Total costs	4,476,600	5,373,400	8,350,000	18,200,000
Cost per unit of volume	£29.84	£26.87	£23.86	
Absorption costs based on equal allocation				
Variable costs	3,000,000	3,400,000	4,900,000	11,300,000
Fixed expenses	2,300,000	2,300,000	2,300,000	6,900,000
Total costs	5,300,000	5,700,000	7,200,000	18,200,000
Cost per unit of volume	£35.33	£28.50	£20.57	

While there is not much difference between using sales value and equal allocations for overhead, the volume method leads to lower costs for Products A and B and higher costs for Product C. The important point here is that different methods of overhead allocation (of the same value of overhead) can lead to different costs for products and services.

Breakeven
See Table A2.21.

Table A2.21

	A	B	C	Total
No. units	150,000	200,000	350,000	700,000
Sales revenue	7,500,000	7,000,000	8,750,000	23,250,000
Variable costs	3,000,000	3,400,000	4,900,000	11,300,000
Contribution (total)	4,500,000	3,600,000	3,850,000	11,950,000
Average contribution per unit of volume				£17.07

Fixed costs	£6,900,000	404,218 units of volume
Contribution per unit	£17.07	

Maintaining the same sales mix, the breakeven sales units of each product are:

86,619 of A
115,490 of B
202,109 of C

SOLUTIONS FOR CHAPTER 14

14.1 Formula for present value = +NPV (16%, C3 : E3). The cash flows are entered in columns C (Year 1) to E (Year 3). See Table A2.22.

Table A2.22

Col A	Col B Year 0	Col C Year 1	Col D Year 2	Col E Year 3
Cash flows		10,000	10,000	10,000
Present value	22,459			
Initial investment	−18,000			
NPV	4,459			

To calculate IRR using the spreadsheet function, a negative figure (the initial cash investment) must be part of the range of values. Formula for IRR = +IRR (B3 : E3).

	Year 0	Year 1	Year 2	Year 3
Cash flows	−18,000	10,000	10,000	10,000
IRR	31%			

14.2 See Table A2.23.

Table A2.23

	Year 0	Year 1	Year 2	Year 3
Cash flows		1,000	800	700
Present value	2,029			
Initial investment	−2,000			
NPV	29			

14.3 Payback

Project A	2.5 years	$(100 + 200 + 1/2 \times 50)$
Project B	3 years	$(40 + 100 + 210)$
Project C	2 years	$(200 + 150)$

Accounting rate of return

	Total cash flow	Depreciation	Profit	Average profit	ARR
Project A	640	350	290	58	33.1%
Project B	770	350	420	84	24%
Project C	630	350	280	56	16%

Average investment £350,000/2 = £175,000

$$\frac{\text{ARR is average profit (profit/5 years)}}{\text{Average investment}}$$

NPV

See Table A2.24 (overleaf).

On a payback basis, the ranking of projects (with preference to the quickest payback) is C, then A then B. The accounting rate of return method favours B, then A then C. The NPV method ranks B followed by C then A. The IRR suggests that Project C has the highest return (as the cash flows are returned more quickly). No absolute preference is clear, although Project A is slightly less attractive. As the accounting profits are likely to be important in terms of satisfying shareholders, this may be the optimum solution.

Table A2.24

Project A	Year 0	Year 1	Year 2	Year 3	Year 4	Year 5
Cash flows		100	200	100	100	140
Present value	499					
Initial investment	−350					
NPV	149					
Project B	Year 0	Year 1	Year 2	Year 3	Year 4	Year 5
Cash flows		40	100	210	260	160
Present value	571					
Initial investment	−350					
NPV	221					
Project C	Year 0	Year 1	Year 2	Year 3	Year 4	Year 5
Cash flows		200	150	240	40	0
Present value	523					
Initial investment	−350					
NPV	173					

IRR	
Project A	24%
Project B	26%
Project C	33%

14.4

	1	2	3
NPV	1.7	1.1	1.0
Outlay	3.0	2.0	1.5
PI	0.57	0.55	0.67
	57%	55%	67%
Ranking	2	3	1
Select	All	Part	All

Ranking 1	Project 3 requires	£1.5 million
Ranking 2	Project 1 requires	£3 million
Ranking 3	Project 2	£0.5 million available (25% of project)
Total investment		£5 million

14.5 **Payback period**
End of year 4, i.e. £200,000.

Return on investment

	1	2	3	4	5
Investment	200	160	120	80	40
Cash flows	45	50	55	50	35
− Depreciation 20%	40	40	40	40	40
Profit	5	10	15	10	−5
ROI	2.5%	6.25%	12.5%	12.5%	−12.5%

Over the 5 years:

Profit £35/5 = £7   Investment £200/2 = £100
ROI 7/100 = 7%

NPV

	Inflow	Outflow	Net	Factor	PV
Year 1	75,000	30,000	45,000	0.9091	40,910
Year 2	90,000	40,000	50,000	0.8264	41,320
Year 3	100,000	45,000	55,000	0.7513	41,321
Year 4	100,000	50,000	50,000	0.6830	34,150
Year 5	75,000	40,000	35,000	0.6209	21,731

PV of net cash flows	179,432
Cash outflow	−200,000
NPV	−20,568

Although the project has a payback of four years and an ROI of 7%, it should not be accepted as the NPV is negative, i.e. the cash flows do not cover the cost of capital.

SOLUTIONS FOR CHAPTER 15

15.1

	Original	Additional	New
Investment	10,000	2,000	12,000
ROI	15%	14%	14.8%
Profit	1,500	280	1,780
Cost of capital 12%	1,200	240	1,440
RI	300	40	340

15.2

	Original	Additional	New
Investment	10,000,000	2,000,000	12,000,000
ROI	15%	14% (£280/£2000)	14.8% (1,780/12,000)
	1,500,000	280,000	1,780,000
Cost of capital 9%	900,000	180,000	1,080,000
Residual income	600,000	100,000	700,000

15.3

	Current	Additional	After
Controllable investment	750,000	100,000	850,000
Profit	150,000	15,000	165,000
ROI	20%	15%	19.4%

Green may not want to accept the investment as it decreases the divisional ROI, but for Brummy the project is better than the cost of capital (15% compared to 12%) and will increase shareholder value.

	Current	Additional	After
Controllable investment	750,000	100,000	850,000
Profit	150,000	15,000	165,000
Cost of capital 12%	90,000	12,000	102,000
RI	60,000	3,000	63,000

Using residual income, both Green and Brummy see an increase and will support the investment.

15.4 Compax

	1	2	3	4	Total
Cash flow	2.4	2.4	2.4	2.4	9.6
Depreciation	1.6	1.6	1.6	1.6	
Profit	0.8	0.8	0.8	0.8	3.2
Asset value					
Opening	6.4	4.8	3.2	1.6	
Closing	4.8	3.2	1.6	0	
Cost of capital 16% of opening asset value	1.02	0.77	0.51	0.26	
RI	−0.22	0.03	0.29	0.54	0.64
ROI	12.5%	16.67%	25%	50%	

Average ROI

Average profit $3.2/4 = 0.8$
Average investment $= 6.4/2 = 3.2$
Average ROI $= 0.8/3.2 = 25\%$

Newpax

	1	2	3	4	Total
Cash flow	2.6	2.2	1.5	1.0	7.3
Depreciation	1.3	1.3	1.3	1.3	
Profit	1.3	0.9	0.2	−0.3	2.1
Asset value					
Opening	5.2	3.9	2.6	1.3	
Closing	3.9	2.6	1.3	0	
Cost of capital					
16% of opening					
asset value	0.83	0.62	0.42	0.21	
RI	0.47	0.28	−0.22	−0.51	0.02
ROI	25%	23%	7.7%	−23%	

Average ROI

Average profit $2.1/4 = 0.525$
Average investment $= 5.2/2 = 2.6$
Average ROI $= 0.525/2.6 = 20.2\%$

The NPV calculations show that Compax has a higher NPV at £315,634, giving a cash value added of 4.9% (315,634/6,400,000). Newpax has an NPV of £189,615 and a cash value added of 3.6% (189,615/5,200,000).

Overall, Compax has a higher ROI, a higher RI and a higher cash value added based on the NPV. This is the preferred investment. However, it is important to realize that the returns for Compax are in the third and fourth years. Newpax looks more appealing in the first two years, when both its ROI and RI are higher. This may make Newpax more attractive from a divisional perspective or if Anston has a short-term focus.

15.5 See Table A2.25 (overleaf).

Before the new investment, Divisions A and C have the highest ROI and Division C has the highest residual income. The additional investment achieves the same ROI and RI for each division. After the new investment, Division A has the highest ROI and Division C the highest RI. Division B has a negative RI before and after the new investment because the current ROI of 6% is less than the cost of capital of 7%. The additional investment improves that position, but Division B still erodes shareholder value.

Table A2.25

	Division A	Division B	Division C
Original investment	1,000,000	1,500,000	2,000,000
Original net profit	75,000	90,000	150,000
Original ROI	7.5%	6.0%	7.5%
Cost of capital 7%	70,000	105,000	140,000
Original RI	5,000	−15,000	10,000
Additional investment	500,000	500,000	500,000
Additional profit	40,000	40,000	40,000
Additional ROI	8.0%	8.0%	8.0%
Cost of capital at 7%	35,000	35,000	35,000
Additional RI	5,000	5,000	5,000
New investment	1,500,000	2,000,000	2,500,000
New profit	115,000	130,000	190,000
New ROI	7.7%	6.5%	7.6%
New cost of capital	105,000	140,000	175,000
New RI	10,000	−10,000	15,000

SOLUTIONS FOR CHAPTER 16

16.1

Cash received in:		Jan	Feb	Mar	after	never
Sales made in:						
Jan	100	30	60	8	–	2
Feb	120		36	72	9.6	2.4
Mar	110			33	74.8	2.2
	330	30	96	113	84.4	6.6

Cash received in March £113,000
Debtors at end of March 84.4 + 6.6 = £91,000

16.2   Profit
See Table A2.26.
Note: Depreciation is £2,400 p.a. or £200 per month.

Cash
See Table A2.27.
Note: Depreciation does not involve any cash flow. The opening bank balance is the capital of £20,000 less the equipment purchased of £7,500.

Table A2.26

	July	August	September	Total
Sales	20,000	30,000	40,000	90,000
Purchases	8,000	15,000	20,000	43,000
Gross profit	12,000	15,000	20,000	47,000
Wages	3,000	4,000	5,000	12,000
Other expenses	2,000	2,000	3,000	7,000
Depreciation	200	200	200	600
Operating profit	6,800	8,800	11,800	27,400

Table A2.27

	July	August	September	Total
Receipts		20,000	30,000	50,000
Payments to creditors	−5,000	−10,000	−20,000	−35,000
Wages	−3,000	−4,000	−5,000	−12,000
Other expenses	−2,000	−2,000	−3,000	−7,000
Net cash flow	−10,000	4,000	2,000	−4,000
Opening balance	12,500	2,500	6,500	12,500
Closing bank balance	2,500	6,500	8,500	8,500

Balance Sheet

Fixed assets	7,500	
Less depreciation	600	6,900
Current assets		
Debtors	40,000	
Bank	8,500	48,500
Less creditors		8,000
Net current assets		40,500
Total assets less current Liabilities		47,400
Capital		20,000
Plus profit for period		27,400
		47,400

Note:

Debtors 90,000 − 50,000	40,000
Creditors 43,000 − 35,000	−8,000

16.3 See Table A2.28.

Table A2.28

Budget in £'000	Apr	May	Jun	Jul	Aug	Sep	Oct	Nov	Dec	Jan	Feb	Mar	Total
Revenue	225	225	225	225	225	225	150	150	150	150	150	150	2,250
Variable operating costs	68	68	68	68	68	68	45	45	45	45	45	45	675
Fixed operating costs	35	35	35	35	35	35	40	40	40	40	40	40	450
Total operating costs	103	103	103	103	103	103	85	85	85	85	85	85	1,125
Gross profit	123	123	123	123	123	123	65	65	65	65	65	65	1,125
Overheads													
Sales charge	15	15	15	15	15	15	12	12	12	12	12	12	162
Salaries	25	25	25	25	25	25	25	25	25	25	25	25	300
Depreciation	5	5	5	5	5	5	5	5	5	5	5	5	60
Rates	8	8	8	8	8	8	8	8	8	8	8	8	96
Heat, light and power	3	3	3	3	3	3	2	2	2	2	2	2	30
Total overheads	56	56	56	56	56	56	52	52	52	52	52	52	648
Operating profit	67	67	67	67	67	67	13	13	13	13	13	13	477

The gross profit is 55% in the first half year and 43% in the second half year, because an increased fixed cost is spread over a lower volume of sales.

16.4 See Table A2.29.

16.5 The known information is:

	Current year £ mill	Next year £ mill
Sales	586	791 + 35%
Cost of sales	486	
Gross profit	100 17%	
Overheads	−19	22
Operating profit	81 13.8%	119 15%

Therefore, gross profit can be calculated as 141 or 17.8% of sales.

Sales	586	791 + 35%	
Cost of sales	486	650 (791 − 41)	
Gross profit	100 17%	141 17.8% (119 + 22)	
Overheads	−19	−22	
Operating profit	81 13.8%	119 15%	

Table A2.29

	Qtr 1	Qtr 2	Qtr 3	Qtr 4	Total
Budget					
Volume (tonne)	100,000	110,000	105,000	120,000	
Selling price (per tonne)	300	300	310	310	
Variable costs (per tonne)	120	125	125	130	
Budget in £'000					
Sales and production	30,000	33,000	32,250	37,200	132,750
Variable costs (raw materials)	12,000	13,750	13,125	15,600	54,475
Contribution	18,000	19,250	19,425	21,600	78,275
Fixed costs:					
Salaries and wages	3,000	3,000	3,300	3,300	12,600
Maintenance	1,500	1,500	1,500	1,500	6,000
Rates	400	400	400	400	1,600
Insurance	120	120	120	120	480
Electricity	1,000	1,000	1,000	1,000	4,000
Depreciation	5,400	5,400	5,400	5,400	21,600
Other costs	2,500	1,800	1,800	2,500	8,600
Total fixed costs	13,920	13,220	13,520	14,220	54,880
Operating profit	4,080	6,030	5,905	7,380	23,395
Interest expense	600	600	600	600	2,400
Profit after interest	3,480	5,430	5,305	6,780	20,995
Budget					
Cash flow					
Profit after interest	3,480	5,430	5,305	6,780	20,995
Add back depreciation	5,400	5,400	5,400	5,400	21,600
	8,880	10,830	10,705	12,180	
Less capital expenditure	6,500	2,000	1,000	9,000	18,500
Less dividend			10,000		10,000
Less debt repayments	1,000	5,000	4,000	3,000	13,000
Net cash flow	1,380	3,830	−4,295	180	1,095
Cumulative cash flow	1,380	5,210	915	1,095	

The company plans to increase sales substantially and improve margins through better purchasing and/or higher prices, and will incur significant costs in store openings, warehousing and IT systems while maintaining only a 15% increase in corporate overheads.

A detailed budget projection would need to support these broad figures. The budget should identify, as a minimum:

- The sales mix by whatever categories are relevant (products, geographic sales, type of customer etc.).
- The margins on different categories of sales.
- The cost of materials, retail store salaries and property costs that are deducted to arrive at gross profit.
- The warehousing and distribution costs.
- Central overhead costs.

In terms of marketing, there are three distinct market strategies in existence:

- Increasing sales to existing customers through direct mailing.
- Winning market share through television advertising.
- Increasing sales in new geographic areas through opening new stores.

The information needed to support these strategies is the expected contribution from each strategy, drawing from past experience. Questions to be asked include:

- What is the cost of TV advertising and what additional sales and margins does it contribute?
- What is the cost of catalogues and direct mailing and what sales and margins does it contribute?
- What is the cost of store openings and what is the impact on capital investment (and therefore on cash flow) and the effect on running costs (especially salaries and property costs, including non-cash depreciation)?

The cost effectiveness of operations may improve by investing in warehousing and distribution facilities and IT systems, but the cost/benefit of this needs to be demonstrated. Questions include:

- What is the current stockholding and delivery lead time and how much is this expected to improve through new warehousing and systems?
- How does this saving compare with the additional capital investment?
- What is the impact of additional capital investment on operating costs?

This information needs to be modelled to determine whether the strategies will in fact lead to the desired profit target. The impact on capital investment, cash flow and financing also have to be determined.

Non-financial issues include whether the existing staff in stores, distribution and head office will be able to cope with the extra volume of business that is expected while retaining at least current standards of customer satisfaction, delivery lead time and product quality.

SOLUTIONS FOR CHAPTER 17

17.1

	Budget	Flex	Actual
Units	2,000	1,800	1,800
@	£3	£3	£3.20
Cost	£6,000	£5,400	£5,760
Variance			£360 – adverse

17.2

(Standard price – actual price) × quantity purchased
(3.10 – 3.05) × 5200
= 260 favourable

17.3 (a) See Table A2.30.

Table A2.30

	Budget	Actual
Sales unit	10,000	11,000
Price per unit	£37.10	£36
Sales revenue	371,000	396,000
Direct materials		
Magna – per unit	40,000 kg @ £1.50/kg	46,500 kg @ £1.45
– total	60,000	67,425
Carta – per unit	10,000 kg @ £5/kg	11,500 @ £5.10
– total	50,000	58,650
Labour – per unit	25,000 hours @ £7	26,400 hrs @ £7.10
– total	175,000	187,440
Total direct costs	285,000	313,515
Contribution margin	86,000	82,485
Fixed costs	75,000	68,000
Profit	11,000	14,485

(b) See Table A2.31.
(c) See Table A2.32.

Table A2.31

	Budget	Flexible budget	Actual
Sales units	10,000	11,000	11,000
Price per unit	£37.10	£37.10	£36
Sales revenue	371,000	408,100	396,000
Direct materials			
Magna – per unit	60,000	11,000 × 4 = 44,000	67,425
– total		@ £1.50 = 66,000	
Carta – per unit	50,000	11,000 × 1 = 11,000	58,650
– total		@ £5 = 55,000	
Labour – per unit	175,000	11,000 × 2.5 = 27,500	187,440
– total		@ £7 = 192,500	
Total direct costs	285,000	313,500	313,515
Contribution margin	86,000	94,600	82,485
Fixed costs	75,000	75,000	68,000
Profit	11,000	19,600	14,485

Table A2.32

Sales price variance
(Actual price – standard price) × actual quantity
(36 – £37.10) × 11,000   12,100 Adverse
Sales quantity variance
(Budget quantity – actual quantity) × standard margin
(10,000 – 11,000) × £8.60   8,600 Favourable
Standard margin: selling price £37.10 – variable costs £28.50

	Standard quantity × standard price	Actual quantity × standard price	Actual quantity × actual price
Magna	11,000 × 4 = 44,000 kg @ £1.50	46,500 kg @ £1.50	46,500 kg @ £1.45
	66,000	69,750	67,425
Variances	Quantity 3,750 A		Price 2,325 F
Carta	11,000 × 1 = 11,000 kg @ £5	11,500 @ £5	11,500 @ £5.10
	55,000	57,500	58,650
Variances	Quantity 2,500 A		Price 1,150 A
Labour	11,000 × 2.5 = 27,500 hrs @ £7	26,400 @ £7	26,400 @ £7.10
	192,500	184,800	187,440
Variances	Quantity 7,700 F		Price 2,640 A
Fixed costs	75,000	75,000	68,000
Variance			7,000 F

(d)

Budget		11,000
Variances		
Sales price	12,100 A	
Sales quantity	8,600 F	
Magna price	2,325 F	
Magna quantity	3,750 A	
Carta price	1,150 A	
Carta quantity	2,500 A	
Labour price	2,640 A	
Labour quantity	7,700 F	
Fixed costs	7,000 F	3,485 F
Actual		14,485

APPENDIX 3: CASE STUDIES

The case studies contained in this chapter provide the reader with the opportunity to interpret and analyse financial information produced by an accountant for use by non-accounting managers in decision-making. Each case study is identified with the chapter numbers that will aid in understanding, interpretation and critical analysis of the case.

Appendix 4 contains a suggested answer for each case, although the nature of such cases is that there is rarely a single correct answer, as different approaches to the problem can highlight different aspects of the case and a range of possible approaches are possible.

Case study	Title	Chapters
1	Paramount Services PLC	7
2	Swift Airlines	10 and 11
3	Holly Road Farm Produce Ltd	12
4	Call Centre Services PLC	11 and 12
5	Cryogene Corp.	13
6	Serendipity PLC	14 and 15
7	Carsons Stores Ltd	16
8	White Cold Equipment PLC	17

Case Study 1: Paramount Services PLC

Paramount Services provides a range of business consultancy services. Its financial statements for the last year are given in Table A3.1.

Table A3.1 Paramount Services PLC

Income Statement in £'000	2002	2001
Income	34,000	29,000
Less expenses	16,500	13,000
Operating profit before interest	17,500	16,000
Less interest expense	4,000	2,700
Profit before tax	13,500	13,300
Income tax expense	5,400	5,320
Net profit after tax	8,100	7,980
Less dividends paid	4,000	3,750
Retained profits	4,100	4,230
Number of shares issued	10,000,000	10,000,000
Earnings per share	£0.81	£0.80
Dividend per share	£0.40	£0.38
Market price of shares	£8.55	£10.20

Balance sheet in £'000	2002	2001
Fixed assets	21,933	17,990
Current assets		
Debtors	7,080	4,750
Bank	377	1,250
	7,457	6,000
Less creditors due within one year		
Creditors	4,300	3,750
Net current assets	3,157	2,250
Total assets less current liabilities	25,090	20,240
Less creditors due after more than one year		
Long-term loans	2,750	2,000
Total net assets	22,340	18,240
Capital and reserves		
Shareholders' funds	10,000	10,000
Retained profits	12,340	8,240
	22,340	18,240

An analyst has produced the following ratio analysis (Table A3.2) and has asked you to comment on any aspects that you think are important.

This question particularly relates to an understanding of Chapter 7.

Table A3.2 Paramount Services PLC

Ratio analysis

	2002	2001
Sales growth	17.2%	
Expense growth	26.9%	
Profit growth	9.4%	
Interest cover	4.4	5.9
PBIT/Sales	39.7%	45.9%
ROCE (PBIT/SHF + L/TD)	53.8%	65.7%
ROI (NPAT/SHF)	36.3%	43.8%
Dividend payout	49.4%	47.0%
Dividend yield	4.7%	3.7%
P/E ration	10.56	12.78
Asset efficiency (Sales/TA)	1.2	1.2
Days sales outstanding	76.0	59.8
Working capital (CA/CL)	1.7	1.6
Gearing (LTD)/(SHF + LTD)	11.0%	9.9%

Case Study 2: Swift Airlines

Swift Airlines has a daily return flight from London to Nice. The aircraft for the flight has a capacity of 120 passengers. Swift sells its tickets at a range of prices. Its business plan works on the basis of the following mix of ticket prices for each day's flight:

Business	30 @ £300	£9,000
Economy regular	40 @ £200	£8,000
Advance purchase	20 @ £120	£2,400
7-day purchase	20 @ £65	£1,300
Stand-by	10 @ £30	£300
Revenue	120	£21,000

Swift's head office accounting department has calculated its costs as follows:

Cost per passenger (to cover additional fuel, insurance, baggage handling etc.)	£25 per passenger
assuming full load	£3,000 (120 @ £25)
Flight costs (to cover aircraft lease, flight and cabin crew costs, airport and landing charges etc.)	£7,500 per flight
Route costs (to cover the support needed for each destination)	£2,000 (based on 1/2 of the daily cost of £4,000 – balance charged to return flight)
Business overhead	£3,000 (allocation of head office overhead)
Total	£15,500

This results in a budgeted profit of £5,500 per flight, assuming that all seats are sold at the budgeted price. The head office accountant for European routes has advised the route manager for Nice that while the Nice–London inbound leg is breaking even, losses are being made on the London–Nice outbound leg. If profits cannot be generated, the route may need to be closed, with the aircraft and crew being assigned to another route. The route manager for Nice has extracted recent sales figures, a typical flight having the following sales mix:

	% of tickets sold		
Business	60	18 @ £300	£5,400
Economy regular	70	28 @ £200	£5,600
Advance purchase	80	16 @ £120	£1,920
7-day purchase	75	15 @ £65	£975
Stand-by	100	10 @ £30	£300
Revenue		87	£14,195

The route manager has calculated a loss on each outbound flight of £1,305. She believes that there is a market for 48-hour ticket purchases if a new fare of £40 was introduced, as this would be £5 less than the price charged by a competitor for the same ticket. She estimates that she could sell 15 seats per flight on this basis. This would not affect either the 7-day purchase, which is used by business travellers, or stand-by fares, which are usually over-subscribed. The additional revenue of £600 (15 @ £40) would cover almost half the loss. The route manager has prepared a report for her manager asking that the new fare be approved and allowing her three months to prove that the new tickets could be sold.

Comment on the route manager's proposal.

This question particularly relates to an understanding of Chapters 10 and 11.

Case Study 3:   Holly Road Farm Produce Ltd

Holly Road is a farm employing 100 people, 60 of who mare agricultural specialists, 35 unskilled labourers and 5 clerical staff. The salary and related costs are shown in Table A3.3.

Table A3.3   Holly Road Farm produce

		Total costs
Agricultural specialists	60 @ £15,000 p.a.	900,000
Unskilled labourers	35 @ £9,000 p.a.	315,000
Clerical staff	5 @ £7,000 p.a.	35,000
Total salaries		1,250,000
Oncosts	10%	125,000
Total salary and related costs		1,375,000

Due to a decline in business as a result of increases in sales of organic crops by competitors, the company is going to make 40% of its employees redundant, reducing each grade of employee equally. Holly Road will use its remaining employees over the next 12 months to change its production methods to be able to compete with organic crops. Although none of the employees is unionized, redundancy costs will incur three months' salary and no oncosts are applicable to redundancy payments. At the end of the year the company will have to replace and retrain its new agricultural specialists at a cost of £7,500 each in order to have the skills necessary to support the new production methods.

Holly Road's advisers have produced the following information (Table A3.4) to justify

Table A3.4 Holly Road Farm Produce

	Redundancy	Cost savings 40 employees	Continuing costs 60 employees
Agricultural specialists	40% of 60 @ £15,000 p.a. = 24	360,000	540,000
Unskilled labourers	40% of 35 @ £9,000 p.a. = 14	126,000	189,000
Clerical staff	40% of 5 @ £7,000 p.a. = 2	14,000	21,000
Total salaries		500,000	750,000
Oncosts	10%	50,000	75,000
Salary and related costs		550,000	825,000
Less: Redundancy costs	Three months' pay (500/4)	−125,000	
Less: Retraining costs	24 @ £7,500	−180,000	
Actual cost savings		245,000	

their redundancy recommendations, resulting in a net cost saving of £245,000 for the 12-month period when the farm is being changed to support organic crops.

The manager has asked for your comments.

This question particularly relates to an understanding of Chapter 12.

Case Study 4: Call Centre Services PLC

Call Centre Services (CCS) operates two divisions: a call centre that answers incoming customer service calls on behalf of its clients; and a telemarketing operation that makes outgoing sales calls to seek new business for its clients. In the call centre, each operator can handle on average about 6,000 calls per annum.

Although staff are allocated to one division or the other, when there is a high volume of incoming calls sales staff from the telemarketing division assist customer service staff in the call centre division. This is the result of a recruitment 'freeze' being in place.

The finance department has produced the information shown in Table A3.5.

What conclusions can you draw about the performance of the two divisions? This question particularly relates to an understanding of Chapters 11 and 12.

Table A3.5 Call Centre Services

	Call centre	Telemarketing	Total
Number of calls	70,000	25,000	
Fee per call	£5	£10	
Revenue	350,000	250,000	600,000
Less expenses			
Staff costs 10 @ £15,000 p.a. 5 @ 22,000 p.a.	150,000	110,000	260,000
Lease costs on telecoms and IT equipment (shared 50/50)	20,000	20,000	40,000
Rent (shared in proportion to staffing: 2/3, 1/3)	80,000	40,000	120,000
Telephone call charges		20,000	20,000
Total expenses	250,000	190,000	440,000
Operating profit	100,000	60,000	160,000

Case Study 5: Cryogene Corp.

Cryogene is a manufacturer of three products used in genetic biology: Cryod, Genet and Yogen. The company has just finished its first full year of operations and has produced its summary Income Statement.

The company is unsure how its products contribute to profitability. The accountant has produced five versions of a product profitability calculation:

- Absorption costing based on labour hours.
- Absorption costing based on machine hours.
- Activity-based costing.
- Throughput accounting.
- Target costing.

Table A3.6(a) shows the contribution for each of the three products, with overhead unallocated.

Table A3.6 Cryogene Corp.

(a)	Cryod	Genet	Yogen	Total
Sales units	3,000	2,000	1,000	
Price (£)	1,500	1,150	2,500	
Sales £'000	4,500	2,300	2,500	9,300
Unit costs:				
Direct materials	450	600	900	
Direct labour				
Design @ £10	50	20	30	
Manufacture @ £20	240	60	160	
Assembly @ £15	60	90	60	
Total direct labour	350	170	250	
Prime costs per unit	800	770	1,150	
Total variable costs	2,400	1,540	1,150	5,090
Contribution margin	2,100	760	1,350	4,210
Manufacturing overhead				3,500
Gross profit				710
Less non-mfg overhead				600
Net profit				110

(b)	Cryod	Genet	Yogen	Total		Cryod	Genet	Yogen	Total
Product profitability 1: labour hours									
					Direct labour hours				
Sales £'000	4,500	2,300	2,500	9,300	Design	5	2	3	10
					Manufacture	12	3	8	23
Contribution margin	2,100	760	1,350	4,210	Assembly	4	6	4	14
						21	11	15	
Mfg overhead allocation	2,205	770	525	3,500					
					Labour hours	63,000	22,000	15,000	100,000
Gross profit	−105	−10	825	710					
Less non-mfg overhead				600					
Net profit				110					
Profuct profitability 2: machine hours									
Sales £'000	4,500	2,300	2,500	9,300	Manufacture	12	3	8	23
Contribution margin	2,100	760	1,350	4,210	Machine hours	36,000	6,000	8,000	50,000
Mfg overhead allocation	2,520	420	560	3,500					
Gross profit	−420	340	790	710					
Less non-mfg overhead				600					
Net profit				110					

(c)
Product profitability 3:
activity based

Driver	Total cost	No.	Cost each		Cryod	Genet	Yogen	Total
Purchase orders	700	100	7		40	10	50	
(orders)					280	70	350	700
Set-ups	1,000	20	50		10	5	5	
(batches)					500	250	250	1,000
Scheduling	1,000	40	25		10	20	10	
(work orders)					250	500	250	1,000
Despatch	800	50	16		30	10	10	
(deliveries)					480	160	160	800
Total					1,510	980	1,010	3,500

	Cryod	Genet	Yogen	Total
Sales £'000	4,500	2,300	2,500	9,300
Contribution margin	2,100	760	1,350	4,210
Mfg overhead allocation	1,510	980	1,010	3,500
Gross profit	590	−220	340	710
Less non-mfg overhead				600
Net profit				110

(d)
Product profitability 4:
throughput

	Cryod	Genet	Yogen	Total			Cryod	Genet	Yogen
Sales £'000	4,500	2,300	2,500	9,300		Sales	1,500	1,150	2,500
						less:			
Contribution margin	2,100	760	1,350	4,210		Direct materials	450	600	900
						Throughput value	1,050	550	1,600
Mfg overhead allocation	0	0	0	3,500					
						No. machine hours	12	3	8
Gross profit				710		Throughput per	87.50	183.33	200.00
						machine hour			
Less non-mfg overhead				600		T/A ranking	3	2	1
Net profit				110					

Product profitability 5:
target

	Cryod	Genet	Yogen	Total			Cryod	Genet	Yogen	Total
Sales £'000	4,500	2,300	2,500	9,300						
						Investment	3,000	1,000	4,000	8,000
Contribution margin	2,100	760	1,350	4,210		Required return	300	100	400	800
Mfg overhead allocation	0	0	0	3,500		10%				
Gross profit				710						
Less non-mfg overhead				600						
Net profit				110						

Table A3.6(b) shows product profitability, with overhead allocated first on labour hours and second on machine hours.

Table A3.6(c) shows product profitability based on activity-based costing principles.

Table A3.6(d) shows a ranking of products using throughput accounting and the target return on investments required based on the capital investment that supports each product.

Assuming that you have been presented with these financial reports, contrast the five methods of calculating product profitability. What are the assumptions behind and the limitations of each method? Consider how the information provided in each report might inform management decision-making. What criteria should the business use in any decision to discontinue its least profitable product?

This question particularly relates to an understanding of Chapter 13.

Case Study 6:   Serendipity PLC

Serendipity is an Internet service provider that has a major investment in computer and telecoms equipment, which needs replacement on a regular basis. The company has recently evaluated a £5 million equipment-replacement programme, which has an expected life of five years. The proposal is supported by the data in Table A3.7.

As the ROI and NPV look healthy, the investment proposal will be submitted to the board for approval. Prior to the above figures being submitted, you have been asked for your comments.

This question particularly relates to an understanding of Chapters 14 and 15.

Table A3.7 Serendipity PLC capital investment evaluation

in £'000	Year 0	1	2	3	4	5	6
Capital investment	5,000						
Depreciation 20% p.a.		1,000	1,000	1,000	1,000	1,000	
Asset value end of year		4,000	3,000	2,000	1,000	0	
Profit							
Additional income		1,500	2,000	2,500	2,500	2,500	
Additional expenses		−150	−350	−500	−500	−500	
Depreciation		−1,000	−1,000	−1,000	−1,000	−1,000	
Profit		350	650	1,000	1,000	1,000	
Tax @ 35%		−105	−195	−300	−300	−300	
Profit after tax		245	455	700	700	700	
ROI		6.1%	15.2%	35.0%	70.0%	n/a	
Cash flow							
Capital investment	−5,000						
Cash receipts		1,500	2,000	2,500	2,500	2,500	
Additional expenses		−150	−350	−500	−500	−500	
Tax @ 35%			−105	−195	−300	−300	−300
Net cash flow	−5,000	1,350	1,545	1,805	1,700	1,700	−300
Discount rate	8%						
Net present value	£1,225						

Case Study 7:   Carsons Stores Ltd

Carsons is a retail store that has given the task of preparing its budget for next year to a trainee accountant. The budget is prepared in quarters. Table A3.8 is the profit budget report produced by the trainee.

A cash forecast has also been prepared (see Table A3.9).

What are the questions you would want to ask the trainee accountant in order to satisfy yourself that the budget was realistic and achievable? Can you identify any errors that have been made in the budget or cash forecast? If so, make any corrections that you think are necessary and comment on any problems you have identified. This question particularly relates to an understanding of Chapter 16.

Table A3.8 Carsons Stores Ltd

In £'000	Quarter 1	Quarter 2	Quarter 3	Quarter 4	Year total
Sales	100	110	110	120	440
Cost of sales	40	44	44	48	176
Gross profit	60	66	66	72	264
Expenses:					
Salaries	10	10	10	10	40
Rent	20	20	20	20	80
Depreciation	5	5	5	5	20
Promotional expenses	10	11	11	12	44
Administration expenses	5	5	5	5	20
Total expenses	50	51	51	52	204
Net profit	10	15	15	20	60

Table A3.9 Carsons Stores Ltd

In £'000	Quarter 1	Quarter 2	Quarter 3	Quarter 4	Year total
Cash inflow from sales	100	110	110	120	440
Purchases		40	44	44	128
Expenses	50	51	51	52	204
Capital expenditure		20			20
Income tax			20		20
Dividends		15	20	25	60
Cash outflow	50	126	135	121	432
Net cash flow	50	24	9	8	

Case Study 8: White Cold Equipment PLC

White Cold Equipment (WCE) makes refrigeration equipment for the domestic market. It sells all its production wholesale to a large retail chain. WCE's budget versus actual report for a recent month was as in Table A3.10.

Management was concerned about the significant shortfall in profits of £8,550 and asked the finance director for more information. The finance director produced a revised report (Table A3.11) based on a flexible budget.

The report showed that by adjusting the budget to the actual volume of production/ sales, the profit was £2,950 higher than expected. The finance director also produced a variance analysis (Table A3.12).

This showed that the gross margin was lower than expected for the 1,000 units actually produced by £3,550, but that selling and administration expenses were below budget by £6,500. Therefore, profits were higher than expected for the 1,000 units actually produced.

On receipt of the finance director's report, comments were sought from the operational executives.

This question particularly relates to an understanding of Chapter 17.

Table A3.10 White Cold Equipment PLC

Budget v. actual report	Actual	Budget	Variance
Sales units	1,000	1,050	−50
Price	700	700	
Revenue	700,000	735,000	−35,000
Cost of production			
Materials per unit		£250	
Materials consumed			
Materials cost	245,700	262,500	16,800
Labour per unit		£150	
Labour consumed			
Labour cost	152,250	157,500	5,250
Manufacturing overhead per unit		£70	
Manufacturing overhead cost	75,600	73,500	−2,100
Total manufacturing cost	473,550	493,500	19,950
Gross margin	226,450	241,500	−15,050
Selling and admin. expense	183,500	190,000	6,500
Net operating profit	42,950	51,500	−8,550

Table A3.11 White Cold Equipment PLC

Flexible budget report	Actual	Flex budget	Variance
Sales units	1,000	1,000	0
Price	700	700	
Revenue	700,000	700,000	0
Cost of production			
Materials per unit	£270	£250	
Materials consumed	910	1,000	
Materials cost	245,700	250,000	4,300
Labour per unit	£145	£150	
Labour consumed	1,050	1,000	
Labour cost	152,250	150,000	−2,250
Manufacturing overhead per unit	£72	£70	
Manufacturing overhead cost	75,600	70,000	−5,600
Total manufacturing cost	473,550	470,000	−3,550
Gross margin	226,450	230,000	−3,550
Selling and admin. expense	183,500	190,000	6,500
Net operating profit	42,950	40,000	2,950

Table A3.12 Variance analysis

Materials price variance	£20
Actual no. units	910
Adverse variance	18,200
Materials usage variance	90
Standard cost	£250
Favourable variance	22,500
Favourable materials variance	4,300
Labour rate variance	£5
Actual no. units	1,050
Favourable variance	5,250
Labour usage variance	50
Standard cost	£150
Adverse labour variance	−2,250
Overhead rate variance	£2
Actual no. units	1,050
Adverse variance	2,100
Overhead usage variance	50
Standard cost	£70
Adverse variance	3,500
Adverse overhead variance	−5,600
Total adverse manufacturing expense variance	−3,550
Favourable selling and admin. variance	6,500
Variance based on actual production volume	2,950

APPENDIX 4: SOLUTIONS TO CASE STUDIES

Case Study 1:   Paramount Services PLC

It is important to remember that ratio analysis is really only useful to identify trends and comparisons. Trends require more than two years' data, while comparisons require either budget data or industry/competitor results that can be used as a performance benchmark.

Nevertheless, although the two years' data is limited, some conclusions can be drawn from the ratios.

Sales growth is high (17.2%) but expense growth is greater (26.9%), suggesting the need to control expenses. Consequently, profit growth (9.4%) has not been maintained at the same level as sales growth. Interest cost has increased due to higher long-term borrowings and consequently the interest cover has fallen, a slightly more risky situation for lenders.

All profitability measures (PBIT/Sales, ROCE and ROI) have fallen, as a result of the above-mentioned reasons. However, dividend payout has increased in total (and consequently per share for a constant number of shares) while the yield has increased, predominantly a result of the fall in the share price. For the same reason (a reduced share price) the price/earnings ratio has fallen.

Asset efficiency is constant at 1.2, although Paramount does appear to have a very high level of investment in fixed assets in relation to its income from services. Days' sales outstanding have increased significantly from 60 days to 76 days, a reflection of a credit control problem. Although creditors have also increased, the working capital ratio has increased and is adequate at 1.7. Gearing has increased, but the level of long-term debt is quite low in comparison to the fixed asset investment, an indication that a substantial part of the capital and reserves has been invested in fixed assets, possibly real estate.

Perhaps the major area of concern is whether the large fixed asset investment can be justified in terms of the business services that the company carries out.

Case Study 2:   Swift Airlines

By separating the controllable and non-controllable costs for the route, which the route manager has not done, we can see the true position (Table A4.1).

Contrary to the route manager's belief, the loss is £480, not £1,305. This is because she did not take account of the per passenger variable cost of £25. This reduces the costs by £825 per flight (120 − 87 = 33 @ £25).

While the additional revenue of £600 would help, the route manager has

Table A4.1 Swift Airlines

	Outbound	Inbound	Total
Revenue	14,195	15,500	29,695
Costs per passenger	87 @ £25	120 @ £25	
	2,175	3,000	5,175
Costs per flight	7,500	7,500	15,000
Costs per route	2,000	2,000	4,000
Controllable costs	11,675	12,500	24,175
Contribution to head office overhead	2,520	3,000	5,520
Head office costs	3,000	3,000	6,000
Profit/-loss	−400	0	−480

also overlooked the additional per passenger variable cost of £25. Each passenger would therefore contribute £15 to profits (£40 − £25), a total of £225, although this is only half the loss.

It is important to identify the relevant costs. On a per passenger basis, the relevant cost is £25 as that is the only extra cost to cover the additional fuel, insurance, baggage handling etc. The relevant costs for the Nice destination are the flight costs of £7,500 (£15,000 for the outbound and inbound legs) and £4,000 for the costs that support each route. If the route were discontinued, Swift would save £11,500, particularly as it could reassign the aircraft and crew costs to another route. The £3,000 allocation of business overhead (£6,000 for the return flight) are not relevant costs as those costs would not be saved, but would have to be reallocated to other routes.

Importantly, the route still makes a positive contribution to the recovery of head office overheads, which are allocated over each route. The route manager still needs to address the capacity utilization problem and the average price needed to generate a profit on each flight. The average price based on Swift Airlines' model is £175 (£21,000/120). The average price being achieved on the outbound route is £163.16 (£14,195/87). There is a likely trade-off between price and volume (of passengers).

The breakeven per flight can be calculated based on fixed costs of £12,500 (£7,500 + £2,000 + £3,000) and variable costs of £25 per passenger. A range of breakeven prices can be calculated.

The breakeven price for 120 passengers is:

$$\frac{12,500}{120(P - 25)}$$

$$P = £129.17$$

The breakeven price for 100 passengers is:

$$\frac{12,500}{100(P - 25)}$$

$$P = £150$$

Using Swift's business model average price of £175, the breakeven number of passengers is:

$$\frac{12,500}{(175 - 25)n}$$

$$n = 83.3 \text{ or } 84 \text{ passengers}$$

Using a range of volume/price scenarios, the route manager should be able to present a report to head office asking for additional time to reduce the losses, emphasizing the small size of the loss, the positive contribution to head office costs being made, and how flexibility in pricing and capacity utilization could overcome the current problem.

Case Study 3: Holly Road Farm Produce Ltd

The high cost of redundancy and retraining of skilled employees erode the cost savings. Given the salary differential between agricultural specialists and unskilled labourers (£15,000 compared to £9,000), it would make more sense to make the unskilled labourers redundant and to use the agricultural specialists to do all the work necessary to convert the farm to organic crops. As unskilled labourers have lower salaries the redundancy payments would be less, and as all the agricultural specialists are retained there would be no retraining costs.

Table A4.2 shows the potential cost savings if this strategy were adopted. This would of course require the agricultural specialists to undertake labouring work, but in the absence of unionization, their interest in retaining their jobs and on-the-job learning about crop changeover could have a motivational effect, which will also benefit the business. The cost savings of £279,650 exceed the across-the-board redundancy savings by £34,650. Some of this could be paid to the agricultural specialists as a bonus to cover their changed working conditions for the next 12 months.

Table A4.2 Holly Road Farm Produce

	Redundancy	Cost savings 37 employees (35 + 2)	Continuing costs 63 employees (60 + 3)
Agricultural specialists	60 @ £15,000 p.a.		900,000
Unskilled labourers	100% of 35 @ £9,000 p.a = 35	315,000	0
Clerical staff 40% redundancy	40% of 5 @ £7,000 p.a. = 2	14,000	21,000
Total salaries		329,000	921,000
Oncosts	10%	32,900	92,100
Salary and related costs		361,900	1,013,100
Less: Redundancy costs	Three months' pay 329/4	−82,250	
Less: Retraining costs	None	0	
Actual cost savings		279,650	

Case Study 4: Call Centre Services PLC

The staffing level in the call centre provides a capacity of 60,000 calls (10 staff @ 6,000), but 70,000 calls have been taken. The telemarketing division has subsidized the operations of the call centre.

In the short term, all costs in CCS are fixed costs. The standard cost of a call is £250,000/60,000 calls = £4.17. The standard cost for 70,000 calls is £291,900. It could therefore be argued that a more accurate presentation of the divisional performance is as in Table A4.3.

Table A4.3 Call Centre Services

	Call centre	Telemarketing	Total
Number of calls	70,000	25,000	
Revenue	350,000	250,000	600,000
@ standard cost (£4.17)	291,900	148,100	440,000
Operating profit	58,100	101,900	160,000

Note: Telemarketing expenses have been calculated as total expenses (£440,000) less standard cost for 70,000 calls in the call centre (£291,900).

This shows quite a different picture. However, the telemarketing manager is likely to point out that his staff are paid considerably more than call centre staff (£22,000 compared to £15,000) and that the standard cost is based on a salary of £15,000.

The appropriate staffing for the call centre to handle 70,000 calls is 12 staff (70,000/ 6,000 = 11.7). Given the recruitment freeze, two of the telemarketing staff costs should be transferred to the call centre. Rental costs are adjusted accordingly. It is arguable as to whether the lease costs should be allocated 50/50, but in the absence of more information this is left unchanged. The revised profitability is as in Table A4.4.

Whether based on standard costs or a reallocation of expenses between the divisions, the originally reported profit of £100,000 to the call centre and £60,000 to telemarketing is distorted. As the standard cost and reallocation calculations demonstrate, the call centre is making a much smaller profit and telemarketing a much larger profit than originally reported.

Table A4.4 Call Centre Services

	Call centre	Telemarketing	Total
Number of calls	70,000	25,000	
Fee per call	£5	£10	
Revenue	350,000	250,000	600,000
Less expenses			
Staff costs			
10 @ £15,000 p.a.	150,000		
2 @ £22,000 p.a.	44,000		
3 @ £22,000 p.a.		66,000	260,000
Lease costs on telecoms and IT equipment (shared 50/50)	20,000	20,000	40,000
Rent (shared in proportion to staffing: 4/5, 2/5)	96,000	24,000	120,000
Telephone call charges		20,000	20,000
Total expenses	310,000	130,000	440,000
Operating profit	40,000	120,000	160,000

Case Study 5: Cryogene Corp.

Table A3.6(a) reveals the contribution margins for each product. These are as in Table A4.5.

Yogen, which has little more than a quarter of total sales, has the highest contribution, followed by Cryod and Genet.

Table A3.6(b) shows the gross profit after allocating the manufacturing overhead of

Table A4.5 Cryogene Corp.

	Cryod	Genet	Yogen	Total
Sales £'000	4,500	2,300	2,500	9,300
% of total sales 100%	48%	25%	27%	
Contribution margin	2,100	760	1,350	4,210
Contribution % 46.7%	33%	54%	45.3%	

£3,500,000 (which is very high at 83% of the contribution) based on labour hours. This suggests that Yogen is the only profitable product, with Cryod making a gross loss and Genet almost breaking even. Table A3.6(b) also shows the gross profit after allocating manufacturing overhead based on machine hours. This suggests that both Yogen and Genet are profitable, but that Cryod is making a large loss. Looking at the information on the right-hand side of Table A3.6(b), we can see that Cryod has the highest number of labour and machine hours, which is why the overhead allocation results in that product appearing to be unprofitable. If the high level of manufacturing overhead is a consequence of high labour and/or machine hours, then that result is acceptable. However, if there are other drivers of overheads, such a reported result may be misleading.

Table A3.6(c) shows the allocation of overhead based on activity costing principles, using four cost drivers: purchase orders, batches (set-ups), work orders (scheduling) and deliveries. Contrary to the position in Table A3.6(b), Table A3.6(c) shows that Cryod makes the highest gross profit, followed by Yogen, whereas Genet makes a gross loss. Looking at the information in Table A3.6(c), we can see that most of the overhead is allocated to the Cryod because, on a cost driver basis, that product is consuming more of the four cost pools of overhead. The activity-based approach provides a more accurate allocation of overheads to products because it looks at the causes of costs rather than allocating overheads on an arbitrary basis, such as labour or machine hours.

Table A3.6(d) adopts a throughput accounting perspective, which treats materials as the only variable cost and identifies the 'value added' per unit of the capacity that limits the volume of production. Assuming that machine hours are the capacity limitation, throughput accounting suggests that the maximum contribution can be achieved from the Yogen, followed by the Genet and the Cryod. It is important to remember that while this information is useful, it does not take into account the overheads that are needed to support each product. Throughput accounting is a valuable tool in making optimum use of capacity, but is not a substitute for the other methods, unless overheads are either relatively insignificant or difficult to allocate accurately to individual products.

Table A3.6(d) also shows the profitability using a target pricing approach. Target pricing takes into consideration the capital investment needed to support each product and the cost of capital of the business. Table A3.6(d) shows that the main investments are in the Yogen and the Cryod, which are expected to generate the highest return.

Each presentation of information provides different information. Assuming that activity-based costing provides the most meaningful allocation of overhead costs, then we should maximize sales of Cryods and Yogens. Genets consume more overheads than they contribute. This requires investigation: either the selling price is too low, or costs are too high to support that product. Continued sales of the Genet are likely to reduce the overall profitability of the business. This is despite the low capital investment in the Genet.

The maximum throughput contribution comes from the Yogen and the least from the Cryod. This suggests a need to look at the manufacturing methods for the Cryod to see if productivity can be improved to reduce the number of machine hours needed to make this product.

In terms of target pricing, the gross profit made by the Cryod is almost twice the required return of £300 (10% of £3,000), while the Yogen is a little below target. However, in neither case have non-manufacturing overheads been taken into consideration. This leads to the overall conclusion that overhead costs are very high in the business, resulting in an overall contribution of 45.3% being reduced to a net profit of 1.2% of sales (£110/£9,300). Overhead cost control should be the over-riding consideration of Cryogene Corp. Subject to this and to the above comment about the high number of hours required to produce the Cryod, Cryogene needs seriously to consider dropping the Genet if costs cannot be restructured and increase its sales of the Cryod and the Yogen. It is important to note that if Cryogene used labour hours or machine hours to allocate overhead as the principal measure of profitability, it would be likely to discontinue the Cryod!

Case Study 6:   Serendipity PLC

The first comment to be made is in relation to the accuracy of the expected additional cash inflows and outflows, which are notoriously difficult to assess. The proposer of the capital investment will need to have some information to support the revenue growth projections and expected cost increases.

The ROI calculations are important, although as is common with 'cap ex' proposals, the higher ROIs are in later years. A fuller picture may be seen by looking at the average ROI over the life of the investment. Average profits are £560,000 (total profits/5) and average investment is £2.5 million (£5 million/2). The average ROI is therefore 22.4% (560/2,500).

Given a cost of capital of 8% used in the NPV calculation (which needs to be verified as the weighted average cost of capital for Serendipity), a residual income approach may also present a fuller picture (Table A4.6).

The total RI over the project is £2 million.

The NPV produces a positive £1.225 million at a cost of capital of 8%. Again, to present a fuller picture, an internal rate of return calculation shows the discount rate that equates to a nil NPV. The IRR is 16.8%, which is double the cost of capital, a more meaningful figure than the NPV residual value.

Finally, a payback calculation shows that on a cash flow basis the investment is paid back after three years and two months (Table A4.7).

Table A4.6 Serendipity

		1	2	3	4	5
Residual income						
Profit after tax		245	455	700	700	700
Cost of capital on asset value	8%					
Cost of capital on asset value		320	240	160	80	0
Residual income		−75	215	540	620	700

Table A4.7 Serendipity

	Year 0	1	2	3	4	5	6
Payback							
Net cash flow	−5,000	1,350	1,545	1,805	2,700	1,700	−300
Cumulative	−5,000	−3,650	−2,105	−300	1,400	3,100	2,800

$$300/1{,}700 = 176 \times 12 = 2.1 \text{ months}$$

Provided that payback, ROI, RI, NPV and IRR meet any board criteria, the investment proposal appears to be sound, but inclusion of the additional information should assist in obtaining board approval.

Case Study 7:   Carsons Stores Ltd

The first set of questions to be asked is how the level of sales was arrived at. In particular, have the sales been broken down by department/product? Have managers been consulted to see if the budget sales figures are achievable? Is the seasonal increase over the four quarters consistent with past trends, consumer spending patterns and market share? Does it reflect changing prices and competitive trends?

The second set of questions is in relation to the rate of gross profit (264/440 = 60%). In particular, is this broken down by product or supplier? Is the cost of sales consistent with previous trading? Does it reflect current negotiations with suppliers? Does it reflect changing prices?

The third set of questions is in relation to expenses. Is the salary budget consistent with the headcount and approved salary levels for each grade of staff? Has an allowance for across-the-board (i.e. inflation-adjusted) salaries been built in? Have all the oncosts been included? Is the rental figure consistent with the property lease? How has depreciation been calculated (e.g. the asset value and expected life)? Promotional expenses appear to be 10% of sales – is this consistent with past experience and/or with marketing strategy? Are administration expenses consistent with past experience and any changes that have been introduced in the administration department?

The fourth set of questions is in relation to the cash flow. Are all sales for cash (because there is no assumption about delayed receipts for sales on credit)? Cost of sales appear to be on 30-day terms, but there is no payment showing for Quarter 1 – the payments for purchases made in Quarter 4 of the previous year have not been included. It also appears from the pattern of payments for purchases that there is no increase or decrease in stock – is this correct given the trend of increasing sales over the year? All expenses have been treated as cash expenses, i.e. no allowance has been made for creditors – is this correct? The inclusion of depreciation expense as a cash flow is incorrect. Have the assumptions as to the timing and amount of capital expenditure, income tax and dividends been checked with the appropriate departments?

An adjusted cash forecast, taking into account the missing purchases figure (assume £40,000) and removing depreciation as a cash outflow, would be as in Table A4.8.

The previous cash flow of £8,000 has been increased by the non-cash depreciation expense of £20,000 and reduced by the omission of the estimated Quarter 1 purchases of

Table A4.8 Carsons Stores

In £'000	Quarter 1	Quarter 2	Quarter 3	Quarter 4	Year total
Cash inflow from sales	100	110	110	120	440
Purchases	40	40	44	44	168
Expenses	45	46	46	47	184
Capital expenditure		20			20
Income tax			20		20
Dividends		15	20	25	60
Cash outflow	85	121	130	116	452
Net cash flow	15	−11	−20	4	−12
Cumulative cash flow	15	4	−16	−12	

£40,000. This results in a negative cash flow of £12,000. Importantly, this raises the question as to whether Carsons has an adequate overdraft facility to cover the negative cash flows in the third and fourth quarters. Due to the errors, this was not disclosed by the trainee accountant's cash forecast.

Case Study 8: White Cold Equipment PLC

While the flexible budget provides a better tool for evaluating manufacturing performance, the business cannot ignore the difference between the budgeted level of sales (1,050 units) and the actual level of sales (1,000 units). The loss of margin is shown in Table A4.9.

The full variance reconciliation is as in Table A4.10. This comes back to the variance in the original actual versus budget report for the month.

In explaining the variances, it must be remembered that WCE can sell all its output and that it has failed to produce (and therefore sell) 50 units. This may be the result of a productivity or a quality problem.

Although 9% fewer materials have been used (90/1,000), this has been at an additional

Table A4.9 White Cold Equipment

Loss of gross margin	
Shortfall no. of units	50
Gross margin per unit	£230
Loss of gross margin	11,500

Table A4.10 White Cold Equipment

Total adverse manufacturing expense variance	−3,550
Favourable selling and admin. variance	6,500
Variance based on actual production volume	2,950
Loss of margin on units not produced	−11,500
Total variance	−8,550

8% cost (£20/£250). The overall favourable materials variance may be a result of less wastage or a greater productivity of materials used in the manufacture of the final product. However, the adverse labour and overhead variances cannot be ignored.

Labour cost 3.3% less (£5/£150), which may be the result of lower-paid employees or less overtime. However, 5% more labour units than expected have been used (50/1,000). This may be linked to the lower materials usage, which may have caused quality problems. The overhead rate is 2.85% higher (£2/£70) and, as usage follows labour usage, this is also 5% higher (50/1,000).

Consequently, if the change in materials has caused excess labour to be worked, then the favourable materials variance of £4,300 may be more than offset by the adverse labour usage (£7,500) and adverse overhead usage (£3,500), resulting in an overall adverse variance of £6,700. This is offset by the favourable rate variance on labour (£5,250) less the adverse rate variance on overhead (£2,100). The danger is that the adverse usage variances persist while the rate variances are eliminated. These issues are particularly important if the effect of the variances has been to reduce the actual production volume from 1,050 to 1,000 units! The most important questions are therefore what usage and rates will persist in the future? And is there a quality problem caused by materials that is influencing labour productivity?

Of course, the actual production situation may be something different to what has been described here. In a real business situation, managers would undertake an investigation into the causes of the material, labour and overhead rate and usage variances. In the absence of such an investigation, the above comments may be reasonable conclusions to draw from the variance analysis.

INDEX